THE PARK

ROY ROSENZWEIG   ELIZABETH BLACKMAR

AND THE PEOPLE

A HISTORY OF CENTRAL PARK

AN OWL BOOK

HENRY HOLT AND COMPANY

NEW YORK

Henry Holt and Company, Inc.
Publishers since 1866
115 West 18th Street
New York, New York 10011

Henry Holt® is a registered
trademark of Henry Holt and Company, Inc.

Excerpt from "Central Park" from *Selected Poems* by Robert Lowell.
Copyright © 1976 by Robert Lowell. Reprinted by permission of Farrar,
Straus & Giroux, Inc. As excerpt from *Near the Ocean* by Robert Lowell
reprinted by permission of Faber and Faber Ltd.

"City Greenery" (6 lines from "Our City, Our Citizens or Patience and
Fortitude"). From *EVERYONE BUT THEE AND ME* by Odgen Nash.
Copyright 1962 by Odgen Nash. Copyright © renewed 1986 by Frances
Nash, Isabel Nash Eberstadt, Linnell Nash Smith. By permission of Little,
Brown and Company and Curtis Brown Ltd.

Library of Congress Cataloging-in-Publication Data
Rosenzweig, Roy.
    The park and the people : a history of Central Park / Roy
  Rosenzweig, Elizabeth Blackmar. — 1st Owl book ed.
      p.   cm.
    "An Owl book."
    Includes bibliographical references (p.) and index.
    1. Central Park (New York, N.Y.)—History.   2. New York (N.Y.)—
  History.   I. Blackmar, Elizabeth.   II. Title.
F128.65.C3R67   1994   93-43425
974.7'1—dc20   CIP

ISBN 0-8050-3242-8

First published in hardcover in 1992 by Cornell University Press.

First Owl Book Edition—1994

Printed in the United States of America
All first editions are printed on acid-free paper. ∞

1   3   5   7   9   10 8   6   4   2

This book has been supported by a grant from the National Endowment for the
Humanities, an independent federal agency.

To Deborah,
R. R.

To Bill,
E. S. B.

Contents

Acknowledgments

Like the design of Central Park, this book is the work of two equal collaborators. From the start, we jointly conceived the book's themes and approach, mapped out its research strategy, constructed its analysis, and shaped its narrative. Although we have taken individual responsibility for researching and drafting particular chapters, we have together edited, rewritten, and argued about every page (indeed, virtually every sentence) in the manuscript.

As was true of the realization of Central Park's design, many other people contributed to turning our ideas into a physical reality. Our oldest debt, in fact, goes back to another collaborative project—a documentary film on the history of urban parks that Richard Broadman planned more than a decade ago. The script we wrote for that project led ultimately to our collaboration on this book. We thank Richard for providing the original inspiration.

Although we were never able to raise the necessary money to make the film, we were lucky enough to win the needed financial support to complete this book. Most important was a research grant from the National Endowment for the Humanities, an independent federal agency. We want particularly to thank our program officer at NEH, David Wise, for his continuing encouragement. An NEH College Teachers Fellowship to Rosenzweig, although granted for a slightly different project, allowed him to do the essential groundwork that led to this book. A postdoctoral fellowship at the National Museum of American History of the Smithsonian Institution and summer grants from the Columbia University Social Science Council to Blackmar as well as a study leave and a summer stipend from George Mason University to Rosenzweig provided essential free time for research and writing. In the final stages of the project a fellowship from the John Simon Guggenheim Memorial Foundation to Rosenzweig allowed him to do the research to bring our story into the twentieth century. Additional funds for research expenses were provided by grants from the American Association for State and Local History, the American Historical Association, and from Columbia and George Mason universities. Money from a New York State Historical Association manuscript prize helped us pay for the illustrations. We thank all these organizations and institutions.

Culling literally thousands of articles on Central Park and the city out of New York newspapers as well as myriad other research tasks was greatly expedited by some extremely able research assistants. Kathi Ann Brown, Thomas Weidlich, and especially Kevin Smead displayed particular skill and dedication; their efforts were indispensable to completing this project. Mary Kell, Gerry Thomas, Elizabeth Glenn, and John Miles also provided essential assistance, as did several people who helped us for briefer periods of time: Carrie Hayes, Barbara Smith, Kelly-Anne Jenkins, Vera Scanlon, and Tyler Anbinder.

Other scholars have generously supplied documents, pictures, and research leads. We have relied heavily on the scrupulously edited published volumes of the Frederick Law Olmsted Papers project at American University. The editorial staff also freely opened their files to us, allowing us to consult typescripts of as-yet unpublished letters and documents, to make use of their excellent indexes, and even to borrow some of their illustrations. We thank the heads of the project, Charles E. Beveridge and Charles Capen McLaughlin, as well as Carolyn F. Hoffman and especially Jane Turner Censer and David Schulyer for their exemplary scholarly cooperation. We also thank Herbert Mitchell for graciously making available to us his exceptional collection of stereoscopic views of Central Park. Sara Cedar Miller, the Central Park Conservancy's historian and photographer, generously provided photographs and information. We also thank Renée Friedman, Robert Garafola, and Linda Davidoff for sharing with us their views of contemporary park conditions.

We are indebted to the many librarians and archivists who organize and maintain the collections on which we have relied in our research—particularly those belonging to the Library of Congress, New York Public Library, New-York Historical Society, Museum of the City of New York, All Angels' Episcopal Church, New York City Municipal Archives and Record Center, New York City Department of Parks and Recreation, New York County Clerks' Office, New York State Library, American Museum of Natural History, and Church of Jesus Christ of Latter Day Saints. At an early stage in our research, the parks department's official historian, Mike Siegel, helped us unearth early park scrapbooks and other materials, and his successor, Jonathan Kuhn, assisted us in locating photographs despite the budget cuts that have devastated his office. Bruce Abrams and John Van Nostrand at the Bureau of Old Records and Condemnation Records provided a congenial setting for our research into the acquisition of the park land and the displacement of those who lived on it. Archivists at the Schomberg Center for Research in Black Culture; Archives, Mount St. Vincent, Bronx, New York; Rockefeller Archives Center; Wisconsin

State Historical Society; and Historical Society of Pennsylvania were kind enough to send us necessary documents by mail.

For helping to move the book down the long—and sometimes winding—road from conception to production, we thank Carol Mann as well as the editorial and production staff at Cornell University Press, particularly its director, John Ackerman. Our editor, Peter Agree, has been an enthusiastic supporter of this project from very early on. Judith Bailey copyedited the manuscript with great precision, and Carol Betsch carefully oversaw the book's production.

We presented our preliminary research in a number of settings (from Atlanta to Budapest to Sydney) and benefited from the remarks of official and unofficial commentators at those presentations. Space unfortunately prevents us from individually acknowledging the many people and institutions who hosted us on those occasions. Josh Brown generously provided research leads, copious comments on the full manuscript, and even his skills as a photographer. We also received valuable comments on individual chapters from Jean-Christophe Agnew, David Alpaugh, Jeanie Attie, Deborah Bell, Chuck Blackmar, Michele Bogart, Steve Brier, George Chauncey, Richard Fox, Joshua Freeman, David Glassberg, George Lipsitz, Peter Marcuse, Robert Snyder, and David Thelen, and sound advice from Peter Dimock. And we especially thank the following people, who took many, many hours from busy schedules to read the entire manuscript and offer thoughtful and perceptive comments: Iver Bernstein, Charles B. Blackmar, Daniel Bluestone, Alan Brinkley, Jack Censer, Elizabeth Cromley, Gary Gerstle, Elliott Gorn, Nancy Hewitt, Mark Hirsch, Deborah Kaplan, William Leach, Barbara Melosh, David Rosner, Nick Salvatore, David Scobey, and Mike Wallace. In countless ways their suggestions have improved the organization, style, and argument of this book. Although we lack the space to single out each of their contributions, our thanks are nevertheless heartfelt.

Jeannette Hopkins did a heroic job of incisively editing the manuscript in record time. We thank her for helping us to make this a clearer—and better—book.

Our families—Rosenzweigs, Schkrutzes, Blackmars, Alpaughs, and Kaplans—offered warm support for the project as well as diversion from some of its burdens. Finally, our dedications acknowledge our deep individual and collective obligation to Deborah Kaplan and William Leach, whose intellectual and personal companionship has been an indispensable part of this collaborative effort.

E. S. B.
R. R.

THE PARK AND THE PEOPLE

INTRODUCTION

In 1890 Eugene Schieffelin, a member of an old and wealthy New York family, released eighty starlings in Central Park, so New Yorkers could see the birds mentioned in Shakespeare's plays. Today, their 200 million descendants fill the skies across America. The influence of Central Park similarly spans the country. Thousands of municipal parks are direct descendants of this first landscaped public park in the United States. Its organization, policing arrangements, rules for use, and especially its design have been a powerful model (and sometimes countermodel). Central Park, one popular architectural guide concludes, is "the granddaddy of America's naturally landscaped parks."[1]

Central Park has been, in addition, a symbol of our national culture. In its first decade, the 1860s, the lithographs of Currier and Ives displayed to a national audience elegant New Yorkers riding in their carriages and strolling on the paths. In 1879 the democratic poet Walt Whitman noted the "rich, interminable circus" of the carriage parade "of New York's wealth and 'gentility'" in the park.[2] A century later it appears in films as a place of sophisticated urbanity. Woody Allen's cerebral New Yorkers ponder the meaning of life as they negotiate its walks in *Hannah and Her Sisters*. The "yuppies" of the 1980s in *When Harry Met Sally* sip drinks at the boathouse cafe. In *Wall Street* a young stockbroker confronts a ruthless inside trader on the Sheep Meadow.

But Central Park is also a place where crowds of ordinary New Yorkers gather and play. In the 1890s William Dean Howells marveled at the "spectacle" of the immigrants who jostled on the Mall as they took in "this domain of theirs." A half century later, the musical *Up in Central Park* celebrated the park as the common possession of all New Yorkers—"the big back yard of the city," a place "to laugh, to dream, to love, to roam." In the movie musical *Hair*, dreamers in long hair and Day-Glo clothing roam there. In E. B. White's 1945 children's book *Stuart Little*, no one thinks it odd to cheer a mouse to victory in a model-boat race on the Conservatory Water.[3]

Central Park has been envisioned as a place of romance and of destiny as well. In Edith Wharton's *Custom of the Country*, Undine Spragg seeks out an assignation in the wisteria arbor. Robert Nathan's Eben Adams finds love with a young woman from the past on the Mall and the Lake in *Portrait of Jennie*. In a more sultry key, Billie Holiday sang about "lovers that bless the dark on benches in Central Park." J. D. Salinger's Holden Caulfield watches his sister Phoebe reach for the golden ring on the Carousel. In Isaac Bashevis Singer's "Neighbors," an old man glimpses death in the winter in the park: "The desolate park became a cemetery. The buildings on Central Park South towered like headstones."[4]

Central Park has also powerfully symbolized the redeeming power of nature. In George Loring Brown's 1862 canvas, people are barely visible amid the serene greens and browns of the trees and grass. In the postimpressionist Maurice Prendergast's turn-of-the-century paintings of May Day, the people seem to turn into flowers. W. B. Van Ingen's landscapes have no people at all, only nature. Marianne Moore saw the park through its seasons: "Spring: masses of bloom, white and pink cherry blossoms on trees given us by Japan. Summer: fragrance of black locust and yellow-wood flowers. Autumn: a leaf rustles. Winter: one catches sight of a skater, arms folded, leaning to the wind— the very symbol of peaceful solitude, unimpaired freedom. We talk of peace. This is it."[5]

For all the celebrations of the park's pastoral attractions, perhaps the most compelling image for artists and writers has been the juxtaposition of the city and nature, of New York and Central Park. Photographers have been fascinated by the contrast offered by steel and glass office towers and art deco apartments looming over trees and lakes. Reversing the perspective, Ruth Orkin captures the park from the heights of those same buildings. Other images counterpose the charms of nature to the city's dangers. As early as the 1880s the plot of *The Mystery of Central Park* revolved around a murder in the park, though only two or three murders occurred in the park's first thirty years. In the 1960s Johnny Carson joked about the danger: "It was so quiet in Central Park last night. You could have heard a knife drop." The poet Robert Lowell invoked the fears of violence:

> We beg delinquents for our life.
> Behind each bush, perhaps a knife;
> each landscaped crag, each flowering shrub,
> hides a policeman with a club.[6]

Whether in the form of a one-liner or a poem, these stark hints of urban danger in a pastoral setting have unfairly exaggerated the threat of crime in Central Park. Yet they do remind us that America's most important naturally landscaped park is an *urban* space, best understood in relation to its city. That reminder is particularly important since most nonfiction about Central Park (as distinguished from imaginative representations) has tended to view it as isolated from city life and conflicts, as a landscape of vistas, birds, bridges, buildings, rocks, and trees. Few have written of the *people* who made, maintained, and above all, enjoyed the park that was their own.

Historians have shared the tendency to study this public space apart from the city's people. No full-scale history has been published; most historians concentrate instead on the career and the vision of Frederick Law Olmsted, who designed the park with Calvert Vaux in 1858. The two envisioned it as a pastoral retreat from the pressures and aesthetic monotony of a growing city, and historians and landscape architects have seen it reflected in their eyes, as a work of landscape art.[7]

To be sure, it is impossible to comprehend Central Park fully without understanding its appeal as a designed natural landscape, and we have benefited enormously from the work of those who have explored these dimensions of the park. Nevertheless, our goal in this book is to offer a different perspective on the park's history—one that puts people at the center and relates the park to the city. We tell the story of the park's people—the merchants and uptown landowners who launched the project; the immigrant and black residents who lived on the land seized for the park; the politicians, gentlemen, and artists who disputed its design and operation; the German gardeners, Irish laborers, and Yankee engineers who actually built it; and the generations of New Yorkers for whom Central Park was their only backyard.

We begin this history of Central Park as a social institution and space, an aspect of the city rather than just a natural or designed landscape, by asking a seemingly easy question: What is a "public park"? In its broadest terms, this book is an exploration of the changing meanings New Yorkers have attached to that deceptively simple phrase.

Parks have evolved over the centuries in concept and in form. In medieval and early modern England, a *park* was "an enclosed tract of land held by royal grant or prescription for keeping beasts of the chase," usually deer. More and more of these parks were created in the sixteenth century as English aristocrats and gentry cleared and enclosed large tracts of land around country estates, taking over entire villages and common fields. Eighteenth-century landlords continued what cultural critic Raymond Williams characterizes as the "imposition and theft" of the English enclosure movement, but instead of mere private hunting preserves, these new parks were often artificially constructed scenic landscapes. With the assistance of landscape gardeners such as Humphrey Repton and Lancelot ("Capability") Brown, landlords created "the view, the ordered proprietary repose, the prospect," Williams writes, "a rural landscape emptied of rural labour and labourers; a sylvan and watery prospect, with a hundred analogies in neo-pastoral painting and poetry, from which the facts of production had been banished."[8]

Paradoxically, then, these carefully crafted English landscapes were intended to mimic or improve nature, to present idealized nature so arranged as to disguise human intervention. And since this work "was centered upon the great expanse of land and woods that in the typical large country place was simply called the Park," historian Norman Newton writes, the word *park* came to be attached to an artificially natural landscape. English travelers readily extended this usage to the royal and aristocratic grounds of the Continent, where landscape gardeners arranged nature in a more formal style.[9]

In the late eighteenth and early nineteenth centuries, parks increasingly became identified with cities. German towns turned old fortifications into public gardens. The London public had been admitted, with regulations, to royal grounds such as Hyde Park as early as the seventeenth century, and over the next two centuries other royal lands were opened to public use. By the early nineteenth century municipal and national governments had begun to establish and landscape public parks that represented the romantic ideal of *rus in urbe*— country in the city.

Alongside this formal strand of park development, there has long existed a vernacular concept of public open space, whose tradition is more difficult to document. The cultural geographer J. B. Jackson contrasts "two types of park land": the " 'designed' parks" produced by landscape gardeners and " 'unstructured' playgrounds," where, at least until the late nineteenth century, "the common people and particularly adolescents, could exercise and play and enjoy themselves, and at the same time participate in community life." Jackson finds evidence of these unstructured "parks" in the churchyards of medieval Europe, in the stretches of undeveloped land outside the city walls or along riverbanks (what the French call *terrains vagues*), and in the "grove out in the country near the river."[10]

The dual heritage of designed and vernacular public spaces shaped the development of urban parks in the United States. One strand of the vernacular tradition stretches back to the New England commons—spaces held by the community for shared utilitarian purposes (for example, grazing cattle or gathering fuel) as well for public assemblies, particularly militia drills. New York's own Common served a variety of purposes in the seventeenth and eighteenth centuries—pasture for cattle, the setting for executions, the home of the almshouse and jail, and the site of public festivals and protests. But only in 1797, five years after it was enclosed for the first time, was it labeled "The Park" (rather than "The Fields" or "The Common") on a city map. And the designation "City Hall Park" or "The Park" came into wide use only in the first decade of the nineteenth century when it was landscaped in connection with the construction of City Hall.[11]

Another vernacular strand derives from the early nineteenth-century commercial proprietors who opened private parks such as New York's Vauxhall Gardens, modeled on pleasure gardens in London. More elusive to historical recovery and less structured in their composition were the innumerable open spaces appropriated by youths and adults for sports and games—for example, along the Manhattan waterfront or in vacant lots uptown. On the cusp of the vernacular and formal park traditions in the United States stood "rural" cemeteries landscaped in the English romantic style. In the 1830s and 1840s Cambridge's Mount Auburn, Philadelphia's Laurel Hill, and Brooklyn's Greenwood cemeteries helped to foster a taste for pastoral landscapes and a habit of "country" picnics and excursions within the city.

When New Yorkers created Central Park in the 1850s, they turned to formal landscaped European parks for their model rather than to vernacular traditions—but not without opposition. Even before the city acquired land for a park New Yorkers began to debate how this new public institution should be defined.

Frederick Law Olmsted, who was the park's first superintendent, said that the public would have to be "trained" to use a park "properly so-called," by which he meant a pastoral landscape in the English tradition. But what *was* a "proper" park? New Yorkers repeatedly proposed to alter Central Park's natural design—for example, by adding ornamental gates, formal gardens, or baseball diamonds with spectator stands. Parkgoers created their own paths ("desire lines," as landscape architects call them) and turned meadows into playing fields. When automobiles arrived, administrators responded to the pressure of new uses and new users by rearranging paths and adjusting the drives. City residents also enthusiastically greeted new park features, from statues and restaurants to children's rides and tennis courts, that distracted attention from the natural scenic effects. Through a vernacular process, the meaning of the park, proper or not, evolved. Still a "natural landscape," it also became a social institution and city space.

Just as there are two traditions in the definition of Central Park as a park, its meaning as a public institution also has two dimensions: its political character as property and its cultural character as an open space. *Public*, in one sense, signifies property rights, government ownership and control of land removed from the real estate market. Public property, owned by the government, thus contrasts to private property, owned by individuals or corporations who can exclude others from their land. But public property also differs from common property, that is, land or resources to which all members of a community have unrestricted access. The right to control public property is vested in government officials who determine who has access to it and under what conditions. In a democracy, when land is owned by the "public," government officials are thought to represent the interest of all citizens. In this sense, the people who organize and control a public park constitute the sovereign or political public. Yet the political process of selecting public officials is itself a matter of contest in which not all participants are equal.[12]

In a democratic and capitalist society, municipal politics revolve around difficult problems of distributing and managing public resources. The creation of Central Park as public property initiated a remarkable redefinition and expansion of city government's responsibilities to its citizens. The municipality had long overseen streets and docks for commerce; now it would provide a grand public space for recreation and socializing. Creating Central Park touched on issues beyond its own borders—from city planning and real estate investment to conditions of public employment and the city's fiscal integrity. Taxpayers, landowners, public workers, politicians, and city residents with differing visions of the public sector made particular and often antagonistic claims on the park.

Because Central Park is public property, the management of its grounds has also continually been negotiated through the city's tension-ridden political system. Who has the authority to control the park and define "proper" behavior within it? What sorts of restrictions on use should be set? According to what standards should the park be maintained? Should new facilities be added? What kind? Who is permitted to participate in the public decision-making process? As New Yorkers have debated these questions, they have confronted all the myriad problems and possibilities of managing public property to meet the needs of all citizens.

The *public* of a public park has a cultural and spatial as well as a political and property-based dimension. We think of public spaces as territories open to all visitors. As open, nonexclusive spaces, parks assume their character not through political powers of ownership or control but through patterns of use. The people who claim access to this public space constitute the cultural public. This cultural dimension of a park as a public space overlaps with its political and property-based definition in sometimes confusing ways. Some "public" space can be privately owned, as, for example, a theater or saloon, and proprietors can regulate access by price, if no longer by racial or gender categories. Public spaces defined as territories open to all people suggest the ideal type of the village commons, but historically such common property has served closely knit, homogeneous communities. By contrast, making Central Park a public space has required the remarkable experiment and challenge of creating a large territory open to all people in a capitalist and socially divided city.

Property-based definitions of *public* and *private* tend to be absolute (rooted in legal rights of ownership and control), but the idea of public space as nonexclusive territory is a relative concept. In the modern American city, few, if any, spaces can be said to be entirely open or entirely restricted. Degrees of exclusivity and access are shaped by economics, politics, and culture. A variety of structural constraints determine whether people possess the means to make use of the public space. In the 1860s, for example, long work hours, low wages, the cost of public transportation, and distance from downtown neighborhoods restricted working-class New Yorkers' use of Central Park. Further, formal, prescriptive rules can control access. Rules that forbade commercial wagons on its drives, for example, originally prevented the city's bakers and butchers from taking their families there for Sunday outings. Also, informal rules or codes of social conduct can determine whether particular groups want to use different public spaces and whether they will feel welcome. In the early twentieth century black children who went to the park faced the taunts of white youths. Although Central Park has always been a nonexclusive "public" space, it has not always been equally accessible to all New Yorkers.

Between the mid-nineteenth century and the present, New Yorkers continually debated the political status of Central Park as public property and its cultural value and use as an open public space. The interaction of different views of these two dimensions of the term *public* shaped the park's creation, design, use, and subsequent modification. Conflicts over the meaning of *public*, like those over the meaning of *park*, have thus been part and parcel of the history of Central Park. Debates over what constitutes a public park, in turn, raise difficult questions about the meaning of political, economic, and cultural democracy. Who participates in decisions about the management of public resources? Who benefits from and has the means to make use of public spaces? Can such spaces accommodate people of different classes and cultures? When New Yorkers struggled to define Central Park as a public park, they also struggled over the meaning of democracy.

In part because definitional questions were raised most sharply in the nineteenth century, this book focuses particularly on the park's first half century, but we also trace these themes into the twentieth century. The first section examines how New Yorkers created Central Park as a new kind of public institution. The decision to build the park, although clothed in democratic rhetoric, was fundamentally rooted in the interests of New York's wealthiest citizens—its gentlemen and ladies. Leading merchants and bankers and their families advocated creating a grand public park in order to promote their city's (and their own) cosmopolitan stature. They were joined by uptown landowners, who wanted a park to enhance real estate values. But not all New Yorkers agreed that the city needed such an expensive public symbol of its grandeur, and only after a three-year debate over the necessity, location, and financing of a public park was the site selected. Yet, despite the opposition, the park's gentlemen advocates claimed to represent the entire "public."

Municipal use of the power of eminent domain to take possession of more than eight hundred acres of land for Central Park represented an unprecedented intervention in the real estate market—a precursor to city planning and urban renewal. Chapter 3 examines how land acquisition affected landowners and the people who lived there, reconstructing the world of those forgotten "park dwellers." In choosing a site and taking the land for a democratic public park, the gentlemen swept aside the concerns of poor New Yorkers.

The second section explores the political, aesthetic, and economic conflicts that intersected in the designing and building of Central Park. The power to define the park depended on the political composition of the public, that is, on who had the right to make decisions concerning its management. As Chapter 4 shows, the battle between state Republicans and city Democrats placed control of the park in the hands of a state-appointed board of commissioners dominated by Yankee Republican gentlemen. The board's design competition for Central Park yielded a variety of proposals for how this space should be arranged for public benefit. Some New Yorkers wanted a park that resembled the flexible and eclectic pleasure grounds that dotted the surrounding landscape. Most wealthy New Yorkers preferred European models—the pastoral parks of England or the more formal parks of France and Italy. A combination of political alliances and cultural preferences led to the selection of the Greensward plan submitted by Calvert Vaux and Frederick Law Olmsted. Chapter 5 reconsiders the collaboration of Vaux and Olmsted and explores the designers' shared— and, in certain respects, different—visions of the park as a democratic institution and a work of landscape art.

Chapters 6 and 7 describe construction. For all its natural features, Central Park is not a "natural" landscape; it required the labor of thousands of men to transform the site's swamps and rocky ledges into a beautiful pleasure ground. Commissioners, politicians, park officers, engineers, and workers, moreover, had different ideas about how such a massive public works project should be organized and managed. Although working-class New Yorkers asserted their right to have a say in the conditions of public labor, they were not recognized as members of the political public that governed the park. When the expense of construction triggered public criticism, the park was completed according to new corporate principles of efficiency and labor discipline.

When the park opened for public use between 1858 and 1860, wealthy and middle-class New Yorkers flocked to its drives, paths, concerts, and skating ponds. Part III—Chapters 8 and 9—shows how this select cultural public of parkgoers, along with the exclusive political public represented by the park board, created an "elite park" in the 1860s. Not only did immigrant and working-class New Yorkers live far away from Central Park, but in their limited leisure time they preferred commercial (and less regulated) pleasure gardens that more readily accommodated their familiar habits of public socializing.

After 1870 Central Park began gradually and unevenly to change—to open itself to the city. Part IV examines how New Yorkers went about redefining the park as a more open and democratic institution between 1870 and 1900. In part, this redefinition resulted from the reconfiguration of the political public that controlled the park. A new city charter passed in 1870 brought control back into the rough and tumble of municipal politics. Moving from the ascent of Democratic party boss William Tweed through the 1870s era of fiscal retrenchment to the 1886 mayoral campaign of radical visionary Henry George, Chapters 10 and 11 explore the debates among politicians, taxpayers, public workers, and real estate developers over who constituted the political public and what claims that public could make on city government—and on its parks. In the 1880s, park workers, like other working-class New Yorkers, organized to assert their own rights as members of the public and demanded the leisure time and public space to enjoy recreation.

Chapters 12 and 13 examine the expansion of the park's cultural public in the last third of the nineteenth century through new patterns of use and the introduction of new features. Political changes opened the rules and policies of park management to more contention. Organized political pressure, for example, overturned the strict "keep-off-the-grass" rules and the restrictions on Sunday use imposed by the original board. But the most important pressure for change came from patterns of everyday use as the park became increasingly accessible and appealing to immigrant and working-class New Yorkers. They transformed the elite park of the 1860s into a more eclectic and popular space by the 1880s and 1890s, and by the end of the century Central Park was beginning to fulfill some of the democratic promises implicit in its creation as a public space. This democratization also affected the three cultural institutions situated within the park. The zoo, the American Museum of Natural History, and the Metropolitan Museum of Art drew new crowds to the park, but the museums' trustees sought to control popular uses of "their" institutions by fashioning a novel arrangement that gave private boards control over the management of institutions subsidized by public money.

How did New Yorkers adapt their nineteenth-century park to the twentieth century? Part V looks at the accommodation of new cultural, social, and political pressures in the first four decades of the new century. As Chapter 14 argues, Central Park's publics fragmented in the decades after the 1898 consolidation of Greater New York. Skyscrapers, automobiles, the growth of immigrant neighborhoods, and new ideologies and institutions of play (from playgrounds to commercial amusements)—all impinged on the park's design and use. The steady infusion of the modern city stirred new tensions among parkgoers, modified the landscape, and provoked new controversies over the park's future.

The question of how Central Park would serve the expectations of the twentieth-century public came to a head with the introduction of a new piece of land at its very center. Chapter 15 examines the debate over what to do with the land produced by the draining of the Lower Reservoir. Should the park provide new recreation facilities—playgrounds, playing fields—for the immigrant working-class population of the surrounding neighborhoods, as progressive reformers argued? Should it be redesigned to represent the formal civic aesthetic admired by advocates of the City Beautiful, with plazas, boulevards, and sunken gardens replacing meadows and winding paths? Or should city officials follow the lead of preservationists who urged a reversal of the movement toward a more urban and eclectic landscape, which had occurred over the previous fifty years? Populist politicians and editors, labor leaders and settlement house workers alike resisted both the introduction of classical monuments and the pure preservation of the park intended by the designers, generating a political stalemate over what to do with the site of the Lower Reservoir.

The resolution came only in the 1930s, through the odd combination of the imperial control of park commissioner Robert Moses and the democratic social impulses of the New Deal—the subject of Chapter 16. The greatest democratization of access to public recreational facilities in the city's history was accompanied, ironically, by the most autocratic regime of park management.

The "publicness" of the park—in the sense of democratic access and democratic control—continued to be contested after 1940, as Part VI shows. In these years black and Puerto Rican New Yorkers became more important users of the park, and some New Yorkers, responding to new social tensions, began to associate the park with crime—often in exaggerated ways. Pressure from park users—for example, from West Side mothers opposing a new parking lot at the Tavern on the Green restaurant—gradually eroded the autocratic rule of Moses. Moreover, the cultural experiments and new political currents of the 1960s further opened up the park. For the first time, it became a public space for mobilizing and expressing oppositional politics. The fiscal crisis and resurgent conservatism of the 1970s, however, closed down some of these new democratic uses. Chapter 17 considers the park's volatile history in the four decades after the Great Depression through a series of brief vignettes, one drawn from each decade.

The 1980s, Chapter 18 argues, brought new challenges to the definition of Central Park as a public space; in effect, the park became less "public" as city officials turned to the private sector for money as well as administrative guidance. By the early 1990s, the Central Park Conservancy, a nonprofit voluntary organization, supplied half of the budget and exercised considerable influence on policies for its use. Under the conservancy's direction, a remarkable restoration has reestablished its preeminence as the nation's premier landscaped park. Rehabilitation has also prompted new restrictions on the range of activities permitted. Yet New Yorkers continue to contest the definition of their public park and to demand a say in how it should be managed.

Despite the dramatic changes that have shaped Central Park from the mid-nineteenth century to the present, these fundamental questions have persisted: Is a park best understood as a designed natural landscape or as a common space shaped by ordinary parkgoers? Who constitutes the public, and how does the public participate in making decisions about the park's management and use? How should the park accommodate the conflicting expectations of different groups of parkgoers and city residents? The answers to these questions have changed over the past 140 years. As both a natural landscape and a social institution, the park has gone through seasons of germination and drought, of frost and bloom. Its natural features have been carefully studied, but the people who have fought over its creation, design, use, maintenance, and restoration are what makes the history of Central Park so compelling and complex. These conflicts testify to the vitality as well as the difficulty of this extraordinary experiment in creating a democratic public space within a society driven by the private market and divided by class and culture. We offer this history, then, in the hope of encouraging continuing debate and thought about the past, present, and future of our democratic public spaces.

Bird's-eye View of New York and Brooklyn, 1851

I. CREATING CENTRAL PARK

I

THE GENTLEMAN FROM EUROPE
AND THE IDEA OF A GREAT PARK

"Who was the author of the wise scheme to turn the waste lands in the centre of the island into a city park?" John Punnett Peters, chronicler of St. Michael's Protestant Episcopal Church (the church of the richest and most prominent West Side families), claims authorship for St. Michael's own warden, Dr. A. V. Williams. But there were other contenders for the honor. Antiquarian Charles Haswell credited Andrew Jackson Downing, the leading American landscape gardener of the mid-nineteenth century, for "the birth of the idea." In 1849 and 1850 Downing had written a series of letters from London urging "the necessity of a great Park" for New York City. Allan Nevins believed that the "real originator" of the park was the editor of the *New York Evening Post*, poet William Cullen Bryant, who in 1844 had published an editorial calling for "a new park"; it had preceded Downing's appeal by five years.[1]

The Anonymous Gentleman Who Invented the Idea

As far back as the early 1850s, newspaper editorials, letters to the editor, and testimony before legislative committees offered various accounts of the origin of Central Park, and many shared a common theme: they attributed the idea to an anonymous "gentleman," who, some said, had recently returned from Europe with the vision of a great park. An anonymous letter to the *Journal of Commerce* in June 1851, signed "AA," declared that the park "enterprise" originated "with a worthy and excellent citizen who has no other views in the movement but the public good." This citizen, "on return from Europe where he had been traveling about two years, invited several gentlemen to meet at his house to confer

The "Gentleman from Europe": The wealthy merchant Robert Minturn (1805–1866), urged on by his wife, Anna, called together a committee of gentlemen to lobby for a public park.

together in reference to establishing a large park on this Island similar to parks he had seen in Europe." Two and a half years later at city hearings on the proposed park, three witnesses alluded to the same mysterious gentleman. "The scheme of having a large park in New York," testified Robert M. Hartley, executive secretary of the Association for Improving the Condition of the Poor, "originated from a gentleman who, on visiting Europe, was so delighted with the parks of London, Paris, and Vienna, that he proposed immediately on his return to have one of these large parks in New York. Yes, he came home for the full purpose of laying a train to get a grand park in the centre of the city."[2]

The leader in the project of creating a new public park was indeed, as some had said, a gentleman, who had, as had been rumored, recently returned from Europe. All evidence points to the merchant prince Robert Bowne Minturn—a man eulogized at his death as *the* "American gentleman." In May 1848, so said a privately published *Memoir* by his son, an overworked Minturn and his family headed for an eighteen-month grand tour of England, France, Italy, Switzerland, Germany, Jerusalem, and Egypt. In the winter of their return, 1849–1850, "conversation often turned upon the difference between our own country and city, and those abroad; and the remark was made that there was no want of our city so great as a large park for walking and driving." At an evening gathering at the Bowling Green mansion of the banker Robert Ray, "a decision was made at once to call a meeting of gentlemen to discuss the idea." They convened at Minturn's downtown home and decided not only on a park but on "a large and beautiful grove on the East River," known as Jones Wood, as the appropriate site; whereupon "legislative action [was] taken to secure it."[3]

"The remark was made"—that passive voice in the memoir obscures the identity of the speaker of the crucial remark. It appears, in fact, that the anonymous person was no gentleman at all, but a gentlewoman. A sketch of the Minturn family published in 1897, based on information supplied by Minturn's grandson, describes the "high intelligence and personal charm" of Minturn's wife Anna Mary Wendell and declares that "the agitation for establishing Central Park was initiated by her, and carried to success by her husband and the friends whose interest in the plan she had aroused and inspired."[4]

Whether initiated by a gentleman or gentlewoman, the proposal to create a public park did originate within a circle of elite New Yorkers. After the "gentleman from Europe" called together the "conference" of like-minded citizens to discuss a public park, "a committee was appointed to call upon the owners of the land known as Jones Wood . . . and ascertain if they would sell these grounds for such a purpose and their price and also call upon the city authorities and urge the purchase of said land."[5] So reported the anonymous "AA," probably Alonzo A. Alvord, an uptown landowner and the Whig president of the board of assistant aldermen, who traveled in the same social circles as the gentlemen who had initiated the proposal.

Why did contemporary New Yorkers repeatedly attribute the idea of a park to an unnamed gentleman returning from Europe? Why have subsequent historians credited individuals known for their literary or artistic accomplishments? Both interpretations trace the park's origin to the inspiration of a "great man." Even more important, they invest its origins with disinterestedness and civic-mindedness. But contemporary tales of the gentleman from Europe had another, quite specific purpose. They were used to counter a different, less flattering explanation for the park's creation, namely, that it was the work of speculators out to make a buck. "AA" told the story as proof that "the enterprise did not originate with speculators." Bryant also spoke of a gentleman who had urged him to write editorials for a park, insisting that the movement had been "started by persons who had no more interest in any real estate speculation here, than they have in the regions of the moon." The gentleman who accompanied him to the proposed park site, he added decisively, "never speculates."[6]

Charles Beard was perhaps the only historian to consider the role of real estate development in Central Park's history. In a 1926 article, he called for "a deeper consideration of the economic forces which may be enlisted for or against the dreams and blue prints of artists and engineers, and the precise social and political modes in which those forces operate." "Economic forces" included "subjects not usually mentioned in polite society . . . themes that are usually as tabu in academic circles as sex at a Boston tea party . . . topics vulgarly known as special interests, private rights—acquired and potential—honest graft, and plain graft."[7] To consider the interplay of "special interests" in creating Central Park is not to reduce its history to the story of the narrow pursuit of private gain. Special interests are not simply economic or necessarily individual, just as "gentlemen" and "speculators" are not mutually exclusive categories. And in a democratic society, the members of an elite could not act alone. They had to convince other New Yorkers of the public benefit to be derived from a park—indeed, of its "necessity"—and also of their own lack of special interest in the matter.

Central Park thus emerged out of a complex mix of motivations—to make money, to display the city's cultivation, to lift up the poor, to refine the rich, to advance commercial interests, to retard commercial development, to improve public health, to curry political favor, to provide jobs. No single individual either conceived or carried through the massive public project that, in the end, cost more than $10 million (three times the city's total budget in 1850) and took more than eight hundred acres out of the most expensive and intensely competitive real estate market in the United States.[8]

The First Park Proposal

On May 5, 1851, Mayor Ambrose Kingsland proposed to the common council that New York City create a public park. "The public places of New York are not in keeping with the character of our city," he advised the council's aldermen. Noting the "necessity of making some suitable provision for the wants of our citizens," Kingsland said that no period "will be more suitable than the present one for the purchase and laying out of a park, on a scale which will be worthy of the city." "The establishment of such a park would prove a lasting monument to the wisdom, sagacity and forethought of its founders."[9]

Mayor Kingsland's bold proposal that the common council appropriate public money to establish a large public park was unprecedented. True, the previous year then-mayor Caleb Woodhull had observed that "no well governed city was ever content" without "open squares." "Open squares," however, called to mind not a landscaped park but rather the greens of ten acres or fewer, such as those of the popular promenades of the Battery and City Hall Park or the residential enclaves of fashionable Gramercy Park, Union Square, or Washington Square. For more than two decades, aldermen had endorsed the opening of private squares (such as St. John's and Gramercy parks) and public spaces (such as Tompkins and Madison squares) to enhance the city's beauty and its real estate values. In keeping with this policy, Mayor Woodhull recommended only that the Battery be enlarged to twenty-four acres. He said nothing of a great park.[10]

Private parks such as St. John's Park (located at Hudson Street one block south of Canal and shown here in 1840) were open only to adjacent landowners. Their manicured grounds provided a setting for the promenades of fashionable New Yorkers.

But others questioned the adequacy of the city's seventeen public squares, which comprised fewer than 165 acres. Two-thirds of the designated squares remained unimproved and lay far uptown, and the city devoted few resources to maintaining public spaces in lower Manhattan. "City Hall Park, Tompkins' Square, and Washington Parade Ground, are totally neglected," charged Bryant's *Post* in 1850. St. John's and Gramercy parks were, indeed, "ornaments" to the city, but "these," the *Post* said a year later, "are private gardens" and "no more belong to the public than the houses that surround them." Such squares in no way matched the expansive parks of European capitals where royal grounds had been converted to public use. Others joined Bryant in lamenting, as he put it, the city's "niggardly appropriation . . . for the purposes of public parks." On July 15, 1850, *Herald* publisher James Gordon Bennett conjured up the vision of European parks built on a "scale of magnificence" with "beautifully spacious drives." He concluded, "In New York we . . . must despair of ever having an apology for a Hyde Park."[11]

For more than five years, scattered editorials in Bryant's *Post* and Horace Greeley's *Tribune* had extolled the "beautiful woodland" of the picturesque Jones Wood estate, 150 acres between 66th and 75th streets and Third Avenue and the East River. A number of wealthy New York families, including the Alvords, and the Frederick Primes (who attended Minturn's earliest meetings), owned land and country houses nearby. In the fall of 1850 James Beekman, a Whig state senator and wealthy uptown neighbor of the Joneses and Schermerhorns (who owned the land), lobbied with the aldermen for the park. That winter, the gentlemen's committee probably met again, this time with newly elected mayor Kingsland, himself a scion of a wealthy mercantile family and a Whig, who supported government promotion of such internal improvements as canals and roads.[12]

When Kingsland urged the creation of a large public park, he did not recommend a specific site, but the criteria he identified—"easily accessible and possessing all the advantages of wood, lawn and water, which might, at a comparatively small expense be converted into a park"—would have suggested Jones Wood to those who had read Bryant's *Post* editorials. And as if following a script, one month later a committee of aldermen urged the city to seek state authorization to acquire the Jones Wood land. The committee's resolution quickly passed the boards of aldermen and assistant aldermen with bipartisan (though not unanimous) support.[13]

Jones Wood was, according to the *Tribune*, "better adapted for the purpose than any other they could have chosen." After the common council passed the park resolution, other editors visited the estate and noted the attractions of sea breezes, "undulating lawns," and "charming views up and down the River." The *Courier and Enquirer* reported that the land was the "first unmistakable 'country' on that great turnpike [Third Avenue]" with an "aboriginal woody aspect . . . not to be seen again" until Westchester. From the gate at the southern end of the woods, a visitor could follow "a secluded lane" through an "orchard of blackberries" to meadowland and then upland where the owner's mansion stood "in the thick of high grass."[14]

No "aboriginal" property at all, Jones Wood had been carefully landscaped as a private country estate. In the early nineteenth century, tavern keeper John Jones had purchased the tract from the heirs of a smuggler, David ("Ready-Money") Provoost. In 1851 John Jones's son, James, occupied the old Provoost Mansion on 69th Street. His daughter, Sarah, had married Peter Schermer-

The Beekman family estate, overlooking the East River between 63rd and 64th streets, formed the southern border of Jones Wood.

horn, whose family made its fortune in ship chandlery and real estate, and Schermerhorn added twenty acres of meadowland to his wife's inheritance and built a riverfront country house at 64th Street.[15]

"Nothing is wanted" to transform the Jones Wood into a public park, said Bryant in his editorial "A New Park," "but to cut winding paths through it, leaving the woods as they now are, and introducing here and there a jet from the Croton aqueduct." But when the aldermanic committee interviewed the Joneses and Schermerhorns, they found them unwilling to sell their country estates to create a public park. On June 17, 1851, James Beekman introduced a bill into the state senate to override those objections and authorize the city to take Jones Wood through eminent domain. The bill passed unanimously the next day.[16]

"I give you great credit for the skill and promptness with which you carried the measure through the senate," Robert Minturn wrote Beekman, offering assistance in getting the Jones Wood bill through the assembly, the next step in the process. Minturn circulated a petition, and the *Tribune* printed the names of twenty-five of the most prominent signers to demonstrate "that those who will be called upon to contribute most liberally [through taxes] toward the expense of the new park are most strongly in favor of the measure." Gaining the support of the city's elite merchants and bankers had been part of the committee of gentlemen's strategy from the outset; Alvord reported that they had "consulted . . . Mr. [William] Astor and several other large taxpayers in reference to the new park." All but one of the petitioners appear in Moses Beach's contemporary guide to "Wealthy Citizens" of New York City.[17]

Minturn and his friends did not move much outside their own circles, and some petition signers had attended Minturn's original meeting of gentlemen. The list included leading importers and exporters—Minturn's partner Moses Grinnell and his close friend William Aspinwall—whose packets and steamships traveled to Europe, South America, and China. Others—Frederick and Rufus Prime, Robert Ray, John Ward, and Shepherd Knapp—had moved from international shipping to banking and railroads. Webs of business partnership and marriage bound together many of the signers in a dense social circle. Active in the chamber of commerce, the Episcopal church, and numerous city charities, these gentlemen had established themselves as civic leaders. Not all the signers were Whigs, but the Democrats among them had crossed party lines to support the expansion of the state canal and compromises on slavery.[18]

No doubt influenced by the economic and political clout of these supporters, the Whig-dominated assembly passed the Jones Wood bill on July 11, 1851, and the governor quickly signed it.[19] The bill was law. The idea of a *central* park had not yet surfaced, but the decision to build a large public park had been made.

A Public Space Worthy of Our Great Metropolis

In half a century, New York City's population had grown from ninety thousand to half a million. More than twenty thousand immigrants were arriving at the port each year; by 1850 almost half of the residents were foreign-born. Blocks of houses and stores stretched almost three and a half miles north of the Battery to 30th Street, and ferries linked the city to Brooklyn and New Jersey. The extension of trade lines, the expansion of craft production into sweatshop manufacturing, and the organization of banks and insurance and railroad companies had transformed the port into a national shipping, industrial, and financial center. Not all New Yorkers shared equally in the benefits of rapid economic growth. Signers of the Minturn petition had accumulated massive fortunes, and 4 percent of the city's residents controlled more than 80 percent of the city's wealth. The nation's most prosperous city also had the highest mortality rate.[20]

In the face of these dramatic social changes, New Yorkers had come to feel that their city needed many improvements. Wealthy merchants were calling for more efficient transportation, cleaner streets, a stronger police force, and more honest political leadership. Labor leaders called for steadier employment, higher wages, shorter hours, and more affordable housing. Reformers—among them doctors, manufacturers, merchants, and philanthropic women—campaigned for temperance, sanitary housing, and the protection of new immigrants. Nativists advocated immigrant restriction; Christian evangelists urged a citywide moral revival; abolitionists demanded an end to slavery in the South.[21]

With so many pressing issues, why did New Yorkers decide that a large public park was necessary?

The aldermanic committee that recommended Jones Wood believed that the "necessity" of a park had "long been acknowledged by all classes in the community." But most of the public discussion took place in the narrower community of politicians, merchants, bankers, landowners, and the publishers and editors of New York's more than two dozen newspapers. Universal white male suffrage had opened the political process to a relatively broad spectrum of New York men in 1826, but the park was a project of relatively few gentlemen who saw themselves as representing *the* public.[22] These gentlemen justified a large public park on three grounds: utilitarian claims that it would promote the city's commercial and physical health; social and moral arguments that it would "improve" the "disorderly classes" and foster order among them; and cultural contentions that it would display the cultivation of the leading citizens.

New York, its boosters claimed, had become the "Commercial Metropolis of the New World destined to an expansion to which there really seems no limit." After decades of competition with other American ports, editors, merchants, and bankers had begun to measure New York against European centers of trade. Pointing to European parks, editors insisted that New York required comparable public spaces "worthy . . . of the greatness of our metropolis," as Bryant put it.[23] Most of Minturn's gentlemen had made their fortunes in international shipping and had traveled to Europe for business as well as for pleasure. Returning from Europe, they had found their city sadly deficient in the public grounds of Old World capitals. They felt embarrassed at its lack of refinement.

Gentlemen and ladies were more confident about matching the commercial stature of London or Paris than they were about their cultural achievements. "Few of the civilized nations of our time have made less progress" in the arts, literature, or science, Alexis de Tocqueville had observed after visiting the United States in the 1830s. American democracy produced a restless, materialistic, and individualistic people "passionately bent on physical pleasure" but indifferent to higher cultural pursuits. Other visiting Europeans complained of "vulgarity" and "barbarism." Wealthy New Yorkers winced. "We are tired of having everything boorish and coarse and unfeeling called American," complained George W. Curtis in a *Harper's Magazine* editorial advocating a landscaped park. "Good heavens," exclaimed a New Yorker when he first glimpsed London's grand parks: "And I took some Londoners to the steps of City Hall last summer to show them the park of New York." Comparing the parks of London and Paris to New York's "penurious" allotment, the *Times* found the contrast "mortifying."[24]

Building a grand, landscaped park would be one way to disprove European criticism (and assuage American self-doubt) about the mediocrity and unsettledness of American society. Such a grand public institution would answer

Tocqueville's charge that Americans became involved in civic affairs more out of self-interest and greed than from pride or a sense of duty. "Why," asked one early park advocate, "should monarchy be allowed to do more . . . for its subjects than republican civic policy can achieve for a City of Sovereigns?"[25]

Arguments for the necessity of fulfilling New York's destiny as a great world city intersected with concerns about the city's competitive position within its own emerging metropolitan area. To answer any doubts business readers might have about the relation between a public park and sustained economic growth, the editor of the *Commercial Advertiser* drew a practical analogy: "Many a tradesmen finds it profitable to expend money in extra fixtures and ornaments for his store. . . . to lay out money to bring in money is a common axiom of commerce." Many who lived in Manhattan were now seeking residence and recreation in Brooklyn and New Jersey, the editor explained: "It is to prevent this drawing away of our population and their money that we ought to be concerned."[26]

In 1844 when Bryant first called for a park, the city was still recovering from the ravages of the 1837 Panic and no movement emerged to implement his proposal. The economic boom of the early 1850s directly fueled confidence that the city would be "immensely advantaged pecuniarily" as well as fulfilled in its metropolitan destiny by establishing a great park. But the march of the city's economy had produced grave public health problems that marred New York's reputation as an attractive place to visit, settle, or do business. Here, as in other industrial cities, the staggering mortality rate stemmed from contagion, accidents, malnutrition, exposure, contaminated water, and conditions of childbirth as well as from lung diseases associated with polluted air, but doctors believed it was the bad air of cities that caused disease. In the 1830s and 1840s health reformers in England, proclaiming that parks would serve as "lungs for the city," had launched campaigns for new public grounds as an antidote to the ills of industrial society. New York editors and politicians repeatedly invoked this phrase, urging the healthful benefits of parks for fresh air and exercise. Other measures (better housing and sanitation and more downtown public spaces, for example) would have more directly addressed health problems than a public park. Still, during muggy summer months in a fetid atmosphere of dust, coal smoke, and decaying manure and garbage, many naturally viewed fresh air and tree-filtered breezes as a primary source and certainly the symbol of physical well-being.[27]

To most of the park's promoters, moreover, health represented as much a moral as a biological condition. Disease was associated with "dissipation," and nowhere did dissipation seem more threatening than in such popular male recreations as drinking, gambling, cockfighting, and boxing. A public park would provide a site for "healthy" and "manly" exercise. Bryant and his fellow editors stressed the contribution of parks "to the health . . . and to the morals of the community." In contrast to rough male sports or the temptations of "brightly lighted streets," a *Courier and Enquirer* article said, a park would encourage *family* outings and inspire "home associations."[28]

Park advocates believed that women and children (the two usually linked) would be the particular beneficiaries of a public park, "where the masses can enjoy perambulation, pure air, and exercise in summer." Although women were far from cloistered in nineteenth-century New York City, they had few opportunities for exercise and relaxation. In the 1840s writers had expressed alarm at the sickly condition of American women. Pointing to the burden of domestic duties as well as to constricted middle-class conventions of female dress, Catharine Beecher urged increased exercise; others charged that women's ill health reflected their general lack of opportunity for physical and mental development. A public park, advocates suggested, would "tempt fair pedestrians to . . . healthful and natural exercise." Assertions of its value to women as essentially moral beings also affirmed the essentially "moral" (and hence healthful) character of a public park.[29]

"Good Morals and Good Order"

The appeal to health and virtue does not alone explain the rise of a movement to establish a large, landscaped park as a new *public* institution. Undeveloped lots and uptown resorts, as near to the city's center as the proposed park, could offer New Yorkers open space for fresh air and exercise. So could the extensive pleasure grounds of Hoboken's Elysian Fields, Brooklyn's Fort Green, and resorts on Long Island and Staten Island. Improved and cheaper mass transportation could make such resorts even more accessible. But editors agreed, only city government had the power to remove land from the rapacious Manhattan real estate market; only government could establish a park as a permanent and orderly environment for recreation.[30]

Tocqueville linked Americans' impoverished civic culture to "conditions of equality" in a democracy, but wealthy New Yorkers worried as much about the conditions of inequality that fostered new kinds of social disorder. In 1849 riots had broken out when native-born mechanics protested the appearance of an elite-backed British actor at the downtown Astor Place Theater; the troops brought in to restore order fired into a crowd and killed twenty-two people. The following year, the city's nascent trade unions formed the New York Industrial Congress to coordinate their opposition to employers' degradation of the crafts. New waves of German and Irish immigrants, concentrated in crowded tenement districts, created their own cultural institutions, including beer gardens and corner saloons. The power of the city's merchants and bankers to dictate the terms of economic growth or maintain a unified cultural order was steadily being undermined.[31]

Older conceptions of republican benevolence held that wealthy citizens had an obligation to contribute to the well-being of the community as a whole. But as growing poverty and social conflict strained the conventions of personal charity, wealthy New Yorkers responded with ambivalence. Robert Minturn, who with his wife sparked the idea for a public park, was imbued with a commitment to public service and charitable works that may have derived from his Quaker ancestors or his own fervent Episcopalianism. (The acerbic diarist George Templeton Strong typically found him "too good, *too much* merchant prince and liberal Christian, and glorified donor to charitable uses.") In the 1830s he had been well known for his philanthropy among the poor of his downtown neighborhood, who "fairly thronged" his doorway. But then in 1843, deciding that personal benevolence was a "dangerous species of charity," he helped sponsor the New York Association for Improving the Condition of the Poor, which maintained that the "injudicious dispensation of relief" was the chief cause of increasing poverty. Its agents would separate out the "incorrigible mendicants" (who were to be packed off to the almshouse or the penitentiary) from the deserving poor (who were to be given limited physical relief and ample advice on remedying the character flaws that had landed them in poverty).[32]

Advocates suggested that a park would be a less repressive means of reforming the character of the city's working classes. If the city established the Jones Wood park, Bryant observed a week before the state senate voted on the bill, "there will be fewer inducements to open drinking houses. Give the people the means of innocent and cheap pleasures and they will be less likely to seek for expensive and vicious ones." A park, said Bryant, might promote "good morals and good order" by encouraging virtuous habits of play as well as work. A public park would have the further effect, the *Commercial Advertiser* suggested, of "softening and subduing the asperities that toil and suffering create."[33]

The *Tribune*'s editor, Horace Greeley, who supported the labor movement and especially efforts to develop new institutions such as cooperatives, drew on a republican tradition to argue that "good places of public gathering" would open new opportunities for workers' self-improvement. Greeley's definition of improvement included the "civilized" manners of "milder and more genial excitements." "Much of the rowdyism, the brutality, and the drunkenness we see here," his *Tribune* noted, "may be owing to the want of such humanizing and elegant resorts." With a park that "uplifted" all citizens, the city would bind rich and poor into a single public that testified to the possibilities of an orderly as well as a refined republic.[34]

Rural Embellishments for the "Imaginative and Cultivated Few"

Despite all the commercial and moral arguments, many of the gentlemen merchants who advocated a park were more concerned with serving their own needs. Europeans had not exempted wealthy citizens from their charges of crass American materialism; New York's gentlemen and gentlewomen needed to prove their own appreciation of the values of Old World refinement.

Anna Mary Minturn was a member of what one historian has described as the "simple, serene, well-satisfied circle," of elite "New York Society." But by midcentury this insulated social world was threatened as religion, politics, and economic self-interest put wealthy New Yorkers at odds both with one another and with the city's working people. Through charity organizations, Minturn (who was devoted to the Domestic and Foreign Missionary Society and other causes) and other women of her class could forge ties that overrode their families' competing economic interests and political affiliations; a large public park similarly offered a new kind of space that could transcend emerging social divisions. Although the Minturns never articulated their wishes in these terms, they surely understood that in a grand landscaped park the circle of refined New Yorkers who gathered in their parlor could also expand. Moreover, such a public space of assembly was particularly appealing in a city of rapidly changing neighborhoods. In the 1840s when commerce pressed the aristocratic St. John's Park at Hudson Street, a block south of Canal Street on the West Side, Robert and Anna Minturn moved uptown from that once-tranquil spot to Fifth Avenue and 12th Street. Families like the Minturns could and did reestablish new elite residential enclaves, but controlling the streets through which they traveled was more difficult.[35]

Earlier in the century the late afternoon, early evening, and Sunday promenades of affluent New Yorkers had evolved into parades of high fashion; the wide thoroughfares of Broadway, the Battery, and Fifth Avenue had become a public setting in which to see and be seen. By midcentury, however, the fashionable Broadway and Battery promenades had declined as "respectable" citizens lost control over these public spaces. "The very noticeable change has been produced," a *Post* correspondent explained, "by vast immigration of a foreign population." Modest female promenaders found themselves "stared out of countenance by troupes of whiskered and mustachioed chatterers." "But there is a remedy for all these inconveniences," the *Post* declared: "Let the new park be secured at once."[36]

Husbands, including male reporters and editors, hoped a landscaped park would protect their wives from the impositions of strangers on city streets. Women hoped the park would offer an opportunity for respectable public recreation. Anna Minturn's suggestion of a park represented the claims of ladies for a regulated space for daytime socializing beyond the confines of the parlor and the duties of housekeeping, shopping, and charity work.

Both men and women wanted grander public spaces for a new form of public promenading—by carriage. In the mid-nineteenth century, carriage ownership was becoming a defining feature of urban upper-class status. Affluent New Yorkers "had heard," the *Post* suggested, that the "fashionable part of society in Europe are not in the habit of walking in the streets." And the "generally increasing wealth," it noted, had "supplied most of the class who [once] favored Broadway . . . with equipages." Society, observed the snobbish editor of the *Home Journal*, Nathaniel Willis, consisted of "those who keep carriages, have town and country homes, who give balls and parties."[37]

But where could the "carriage-owning class" take their carriages? Traffic, immigrant crowds, and dirty streets had impinged on the gentility of lower Manhattan promenades by midcentury. The *Herald* complained also that the "swearing, drinking, silly boors" of the Bowery sporting crowd had "destroyed all enjoyment" of drives along Third Avenue or the Bloomingdale Road (later Broadway, north of 59th Street). The Jones Wood park, by contrast, the *Herald* said, "would form a kind of Hyde Park for New York," where the "public" could "enjoy an agreeable drive" without encountering local boors.[38]

To people like the Minturns, who believed in the Protestant work ethic and republican self-improvement, pedestrian promenades and carriage drives seemed rational modes of recreation. "Taking the air" had a special virtue of innocence that came from association with "pure" nature, not the taint, for women, of attending the theater or, for men, of frequenting boisterous (and mixed-class) amusements such as boxing matches or cockfights. And criticism that the "codfish aristocracy" (as the popular press called Yankee merchants) was abandoning the moral precepts of republican simplicity in favor of decadent and tasteless fashion reinforced elite New Yorkers' need to show that they put their wealth and leisure time to elevating ends.[39]

The Minturns and their circle associated parks with an appreciation of landscape aesthetics, which had come to represent a measure of cultural accomplishment akin to enjoying fine art, music, and literature. Like their cousins and business associates in other cities, New York's merchant families had developed new (and privately owned) "rural" cemeteries as places where the public could stroll and admire edifying monuments and pastoral scenery. Genteel New Yorkers had enthusiastically greeted, for example, the opening of the Greenwood Cemetery in Brooklyn in 1838, which they believed surpassed Boston's Mount Auburn and Philadelphia's Laurel Hill as a "grand, dignified" setting that "united the charm of nature and art." In the 1840s and 1850s more and more of the city's wealthiest citizens had landscaped the grounds of their private country residences; framing nature as art, they expressed a nostalgic attachment to the reinvented rural landscapes of their youth. When the Minturns returned from Europe they bought a summer residence at Hastings-on-Hudson, twenty miles from their city house. Robert Minturn joined other "gentlemen-farmers" (including other park petitioners) in organizing the New York Horticultural Society to disseminate information about rural improvements and theories of landscape design. Creating a public park—particularly by approaching an already landscaped private park—was consistent with this new appreciation of nature. It offered an opportunity to incorporate this appreciation

Editors complained that traffic, dirty pavements, and "troupes of whiskered and mustachioed chatterers" kept genteel New Yorkers from promenading on Broadway (shown here at the intersection of Fulton Street in 1860).

of "rural embellishments" into public socializing. The horticultural society lobbied for the new park, envisioning greenhouses and botanical gardens that would enhance "cultivation"—in both senses of the word.[40]

Urban newspaper editors were also surprisingly partial to rural landscapes. Bryant, one of the nation's most popular romantic poets, retreated to a Long Island estate where he could satisfy his passion for long walks through the countryside. He celebrated nature as a unique source of artistic and moral inspiration for his fellow Americans. Horace Greeley owned a model farm outside the city and a seven-acre rural retreat along Turtle Bay (about a mile south of Jones Wood); he was becoming famous for urging young men to "go west" to take advantage of the nation's abundant natural resources. His Turtle Bay estate, reported his friend Margaret Fuller, "is to me, entirely country, and all around is so bold and free."[41]

Sharing this romantic sensibility, the landscape gardener Andrew Jackson Downing nonetheless regarded rural embellishments as a means of taming the republic's boldness so as "to soften and humanize the rude . . . and give continual education to the educated." He designed the country estates of

merchant families, assuring his clients that the enjoyment of artistically arranged nature is the "purest of human pleasures," preserving "moral rectitude"
and "rational enjoyments." A large landscaped park, he believed, would afford
wealthy New Yorkers a public display of their own (and, by extension, their city's
and nation's) cultural accomplishments.[42]

In reprinting, on June 6, 1851, Downing's 1850 letter on London parks
from his *Horticulturalist* journal, the *Commercial Advertiser* implicitly marshaled
his support for the Jones Wood park. Downing had compared the "peculiar and
distinguishing luxury" of the parks of London's West End to "the loveliest
pleasure grounds of the Hudson." In his exhilarating account of Hyde Park
carriages, he described the distinctly unrepublican livery of London coachmen
as "tree-peonias, the most blooming blossoms of this parterre of equipage."
Downing had earlier celebrated parks as democratic institutions ("the pleasant
drawing rooms of the whole population"), but his London letter stressed the
pleasures of wealth and only briefly referred to London's new East End Victoria
Park, which had been built in the 1840s "expressly for the recreation and
amusement of the poorer classes."[43]

Downing appealed to the "imaginative and cultivated few" whose "refined
minds" were capable of appreciating "correct taste in art," but he also advised
leading citizens to influence the tastes of those below them. His writings
expressed the tensions felt by his elite clients, who, as republican patricians,
regarded parks as public institutions to benefit everyone but also as settings to
exhibit their own attainments. Neither Downing nor his clients perceived a
contradiction. The public appropriation of funds for the creation of such a
refined leisure space was justified, in part, because ordinary people would
appreciate (and hence be improved by) such public display of cultivation.[44]

Uptown Property and a "Company of Gentlemen"

Despite broad support among the leading merchants, editors, and politicians, not all New Yorkers welcomed the proposal for a public park. "There is
no need of turning one-half the island into a permanent forest for the accommodation of either gentlemen or loafers," the editor of the *Journal of Commerce*
complained in dissent from the general newspaper support for the park. "It
might suit the interest of uptowners to have the habitable part of the island
essentially diminished as . . . the market would be less plentifully supplied and
prices consequently enhanced," but it appeared to the *Journal*'s editors "that the
grand park scheme is a humbug and the sooner it is abandoned the better."[45]

The *Journal*, which represented the views of downtown merchants and
conservative Democrats, was not alone in its misgivings. Other newspapers
charged that the movement for the Jones Wood park stemmed not from disinterested desire to fulfill New York's destiny as a great and refined republican city

Brooklyn's Greenwood Cemetery, established in 1838, offered landscaped grounds and edifying monuments to New Yorkers who sought a retreat from the city.

but from the speculative interest of a select group of uptown gentlemen. "Will anyone pretend the Park is not a scheme to enhance the value of up-town land, and create a splendid centre for fashionable life, high rents &c, without regard to, and even in dereliction of, the happiness of the multitude upon whose hearts and hands all the expenses will fall?" the land reformer Hal Guernsey asked in a letter to the *Tribune*. Such doubts grew as New Yorkers looked beyond the arguments on behalf of a park to the specific location of Jones Wood and to the proposed method of paying for it.[46]

When the assembly took up the Jones Wood bill, some observers began to question Senator James Beekman's motives in supporting the new park. Beekman shared many of the cultural predilections of the Minturn circle. He too had traveled in Europe. He too worked to display the accomplishments of the rich through the New-York Historical Society and to improve the condition of the poor (within the limits of his nativist outlook) by working for free public schools. But his own landholdings gave him a more direct financial stake in the creation of the Jones Wood park than Robert Minturn. At thirty-five, Senator Beekman was the sole heir of the Mount Pleasant country estate, located between 49th and 51st streets, east of Second Avenue, and as his critics correctly noted, he shared with other Beekman heirs fifteen other acres located one block south of

State senator James Beekman (1815–1877) campaigned for the Jones Wood park, which would enhance the value of his adjacent land.

Jones Wood, as well as other land in the vicinity. "Mr. Beekman our Senator is too deeply interested in the neighborhood of the contemplated Park to be an impartial judge of its feasibility," an anonymous reader charged in a letter to the *Journal of Commerce* while the bill was awaiting the state assembly vote. "He and his family have a large extent of land there which will be greatly augmented in value by this operation."[47]

Like the forebears of many of the largest uptown landowners, Beekman's Knickerbocker ancestors had accumulated real estate and built country houses to give a gloss of gentility to their commercial capital. By the late 1840s the heirs of colonial landowners had been joined by new merchant investors, many of whom had acquired twenty to fifty acres of uptown real estate during the city's periodic commercial booms. Uptown proprietors faced difficulties in managing these large tracts as an investment. Rapidly rising taxes and utility assessments had dramatically raised the carrying costs of real estate, increasing the pressure to bring land into "productive use." Property tax rates had almost tripled (from $0.42 to $1.14) between 1830 and 1850. The Jones and Schermerhorn families and some others had sufficient wealth to cover the annual expenses of country estates used primarily as summer retreats. But for more and more large land-owners taxes became a burdensome cost in the management of real property.[48]

Taxes were not the only expense of owning land. The bane of all large landowners was the special assessments they paid for such public improvements as opening and paving streets and laying sewers. City officials charged proprietors for a new improvement immediately adjacent to or in the general vicinity of their land because they benefited from the traffic or utilities that increased real estate values. But as downtown commercial redevelopment and new streets pushed total assessments from just over $200,000 in 1830 to $1,113,838 in 1837, large landowners organized in opposition to the system of benefit assessments. They maintained that instead of charging nearby landowners a portion of the cost of a street or sewer, the city should finance such public improvements through general taxes, spreading the burden to property owners across Manhattan.[49]

With the recovery of the real estate market in the late 1840s, uptown landowners, who faced assessments for public works north of 40th Street, renewed their efforts to change the benefit assessment system and to free themselves from the expense of building the city's infrastructure. Their champion in Albany was James Beekman. But opposing the assessment system was not the same thing as opposing development. Beekman seems to have shared the opinion of a real estate agent who advised the senator that "if I had uptown property that I wished to dispose of I should improve [it at] the first opportunity." Beekman actively encouraged the introduction of utilities in the vicinity of that part of the Upper East Side estate he was subdividing for lease and sale. But even as he welcomed the new streets, sidewalks, and sewers that would attract buyers, he remained true to his antiassessment principles: when petitioning aldermen to build sewers, he urged that the city bear "a proportion of the cost."[50]

Besides assessment costs, property-owning uptowners also worried about what they called nuisances. New construction, restrictive lease covenants, and especially the price of land below 34th Street had pushed "undesirable" industries and poorer tenants to the periphery of the built city. In 1851 the *Post* denounced the "disgrace" of uptown "suburbs" that were surrounding the city with a "cordon of slaughter houses, milk distilleries, and bone-boiling establishments, hogpens and dung-heaps." The 1849 cholera epidemic, too, drew attention to new uptown sanitation problems. "Nuisances in the shape of 'Hoggeries' and 'Fat Houses'," the agent of an uptown landowner reported to Beekman in 1849, were deterring respectable New Yorkers from moving north of 40th Street. Removal "would materially improve Real estate," another landowner, M. Hopper Mott, thought, for "families would then come up and reside among us." Mott informed Beekman in 1850 that he had "great difficulty in renting houses . . . and I am constantly told, remove that *stench* and we will come up there to reside."[51]

Beekman, like many proprietors interested in controlling neighborhood development, had inserted restrictive covenants against nuisances into his own ground leases, but such private measures had no effect on his neighbors' leasing policies. However much Beekman might complain to the Butchers Melting Association about the "offensive effluvia" coming from their factory near his Second Avenue property, individually he could do little to stop encroachments. The match factories and breweries as well as the "Goat Hill" shanty settlement just south of Beekman's property undermined his hopes of attracting respectable families to his land.[52]

The difficulties Beekman and other landowners faced in regulating uptown development suggested the advantages of coordinating their strategy of response. When private solutions (such as restrictive covenants and letters of complaint) failed, landowners tentatively turned to government. Whigs like Beekman and his neighbor Alonzo Alvord had already endorsed the active involvement of state and national governments in providing canals and roads; now they urged that city government create a public park. By removing territory from the market, by protecting it from encroachments, and most important, by establishing the uniform "character" of the neighborhood, such a park would make private real estate investments more profitable and predictable. New York offered ample precedent for developing public squares to secure and enhance land values in the immediate vicinity by providing light, air, and greenery. That "public improvements of this description are sources of public wealth" was "manifest to anyone who will look at the valuable lots in the vicinity of all the little squares and pieces already set apart by the city," uptown alderman Henry Shaw noted in the summer of 1851. "Wealth clusters around them and defines their boundaries by their palaces." Such public places "increase immensely the aggregate value of the city" and especially the value of neighboring land.[53]

The proposed 150-acre Jones Wood park would offer a new scale for elite residential development in conjunction with a public ground, one reminiscent of the terraced villas facing Regent's Park in London or the private dwellings in Liverpool's Birkenhead Park—a scale appropriate to the extensive neighboring Beekman lands. A *Journal of Commerce* account of the origins of the park movement two years later even suggested that a "company of gentlemen," who had first envisioned Jones Wood as a "sort of park for the use of the public," hoped to purchase the land themselves and build twenty or more villas within its boundaries. Such a private venture would have been expensive and difficult to organize, however, and the opposition of the owners of Jones Wood required the use of eminent domain. We do not know if Beekman participated in any such unsuccessful scheme, but he was one of the earliest advocates of public purchase of Jones Wood for a park and had close ties through the Whig party with both Mayor Kingsland and Alderman William A. Dooley, chairman of the committee that recommended the Jones Wood site and Beekman's uptown neighbor.[54] Dooley had drafted the common council resolution seeking legislative authorization for the Jones Wood park "to be paid for by taxation." Financing a park out of taxes rather than by assessing adjacent proprietors would spread the costs of uptown development throughout the city but leave the benefits for just uptown landowners. If city taxpayers placed a park at his doorstep, Beekman would stand to reap the profits from the sale of park-front villas on his land.

The method of payment for the park quickly emerged as a crucial—and politically explosive—issue and called attention to the uptown gentlemen's interest in the Jones Wood location. Even some Whig gentlemen objected to the novelty of financing the park through general taxation rather than through conventional benefit assessments. When Minturn and Rufus Prime asked U.S. Senator Hamilton Fish to sign their petition, they learned that he had "scruples about the proposed mode of payment"; he would sign only if neighboring landowners paid for at least three-fifths of the cost. The Jones Wood bill encountered difficulties in the assembly centered on the method of financing. Of uptown landowners who joined Minturn in intense lobbying for its passage, the most active were James Crumbie and Timothy Churchill, owners of large tracts on the southern and northern borders of Jones Wood. Other gentlemen petitioners or their families—for example, Alvord, Prime, William DeForest, William C. Wetmore, and Mortimer Livingston—also owned land within as-sessment range of Jones Wood. Such landowners saw no reason that they should bear the cost of an improvement that, they argued, would benefit the city as a whole.[55]

Not all these gentlemen, of course, were motivated by direct calculation of financial gain. For most, the social and cultural benefits promised by the park were more compelling. Even Beekman, Crumbie, Churchill, and others who had significant financial stakes in the Jones Wood location did not see them-selves as narrowly self-interested, any more than the Minturns did in their advocacy of a park that would be heavily used by wealthy New Yorkers like themselves. In both instances, class interests (whether defined in economic or cultural terms) were equated with the *public* interest. *Journal of Commerce* publisher Gerard Hallock captured this point nicely in a response to Beekman's complaints about the charges of self-interest that had appeared in the letters to the editor. "I do not at all doubt," Hallock acknowledged, "that in advocating the measure, you are influenced by a conviction that the *public* interest, as well as your own individual interest, will be promoted."[56]

Beekman indirectly conceded that wealthy New Yorkers saw no contradic-tion between their class interest and the public interest. When, during the senate's consideration of the Jones Wood bill, one legislator expressed hope that "the measure had been attentively considered in relation to its cost and the taxation consequent," Beekman replied that not a single remonstrance had been presented against it, then offered a curious—but strikingly appropriate—characterization of the beneficiaries: "The park will benefit all classes—the holders of large estates, the bankers and lawyers who concentrate in a small sphere like a bee-hive, their work of accumulation." Although in June and July

1851 newspaper editorials continued to explain why New York City needed the Jones Wood park, suspicions were growing about the true beneficiaries. "How many other classes does Dr. Senator Beekman know besides this team of three?" the *Staats-Zeitung* wondered, referring to the "holders of large estates, the bankers and lawyers."[57]

Between the fall of 1850 and the summer of 1851, the proposal for a large landscaped park moved quickly from casual conversation in the parlors where the Minturns gathered with their friends to a state law giving the city the power to take the Jones Wood site. Editors and politicians declared that "all classes" backed the project. Merchant families maintained that the park would establish the city's metropolitan stature, bring order to the lower classes, and certify their own credentials as a metropolitan gentry. Uptown landowners believed the park would ensure the respectable and profitable development of uptown Manhattan. The alliance of these groups seemed to promise that New Yorkers would soon be enjoying seaside breezes at Jones Wood park.

But just as the project seemed close to realization, dissenters from such disparate corners of the city as the *Journal of Commerce* and the *Staats-Zeitung* began to raise troubling questions. Why was the park to be located on the East Side? Why was it to be financed through general tax revenues instead of through benefit assessments on adjacent landowners? Did "all classes" really want the Jones Wood park, and would all benefit from it?

2

"GIVE US A PARK . . . CENTRAL OR SIDELONG . . . A REAL PARK, A LARGE PARK"

On June 28, 1851, two weeks before the legislature authorized purchase of Jones Wood, the *Journal of Commerce* published a correspondence between two city officials suggesting an alternative site for a large park in the middle of Manhattan. Uptown alderman Henry Shaw and the president of the Croton Aqueduct Board, Nicholas Dean, recommended a "Central Park," maintaining that it that would better meet New Yorkers' needs than the "one-sided" Jones Wood park on the East River. Their proposal initiated an intense three-year battle over whether, where, and at whose expense New York would create its grand public park.[1]

Robert Minturn and the other gentlemen argued that city government should provide this new (and expensive) public amenity. But their assertion of unified public support crumbled as other groups of New Yorkers entered the discussion and examined who would benefit from the Jones Wood park. Some New Yorkers—particularly downtown merchants—wanted no park at all, and others especially objected to paying for Jones Wood through general tax revenues. Still others, including land reformers and artisans, asked why there should be a large park uptown and suggested smaller parks in neighborhoods more accessible to a majority of city residents. A number of West Side landowners built their own powerful coalition in behalf of the suggestion for a central park. In the state legislature, advocates of each location resorted to backroom deals and bribes, petitions, and editorials to influence elected representatives.

In urging the creation of a park, New York gentlemen were calling on the state to intervene massively in the private land market and establish a new kind of public institution for its citizens. They were expanding the definition of appropriate state action on behalf of the public good. That the conflicts over

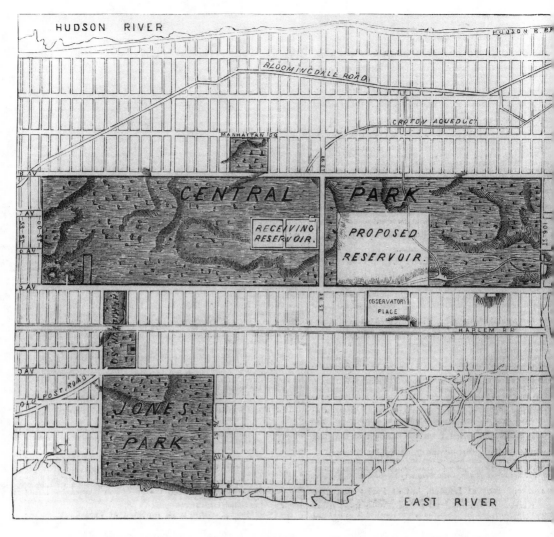

This map, comparing the two proposed sites for a park, first appeared in aldermen Daniel Dodge and Joseph Britton's 1852 report. Hamilton Square (between the two sites) was later sold off by the city.

which park to build focused particularly on costs and even more on who would pay those costs reflects the uncertainty with which those wealthy New Yorkers embraced the concept of a more activist government. In the process they encountered ambiguities in the concept of the "public" in the public park they sought to create. Committing the state or the city to a huge expenditure of resources could only be done in the name of all citizens. The association of a new park with the "public" meant that a much broader cross section of New Yorkers would ultimately claim their rights to this new cultural institution than the relatively narrow groups of wealthy (and often self-interested) New Yorkers who actually carried the proposal for a park through the political process.

"No One-Sided Work Either by Speculators or Officeholders"

The common council's Jones Wood resolution, no doubt influenced by the antiassessment sentiments of Mayor Kingsland, Senator Beekman, and members of the gentlemen's committee in the summer of 1851, sought state legislative authorization to appropriate fifty thousand dollars a year from general tax revenues to pay for the park.[2] Some newspaper publishers and editors maintained that all taxpayers should bear the cost of a public improvement that would enhance the city's reputation, though by tradition, adjacent proprietors who would immediately benefit were to be charged assessments. The debate over who would pay raised the issue of where the park should be.

From the moment the common council ratified the Jones Wood park, the *Journal of Commerce,* representing the views of the city's fiscally conservative downtown Democratic merchants, led the opposition. Although many downtown gentlemen had earlier supported the state's involvement in expanding the canal system to promote trade, they were skeptical of city government intervention in cultural (as opposed to economic) affairs. If the park were an "urgent necessity," the expense could be borne "in prosperous times like the present," the *Journal's* editor Gerard Hallock observed, but he questioned whether New York *needed* a large public park. As an island, the city had plenty of fresh air, and there was access to other resorts: "If downtown people wish to rusticate, they can find Elysian Fields [in Hoboken] within half the distance."[3]

Downtown merchants objected even more strongly to the proposal to pay for Jones Wood through general tax revenues. If all taxpayers paid for the park, the First Ward (filled with the city's most valuable commercial property) would bear one-fifth the cost. In Hallock's view such a system involved "pretty much the same principle as if the national government should lay a tax upon cotton to build a railroad for the accommodation of the state of Maine." Letter writers to the *Journal,* moreover, complained that uptowners had been exempted from paying their fair share of taxes for other citywide improvements, including the Croton water system. "Why should those [uptowners] who already enjoyed such manifestly unfair exemption be permitted for their own benefit to lay a tax upon citizens," one indignant letter asked. "Is it equal? Is it just? Is it fair?"[4]

In an earlier generation, when most successful merchants had invested shipping profits in Manhattan real estate, "uptown" and "downtown" taxpayers were essentially the same people. By the late 1840s, however, investments in manufacturing, state bonds, and railroad and bank stocks had created new (and greatly underassessed) sources of personal wealth. Uptown landowners, including Beekman, joined in campaigns to equalize taxes on personal and real property, implicitly viewing their own interests as in opposition to those of wealthy downtowners. Lower Manhattan merchants and manufacturers, in turn, had little sympathy for large landowners whose concentrated holdings drove up rents. Some of these downtowners viewed payment for Jones Wood through general tax revenues as "special legislation for the benefit of land speculators."[5] Yet, a number of prominent downtown merchants and bankers who actively supported the new park had no significant uptown landholdings— Robert Minturn and Moses Grinnell, for example. They thought local government should promote the city's cultural as well as its commercial advancement.

New York assemblymen had endorsed the cultural aspirations of the Minturn circle and, at the same time, responded to the concerns raised in the *Journal of Commerce* about equity in financing. Unlike the aldermen's resolution, the Jones Wood bill the legislature passed in July restored benefit assessments in a compromised form: one-half of the park's cost would come from assessments on property in the uptown and northeastern portions of the city, and general taxes would pay for the other half. A *Sun* editorial wondered why the proprietors immediately *adjoining* the park had not been assessed for the full cost. Senator Beekman had succeeded in protecting adjacent landowners' interest by spreading the assessments among all uptown property owners, including West Side and Harlem proprietors who would derive little direct benefit from a park more than two miles from their own land.[6]

The passage of the Jones Wood bill did not stop New Yorkers from proposing alternative sites for a park in letters to their newspapers. One suggested a space stretching across the island from the east to west shores, another an irregular "serpentine" park winding its way north of 39th Street. Jones Wood was "too far down and one sided," a letter to the *Journal* asserted. We want "no *one sided* work either by speculators or officeholders." The exchange of letters in the *Journal of Commerce* between Nicholas Dean and Henry Shaw proposing a more centrally located park had been commissioned and published by the newspaper as part of its editorial campaign to persuade the legislature to "go slow" on the Jones Wood bill. Shaw recommended a hundred blocks between Fifth and Sixth avenues, reaching from 39th Street to the Harlem River; Dean proposed six hundred acres between Fifth and Seventh avenues, from 58th to 106th Street. But both agreed that a "central park" of whatever boundaries would offer economic as well as cultural advantages over the "mere sectional improvement" of Jones Wood. Dean and Shaw linked their proposals for these alternative sites to the building of a new receiving reservoir, to be, they believed, the city's ultimate achievement. Dean, as president of the Croton Aqueduct Board, had decided that the new reservoir should be located on the city-owned land immediately north of the existing reservoir at 79th Street. Like many New Yorkers, he welcomed its embellishment with a landscaped park. The union of the reservoir and park proposals "would cheapen the cost of both." For the same $1.5 million that had been estimated for Jones Wood, the city could have a much more "ample" park, and one that would more fully accommodate the desires of wealthy families to enjoy drives on a "magnificent country road."[7]

The Dean and Shaw proposals for a central park appealed to those merchants who supported the idea of a new public park but who were worried about its costs. Downtown businessmen, however, were not the only New Yorkers to object to the cost of a large uptown park or to question the motives of the advocates. Although they commanded much less attention in the English-language press, working-class New Yorkers and sympathetic middle-class reformers greeted the prospect of any grand uptown park, whatever the location, with only modest enthusiasm. Two of the four aldermen who opposed the common council's Jones Wood resolution represented downtown wards populated by artisans, shopkeepers, and wage-earning tenants.[8] Their constituents probably had more cause than wealthy merchants to worry about the added tax burden from the fifty-thousand-dollar annual appropriation for the park's purchase. Taxes for the amenity of a park might shave large landowners' profits, but they would cut much more sharply into the budgets of householders already struggling to maintain their economic independence.

"Why will the rich keep loading down the shoulders of the poor," asked Hal Guernsey, a physician and land reformer, who, like other public health activists, focused attention on housing conditions. The "real workingmen of the City," who would disproportionately bear the tax burden, Guernsey wrote in letters to the *Journal of Commerce* and the *Tribune*, "would be the least benefited by a *large* Park, because" of "its remoteness from them" and their lack of leisure time. City and state officials ought to apply the same amount of money (and "accomplish ten times the amount of good") to build cheap residences on public land. One of the few newspapers that claimed to speak for working people, the *Dispatch*—aligned with the popular Democratic politician Mike Walsh—did endorse the Jones Wood proposal as a "boon to future generations." But even as the *Dispatch* celebrated the pleasing "sight of grass, flowers and trees with the purer atmosphere they create," it most energetically supported proposals to enlarge the downtown Battery promenade, stressing that "the masses of people demand it." Working-class New Yorkers, Walsh implied, were less interested in the cultural refinement promised by a large landscaped park than in preserving *access* to existing and nearby public spaces. In the mid-1840s Walsh had dramatized his demand for greater spatial equality by announcing that he often climbed the fence to the private St. John's Park (the onetime home of the Minturns) and walked on its exclusive grounds. The common council, he urged, should "open its gates to the honest and industrious portion of the public."[9]

The New York Industrial Congress was more skeptical than Walsh about the Jones Wood park. Organized in 1850 as a forum to address labor issues, the congress represented an uneasy coalition of trade unionists, middle-class land reformers, small employers, and contractors. Now it raised its voice on the issue of the park: "If the City fathers really want to accommodate the people in the selection of parks," a report adopted at one July meeting noted, "they would better accomplish it by purchasing vacant squares in the more thickly populated districts." It pointed out that for half what the large park would cost, the city could create small parks that would "bring to our doors the blessings proposed." Some members directly condemned the Jones Wood plan. "The Park," argued James S. Smith, "was the offspring of the speculating jobbers in human misery of Wall St.," operating "under color of public spirit and improvement." Real estate speculators expected to reap millions "while nine parts of the people who would have to pay for the Park and this rise of property in rents, would but seldom be enabled to reach or see it, from poverty and want of time to spend." Meanwhile, Smith complained, "those who did *not* pay for it, but lived upon the labors of the many . . . would enjoy it."[10]

Most of the city's newspapers ignored the Industrial Congress and although their editorials supporting Jones Wood directly addressed the objections of downtown merchants, the press failed to respond to working-class complaints about the inequities of the Jones Wood plan. The German-language *Staats-Zeitung,* however, printed the deliberations of the Industrial Congress and, throughout the early 1850s, provided the most aggressive and consistent newspaper opposition to the park proposal. In the *Staats-Zeitung*'s view, the new park was "a mad project" that would benefit only "greedy speculators" and "codfish aristocrats" who would drive through the park in "pompous" and "elegantly decorated carriages." It dismissed as "complete humbug" the notion that the new park would improve health: narrow and dirty streets, not the lack of parks, made New York "the most unhealthy city of our continent."[11]

Many working-class New Yorkers greeted the gentlemen's Jones Wood proposal with opposition or indifference. Unlike the laissez-faire merchants represented by the *Journal of Commerce,* most artisans supported government provision of new public services, including schools and public spaces. But Walsh, the Industrial Congress, the *Staats-Zeitung,* and land reformers such as Guernsey wanted these public institutions to ameliorate social and spatial inequalities. Thus, the *Staats-Zeitung* urged "many smaller parks in different parts of the city," which would be "equally useful and accessible to all citizens," instead of a "mammoth park" that would be used only by "the heirs of the Upper Tendoms."[12]

Despite the emergence of alternative proposals for a central site or for small downtown parks, most of the city's newspapers stood firmly behind Jones Wood. In August 1851, however, proposals for three Manhattan parks collided. The legislature had authorized the taking of Jones Wood for a park; suggestions for a central park had been circulating for two months. But it was the third park—the enlargement of the Battery at Manhattan's southern tip—that shifted local political alignments and opened a wedge for reconsidering the entire matter.

New Yorkers who could not afford to leave the city in the summer flocked to the Battery for evening strolls. If uptowners were to get a large public park, they argued, the Battery should be expanded into the harbor.

"No Enlargement, No Park"

For more than twenty-five years, the ten-acre Battery, with shaded walks along the seawall and the Castle Garden pleasure ground and theater, had been a popular and fashionable promenade. In the late 1840s, when construction of new and larger piers threatened to block the scenic harbor view, aldermen proposed expanding the Battery with fourteen acres of landfill to preserve the city's "great ornament." The crowds on the Battery, however, were changing almost as rapidly as the view as wealthy New Yorkers moved uptown. But the Battery remained a favorite resort of working people who wanted an evening stroll or could not afford the time or fare to go to Hoboken's pleasure grounds. Genteel New Yorkers bemoaned its decline as a fashionable promenade, and some downtown gentlemen, who still went there from their offices during the day, supported its enlargement in order to provide more elbow room between themselves and the crowds of "loafers," as one letter writer to the *Courier and Enquirer* put it.[13]

Popular support for the expansion confronted the opposition of merchants convinced that the landfill would threaten harbor channels and safe dockage.

The northward migration of population (and particularly of "respectable" households), they insisted, eliminated the need to expand or improve downtown public spaces. Valuable shoreline property should be used instead for railroad tracks, wharves, or warehouses.[14]

The day after the city aldermen endorsed the Jones Wood park on the East River—and perhaps not coincidentally—they also unanimously approved enlargement of the Battery. Merchants lobbied the mayor to veto the Battery resolution, and throughout the summer of 1851, virtually every newspaper editorial that supported Jones Wood opposed expansion of the Battery. The two exceptions were papers with certain working-class sympathies. Mike Walsh's *Dispatch* and Horace Greeley's *Tribune* advocated both expanding the Battery and taking Jones Wood for a public park. "Residents in the lower wards in favor of the enlargement," the *Tribune* reported, "say that, with the new park uptown, it is not much to ask that so very cheap and beautiful addition [be made] to the public grounds in their section of the city." Three days later the *Dispatch* more roundly denounced "speculating dollar and rent merchants" who wanted "to get hold of the Battery, and erect their warehouses on that sacred spot." The editor, who visited the promenade on an August Sunday, found it "excessively crowded" with five thousand people, "the 'bone and sinew' of our city." Wealthy families were moving uptown or out of town, the *Dispatch* observed, "but when . . . [the] lower part of the city is surrendered to the laboring classes, there will be still greater necessity" for the Battery improvement.[15]

On August 5, Mayor Kingsland responded to the merchants' opposition and vetoed the aldermen's Battery enlargement resolution, whereupon the Battery's supporters retaliated by forming a coalition with those aldermen who opposed (for fiscal reasons) any large public park and those, like Henry Shaw, who were beginning to favor a central site. The coalition of aldermen halted action on Jones Wood by forming the Special Committee on Parks to consider "whether there be not a better locality for such a park" that might also include the new reservoir. In effect, the Battery's supporters took the Jones Wood bill hostage to win their own demands for the improvement of the downtown park. "'No enlargement, no park,' is their war cry," the *Staats-Zeitung* explained. The strategy worked. On September 10, 1851, the corporation counsel, Henry Davies, found a technical reason to declare the Battery veto unconstitutional. That same evening, with the Battery's advocates satisfied, the aldermen (with Jones Wood opponents still dissenting) directed the corporation counsel to petition the court to appoint commissioners of estimate to take the Jones Wood land through eminent domain. The aldermen's special committee, according to the *Post*, continued unabated "examining and comparing the relative merits" of various park sites.[16]

Although the common council had now moved ahead, the battle of the Jones Wood site had only begun. In the fall of 1851, having refused offers to purchase their estate from both private developers and city officials, and faced with losing their land to eminent domain, the owners of Jones Wood, the Jones and Schermerhorn families, went to court. Both families had downtown residences, but they were attached to their country estates and had fought earlier public improvements in the vicinity, including the opening of Second Avenue. On December 1, a district supreme court judge for New York County declared the Jones Wood law unconstitutional because its last section gave the common council the power to accept or reject the commissioners' awards "while at the same time there is no such privilege granted to the owner."[17] Nervous about the proposed novel city intervention in the private land market and about how much the city should be spending on such an amenity, the drafters of the Jones Wood bill had inserted an "escape clause" that would have allowed the city to back out of the deal. But since the owners would be given no such option, this clause was held to violate the principle of due process.

"Grounds . . . Useless for Building Purposes"

With the proposal for Jones Wood temporarily blocked by the courts, in January 1852 the Special Committee on Parks recommended creating a central park on a site similar to that proposed by Nicholas Dean: between Fifth and Eighth avenues, from 59th to 106th Street. The authors of the report, Daniel Dodge, a Democrat from a downtown ward filled with leading mercantile houses, and Joseph Britton, a Whig from the city's wealthiest residential ward, emphasized the economic advantages of the central site—a clear response to taxpayer opposition that had emerged in the preceding seven months. Although the central site was five times the size of Jones Wood, its irregular topography— "numerous abrupt and rocky elevations, intersected constantly by ravines and gentle valleys"—would reduce its per-acre purchase price. "Central Park will include grounds almost entirely useless for building purposes, owing to the very uneven and rocky surface, and also to its lying so far below the proper grade of the streets as to render the grading very costly." Not only would taking the land for a park save the enormous expense of opening streets through the area, the land's very undesirability for private development made it relatively cheap.[18]

If the central site's rugged terrain was the key determinant of its cost, the committee also pointed out that the municipal corporation already owned 135 acres of common land in the area and would not need to purchase land allocated for the reservoir. The extent and centrality of Central Park, as Dodge and Britton had now named it, meant there was more fronting property to be assessed. Attributing an unusual magnanimity to uptown landowners, the report optimistically suggested that in exchange for the benefit of a park in their neighborhood, "the owners of property would probably come forward themselves and cheerfully subscribe a large portion of the purchase money and not feel it." The committee's dollar-and-cents calculations—displayed in elaborate (though somewhat questionable) tables—sought to win over the fiscally conservative merchants who had objected to the costs of the new park. But Dodge and Britton also appealed to the vision of cultural ascendancy that had first mobilized Robert Minturn and his friends. *"Central Park,"* they boasted, "would probably be one of the largest parks in the world, but not too large for the use of a city destined, in all human probability, to equal, and perhaps to exceed in population every other." The central site—unlike the "limited" Jones Wood— would accommodate "the most beautiful feature of a large park," a "very great length of serpentine road" offering a "very long drive through constantly varying scenery."[19]

To convince readers that land previously described as worthless rock and swamp was capable of greater "improvement and adornment" than the already landscaped Jones Wood, Dodge and Britton shrewdly suggested how the completed Central Park would look from a carriage: the "most beautiful and varied roads" would transcend existing ravines, pass artificial lakes retrieved from swamps, beautiful groves in the place of stumps of trees cut for firewood, and "velvet lawns decorated with sparkling fountains," extending across fields once covered with hogpens and vegetable gardens. Their fanciful trip over hill and dale culminated with a magnificent ascent to "the highest land on the island south of Fort Washington . . . from which a magnificent view is presented to the beholder in every direction." Neglecting to mention the cost of transforming this landscape, the committee concluded that Central Park could be possessed "at a comparatively trifling expense" and would "compare favorably with the most celebrated grounds of Europe." Only the latter prediction proved true.[20]

By the winter of 1851–1852, Jones Wood supporters confronted not only the court decision striking down the 1851 authorization bill and the Dodge-Britton report recommending the central site but also the persistent opposition of the Jones Wood landowners, fiscally conservative merchants, and members of the common council. Newspaper editorials and petition campaigns focused on the need for a landscaped park and on which park best satisfied that need, while, behind the scenes, circles of New Yorkers with specific interests in the park's location and financing moved to control the legislative process. In that process, Central Park proponents were to build a growing—and ultimately successful— coalition during the spring and summer of 1853.

The supporters of Central Park were slow to mobilize, however. Meanwhile the advocates of the Jones Wood park tried compromises to salvage their own project. The Schermerhorns suggested shifting the park's boundary north to 68th Street, a move that would protect their lands. But one landowner, James Crumbie, who was lobbying for Jones Wood, objected that Schermerhorn land between 66th and 68th streets was the "most desirable" in the entire plot. Crumbie wanted *his* land, which fronted East 66th Street, to be directly across from the new park. The 66th Street border, he reminded neighboring landowner Beekman, "is [in] your individual interest as well as ours to maintain."

The proposal for a more northerly boundary also disturbed the Schermerhorns' own Jones cousins, since the site would still encompass the Jones family compound.[21]

Whig state senator Edwin Morgan, who had introduced the Jones Wood bill in February 1852, began to waver in the face of these and other problems. A politically ambitious merchant and railroad president, he could not afford to offend too many voters or too many powerful interests. By April 1 he was spelling out his growing reservations to Robert Minturn, a fellow Whig and a fellow director of the Bank of Commerce. "If it should be thought best to make an effort for *Jones Wood* and the southern boundary is fixed at 66th street, the family of Peter Schermerhorn will oppose it. . . . If 68th street, the Schermerhorn family will not but General Jones *will* oppose it strongly. Another difficulty will arise in the manner of the assessment. The park being on one side, the city at large can hardly bear more than half of the tax and not contentedly so much." "I am quite desirous of carrying into effect the wishes of our citizens, especially the taxpaying portion." But the common council had also withdrawn its support from the Jones Wood park, and Morgan had begun to look more favorably on Dodge and Britton's Central Park. Morgan's shift blocked the new Jones Wood bill (revised to meet the constitutional objections), and it died along with the state legislative session in mid-April 1852. In letting the bill expire, Albany lawmakers tacitly acknowledged city politicians' opposition to Jones Wood. The Democrats had swept the city elections in the fall of 1851, and the new Democratic-controlled common council had overwhelmingly endorsed resolutions asking the state legislature to suspend action on Jones Wood until the aldermen determined "whether a city park should be in the centre or on one side of the island."[22]

More than a year later, Jones Wood advocate James Hogg declared that legislative inaction in 1852 had stemmed in part from the "desire of some speculative members of Common Council to get the Central Park." Senator Morgan, Aldermen Ashabel Denman and Joseph Britton, and Assistant Alderman Daniel Tiemann were "considerably interested in Central Park property," said Hogg. The *Times* also charged "shameless speculation" in and around the central site.[23]

The evidence of public officials' land speculation is ambiguous, however. Morgan (who himself complained about the "speculation that will take place") owned no property either within or near the proposed central site; Denman and Tiemann *did* own property in upper Manhattan and probably favored uptown development, but they had not recently speculated in land. Britton, coauthor of the aldermen's report recommending Central Park, had a more tangible, albeit modest, stake in the central site: between 1851 and 1852 he made a quick $4,800 in buying and selling ten lots at 82nd and Fifth Avenue. Assistant Alderman S. Benson McGown, whose family owned about forty-five acres of land between 97th and 106th streets, immediately east of the central site, was no speculator: the land had been in his family since the early eighteenth century. Nevertheless, he stood to benefit greatly from Central Park.[24]

Some aldermen might have benefited not from landownership as such but from bribes paid by others with a financial interest in the park plans. Such graft was what Timothy Churchill had in mind in 1853 when he charged that "the Central Park has a large body of interested supporters and they are better organized and have the present common council with them who have been laying pipe for the last year." Churchill's phrase "laying pipe" resonated quite sharply in the 1850s as a term for patronage and corruption associated with the construction of the Croton aqueduct. Nor would it be unreasonable to suspect that bribes influenced a body that came to be known as "the Forty Thieves" after some of its members were indicted by a grand jury for their corrupt streetcar dealings. Although the evidence of aldermen's self-interest is not conclusive, the political shift is: New York City Democratic aldermen, who had not previously opposed the Jones Wood park, in 1852 became its explicit adversaries and thus Central Park's implicit supporters. The strategy of the Whig gentlemen who had originally suggested a park was in disarray.[25]

No bill authorizing a central park had yet been introduced in the legislature, but in the spring and early summer of 1853 a group of leading Upper West Side landowners endorsed the central site. A signer of one petition, the landowner and Whig lawyer Gerrit H. Striker, persuaded the board of aldermen to pass its first resolution endorsing the central site in June 1853. Striker also apparently drafted the Central Park bill, which Morgan introduced in the state senate on June 21, 1853. West Side landowners, ironically, were following the development strategy East Siders had pursued in advocating Jones Wood. A park, they believed, would raise and stabilize property values and help establish their neighborhood as an elite residential enclave. As early as 1850, an unnamed "private party," according to a *Tribune* story, had contemplated creating a fifty-acre private residential park in the vicinity of the central site "upon the plan of the Regent's Park in London, with road and pathways, ponds, shrubbery, etc." The failure of this private park scheme (and the similarly unsuccessful East Side villa plan) surely helped persuade many large West Side landowners that government intervention was necessary for the coordinated, profitable, and "respectable" development of their neighborhood.[26]

Much of the land on the central site—particularly the western portion of it—was occupied by poor Irish, German, and black families, who raised vegetables and tended hogs. Large West Side landowners undoubtedly shared the concern of their uptown assistant alderman (and future mayor) Daniel Tiemann, who warned that unless this land were used for a park it would soon "be covered with a class of population similar to that of Five Points," the city's poorest Irish and black neighborhood, four blocks north of City Hall. A few years later, the *Sun* echoed, albeit from a more critical vantage point, Tiemann's suggestion that Central Park would act as "a breakwater to the upward tide of population," raising uptown land prices and rents and forcing "persons of limited means" to seek homes elsewhere. Indeed, one version of the park's origin suggests that John A. Kennedy (later police commissioner), in proposing the central site to an alderman, noted that it "was covered with shanties and filled with the most degraded of our population."[27]

The central site now won support from Whig bankers and international shippers who had formerly backed the Jones Wood park and from fiscally conservative and laissez-faire Democratic merchants, who had strenuously objected to the costs and the method of payment. More than half the signers of one pro–Central Park petition were downtown merchants, and the rest were brokers, bankers, or lawyers, some of them—merchant William DeForest, landowner William Astor, and bankers Shepherd Knapp and George Newbold—initial supporters of the Jones Wood park. Although we don't know whether Minturn himself responded favorably to Senator Morgan's suggestion that he consider the alternative site, many of his closest friends did switch over by 1853. At the same time, some of the more fiscally conservative merchants apparently followed the *Journal of Commerce*'s lead in moving from adamant opposition to Jones Wood to grudging acceptance of Central Park. "If either must be forced upon us," the *Journal* editorialized in early July 1853, "the city will greatly prefer the central position." (*Journal* readers also responded to arguments that the Jones Wood "*river front* will soon be needed for commercial purposes," as one petition put it.)[28]

The petitioning merchants emphasized that since the city already owned "the greater part of these grounds" (a misrepresentation, as it happens) and the land was poorly adapted for private development, Central Park would cost less per acre than Jones Wood. Lest anyone miss this point, carefully added to the bottom of this printed petition was a handwritten proviso indicating that the signers' support was contingent on the park costing no more than $1.5 million. Yet, if costs quite literally became the bottom line for the city's merchants, they also invoked the original arguments for a park. Noting the site's great "extent," one bankers and merchants' petition argued that Central Park "would constitute one of the largest . . . parks in the world; and one which alone would be worthy of the future greatness of this city." And in more than one petition, merchants and landowners projected the pleasures of driving their families and out-of-town clients and friends through a park "sufficiently extensive to afford ample room for riding and driving therein with Horses and Carriages."[29]

A final factor in the growing elite backing for the central site was the support mobilized by that particularly important family of downtown merchants, the Schermerhorns. The owners of part of Jones Wood had become increasingly rigid in their opposition to the Jones Wood proposal, possibly because of the death of the family patriarch, Peter Schermerhorn. (Diarist George Templeton Strong commented that a "chronic disease—enlargement of the bank account . . . shattered his nervous system.") Thirty-one-year-old William C.

Schermerhorn reasserted the family's belief that government existed only to protect private property—or at least "the undisturbed enjoyment" of *their* property. "We shall be found as firm as our Father was before us," he told Beekman, "in opposing a measure which we look upon as a persecution." They were apparently less concerned with the rights of owners of the Central Park land. James H. Banker, son of the Schermerhorns' former business partner, headed the list of merchants signing a May 1853 pro–Central Park petition, and virtually all the signers worked in the area along South and Wall streets where the Schermerhorns had long operated.[30]

The central site (in part because of its very size and location) was now building a much more diverse alliance of supporters than had Jones Wood: West Side landowners attempting to "gentrify" their district, gentlemen seeking to symbolize the city's (and their own) greatness, downtown merchants seeking a cost-effective solution to the "public" demand for park space, New York City Democrats opposed to a scheme that originated largely in Whig circles, supporters of the Croton reservoir who wanted to combine the two projects, and members of the Schermerhorn and Jones families eager to protect their own land.

The emerging coalition alarmed James Beekman and his allies; and when the state legislature reconvened for its 1853 session, the Jones Wood advocates resorted to devious tactics. In contrast to the two preceding years, for example, they introduced their bill in the assembly. It seemed a peculiar strategy, for the Democrats (who had opposed Jones Wood in the 1852 common council) now controlled the lower house. But at a late-night session and in the midst of a debate on a different matter, Democratic assemblyman Moses Gale, apparently a recipient of a nice patronage plum from Beekman's allies, slipped through the Jones Wood bill. Many New York City assemblymen may have been unaware of what they were voting for—or so the *Journal of Commerce* later charged—and the Jones Wood forces were not eager to advertise their ploy. Court testimony subsequently revealed that they persuaded (or perhaps bribed) the clerk who reported the assembly's proceedings to omit mention of the bill's passage from his telegraphic reports to New York City newspapers. The fancy maneuvers continued in the upper chamber. The senate had referred the bill to a select committee composed of the four New York City senators, who were evenly divided on the park question, but Beekman managed (again thanks to late-night confusion) to get the bill referred to a special three-man committee chaired by him and including at least one other firm Jones Wood supporter. Beekman's committee heard testimony from a series of horticultural experts who, with one exception, endorsed the Jones Wood site.[31]

But Democratic senator James Cooley ignored the expert testimony when he issued his minority report and introduced yet another argument on behalf of Central Park. Cooley's objections to Jones Wood focused on the danger of "disorder and anarchy" in a waterfront park accessible by ferries to working-class and immigrant crowds. Nativist New Yorkers well remembered an 1851 riot that had marred a German social club outing to Hoboken's Elysian Fields. Cooley invoked these "scenes of disorder of Hoboken" to capitalize on their fears. One wealthy landowner, Thomas Suffern, echoed Cooley, warning Beekman that "depravity, licentiousness and confusion" would ruin any East River park. "No, No, beware of proximity to either shore."[32]

The Jones Wood advocates continued their heavy-handed lobbying. James Hogg (whose family owned an Upper East Side nursery near Jones Wood and who doubtless anticipated business from the new park) concentrated on maintaining press support. On a single day in late June, he bent the ears of editors of six different New York newspapers.[33]

Clearly, local newspapers were crucial to the park debate. In the absence of public opinion polls, the press could claim to represent the undefined "public." The newspapers organized petition drives that may have netted as many as twenty thousand signatures on behalf of one or the other of the two sites. (Partisans on each side further demonstrated their ardor by apparently forging at least 10 percent of the names.)[34]

"A stranger to our city would be led to suppose," observed the *Journal of Commerce* on July 7, 1853, "that a strong feeling was manifested here in favor of Parks," but "the zeal exhibited is chiefly the offspring of selfish interest and embraces but a small portion of our citizens." The *Journal*'s general skepticism about the potential cost to taxpayers obviously colored its analysis, but the ardently propark *Tribune* made a similar point about the narrow basis of *active* support. Attributing the park momentum to "a mere handful of liberal, farseeing men—of philanthropists and artists," Horace Greeley's *Tribune* lamented that they had operated "without any aid from the masses for whom they have labored." "Will not mechanics and laborers move on this matter?" it asked, implying that workers ought to reciprocate Greeley's support for labor reform.[35]

But the political system offered few ways for "mechanics and laborers"—or most professionals and shopkeepers, for that matter—to affect the decision-making process. New York City voters (not to speak of the majority of the adult population—women, most black and some immigrant men—who could not vote) had limited access to the politics of park making. At least some German New Yorkers opposed either park, but they were only just emerging as a political bloc. Lawmakers ignored the *Sun*'s editorial suggestion that the park question be resolved through a referendum. Even New Yorkers who wanted a large public park knew relatively little about the comparative merits of the two sites, both of which were quite far from the city's population center. The *Commercial Advertiser* may have spoken for many in the summer of 1853 when it threw up its hands at the debate and declared simply "Give us a park, be it central, or sidelong, here, there, anywhere, . . . a real park, a large park."[36]

The Showdown

Senator Beekman, aware that an increasingly powerful alignment of interests backed Central Park, knew that his own bill would have trouble passing the
senate. Thus he proposed a compromise amendment to the assembly bill.
Under it, the common council would appoint a commission to choose either or
both sites for a park. Beekman's collaborator James Hogg understood the
compromise as just another political gambit, "eminently wise as it has given us a
character for disinterestedness and fairness which the opposition cannot get
over." Hogg had no intention of carrying out the compromise and urged
Beekman to "throw the amendment over if possible." If not, he was confident
they could defeat the central site by stacking the commission or by crying " 'mad
dog' at the Central Park, extravagant cost and all that sort of thing."[37]

Beekman introduced his amended version of the Jones Wood bill to the
senate on June 21, 1853, the same day Morgan presented the Central Park bill
for consideration. The choice would hinge on the strength of the political
coalition that both sides had been able to build and on the astuteness of their
sponsors. Beekman and his allies had already proven themselves shrewd operators by finessing—temporarily at least—the troublesome assessment question.
In contrast to the first Jones Wood Act, the 1853 bill would finance the park out
of general tax revenues and impose *no* assessments at all, just as Beekman's
landowning friends in the antiassessment movement had wanted all along.
Beekman managed to make this crucial change without arousing his opponents'
notice. Central Park advocates, too, finessed the assessment problem. Morgan's
Central Park bill required assessments on property adjoining the park, but the
amounts and method of assessment were left up to the commissioners who
would value and take the land. With the issue of financing swept under the rug,
the Central Park proposal won overwhelming approval from both legislative
houses. Immediately afterward Jones Wood came up for consideration and
failed to win a majority of votes in the senate. With the legislature about to
adjourn in July 1853, the Jones Wood park seemed dead and Central Park
victorious.[38]

But then the battle of the parks took another curious turn. The senate
version of the Central Park bill had a technical flaw in its drafting and therefore
had to be reamended and repassed by both branches of the legislature after the
dinner break. When the senate once again approved Central Park, Beekman
promptly moved for reconsideration of the Jones Wood bill. The ensuing debate
was far from courteous. It was, after all, the end of a long day and a long
legislative session. Senator Cooley denounced Jones Wood as an "outrage" and,
in a pointed reference to Beekman and his friends, claimed that it was "urged
from interested motives." His charges backfired, and evading the specific
allegations, Beekman urged a pro–Jones Wood vote as a vindication of his honor
as a gentleman. He later recalled that a "personal attack on me on that occasion,

secured by its violence" passage of the bill. After three years of debate and maneuvering, the legislature had now authorized *two* large public parks in New York City.[39]

Most legislators assumed that they had passed Beekman's amended bill, which left it up to the common council through an appointed commission to decide whether to create the Jones Wood park. Indeed, newspapers reported the following day that lawmakers left it "optional with the city . . . to take action on" Jones Wood. But when the bill had briefly returned to his select committee, Beekman had covertly revised it. The law passed by the legislature *required* the city to apply for appointment of commissioners to take the Jones Wood land for a park. The gentleman Whig James Beekman had outfoxed his opponents. The Schermerhorns' only recourse was to go to court, as they had done in 1851, to overturn the Jones Wood legislation.[40]

When the case came up before the district supreme court judge James I. Roosevelt, a Democrat, in December 1853, most of the courtroom debate centered on the absence of any provisions for assessments on neighboring property owners. The financial issue that had opened the way to the Central Park alternative finally closed the gate on Jones Wood. Judge Roosevelt suspended any action on the law until the new state and city legislatures had the opportunity to "remove its objectionable and perhaps unconstitutional features," particularly Beekman's plan to have the park financed entirely through general taxation. The Jones Wood legislation, Roosevelt wrote in his decision of January 9, 1854, "is a private act, its effect is to transfer by local taxation the property of one portion of a limited community to another." Using an initial that most people involved in the park battle would readily recognize as referring to Beekman, Roosevelt declared that the bill "provides a garden for B's lot in the Nineteenth Ward, quadrupling its value, and takes A's garden in the Fifth Ward to pay for it." With these words, he confirmed that Central Park alone would become New York's public garden.[41]

The judge's opinion outraged Beekman and his friends. Timothy Churchill, for example, had previously "entertained a very high opinion of Judge Roosevelt"; he knew him "to be wealthy and supposed him to be an upright honest and honorable man," but this decision was an "electioneering circular" that made the judge "unworthy of his high position." Politics maybe, but loyalty to party was breaking down in the collapse of the second party system in these years before the Civil War. Roosevelt (the great-uncle of the future Republican president) was a prominent Democrat, but his decision, in effect, endorsed the Central Park Act, which had won the support not only of the Democratic-dominated common council but also of such prominent Whigs as Edwin Morgan, who would go on to become the state's second Republican governor.[42] Further, Beekman's move—whether out of greed or principle—to abandon benefit assessments had offended powerful taxpayers and editors who remained ambivalent about the costs of this new kind of public improvement. The advocates of Central Park acknowledged this ambivalence even as they built support for a far grander public park. In the final outcome, the political and judicial system ultimately gave wealthy New Yorkers the sort of park they wanted: a location that benefited the largest number of property holders, a size that advertised the city's greatness and accommodated elegant carriage drives, and a compromise in the mode of financing (both general taxes and benefit assessments) that satisfied the merchants and landowners. Central Park had proven itself "central" in politics and economics as well as in geography.

The "One Creditable Act" of Fernando Wood

Just as the Jones Wood park was finally being laid to rest, Central Park faced some new problems of its own. In 1853 a reform movement led by the city's wealthiest men had begun to decry excessive government spending, in part in reaction to skyrocketing taxes, which had jumped 54 percent in just the past three years. Grand jury revelations of widespread corruption on the common council heightened such concerns. Reformers mobilized and ran the Democratic incumbents out of office, electing in their place a combination of Whigs and reform Democrats committed to "economy" in government. Meanwhile, by January 1854 the city's economy had started on a downward slide that would end in the Panic of 1857.[43]

In this climate of fiscal retrenchment, Mayor Jacob Westervelt, a reform Democrat and shipbuilder, proposed to reduce the size of Central Park. The newly established board of councilmen (which a reform charter substituted for the old board of assistant aldermen as the lower chamber of the common council) initiated hearings on the proposal. Westervelt, who had supported the Central Park bill, had second thoughts about the dramatic expansion of state power and especially the public spending entailed by the new park. But some predictable voices defended the Central Park boundaries. Jacob Harsen, descendant of one of the West Side's most prominent landholding families, cited the value of the park as a place for the affluent to drive their carriages and as "one of the greatest devices of attracting wealth to the city of New York." Harsen had one concern: assessments to be levied on neighboring property owners like himself. But in the spirit of the day, he offered a cost-cutting solution: use "gangs of convicts from Blackwell's Island, and paupers from the station houses" to construct the park.[44]

Certain other uptown landowners had misgivings, too, depending on whether their land fronted the park or was included within its borders. Several property owners in the lower portion of the park (mostly land speculators, it seems) spoke out for pushing its southern boundary up to 72nd Street, worried that the downturn in the real estate market would lower the price the city would pay for their land. Those owning land within the park did not stand to benefit in the same way as those like Harsen whose property fronted it and who would reap its benefits through development when the real estate market improved.[45]

The pro-working-class *Dispatch,* which six months earlier had advocated both park sites, now expressed anxiety about the cost to those "on whom the burden of all taxation falls," charging that "the secret operation of speculators," not "the working masses," had determined the outcome of the park debate. Others, Robert Hartley, executive secretary of the Association for Improving the Condition of the Poor, for example, feared that the new park would exacerbate the city's housing problems. Removing such a large tract from the real estate market would further "diminish the channels for public health" by increasing rents and hence crowding. Even the "gentleman from Europe," Hartley claimed, now had come to oppose the park.[46]

Seven months earlier, Hartley's fellow health reformer Dr. John H. Griscom had gone even further and echoed the *Staats-Zeitung*'s largely ignored alternative to a large uptown park, a number of small downtown parks. If lawmakers "compel us to reserve so large a portion of our restricted area from more useful purposes," Griscom wrote, "we beg them to give it in *divided doses,* and instead of one plot of 800 acres, whose healthful influence cannot possibly be proportionate to its size, give eight parks of 100 acres each, or sixteen of 50 acres, and *disperse* them over the island. . . . This would certainly be less aristocratic; more democratic, and far more conducive to the public health." But neither public health nor the living conditions of the working class had ever been at the heart of the park movement.[47]

The majority and the minority reports to the common council rejected these proposals to abandon Central Park, but they did recommend that the council ask the legislature to diminish its size substantially (differing only in whether to chop off the land below 72nd Street or four hundred feet along each side). The majority report—perhaps reflecting the common council's greater responsiveness to ordinary citizens—accepted much of the logic of Griscom's critique. It declared, for example, that a grand-scale park with carriage drives to "display dazzling equipages to the admiration and awe of the outside multitudes" violated "the very spirit of our institutions . . . [by] ministering to the indulgence or vanity of the few at the cost of the many." Calculating the size of Central Park as equivalent to seventy-four Tompkins Squares, it insisted that "squares such as we now have, are in every respect, more convenient and ornamental, and much preferred by all classes." Urging the claim of "equal and exact justice," it advanced a broader definition of the public than had previously prevailed in the park debate: "The wealthy, as a class . . . have facilities for pleasure, and . . . have no particular claim on the public for such, at the public's expense."[48]

In part because of the differing reduction proposals in the common council, city lawmakers remained stalemated for the rest of the year. Then, in the winter of 1854–1855, the New York economy slipped further. More than fifteen thousand people were out of work; rich merchants set up soup kitchens to feed twelve thousand people per day; and unemployed workers held almost daily demonstrations in City Hall Park to demand jobs. More New Yorkers wondered whether a large park was a good idea.[49]

In March 1855 the board of councilmen resumed hearings on a cutback, and in the chilly economic climate of the winter of 1855, the board of aldermen voted fourteen to three to cut both the lower twelve blocks (from 59th to 72nd streets) *and* four hundred feet from each side. But on March 23, the new Democratic mayor, Fernando Wood, saved Central Park by vetoing the measure.[50]

Wood, member of a Philadelphia Quaker family, had started his business career as a grocer, liquor dealer, and stevedore's paymaster. He had been elected to Congress at twenty-eight. By 1847 he owned eight ships and extensive real estate. Described by one contemporary as a "brilliant desperado," he quickly became a controversial figure, charged with business dishonesty as well as political demagoguery. Wood often invoked the militant rhetoric of the workingmen's movement to advance his policies, and during the Civil War, he would lead the rabidly racist secessionist movement in New York City. Most historians cite saving Central Park as his only "heroic" act. "Mr. Wood's public record is every way so unhandsome," wrote art critic Clarence Cook in a typical account, "that we are glad to be able to give him credit for at least one creditable act."[51]

But Wood was no more a disinterested spokesperson for an abstract "public" than Minturn, Beekman, Shaw, Hogg, Crumbie, Striker, Schermerhorn, Harsen, and many others who figured prominently in the story of park making. He was, in fact, a major West Side landowner, whose property was likely to benefit greatly from the building of Central Park. Part of his considerable wealth had come from shrewd dealings in upper Manhattan real estate. No less an authority than Boss Tweed once commented: "I never yet went to get a corner lot that I didn't find Wood had got in ahead of me." Tweed was right to be envious: lots fronting Central Park that Wood bought for a few hundred dollars would be worth ten thousand dollars each by 1860.[52]

Still, Wood was already a wealthy man, and as mayor, he had plenty of other opportunities to fatten his bank balance. Political considerations probably figured at least as strongly as economic gain in his veto of the bill to cut Central Park. Fashioning himself as a reformer and leader in New York's rise to greatness, he won the support of gentlemen such as Robert Minturn, William Astor, and William Aspinwall in the mayoral election of 1854, and he needed to keep this elite support if he was to turn back a move in Albany to pass a police reorganization bill that would, in his view, threaten the city's autonomy and his personal channels of patronage. Wood also needed the votes of the working classes, particularly the immigrant communities, to stay in power locally. Thus, he was in the vanguard of Democratic efforts to organize and mobilize immigrant voters. Many immigrant working-class New Yorkers may have shared the

Fernando Wood (1812–1881)—one of New York's most controversial mayors—blocked the effort to reduce the size of Central Park, claiming that it represented the city's "destiny now opening so brilliantly before us."

Staats-Zeitung's preference for small, downtown parks, but they also had a stake in the "mammoth park" project as a source of jobs during a recession. Building the park, it was becoming clear, would employ thousands of unskilled (and politically active) Irish workers. And just two months earlier, a mass meeting of German workingmen had pressed for an immediate start to the building of the reservoir within Central Park to "furnish employment to those who do not covet the degradation of beggary." Wood invoked the benefits of the park as a public works project in his message vetoing the reduction plan. If it were not for all the delays, he noted, "many hundred workmen and laborers would now be employed toward its completion."[53]

Like Robert Minturn and other gentlemen merchants, Wood did not perceive any conflict between the public interest and his self-interest. A park that symbolized New York's rise to greatness would benefit the "public" and his own substantial, almost imperial political ambitions. Like Minturn, Wood had been in Europe in 1849, where, as he later told an acquaintance, he had seen "the importance of such breathing spots to the people of a great city." He returned home determined "to bring about a park above 59th Street." Although the recession may have given Robert Minturn second thoughts about the park, Wood, the *other* "gentleman from Europe" buoyantly proclaimed that New York contained the "inherent seeds . . . of a growth far beyond the comprehension of the visionary enthusiast." "To assert that this [park] will be too large, is," he declared in his veto, "entirely unworthy of even the present position of this metropolis, to say nothing of a destiny now opening so brilliantly before us."[54]

Wood's defense of this "intelligent, philanthropic and patriotic public enterprise," as he called it, embodied the contradictions of the entire battle over the park. As New Yorkers persuaded themselves to expend a substantial portion of their relatively meager municipal resources on something that they had never had before—a large public park—they talked repeatedly of its benefits to the abstract "public." Yet the actual political struggle to establish it was fought out among much narrower groups of New Yorkers: gentlemen merchants and newspaper editors advocating metropolitan greatness, cultural uplift, and rural taste; large landholders eager to develop respectable uptown neighborhoods; conservative downtown taxpayers worried about the costs of such a vast public enterprise. Middling and working-class New Yorkers had at times entered the fray—some welcoming the vision of a public park, others wondering whether alternative arrangements might not be more beneficial and democratic—but their opinions were seldom acknowledged in the public debate.

In the end, it was primarily wealthy New Yorkers—motivated by a combination of private greed, class interest, and a sense of duty as the city's "leading citizens"—who carried the day. Gentlemen and gentlewomen had "invented" Central Park as a new kind of public institution, a space permanently removed from the private real estate market. The gentlemen who saw the project through to law challenged the laissez-faire principles championed by the *Journal of Commerce* and, in place of William Schermerhorn's conviction that the state existed only to protect private property, offered an expanded vision of positive government action. The gentlemen who proposed the park now, of course, expected to control it. But precisely because the park was to be public, its creation offered New Yorkers the possibility of a broader, more democratic conception of government's responsibilities to its citizens. As New Yorkers socialized private land for a park, they entered into new kinds of negotiations over the meaning of the "public good."

3
PRIVATE TO PUBLIC PROPERTY

In the midst of the battle over the park site, Senator James Beekman scribbled a few notes for his ally James Hogg. "The great objection to be overcome," he wrote, "is this: A park is not of sufficient public necessity to justify its being taken by the State in opposition to the wish of the owners by the violent exercise of eminent domain." For all his zealous advocacy of the Jones Wood park, Beekman, himself a major landowner, was deeply troubled by coercive state intervention in the private land market. "Cemeteries," he noted with an eye to an institution that contemporaries saw as similar to parks, "are never taken by this method—always by voluntary sale."[1]

But the state was not confiscating anyone's property; it was taking it through a judicial procedure and only after payment of suitable compensation. The assessment of surrounding lots for a portion of the park's cost, which Beekman opposed with even greater vehemence, was also to be safeguarded by principles of due process. Still, such massive state intervention in the private land market was highly unusual though not unprecedented (building the Croton aqueduct, for example, had required powers of eminent domain). The 778-acre Central Park (expanded to 843 acres in 1863) would be almost five times as large as all the existing parks and squares in the city combined. And the use of eminent domain for a large public park *was* unprecedented; it marked a gradual redefinition of the relationship between the state and the private economy. State action would dramatically reshape the uptown Manhattan landscape and draw new lines of land use and land value.

Beekman and his allies had advocated a Jones Wood park precisely because they hoped it would create new value—and increase the worth of their own landholdings. But Beekman realized that a state that could create value could also diminish it. He simultaneously, and contradictorily, believed that the government should build a park to promote uptown real estate development *and* that the state should protect the rights of private property. Decisions on costs and benefits would, of course, determine whether a particular individual would view the process as beneficence or violence. If public authorities were to intervene in the private land market, whom would they benefit? How would the city balance the competing interests of landowners and taxpayers, of proprietors whose land would be taken, landowners whose property would benefit, and people who would have to pay for the project?

The group with the greatest reason for seeing the creation of Central Park as a violent act—the sixteen hundred or so people who lived on the land and would lose their homes—had not figured in the considerations of public officials. The only ones who had entered into discussions of the park scheme at all were those who owned the land. Prior-use claims did not loom as large as ownership rights in mid-nineteenth-century New York, and those who dwelled on the park site, mostly poor immigrants and African Americans, had no power to make or influence policy decisions.

Yet despite their lack of power or public voice, "park dwellers," by their possession and use of the land, joined taxpayers, absentee owners of park land, and owners of nearby land as key actors in the next scene of the drama. In the fall of 1853, New York City still did not have a grand landscaped park—only a law authorizing one. Before the rocks and swamps covering the two and a half miles between 59th and 106th streets could be transformed into a scenic "natural" park, New York City would need to take the land, finance that acquisition, and remove the people who lived there. In the process, the physical and social landscape of upper Manhattan would be permanently reshaped.

The Eighth Largest City in the Nation

The city above 40th Street comprised the Twelfth, Nineteenth, and Twenty-second wards, widely called the "rural districts." The appellation was unjustified. Although fewer people lived uptown than downtown, the land could hardly be called rural. In 1855 almost sixty thousand people lived in the three outer wards; by 1860 those wards, if a city, would have ranked as the eighth largest in the United States. This "city" was really a series of relatively discrete and autonomous settlements: Harsenville (in the west 60s and 70s), Strikers Bay (in the west 90s), Bloomingdale (in the west 100s, but also a general term for the Upper West Side), Yorkville (on the East Side from 76th to 100th streets); and Harlem, Manhattanville, and Carmanville above 110th Street. In certain respects, uptown Manhattan resembled the rest of the city. Its proportion of immigrant (53.6 percent) and black residents (1.89 percent) almost precisely mirrored citywide levels. By some measures (for example, per capita personal wealth) uptowners were less affluent than other New Yorkers, by others (for

Manhattan north of 57th Street in 1854 included a mixture of country estates, asylums, and small villages such as Yorkville at East 85th Street. The rectangular Croton Reservoir later became part of Central Park, as did the Mount St. Vincent convent (far left) and the turreted New York State Arsenal.

instance, percentage of people owning land or numbers of people per dwelling), they were slightly better off. These figures undercut two other often-repeated, contradictory characterizations of uptown: that it was a slum or shantytown of twenty thousand squatters or that it was a bucolic watering place of the elite.[2]

Wealthy New Yorkers who built country estates along both river shores in upper Manhattan were never more than a small minority of the uptown population, though their social prominence—and the prominence of their dwellings—rendered them much more visible in both contemporary and historical accounts. In 1855 at least twenty-three hundred industrial workers in the "rural" districts toiled in sixty-four mostly small shops, including fourteen carriage- and coach-making establishments and various "nuisance industries" (soap, wax, paint, match, chemical, and bone-boiling plants). The uptown farms and gardens were also small; only the northernmost corners of the island retained intensive agriculture, with a total of perhaps a thousand acres actively cultivated for oats, potatoes, turnips, and other crops.[3] Uptown Manhattan was, thus, less agricultural and more industrial than standard accounts suggest.

But the most distinctive uptown feature—the profusion of orphan asylums, hospitals, old age homes, and lunatic asylums—has rarely been noticed at all. A startling 15 percent of the population of the upper three wards (perhaps as many as nine thousand people) lived in such institutions, presumably because land was relatively cheap, because a "country" atmosphere was seen as rehabilitative, and because paupers, "lunatics," and criminals were considered undesirable neighbors.[4]

At midcentury, then, uptown Manhattan was a "suburb" in the sense of a settlement outside the densest urban concentration. But it was the opposite of the modern sense of a suburb as a regulated residential environment. Instead, it was a jumble of small craft shops, large factories, tiny garden patches, two-hundred-acre farms, plank shanties, country estates, and institutional homes for the poor, criminal, and disabled. Between 1840 and 1855, the population above 40th Street multiplied five times, twice as fast as the rest of the city.

Many newer residents clustered in the areas made accessible by the emerging transportation system, which favored the East Side over the West Side. In 1834 regular runs of the New York and Harlem Railroad to 86th Street and Fourth Avenue attracted skilled American, German, and Irish workers and clerks to Yorkville, as did the opening of upper Third Avenue around the same time. Three years later, the railroad extended its range (and its impact) to Harlem; by the end of the decade it was carrying one million passengers per year just within Manhattan alone. On the West Side, the limited service of the Bloomingdale stagecoach line retarded West Side development. New transportation accelerated the exit of some older inhabitants. The Hudson River Railroad's appearance on the far West Side in the late 1840s, observed longtime resident John Punnett Peters, "drove the occupants of those old homes to other regions." But actually, the destruction of the West Side's rural ambiance began in the previous decade with the laying of the Croton aqueduct, which cut through several of the old country estates and obtrusively ran pipes above ground between 84th and 113th streets.[5]

Disease also undermined the West Side elite's gentry ideal. Wealthy New York merchant families had built uptown summer residences to escape the port's yellow fever epidemics, but by the 1840s uptown no longer offered safe refuge from downtown diseases. In 1849 cholera appeared in the upper wards, hitting as one of its victims the wife of the minister of St. Michael's Protestant Episcopal, the church of wealthy West Siders. Uptown residents such as Horace Greeley (who lost his only son to cholera) blamed the epidemic—inaccurately—on the arrival uptown of twenty thousand hogs that had been driven out of downtown by city police that summer. The intrusion of cholera as well as charitable institutions, railroad tracks, and aqueduct pipes prompted

Bloomingdale's elite to move their summer homes farther from the city—to be replaced, Peters writes, by "a poorer, if more numerous, class of residents."[6]

With the city's outer wards undergoing rapid changes, some uptown land-owners had begun to lobby for a large landscaped park within their district in the hope of shaping these powerful forces of development. A park, they thought, would eliminate the "nuisance" of workshops, hogpens, and asylums by replacing them with a new kind of suburb organized around private resi-dences—the "garden, villa, and village settlement" that some uptown real es-tate investors promoted. "If the opening of the Park raises the actual or specula-tive value of lands in its vicinity," the *Sun* pointed out in 1855, "it is certain that the poorer class of citizens will not settle them extensively when homesteads can be obtained cheaper elsewhere." Uptown landowners saw the park both as a way of screening out new poor residents and their associated trades (an early form of zoning) and as a means of removing the existing poor population (an early form of urban renewal). "We want a park up town," one citizen declared at a public hearing, "to remove the hog pens and filth that crowd people in the up-per part of our city together," but such uptown representatives as landowner and future mayor Daniel Tiemann privately admitted the concern was at least as much about a disagreeable urban population as about the disagreeable urban industries. West Siders, not coincidentally, advocated a park precisely in the territory with the largest concentration of poor uptown residents.[7]

In contemporary and historical accounts, those who lived in Central Park before it became Central Park have generally been unrepresented or misrepre-sented, either ignored or disparaged as a debased population of savages. Legis-lative discussions and public reports contain only indirect hints that anyone at all lived on proposed park land. Guides to the city that described East Side settlements like Yorkville and Carmanville made no mention of the equally large community of park dwellers. A few newspaper reporters evinced slightly more interest, none of it sympathetic. On March 5, 1856, a *Times* reporter drew on the recurrent New York motif of a dual city of "sunlight and shadows" to contrast the "human misery" in its "lowest and filthiest depths" within the park boundaries to "the luxury and elegance" that he expected to flourish when the finished park rivaled the Champs Elysées. He described the residents as "prin-cipally Irish families" living in "rickety . . . little one storie shanties . . . inhabited by four or five persons, not including the pig and the goats." The *Evening Post* wrote that the duties of the new Central Park police would be "arduous," since the park was the "scene of plunder and depredations," "the headquarters of vagabonds and scoundrels of every description," and the location of "gambling dens, the lowest type of drinking houses, and houses of every species of rascality." An even more pervasive charge (really, an assumption) was that the park dwellers had stolen the land itself, that they were squatters.[8]

Most subsequent writers have drawn their information (often embellishing along the way) from a single paragraph written by the park's first engineer,

Egbert Viele, who from the distance of forty years recalled the park as "the refuge of about five thousand squatters, dwelling in rude huts of their own construction, and living off the refuse of the city." "These people who had thus overrun and occupied the territory were principally of foreign birth, with but very little knowledge of the English language, and with very little respect for the law. Like the ancient Gauls, they wanted land to live on, and they took it."[9]

The "pre-parkites," as one commentator called them, left no firsthand accounts to counter these scornful reports, but it is possible to piece together an alternative portrait of the roughly sixteen hundred residents from manuscript censuses, city directories, tax lists, land records, church registers, and the maps and petitions generated by the acquisition of the park land. More than 90 percent of those who lived on that land were immigrants—mostly Irish or German—or African Americans, compared to about half of the overall population of the city and also of uptown Manhattan. More than two-thirds of the adults worked at unskilled and service jobs—as laborers, gardeners, domestics, and the like—and most of the rest as tailors, carpenters, masons, or in other skilled trades. About one in ten ran a small business—a grocery or a butcher shop, for example.[10]

These aggregate figures challenge the existing portraits of the "pre-park-ites" as criminals and vagabonds, but they hide much of the complex reality of life in the park. To uncover some of that reality, we need to look more closely at a particular park settlement known as Seneca Village.[11] The densely settled area between 82nd and 88th streets and Seventh and Eighth avenues had least three times as many people per block as the rest of the park. Atypical in its racial composition and its length of settlement, it deserves close scrutiny both because

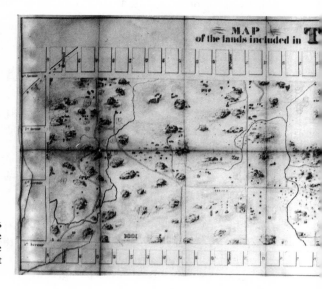

Nearly 1,600 people lived in shanties and farmhouses scattered across the swampy and rocky terrain of the future park. Topographical map by Egbert Viele, 1856.

it was the largest of the park settlements (with more than one-sixth of the area's residents) and because its story contests what we have been led to believe about the prepark era.

Seneca Village

In September 1825 cartman John Whitehead and his wife Elizabeth began selling off parcels of the farmland they owned, which lay roughly between 83rd and 88th streets and Seventh and Eighth avenues. The first purchaser was Andrew Williams, a twenty-five-year-old African-American bootblack, who bought three lots for $125. Epiphany Davis, a black laborer and a trustee of the African Methodist Episcopal Zion church, purchased twelve lots for $578 that same day. (AME Zion had been organized in New York in 1796; a contemporary described it as the "largest and wealthiest church of the coloured people in this city, perhaps in this country.") Within a week of Williams's and Davis's purchases, AME Zion bought six lots from the Whiteheads. Over the next three years three or four other church leaders—trustees, deacons, and preachers—purchased lots in the Whitehead tract. Between 1825 and 1832 the Whiteheads sold fifty land parcels, no fewer than twenty-four of them to black families.[12]

By 1829 at least nine houses dotted this landscape, including one belonging to Andrew Williams. The other houses also seem to have been owned by African Americans. We might, then, suspect that black settlement of Seneca Village began in 1825 with these initial purchases, but it may have begun even earlier in this general area. By the second decade of the nineteenth century, free

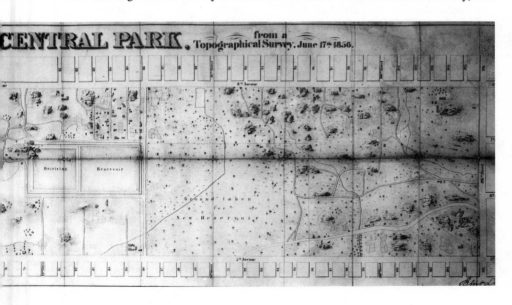

African Americans had apparently developed a community on York Hill, an elevation located almost precisely in the middle of the future Central Park, on the blocks just west of the Whitehead tract, between 79th and 86th streets and Sixth and Seventh avenues. It gave its name to the village of Yorkville, then being settled in that vicinity and farther north and east. One account describes Bill Dove, a young runaway slave from Virginia (and later a family retainer for Boss Tweed), who spent 1819 hiding out among black families who lived in this vicinity. In the early 1830s, St. Michael's Episcopal Church briefly conducted a mission Sunday school "among the colored people" on this site. Although the city owned most of York Hill, by the late 1830s William Matthews, a young black man from Delaware, may have held almost five acres.[13]

The building of the first reservoir in the late 1830s and early 1840s disrupted York Hill's black community. In 1838 New York acquired the thirty-seven-acre York Hill tract as a receiving basin for the new Croton water system. Some families probably moved directly west and joined those who had begun to settle the Whitehead tract, where ten more houses were added between 1835 and 1839. In the late 1830s the African Union church, which William Matthews served as minister and trustee, bought land in Seneca Village. By 1840 the former Whitehead tract was home to more than a hundred people. By the next decade, Seneca Village (reflecting the virulent racism of the day) was known as "Nigger Village." But as the neighborhood more than doubled in population, its composition changed; by 1855 when at least 264 people lived there, Irish Americans made up about 30 percent of the community.[14]

Among the earliest Irish residents of the area was its most famous native. In 1842 Sara Plunkitt, wife of Irish immigrant laborer Pat Plunkitt, gave birth to twin sons, one of whom grew up to be the celebrated West Side Tammany boss George Washington Plunkitt. Years later Plunkitt recalled that he was born on "Nanny Goat Hill," just "twenty feet inside the Central Park wall at [West] Eighty-fourth Street" and right on the edge of what he called "Nigger Village." Within the next seven or eight years, the Plunkitts moved farther south, although still perhaps within the borders of the future park. Plunkitt may not have been the only future Tammany boss to spend his early years on the western edge of Seneca Village. In 1846 the Croker family—including three-year-old Richard—fled famine-ridden Ireland and took up residence, according to one biographer, "in a dilapidated dwelling in what is now the western portion of Central Park." Young Richard's father plied his trade as an itinerant veterinarian among the horses, cows, and pigs of the park dwellers. Although some other white residents—police officer William Evers and milkman Philip Dunn, for example—settled in Seneca Village in the 1840s, most came after 1850, seeking cheap housing in an increasingly crowded and expensive city.[15]

Seneca's white population generally faced the same contempt leveled at their black neighbors. The commingling of whites and blacks sparked fears and fantasies of miscegenation and "amalgamation." Working from the notes of his father, a missionary to the Seneca Village residents in the 1840s and 1850s, John Punnett Peters of St. Michael's described the park in the late 1840s as a "wilderness" filled with "the habitations of poor and wretched people of every race and color and nationality." "This waste," he continued, contained "many families of colored people with whom consorted and in many cases amalgamated, debased and outcast whites. Many of the inhabitants of this village had no regular occupation, finding it easy to replenish their stock of fuel with driftwood from the river and supply their tables from the same source, with fish."[16]

Were the residents of Seneca the "wretched" and "debased" floating population that Peters and other observers described? The origins of the village in purchases from the Whitehead tract as well as in the earlier settlement at York Hill suggests that this community had a much longer and more continuous history. Three-quarters of those residents (or their families) who were taxed in 1840 were still there fifteen years later. Virtually every black family in Seneca Village recorded by the 1850 census was still there five years later. Such figures acquire special significance when we consider that 40 percent of Boston's population moved in those same five years, that other cities had similarly high mobility rates, and that African Americans, in general, showed significantly less residential stability than other city residents.[17]

Other evidence reinforces this picture of unusual stability. Although few Seneca Village black heads of household were New York City natives, by 1855 they had been in the city an average of twenty-two years, a sharp contrast to the area's Irish residents. Some black residents had much deeper roots specifically in Seneca Village; at least nine individuals or families could trace their ties back more than two and a half decades.[18] Over those years they developed dense webs of interconnection.

Between 1825 and 1827 Diana and Elizabeth Harding (probably mother and daughter) purchased land in Seneca Village from the Whiteheads. Sometime before 1835 Elizabeth Harding married Obadiah McCollin, a cook born in Westchester County, who had already acquired at least two lots of Seneca Village land from James Newton, who had purchased it from the Whiteheads in 1825. Despite her marriage (and in seeming contravention of the common law of married women's property rights that prevailed in New York until 1848), Elizabeth Harding McCollin continued to hold some Seneca Village land in her own name. In the course of the next three decades, the McCollins forged ties and alliances with other families. In 1855 their household included six-year-old Frederick Riddles; Frederick's parents, Peter and Angelina Morris Riddles, are not listed in that year's census, but they were present five years earlier when they buried his nineteen-month-old brother and his grandmother, Nancy Morris, in the AME Zion graveyard. Nancy Morris had purchased land in Seneca Village back in 1827, and her daughter Angelina remained a landowner there thirty years later, even after she and her husband had moved out (and left their young son in the care of their neighbors, the McCollins). Also still present in Seneca Village was Nancy Morris's other daughter, Charlotte, who had married William Godfrey Wilson.[19]

Such examples of intermarriage and interconnection can be multiplied even on the basis of the limited surviving evidence. Elizabeth Harding McCollin's father, Samuel Harding, for example, boarded for a time with his daughter and previously with Elizabeth and James Thompson, the son of Ada Thompson, another long-standing resident. And William Godfrey Wilson (Nancy Morris's son-in-law) may have been the son of Sarah Wilson (also a longtime Seneca Villager), who later adopted Catherine Treadwell, daughter of another of the original purchasers of the Whitehead land. These instances of kinship and neighborhood ties stretching over at least four decades may seem unexceptional; yet they defy the stereotype of the park dwellers as a drifting population of criminals. So does information on their housing, jobs, property holdings, and community institutions.

Most observers described the humble dwellings of Seneca Village residents as "shanties." In part, the word accurately describes small, one-story, six-to-ten-foot-high dwellings usually built out of unpainted rough board and not professionally constructed. Ishmael Allen, for instance, shared his nine-by-eleven-foot dwelling on 83rd Street with his wife, four children, and a boarder. Yet the word *shanty*, as a cultural term, often describes (and demeans) a building's occupants as well as the building itself. Although many lived in crowded circumstances, their conditions were often significantly better than thousands of other poor immigrant and black families living downtown in cellars, garrets, or eight-by-ten-foot tenement rooms. Park dwellers also had considerable outdoor space, an amenity in short supply in the downtown tenement districts. Given what we know about the length of residence of so many Seneca Village black families, it also seems unlikely that their shanties were the rickety structures described by outside observers. Some perhaps more closely resembled rural cabins. Certainly park dwellings were valuable enough to cause disputes over ownership when the city took over the land. In seeking permission to remove a two-room "little house" he had erected at his own expense, Irish Seneca Village resident John Wallace pointed out that it "is to me of considerable importance having a wife and four little children to support." The quality of housing, moreover, varied considerably. Not too far from the Allens lived the four-person McCollin household in an ample, nine-hundred-square-foot, two-story frame house, which the census taker valued at four thousand dollars.[20]

One should not exaggerate the wealth of even the McCollins, one of the best-off Seneca Village families, whose substantial dwelling no doubt reflected savings accumulated over more than one generation as well as perhaps their own construction labor. Obadiah McCollin could not have earned a very large weekly salary as a cook, one of the few occupations open to African Americans in antebellum New York. Like their counterparts elsewhere in the city, virtually

Poor New Yorkers often leased or purchased land and built their own houses on the property that became Central Park.

all black Seneca Villagers earned their living in the service trades—as domestics or waiters, for example—or as unskilled laborers. The same could be said of their Irish neighbors, most of whom were laborers earning perhaps a dollar per day. Among Seneca residents, only German grocer Henry Meyers, black grocer William Pease, and New York–born innkeeper John Haff could even loosely be considered occupationally "middle class."[21]

The economic activities of women and children supplemented the earnings of male household heads. Many black women worked as domestics or laundresses. Wives also contributed to the household economy through housework: sewing, economizing on meal preparation, and especially scavenging for food, clothing, fuel, and implements that could be used by their own households or traded in New York City's extensive secondhand market.[22]

Such activities throw a different light on the repeated references to "living off the refuse of the city," gathering "rubbish of all description," and denuding the park's forests for firewood. For contemporary commentators, the scavenging of the park dwellers was a mark of sloth, of lack of "regular occupation."[23] Yet it might as easily have signified the reverse—the energy and resourcefulness with which park dwellers supplemented paltry wages with food, fuel, furniture, and clothing that could be obtained without cash. On the urban fringe in upper Manhattan trees offered a free source of fuel for warmth and cooking. It was only a short walk to the river, where driftwood and fish could be gathered much more easily and with less competition than downtown. There were economical uses for refuse that could not be recycled for human consumption: unused garbage fed the pigs and goats that some park dwellers raised; the bones of dead animals fueled the two bone-boiling plants located at 66th and 75th streets, a short walk south of Seneca Village. A few residents had fairly extensive gardens as well as their own stables and barns. Others—such as eighty-eight-year-old Henry Garnet—kept small gardens out of which they supplemented their diets. The ability to raise at least some of their own food and to take advantage of the larger urban and natural ecology were among the advantages Seneca Village residents had over downtown poor families.

Most important, many of the black Seneca residents had something denied to most of their compatriots elsewhere in the city: security of tenure based on landownership. Throughout the city, few black New Yorkers owned land because of the barriers imposed by limited financial resources, a state law that prohibited black inheritance as late as 1809, informal racial bars on land sales, and the high price of downtown Manhattan real estate. In 1850 census takers counted only seventy-one black property owners; ten years later the number had grown only slightly to eighty-five. In this context, Seneca Village, where the Whiteheads willingly sold land to African Americans and where land was cheap by New York standards, offered an unusual opportunity for blacks who had some savings and wanted to become landowners. At least some black Seneca Village landowners actually lived downtown. Joseph Marshall, a hardworking house painter and AME Zion church member, owned five lots in Seneca Village as well as his house on Centre Street in lower Manhattan.[24]

Among black Seneca Village residents, landownership rates were extraordinarily high. With more than half the black households in Seneca Village in 1855 owning property, African-American residents there had a rate of property ownership five times as great as New Yorkers as a whole.[25] In 1850 black Seneca Villagers were thirty-nine times as likely to own property as other black New Yorkers. Seneca Village's Irish households were not equally fortunate: only three of twenty-one owned property, and none of the recent Irish arrivals did. Irish immigrant settlers of Seneca Village in the 1850s faced some of the same problems as did black migrants to the north a century later: a narrowing of opportunities, in this case, less available land and higher prices.

The high levels of property ownership and residential stability among black Seneca Villagers allowed them to reinforce and develop their own community institutions, particularly churches. A settlement centered on four city blocks and comprising around sixty households included two African-American Methodist churches (AME Zion and African Union) and one racially mixed Episcopal church (All Angels', an affiliate of St. Michael's). AME Zion church

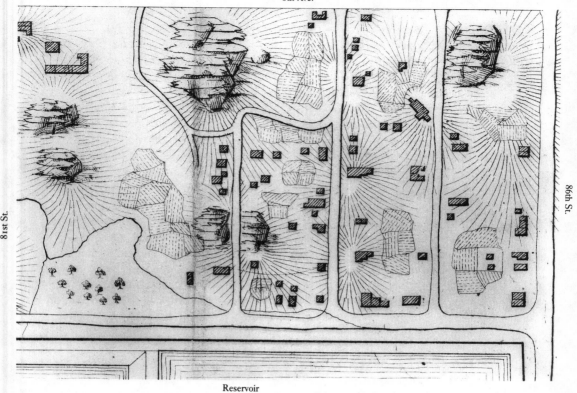

81st St.

86th St.

Reservoir

This section of Viele's topographical map shows the cluster of small houses in Seneca Village (between 81st and 86th streets near Eighth Avenue), one of the city's best-established black communities, with three churches and a school.

had purchased land from the Whiteheads in 1825 and 1827, and in 1827 when the city transformed the Potters Field into Washington Square, thereby eliminating the burial ground used by AME Zion, it began to use some of its Seneca Village lots as a cemetery. Not until 1853 did AME Zion begin construction of a church, although a congregation—with a hundred weekly worshipers—predated that building by as much as five or six years. In downtown Manhattan, where most black New Yorkers lived, AME Zion had faced competition from three other Methodist churches, and one of those rivals now competed with AME Zion in Seneca Village. The trustees of African Union Methodist Episcopal church had purchased land only a hundred yards from AME Zion in 1837, although in 1855 they claimed to have "been in possession of said lots and meeting house thereon for more than twenty years." The African Union Church also housed another important local institution, Colored School No. 3, set up in the 1840s, one of only a handful of black schools in New York City.[26]

St. Michael's at Broadway and 99th Street created Seneca Village's third church in 1846 as a mission to the poor residents of the park. First, it set up a Sunday school and then held services in the home of a white policeman, William Evers. Thomas Peters greatly expanded the missionary work, and by 1848 he arranged to build a wooden church on West 84th Street with subscriptions raised among wealthy white parishioners of St. Michael's and other philanthropic New Yorkers—Robert Minturn, for example. Known as All Angels' Church when it opened in 1849, it ministered to an unusual congregation. Black parishioners came largely from Seneca Village, white parishioners from Irish and German settlements located within a mile of the church.[27]

African Americans numbered about two-thirds of the names in All Angels' register and were some of its most loyal and active members. Ishmael Allen, who lived next door, not only served as church sexton but named his first son after the Reverend Mr. Peters. The widow Ada Thompson, a domestic worker born in Virginia in 1796, lived just across "old lane" from the church. In September 1849 Peters came to her small house to baptize her first grandchild, who was named (like four other black Seneca Villagers) after the late president William Henry Harrison. Over the next six years, Peters baptized three more of Thompson's grandchildren and buried her son and a fourth grandchild. Four children of ragpicker and sailor John White were baptized through All Angels'. A fifth was buried in the graveyard in Astoria, Queens, that Peters established for the church after burials were banned below 86th Street in Manhattan. But although All Angels' was the best-endowed and largest of Seneca Village's three churches, only about thirty people seem to have attended its weekly services. Many black residents may have preferred to worship in all-black churches. African Union, with only half the capacity of All Angels', had fifty regular congregants, and AME Zion seems to have been twice as large as that.[28] In a community of perhaps only 260 inhabitants, 180 people attended church each week. Even allowing for some exaggeration and for the attendance of some people from outside Seneca Village, this community was exceptionally devoted to its churches.

The community involvement suggested by these high levels of church attendance was reflected in politics as well, although here the evidence is somewhat sketchier. In the mid-nineteenth century, black New Yorkers faced formidable and unique obstacles to voting: a $250 freehold estate and three years of residency in the state were required. As late as 1845 (the last time citywide statistics were collected) only 91 of 13,000 black New Yorkers had the franchise, and ten years later, with the city's black population just below 12,000, the number of voters was still under 100. Of that tiny cadre of black voters, 10 lived in tiny Seneca Village; thus, that community's residents were several times more likely to have voting privileges than black New Yorkers in general. Some black men who lived downtown had also qualified to vote based on landownership in Seneca Village; indeed, land purchases there may have been a deliberate stratagem to meet the property qualification. At least three of those "absentee" owners took a prominent role in New York politics. Timothy Seaman, who owned a lot on 87th Street, and James N. Gloucester, a minister who held a lot on 88th Street, were both leaders in the campaign for unrestricted black suffrage. Charles B. Ray, who owned three lots a half mile south of Seneca Village, was a well-known abolitionist clergyman and president of the New York Society for the Promotion of Education among Colored Children. Ironically, a settlement that contemporary and historical accounts depict as disorganized and degraded may have been one of the pillars of New York's antebellum black community.[29]

Pig Keepers, Gardeners, Sisters, Bone Boilers, and Squatters

Other, less-established settlements clustered through the area of the future park. The southeastern corner, which the *Journal of Commerce* called "Pig-town," was home to about fourteen households, roughly three-quarters of them Irish. A larger concentration of Irish families could be found farther north and west (between 68th and 72nd streets and between Seventh and Eighth avenues) with about thirty-four households, two-thirds of them Irish. Although these Irish-American park dwellers did not develop the same sorts of institutions within the boundaries of the future park as did black Seneca Villagers, they did join in the community life of surrounding Irish-Catholic settlements. Some attended St. Lawrence O'Toole Roman Catholic Church in Yorkville built in 1851 (now Church of St. Ignatius Loyola). Others apparently walked to the slightly more distant Catholic churches on 50th and 117th streets.[30]

The park site allowed Irish immigrants, many of whom came from rural areas, to grow food or keep hogs and goats as they had back home. Immigrants who wanted to tend animals were much more likely to live uptown when restrictions tightened on such activities downtown after the 1849 cholera epidemic. Most kept pigs or raised food to supplement their wages as day laborers on the road gangs building uptown streets. German immigrants lived alongside the Irish in these areas but developed distinctive settlements. One dominated the northern end of the park, the other the southwestern corner between 69th and 79th streets and Sixth and Seventh avenues, below the reservoir. One 1855 census taker, apparently referring to Germans who lived in the middle of the park, noted that "a majority of the deaths that are recorded on this page are among the children of the 'German' population who have been in the Country but a short time, very poor, having no visible means of support except picking rags, gathering cinders, etc., located in a 'Swamp,' which is continually wet, and

FASHIONABLE DENIZENS.

In the fall of 1857, *Harper's Weekly* magazine satirized Irish shanty dwellers and their pigs as the "fashionable denizens" of Central Park.

subject to 'Fever and Ague.' " Counting the population farther north in the park, a different census taker wrote: "Germans cultivate small patches for gardens and make out to raise enough to live upon in their way. But nothing more."[31]

Compared with Seneca Villagers, as the census takers' comments show, the German ragpickers and gardeners were even more closely tied to the park land for their subsistence. Many of the thirty-nine gardeners—all but six of them German immigrants and the second largest occupational group in the park after laborers—eked out a marginal existence, but a few had modestly prosperous spreads. A German-born music teacher with the colorful name of Jupiter Zeuss K. Hesser began cultivating seven lots near Seventh Avenue and 100th Street around 1852, which he called "Jupiterville." By 1855 he had erected a "neat two story house . . . with fine hard walls," a chimney, a "very nice cellar," and a "good sewer 4 or 5 feet deep"; he had cleared the ground of stones, bushes, and woods, laid down manure, dug a ten-foot well with the "most excellent water," fenced in his gardens, and built a barn, chicken coop, and goat stable. Within five blocks of Hesser lived Henry Ellerman, who had arrived from Germany in the late 1840s. Assisted by his father-in-law and three German immigrant boarders, Ellerman cultivated eight acres and produced two thousand dollars worth of crops in a year.[32]

Though most German and Irish park dwellers had been in New York City considerably less time—twelve years on average—than their black neighbors, at least some could claim longer tenures within the park. In 1836 Catherine and William Coggery, for example, arrived in New York well in advance of the famine-driven wave of Irish immigrants in the 1840s, and within nine months, they settled on 93rd Street near Seventh Avenue. Several other Irish families joined them in the next ten years. When asked in an 1857 court case about her familiarity with a tract of land in the upper park, Catherine Coggery replied: "I . . . have been looking at it for 20 years."[33]

The area of the park under longest continuous settlement was probably the northeast corner, where the old Boston Post Road made its way between two rocky ridges. By the 1750s Jacob Dyckman had built a tavern on a hill in the vicinity of 105th Street and Fifth Avenue. It soon passed into the McGown family, which owned the tavern and the surrounding land for most of the next century. During the Revolutionary War, Hessian mercenaries occupied McGown's Pass, as it had come to be called, and in 1814 sixteen hundred militiamen guarded the area against a threatened British invasion. (The stone blockhouse at West 109th Street, the oldest building in the park today, is a surviving relic of the chain of fortifications built then.) In 1847 the Sisters of Charity of New York purchased a dilapidated frame house surrounded by pools of water on the site of the abandoned tavern; they took turns cooking their meals on a small coal stove and carried water from the nearest spring. "I have heard of poverty, but I never saw such a picture of it before," a young candidate for the order said to herself when she arrived in 1849. Within a few years, the sisters had constructed a flourishing religious community on what they called Mount St. Vincent. By the mid-1850s, their convent, with seventy sisters (half of them Irish-born), eleven Irish female servants, and nine Irish male employees, encompassed several substantial buildings including a laundry, a large brick chapel, a boarding academy for two hundred "young ladies," and a free school for fifty or sixty children from surrounding areas.[34]

The religious buildings at McGown's Pass were not the only impressive structures within the proposed park boundaries. In 1848 the State of New York had erected the Arsenal on ten acres of land at 64th Street and Fifth Avenue. About fifteen blocks north the wealthy Wagstaff family maintained an old farmhouse at Fifth Avenue and 79th Street, one of the few paved streets in the area. And at around 68th and Sixth, the broker Peter B. Amory and his family of ten occupied the Amory family homestead.[35]

On the western side of the park, a world away from the Amorys and the Wagstaffs, were the bone-boiling plants of George Moller and William Menck. Such "nuisance" industries were being driven out of lower Manhattan by ordinances, restrictive covenants, and public pressure. Leather dresser Benjamin Beaman, butcher Ludwig Sheff, and soap boiler Charles Lucke also faced fewer restrictions on their trades here than downtown. Some park dwellers helped to gather the thirty-four thousand bushels of animal bones that Moller and Menck required each year; others found the dollar-a-day wages offered at the plants attractive; and the rest were willing to tolerate (or at least lacked the resources to complain about) the noxious odors released when bones were boiled to produce fuel for sugar refining.[36] (The current occupant of the

The Sisters of Charity founded the Mount St. Vincent Convent, perched on a hill at 105th Street and Fifth Avenue, in 1847. Park officials later turned the convent into a restaurant and the chapel into a museum.

site of the Menck bone-boiling works at West 66th Street—the swank Tavern on the Green—posts no commemoration of its distinguished predecessor.)

Others in the future park engaged in businesses that were conventionally viewed as illegal. Most of the evidence on such crime comes from observers with little understanding of and still less sympathy for the park dwellers. The press repeatedly accused them of "theft" between 1855 and 1857, but such charges often recorded their removal of their own property from the park before the onset of construction. Other charges reflected differing perceptions of customary rights. "Some of the people living in that vicinity," the *Journal of Commerce* reported on June 28, 1856, "are in the *habit* of cutting small limbs from the few remaining trees" to use in drying hops for beer. That being said, it would hardly come as a surprise that people who did steal food, fuel, furniture, or clothing (or whose scavenging sometimes crossed the thin line separating it from theft) found the park a convenient place to avoid legal scrutiny, particularly given the scarcity of police in upper Manhattan. This same absence of close police surveillance probably encouraged other illegal pursuits. Some Irish widows with no visible means of support may have operated illegal liquor outlets, or *shebeens*—a traditional trade for such women in their native Ireland. In March 1855 when a police officer broke up a Sunday morning boxing match at a location just south of the park, the participants reassembled in "Pigtown" near 65th Street. And when police first arrived in Central Park in 1856, they cracked down on "disorderly" (and presumably unlicensed) dance houses, which had probably operated for years.[37]

Of course, the most common charge against park residents was that they illegally occupied the land by "squatting" there. As a broad generalization, the term *squatters* could not apply to the one-fifth of the residents who owned their own land and who as a group had a level of property ownership 50 percent above the average for the city. Of the four-fifths who did not own property, nine families appear in the city tax lists, indicating that they held ground leases requiring them to pay the taxes. The majority of park dwellers appear in neither land nor tax records, but some "squatters" probably had formal or informal arrangements with landowners that permitted use of the land. In the early 1840s, for example, landowner Abraham Higbe allowed Nicholas Ray and John Donnelly to settle their families and grow corn, potatoes, and other vegetables on his land in return for their clearing it of brush. After the mid-1840s, Donnelly apparently began to pay a cash rent of twenty-five dollars per year, but the landlord's agent did not always make the annual collection, perhaps because the sum seemed so small to him. Donnelly, meanwhile, collected rents from subtenants on the same land. When Donnelly moved from the area, rent collection became even more casual. One resident, widow Mary O'Donnell, had to enlist the help of a local policeman to locate the current landlord. When they found him, he was willing to accept whatever cash she offered as that year's rent.[38]

The *New York Sun,* one of the few newspapers even mildly sympathetic to the so-called squatters, noted on May 6, 1857, that of the "many persons who have erected shanties in the swamps and on the rocks" of northern Manhattan, "most . . . seek the permission of the owners of the land before erecting their shanties, or they squat on lands whose owners are unknown. Not a few of them have been paying a small ground rent, and raising fruit and vegetables on patches of land which would otherwise have been unproductive." In other words, most New York landlords, even of marginal lands in the future Central Park, kept track of who lived on their property, even if they did not always collect regular rents from them. Thus, the park dwellers most accurately called squatters were the few who made their homes on lots whose owners were listed as "unknown." Like the word *shanty,* in mid-nineteenth-century New York the term *squatter* was more of a cultural category than a formal legal description, a convenient shorthand for the sort of poor people more affluent New Yorkers preferred to remove from their neighborhoods.[39]

Eviction of all these people—landowners and squatters alike—would begin when the commission of estimate finally issued its Central Park report in the fall of 1855.

The Landowners

In September 1853 the antagonistic parties involved in the acquisition of the land that would become Central Park, the city and the owners, had appeared in court to present alternative slates of commissioners of estimate; the commission was to arbitrate between the public interest in acquiring land as cheaply as possible and the landowners' interests in receiving fair value. The usually dry and routine court procedure attracted, as the *Post* reported, "unusual interest," reflecting "the unexampled magnitude of the proposed appropriation . . . the still greater pecuniary benefits, direct and indirect, to be diffused by opening such a Park—and, above all, its ever-enduring influence in adding to attractiveness and elevating the character of the metropolis, and thus fitting it for high destiny."[40]

The lawyers who appeared on behalf of some of the city's largest property holders had money, not destiny, on their minds: how much their clients would be paid for their land or how much they would have to pay in benefit assessments. Most of the major uptown landowners coordinated their nominations for commissioners, convinced that the biggest landowners should have the biggest say in the process. Judge William Mitchell chose three from a slate nominated by the city and two from lists proposed by large property owners. The two groups of commissioners resembled each other much more than they differed. They were all, as the *Tribune* put it, "eminent gentlemen"—retired judges, large landowners, and civic leaders who were expected to understand the real estate market and command respect. Although Corporation Counsel Robert Dillon argued forcefully that the commissioners should speak for "the great body of my fellow citizens," the five men chosen were to mediate largely among the interests of taxpayers (primarily downtown landowners), the owners of park land, and owners of property to be assessed a portion of the park's cost.[41]

The new commission of estimate faced an enormous and not wholly defined task. They needed to decide on the value of each of the 7,520 lots and the 300 or more structures on the site of Central Park and to develop a system for assessing surrounding property owners who would help to pay for this land. In this task, the Central Park Act provided remarkably little guidance, specifying neither what proportion of the cost should be paid by assessments nor which surrounding lots (just those facing the park? throughout uptown Manhattan?) were to be assessed. The commission needed first to determine who owned what. Its comprehensive survey of uptown real estate offers a fine-grained snapshot of uptown landholding. Surveyors recorded on their maps the names of literally hundreds of property owners, but most land was held in relatively few hands. Of the 561 different landowners, only 21 controlled half the park land, and 3 families alone—the Watts, the Wagstaffs, and the Talmans—one-fifth. Big landholders owned most of the land surrounding the park as well. Five families—Lenox, Harsen, McGown, Amory, and Hopper—together owned more than 250 acres; many others had relatively small holdings. The most striking difference between the land inside the park's boundaries and that outside was the considerably greater number of lots (410) inside whose actual owners were unknown, a reflection of the lower value of the rough terrain.[42]

Uptown property had been changing hands for close to two centuries, and it was continuing to do so right under the noses of the commissioners. In 1854 alone, the city clerk recorded 142 transactions involving Central Park land. Owners of uptown property had acquired their holdings at different historical moments and for different (and sometimes changing) purposes. This history ultimately shaped the degree of any landowner's gain (or loss) from the creation of Central Park. Some of the largest uptown landowners inherited their land from the proprietors of eighteenth-century farms. Tracts ranging from one hundred to three hundred acres had passed to the current generation through complex webs of intermarriage, inheritance, and estate division. Dr. Jacob Harsen, a vigorous advocate of Central Park and the owner of about fifty acres to the west of the park and four acres within it, owed his substantial holdings to an estate originally purchased by his ancestor Cornelius Dyckman in 1701. Dyckman property descended to other major uptown landowners as well—the Kortwrights and the interrelated Hoppers and Strikers and Somarindycks and Talmans. On the east side of the park, equally ancient land claims could be made by Assistant Alderman S. Benson McGown, whose forty-five acres could be traced in part to a larger tract first acquired from one of Harlem's earliest settlers in 1706.[43]

In the first half of the nineteenth century when new merchant investors wanted to acquire uptown real estate, they either purchased from one of the old families who were selling parts of their estates or bought portions of city-owned "common" land. Beginning around 1818 Scottish merchant Robert Lenox, one of the city's wealthiest men, purchased what came to thirty acres between Fourth and Fifth avenues and from 68th to 74th streets both from private owners and from public authorities. Two decades later, he passed the land on to his son James. Lenox, like old Knickerbocker families who viewed their estates both as homes and as repositories of family wealth to be handed on from one generation to the next, invested in uptown property with an eye to long-term gain. In the forty years after he acquired it, neither Lenox nor his son made any move either to sell or to develop the land, beyond building a country estate as a retreat from the distempers of downtown life.[44]

Archibald Watt bought his own seventy-five acres at Harlem common land sales and from old Harlem families. In contrast to Lenox, he viewed his uptown land less as a symbol of gentry status or a long-term investment than as a commodity to be bought cheap and sold dear. Watt had "purchased at Harlem . . . for investment," he later explained, then began buying "largely on speculation, for an early sale at good profit." When immediate buyers proved scarce, Watt had shifted to a land-development strategy, and around 1834 he began what he called "an Enterprise to be of long duration and distant fruition" to "encourage garden, villa, and village settlement." His dream had foundered on the shoals of the Panic of 1837, but he revived his schemes in the late 1840s as the economy revived.[45]

Other New Yorkers began to cast a speculative eye toward uptown land in the late 1840s and early 1850s as memories of the "Revulsion of 1837," as Watt called it, faded. By 1852 and 1853 sales had exceeded the previous peak of the mid-1830s, and with increased sales came increased prices. The Croton Aqueduct Board, worrying about its projected site for a second reservoir within the park's boundaries, said in 1852 that land "has probably doubled in value within the last two years, and is still advancing with almost unexampled rapidity." The rising prices drew even old Knickerbocker families into the maelstrom of the market. Jacob Harsen sold forty-two parcels of Central Park land in 1850, and banker and Somarindyck heir John Talman moved decisively into real estate two years later. The need to settle a family estate led to the Amorys' large-scale sales (close to 450 transactions) between 1852 and 1854.[46]

The other big seller of uptown land, particularly within the boundaries of Central Park, was the city of New York; it disposed of eight hundred lots there in 1852. The sale, which came just as the central site was emerging as a viable alternative to Jones Wood, seems odd, but it was part of a larger divestment through which the city moved out of the private land market. Royal colonial charters had endowed the municipal corporation with common lands, which it used to produce operating revenues. These lands were public property but were not commons in the sense that all citizens shared equal access. Before the mid-nineteenth century, the municipal corporation managed real property like other proprietors to generate income; but around 1844, it began to sell off its common lands (partly to reduce the municipal debt and increase the amount of property on the tax rolls), turning instead to tax and bond revenues to support its operations. Thus, the city simultaneously withdrew from the land market as an active owner of property and took a more active role in that same market through projects like the park.[47]

In this process, the city altered its relationship to both public and private land. The park represented a new concept of public property held in trust for the community's cultural rather than its economic benefit. Whereas in the eighteenth century city government principally concerned itself with maintaining a landscape and public order conducive to commerce, now citizens looked to government to provide and administer resources for a common good that included the benefits of recreation. But the city was not just reserving land from private exchange, it was also altering the shape of the market itself. Preventing more than seven hundred acres from being sold and fixing that land's use would have a profound effect on uptown land values; it was thus an experiment in city planning that might offset the unpredictability brought on by unrestrained private competition.

The people who bought Central Park land in the speculative boom of the early 1850s, unlike the old Knickerbocker families with their inherited estates and the Yankee merchants with their large purchases, generally bought parcels of one acre or less, sometimes just a single lot or two. Most ran small businesses, whereas merchants, brokers, lawyers, bankers, and doctors owned the largest tracts of park land. The proprietors of dry goods, clothing, shoe, cigar, and grocery stores dominated the city's common land sales and the ranks of the holders of small parcels.[48]

The more recent and less substantial owners of uptown real estate were likelier to share Archibald Watt's view of land as a commodity to be bought and sold according to the dictates of the marketplace. Many were looking for a quick profit. Close to 40 percent who bought park lots from the city in April 1852 seem to have resold them before the commission of estimate issued its report in 1856; 5 to 10 percent made their living buying, selling, and developing land. Still, some recent buyers regarded uptown land as a safe long-term investment. And leather dresser Benjamin Beaman, laborer William Mulligan, and others bought common lands in the early 1850s simply as a place to live and work rather than as land to invest in or speculate on.

Value, "A Very Indefinite and Latitudinarian Term"

For almost two years, beginning in the fall of 1853, the commission of estimate surveyed and assessed the thirty-four thousand lots in and around the Central Park site.[49] No doubt the massive size of the task prolonged their labors, but the commissioners may also have hesitated to release a report some New Yorkers would find unsettling. Central Park, it turned out, was going to cost a good deal more than the public had been led to believe, and the benefit assessments were going to cover a good deal less of the price.

When the commission finally deposited its report for public examination on October 4, 1855, taxpayers learned that they would be paying $5 million just for the park land, more than three times what they had been told the completed park as a whole would cost. At the same time, the portion of the bill covered by assessing adjacent landowners—$1.7 million, or one-third of the purchase price—would be considerably less than the more optimistic of the earlier estimates. But if taxpayers believed they were paying too much, owners of park land thought they were receiving too little. Many considered the seven hundred dollars per lot (on average) the commission offered inadequate; just two years earlier some of them had suggested that they expected about eight hundred dollars. Adjacent landowners who were charged benefit assessments had the least to complain about. The commission had kept their share to one-third of the cost and spread that expense over a considerable area, running roughly between 34th and 120th streets and almost to Second and Eleventh avenues.

The size of the assessment area angered those on its far fringes, who doubted they themselves would receive any immediate benefit from the park. Uptown landowners also worried about having to pay benefit assessments later for opening and grading uptown streets.[50]

Within days after the report's publication, the *Sun* noted that crowds had gathered to examine its content and that many departed with "most rueful countenances." Given the volume of petitions that poured into the commission in the next few weeks, at least some landowners must have headed directly for their lawyers' offices, while others with more modest resources went home to scratch out less legally formidable complaints. More than two hundred landowners filed petitions objecting to the commission's findings, almost two-thirds from people unhappy about what they were being offered for their land; the rest divided between those complaining about assessments and those disputing land titles. The 130 or so landowners who complained about their awards controlled close to 40 percent of the land within the park boundaries. Their voluminous complaints fundamentally turned on the question of land *value*, which, as one of the most persistent and vituperative of the petitioners admitted, was "a very indefinite and latitudinarian term," especially when applied to vacant and unproductive "lots suburban to the city."[51] Essentially, park landowners countered the commission's valuations with calculations rooted in their own estimation of the market, in some more abstract measure of justice or fairness, in the immediate use of the land, or sometimes in a combination of all three.

Those basing their appeals on the market testified about higher offers for the same land, about the price paid for other similarly situated land, about what neighbors or real estate agents considered the land to be worth, or about the particular advantages of their lots for development. Grocer Peter Doremus, for instance, declared that the $1,240 the city offered him for his three lots at 82nd Street and Seventh Avenue "is much below what I could have sold them for two years ago." Printer Daniel Farnshaw assembled fourteen neighbors to testify that his eleven lots at 100th Street and Fifth Avenue were worth more than the $5,925 to be awarded.[52]

Both Doremus and Farnshaw realized that they were arguing about potential as much as current values. Many complaints similarly spun out the owner's vision of what his or her property *might* be worth if, for example, settlement moved uptown or the Sixth Avenue railroad were opened. By far the most elaborate of these fantasies of future gain came from Archibald Watt, the largest owner of park land and the author of complaints that totaled close to forty typeset pages. Detailing his long-standing plans for an uptown suburban development, Watt demanded compensation, because the park would "disappoint his Adventure . . . defeat his Plans . . . destroy his Enterprise." "War," Watt wrote, reaching for what seemed to him an appropriate analogy, "enhances the cost of the munitions of war and the results of victory. You, in conquering the park for the behalf of the municipality . . . must fully meet the consequences entailed by your disturbances and draughts on those materials."[53] Claims based on the potential and future value of land rather than its current market price obviously shaded over into arguments rooted in the owner's own notions of justice or fairness. The largest group of complainants who talked of the injustice of the commission's awards seemed to have a fairly compelling case. They had purchased their land from the city less than three years earlier and now were being asked to sell that same land back to that same city government at a lower price than they had paid.

Recall that in April and December of 1852, before the Central Park bill had been passed, the city had auctioned off eight hundred lots within the park's boundaries. By December 22 the *Times* would report that the city real estate market had reached a "fever heat" of speculative "mania." Purchasers bid up the lots to three to four times the valuation the city's comptroller had put on them just a year earlier. Most of the buyers were small investors and speculators; many later said they were unaware of proposals to turn the land into a park. Almost immediately after the sale, the booming real estate market began to sour and nearly half of the buyers never completed the deals. The rest were not so smart. They watched the real estate market weaken further while the commission of estimate was making its valuations. Even if those who purchased land at the corporation land sales had received back exactly what they had paid, they would still have taken a loss, given their mortgage interest and taxes.[54]

Faced with these circumstances, at least half of those who had bought land at the December 1852 corporation land sale now in late 1855 filed complaints with the commission. Thomas Shepard, who received $4,700 less than he paid for eleven city lots, submitted a six-page letter charging fraud. Writing "not to beg relief—but to demand justice," he closed his plea by making the first known proposal for a Central Park statue. If justice were not done, "a lasting monument of brass on which shall be inscribed the complete history of this transaction" should be erected in the park as testimony to the city's lack of "honesty" and its "sharpness in driving a bargain."[55]

Those who lived on land that was being acquired for the park often rested their complaints on its current use value. Butcher Sheff, for example, complained that the commission's price ignored the "large amount of money and labor" he had spent "to improve the property for a home for my family and for carrying on my business." Others, worried that the park would disrupt their lives and livelihoods and that the commission had overlooked their personal investments, provided detailed lists of expenditures for constructing homes, shops, stables, fences, and privies; digging wells and sewers; clearing rocks; and planting trees, shrubs, and grapevines—sometimes including their own labor time as part of the calculation.[56]

One of the most eloquent pleas came from the music-teacher-turned-gardener, Jupiter Zeuss Hesser. Detailing and costing out the work he had done in improving "Jupiterville," Hesser professed his deep reluctance to "give up that place as my finished homestead," of which he was only now finally "enjoying the pleasures." While he acknowledged the overriding public benefit of a park for the "enjoyment for poor and rich, young and old, great and small and all kinds of religious and political believers in one union of happiness in the true [love] of nature," he insisted on the "true justice" of "proper compensation" for himself and closed with a plea on behalf of less articulate park dwellers. "A very great number of poor families," he wrote in a postscript, "who worked a number of years on these [lots], squatters and leaseground, will be entirely ruined when they must give up their cultivated land and move away without compensation. Please to have mercy on the Poor, then the Lord will have mercy with you." The Lord's mercy held little sway in the commission of estimate office. Hesser's petition, which he submitted within six weeks of the original report, was marked "too late" and filed away.[57] Very few complaints about land valuations resulted in any change in the commission's awards. The commissioners' notion of "value," rooted in the current market price of land, was the one that determined all payments.

The forty or so proprietors of land bordering the park who complained about the assessments they faced in exchange for the "benefit" of Central Park were slightly more successful than park landowners in winning adjustments from the commission. Not surprisingly, many complaints came from large landowners such as Jacob Harsen and Gouverneur Wilkins and once again raised abstract questions of how to value land in advance of settlement. They disagreed with the commission's mapping of which lots would be most benefited by the park.[58] In drawing its assessment maps, the commission was redrawing the map of the uptown real estate market. Park assessments were thus a self-fulfilling prophecy, in part because assessment costs would be passed on in the selling price. Most obviously, both the existence of the park and the consequent higher assessments established lots along the yet-unbuilt Eighth and Fifth avenues as valuable real estate. Lower assessments on lots farther north reflected expectations for the sequence of development from south to north.

Although the commission made some modest adjustments, it rejected the bulk of the assessment complaints as it had virtually all the valuation complaints. So the landowners, accompanied by an army of lawyers, headed for a courtroom showdown. By law, the state supreme court, a lower court in New York, had to confirm the commission's report. But locally elected district justices in New York County saw the case as too hot to handle, particularly considering some downtown merchants' continuing concern about the burden of the park's cost to taxpayers; and through December and early January, some delayed a ruling and others disqualified themselves. Finally, Governor Horatio Seymour, apparently responding to lobbying by park supporters, appointed Justice Ira Harris of the Albany district to expedite the case. The selection of Harris, the *Sun* reported, "gave great satisfaction to the advocates of the Park," who expected a favorable verdict. Indeed, though acknowledging some of the injustices raised by the lawyers, Judge Harris approved the report.[59]

It had required an out-of-town judge to resolve the contradiction that had troubled Beekman back in 1853. State action to create a public park could serve the cultural and economic interests of wealthy New Yorkers as a class, but a number of wealthy individuals and factions saw this state action as a "violent" seizure of their private property.

The Profit and the Loss

In the months following Judge Harris's decision, the city finally took control of the park land. A few final hitches developed. A clerk in the finance department embezzled two thousand dollars by making out an award check to a non-existent landowner. More seriously, the city encountered cash-flow problems when it attempted to acquire the park land from its owners before receiving the assessment payments or selling the bonds that would pay for the other two-thirds of the cost. By the fall of 1857, however, the city had paid off most of the owners, collected most of the assessments, and cleared the park of most of its residents and structures.[60] What did these changes mean for the groups affected?

With the exception of purchasers at the earlier sale of city land, almost all those whose land was taken by eminent domain for the park made a profit. And given the long-term rise in the value of Manhattan real estate, those who had owned park land for the longest time collected the greatest profits. Many of those long-term landholders had paid nothing for their land, having inherited it. Those who had bought their land earlier in the century also made enormous profits. Archibald Watt, for example, who acquired most of his uptown land in the late 1820s and early 1830s for between $16 and $25 per lot, received $350 per lot from the city less than thirty years later. Why, then, did Watt complain so bitterly about a transaction that apparently netted him a 2,000-percent profit? One reason was that landholders like Watt claimed to have endured substantial carrying costs—taxes and mortgage interest charges. But even considering such costs, Watt's profits still probably exceeded 1,500 percent.[61] Watt never actually objected that he would lose money on the park transaction; his real complaint was that he would not make *more* money. He measured his park profits against still larger profits that he expected on future development of the land. The same was true for those landholders who inherited their land, endured only modest carrying costs, and made even greater profits than Watt. They believed they deserved more.

Some park landowners also measured their profits against the profits that they *would* have made if they had been smart enough to sell their land three years earlier when the land market was at its peak. These landowners looked enviously at neighbors like the Talmans and the Amorys who had sold off their holdings in the fall or winter of 1852. Mayor Fernando Wood, always a shrewd dealer in uptown property, was such a major seller during 1852, although he retained some choice parcels directly bordering the park.[62]

If the biggest winners were those who sold in the fall and winter of 1852, the biggest losers were those who bought at that same moment, especially those who bought Central Park land at the December corporation auction. These buyers had played the real estate market and lost. As is often true in such circumstances, the smaller investors—the grocers like Diederick Knubel or Abraham Clark—lost the most and could least afford to lose it.

The experience of those who had to pay park assessments also varied according to the market and their financial resources, as well as the particular location of their property. Because an 1840 law limited benefit assessments to no more than one-half of the property's taxable value and much uptown land was underassessed for taxes, many landowners paid considerably less in benefit assessments than their actual gain from the park. Put more simply, J. M. Wooly's lots facing the new park at Fifth Avenue and 80th Street jumped a great deal more than $258 in value because of the building of the park, but that amount was about all he could legally be charged. As a result, owners of lots *not* facing the park paid a proportionately greater share of the benefits assessments than might otherwise have been fair. In just three years' time each dollar paid in park-front assessments at 80th Street and Fifth had yielded a two-dollar gain in land value; each dollar paid in assessments off the park (around the corner on 80th Street) had yielded only a fifty-cent gain.[63]

Despite the unequal benefit bestowed on the park-front lots, the ceiling on their assessments kept down assessments for all other lots in the park vicinity. Moreover, those who benefited and lost from this inequality were often the same people. Wooly, for example, owned the entire block on 81st Street between Fourth and Fifth avenues. Most large landowners surrounding the park got exactly what they wanted at a relatively modest price: a large landscaped park that would shape uptown development and increase their real estate values. Of course, the ability of landowners to reap the rewards of those increased real estate values, to experience the "benefit" promised by the park and taxed through benefit assessments, depended on their financial resources. The assessments charged large landowners Wooly, Harsen, and Lenox were substantial but hardly beyond their means. Lenox paid almost $75,000 in park assessments, but he was worth at least $5 million. For small landowners who lived on their land and perhaps operated a grocery or carpenter's shop, by contrast, a $258 assessment could be formidable. "We fear," the *Sun* had commented just after the commission's report was released, "that many poor men . . . will look with dread upon the Park assessments, and should they be obliged to sell, they must, in the present state of the real estate market, do so at a ruinous sacrifice. The speculative value which the Park opening may give to lots held by persons able to meet all expenses, will hardly be realized by poor lot owners forced to sell."[64]

Fourteen months later, when the assessments were coming due, the *Sun* returned to the same theme. "One would suppose," it suggested, "that the arrangement was intended to compel poor men who may own a lot or two in the vicinity of the Park to sell out for the benefit of speculators and rich men." "Was there a deliberate purpose," the paper asked rhetorically, "to drive away from the neighborhood of the Park, the class who cannot meet at once these heavy assessments?" Whether or not the purpose was deliberate, the predictions were accurate. On a three-block stretch between what would become Fourth (later Park) and Fifth avenues and 83rd and 84th streets, for example, seven of the eighteen owner-occupants (all of them apparently small landholders) sold out between 1855 and 1858.[65]

The large landowners' real advantage was not so much their resources to pay assessments and higher taxes as their ability to hold their land off the market until the right moment. The park plans sparked a speculative boom in surrounding real estate. Anticipating large crowds, a few entrepreneurs purchased lots to erect "public houses and places of amusement," but most who responded to the ads featuring "a lot of ground opposite the Central Park" anticipated, as the *Herald* put it in February 1856, that "some of the most splendid private residences in the world" would soon fill their property. By the summer of 1857 lots in the vicinity of the park were commanding what one newspaper called "fancy prices." Although the panic that began that fall reduced prices, park-front lots, by some estimates, had multiplied ten or more times in value between the late 1840s and the late 1850s. The true bonanza profits came to those landowners who waited until the late 1860s and early 1870s to sell. In 1872 when one real estate agent was offering fifty thousand dollars "for any inside lot on Fifth Avenue fronting Central Park" below 73rd Street, those who had paid less than three hundred dollars in assessments for such lots probably no longer had any complaints about the costs of the park.[66]

Even such landowners as James Beekman, who would have preferred an East Side park, profited from the new Central Park. "You are a richer man now" than two years ago, a correspondent told him in May 1856; "true your [park] assessments have been enormous but the increase in value has more than kept pace with them." The so-called violent exercise of eminent domain had quietly enriched Beekman.[67]

The commission's report probably had been as evenhanded as could have been expected; it had crafted a compromise that was calculated to satisfy most well-to-do New Yorkers. Despite the fairness and even conventionality of the report, those like Beekman who had worried that the exercise of eminent domain would be violent were right in one sense. The commission's actions—

and more generally the creation of the park itself—embodied a sort of figurative violence in the force with which they reshaped the uptown landscape. The commissioners had both clarified and established new boundaries for uptown real estate by focusing speculation around the park. Moreover, they had removed more than seven thousand lots from the uptown land market, thus increasing the value of the remaining land and making it more likely that such property would attract wealthier buyers and settlers.

The greatest impact of the coming of the park on uptown real estate, however, was to accelerate two developments that were already well under way. The first was the specialization and regulation of land use. The heterogeneous pattern of settlement on the city's uptown fringe—the mix of country estates, lunatic asylums, bone-boiling plants, subsistence gardens, carriage factories, and black churches—was coming to an end. In downtown Manhattan nuisance industries and pigs had already been banned, and the housing market was shaping specific neighborhoods by class and ethnicity; now a similar process of specialization and regulation spread uptown. To be sure, Archibald Watt's dream of turning upper Manhattan into his version of the modern residential suburb would never be fully realized. Nor would the regulation of uptown Manhattan proceed at the pace the park's advocates hoped. Nevertheless, the park established the expectation of specialized residential land use that in turn affected the strategies of investors—and the living patterns of future generations.

The other change accelerated by the coming of the park was the tendency to regard land as a commodity to be bought and sold. In this respect, the ambitions of landowners who advocated Central Park contrasted with the dreams of contemporary land reformers who wanted to distribute public land, including perhaps the park territory itself, for homesteads. But those who valued land for profit rather than as a means for making a living generally derived the greatest benefits from the coming of the park. Considering how the land market operated and who wielded power within the city, the largest landowners and the owners directly facing the park (who had, of course, backed a park most strongly in the first place) profited the most. If Watt was right to see the taking of the park land as a "war," then it was a war that ratified (albeit sometimes rearranged) more than it overturned existing arrangements of economic and political power.

Those same configurations of power meant that the commission's "judicious" report had little to offer—indeed barely acknowledged—the poor people who lived within the park, although the 20 percent of the park dwellers who owned land, as well as a few others with long-term leases, did receive compensation. Seneca Village pioneer Andrew Williams had bought his three lots on 85th Street for $125 in 1825; thirty years later the city paid him $2,335 for the same three lots plus his modest two-story frame house. Although Williams protested that he had been offered $3,500 for his property and although the commission gave Watt a substantially better rate of return on an investment made around the same time, the black Seneca Village resident did profit handsomely on his purchase of land from the Whiteheads three decades earlier. But for men like Williams there was much more at stake than money. Adjacent to Williams's land was the AME Zion church. On August 4, 1853, just two weeks after the Central Park bill had been passed, his neighbors—apparently unaware of the "improvement" soon to come to uptown Manhattan—gathered to break ground for a new church building. Although blind and aging by this time, Bishop Christopher Rush journeyed uptown to deliver the sermon and lay the cornerstone. A collection was taken up to pay for the new church. During the same months that the sturdy building was being raised and its wood frame was being painted white, the commission of estimate was pondering the "value" of the lots and buildings in Seneca Village and the other precincts of the park.[68] Two and a half years later Bishop Rush would make another journey. This time to the courtroom presided over by Judge Harris to protest (unsuccessfully) the award made to the estate of Seneca Village founder Epiphany Davis in the condemnation proceedings.

By the end of the fall of 1857 the AME Zion church had vanished without a trace. So had the nearby African Union church and Colored School No. 3. The only institutional remnant of Seneca Village was All Angels', which relocated a few blocks west of the park. But "as a result of the condemnation of the Park," the church historian later recorded, "the entire old congregation was scattered and a new congregation organized, only one person in which belonged to the original congregation of All Angels'."[69]

One grim reminder of Seneca Village lingered in the park for the next century. In 1871 laborers digging up trees at 85th Street and Eighth Avenue uncovered the coffin of a "negro." More than fifty years later, a park gardener named Gilhooley was turning up soil in the same area and encountered first a human skull and then an entire graveyard. Reporting jocularly on what had become known as "Gilhooley's Burial Plot," the *New Yorker* described it as "filled with the bones of tramps and squatters who lived in the Park a hundred or so years ago."[70]

Seneca Village, which had been an important pillar of New York's African-American community, disappeared at precisely the moment when that community faced challenges of racism that mounted with the coming of the Civil War. This was not the first time (nor would it be the last) that black New Yorkers were the targets of campaigns of "redevelopment" and "public improvement." In the 1830s the city's first "slum clearance" effort had focused on the poor and racially mixed Five Points community located just northeast of City Hall. And some black Seneca Villagers had already been uprooted a decade and a half earlier when the city chose York Hill as the site for the Croton receiving reservoir.[71]

The other park community built around religious institutions—the Roman Catholic Sisters of Charity convent and school—had also expanded at the same

An 1858 view southwest from Vista Rock (in the vicinity of 77th Street and Seventh Avenue) toward the swampy land that became the Lake. Note the former park dweller's house.

time the plans for the park were moving forward. In March 1855 twenty-one priests joined the sisters and their two hundred boarding students, in their blue uniforms and white veils, to dedicate a stately new brick chapel and dining hall at 105th Street near Fifth. The sisters did get to stay on longer than other park residents, but in 1859 the park commission took over their buildings to use as offices. The Civil War brought their temporary return: between 1862 and 1865 the religious order operated a military hospital in their old buildings. Soon after the war, a park restaurant replaced the hospital and a statuary gallery occupied the chapel. Both were destroyed by fire in 1881.[72]

In the less settled areas of the park, residents had perhaps less to lose than did the Sisters of Charity or the Seneca Villagers. Yet the grocers, founders, milkmen, gardeners, rope makers, bone boilers, leather dressers, and hog keepers lost their workplace as well as their homes. Some, like Edward Snowden, who moved his foundry a few blocks east, reestablished their businesses elsewhere. For others, particularly those who kept animals or worked the land, the upheaval was more traumatic. Moreover, whereas landowners received some compensation from the city, those whose status rested on informal leasing arrangements, those who had "squatted" for years on land whose owners were unknown, and those whose improvements were difficult to value had to start over from scratch, some apparently taking refuge in the "squatter" settlements located in the rocky and swampy land to the west of the park. As Jupiter Hesser feared, the commission provided no "allowance" for the work these people had done in cultivating and improving the park land. "The cultivators (Poor Creatures!)," he had sadly forecast, "had to work for the benefit of the rich. Noble charity that!"[73]

Park residents experienced the end of their world in stages. First came the orders in the late spring of 1856 that they would henceforth have to pay rent to the city if they wanted to remain even temporarily in the houses and on the lots they had long occupied. Then almost simultaneously the city's invading troops appeared—the nineteen members of the newly organized Central Park police assigned to "protect" what was now city property. With the police came a crackdown on practices that had been customary among park dwellers. The resident arrested in the summer of 1856 for selling the "park's stones," which he had broken up as street paving, was engaging in a "business" no one would have questioned six months earlier. Other park dwellers were probably similarly bewildered to find that cutting down trees for firewood was now considered a "crime." So too were the patrons of a dance hall in the upper park bewildered by a 3:00 A.M. raid by Central Park police.[74]

When the city inspector ordered "the removal of the piggeries and other nuisances now existing on the Central Park grounds," a *Times* reporter found the Irish hog keepers reluctant to leave. He commented that "the Policemen find it difficult to persuade them out of the idea, which has possessed their simple minds, that the sole object of the authorities in making the Park is to procure their expulsion from the homes which they occupy." Although the owners of piggeries faced eviction in the summer of 1856, other residents were allowed to stay on while the city tried to decide how it was going to go about financing the park's construction. The final eviction orders came at the worst possible moment. On October 1, 1857, the newspapers were filled with reports of the deepening panic and mounting unemployment but made no mention of the eviction of the park dwellers. The residents—quietly and without violence—left their homes.[75]

Building Central Park, 1858

II. DESIGNING AND BUILDING CENTRAL PARK

4

THE DESIGN COMPETITION

On October 13, 1857, just two weeks after the park dwellers left their homes, the Board of Commissioners of the Central Park offered prizes of four hundred to two thousand dollars for the four best proposals for "laying out the park." This notice for the first important landscape design competition in the United States elicited thirty-three varied proposals, which revealed the influence of English and continental traditions of landscape design as well as more eclectic vernacular ideas about what would make this public place appealing. But when the commissioners opened the proposals six months later, they found one curious entry. Plan 2 by an anonymous contestant was nothing but a pyramid.[1]

This mocking gesture of dissent may well have come from someone unhappy with the outcome of the political struggle that had empowered the board of commissioners to decide how Central Park should be designed and run. The board was not a democratic body directly accountable to the citizens of New York but a self-perpetuating entity appointed by the state legislature. This novel arrangement for administering the city's great park was a by-product of the larger national struggle over slavery. The realignment of political parties pitted New York State against New York City, threatened the principle and custom of home rule, and brought the Republican party to power, whereupon a Republican-dominated legislature removed control of Central Park from the city and invested it in the hands of eleven gentlemen. Elite New Yorkers wanted a park that would match the standards of beauty and order they associated with Old World public grounds, and a board of gentlemen could be trusted to choose a tasteful design. The pyramid entry may have been a wry symbol of imperial rule over a democratic public institution.

The State versus the City

Few precedents existed for administration of a municipal public works project of the scale or projected cost of Central Park. To be sure, for more than a decade, the party in power had tossed control of the Croton water system back and forth from state to city commissions, but the aqueduct required coordination of land and labor under the overlapping local jurisdiction of three counties. Central Park, by contrast, clearly belonged to the municipal corporation—defined by the city's charters as the "Mayor, Common Council, and Commonalty." Thus in the spring of 1856, city officials sought authorization from the state legislature for the mayor to appoint, with common-council approval, a five-person commission to administer the park and for the common council to appropriate bond revenues for its construction.[2]

Such a bill would ordinarily have passed with little debate. The 1846 state constitution explicitly provided for local authorities (street commissions, for example) to be selected by local constituents or elected officials. But in 1856 the two-party system in New York was splintering as large numbers of New Yorkers rallied to the antislavery banner of Whig senator William Seward. The Democrats had long been a quarrelsome group, and the formation of the nativist American, or Know-Nothing, party, which stressed the "immigrant problem" rather than slavery, further divided legislators into factions. In addition, the city had fallen out of favor with state representatives in the wake of the 1853 scandal about the "Forty Thieves" common council. Nativists, Whigs, and temperance advocates blamed political corruption on Irish and German immigrant voters who had brought Democrats to power in New York City. Lawmakers were thus suspicious of any bill that would empower Democratic mayor Fernando Wood, who had been elected with the support of Irish and German voters and had evaded enforcing antiliquor laws. The legislature left the city's request for authority to govern Central Park on the table when it adjourned at the end of its 1856 session.[3]

Mayor Fernando Wood was not a man to let the state interfere with his plans. Wood, after all, claimed credit for saving the park from cost-cutting fiscal conservatives. He regarded it as the emblem of a great city destined to propel him to the White House. He persuaded the common council, in the absence of any state action, to bestow authority to govern Central Park on a park commission made up of the mayor and the street commissioner. In June 1856 Wood appointed a park police force, surveying teams, an office staff, and a board of consultants, made up of gentlemen of taste, to advise him on design. Some, William Cullen Bryant and Robert Dillon among them, refused to lend their prestige to the mayor's scheme to circumvent the legislature. But others, including the novelist Washington Irving; the historian George Bancroft; a banker, Stewart Brown (one of Minturn's gentlemen petitioners); and a book auctioneer and former state senator, James E. Cooley, signed on. The consultants elected Washington Irving chairman.[4]

Most newspaper editors in the city welcomed the mayor's initiative and predicted that the consulting gentlemen would elevate the project above political jobbery. But Tammany Democrats worried that the mayor's system of personal patronage—and particularly his influence over city police—threatened their own control of the party organization. When the Tammany corporation counsel went to court to block the first park commission, newspaper editors backed off and conceded that the building of Central Park required the state legislature's authorization of its financing and administrative structure.[5]

The formation of the New York Republican party offered an even more ominous portent for Wood's plans. In April 1856 a committee of gentlemen—including a number of "Seward Whigs" in Robert Minturn's social circle, free-soil Democrats, and disaffected Know-Nothings—established the state branch of the new antislavery party. And in the fall of 1856 when Wood narrowly won reelection, state voters took their stand against slavery's expansion by electing a Republican governor and majority to the assembly.[6]

The leaders of the infant Republican party faced the difficult task of consolidating their organizational position in state politics. Control of Central Park, like control of the city police force, served this end nicely. If power could be wrested from Mayor Wood, jobs could be strategically conferred on loyal supporters and friendly allies to establish a new channel of party patronage. Republican politicians were wary; one partisan advised the Republican strategist Thurlow Weed that if appointment of the park board were "left to Mayor Wood a class of men will be selected who will use the $100,000 [actually $1.5 million] much to our disadvantage." Whereupon, the Republican-dominated legislature removed Central Park and the police from city politics and placed them under state-appointed commissions. Although Republicans portrayed these laws (as well as kindred acts restricting liquor licenses and sales) as "reform" measures, they fit into a larger Republican strategy of curtailing the power of New York City Democrats and courting the support of nativists and temperance activists. Ignoring the issue of the constitutional legitimacy of the legislature's appointment of local officials, in April 1857 lawmakers installed the eleven-man Board of Commissioners of the Central Park—six Republicans, four Democrats, and one Know-Nothing who would soon become a Republican.[7]

The Gentlemen of the Board

Three of the gentlemen of the park board were veterans of five years of park politicking, although sometimes on different sides: James E. Cooley (who had endorsed Central Park over Jones Wood and later served on Mayor Wood's consulting board), former corporation counsel Robert Dillon (who had carried the legal battle to secure the land), and that redoubtable English-born nursery-man and ardent Jones Wood supporter James Hogg, who had joined the state Republican party at its inception. Hogg lobbied for a commissioner's seat by advising Thurlow Weed that he could capture nativist votes in the Nineteenth Ward, adjacent to the park, by extending patronage to men to be "employed on the improvement." He had little else in common with the rest of the board—lawyers, merchants, businessmen, and bankers—the kind of gentlemen one assemblyman had promised would be selected by state officials, gentlemen "of more mark, taste, and acquisition than would be chosen by local authorities."[8]

The four Democratic park commissioners represented a careful balance of factions. Cooley and Dillon satisfied the more conservative state wing of the party; Thomas Fields was an ardent Tammany lawyer; and Andrew Green, also a lawyer and former president of the city school board, was a reform-minded Democrat, probably recommended by his mentor and law partner Samuel Tilden, a leading Democratic fund-raiser (and future presidential candidate). Green took a nonpartisan stance and frequently aligned himself with the Republican commissioners. He was to become a major power on the new park board.[9]

The Republicans on the board, were, of course, new to their own new party. Charles Russell and John F. Butterworth, who were merchants, had been big financial contributors to the Whig party; John A. C. Gray, a banker, and William Strong, a wool merchant, had defected from the free-soil Democrats. Waldo Hutchins was a former Democrat temporarily residing in the Know-Nothing party on his way to becoming a Republican; Charles Elliott, who was a vice-president of the city Republican party, had studied with Andrew Jackson Downing and spent eight years as a landscape gardener before entering the iron-making business. He represented the new party's more progressive wing: a free-soiler for nearly a decade, he admired Fourierist principles of cooperation and had written a sympathetic biography of the Haitian revolutionary leader Toussaint L'Ouverture.[10]

The new commissioners resembled the gentlemen who first advocated creating a park. Although Robert Minturn turned down an appointment to the board, his business partner Moses H. Grinnell would join the commission in 1860. They were all, except Hogg, wealthy. Many of the commissioners divided their time between the city and country estates or lengthy European tours. In the nativist climate of the 1850s, the board's old-stock background and rural attachments reinforced their claims to being "well-bred" gentlemen. The majority of the new Central Park board were also genteel, Protestant, and predominantly of rural roots. Elliott, Green, Russell, Strong, Hutchins, and Butterworth came from old-stock New England and upstate New York families; like so many "Yankees" after 1825, they moved to New York City to renew or expand their family fortunes. Only two commissioners, Gray and Dillon, had been born or raised in New York City. Dillon, the son of an Irish immigrant, was the only Catholic member and he was far from a typical Irish-American Catholic. His father had arrived well before the famine migration, and Dillon himself was a wealthy lawyer at a time when there were only forty Irish-born lawyers in the entire city.[11]

The new board turned out to be a factious congregation of disparate personalities, political affiliations, and personal views about parks. Nevertheless, the commissioners shared a collective identity as "public spirited and cultivated gentlemen" who, the *New York Times* suggested, would work without pay "for the mere gratification of rendering a service to the public." This concept of stewardship came from classical republican thought—those who obtained wealth should return it to the community through public service. In the 1850s and 1860s, as professional politicians took over the management of elections, many wealthy men eschewed elective office and the fray of campaigning. At the same time, "gentlemen" regained control of critical city institutions through state bodies removed from direct democratic control. State legislators created commissions to control not only the New York City police and park but also, in the 1860s, the public health and fire departments. The Republican-led move to separate crucial public offices from city politics linked the issues of party and class power.[12]

Amid fears that Mayor Wood would challenge the constitutionality of the park board as he was doing in his suit against the new state-appointed police board, the Board of Commissioners of the Central Park assembled on April 30, 1857, to organize themselves into a body analogous to a corporate board of directors. They elected the Democrat James Cooley as president, but gave Republicans control of the most important committees.[13] In mid-May, the commissioners turned to the crucial questions of how the park would be designed and built. What, after all, was a public park? What should it contain? What should it should look like? How should it be arranged for public use?

The First Design

The romantic poet and *Post* editor William Cullen Bryant had envisioned the park primarily as a piece of conserved nature. The commissioners should arrange to plant trees, build roads, walks, and a fountain, and let people find their own relief from city cares in an otherwise unembellished "rural" landscape. Others saw the park as the public equivalent of the private Hudson Valley estates Downing had designed. When Aldermen Daniel Dodge and Joseph Britton advocated the central site, they conjured up dramatic scenic views alongside "architectural works of every order and variety." Alderman Henry Shaw hoped for magnificent architectural structures—museums, colleges, concert halls, and private dwellings—framing park grounds that would be embellished by fountains, statues, and gardens.[14] Many early proposals put design second to what designers today would call the program for the use of the space, but all agreed that Central Park must be beautiful, even magnificent, and it must measure up to European models as a worthy emblem of the city's progress.

Most politicians and newspaper publishers invoked European models to explain to New Yorkers what a park should be. Like Hyde Park in London or the Bois de Boulogne in Paris, the *Herald*'s James Gordon Bennett insisted, Central Park should offer a grand concourse for a "varied, animated and attractive promenade . . . crowded with the beauty and fashion of our city." Horace Greeley of the *Tribune* felt sure the republican application of European models would instruct and elevate citizens. "The workingman and his working wife and working children after their daily toil," instead of resorting to saloons, would find relief "amid lamps, fountains, verdure; enlivened by music; softened by the beauty of the scene; civilized by the good manners which would spontaneously be the rule, and be enforced when wanting."[15]

But some new voices now entered the discussion. The *Irish News*, looking to a model closer to New York, suggested that a public park should have two parts: a landscaped "pleasance" with drives and walks and a "commons" or "public diversion ground," open terrain like Hoboken's Elysian Fields that could flexibly accommodate picnics, sports, games, ice skating, and militia drills. "New York wants a place to play leap-frog in," the *Irish News* urged, "not a mere ornamented place to pass through."[16]

With abundant suggestions promulgated through the press, Egbert Viele, whom Mayor Wood had appointed to oversee the topographical survey, produced the first plan for the park. Viele, at thirty-one, was an engineer and a veteran of the Mexican War. On his own initiative in the summer of 1856,

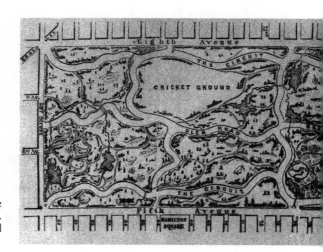

In his 1856 plan, Viele provided ample space for a cricket ground and parade. His "circuit drive" closely followed the park's topography.

before the legislative appointment of the new park board, he presented a design to Wood's consulting board.[17]

Viele's plan provided "open spaces for fresh air and exercise," which would extend "rational enjoyment . . . as a great preventive of crime and vice." He proposed drives through rural scenery, a fifty-acre parade for militia drills and civic assemblies, open fields for "manly" recreations such as cricket, and a botanical garden for popular instruction. In contrast to Europeans, who considered parks to be "appendages of grandeur to rank . . . which the people enjoy at the discretion of their possessors," those who design an American park, according to Viele, should "seek to know the peculiar wants of all classes, and to endeavor to gratify them at every step with due respect to the principles of art, and an economical expenditure of money."[18]

Viele's plan was pragmatic and naturalistic with few architectural embellishments. Describing the irregular lay of the land, the engineer directed public attention to the basic topographical preconditions of any landscape design. He suggested an intricately winding circuit drive that closely followed the terrain, and he logically placed lakes and streams on the site of existing swamps and springs. Viele also invoked the "correct ideas of natural beauty" found in the latest literature of landscape gardening; in contrast to "earlier efforts . . . to make nature assume a strictly artificial appearance, giving to every scene an air of formality and symmetry," the "modern style's" rule was that "the greatest art is to conceal art." Arranging the park's features in relation to topography would be an economical approach, and Viele's plan might have been constructed within the $1.5 million dollars the legislature had authorized.[19]

The presentation and implicit endorsement of Viele's plan in January 1857 in the Wood Park commission's only annual report prompted little public criticism. Five months later, however, the new state-appointed board jettisoned

Viele's design. The commissioners did reappoint Viele as chief engineer but restricted his responsibilities to completing the topographical survey. Neither the Republicans nor the reform-minded Democrats on the board wanted to empower a Wood appointee to design the park and then oversee a construction project that would lead to thousands of patronage jobs. Gentlemen merchants and bankers had promoted the park as an emblem of the city's and their own refinement. Why endanger this powerful symbol with a plan produced by a home-bred army engineer with no experience in designing artistic landscapes? Moreover, Viele had a reputation among gentlemen for poor manners—for swearing and insulting ladies. The board endorsed the recommendation of Commissioner Charles Elliott, a former landscape gardener himself, that it set up a competition and award prizes to the four best designs.[20]

An English architect, Calvert Vaux, helped persuade the commissioners of the aesthetic deficiencies of Viele's plan and the desirability of holding a competition. Vaux, who had emigrated to work with Andrew Jackson Downing and, after Downing's death in 1852, inherited his practice, had good connections with the board. He had designed both a Fifth Avenue house and the Bank of New York building for Commissioner Gray, and he knew Commissioner Elliott, who had himself written for Downing's *Horticulturalist*.[21]

Evaluating a plan aesthetically required a trained eye. When Viele went to court in 1864 to get compensation for the work he had done, Vaux was called to testify. In his critique of the engineer's plan, Vaux stressed two artistic defects. One was that the design incorporated both the views and the traffic of the surrounding city. Indeed, with four commercial surface roads crossing the park, Viele's plan would have brought the city directly into the landscape. It was a simple solution to the problem of crosstown traffic that would also extend the park's benefits to a wider constituency. "A man who was driving along there on business," Viele's attorney noted, "would pass through the park and have an equal chance with those who drive for pleasure" to enjoy its scenes. But such roads, Vaux thought, would intrude on the park's scenery.[22]

Viele's design, Vaux also observed, lacked an "artistic conception," and without a "central idea" or focal point to capture visitors' attention, one part of the park would look like another. The parkgoer, taken as a park *viewer*, would find no "picture." Establishing a line of vision and framing landscape pictures required creating the illusion of distance. The pragmatic route of Viele's drives sacrificed a feeling of breadth on either side; and his small ponds lost the effect of distance that would be supplied by large sheets of water separating the viewer from the eye's object. Nor did Viele have any aesthetic objections to the old rectangular receiving reservoir. Indeed, Viele considered the reservoir worthy of attention as a major engineering feat, and his plan emphasized it by adding a terrace to the walls, from which spectators could observe militia drills. An editorial in *Harpers Weekly* commended Viele's plan for such attention to popular

Egbert Viele (1825–1902) oversaw the topographical survey of Central Park and drew up the first plan. He later served as a Civil War general and U.S. congressman.

interests, but trained criticism of the engineer's taste reinforced the commissioners' decision to reopen the design question.[23]

Pleasure Garden? Civic Monument? Pastoral Eden?

Four aesthetic sensibilities framed the possibilities for Central Park's design. Two—what might be called "republican simplicity" and "popular eclecticism"—derived from vernacular design traditions and found their clearest expression in the city's streets and commercial pleasure gardens. The other two possibilities—romantic naturalism and "artificial" civic display—were closely associated with the formal landscape design traditions of English parks and continental European public spaces.

In February 1856 an anonymous correspondent to the *Tribune* attempted to structure public discussion of design. A new name should set the park apart from the city streets. Of the name in popular use, he said, " 'Central' belongs to geometry, it savors of business"; and "park," because of "local circumstances," summoned up in New Yorkers' minds "a small rectangular enclosure shut in by houses" like City Hall Park or Tompkins Square. The new park's designer, therefore, should observe "one essential principle": remove the visitor's "recollection" of the streetscape.[24]

To the designers of the 1811 street system, the grid had embodied virtues of republican simplicity—rationality, economy, and convenience. By the mid-nineteenth century, however, critics were denouncing the aesthetic monotony of rectilinear streets and also the vulgarity of bold advertising signs on commercial blockfronts. Such vernacular design traditions of simplicity emboldened by promotion was too closely linked to the necessities of work and pressures of the marketplace. At a time when the ordinary was seldom celebrated as beautiful, most New Yorkers agreed with the *Tribune* correspondent that the specialness of Central Park as a civic institution rested on its opposition to the commercial utility of the street grid.[25]

With traffic, dust, noise, crowds, and peddling subverting the grid's expression of republican values, wealthy New Yorkers especially stressed that the park should be designed to represent the city at its best. An artistic public space, cleansed of the street's commercial excesses and social disorders, would offer a symbolic statement of shared civic goals that transcended emerging social conflicts. Then too, a park with beautiful scenery or magnificent architecture and without commercial traffic would provide a proper setting for carriage drives or promenades, for rituals of social decorum and aesthetic display. Genteel New Yorkers saw themselves in such a space as the city's "representative class" and indeed as its "public." Seeking to distinguish this conception of the park from any "aristocratic" European taint, Horace Greeley and other editors explained that as an example of American art the park would elevate and refine the common people.[26]

But, as the *Tribune*'s correspondent recognized and regretted, another vernacular design tradition—popular eclecticism—competed with Europe's artistically landscaped grounds as a model for the park. Formally designed for entrepreneurial profit, commercial pleasure gardens liberally mixed all styles of art and decoration to create recreational spaces that responded to popular desires for novelty and diversion, not with an overarching composition but with an abundant array of showy works of art and nature. Each smaller than two city blocks in area, the Palace Gardens and Niblo's, for example, featured ornamental gardens with promenades, pavilions, grottoes, arbors, fountains, flower beds, topiary art, and inspirational statues, as well as temporary exhibits of panoramas and scenic transparencies. The proprietors of pleasure gardens constructed stages and circus rings and entertained their visitors with elaborate theater programs, concerts, equestrian acts, and fireworks. Variety, flexibility, and unpredictability in arrangement and use of space similarly characterized the

The Pleasure Garden: Popular resorts like the Palace Garden, located at Sixth Avenue and 14th Street, eclectically decorated their grounds with statues, fountains, and bandshells.

eclectic aesthetic of larger pleasure grounds such as Hoboken's Elysian Fields or Harlem Gardens, where lively crowds engaged in picnics, festivals, and sports in the shady groves and open pastures of former farms or gentlemen's country seats. At Elysian Fields, visitors came by ferry from New York to admire sweeping views of the Hudson River, but their attention was also drawn to the inviting foreground of human activity and a landscape decorated with temporary facilities (from tables and benches to tents and carnival booths).[27]

Although the *Tribune*'s letter writer acknowledged that many New Yorkers who enjoyed nature might be "discontented with her simplicity and tameness," he rejected the aesthetic of commercial pleasure gardens as evidence of "poor taste" and pled with the park's future designer to spurn any impulse to "tickle the fancy" by adding a "thousand contrivances," the "spicy ingredients" of Chinese pagodas, Indian wigwams, "nymphs and mermaids and dancing fauns, . . . grottoes, and labyrinths, artificial ponds and innumerable cascades." New Yorkers had been "led astray by the claptrap and gewgaw" of pleasure gardens. Rejecting such vernacular design influences, the *Tribune*'s correspondent con-

New Yorkers traveled by ferry to Hoboken's Elysian Fields for large group picnics, festivals, and baseball games like this one shown at the bottom of an 1866 print.

sidered two formal landscape traditions more appropriate models for Central Park: the English naturalistic tradition or the continental style of artificial civic display.[28]

Of the two, the correspondent preferred the romantic naturalistic tradition. As art criticism and landscape gardening gained influence within upper-class

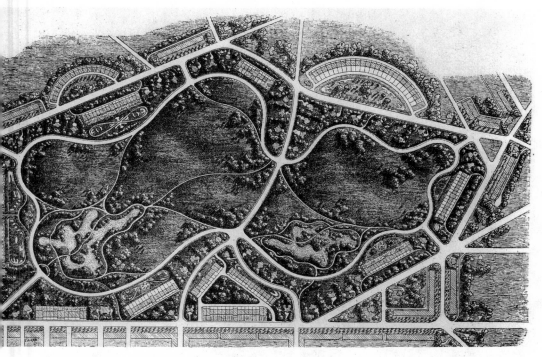

The Romantic Pastoral Park: Many New Yorkers admired Liverpool's Birkenhead Park, designed by Joseph Paxton in the early 1840s. Rectangular lots were set aside within the park for private villas.

circles in the 1840s and 1850s, the unity of aesthetic conception was put forward as the key to the moral purpose of art. Popular romantic critics Andrew Jackson Downing and John Ruskin (whose writings were widely distributed and read) challenged classical landscaping traditions that celebrated the human capacity to "improve upon nature" by featuring, in Downing's words, "regularity, symmetry and the display of labored art." Instead, these self-styled "moderns" advocated art that would reveal the more powerful, spontaneous, irregular, and yet harmonious hand of God in nature. Downing followed the English landscape gardeners (Humphrey Repton and John Nash and later John C. Loudon and Joseph Paxton), who introduced flowing curves, open vistas, and picturesque plantings into the formal, geometric spaces of English parks and private country estates. He also tutored American readers in the different styles within the romantic tradition: "The Beautiful"—what others called the pastoral—"is an idea of beauty calmly and harmoniously expressed; the Picturesque an idea of beauty powerfully and irregularly expressed." In landscaping "rural" cemeteries and their own country houses, wealthy Americans had embraced this naturalistic aesthetic, particularly its pastoral expression.[29]

So did the *Tribune*'s correspondent, who urged the future designer to

Artificial Civic Display: Parisian public grounds like the Garden of Luxembourg featured classical sculpture and formal geometric designs.

develop the park's "chaste and simple" natural features. "What we seek when we emerge from [the city], is repose. We want an extent—an apparently boundless extent of rural landscape . . . broad, expansive and tranquil." The "ample scene" of such an "unadulterated" landscape would rejuvenate parkgoers' moral imaginations and inspire "fresh gratitude" for a "beneficent" republican government. The perception of rural scenery was tinged with nostalgia for an imagined, simpler past. "The captured *Rus in Urbe,*" one editor suggested, "greets us as we tread about our business ways like touches of nature, reminiscences of a lost Eden, jewels which a bounteous but departed mother has hung upon the breast of an ungrateful and degenerate child." And like a bounteous mother, a benevolent government could regenerate its citizens by recreating Edenic harmony in its pastoral public park.[30]

The Crystal Place, built at Sixth Avenue and 42nd Street for the New York Exhibition in 1853, seemed to represent the pinnacle of human progress. Some contestants in the design competition proposed constructing a similar palace of glass and iron in Central Park.

The challenge to a romantic naturalistic park came from those who associated the beautiful with the works of human progress, with what the naturalists labeled "artificial" civic display. The park's designer should beware, the *Tribune* correspondent warned, of following the advice of such advocates, "who would devote the funds to architectural decorations, to arches, columns, or elaborate water-works . . . who would prefer stately and geometrically straight avenues . . . who in short would have it an elegant parade ground—perhaps even a race course." These would display the "vitiated tastes" of "formal and elaborate" continental public spaces. Although he condemned French (as well as German) parks as monuments to "an age of corruption," he excepted the Bois de Boulogne, which had recently been redesigned in the naturalistic style. (Despite the change, the Bois still retained its formal promenandes and its racecourse.)[31]

New Yorkers like Egbert Viele, who saw beauty in civic engineering triumphs, admired the city's waterworks—its aqueduct and reservoirs—as artistic American achievements merging grandeur with utility. In seeing the park as part of a constellation of other public institutions, including the Crystal Palace at 42nd Street or the recently built Cooper Union farther downtown, other admirers of the artificial civic style linked the benefits of the city's prosperity to popular education. Nature and art could be arranged through museums, botanical gardens, and arboretums to further practical knowledge, to instruct park-goers' intellects as well as inspire their moral imaginations.[32]

Yet most admirers of civic display shared the naturalists' distrust of eclectic decoration. As a public work, they thought, the park should present a dramatic institutional statement of the city's accomplishments, encouraging optimism in the material progress of a society committed to individualism. But the emphasis on more formal spaces also suggested that civic display could bind individual citizens together in collective rituals. Personal display along elegant promenades, for example, could inspire respectful deference, decorum, and good manners. As a civic center, basking in the city's reflective light, yet cleansed of its tensions and ambiguities, a park designed in the artificial tradition would restore citizens by linking self-improvement with social improvement.[33]

Naturalists like the *Tribune*'s correspondent thought an "artificial" design that encouraged displays of architecture or fashion risked being corrupted by aristocratic pretensions, inspiring envy or resentment. Although the creation of rural scenery through landscaping was no less costly and artificial than crystal palaces and stately avenues, to the romantic critics, nature itself represented an antidote to the materialistic ambitions they associated with city life.[34]

New Yorkers' different aesthetic sensibilities cannot be easily identified with any particular social group. The pastoral vision of the park may have resonated with New Yorkers of New England stock—most of Minturn's merchant gentlemen and the new park board—whose Calvinist upbringings had taught them to distrust artificial embellishments associated with aristocratic waste or Catholic ritual. The *Tribune*'s correspondent had identified a preference for a naturalistic design with American "adoption" of the English Protestant "system of social and domestic comforts." New Yorkers less invested in Protestant moralism who admired continental fashions and styles may have been more deeply impressed by the civic grandeur promised by Baron Haussmann's new Parisian boulevards. Or those who admired the artificial style may have felt exhilaration at the prospect of grand utilitarian projects as symbols of republican progress.[35]

Yet both of these two formal design traditions differed less from each other than from the flexible aesthetic of pleasure gardens. Whatever their particular tastes, most refined and elite New Yorkers shared the conviction that the city's new public space should express a unified artistic and social purpose. Whether citizens went to the "avenue" or the "woods," the view should be framed, the approach fixed by drives and walks, and the setting insulated from both the novelties of pleasure gardens and the social unpredictability of the streets.

Whatever the wisdom of formal aesthetic theory, many ordinary New York-ers delighted in the eclectic commercial recreational spaces. "Central Park was intended, not as a luxurious promenade for the rich," the *Irish American* pro-tested (picking up on gentlemen's own arguments as to its benefits), "but as the 'lungs of the city' for the working classes." These New Yorkers may have equally welcomed beautiful vistas and the prospect of new civic institutions such as museums and botanical gardens, but they worried less about the possible aesthetic incompatibility of park features (pastoral scenery and formal prom-enades, for example) than about the possible exclusion of popular attractions. In 1856 a *Zeitung und Herold* editorial envisioned "a large, beautiful, and separate portion of the Central Park" set aside for "popular festivals" to introduce New Yorkers to "the hilarious art" of gymnastics and "its consequent sociability." The *Irish News* considered Central Park big enough to accommodate both a popular "commons" and a grand formal "pleasure ground."[36]

In articulating the unified aesthetic motive of their plans, contestants work-ing within either formal design tradition would assume a unified social motive for parkgoers as a "public" that would appreciate an artistic composition. The unity of this aesthetic conception, in turn, would require exclusion of inap-propriate alternatives, implicitly any view of the park as a public space that would accommodate and celebrate the aesthetic variety and unpredictability of the city itself.

The Competition and the Entries

Although the park commissioners themselves expected a unified aesthetic conception of the design, their specifications mandated a mix of facilities. They provided each competitor a copy of Viele's topographical map with instructions that construction cost no more than the $1.5 million authorized by the legisla-ture. Certain details Viele had defined as part of his park also appeared in the board's specifications: four or more cross streets connecting Fifth and Eighth avenues along the park's two-and-one-half-mile length; a twenty- to forty-acre parade ground (significantly reduced from Viele's fifty acres) with "proper arrangements for the convenience of spectators"; and three playgrounds, three to ten acres each. Responding to suggestions from Greeley, Bennett, and other editors, the commissioners also specified sites for an exhibition or concert hall, a flower garden, a winter skating lake, a prominent fountain, and a lookout tower. The requirements thus included at least one institution of cultural uplift or practical knowledge, playgrounds for healthful exercise, and a parade ground for the civic function of militia drills.[37]

There were thirty-three official entries in the design competition, as well as two additional plans submitted by a landscape gardener and a team of engineers who wanted to make suggestions but did not want to compete. Of the thirty-three formal entries, the actual plans in sepia or india ink of three survive. For the other thirty plans, only verbal descriptions are available now. It is impossible to assess their visual composition, and even interpreting the descriptions presents problems, including the limited literary skills of men like landscape gardener J. Lachaume, who explained apologetically that he was "more of a working man than a writer." Still, literary skill—the ability to invoke aesthetic principles of landscape design and to explain a plan's intention or "motive"— did play a crucial role in persuading the commissioners of a designer's professional competence to handle a public work of such dimensions and importance. Entries came from both professional and amateur designers—from landscape gardeners familiar with the theories and rules of their trade; from engineers who were attuned to the topographical problems of building roads, lakes, and scenic effects; and from general enthusiasts with ideas about landscape beauty or the kinds of amusements that should go into a park but with limited practical experience in laying out extensive grounds.[38]

Although the commissioners had hoped to attract European experts in landscape design, all but two of the entrants who can be identified were Americans. At least half were from New York City, with nine proposals submitted by officers, engineers, surveyors, gardeners, or foremen who had been hired by the new park commission during its first eight months in office, or by its predecessor. The surviving verbal descriptions demonstrate that the contestants recognized common problems with the park site and, in many cases, offered similar solutions. Most entries, for example, embraced the logic of ordering the park—particularly the drives and lakes—in conformity with the natural topography. This principle required particular ingenuity for the ardent land reformer (and ex-Owenite) Lewis Masquerier, who suggested the entire park should be laid out as a living map in the shape of the continents, with the swamp near 59th Street converted into Atlantic Ocean lakes, and the hilly area south of the reservoir corresponding to the Rocky Mountains. He regretfully conceded that the Caribbean and Gulf of Mexico on intervening table lands would have to be represented by a meadow. Only H. Noury—apparently a French architect—balked at following the configuration of the land and abandoned all constraints of practicability. In one of the most extravagant plans of the contest, he announced that the new reservoir would simply have to be moved so that a grand parade ground, a *champ de mars*, could be placed on its site.[39]

Virtually all the designers recommended that the park north of the existing receiving reservoir and the planned new one be treated naturalistically, with scenic carriage drives and walks generally following the contours identified by Viele. Modifying the rugged terrain northwest of the reservoirs would be prohibitively expensive, and the territory from 85th to 106th streets was largely inaccessible to park visitors arriving by public transportation. Several contestants took up a theme already sounded by the commissioners and the press and

Design contestant Roswell Graves, who worked as an engineer on the park, submitted this drawing with his proposal for a pastoral design.

proposed that the park boundary be extended northward from 106th to 110th Street to encompass the high point of the northwest rocky ridge. (The suggestion was implemented in 1863.)[40]

The plans differed much more dramatically in the design of the lower half of the park. Although all contestants included the required parade ground, formal garden, major fountain, and an exhibition or concert hall, each pursued a different approach in treatment of these features in relation to the natural setting. Roughly two-thirds of the proposed plans highlighted the natural landscape itself. Working primarily within the naturalistic tradition, these plans provided relief from the city amid pastoral scenery of artistically arranged rocks, trees, lawns, lakes, and streams. The other one-third emphasized an artificial civic display of formal avenues, exhibition halls, museums, fountains, statuary, and zoological or botanical gardens, intended simultaneously to instruct and inspire their viewers in the accomplishments of civilization.[41] A cluster of proposals within each of these dominant modes showed the influence of "popular eclecticism," some stressing the diverting ornamentation of the natural landscape, others emphasizing the parade and playgrounds as popular features accommodating large crowds of spectators and participants. And one particularly ambitious plan tried to merge all these impulses.

Given the popularity of his writings, Downing's overwhelming influence is not surprising. Yet, it is hard not to sympathize with the engineering team who complained that "parrots and magpies" had "learned to repeat . . . stereotyped phrases" from Downing in defense of their conceptions of correct taste. The naturalistic plans repeatedly recommended "planting out" the park boundaries and the "ugly," "artificial," "uncouth," "horrid," and "discordant" distraction of the reservoirs in order to reinforce the sense of natural expanse. They stressed arranging plants in relation to the terrain—"alpine" evergreens and larches amid prominent boulders; lush willows, magnolias, and vines in the alluvial valleys; stately elms bordering level promenades; and pastoral groves of oaks and maples around open fields. Reminding their readers that Downing had found the artistic treatment of water "particularly difficult," contestants working within the naturalistic tradition explained how to conceal the limits of lakes with undulating shores. They pointed to the intricacy of light and shade achieved through strategic planting, highlighted the park's rocky outcroppings as the "peculiar and characteristic feature of the ground," and explained how to balance the picturesque and pastoral to avoid "monotony" while maintaining harmony. At least four plans noted the particularly dramatic qualities of Vista Rock as a natural focal point in the lower park.[42]

Some landscape gardeners were purists who, like the *Tribune*'s correspondent, argued that nature should be kept "chaste and simple." "Some parts of the ground are already so beautifully dressed by nature's frolicsome humor," noted a contestant who had been a gardening foreman on the park, that "man can only spoil but never improve it." Others who favored a romantic aesthetic were less confident of the sufficiency of unembellished nature and introduced a stunning array of statuary and structures—from classical columns to a series of Chinese, Norwegian, Italian, and Swiss keepers' lodges—to provide "interest and variety." John Deutsch from Tarrytown scattered his imagined landscape with statues and fountains of Diana, Neptune, and Apollo, but he also argued for the principle of simplicity by urging the commissioners to ban carriages from the park. "My idea is to bring the public here on a common level; let visitors enjoy themselves on foot." Noting that though the park's abandoned shanties were "picturesque" they were not "appropriate," two former park surveyors suggested that the Arsenal (at Fifth Avenue and 64th Street) be partially destroyed and planted with ivy to create picturesque ruins.[43]

The anonymous author of plan 13, signed "Ars Longa, Vita Brevis Est" (art is long, life is short), understood the rules of naturalistic landscape design but complained that the fragmented terrain lacked a natural focal point. He proposed an elaborate Italianate concert hall, with terraces and fountains, to remedy the site's limitations and create an artistic center. Other contestants who emphasized museums, exhibition halls, and botanical, zoological, and geological gardens considered these attractions the defining rather than the auxiliary features of a public park. A prominent crystal palace—to be placed at the entrance between Sixth and Seventh avenues, or on the peak of the hill over-looking the reservoir, or on the central table land, and to be surrounded by terraces, formal gardens, fountains, and a carriage concourse—emerged as a recurrent motif of the plans that stressed civic display or instruction. These designers wanted to advertise civic progress, suggesting, for example, a column of water (visible from four to five miles away) appropriate to the engineering aesthetic of "this land of enormity"; or a massive fresco mural on the reservoir walls recording the history of the American Revolution; or an arcade for busts of "civil and military patriots" comparable to German Prince Ludwig's Valhalla. The triumphal arches that appeared in more than one plan underscored the park's identity as a monument of civic pride.[44]

The advocates of artificial display differed on whether the park's primary civic purpose ought to be cultural uplift or sociability and amusement. Some contestants stressed the improvement of parkgoers and the dissemination of "practical knowledge" through arboretums, museums, and botanical, geologi-cal, and zoological gardens. The ardent republicans Pliny Miles and John Da-vidson envisioned this public space as a "Grand School of Science," with a geol-ogy museum displaying dinosaur models and a museum of "economic botany" in the Mount St. Vincent convent buildings, where artisans could learn about natural materials. Another amateur designer opted for botanical theme gardens with plants mentioned in classic texts or from the homes of famous men and women (Florence Nightingale and Catharine Sedgwick, for example). Other contestants saw their goal as creating an appropriate setting for refined socializ-ing, fashionable promenades, and holiday spectacles. William Benque and Charles Ravolle (in an unofficial entry) predicted that their promenade would "be the most visited place in the park." Still other plans stressed that "artificial" features such as labyrinths or zoos would offer diversion and amusement.[45]

Those contestants most amenable to accommodating popular amusement elaborated on provisions for the parade and playgrounds. One gardener, Rich-ard Dolben, viewed the parade ground as the park's "principal and most sublime object" and proposed surrounding it on three sides with ten- to twelve-foot spectator terraces. John Rink, who had already worked as a gardener on the park, elevated his own parade terraces on the east side of the receiving reservoir to twenty-five feet with public buildings on top of that. He also recommended cutting a one-third-mile channel through rock on the park's west side to create a three-tier shooting gallery for cannons, muskets, and pistols. Plan 22 provided for ten thousand spectators. By contrast, the "Ars Longa" plan warned that the parade was "certain to be a place for frightening horses and ladies, attracting a constant mob and annoying just the class most fitted by education to enjoy the beautiful in nature and art." George Waring (the park's drainage engineer) suggested locating the parade at 72nd Street, far "from those parts on [Eighth] avenue where drinking shops will be most likely to locate."[46]

The parade ground, besides accommodating the crowds that enjoyed the spectacle of marching men, represented a ceremonial space that affirmed the civic obligation of citizens to defend the republic. Several plans, therefore, linked the parade to formal avenues that would permit a review of the troops and to shaded arcades where "retired military" men could walk and, of course, parade under triumphal arches. The land reformer Masquerier thought his parade ground ample enough to accommodate "all kinds of sports, parades, and mass meetings," a provocative vision in a city that had just weathered five months of demonstrations by unemployed workers. Indeed, he was the only contestant to envision the public park as an arena of democratic political assembly.[47]

The playgrounds also elicited widely varying responses, the majority of contestants limiting themselves to setting aside level fields that could double as scenic meadows. But some planned extensive playgrounds for cricket and baseball, for which one competitor noted, "so many clubs have lately been formed and whose mutual trials of skill attract large numbers" of spectators. Other contestants suggested furnishing playgrounds with gymnastic apparatus. Two designers set aside a special lawn playground for women, equipped for gymnastics and archery and screened by shrubbery from any intruders. Miles and Davidson proposed women's and men's bathing houses for parkgoers who went swimming in the lakes. In several plans children figured as a particular park constituency: Adam Gigrich proposed a carousel, swings, and a miniature railroad; Samuel Gustin, a dairy to supply fresh milk. A fair number of designers, however, warned that innocent children and vulnerable women would need to be vigilantly protected in this new public space. "Arcadia" recommended mounted police and a system of surveillance, with telegraph stations at every gate so the course of rowdies through the park could be "marked, followed, watched, and annoyed in every way by the authorities" until they either left or adopted more refined manners.[48]

Despite the popularity of horse racing among the city's cross-class sporting crowd, only three entries accommodated this sport. One placed a hippodrome, an open-air stadium for horse races, in the center of a nine-acre flower garden, and two others suggested racing roads where, as the contestant James Warner put it, "Young America could take a 'good blow'!" But the circuitous route of drives and rides in most of the naturalistic plans discouraged—as the winning design noted explicitly—trotting matches or racing. Instead, several plans pointed to European models in explaining that their equestrian paths would form an inducement to respectable and healthy exercise for women as well as men.[49]

In its advocacy of the park as a flexible, multipurpose civic center, one plan stood at the opposite extreme from the purist pastoral designs and came closest to crossing over from an artificial design tradition to an urbane version of popular eclecticism. Susan Delafield Parish, descendant of an old and prominent New York merchant family, the wife of a wealthy insurance executive, and a member of the Minturns' social circle, was the only female competitor. Although her brother John Delafield, a banker, was, like Minturn, active in the horticultural movement, her plan transcended naturalistic conventions when she proposed a park for "pleasure, amusement, beauty and instruction." Parish's crystal palace had, in addition to an aviary, conservatory, aquarium, and exhibitions of geology, botany, and "coneology," "*a spacious cage for monkeys, particularly diverting to persons of all ages.*" A "spectacular" iron verandah around the reservoir would overlook spacious parades and playgrounds; platforms cut into the rocks of the surrounding hills would accommodate the "various vocal and musical societies now existing and rapidly forming" and also horticultural and floral displays. Her two-and-a-half-mile "Elm Avenue" along the east side would be a "pleasing resort where friends can meet, can see and be seen by one another which may not be in the winding or circuitous road." The Arsenal was to be converted into a concert hall with lecture and reading rooms. And in the midst of a formal flower garden, Parish placed a dance platform surrounded with turf seats; she suggested that people "bring their own music." Taking a more generous view of parkgoers' manners than many contestants, she proposed that china roses "should be cultivated so profusely as to *give* to anyone" who might want them. "In this way taste and love of flowers may be encouraged at little if any additional expense and be the means of protecting the flowers and plants on the grounds."[50]

Although Susan Parish perhaps came closest to embracing the eclectic urban pleasure garden, a handful of other designers incorporated elements of that tradition, stressing the park's value as an institution of popular amusement and diversion. But most contestants believed the great new park should offer a unified aesthetic conception of rural scenery or civic institutions to refresh, instruct, or refine their viewers. On April 28, 1858, the commission gave one plan first prize, and three others, second, third, and fourth place.

The Victors

First prize went to plan 33, the "Greensward" plan, submitted by the park's superintendent, Frederick Law Olmsted, and the English-born architect Calvert Vaux. This decision would later be hailed as a landmark in the history of landscape architecture. And certainly it was. Yet accounts that emphasize its unique genius imply that artistic judgment alone governed the selection of the design. From the commissioners' perspective, more than aesthetics was at stake; politics as much as artistic merit determined just how the nation's first and most famous landscape park would be designed and built.

The commissioners left no record other than their votes of their criteria for selecting the four prizewinners. We might infer certain aesthetic preferences in Robert Dillon's motion to invite J. C. A. Alphand, the designer of the recently redone Bois de Boulogne, to visit and advise the board or in John Gray's amendment to extend the same invitation to the superintendent of Liverpool's Birkenhead Park. The Bois, though revised in naturalistic English style, was more formal in its design, with a central avenue bisecting the park. Birkenhead Park featured the undulating meadows, groves, lakes, and wandering paths characteristic of the pastoral style. Constructed within the previous decade, both represented the latest European fashions in landscape design. Yet neither park designer came to advise, and the commissioners were left to their own standards of taste.[51]

Two obvious criteria were the visual effectiveness of the plan itself and the authority of the accompanying description. Eleven contestants included portfolios of drawings that suggested "before" and "after" effects, detailed the design of particular features—gardens, gates, fountains, or concert halls—and added, as one contestant put it, "the fascinations of green tint" to plans drawn in sepia or india ink.[52] The commissioners could ill afford to deal with amateurs in selecting a plan that might cost millions of dollars.

The award of prizes suggests that the majority of park commissioners preferred a rural scenic park as well as a professional plan. Yet they were far from united or consistent in this preference. In nine ballots, eight different plans received some votes; of these, five worked within the naturalistic Downing tradition, but two prizewinning plans took their cues from the "artificial" or continental conventions of civic embellishment. Plan 22, which mixed natural scenery with a variety of popular diversions, received two votes in the balloting, but none of the commissioners voted for the decidedly more eclectic design submitted by Susan Parish.[53]

The four winners had little in common. The first-place Greensward plan was one of the most professionally executed designs and worked within naturalistic conventions to produce rural scenery. Second prize went to plan 30, submitted by Samuel Gustin, the park's landscape gardener at the time of the contest. Providing a centrally placed oval parade to be approached by a straight avenue, his design departed from the Downing school of correct taste, seeming to take its authority from an extract of the new Bois de Boulogne plan, which he reprinted in his description. Third prize went to Michael Miller and Lachland McIntosh, the property clerk and the dispersing clerk of Central Park, for plan 27, which provided one of the briefest descriptions announcing as its goal simply to produce unelaborated scenery as quickly and as cheaply as possible. Fourth prize went to Howard Daniels (plan 26), a New York landscape gardener who had worked on the New Jersey rural suburb of Llewelyn Park and later designed Baltimore's Druid Hill Park. Daniels's design drew on English as well as continental schools of landscape gardening; but with formal entrances and adjacent terraces that converged into a grand central avenue, it was the plan's "artificial" style that most impressed its viewers.[54]

As editors evaluated the skill and artistic conceptions of the winning plans, they also acknowledged that art was not the only issue in the contest. Even before the commissioners announced their decision, the *Times* predicted that each contestant in the "grand struggle" would "have his friends and agents wire-pulling for him"—cynicism not ill-founded. A Boston newspaper editor complained about blatant favoritism. Despite the requirement of contestants' anonymity, the commissioners knew for whom they were voting. The first three prize-winning plans had been submitted by employees of the park board and the fourth by a locally known landscape gardener. Park employees, of course, had the advantage of having seen the actual topography, particularly valuable given widespread complaints about inaccuracies in Viele's map. More important, the winning contestants knew and were known by the commissioners. To view the awards in a positive light, the park board had already established trust and confidence in these contestants and could expect to work effectively with them in implementing the design. From a more cynical viewpoint, the commissioners may simply have taken the opportunity to give their own employees a bonus.[55]

These park employees had also been appointed in the first place for political reasons that went back to the park board's own partisan composition and early distrust of Viele. The first-place designers, Olmsted and Vaux, both had close ties to the Republican park commissioners. Olmsted had been recruited by Charles Elliott in August 1857 to apply to be the park superintendent, with the suggestion, as Olmsted later recalled, that he would be a "Republican the Democrats could live with." Although subordinate to Chief Engineer Viele, a Democrat neither Republicans nor reform members of his own party could live with, Olmsted noted that some commissioners had sought to advance his position at Viele's expense that fall by requesting that he (Olmsted) submit reports on drainage and planting. Calvert Vaux, who had earlier pointed out the artistic limitations of Viele's plan to Republican acquaintances on the board, carried the further cachet of having been Downing's partner.[56]

Second-prize winner Samuel Gustin was a Democrat whose appointment as the park's landscape gardener had allowed commissioners to satisfy the expectation of bipartisan cooperation, a point that was particularly important the preceding fall when they were seeking appropriations from the Democratic-controlled common council. As for the third-place winners, personal connections may have been more important than politics. Miller, the park's property clerk, was apparently Commissioner William Strong's nephew or son-in-law. The *Times*, the *Post*, and the *Horticulturalist* could find nothing worth commending in Miller and McIntosh's design for a rural scenic park.[57]

Before the meeting to decide on the awards the board's Democrats, and even one Republican, seemed to expect a "fix." James Hogg, who had already had several run-ins with fellow Republicans, started the meeting by proposing that Olmsted and Vaux's plan 33 be eliminated from consideration because it had been submitted the day after the April 1 deadline. Hogg did not vote for his own resolution, but two Democrats did and two other Democrats abstained.

When Commissioner Robert Dillon (a Democrat) moved that no plan "by reason of its marked superiority" was entitled to first prize, and that therefore the awards should be confined to the lower three places, his motion lost by a seven-to-four vote, identical to the vote of first prize to Olmsted and Vaux.[58]

The six Republican commissioners and one Democrat, Andrew Green, voted for Olmsted and Vaux's Greensward plan; the three other Democrats, for Samuel Gustin's plan, and Know-Nothing Waldo Hutchins for Howard Daniels's plan. Three weeks later Commissioner Thomas Fields charged in the *Herald* that the Republicans on the board had caucused before the meeting to agree on their vote; considering the unreliability of James Hogg's support (suggested by his efforts to disqualify the Greensward plan), the Republicans may have appealed to Andrew Green, who as treasurer had already found Superintendent Olmsted sympathetic to his own particular agenda of efficient labor management. But contrary to the *Herald*'s later charges, the votes for the other three prizes did not follow party alignments, and even individual commissioners were far from consistent in their aesthetic judgments. Perhaps the most important subsequent vote was Robert Dillon's; after Gustin was rewarded with second prize, Dillon voted for Daniels's plan for third and then for fourth prize. Immediately after the awards, Dillon drew on the elements of civic display in Daniel's plan to challenge the first-place winner, expose what he regarded as the politics of that selection, and reopen public debate over the park's design.[59]

Empowered to select a design for Central Park, the commissioners had looked to the cultural authority of formal landscape design traditions and rejected the diverting eclecticism of commercial pleasure gardens. The majority voted for a design that most immediately reflected the tastes of those— mostly affluent—citizens who, like themselves, would feel at home in a beautiful "rural" park where they could admire the scenery and one another. The choice of the Greensward plan reflected the preference of the board's Yankee Republican majority for the English naturalistic design tradition as well as for designers they felt at ease with. The contest over Central Park's design did not, however, end with the decision of the commissioners.

5

THE GREENSWARD PLAN
AND ITS CREATORS

"I have not much faith in the 'individual' theory as applied to architecture and landscape gardening," a park contestant observed in May 1858, a week after the prizes were awarded. "The greatest works of art have been produced by many unknown hands," and "individual talent is but a drop in the swelling fountain." Charles Follen concluded that "if well done," Central Park "will be the work of long time and will embody the work of many minds by the patient toil of many hands."[1] In rejecting individual genius as the source of greatest art, Follen was running against the dominant romantic current of his times. Instead, he echoed the art critic John Ruskin and compared Central Park to magnificent European cathedrals constructed and reconstructed over several centuries. The design of the park was an organic and social, not only an artistic process. Trees and shrubs would grow and assume unforeseen shapes, aesthetic tastes would change, succeeding generations of New Yorkers would bring new needs and expectations to their park, and those who were put in charge of it would adjust its design to meet these demands.

Few historians of Central Park, however, have shared Follen's sense of great art as a collective and historical process; most have stressed the unique genius of one man, Frederick Law Olmsted, allowing even his codesigner, Calvert Vaux, to recede from view. "Olmsted's name came first in the partnership title," one historian tells us, and "the actual design work in the park was functionally divided—Vaux handled all the structures—pavilions, boathouses, bridges; Olmsted handled all the rest." Vaux had "deferred to Olmsted in areas of aesthetic decision. . . . In the final analysis, it is correct to think of Central Park as the extraordinary creation of this extraordinary man." That is, it was Olmsted's park.[2]

The effacement of Vaux as codesigner began as early as May 1858 when the

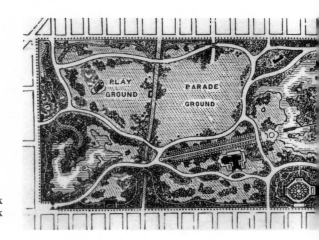

The Greensward plan by Frederick Law Olmsted and Calvert Vaux took first place in the design competition.

Central Park commissioners conferred the singular title of architect-in-chief on Olmsted, who had since September 1857 been superintendent, and began paying paid Vaux a daily wage as his assistant. (Not until January 1859 would Vaux receive the title of consulting architect). Olmsted presented himself thereafter as Central Park's "representative man." It seemed, Vaux protested to Olmsted in 1864, "that I had brought as much as you to the park[,] that I brought education[,] special fitness to take up new problems[,] a love of the [human] race, a love of the park and all it meant intellectually and that I had worked faithfully and fraternally with you throughout. It seemed to me you must be wrong in not accepting me as an equal partner in [the park] heartily." But gradually Central Park appeared—as Vaux predicted it would in another letter a year later—"as an ornament among many ornaments in the watch chain of Frederick Law Olmsted."[3]

Had Olmsted worked alone, had Vaux deferred to his partner in "areas of aesthetic decision," the Greensward plan would not have included some of its most distinguishing features. And had the plan actually fixed the park, like a landscape painting, as an unchanging work of art, it would have failed as a democratic public institution.

Designing Central Park was a process that began with Vaux and Olmsted's shared aesthetic vision in the Greensward plan. Yet, they also modified their design of the park to accommodate the demands of the commissioners and public critics. As the partners came to terms with these demands, they also came face-to-face with their own different definitions of their goals and responsibilities as public servants. "I believed," Vaux explained to Olmsted, "this work was chiefly an example of the art of design, incidentally the art of administration. You thought the administration all inclusive and the design secondary."[4] Despite the unity of their aesthetic conception, the tensions in the collaboration

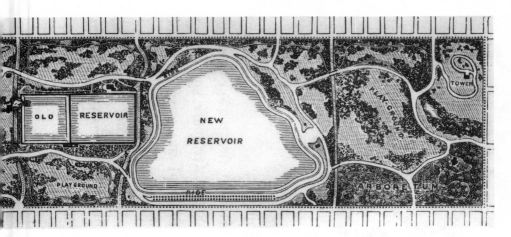

reflected the different understandings of an artist and a gentleman as to how their own work contributed to the making of a democratic public space.

Calvert Vaux, Craftsman and Artist

At thirty-three and thirty-five in 1857, Calvert Vaux and Frederick Law Olmsted had much in common. Both had come from secure social backgrounds, both had recently published books, and both saw in the design competition for Central Park a prime professional opportunity. They also shared a sense of their "fitness" to serve the public—not, they claimed, out of personal ambition for fame or money but out of their commitment to an aesthetic and social vision of what a democratic public park ought to be.

Their personal histories were, however, quite unlike. There is little record of Vaux's childhood and youth in England. His father, a surgeon who died when Vaux was nine, struggled to support his family. Vaux attended a private primary school on scholarship and at fifteen began architectural training as an apprentice in the London office of Lewis N. Cottingham, an early advocate of the revival of Gothic architectural styles. Vaux became a skilled draftsman, and in 1850, a London gallery exhibition of his watercolors of continental landscapes attracted the attention of Andrew Jackson Downing, who had come to England to find an assistant to run a new architectural department in his own thriving landscape gardening practice. He recruited Vaux, then twenty-six, who seems to have welcomed the opportunity to escape the relative rigidity and stuffiness of English society.[5]

During the two years that Vaux worked with Downing in Newburgh, New York, up the Hudson from Manhattan, he devoted most of his energy to

The English architect Calvert Vaux (1824–1895), shown here about 1860, emigrated to the United States in 1850 to join Andrew Jackson Downing's landscape gardening firm. At the time of the competition, he was working as an architect in New York City.

designing "rural" house plans (thirteen of which are included in his 1857 book, *Villas and Cottages*). The "rustic" style of these houses (with pitched roofs, picturesque porches, and ornamented stone and wood work), complemented the "rural scenery" of Downing's broad sweeping lawns, carefully placed specimen trees, and massed border plantings of shrubs and flowers. Vaux, who became Downing's partner, also helped prepare plans for more formal public grounds at the Smithsonian Institution in Washington, D.C., a project that probably inspired an article he wrote in 1852 for the *Horticulturalist* in which he called for government recognition and support of the arts. That summer Downing drowned in a steamboat accident. Vaux carried on his mentor's architectural practice, working with another English architect, Frederick Clarke Withers. He married Mary McEntee, the sister of a Hudson Valley painter, then moved to New York City in 1856, where he became identified with the city's artistic community—"the guild," as he called it. He joined the National Academy of Design and the Century Club and in 1857 was a founding member of the American Institute of Architects.[6]

Vaux's letters and published writings show him as a genial man who might cheerfully enjoy a few glasses of sparkling Moselle during a midday visit to Delmonico's. He liked to entertain his friends with amusing stories, but his teasing manner could turn to caustic irony when his passions were aroused. Although he had worked steadily since his youth, he had little use for "the stereotyped idea that man is a hack and life is a treadmill." Yet Vaux could become so "absorbed" in a design problem, an associate later remembered, that "time and place seemed nothing to him. People could not understand his ways and set him down as eccentric, gentle and courteous always, but nevertheless an oddity."[7]

Vaux's architectural writings followed the nineteenth-century aesthetic convention of judging a building or work of art according to the social meanings it expressed and the moral feelings it inspired. "Correct taste" was less important to him than such qualities as warmth, generosity, agreeableness, and "liberal hospitality." The often sentimental Downing had identified good design with domestic settledness, but Vaux also celebrated the aesthetic satisfactions of a human "well-balanced irregularity." "Human nature, when allowed a free, healthy scope, loves heartily" those qualities that made "the stirring, unconventional, free-spirited man so much more interesting than the cold, correct and somewhat unsympathetic gentleman," he said. The design of buildings should overcome architectural conventions that called for "formality and restraint," lest genuine artistic expression be inhibited. While many "cultivated" Americans (including Downing) were arguing that the republic needed to develop art to refine its rough citizenry, Vaux thought that art ought be valued as an end in itself. Typically, he explained that good architecture was worth having "simply because it is *worth* having" and art should be enjoyed for its intrinsic value just as a good meal should be enjoyed as a means of satisfying a basic human appetite.[8]

To his advocacy of an American architecture that personified spirited "character," Vaux brought the confident respectability of a bourgeois English upbringing and a deep personal respect for craft and skill. His *Villas and Cottages* reveals his intellectual debts to Ruskin and to Ralph Waldo Emerson as well as to Downing. Vaux, a personally devout man, became a liberal Unitarian. Like Ruskin's, his appreciation of art and nature was grounded in their moral attributes, and like Ruskin, he believed that a skilled craftworker could express genuine artistic inspiration. But Vaux rejected Ruskin's pessimistic assessment of the decline of art and craft in industrial societies and instead embraced Emerson's optimism in the "self-reliant" capacity of Americans to create a new and vital culture.[9]

Vaux was strongly committed to his own artistic work and in particular to helping to establish architecture in America as "an honorable calling." The democratic capacity for art, he argued, lay as much in the nation's "industrious classes" as in its patrician class, though only the "sons of rich men" could become architects because "poor men can scarcely afford" such low-paying work. The architectural profession needed to be put on a firmer financial ground; "a class of employers" who did not respect artistic work and thus were unwilling to pay for it, had to be educated to its value. To that end, Vaux had placed his own charges (5 percent of construction costs, or about $375 for a $7,900 house) "with considerable prominence" in his 1857 book of house plans. The move was "a little misunderstood," he explained later to Olmsted, by critics who "said I advertised now that I was [proffering] my card &c rather vulgarly. It touched me & I asked myself . . . if I was showing myself into notice under the impression that I was strengthening the best interest of the profession." The criticism appears to have been chastening for a man who believed that "every attempt to force individual buildings into prominent notice is evidence either of a vulgar desire for notoriety at any sacrifice, or of an ill-educated eye and taste." Designing the park was important to him, Vaux explained to Olmsted, not merely for the enhancement of his personal reputation but for the opportunity it offered to fulfill his "earnest convictions" that he had a duty "to help artists take a true position" in relation to "money men" and thus "to be a benefactor in this matter to the people generally."[10]

Stung by the criticism that he had been overweening in calling attention to himself, Vaux later explained that in the Central Park collaboration with Olmsted he was particularly conscious of not "seeming to insist at the outset on personal prominence." He avoided attending park board meetings lest his own professional independence undermine the confidence of his partner, who was junior to him in experience though two years senior in chronological age. Yet, however much he clothed his personal ambitions in the rhetoric of service to art and the profession, in 1857 Vaux surely recognized that the award of the Central Park design would establish his own credentials not simply as Downing's former partner but as his proper heir. In dedicating his book to Downing's memory and to his widow, in repeatedly advocating the construction of monuments to Downing, and in naming his eldest son Downing, Calvert Vaux affirmed his spiritual descent from America's greatest popularizer of a naturalistic aesthetic.[11]

Frederick Law Olmsted, Gentleman Farmer and Literary Man

Olmsted arrived at the Greensward collaboration by a more erratic route. He spent his first two adult decades searching for a calling while remaining financially dependent on his father, a prosperous dry goods merchant and descendant of a prominent Puritan family in Hartford, Connecticut. (Raised a Congregationalist, Olmsted avoided organized religion in later years.) He was driven by a sense of duty but found pursuing a career for money distasteful. Because a case of sumac poisoning weakened his eyes, Olmsted's formal education—a combination of common and boarding schools—ended when he was eighteen. While his brother and closest friends were attending Yale, he tried a year as a clerk in a New York dry goods house and another year at sea. Neither pursuit proved agreeable. In the mid-1840s he prepared for what he thought would be a suitable profession as a gentleman farmer by living and studying with several prominent agriculturalists, among them George Geddes, whose upstate New York farm had won the state agricultural society prize for exemplary management.[12]

When his father bought him farms first in Connecticut and then on Staten Island, Olmsted envisioned himself as a "country squire" with a responsibility to disseminate scientific knowledge and rural taste. In an era when many people who depended on farming for their livelihood migrated west, Olmsted nostalgically celebrated country virtues untainted by market pressures. Insisting to his brother that "no man of respectable mind" could be satisfied with commercial pursuits characterized by incessant competition, Olmsted thought "rural pursuits tend to elevate and enlarge . . . ideas" without giving "occasion for anything vulgar or offensive." Furthermore, "scientific men of the highest distinction" were working to advance agricultural methods.[13]

As a youth, Olmsted traveled through the New England countryside with his father, who admired rural scenery; and as a young gentleman farmer, he read the latest literature on art criticism (including Ruskin's *Modern Painters*), on horticulture, and on English landscape gardening. He wrote articles for Downing's *Horticulturalist* on pear and apple farming and another on the attractions of Liverpool's Birkenhead Park. With the rural improvement movement at its peak, he also helped organize an agricultural society on Staten Island for the promotion of rural tastes and scientific agriculture. But while Olmsted learned the art of landscape appreciation and the latest theories in rural improvement, he gained little experience in the work of design.[14]

In what was to become a leitmotif of Olmsted's life, his exuberant enthusiasm for farming was not matched by complete practicality. His father, brother, and friends all worried about his lack of attention to businesslike procedures. "Had I better send you a treatise on bookkeeping forms," his father typically wondered, "you seem singularly deficient." Just as his partner-to-be, Vaux, met accusations of personal advertising with a heightened, self-conscious modesty, Olmsted responded to such criticisms of his deficiencies in practical management with what George Templeton Strong later described as a "monomania for system."[15]

In the 1850s, while Vaux was gaining a reputation as an architect in partnership with Withers, Olmsted abandoned model farming for journalism, another field in which he hoped "to take up and keep a position as a recognized literateur, a man of influence in literary matters." Following a trip to England, he published *Walks and Talks of an American Farmer in England*, which combined observations on the English social landscape with sentimental invocations of "Old England for ever!—Amen." He took several journeys through the American South and sent a series of letters to the *New York Times* that formed the basis for his three influential books on southern mores and the economic conditions of slavery. In 1855 Olmsted became both a managing editor of *Putnam's Magazine* and a partner (again through his father's investment) in the publishing house of Dix and Edwards, which was publishing his second book. Appealing to his father for a loan to assist him in "private advertising" for his first book on the South, Olmsted explained, "There is a sort of literary republic, which it is not merely pleasant & gratifying to my ambition to be recognized in, but also profitable. It would for example, if I am so recognized and considered, be easy for me, in the case of the non-success of this partnership, to get employment in the newspaper offices or other literary enterprises."[16]

The "non-success" soon came to pass when the Dix and Edwards firm became an early casualty of the 1857 depression. A family friend, Park Commissioner Charles Elliott, encouraged Olmsted to apply for the post of park superintendent, and he did so. (Elliott came from the same circle of prominent Connecticut families and had known Olmsted's brother at Yale). In his application, Olmsted stressed that for the "past 16 years my chief interest and occupation has been with those subjects" most pertinent to managing the park labor force. He cited his published writings on "economy in the application of agricultural labor," "the direction and superintendence of agricultural laborers and gardeners," and visits to European parks.[17] It was a claim that could be supported only weakly. The ten to twelve laborers he supervised on his Staten Island farm were a small responsibility compared to Central Park's labor force of more than a thousand, and in his European tours "as a student" of landscapes, Olmsted had set his own curriculum. But he used old social connections and his recently established literary reputation to good advantage. Further, his letters from the South to the *Times* and his promotion of a free-labor, nonslave colony in Texas established his credentials as a Republican, but one whose limited identification with the local party organization made him palatable to the park board's Democrats.

Olmsted solicited the signatures of some prominent men, Washington Irving and Peter Cooper among them, for petitions that recommended his appointment. Olmsted, the *Evening Post*'s editor, Parke Godwin, advised the commissioners, was "a practical farmer, a man of exquisite tastes, most delightful habits and decided character." As initially prescribed by the board, the superintendent, subordinate to the chief engineer, was to oversee the work force and "have charge of the general police of the Park to see that the ordinances of the Board are respected & obeyed." But preferring both his politics and character to those of Chief Engineer Egbert Viele, some of the commissioners, Olmsted reported to his father in the fall of 1857, "strive to advance me— withdraw responsibility from him & confer it on me."[18]

There is no satisfactory account of how Vaux and Olmsted became partners in the design competition for Central Park. Vaux (who had suggested the competition to the park board) had met Olmsted at Downing's home in New-

Frederick Law Olmsted (1822–1902) was serving as superintendent of park workers when he and Vaux entered the design competition. At the time this photograph was taken in 1860, he held the position of architect-in-chief.

burgh. He noted in a memo written shortly before his death that he had asked Olmsted to collaborate on the design partly because he admired Olmsted's discussion of the English landscape in *Walks and Talks* but "mainly" because Olmsted's "days were spent on the Park territory," and he thus "could bring . . . accurate observations in regard to the actual topography which was not clearly defined on the survey." Vaux had not, he explained to Olmsted, attached much importance to his partner's *position* as park superintendent. (This underestimation, as Olmsted viewed it, led to later difficulties between them.) Rather, Vaux reported that he had seen in Olmsted a fellow artist who gave him confidence to undertake a project for which he felt "very incompletely educated." Twenty years in architecture had taught Vaux respect for the skill involved in good design work; he was aware that designing a landscaped public park differed in scale and in kind from planning a house and grounds.[19]

Olmsted later stressed to Vaux that he himself had entered into their collaboration with "*no regard for Art or fame or money,*" but rather to fulfill his "special instinctive passion" for parks, a passion that, in part, compensated for personal frustrations, for "disappointed love, unsatisfied romance, and down-trodden pride." (In June 1859 he would dutifully marry his brother's widow, Mary Perkins Olmsted, with whom in later years he was to find comfortable companionship.) But however great his compensatory passion for pastoral landscapes, Olmsted admitted that he had linked the design competition to a personal "ambition, purpose, plan of life" to be the park's sole administrator, a goal that in his mind subsumed the mere work of design. "If successful," Olmsted reported to his father at the time of the competition, trying to reassure him about practicalities, "I should not only get my share of $2000 offered for the best [plan], but no doubt whole control of the matter and my salary increased to $2500."[20]

Landscape Art and the Natural Aesthetic

Although both men "had other work on our hands," Vaux recalled, the Greensward plan "occupied our minds, more or less continually" starting in November 1857. "We looked at the map and the ground and went to look in our own way," Vaux laconically reported. Then Olmsted "came to my house [on 18th Street] nearly every evening and we consulted and worked together in that way."[21]

Whatever their later differences over their specific contributions, both men knew neither could have done the design alone. Olmsted, he and his partner agreed, showed little interest in the details of plans on paper. Vaux, relying on his skills as artist and his experience as draftsman, drew the plan itself, provided the portfolio of sketches and watercolors to demonstrate the vistas that they would create, and later explained most concretely just how the park's spatial layout contributed to particular visual effects. Olmsted provided knowledge of the park's terrain and its natural features. Vaux's "limited education" in park design was most apparent in horticultural matters, and he praised Olmsted's knowledge of "agriculture in its finer sense," including familiarity with specific trees and plants. Both men understood the theories of creating landscape effects—for example, the selection and placement of trees and shrubs to create a visual sequence that would lead the eye from a darkened foreground to an undefined distant view. But the key to the park's design lay as much in the placement of viewers in the landscape as in the details of the view.[22]

The premise of the Greensward plan was that Central Park should express an overarching aesthetic motive. In criticizing Viele's plan, Vaux stressed its lack of an "artistic conception" that would give shape and coherence to the viewer's experience. The goal of Vaux's entire professional career had been to arrange "useful and necessary forms" to "suggest the pleasant ideas of harmonious proportion, fitness, and agreeable variety to the eye." For Vaux to have accepted the unplanned and eclectic aesthetic of commercial pleasure gardens would have meant surrendering his judgment as an artist. Olmsted, who admired the harmonious composition of English parks, found spontaneous manners as well as eclectic design distasteful. The partners envisioned the future Central Park as a unified work of landscape art.[23]

Vaux and Olmsted's artistic conception further rested on a shared belief in the moral superiority of a natural aesthetic. Americans' "innate homage to the natural in contradistinction to the artificial—a preference for the works of God to the works of man," Vaux had suggested in *Villas and Cottages,* furnished "valuable proof of inherent good, true and healthy taste." Nature, the most "inherently" satisfying source of artistic inspiration, "ministered" to the eye "with the infinite host of progressive ideas, to which it acts as the mysterious portal." Vaux celebrated the delights of both art and leisure for their own sake and contrasted the satisfaction of natural beauty to the aesthetically deprived vernacular landscape that had been produced by Americans preoccupied with *making* more than enjoying material wealth. For Olmsted, the power of natural beauty lay in its social influence as well as aesthetic pleasure. An artistically designed landscape would provide a refreshing antidote to the city's competitive pressures and dreary buildings and would also, as he later explained, exercise "a distinctly harmonizing and refining influence upon the most unfortunate and most lawless classes of the city,—an influence favorable to courtesy, self-control, and temperance."[24]

To create an artistic pastoral landscape, Vaux and Olmsted intended to insulate Central Park visually from the city's "confined and formal lines" and its busy traffic. Only if the park were clearly separated from the city could its designers control the landscape and the "motive" of those who visited it, so that the park would become a special place and going there a special occasion. Thus, the description that accompanied the Greensward plan began with a discussion of the "general suggestions" of the park's terrain that supported a naturalistic treatment, the handling of its borders to "plant out" the city, and the placement of new transverse roads to preserve a unified parkgoing experience.[25]

Most contestants shared Olmsted and Vaux's ambition to design the park as a self-contained environment, but most other plans treated the roads that were to connect Fifth and Eighth avenues as scenic drives following the contours of the ground. These plans in effect, if not by intention, integrated the park and the city, extending the refreshing qualities of shade and clean air to those who could not stop to consume its views. But Vaux and Olmsted worried that "a turbid stream of coarse traffic" bisecting the park would destroy the sense of unity and expanse that should envelop a visitor whose prime object was to contemplate natural scenery. Thoroughfares crowded with "coal carts and butchers' carts, dust carts and dung carts" or the "frantic zeal" of fire engines "have nothing in common with the park proper . . . [and] those agreeable sentiments that we should wish the park to inspire." Although one contestant, Susan Parish, recommended tunneling a transverse road at 79th Street, another

The park commissioners' third annual report illustrated how the transverse roads would preserve the designers' conception of the park as a pastoral retreat by channeling ordinary city traffic below the park's surface.

suggested gates, and a correspondent to the *Sun* advised bridges at the intersections of trade streets and pleasure drives, Olmsted and Vaux's plan went farther: it sank all four commercial transverse roads eight feet beneath the park's surface so that neither bridges nor traffic would obstruct movement and views through the park. Reinforcing their design with the suggestion that commercial vehicles be excluded from the park drives, Vaux and Olmsted affirmed the separation of work and leisure as distinct pursuits, each of which required a distinct environment. They then undertook to orchestrate the experience of leisure by artistically arranging nature within the park.[26]

Since New Yorkers who came to the park would arrive with the clear intention of enjoying its scenery, Vaux explained, the principal Fifth Avenue drive would run into the park diagonally from 59th Street to withdraw attention from the boundaries and take people "out of the city into the park with the least delay possible." But once the parkgoer was at the center, the designers faced the problem of how to treat the site's "irregular disconnected featureless conglomeration of ground" so as to establish lines of vision and frame scenes that would reward the visitor. Some contestants placed prominent architectural structures at the center, but Vaux and Olmsted, like other contestants who were working within the Downing tradition, stressed that natural scenery should remain the chief attraction: "Artistically the point for study was what prominent features of the landscape could be laid hold of and exaggerated and made into a point of importance to give distance." Although they would have preferred the dramatic scenic emphasis of "a mountain or a rock," Vaux later explained, the designers decided the hilly "ramble should be the picture that people would come to see." They identified Vista Rock (at the top of this hilly area between 74th and 79th streets, which came to be known as the Ramble) as a natural focal point and proposed filling the low ground to the south with water, letting the new Lake give "dignity and distance" to the view beyond.[27]

Olmsted and Vaux also proposed siting a "Promenade" (later called the Mall)—the "open air hall of reception"—in relation to the Lake and the Ramble in such a way as to accommodate socializing while also directing visitors' attention toward the park's natural features. A "grand promenade" was "an essential feature of a metropolitan park," the designers acknowledged, yet its formal symmetry—like all architecture in the park—must be rendered "subservient" to the natural "view as the ultimatum of interest." Comparing their promenade to the place of a house in a private estate—the visitor's logical goal—they terminated it at the northern end "with a landscape attraction of considerable extent" that would keep "the idea of the park itself" "uppermost in the mind of the beholder."[28]

A terrace would lead down from the Promenade to the Lake. In the original plan the designers suggested that this architectural feature was "not absolutely necessary," though they thought it "would add much to the general effect." But as the plan evolved, Vaux became especially proud of the Terrace (later the Bethesda Terrace), the only part of the plan he privately claimed as "an original conception of my own in its entirety." He thought the success of its design rested on his mastery of "light and shade and play of line . . . the weaving of the L[andscape] into the A[rchitecture] and the A[rchitecture] into the L[andscape]." Artificial structures were subordinate throughout the park, he later explained to the *Tribune's* art critic, Clarence Cook, "not because the citizens have not money to spend [or] are mean but because the art idea requires it. Nature first 2nd and 3rd—architecture after a while." But at the Terrace, which was "rich for a Terrace—liberal for a terrace and in the absence of a mountain or a rock—will do," the hospitable Vaux "would let the New Yorker feel that the richest man in N.Y. or elsewhere cannot spend as freely as is here spent just for his lounge—*here* he may lounge by the week if he pleases, entirely acclimated—his eye all purified—his reminiscence of arch[itecture] all wiped out," his attention drawn toward a distant prospect.[29]

For the designers the key to the park's enjoyment lay in the healing release that would come from such visual experiences. The architectural arrangement of the Terrace, Olmsted explained in 1861, "invites observers to leisurely contemplation." Similarly, they created open stretches of "greensward" over

The Greensward plan included "before and after" studies of the park landscape. The photograph looks northeast toward Vista Rock from the Cherry Hill concourse. Vaux's drawing suggests how the low swampy ground in the foreground would become the Lake.

which the eye could range and introduced "charming" paths through the Ramble with openings for views of the water. The serenity of the park's vistas would inspire a refreshing sense of possibility. Nature itself required that people daily set aside their "utilitarian" cares and strivings, Vaux wrote, and "cheerfully subscribe something to [their] ideal life." Gazing into the landscape, parkgoers could realize their distinctly human "capacity to see and fully appreciate the beautiful." In America, Vaux believed, the "sensation of freedom" itself "commands a boundless prospect, and no fitting or enduring edifice can be erected on [American liberty] that does not include the most liberal manners, the most generous aspirations, and the most noble institutions, and the most pure and beautiful arts that unfettered humanity is capable of conceiving." Through the design of the Terrace in particular, Vaux sought to honor boundless democratic aspirations that included the human "craving for beauty."[30]

Lest pastoral vistas alone become monotonous, the two designers varied the landscape by their picturesque treatment of the Ramble and the rugged northern park. Olmsted was especially attached to the intricacy of the Ramble's plantings, which he thought might inspire a "sense of the superabundant creative power, infinite resource and liberality of Nature." He contrasted this "childish playfulness and profuse careless utterance of Nature" to the "emotion sought to be produced in the Mall and playgrounds regions—rest, tranquility, deliberation and maturity."[31] Like so many romantics of their day, the designers projected onto nature qualities that seemed absent from their own society. Discovering these qualities in the park would revive visitors' weary imaginations.

The creation of visual effects remained foremost in the partners' thinking about design, but they also arranged features for parkgoers' comfort. Vaux, his partner recalled later, "was absolutely the most ingenious, industrious and indefatigable man in his profession . . . for the study of *plans* to meet complicated requirements of convenience." In a park "convenience" required close attention to the system of circulation; the accessibility of particular attractions; the grades, curves, and paving of walks and drives; and drainage and water systems that would support plantings and keep parkgoers' feet clean and dry. Olmsted's knowledge of rural improvements and Vaux's experience with domestic utilities gave authority to their discussion of the park's infrastructure. Their detailed appendix on drainage and country road building—features that would free visitors to enjoy the park's artistic conception—no doubt impressed those commissioners who were concerned about practicability.[32]

While preserving an overarching definition of the park as rural scenery, the designers also located specific features to serve visitors' needs. They placed the mandated cricket playground near the West 59th Street entrance so it would be near the Sixth and Eighth Avenue railways. Convenience also dictated their location of paths alongside the drives to satisfy parkgoers' gregarious desires. "It is hardly thought that any plan would be popular in New York that did not allow of a continuous promenade along the lines of drives, so that pedestrians may have ample opportunity to look at the equipages and their inmates," the designers explained.[33] They recognized the attraction that crowds would create in the park but did not anticipate that pedestrians, tired of battling the street's traffic, noise, and dust, might prefer to separate themselves altogether from the horses and carriages on the park drives.

"Translating Democratic Ideas into Trees and Dirt"

Vaux had told Clarence Cook that the Terrace was "essentially Republican in its inspiration and general conception." The question in retrospect, of course, is how was the Terrace—and indeed the park as a whole—essentially republican in its design? How did Vaux and Olmsted move from defining pastoral scenery as the aesthetic goal of a public park to a larger social philosophy that claimed, as Vaux put it, to "translate Democratic ideas into Trees & Dirt"? At the time of the competition, Vaux and Olmsted did not find this question particularly problematic. The partners were confident, as Vaux later said, that they "represent[ed] the people and the good part of the people."[34]

Even before the competition, both men had advocated government support of culture and the arts, and they viewed a public park as one public institution among many—schools, museums, libraries—that could enhance the lives of free citizens. Central Park would be a democratic institution by virtue of the mixing of classes within its boundaries. And the Greensward plan itself postulated what individuals from all social backgrounds would do there: admire the artistically composed scenery, enjoy the spectacle of the crowd on the Promenade, and engage in the wholesome exercise of driving, riding, walking, skating, or—for those who played cricket—competitive sports.

Despite their common vision, however, Vaux and Olmsted understood the work of design and the workings of a democratic culture in different ways. The tension that was to arise in their collaboration derived from these differences. Vaux had the perspective of an independent English émigré who, as an artist, identified most strongly with his "guild"; Olmsted, the perspective of a descendant of an old-stock Yankee family intent on fulfilling his inherited social duty as a gentleman.

To Vaux the park represented the "big art work of the Republic," of a society in which citizens created their own public institutions. In contrast to the rigidly stratified English society from which he had come, "true and intelligent republicanism," Vaux wrote, "clearly points to a state of society in which the private possession of great pecuniary wealth ought to be a comparatively unimportant matter, because it should yield to its possessor but little more comfort, or even luxury, than can be readily acquired by every industrious man." Through *public* institutions, a "man of small means *may* be almost on the same footing as the millionaire." Public schools, gymnasiums, music halls, libraries, parks, gardens, museums, baths, and "everything that is needful for the liberal education of an intelligent freeman's children can easily be obtained by the genuine republican," Vaux insisted, "if he will only take the trouble to *want* them." Such institutions derived their vitality from the commitment of all citizens to realizing the benefits of social progress, including the pleasures of art.[35]

Eighteenth-century Americans, Vaux explained, had regarded works of art "as pomps and vanities so closely connected with superstition, popery, or aristocracy that the spirit of republicanism refused to acknowledge the value of art as it then existed, a tender hot-house plant ministering to the delights of a select few. The democratic element rebelled . . . and . . . demanded of art to thrive in the open air, in all weathers, for the benefit of all, if it was worth anything." Vaux found this democratic hostility to art a "severe course," but one that "after all had truth on its side." Artistic taste would advance only when artisans, laborers, and professional designers as well as an "appreciative and able" public encouraged by the press, all shared in a "liberal education" that valued aesthetic sensibilities and skills as well as practical ones. The goal of this liberal education would be to empower each individual with the confidence of personal aesthetic judgment, to encourage a liberating "self-reliance" that drew its authority not from European canons of taste but from people's own love of beauty.[36]

Confident in their own "untrammeled" tastes, Americans of all walks of life, Vaux believed, could contribute to the work of artistic production. Vaux never identified directly with the labor movement, but he did invoke the language of artisan cooperation in envisioning democratic citizens as the makers of their own government and of their own public art. Whereas John Ruskin regarded the artistic craftworker as a relic of a more organic medieval society, Vaux believed that republican progress brought with it a liberation of artistic capacity. Without "widespread appreciation of the possibilities that are within reach of every class," Vaux thought, "galvanized action is worthless, however smartly it may be got up; there must be genuine life-blood flowing through all its members, freely and vigorously, or nothing good will be achieved." Enumerating twenty-two trades involved in the work of building (from quarry workers and masons to gasfitters and carvers), he concluded, "It is only as these trades improve that the art improves."[37]

Vaux earnestly pursued his faith in artistic craft production. With his "imperturbable good nature veiling an inflexible will," one friend recalled, the architect had "astonished" the masons and carpenters of Newburgh when he criticized the quality of their work and then attempted to "set them in the right way" by urging finer workmanship. Believing that artisans and artists must work together in the spirit of republican cooperation, Vaux tried unsuccessfully to persuade fellow members of the American Institute of Architects to admit craftworkers to their "professional" organization. He occasionally used the term "manliness" to refer to the qualities of energetic independence and conviction that he most admired, but his vision of the makers of a vital democratic culture included women, who, he thought, lacked only for "opportunity" to realize the "inventive capacity and artistic feeling latent among them." Explaining that a customer's wife had suggested "the leading idea" of one of his house plans, Vaux urged that women's "good abilities" be granted "a much wider outlet" in the work of architecture and design.[38]

In contrast to the broad participatory strain in Vaux's concept of progressive republicanism, Olmsted had arrived at his initial argument on behalf of state involvement in culture from a more defensive class posture. The problem of democratic culture, as he saw it, lay in "the rowdyism, ruffianism, want of high honorable sentiment & chivalry of the common farming and laboring people of the North" and the failure "of the thorough-bred gentleman" to set a better example. His concept of the responsibilities of "gentlemen" emerged from deep-seated New England (and Federalist) values that favored a hierarchical sense of social duty over the competitive individualism of a "low, prejudiced, party enslaved and material people."[39]

Olmsted had developed his arguments in support of government "encouragement" of cultural institutions in response to southern slaveholders' charges that "the mass of people in the North" lacked those "qualities of character" associated with the "well-bred" gentleman. During his tour of southern states, Olmsted reported to his friend Charles Brace his "melancholy" feelings at being "made" to acknowledge the deficiencies of northern society. Although Olmsted criticized slavery, he admired "true and brave Southern gentlemen" with their "honest and unstudied dignity of character, the generosity and the real nobleness of habitual impulses, and the well-bred manly courtesy." But for every "one true gentleman . . . [in] the South," he noted in his article for the *Times*, "there are two whose whole life seems to be absorbed in sensualism and sickly excitement." These latter slaveholders, Olmsted believed, were "the dangerous class at present of the United States."[40]

Still, in order to answer and confound slaveholders' charges that northerners were governed only by "a regard for self-interest," Olmsted thought gentlemen had a duty to improve the character of democratic society. "The poor need an education to the refinement and tastes and the mental & moral capital of gentlemen," he wrote, in order to protect democracy from that "excessive materialism of purpose in which we are, as a people, so cursedly absorbed" and which threatened to destroy the "simple and sensible social life in our community." Olmsted—like Horace Greeley, who had been stressing the "elevating influence" of a public park for three years in the *Tribune*—argued that "the aesthetic faculties need to be to educated—drawn out. . . . there need to be places and times for *re-unions*" where "the rich and poor, the cultivated and *well-bred* and the sturdy and self-made shall be attracted together and encouraged to assimilate." In such places, the merchant and the laborer alike would come to appreciate gentlemanly values expressed through personal refinement. And in Olmsted's mind, government "ought to assist in these things" for the same reason that it provided public education and supported agricultural societies: to improve its citizens and give them a higher sense of moral and civic purpose.[41]

Olmsted did not have Vaux's regard for independent craft and skill as a foundation of a vital democratic culture and art. Instead, he stressed the economic "advantages" of "combination . . . when efficiently controlled and judicially directed by a central administration." Arguing that the "occupation of laborer does *not* necessarily prevent a high intellectual and moral development," Olmsted nonetheless thought that in an orderly democracy gentlemen must lead the way. He felt it his duty as a gentleman to train the poor and the uneducated, whom he did not entirely trust, in the tastes and manners he had inherited. He shared with members of the park board the concept of stewardship that assumed that they knew what was best for the people. All that was needed was "to force into contact the good & bad, the gentlemanly and the rowdy," Olmsted suggested to Brace, for the "good" and "gentlemanly" to prevail.[42]

The Architect-in-Chief and the "Clerk"

Vaux and Olmsted believed that Central Park would be democratic because public institutions could give all people access to cultural resources otherwise available only to the wealthy. For Vaux, this democratic art—produced through the efforts of all citizens and thriving "in open air . . . for the benefit of all"—had intrinsic value; for Olmsted, the park was a means to a larger end, a way of bringing people together so that those who lacked "mental & moral capital" could gain it. But what if the majority of New Yorkers did not want the particular cultural resources or mental capital the designers proposed to give them? What if they wanted in the new park a grand avenue, a pleasure ground, or a racetrack instead of rural scenery? Vaux's and Olmsted's conception of Central Park as a democratic work of art posed the larger issue of their cultural authority to define the true, the good, and the beautiful for others.

From the first, Vaux defended their conception of the park as that of artists. Confronted with alternative visions, Vaux acknowledged a difference of opinion and set out to make the strongest case possible through the press. Open-air criticism and debate were part of an educative process that made a democratic culture strong, and he trusted that all Americans did share his love of natural beauty. Thus, Vaux saw public appreciation of the park as an ongoing process that depended less on enforcing correct conduct and taste than in making resources available. The park itself, if well designed, would offer an "art education," its very existence "teaching its lesson of possible magnificence for the poor." Not even vandalism could shake his faith. Any damage, he argued, "should be carefully repaired *at once* and costs & charges set down to profit & loss as part of the necessary expense for the art education of the people[.] More costly today because it was neglected yesterday. Less costly tomorrow if attended to now. The city [is] to blame for not giving the opportunity to acquire good manners long ago and must take the consequences good humouredly."[43]

Olmsted had little good humor with respect to abuses of the park, and he was far more worried than Vaux about educating the public to its proper enjoyment. In order for the park to exercise its "harmonizing and refining influence," the public needed not just firsthand contact with natural beauty but also "efficiently controlled and judiciously managed" supervision and guidance. Olmsted believed his duties as superintendent stood apart from and above his contribution as an artist to the park's design.[44]

The tension in the designers' understandings of their contribution to the park came to the forefront in an exchange of letters in 1863 and 1865. Distressed that newspaper articles (written by Olmsted's close friends) described Olmsted as the sole designer, Vaux sought a clarification of the true nature of their collaboration. Olmsted responded by elaborating their respective "properties" in Central Park. They equally shared the "general design" and its details; the "architectural design" belonged "wholly" to Vaux, the management of the construction primarily to Olmsted. But Olmsted considered "administration and management of the public introduction to and use of the park" his own "most important property" and the one that had made the park's success "much more complete and permanent and unquestionable and advantageous to us."[45]

The relation of design to use, Olmsted acknowledged to Vaux, was "vague but intimate, dependent upon the fittingness of the design for an easy, safe and convenient habituation of the public to the customs desirable to be established in it, and especially to gaining the public regard and respect to it. . . . Therefore in one sense this belongs to you equally with me—but so far as this can be disregarded, I mean that you have had little to do with the last division of our service": superintendence. The park would have been "shipwrecked again & again," Olmsted insisted "if it had not been for my intense sympathy with and fore-reaching for the best use which the people would, properly introduced and led along and prepared for, find the park to be to them." It was through his "natural gift" for such superintendence that Olmsted believed he had "been worth most to the park."[46]

Olmsted's letter made Vaux "sick and sad," for the very metaphor of "property" violated his sense of their work as a shared and equal endeavor. In assigning preeminence to superintendence and suggesting that design could in any sense be "disregarded," Olmsted devalued his partner's and his own artistic contribution. Only if the park was well designed, Vaux believed, could it inspire the respect of those who used it. Olmsted had created a false hierarchy and violated the park's spirit when he said that its success rested on his training of parkgoers. A "liberal" or "extended" definition of design, Vaux argued, would include the process of "working out our plan" and the cooperative values such a process entailed. "I think the last analysis would show," he added, "that after all I have a share in [superintendence] having included it in my estimate of [design] and that in both together[,] that is[,] in the Park not as a work of the arts of architecture and landscape gardening only but of the art of administration and good government in its extended sense we stand as co-workers."[47]

Olmsted's belief in the supremacy of superintendence over design left his partner in a bind. The two men had met shortly after they won first prize in April 1858 to divide the premium, Vaux recalled, and at that time he had suggested that they might logically terminate their partnership. As long as he received equal credit for the design, he was glad to entrust Superintendent Olmsted with executing the plan, for he found "bossing jobs is one thing and art another—and I have an instinctive hate to anything of the Napoleon III sort." Olmsted had insisted that he could not fulfill the design without Vaux's assistance, a recognition readily confirmed as they faced demands for modification of the plan. But Vaux soon discovered that preserving the partnership for purposes of preserving the design did not mean the same thing to the two partners.[48]

Those park commissioners who had for ten months sought to shift Viele's responsibilities as the park's chief executive officer to Olmsted saw in their selection of the Greensward plan the opportunity to complete the process by firing Viele and appointing Olmsted architect-in-chief. Although the Democratic press criticized the move, Olmsted eagerly accepted the position, and Vaux was hired as his assistant at five dollars a day. Olmsted viewed the title, he later told Vaux, as "a mere enlargement and dignification of my previous office [superintendent], with which you had nothing to do." Knowing that Olmsted was sensitive about his authority on the park, Vaux in turn regarded the arrangement as an expediency to get work started. If challenged by his own partner, Olmsted would not have "work[ed] efficiently," Vaux thought, and the designers would risk losing all artistic control. Under these circumstances, it was "impossible," Vaux observed, to make Olmsted see that by assuming the title of architect-in-chief he was also claiming public credit for the design. "Knowing the state of art and the position of artists and the need of every strength being brought to bear[,] it was of course somewhat difficult to countenance the idea of an established arch[itect] serving as clerk for . . . a new man who chose to call himself or be called arch[itect]." Yet Vaux felt Olmsted's "cooperation [would be] greater if it could be secured to the public at any price the work or I might be called on to pay for it."[49]

Vaux saw Olmsted's insensitivity on the matter as an "intellectual" rather than a "moral" mistake, a misconception of their responsibilities as artists that stemmed from Olmsted's professional inexperience. But Vaux was increasingly pained to see his own contribution erased. He had "sacrifice[d] [his] professional rights for the good of the common cause . . . of the park and all it meant in its best sense," while Olmsted had in effect declared, as Vaux put it in an 1865 letter, "all theirs is ours[,] all ours is mine—and all mine is my own. . . . I will work for the Park but I must have the reputation and I must have it all and I must have it immediately and I must have it always." Olmsted, for his part, repeatedly tried to convince Vaux that his work as superintendent had protected their shared artistic conception of the park. He agreed that he lacked Vaux's "professional training, experience, esprit de corps, and class interests" as an artist, but without his own "real instinctive devotion and enthusiasm," Olmsted claimed, "there was no . . . sympathy with us or courage or greatness of purpose or good taste, or personal respect for us on the Commission."[50]

Olmsted's sense of lack of "respect" from the board referred specifically to the protests of two Democratic commissioners, which, when taken up by the press, opened the designers' definition of the park to a wider public negotiation. Yet, despite Olmsted's claims that the park board did not fully appreciate his and Vaux's vision of Central Park, a majority of commissioners responded to public pressures by requesting changes in the plan that ultimately reinforced the park's definition as rural scenery.

The Debate over the Greensward Plan

Not all New Yorkers shared Vaux and Olmsted's assumption that the "popular idea of a park is a beautiful open green space." That fact became apparent in the weeks after the award was announced. Critics for the *Horticulturalist* and the *Crayon* (a Ruskinian art journal) heartily endorsed the selection of the Greensward plan, but the *Herald*'s James Gordon Bennett found it "impossible to make head or tail" of the winning plan and attributed its selection entirely to politics; *Frank Leslie's Illustrated Weekly* admired the winning plan but primarily the Parade, playgrounds, Mall, and concert hall, ignoring the naturalistic landscape effects; and even the *Times*, *Post*, and *Courier and Enquirer*, which all agreed that the first prize was deserved, hoped that the plan would be modified by "valuable hints" that appeared in some of the losing plans.[51]

Although the park commissioners arranged a public exhibition of the plans, they also attempted to preempt public discussion of the design. A week after the awards, a committee (Andrew Green and Charles Russell) consulted with Superintendent Olmsted and proposed three modifications: first, thirty-foot roads with a fifteen-foot pedestrian walk on one side and a twenty-foot bridle path running for three miles on the other to save paving costs and to satisfy the expectations of equestrians (the Greensward plan itself pointed to the example of the Vienna Prater and the Bois de Boulogne in proposing sixty-foot carriage drives, flanked on either side by twenty-foot walks); second, a cost-saving "footway" instead of the carriage entrance between Sixth and Seventh avenues; and third, drawing the western drive deeper into the park, thereby reducing the Parade.[52]

This third proposal marked a shift in the board's own definition of what a public park should contain. Vaux and Olmsted had shown some ambivalence about militia drills in a "park proper," but the specifications called for a parade ground. Nearly half of the contestants had followed Viele in placing a forty-five- to fifty-acre parade on the east side of the old rectangular reservoir facing Fifth Avenue (between 82nd and 85th streets, the present site of the Metropolitan Museum). The Greensward plan set aside just twenty-five acres on the park's west side between 66th and 71st streets (today called the Sheep Meadow). Olmsted and Vaux had apologized for its contracted dimensions but tried to recognize the Parade's civic function and create a "picturesque approach" by providing a "portcullis gate" (like that on a castle drawbridge) through which the militia could march. Green and Russell, however, saw no advantage to such a ceremonial gate for militia marches. The western drive would be "more agreeable," they thought (and the Parade further reduced), if it were swept closer into the park's interior, eliminating the gate. The commissioners seemed to share the contempt expressed by the author of plan 13, who warned that "not one parade in fifty, possibly not one in one hundred, would attract the class of people who would make use of the drive." The "public" the park board wished to welcome came close to what plan 13 had identified as that "class most fitted by education to enjoy the beautiful in nature and art," a class that the commissioners themselves believed to "represent" the city.[53]

Parade grounds like that envisioned by the 1811 street plan served a traditional republican concept of civic duty. They provided space for citizens to demonstrate their commitment to defense of their government. But with the rise of political parties and the growth of immigrant communities, the participatory male ritual of militia drills, with crowds of admiring spectators, had come to entail raucous entertainments of fire companies, political clubs, and target companies. A parade ground, moreover, resembled the unregulated space of pleasure grounds. A majority of the gentlemen on the board wanted to exclude uses of public space, however linked to republican traditions, that undermined their own concept of civic order achieved through the refinement of taste.[54]

The week after it endorsed these changes, the park board fired Viele and transferred his responsibilities to Olmsted. But then Commissioner Robert Dillon issued thirteen further suggestions for modification. His opposition to the Greensward plan had political as well as aesthetic roots. As a lifelong Democrat, Dillon seems to have instinctively distrusted the motives of the board's Republicans; as a wealthy Irish-American Catholic (and an organizer of the Irish Emigrant Society and the Immigrants Savings Bank), he expressed little fondness for English traditions of landscape gardening. It was Dillon who had urged the board to appropriate a thousand dollars to invite the designer of the Bois de Boulogne to visit and advise.[55]

In his campaign to modify the winning plan, Dillon recruited the board's newest member, financier August Belmont, also a prominent Democrat. Belmont had been born into a German-Jewish landholding family and had expanded his family's already substantial fortune by becoming the Rothschild banking firm's American representative. In appointing him to the board in March 1858, other commissioners doubtless hoped that he would prove useful in floating park improvement bonds. Known throughout the city for his cosmopolitan and sporting ways, Belmont shared Dillon's admiration for continental public spaces.[56]

Dillon and Belmont invoked the design tradition of artificial civic display when they announced their "dissent entirely" from the Greensward plan's naturalistic aesthetic. "The Central Park, as its name imports," they argued, "is to be in the very center of an immense City . . . and surrounded by the highest forms of artificial or civilized life, erected by the wealth and designed by the genius of man." How could "rustic" taste be reconciled with a sense of progress that took satisfaction in the attainments of "civilized" life? Dillon and Belmont warned that the "sudden and violent" contrast between the city and a rural park would be "grotesque."[57]

The two commissioners thought that the park would be more urbane if its circulation system allowed for more intensive use of the grounds. With Belmont's public support, Dillon proposed the separation of drives, walks, and rides as a "cardinal" design principle both for practical and for aesthetic reasons. To install paths on either side of the drives would expose pedestrians to "the distractions, noise, dust, and dangers of horsemen and carriages." And in place of the Greensward proposal for a equestrian path only around the reservoir, Dillon suggested a separate ride running the length of the park "to accommodate manly and invigorating horsemanship." His second major proposal extended the logic of separate systems of movement through the park. "Meandering paths" and a promenade only six city blocks long would be "inadequate to meet the habits, tastes, or expectations of the people." Borrowing suggestions from Howard Daniels's plan, Dillon proposed an alternative two-mile "Cathedral Avenue," which would lead pedestrians from 59th Street, over a suspension bridge at the Lake, around the top of the reservoirs and north to a grand concourse at Observatory Hill (now called the Great Hill, at 106th Street on the west side). Such a "stately" promenade would be the park's "main and most distinguished feature because it will give more pleasure and more health than other forms in which the Park can be used" and "like any grand erection in architecture excites elevation of mind and promotes order and good manners."[58]

Dillon's routing of the Cathedral Avenue around the reservoirs further emphasized his vision of a park that displayed civic accomplishments. The Greensward plan drew attention away from the "artificial" reservoirs and camouflaged their walls with plantings. Dillon and Belmont thought the reservoirs ought to be "treated and used as the jewels of the park," encased in a "casket" of marble walls and staircases that would lead the parkgoer to a view of "immense artificial lakes, unrivaled in extent." The Croton aqueduct, they proclaimed, was "one of the greatest works of modern times," particularly "suggestive of the wealth, the enterprise, the science and sagacity of the people of New York."[59]

A majority of the board rejected Dillon and Belmont's proposals for enhancing the park's grandeur and endorsed Olmsted's rebuttal that a grand avenue would "destroy scenery at great cost" and that "straight lines of trees or stately architecture . . . belong not to parks for the people, but to palatial gardens."

Another bias underlying the predominantly Yankee board's response to the elite continental tastes of its only Catholic and Jewish members, however, became apparent as the *Post* attacked the dissenters. With thinly veiled anti-Semitism, the *Post* criticized Belmont for publicly airing his disapproval of the winning design when he had only been on the park board one month and owed his election to the other commissioners: "We are willing to make reasonable allowances for that want of modesty which seems to be constitutional with certain tribes of the human family, but we do not remember when our charity has been tested by a case of more flagrant presumption than this."[60]

A lively discussion ensued in the press as editors and letter writers reflected on what they themselves wanted in a public park. Some correspondents sided with Dillon and Belmont in rejecting natural scenery as a primary goal, complaining, for example, of the "unfinished look" of open meadows. These correspondents believed New Yorkers were less interested in nature than in one another and their city. The Greensward plan, making room for the spectacle of fashion, saw no inherent contradiction between this personal display and the appreciation of nature; rather, Vaux and Olmsted hoped to tempt those who socialized on the Promenade into the contemplative reaches of nature through the inviting distant view. But New Yorkers who found the park's urban qualities most attractive supported a more continental design that would emphasize "the brilliant spectacle of handsome equipages and gaily dressed company" even though it wasn't "very rural or country like," as an "Artist" wrote in a letter to the *Tribune*.[61]

By publishing their suggestions for modifying the Greensward plan, Dillon and Belmont brought a wider public into the design negotiations and recruited both the *Herald* and the *Tribune* to their call for more ample rides and walks and the "convenience" of their separation. Since many historians have identified the separation of ways as one of the most praiseworthy elements of Central Park's original design, it is worth stressing that without Dillon and Belmont's public protest, this feature would not have been adopted. Although the Republican commissioners and Green easily outvoted Dillon, Belmont, and Fields, the three Democrats had appealed to the public and recruited the common council to their side. By the end of June, however, Republican commissioners successfully closed further public debate and fixed the park's definition as rural scenery. Then, apparently without a formal resolution, they directed Vaux and Olmsted to rework the circulation system into the separate ways advocated by the Democratic commissioners and the press.[62]

The designers ingeniously responded to the commissioners' demands in such a way as to accommodate the convenience of parkgoers and to give the natural landscape even greater emphasis. Not only did they design winding rides and walks separated from the drive, they introduced more than thirty bridges to carry the various routes over each other. In a technique that Vaux, as architect, appears to have most fully mastered in the later design of Brooklyn's

These 1858 and 1868 maps show modifications in the Greensward plan requested by the park commission. Note the reduced size of the Parade (called the Green in 1859 and later, the Sheep Meadow), the substitution of a pedestrian for carriage entrance at 59th between Sixth and Seventh avenues, and the introduction of winding pedestrian and equestrian paths separate from the drive. The later plan also included land between 106th and 110th streets, added in 1863.

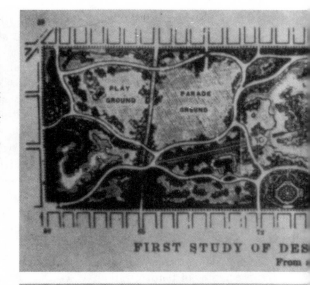

FIRST STUDY OF DES
From

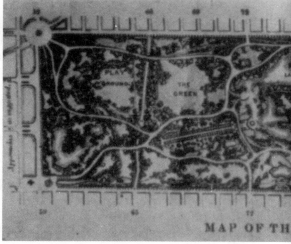

MAP OF TH

Prospect Park, bridges themselves became graceful frames for landscape scenes beyond.[63]

In *Villas and Cottages*, Vaux had argued that only by being invited to "criticize freely" could citizens clarify their own aesthetic values. Although he readily and aggressively defended the essential elements of the Greensward plan, particularly the subordination of "artificial" to natural features, Vaux relished the opportunity to explain (and defend) the design's intentions. As a professional architect, he was used to hearing and addressing a client's dissatisfactions with the details of a plan. Olmsted, by contrast, found debate over the Greensward plan personally threatening to his own ambitions as the park's chief executive

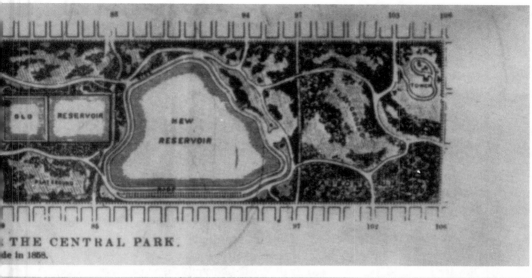

THE CENTRAL PARK.

de in 1858.

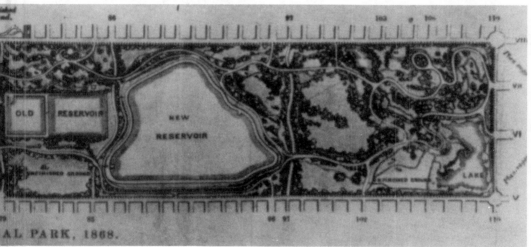

AL PARK, 1868.

officer. Turning to his connections in the "literary republic," he privately recruited journalists from the *Courier and Enquirer, Post,* and *Times* to help him correct "misrepresentations" of the plan. The *Courier and Enquirer*'s "timely" endorsement was particularly "gratifying to my pride," Olmsted informed one of the paper's editorial writers, Richard Grant White.[64]

The sheer number of newspapers and the willingness of editors to take up crusades both in support of and in opposition to the Greensward plan did introduce, as Vaux had suggested, a certain vitality to the process by which New Yorkers formed and expressed their own conceptions of a public park. But Olmsted was anxious to counter such criticism in the summer of 1858 as he set about establishing his executive authority over the park. Understanding his partner's fear that he "would get no reputation at all," Vaux "set the example of subordination" for other park officers and workers. He worked with Olmsted in two "characters," Vaux recalled, seeing him, on the one hand, as a fellow artist "with whom I could heartily act and sympathize" and, on the other hand, as "the bureaucrat and imperialist with whom I never for a moment sympathized."[65]

The differences between the two partners could be attributed in part to temperament, but they also hinted at larger debates regarding the future of a republican society. Vaux clung to his romantic faith in a society that would respect the artistic capacities of all citizens and in republican progress through cooperation. Like so many craftworkers in the mid-nineteenth century, he resisted hierarchies that devalued the skills of individual workers. He regarded Olmsted's claims for the priority of administrative power over the work of design as upside-down and "semi-barbarian." Vaux spoke with great scorn of the "conversion of this many sided, fluent, thoroughly American high art work into a machine—over which as Frederick the Great, Prince of Park Police [Olmsted] should preside, and with regal liberality dispense certificates of docility to the artists engaged in the work."[66]

Olmsted's concept of stewardship looked to gentlemen for disinterested civic leadership in fostering the values and manners that would improve the character of a democratic society. But in superintending park work and park use, he also helped shape a new corporate ideology that found progress and order in the hierarchy of management. When Olmsted reported to his father that he had gotten the park into "capital discipline, a perfect working system, working like a machine," he saw no loss to republican principles in this achievement. And in the end, Olmsted's treatment of his partner differed little from his treatment of park workers—whether engineers or laborers—on whose skills he depended. As the design and building process proceeded, the artist and the gentleman represented the clashing visions of the artisan and the manager.[67]

Ironically, Vaux's angriest letters to his partner came in 1865, as he recruited Olmsted back to their landscape architecture practice. Vaux tried to appeal to his "humble artist spirit" and then dared Olmsted to prove him mistaken in a less flattering interpretation of his partner's behavior. Olmsted, Vaux speculated, might after all be "Nap[oleon] III in disguise . . . a selfish fellow who would like to get power and reputation on other men's brains." Respecting Olmsted's aesthetic judgments, Vaux through much of their thirteen-year partnership suspended his reservations about his partner's "insatiable egoism" and imperial managerial style. Olmsted told Vaux when they launched their partnership again in 1865, "If I don't wholly adopt or agree with all you say, at least I respect it very thoroughly and feel that I have not altogether done justice to your position heretofore." In later years he tried, albeit with little success, to make sure Vaux was recognized as Central Park's codesigner. Still, the tension of their different conceptions of their collaborative work in designing a democratic park

persisted. Vaux suspected that he would never win Olmsted to a "fair subscription of *the power* that each is capable of exercising . . . because it involves the idea
of a common fraternal effort [and] it is too republican an idea for you, you must
have a thick line drawn all around your sixpen' worth of individuality."[68]

Without Vaux's encouragement and teaching, Olmsted would never have
achieved his success as an artist and a parkmaker. At the time of the Greensward collaboration, "the higher ambition" of artistic work to which your "com-
radeship afterwards brought me," Olmsted later told Vaux, "was less instinctive
in character, less engrossing and permanent" than the ambition to serve as park
superintendent. As he turned to managing construction, Olmsted insisted on
the subordination of the process of design to administration, the subordination
of his partner's claim as an "equal worker," and above all, the subordination of
the artisans and laborers who turned the Greensward plan into a public park.

6

BUILDING FOR "THE
PUBLIC AND POSTERITY"

In the early 1860s, Horace Greeley went up to look at the new Central Park. "Well, they have let it alone better than I thought they would," he said, as Calvert Vaux remembered it. But Vaux knew better. "We concealed the processes from him," he wrote. "But there were processes and nearly all was intended and foreseen." The devout Vaux then corrected himself: when God "acts as contractor one cannot reckon on the specifications being very exactly followed."[1]

Whether or not God did the general contracting, men turned the earth. It took a massive human effort to transform the rocky and swampy site that the city had purchased in 1856 into a landscaped park. By the time Central Park was completed, workers had gone over every foot of ground, raising or lowering the surface; they had transformed natural drainage courses into artificial subterranean waterways and created the illusions of picturesque abundance and distant prospects. In the first five years, laborers excavated, moved, or brought into the park nearly 2.5 million cubic yards of stone and earth—enough to raise the level of a football field eighty stories. With pickaxes, hammers, shovels, and 166 tons of gunpowder (more than the amount fired at the Battle of Gettysburg), they cut through more than 300,000 cubic yards of gneiss rock veined with granite. Stone breakers crushed 35,000 cubic yards of this rock into paving stone. Contractors supplied 6 million bricks, 35,000 barrels of cement, 65,000 cubic yards of gravel, and 19,000 cubic yards of sand. Gardeners fertilized the ground with more than 40,000 cubic yards of manure and compost and planted 270,000 trees and shrubs. Out of this immense expenditure of labor and materials— 20,000 men and $5 million by 1866—emerged the park's drives, paths, bridges, hills, lakes, lawns, and scenic vistas.[2]

This massive production process rested, in turn, on a highly contested political process. Central Park's creation coincided with intense partisan conflict, a dramatic expansion of the public sector, the rise of a new class of professional managers, and growing labor militancy. With so much money and power at stake, building the park became a field of contention: state and city representatives fought over which party would control the project, and commissioners debated how to manage it. Meanwhile workers were demanding jobs, the park artisans were asserting traditional craft prerogatives, and park laborers were seeking equitable wages. And yet when all the pulling and hauling was over, Central Park—the result of these intensely social "processes"—would, ironically, be described as "natural."

"We Want Work"

In November 1857 (six months before the selection of the Greensward plan), more than two thousand angry workingmen gathered at the office of Superintendent Frederick Law Olmsted to demand jobs building Central Park. "As I worked my way through the crowd, no one recognized me," Olmsted recalled later. "I saw & heard a man then a candidate for reelection as a local magistrate addressing it from a wagon. He urged that those before him had a right to live; he assumed that they could live only through wages to be paid by the city; and to obtain these he advised that they should demand employment of me. If I should be backward in yielding it—here he held up a rope and pointed to a tree, and the crowd cheered."[3]

Contemporary newspaper accounts partially sustain Olmsted's story, but where he recalled an "organized mob," a *Herald* reporter saw a crowd of "sober, industrious and well inclined" workingmen. Olmsted remembered a threatening sign demanding "Blood or Bread"; journalists recorded white muslin banners of "WORK/ARBEIT" and "We Want Work." In the middle of the severest depression in twenty years, unemployed workers had turned to city government for jobs. To New York City's laboring families, the park in 1857 represented a place of work, not a playground.[4]

At the time unemployed laborers took to the streets, the park project was stalled. Surveying teams appointed by Mayor Fernando Wood's premature park commission had been at work since the summer of 1856. But in order to start building the park, the new Board of Commissioners of the Central Park, appointed by the state legislature in April 1857, had to persuade the common council to appropriate the bond revenues authorized by the legislature. A mass meeting of twenty thousand New Yorkers in City Hall Park in mid-May denounced the Republican-dominated legislature's creation of the Central Park board (as well as the Metropolitan Police Board and new liquor license regulations); such unprecedented intervention in local affairs was "grossly insulting to the people of this City." To create "a new form of government without submitting its provisions to those who are to be governed by it," a resolution signed by Democratic leaders declared, "outraged the constitutional rights of freemen."[5]

Encouraged by this public support for home rule, the common council's Democratic majority initially ignored the park commissioners' request for construction funds. Meanwhile, the new board sought to assert its unilateral sovereignty over Central Park in the summer of 1857. Rejecting the proposal of some Democratic members to open meetings to the public, the commissioners adopted a policy of closed sessions and decided, further, to omit members' names from the minutes handed out to the press. Unlike elected officials or even members of other state boards that held open meetings, commissioners could not be held publicly accountable for their actions. The park board also overlooked the city charter's requirement that public works be contracted out to private builders and began to hire laborers directly. But in order to overcome the resistance of local politicians, the commissioners apparently struck a deal with Mayor Wood. When the common council finally appropriated park improvement bonds in late August, Wood's appointee, engineer Egbert Viele, was allowed to hire the first group of nearly 650 laborers—"nine-tenths of [them] Wood Democrats."[6]

New obstacles stood in the way. The city comptroller tried to sell the park bonds, but there were no buyers; then in late September the financial crisis that had been building for months broke, and firm after firm declared bankruptcy. Newspapers proclaimed Wall Street in panic. When, on October 8, the *New York Times* surveyed the "effect of the hard times . . . on hundreds of mechanics, 'shop girls,' sewing women and day laborers," Central Park's laborers—"Irishmen and Germans . . . a few who were Italian"—led the list of those laid off. The park board submitted a request for new appropriations to an unsympathetic common council. Then in late October, with editors predicting a grim winter of evictions and soup kitchens, Mayor Wood told the aldermen that fifty thousand people would be unemployed by midwinter. "Not a few" of these men and women, he said, would "resort to violence" rather than face the "precarious and humiliating dependencies" of charity. To maintain peace, city officials should hire unemployed workers on public works. But Democrats on the board of councilmen continued to oppose funding the state-appointed and Republican-dominated park commission.[7]

Unemployed laborers took matters into their own hands in the first week of November: they mounted demonstrations in Tompkins Square, the ten-acre park in the middle of a Lower East Side working-class district. On November 5, six thousand protesters marched to the Merchant's Exchange in the heart of the financial district and on to City Hall. "Every human being has a RIGHT to live, not as a mere charity, but as RIGHT," a committee of the protesters declared in a resolution to Mayor Wood, "and governments, monarchical or republican, MUST FIND work for the people if individual exertion prove not sufficient." Month-long "Bread and Work" demonstrations united Irish, German, and native-born New Yorkers, who cheered when James McGuire reminded them that "if one man suffer, it don't matter whether he is an all American or a foreigner—they all suffer." "The working men have made capitalists and aristocrats of this country rich by the sweat of their brows," the blacksmith William Bowles told the crowd, "and now it was no more than just that the working men should in turn receive their rights at their hands."[8]

In asserting their claims as a class on city government, unemployed laborers raised the larger issue of their membership in the public. Throughout the 1850s, the city's trade union movement had debated whether and how workers should engage in politics. Only if they organized into an independent political movement, some radicals argued, would working people be heard. More cautious union leaders, viewing all politicians with contempt, urged workers to concentrate on securing economic demands against employers. The unemployed demonstrators included activists who advocated a far-reaching program of "labor reform" and workers who during "good times" looked to political patrons for employment. Brought together by the extremity of the depression, the workingmen put forth a plank—the right to earn a living—not found on any party platform.[9]

On November 9, with hundreds of workingmen crowding the chamber at City Hall, the board of councilmen agreed to the Central Park appropriation. The next day, Tompkins Square speakers, in a brief victory celebration, called on laborers "to create political capital out of the movement" and to organize "to protect themselves as did other classes." City politicians and park officials, seeking to contain the unrest, tried to bribe the movement's leaders with jobs on the park. But they largely ignored the names of job seekers gathered by rank-and-file demonstrators.[10]

The workingmen moved their demonstrations to the park itself with demands that men be hired from their ranks. On November 20, a *Sun* reporter wrote that "some of the crowd . . . threatened to go in, thrash the men who had been set to work, compel the clerks under pain of being throttled, to take down the names of all who wanted work, and they would seize the tools, and all go to work." But once the unemployed laborers had successfully pressured the councilmen to appropriate funds, their greatest political bargaining chip was not rhetoric or even need but rather their votes, and here they competed with others who sought the same jobs. More than four thousand letters from job seekers (many listing thirty or forty names) came in to the park commissioners, and with an eye to the upcoming municipal election and securing future appropriations, they divided the patronage of park jobs among themselves and local politicians.[11]

Most commissioners—hoping to fashion the park board's reputation as a nonpartisan body—deployed their patronage discreetly. But Commissioner James Hogg freely admitted that he had "called together the foremen and told them plainly that the continuance of the work depended upon the defeat of Mr.

Wood." Nativists and Tammany Democrats, who blamed the mayor for the past year's civil disturbances and who resented his usurpation of patronage, united with Republicans like Hogg to elect a reform Democrat.[12] As a result, the state-appointed park commission no longer had to deal with the troublesome Mayor Wood or his followers in the common council. For unemployed workers, the outcome of the fall struggles were more equivocal. Their protests finally launched the construction of the park, but they gained little control over park jobs.

Patronage versus Professional Management

More than anything else, political expediency determined the Central Park commissioners' initial strategy for organizing construction. The gentlemen of the state-appointed board, concerned for its future, capitalized on the turmoil of the workers' demonstrations to establish the park's indispensability to the city. Through their control of the largest public works project in New York, the commissioners temporarily circumvented the deep-seated local hostility to state-appointed management of the city's park. The question of how the board would organize construction, however, was not resolved in the fall of 1857. Even as they won a tactical victory and secured appropriations, commissioners debated among themselves how far they would take their coup. Staunch Republican partisans on the board saw an opportunity to reassign the spoils to their own party. Other members perceived control of the park as an opportunity to implement a reform agenda that would not only break the local Democrats' grip on patronage but also demonstrate to the city an entirely new system of labor management.[13]

The commissioners' debates reflected both the ideological and the practical conflicts that had arisen with the massive expansion of public works in the first half of the nineteenth century. Through the 1840s, lawmakers had relied on the competitive contract system to preserve the laissez-faire foundation of governmental promotion of internal improvements. According to the logic of the free market, the profit motive would prompt the private contractors who directed the building of canals and railroads to manage the work efficiently, albeit often at the expense of customary work rules that gave workers some control over their labor. But pitched battles had erupted as laborers contested contractors' low wages and strict rules. Organized workingmen regarded the contract system, whether in the public or private sector, as exploitative. Denouncing contractors' "exactions"—the profits that stemmed from paying workers less than the labor costs cited in their bids—workingmen campaigned for the abolition of the contract system on public works and, failing that, for ordinances requiring public contractors to comply with the wage rates and work rules "established by the trade." Meanwhile, railroad directors responded to the turmoil between contractors and workers by placing their own officers in direct charge of supervising construction.[14]

On the local level the contract system fed the patronage system and reinforced party rule. Despite requirements in the city charter that public contracts go to the lowest bidder, politicians made sure that contractors contributed to campaign coffers and guaranteed election turnouts in exchange for public contract awards. Street contractors, feeling confident of politicians' tolerance of cost overruns, did not always push or discipline their workers—or so it seemed to city taxpayers who complained about delays and added expenses on local public works. Yet, few New Yorkers in the mid-nineteenth century regarded patronage as inherently unethical. The American party system, after all, had been built on the exchange of favors. Public jobs, like private employment, were distributed through clientage relationships. But some taxpayers did worry about the rising costs of local public works and blamed politically connected contractors and their "inefficient" laborers.[15]

The new park board was attuned to taxpayers' worries about costs. In September 1857, before the unemployed demonstrations, reform-minded commissioners sought to advance efficient administration by hiring their own "nonpartisan" officer—Superintendent Olmsted—to manage park workers. In later years, with a somewhat bitter irony, Olmsted credited his selection as superintendent to a reputation for being an "unpractical man," by which he meant a man without conventional political ties. John Gray, president of the park board, and Andrew Green, treasurer, were relieved, Olmsted recalled, to discover that he had "no experience in practical politics, even no personal acquaintance with Republican leaders in the city." Furthermore, Olmsted "responded warmly to virtuous sentiments with regard to corruption in both parties."[16]

Olmsted contrasted his supposed "unpractical" principles to Chief Engineer Egbert Viele's tolerance for a park regime in which lazy foremen, appointed through political connections, could insult their boss with impertinent remarks. "Hallo Fred—get round pretty often, don't you," one foreman had greeted the new superintendent after looking up from his newspaper. Although the board had let Viele supervise the workers hired in August, in late November—with Mayor Wood and his followers out of office—it placed Olmsted in charge. No man who "is not disposed to give a full measure of work," he assured the board, would be retained.[17]

The following June, after the park commissioners adopted the Greensward plan and promoted Olmsted to architect-in-chief, Democratic members challenged the ad hoc arrangements for organizing the park's construction through direct hiring rather than contracts. "If the history of public expenditure establishes one truth more clearly than another," Commissioner Robert Dillon insisted, "it is that no work should be undertaken by the Government, which can be done by individuals, and that all public work should be executed by contract to the lowest bidder." Only by turning public work over to the private sector, he said, could park officials determine the fixed (that is, contracted) costs and guarantee "vigilant supervision which springs alone from private and individual interests." Laissez-faire principles were a mainstay of Democratic party rhetoric, but Dillon also had a strong personal stake in limiting the expense: as corporation counsel in 1856, he had promised taxpayers that the *total* cost of the park would not exceed $5 million, an amount already surpassed in acquiring the land. He had, in addition, drafted the bill that limited construction funds to $1.5 million. "This *covenant with the people,* thus enforced by positive law, should be most religiously observed," he insisted, "and there is no security against its violation except the adoption of the contract system in the execution of the plan."[18]

Republican commissioners Charles Elliott, an iron manufacturer, and John Gray, who served on the boards of directors of numerous railroads, associated the traditional contract system with inefficiency and patronage. They preferred the new centralized and hierarchical system of administration developed by the railroads and urged the board to continue to hire "day labor" directly. "A constant economy of labor" could be obtained, Commissioners Gray and Elliott argued in a joint report, "from the judicious management under one general head, which a dozen contractors would not and could not practice or contemplate." Gray and Elliott's advocacy of day labor also rested on another consideration—the demands of the city's labor movement. Private contractors submitting the lowest bids, they warned, "could only make money by in some way oppressing the working man." It would not be a "wise policy" for the board to permit any "intermediate parties [to] profit by any exactions upon" laborers. Optimistically recasting the experience of the unemployed demonstrations, they suggested that "the wages paid to the working man is an item in our City expenditures never objected to by the taxpayers." The board's aim, therefore, "should be to have faithful laborers at fair wages."[19]

This policy acknowledged the practical power of the city's workers in pressuring politicians for appropriations. Republicans such as Elliott also saw an opportunity to recruit workingmen from the ranks of the Democratic party by supporting labor reform. Yet, reform had its own contradictions. Workers were spared the contractors' exactions on their wages but had to face park officers' expectations of what constituted a "faithful" worker. For the private sector's traditional equation of economy with competition, the commissioners were proposing a new public works equation of economy with discipline.[20]

Olmsted endorsed this view of public works management and linked the policy of direct hiring to his own ambitions as the park's chief executive officer. He shuddered at the alternative prospect of "bodies of laborers, under a different government, with different wages, hours of work, privileges, requirements and customs from those which belong to the regularly hired laborers of the commission." By retaining the power to hire and fire his own workers and to move gangs "from one branch of the work to another, as from day to day may be found best," Olmsted would be able to maintain his own "capital discipline" for construction, and he would be free, as architect-in-chief, to "improve the plan as the work progresses." Indeed, it was the "custom of many landscape gardeners to make no special preliminary surveys . . . but to fix curves and grades definitely only day to day, as point after point is reached." Arranging his own day-to-day schedule to permit him to deploy several thousand laborers "from one branch of work to another" while at the same time refining "moderately exact preconception[s]" of design, however, would prove a great deal more difficult than Olmsted had imagined.[21]

In August 1858 after intense debate over the system of labor the board granted Olmsted a trial period to prove his skills in the "judicious management" of thousands of day laborers.[22] Central Park thus became the largest and most visible American experiment in the centralized corporate model for building public works. But because it was an experiment, the "specifications," as Vaux noted and Olmsted predicted, were not always "exactly followed." Olmsted and the engineers who tried to implement the board's managerial principles encountered the resistance of workers and even of commissioners and fellow park officers with a stake in Central Park other than its efficient production alone.

Despite Olmsted's insistence on his own rules for hiring, the commissioners continued to make appointments with an eye to political pressure and to their obligations as partisans and patrons. Commissioner Hogg typically explained in a note to Olmsted that although one man he recommended for assistant foreman was "not used to out of door work," his name had been forwarded by a delegate on the Republican state central committee. "There will have to be some men put on for the Aldermen and Councilmen," the property clerk B. F. Crane gently reminded Olmsted in the spring of 1860, "or we will have trouble when we apply for money." Even the reform-minded Charles Elliott was not above such concessions. Alderman John Brady, Elliott advised Olmsted, "had not a single foreman or assistant on the Park while other members of the Board have three or four each." Brady was an influential man, "one whom it is hardly worthwhile to offend unnecessarily."[23]

Patronage and the exchange of personal favors was as much a part of the culture of gentlemen as it was of local politicians and contractors. Commissioners intervened, for example, on behalf of an assortment of needy individuals or families. Elliott forwarded a letter from R. S. Watson in Boston requesting a job for his nephew "of course not requiring hard lifting work"; Commissioner William Strong urged Olmsted to hire a Michigan lawyer with the resounding name of Dewitt Clinton Bancroft, who had lost his fortune in an Illinois land speculation deal. Even Olmsted himself was not above such favors: one summer he placed his fifteen-year-old cousin George Putnam (also his publisher's son) on the gardening staff during school vacation.[24]

Olmsted considered interventions from politicians and commissioners an intolerable threat to his authority as chief executive officer. During his four years of superintending construction, he railed against the board's subversion of the new system of public works administration. Though proud "to claim the credit of conducting its work free from the vice of politics," as Olmsted put it, the commissioners were nonetheless unwilling to abandon either the privileges of their class or the park's advantages to the fledgling Republican party.[25] Carrying forward the lessons of their 1857 negotiations with local politicians, the Republican and the Democratic commissioners alike also sought to avoid "unnecessarily" offending local Democrats, for whom the board remained an "alien body" that had usurped power and had violated the fundamental principle of democratic home rule. Yet, if the board failed to abolish patronage, it did succeed in consolidating and centralizing management in a way never previously tried on a public works project.

The Engineering Corps

Central Park's engineering "corps," as its members called themselves, primarily determined how the building of the park would be organized and managed. As salaried employees, engineers occupied a position midway between a new class of corporate employers (who oversaw massive construction projects on behalf of "public" shareholders) and independent contractors (who negotiated work rules with local labor groups to secure their own private interests). The building of canals, water systems, and especially railroads had made engineering the fastest growing American profession in the mid-nineteenth century. The engineers generally came from prosperous old-stock families who were able to educate their sons; they brought to the park a professional ideology that linked expertise to efficiency, and like Olmsted, they valued discipline and "duty."[26]

In later years Olmsted would take full credit for organizing the park into an efficient "machine," but when the *Herald* complained in the late spring of 1858 that the architect-in-chief "knows nothing at all about engineering," it was pointing to a real limitation. Olmsted's inability to attend to his own finances was symptomatic of his impatience with keeping track of costs for the park. The same man who explained to his father in February 1858 that he could not account for his personal debts "because I have had too much on my mind & been too absorbingly occupied to keep systematic accounts," proposed to the park commissioners the following May that only a "moderately exact preconception" of a road's grades and curves would be required before launching construction. He depended on the engineers both for precise calculations and for implementing and enforcing the management principles and work discipline that established Central Park's reputation as a model public works project.[27]

Most of the engineering corps (thirty-one men at the peak of construction) arrived on the park with prior experience on railroads, canals, or water systems. A youthful group—most in their twenties and thirties—they had usually begun professional training after a year or two of high school or college. Chief Engineer William H. Grant—Viele's replacement—had attended Ithaca College for two years and then apprenticed himself as a surveyor on the New York and Erie Railroad. Grant's nine-year stint as assistant engineer on the Erie Canal enlargement initiated him into the "systematic and thorough going course of [public works] management" advocated by his mentor, John B. Jervis. He was now forty-two.[28]

Within a month of his arrival, Grant had organized the park into four divisions, appointed assistants in charge of each section, and established a hierarchical chain of command for the rest of the engineering corps. Montgomery A. Kellogg, then twenty-eight, who (like Grant) had worked on the New York Central and Hudson Railroad, was put in charge of job assignments and set a high standard for his subordinates. When Kellogg died in 1898, his obituary noted that "his last illness was caused by overwork. He had not taken a vacation in twenty years." J. H. Pieper—described by the architect-in-chief as "a sturdy hard-headed German, tough as a pine knot, and able to do more work than almost any man I know"—assumed responsibilities as the superintending engineer for the four division assistants. Pieper, thirty-four, had learned his profession at a German polytechnic college, but he himself trained two young division engineers, Francis T. Hawks, who had come to New York from the South, and John Bogart, twenty-two, the son of a prominent Albany merchant, who had worked several summers with the New York Central engineering corps.[29]

In contrast to the surveying engineers hired by Viele, most of the construction engineers came from outside New York City. Their first loyalty was not to a local community but rather to their profession and to an abstract "public" that would benefit from their work. Free of political obligations in gaining their jobs, many of the engineers probably shared the sentiments of A. W. Craven, who was overseeing private contractors building the city's new reservoir within the park. When in 1860 the mayor tried to fire him for "insubordination" (for failing to follow directives on hiring), Craven explained that he had little interest in the local conventions of patronage, "for even if I had friends to provide for, all personal feeling would be secondary to my duty to the public as Engineer."[30]

At least at times, the engineers' concept of professionalism clashed with Olmsted's ideas about an "artistic" approach to building a park. In Grant's earliest memos to the division assistants, he provided minute specifications and procedures for grading roads, organized a system for returning daily reports to his office to account for any delays, and elaborated on the engineers' supervisory responsibilities over foremen and work gangs. Whereas assistant engineers especially worried about their calculations and estimates for materials, the general foremen (most of whom also came from outside the city and had experience with large public works projects or railroads) focused on supervising particular tasks. Cornelius Ryan, for example, oversaw nine blasting gangs, and C. D. Clark kept track of the grading gangs. "If a man does not work up to the general standard," Clark later testified to a state senate committee, "he is reported to me by the foreman, and I dismiss him; if the foreman does not report such men to me, I dismiss the foreman."[31]

The general foremen and engineers alike maintained their distance from the networks of personal obligation so characteristic of the city's building trades. As outsiders, most had (as Craven put it) few "friends to provide for" within the city and little to gain from any exchange of favors. Rather, their own ticket to job security lay in loyally following the work orders outlined by Olmsted, Grant, and the head engineers. Olmsted may have set the tone, marching through the park (as Vaux recalled sardonically) with ten foremen's reports in "each pocket and one in [his] mouth" and "never . . . a word to say to a friend." But the engineers created their own esprit as they worked the long hours Grant told Olmsted were customary for managers on public works projects. With both affection and irony, the engineer John Culyer, Grant's office assistant, signed one of his countless memos to assistant engineer Hawks, "Yrs 4 ever."[32]

The managerial hierarchy did not entirely succeed in rationalizing and reforming the prevailing system of labor. As in any bureaucracy, personal intrigues undermined the model system as each man looked over his shoulder to determine his standing with those above him in the chain of command. Even Chief Engineer Grant was suspected of violating professional seniority rules and playing favorites among the engineers. The requirement for daily reports and accounting spawned anxiety along with discipline: divisional engineers and general foremen surveyed one another as well as their subordinates and reported the causes of any delays. The engineers, after all, were only middle management. Above the chief engineer, the assistant engineers, and the general foremen stood the architect-in-chief, anxious about his own authority, and the board of eleven commissioners whose understandings of their duties as public officials and as gentlemen were frequently at odds with professional ideals of rational administration. And below them stood thousands of laborers committed to their own local customs and work rules.[33]

Clearing the Ground

Central Park was soon turned into a vast construction arena with blasting teams, stone breakers, road-building gangs, masons, blacksmiths, carpenters, stonecutters, gardeners, wagon teams, and cart and wheelbarrow gangs working side-by-side. At the peak of construction in 1859 and 1860, the Board of Commissioners of the Central Park was one of the city's largest employers, hiring an average of four thousand workers each year, with as many as thirty-six hundred laborers working on a single day at the peak of construction in early September 1859.[34]

Building had begun in the summer of 1856 when Mayor Wood appointed surveying teams under the supervision of Egbert Viele. Four surveyors, assisted by twelve axemen and chainmen, trudged through swamps, hacked away under-brush, and climbed rocks to map the lay of the land. Large parts of the uneven terrain had, of course, been cleared earlier and occupied for more than thirty years, but the rocky hillside and bogs just below the rectangular receiving reservoir at 79th Street and the rugged western high ground north of 102nd Street remained sparsely settled. Dirt cartways, old post roads, and partially built city streets led to stone-bounded pastures and past clusters of cottages, pigpens, and bone-boiling plants—all of which would have to be cleared.[35]

Park dwellers had cut down many mature trees for firewood, but more than 150,000 saplings and shrubs, heavily laced with poison ivy, still covered the land. Surveyors found the vegetation below 72nd Street sparser than on the rugged northern ground, which was "thickly covered with undergrowth where, among thickets of besetting thorns and briars, many valuable shrubs and young trees are struggling for life." Elm, beech, sugar maple, sweet gum, and black walnut trees were scattered through the valleys of the upper and lower park. A thick brush of bayberry, common alders, privets, andromeda, clematis, sweet pepper bushes, and honeysuckle vines covered low and often swampy ground. On the rocky hillsides sassafras and witch hazel shadowed the dense brush of choke cherry, wild filbert, mountain cranberry, fox grape, and American ivy vines. Near farmhouses, former residents had planted poplars, mulberries, and ornamental flowering honey locusts and catalpas.[36]

The 778-acre stretch of irregular terrain (including the reservoirs) had recommended itself to city officials as a site for a public park in part because it offered so many obstacles to systematic private development. Indeed, surveyors had difficulty even in providing a systematic description of the "exceedingly diversified and abrupt appearance" of the land. "Bold, rocky, and precipitous" outcroppings—some rising as high as ninety feet—punctuated a terrain of alternating ridges and undulating plateaus. Elevations ranged from 11.5 feet above sea level at McGown's Pass to 134 feet at Summit Rock (83rd Street and Eighth Avenue). Only with enormous effort had Viele's engineering team been able to map the topography by the fall of 1857. The contours of the Greensward plan followed the "general suggestion" of the land. But in emphasizing unob-structed vistas that would give visitors a sense of expanse, Vaux and Olmsted introduced a particularly difficult and expensive plan to construct.[37]

In late August and September 1857 workers hired by Viele under the new park commission began the "herculean task" of transforming the park ground below the old reservoir at 79th Street. Toiling ten hours a day in the hot late-summer sun, twenty-six gangs of fifteen to twenty men each stripped the land of its social and natural history, dismantling stone walls, clearing out old pig yards, digging up small boulders, and ditching clay mud. One hundred and thirty cartmen and drivers of fifteen double trucks (pulled by two horses) carried rocks to the park's periphery, where an experienced wall builder was directing the construction of a temporary wall. "Other gangs of men are engaged in the delightful occupation of 'grubbing,'" the *Times* reported, "removing the bushes that grow rank and worthless in the vicinity of the odoriferous swamps." Fifty German-born gardeners led the way through the underbrush, identifying plants worth saving and turning the rest over to the grubbers, who followed behind with brush hooks and shovels to dig out roots.[38]

The grubbers did their best to avoid contact with the poison ivy they were digging up and burning. But fifteen or twenty laborers in the vicinity of the bog southwest of Vista Rock (at 79th Street), which was described as "very deep and filled with mud and filthy yellow water," came down with "ague" and abandoned the job. By early October, Superintendent Olmsted was reporting that nearly one-seventh of the laborers "have been attacked with intermittent fever during the last fortnight." Laborers also got sick and developed itching rashes as smoke from the burning ivy spread the oil; others suffered sunstroke. Still, during the severe economic depression, they were lucky to have any employment at all.[39]

The battle over appropriations halted the preliminary work in September, but in November a new force of a thousand workers resumed the clearing of the ground. Laborers carted some ten thousand loads of loose stones to the periphery. Olmsted placed the men he judged "best fitted for hard work" on stone-blocking gangs, which sledgehammered boulders; five other gangs then pounded these blocks into two- to six-inch paving stones. Stone breakers were paid nine cents per cubic yard, and Olmsted directed foremen to check carefully that they did not practice the "knavery" of mixing rubbish in with the broken stones to increase the volume and, hence, their pay. On the cleared ground, 120 men prepared a nursery for a late fall planting.[40]

In retrospect Olmsted remembered the early days of building as an entrenched battle in which he single-handedly transformed "a mob of lazy, reckless, turbulent and violent loafers" into "a well organized, punctual, sober, industrious and disciplined body." Although the superintendent told a common council investigating committee in 1857 that he "desired" that the workers hired for unemployment relief should make a living wage at the unfamiliar task of breaking stone, he later spoke with pride of having made "idle, incompetent paupers" "take 30 or 40 cents a day, that being the exact value of their service in the open market, instead of a dollar and a quarter a day, which they demanded." Still, Olmsted could not impose all his disciplinary ideas: by late winter he had modified his strict absentee rule of dismissal after two days' absence to permit workers to miss three days' work before they risked being fired.[41]

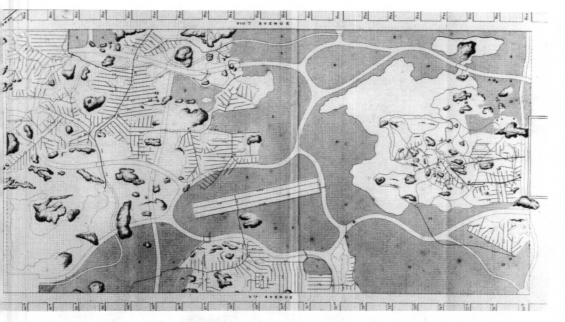

To help the public understand the massive process of the park's construction, the park commission published this map of the field drainage system designed by George Waring. The diagonal lines represent the clay tiles placed three to four feet under the surface to collect and carry off excess rainwater.

Draining, Moving, Blasting, and Grading

With warm weather as well as a hot political climate in the wake of the depression, the park board was able to keep most of the thousand men hired in November and December 1857 employed through the winter. In the spring laborers began the most important step of construction, a thorough drainage of the ground.

In his 1856 report to Mayor Wood's park commission, Chief Engineer Viele had warned that unless it were drained, the park would remain "a pestilential spot, where rank vegetation and miasmatic odors taint every breath of air." Clay soils and street embankments (built by the city before the land was acquired for the park and rising as high as eight feet above the surrounding ground) trapped stagnant pools of water. More important, thorough drainage was essential to maintain the loose and fertile subsoil necessary to support the new plantings. Only swamp plants could thrive on the existing mire, Olmsted observed in his own report on drainage, and during droughts, the puttylike soil would harden and "interpose a hydraulic floor between the thirsty roots in the surface soil" and the moisture of "the cool earth below."[42]

Twenty-four-year-old George Waring, who had studied with a leading

At the same time that Central Park was being built, contractors constructed the curvilinear reservoir at its center (85th to 96th streets). This 1862 photograph shows the laying of the aqueduct pipes.

expert in "agricultural chemistry" and had managed both Horace Greeley's and Olmsted's "model farms," was placed in charge of the park's drainage. In June, Waring's team of four hundred laborers removed barriers or dug ditches to open the natural streams and clogged pools, then excavated trenches three to four feet deep at forty-foot intervals across the entire park, and laid one-foot sections of joined clay pipes or tiles. Placed at a proper slope, the well-fitted pipes would draw surface water downward to collecting drains, which then would channel it through brick sewers to the lakes. Where several collecting drains came together, the teams built three-foot silt basins with iron covers that could be opened to remove the sediment.[43]

At the end of six months (December 1858), the drainage gangs had laid twenty miles of drain tiles in the southern portion of the park. They had also accomplished the more dramatic feat of filling the twenty-acre lake south of the

Ramble in time for the winter skating season. While drainage gangs laid pipes to direct the Ramble's runoff rainwater into the Lake, other laborers excavated the former bog to a seven-foot center depth and built a terraced shore that permitted park officers to reduce the water level to four feet for safer ice skating. Filling the Lake helped appease impatient newspaper demands for some immediate public benefit from the park, though some editors were also aware of other, more hidden achievements of the first year's expense and labor. The *Tribune* especially commended the drainage work, which would "prove instructive to thousands who have, if not farms, at least gardens, lawns and walks, which they would gladly render dry and solid at all times."[44]

Waring hoped to use such praise to secure the new title of "aquatic engineer," but the principal engineers viewed his claims to professional status with skepticism. The cocky young rural improver had been able to maintain his independence from Chief Engineer Grant's chain of command. So when the trenching gangs (who were following the drainage gangs, turning up the subsoil to prepare for planting) unexpectedly broke the new drain tiles, the division engineers blamed Waring for "discrepancy in the depth as represented to [them]." Furthermore, although Waring drew up drainage maps for the board's early annual reports, he seems not to have reliably filed his later notes on the placement of what Grant disdainfully called "Waring's pipes." Drainage problems remained chronic, and twenty-five years later, in 1883 when these problems triggered fears of malaria, park officials again complained of the lack of systematic records.[45]

While Waring went his independent way, the four division engineers spent their first year in Central Park directing the grading and trenching of the southwestern Playground, the Promenade, the Parade, and many roadbeds. To remedy what the park's designers considered the "natural defect" of the "ceaseless repetition of rocks and hillocks with meager depressions of surface between them," gangs of workers reshaped and sculpted the lower park's topography. To produce the roughly thirty acres of "level or but slightly undulating ground," for example, that encompassed the site of the Parade (today called the the Sheep Meadow), it was necessary to fill in ten acres of boggy land an average depth of two feet, blast out protruding boulders, reduce the height of intervening outcroppings, fill in the remaining depressions, and cover the entire transformed terrain with two feet of topsoil. Blasting reduced a rocky ridge to the northeast by sixteen feet, and the loosened rock and soil was used to fill swampy land east of the Parade. With the addition of four feet of topsoil, part of the filled land became the Promenade (later called the Mall), separated by a drive from the Parade. Grading the lower park involved some of the heaviest and most dangerous work.[46]

Grant and Olmsted created special rock gangs and established careful procedures for the dangerous task of blasting out ridges and boulders. Blasting foremen earned an extra twenty-five cents a day for the risks and the respon-

Workers graded the entire surface of the park to create the landscape effects proposed by the Greensward plan. This 1858 lithograph shows cartmen and laborers removing stone and dirt to create the Mall.

sibilities of this job. No rock foreman was permitted to set a charge without two hours' advance notice plus a written order from an engineer or the general foreman of blasting. Red flags on the bell tower signaled a blast, and all gangs were required to stop work until a white flag went up to signal that the blasting was over. Laborer Luke Flynn became the park's first casualty when he was killed by an explosion in the fall of 1858. A year later, the *Irish News* reported that Timothy McNamara had been "instantly killed . . . by being struck in the head with a large stone thrown from a blast" five hundred feet away. During the entire course of construction, five men were killed. Considering the frequency of gunpowder blasts, this impressively low number is evidence of effective precautions. There was little compensation for the survivors of those who died, however. When one widow petitioned the board for compensation, she received only fifty dollars for her husband's life, and not even an expression of condolence. The deaths, an annual report said, resulted from the workers' own "imprudence."[47]

Once massive boulders had been blasted out of the ground, derrick gangs used cranes to load them onto two-horse trucks. And when derricks and trucks proved inadequate for the largest masses of rock, the superintendent hired house movers, who were experienced at loading two-story brick houses onto stone flatbeds to move them to new locations. Meanwhile, carts and wheelbarrows, also used by grading gangs, formed a steady stream of traffic transporting fieldstone and rubble to the stoneyards or other locations in the park.[48]

Managers and workers skirmished over the pace and standards of grading. Despite Grant's efforts to fix specifications before work began, last-minute changes were not uncommon, and engineers worked gangs at night in order to correct "mistakes" on daytime work that had failed to satisfy the architect-in-chief. Exhausted workers excavating rock occasionally ignored the specifications, leaving the roadbeds several inches above the stipulated subgrade. Grant also warned the engineers to make certain that "no useless work [was] being done" by the laborers such as "trimming the side slopes and smoothing off grounds where no special directions have been given." Such insistence on maintaining the hierarchy of "mental" and "manual" labor was key to the new system of labor for public works.[49]

Drives and walks in the lower park having been graded during the 1858 construction season, workers turned to paving them the next year. Like agricultural drainage, the best paving technique had become a lively topic of debate in rural improvement journals. Park officers quickly ruled out the cobblestone or macadamized paving used on city streets. Although durable and easy to maintain, such hard, compact surfaces would be too noisy for "rural" drives. Instead, after experimenting with different types of gravel roads, Grant devised his own low-cost method of paving.[50]

A well-laid road would withstand frost heaves that could reach under the twelve inches of paving materials and push rocks to the surface, causing ruts and potholes. Laborers manually wedged together rectangular foundation stones to create an even surface at a depth of seven to eight inches. After rolling this substratum, they added a five-inch layer of smaller stones supplied by the stone breakers, a layer designed to relieve the foundation from the compacting effect of surface traffic. Special gangs of pavers, paid ten cents a day more than laborers, topped the middle stratum with a one-and-a-half-inch layer of finely screened gravel (intermixed with moistened loam and sand as binders), and this was rolled and compacted by a six-and-a-half-ton cylinder pulled by eight horses. At the edges road gangs built gutters and laid drain tiles to keep new drives from flooding.[51]

Walks and bridle paths were built in similar steps. Walks required trenching and grading the bed, laying drain tiles and building gutters, putting down a substratum of broken field or quarry stone, and adding and rolling a three-inch surface layer of gravel. By June 1859 workers had finished the walks through the fifty-acre Ramble, the second park attraction to be opened to public use.[52]

Graders in Central Park used horse-drawn cylinders for the last step in paving a road or smoothing out a meadow. This photograph is from the early 1870s.

The laborers were familiar with the work of grading and paving drives and walks, but the transverse roads, running eight feet below the park's surface, presented unusual construction problems. When the Greensward plan was adopted, some engineers had pronounced the sunken transverse roads "unpracticable," predicting flooding and a dangerous erosion of side embankments. The engineer J. H. Pieper took up the challenge. In consultation with William Grant, he experimentally and effectively designed the transverse roads and their bridges as the work proceeded.[53]

The engineers took a problem-solving approach to other aspects of construction as well, adjusting road lines, grades, and foundations when they encountered intractable seams of rock, particular problems of drainage, or—in the case of the Dalehead Arch on the west side near 64th Street—quicksand. Memos and instructions—often torn from a longer list and pasted to another sheet with sketches, additional notes, and hastily scribbled pencil calculations—passed down the chain of command. Division engineers instructed their foremen, carefully added up the amounts of brick, cement, sand, and asphalt needed from contractors, and dispatched orders to the stoneyards on the park's edge where stonecutters faced the stones used on foundations and bridges.[54]

Where applied science could not solve the problems or where there was a risk of poor workmanship, the engineers turned to homespun remedies. When, for example, contractors sold them cement adulterated with salt, Grant sent out a recipe he concocted for testing its purity: Form a two-ounce ball of cement, "put the ball carefully in a cup and set in the air (not sun) ten minutes by a watch. Then fill cup gently with water so as not to disturb the ball in any way. If no effervescence or bubbling takes place and the ball keeps its shape and is well set at the end of ten hours or overnight, the cement may be used." Living in a four-dimensional world of cubic yards and "ten minutes by a watch," the engineers were intensely aware of the volume of material and pace of labor necessary to complete each feature. Recognizing as much, the commissioners gave them wide latitude in the first year and a half of construction.[55]

By the summer of 1859 the board's executive committee (which oversaw costs and operations) observed, "Very much that was experimental and untried assumes the character of reality" and "offers guidance for the conduct of future operations." But not all the commissioners were satisfied with the engineers' management of construction. Commissioner John Butterworth complained that the work on the 79th Street Transverse Road (which ran under Vista Rock) was too expensive and proposed that the job be turned over to a railroad contractor. Park workers steadily blasted, drilled, and sledged their way under Vista Rock all the same, and by August they had opened a forty-foot-wide and eighteen-foot-high tunnel for the transverse road.[56]

From all contemporary reports, it appears that the quality of work on the drives, walks, and transverse roads was high—too high to keep within the original construction budget. The optimistic predictions of great cost savings from recycling the site's boulders into paving materials failed to take account of the labor costs of stone-breaking. Furthermore, the diorite stone in the boulders was "very hard and tough and very expensive to break by hand." The first experiments with stone-breaking machines failed to reduce expenses, but beginning in 1860, a new machine saved the park, Olmsted estimated, the labor of ten men a day. By the next year, Grant reported that machines had reduced the cost of such labor by 25 to 30 percent.[57]

Despite the mechanization of stone breaking, it was the muscle and sweat of what George Templeton Strong in his diary described as a "small army of Hibernians" that slowly transformed the "shapeless" landscape into Central Park. When he visited the lower park in June 1859, Strong found it still in a "ragged condition: long lines of incomplete macadamization, 'lakes' without water, mounds of compost, piles of blasted stone, acres of what may be greensward hereafter but is now mere brown earth; groves of slender young transplanted maples and locusts, undecided between life and death, with here and there an arboricultural experiment that has failed utterly and is a mere broomstick with ramifications." Yet the work "promise[d] very well." "Celts, caravans of dirt carts, derricks, [and] steam engines," Strong concluded, "are the elements out of which our future Pleasance is rapidly developing."[58]

The Artisans

Nearly one-fifth of the construction workers employed on the park in June 1859 were skilled or independent artisans who tried to maintain the standards of their own trades within the new system of management. The more than three hundred independent cartmen who owned their wagons and horses, for example, successfully blocked Olmsted's move to permit the subcontracting of carts not driven by their owners. They also flouted orders requiring them to drive "briskly," to "carry full loads," and to refrain from "loitering" at the dumps. And as the drives took shape in the fall of 1859, Grant was distressed to discover that cartmen themselves were enjoying the facilities they were helping to construct. Any employee found riding or driving a horse or vehicle "*faster than a walk* on any of the drives that are completed or are in progress," he announced, would be promptly dismissed.[59]

The thirty or so blacksmiths and their assistants who operated the park's repair shops (fixing broken carts, tackle, and tools), were equally unruly and, Grant complained to Olmsted in May 1859, prone to "delays and bad work." The blacksmiths sometimes played quoits (a predecessor of horseshoes) in the workshops, and one foreman, Joseph Lynees, confessed that he had had four quoits made by his shop. During "spare" hours, blacksmith Joseph Baddanock reported, he had seen men in his shop using park materials to make objects "that were not intended for use on the park"—"butcher knives, oyster knives, hatchets, carving forks and various other things, besides rivet bolts." When they realized that blacksmiths did "not know at the time that it was wrong to make" these things for customers of their own, the commissioners introduced a new rule requiring written work orders for every job.[60]

The blacksmiths were not alone in their understanding of customary ethics that departed from the board's program for tight management. Mary Petrarchi, the wife of the park timekeeper, for one, "borrowed" coal and lumber from the park. In response to such ambiguous loans, more frequent tool and material inventories were required. In this, too, Central Park's management differed from that of many other construction projects: on the reservoir, foremen regularly "borrowed" powder and fuses for weekend and evening blasting jobs.[61]

The best-organized and most militant craftworkers were the roughly 160 stonecutters who chiseled and sawed stone for foundations and bridges. For years city stonecutters had resisted the degradation of their craft by stonemasons, who, whenever possible, subcontracted out the preparation of the stone to less skilled (and cheaper) workers. The stonecutters brought this battle to control the conditions of their trade to the park.[62]

In October 1858 the board had agreed that stonecutters, like other artisans on the park, should be hired at "customary rates." During the 1857 depression, that rate had dropped to $1.75 a day, but with economic recovery, stonecutters off the park had raised their rates. In May 1859 seventy-nine "stonecutters

The Denesmouth Arch at 65th Street and Fifth Avenue: Commissioners worried about the expense of the stonecutters' work on this and other bridges.

working on the bluestone in the Central park," as they signed themselves, politely petitioned the board "in behalf of our rights[,] feeling aggrieved by the reduction of our wages. We as a body think we ought to receive as much for our labor as those working on Dorchester stone [outside the park] who have a comfortable shop to work in while we are exposed to both sun and rain." The bluestone cutters objected to the stint set by their foreman and to the supervision of an outside stonemason whose firm had been hired to oversee work on the bridges. Referring the commissioners to a master stonecutter who would "inform [them] what our labor is worth," the stonecutters won their point. By the following year, their wages rose to $2.25 a day, with an additional 14 to 18 cents allowed for supplying their own tools.[63]

Park officers and skilled workers did not quarrel only over pay, discipline, and working conditions. When it came time to prepare the ground for planting, the engineers discovered that the gardeners considered it *their* primary duty to the public to make the park as beautiful as posssible rather than to save money in its construction. The gardeners took orders only from their own foreman, Ignaz Pilat, an Austrian-born landscape gardener. Pilat had studied botany at the University of Vienna, launched his practice as a gardener at private estates, served as assistant director of a Viennese botanical garden, and emigrated to the United States after the failed 1848 revolution. He was hired in 1858 as a general foreman of park gardeners at $1.50 a day, but as he told Olmsted, "to occupy the position of a mere foreman . . . is far from being grateful to my feelings." Three years later, as chief gardener, Pilat supervised the shaping of slopes and arrangement of boulders; the trenching, fertilizing and planting of lawns; and the selection, placement, and transplanting of trees and shrubs.[64]

Pilat commanded the respect and loyalty of the German immigrants who were heavily concentrated in the gardening department and who, from the early days of clearing the ground for the park, maintained their own communal ties. During the grubbing, for example, they erected "a long table and seats of rough boards, in the thick shadows" of a locust grove to enjoy their midday meal out of the sun. Pilat's directions to the gardeners often clashed with those of Grant's engineers, who remained focused on cost. "I have frequently found," assistant engineer Francis Hawks advised Grant, "that in order to produce the desired effect, material has been deposited, moved and removed then more material deposited until in the end" the expense far exceeded the estimates. Gardeners "do not fully appreciate the value of a cubic yard. Therefore it is useless to tell them that this or that slope must not exceed so many cubic yards. Let them be told they can have so many cart loads or so many barrow loads to form a slope or mound, so many and no more." Grant responded by requiring the gardeners to explain to the assistant engineers the "general form or outline of surface" that they were creating; then he forbade them to make further modifications "more than a spade's depth."[65]

Tensions between the engineers and the gardeners extended beyond costs to disputes over aesthetic judgment. Pieper was particularly worried that Pilat's directions to a gardening foreman to uncover a large mass of rock "would produce an exceedingly ugly feature." "Please see Mr. Pilat," Pieper directed Hawks, "with reference to some alterations there and especially to see that some of the rock now uncovered is filled over again."[66]

Disciplining Foremen and Laborers

Almost three-quarters of the construction funds went to pay artisans and laborers. Since machines could not replace labor on most of the construction, the architect-in-chief and engineers regarded the discipline of park workers as the most important method for achieving efficiency. Olmsted, who described park laborers to Charles Loring Brace as members of "the poorest or what is generally considered the most dangerous class of the great city's population," had little faith in their sense of duty. From the earliest days of construction, the superintendent did his best to transform the customary organization of heavy construction work. Some of his reforms made the park board a more attractive employer than private contractors. Workers building the new reservoir (which had been contracted out by the city at the same time the park was being built), for example, received wages only monthly and often had to purchase necessities on credit from the contractors' own store. By contrast, the park board paid semimonthly, and in cash.[67]

Other park rules aimed at "disciplining" foremen, many of whom were used to exercising the personal prerogatives of contractors or foremen on street gangs. Following the unemployed demonstrations of 1857, German working-men's committees had complained, for example, that park foremen expected laborers to treat them to a drink or to pay two dollars for a place on the gangs. "Rumors have frequently been circulated," Olmsted acknowledged in a hand-bill a year later, "of Foremen on the Park imposing upon the ignorance of their men to collect money or obtain services for other purposes than Park work." He repeated the rules that any foreman found taking "gratuities" from laborers, or acting as a boardinghouse agent, collecting debts for third parties, or encouraging his men to purchase raffle tickets would be fired. Foremen (and even park officers) found discussing politics on the job also risked immediate dismissal.[68]

Although Olmsted's rules limited their traditional powers, park foremen did not entirely follow the board's prescriptions for sober, dutiful, and industrious employees. Foreman J. H. Millard, for example, arranged an "evening entertainment," a ball for park workers at the porterhouse of the park timekeeper's mother-in-law. When confronted with this indiscretion, Millard strenuously denied receiving money from the ball or threatening workers with dismissal if they did not take a ticket for the affair.[69]

Olmsted also tried to control foremen and laborers by elaborating treasurer Andrew Green's system of accounting, particularly the careful recording of laborers' work time. In the spring of 1858 laborers often circumvented the strict attendance rules by answering "present" for one another during roll calls. To ensure that foremen would not permit such tricks, Olmsted introduced a quasi-military drill. Twice a day at a signal from the bell tower, the men lined up by gangs and each stepped forward two steps when the foreman called his name; assistant foremen were instructed to become familiar with names and faces, look the men in the eye, and make sure the name and face matched. Any man who quit "his work without orders and [did] not return within five minutes, no matter what the cause of his leaving," lost his pay for the entire day and was not permitted to return until the next day; any man who left work more than once in

CENTRAL PARK.

NOTICE TO MEN EMPLOYED.

EVERY man should distinctly understand that he is employed solely to work on the Park for his regular wages, and for no other consideration whatever. Nothing but his labor, compliance with the rules of the Park, and a civil behavior to all engaged on it, can be required of him.

No one has a right to receive a payment, in any form, for having procured any man's employment, or for retaining any man on the work. If any such payments are made, or any presents or treats are offered, which can be considered as payments or bribes for such favors or services, they will be deemed proper ground for the discharge of the person offering them.

It is entirely contrary to the intention of employing men on the Park that any influence of any sort should be brought to bear upon their political opinions or actions. Officers and Foremen on the Park will, therefore, abstain from talking with the men upon political topics, and are distinctly forbidden to solicit their votes for any person or measure, on any pretence whatever. Men are requested to inform the Architect-in-Chief if they are ever told that it is their duty to vote one way or another because they are employed on the Park, or that it is necessary for them to vote one way or another in order to be kept at work on the Park.

Men who consider themselves to have been improperly reported, unjustly treated, or otherwise aggrieved by the action of their Foremen, or of the Architect-in-Chief, or any officer of the Park, or who wish to make a complaint against any one, or to answer any complaint made against themselves, will call at the office of the Architect-in-Chief, between twelve and two o'clock each day.

Foremen will make a return every two weeks of the names of each man in their respective gangs to whose sobriety, industry and general good conduct during the fortnight they can testify. Before sending in this return they will read it to their gangs. Any man whose name is found on his Foreman's "Good Conduct" return for the previous three months may claim a certificate of character whenever he wishes to leave the Park; and the name of any man found during one year upon the "Good Conduct" returns will be printed in an annual Central Park Directory. The men named in this Directory will be considered as a fixed body for steady and permanent employment upon the Park, so far as the nature of the work will admit; but if at any time they wish to leave, they will be furnished with a special certificate and recommendation for other employment from the Architect-in-Chief.

To the Foremen of the Park:

RUMORS have frequently been circulated of Foremen on the Park imposing upon the ignorance of their men to collect money, or obtain services for other purposes than the Park work. To leave no ground hereafter for such reports, and to make sure, as far as possible, that each man understands his rights and the limits of his obligations to the Park; it is ordered that Foremen read the accompanying notice to their gangs, or get their General Foremen, or some other officer, to do so, at least as often as once a month.

FRED. LAW OLMSTEAD,
Architect-in-Chief.

Frederick Law Olmsted and Chief Engineer William Grant distributed numerous handbills spelling out rules for park workers.

a half day was "to be considered as unfit for work and sent away." Lest the foremen themselves be lax, Grant required division engineers to observe the roll call at least once a day.[70]

Although Olmsted later claimed credit for revolutionizing the management of public works with his daily reports and attendance taking, he complained privately that the system didn't work: "Many of the foremen are ignorant, some of the best can barely write and are quite unable to make any but the simplest entries. These reports, therefore, are too indefinite and untrustworthy to furnish a proper basis for accurate calculations." The time books had to be turned over to clerks to add up hours and calculate wages.[71]

Whatever management's problems with making its system work, some laborers perceived the attendance and disciplinary rules as a sharp departure from local customs. In the spring of 1858 the *Leader,* a pro-Tammany newspaper, charged that the park commissioners were insulting workers' "manhood and independence" by refusing to employ those who were unwilling "to become subservient to the caprices of mushroom officials." "Toadyism" and a "cringing sycophancy," were the chief qualification for employment on the park under a "system requiring the utter surrender of all the best attributes possessed by every honorable man." One apparent object of the *Leader*'s attack were "docile" laborers, recent immigrants from Italy who had been hired instead of "citizens and residents of this city."[72]

Olmsted replied that the majority of park workers were "residents," circumventing the question of nationality or citizenship or how long they had lived in New York. He defended the Italians as "among the most faithful and industrious laborers," and he "supposed [them] to be chiefly persons who have been banished for their resistance to an absolute government." But in the view of the *Leader,* park workers who were not "citizens by naturalization" broke the implicit Democratic party contract of jobs for votes. Indeed, breaking this pact may have been one of the motivations behind the commissioners' patronage of Italian workers, few of whom in this period settled permanently in the city. Although the board defeated a resolution put forward by Tammany commissioner Thomas Fields to require that park keepers be citizens, when the *Leader* objected to a Scottish head of park police, the commissioners moved him to a less visible job. Even the English-born James Hogg felt it necessary to answer a "hint" from Olmsted and assured him that one man he recommended for a job was "perfectly American."[73]

Despite occasional board concessions to nativist pressure, first- and second-generation Irish, more than 80 percent of the city's laborers in 1855, constituted the largest proportion of park workers. Discrimination concentrated Irish immigrants in poorly paid construction jobs, but those jobs also opened up a route of upward mobility for the few who moved into the ranks of contractors. No doubt some of those contractors took foreman jobs on the park, since, by a rough count, one-fourth of Central Park's construction foremen had Irish surnames.[74]

Irish park workers showed a proud independence and deeply resented the park board's attempt to display its model employees by insisting that park workers march during the Atlantic cable parade in August 1859. Irish immigrants saw little reason to celebrate a cable "submerged between Queen Victoria's two provinces," Ireland and Newfoundland. Indeed, the *Irish News* commended the longshoremen's society which had resolved "not to make fools of themselves, in other words not to turn out" for "imperial fêtes." The "stalwart" dock workers had "no task masters—no political buncombe-seekers to parade them through the streets with pick-axes, shovels, tattered garments and labor-stained faces, to be gazed and laughed at by the multitudes. . . . It was humiliating to see the Central Park laborers driven like niggers through the streets—paraded like a lot of human livestock." If ever the commissioners tried to "repeat the farce," the *News* advised park workers to assert their "dignity and refuse to obey any degrading mandate no matter whence it many emanate or what the consequences."[75]

The comparison of park workers to "niggers" exposed deep antipathies on the lowest rungs of the occupational ladder. In an era when white dock workers and waiters frequently walked off their jobs to protest the hiring of black workers, the commission apparently chose to avoid such a confrontation. And although workers believed that "Black Republicans" (as they were called by the Democratic press) held special sympathy for African Americans, no black workers were employed on the park. Customs of occupational segregation also excluded women from the park work force. Mary Tague hired out a cart on the park; the only other women on the payroll cleaned the commissioners' and superintendent's offices or served as washroom attendants.[76]

Although experienced foremen reported that laborers were made to work harder on Central Park than on any other project, the job offered steady, if seasonal, wages and was in the city. For a few workers—ten in 1860—there was also the possibility of moving into the ranks of foremen or assistant foremen. And despite high turnover, the property clerk B. F. Crane complained of the mob of job applicants who assembled at the park office each spring. The city's large reserve of unskilled workers probably served as effectively as the superintendent's rules to discipline park laborers.[77]

By the second year, the seasonal rhythms of park work had been well-established. The commission hired roughly two thousand workers in April and May and then gradually expanded the ranks to as many as thirty-five hundred by late August. In October gangs were cut back, and in December commissioners suspended work for the winter, retaining only "the most efficient workers" and cutting their pay to as little as forty cents a day. Olmsted favored maintaining a stable work force by rehiring in the spring those laid off for the winter, but many unemployed park workers simply moved on to other jobs. Pay vouchers show that it was not unusual for wives or mothers to collect the wages due a laborer who had since left town. In November 1858, the *Times* reported, nearly five hundred park laborers who faced reduced winter pay or layoff had been recruited to work on a railroad in Central America.[78]

Although Commissioners Gray and Elliott affirmed the park board's policy of paying a fair day's wage, the board had taken advantage of hard times and cut laborers' wages from $1.25 to $1.00 a day in September 1857. Working ten hours a day, from 6:00 A.M. to 5:00 P.M. with an hour off for lunch, park laborers in 1860 earned no more than $282—as much as other unskilled laborers but well below the $600 regarded as necessary for a family's comfort in that year. Some workers supplemented their park wages by moonlighting on other public works, for example, on the Bloomingdale Road. Laborers also earned time and a half by working at night or on Sundays, although some Protestant commissioners thought it prudent to disguise their endorsement of Sunday work by referring to it simply as "unusual times."[79]

A park laborer's average income might pay the rent for one room with sleeping closets in a Lower East Side tenement or for an uptown shanty. Unmarried workers probably found accommodations in one of the city's ubiquitous boardinghouses or with another laboring family. Many lived downtown (aldermen were eager to see men from their own wards employed); the Irish laborers John Flaherty and Michael Kenny, for example, lived in the Sixth Ward (the Five Points district), more than three miles from the southern edge of the park. "At the close of the day's work, the laborers could, if they chose to pay ten cents [an hour's wage], go back to the town by some old mule-driven stage which had been secured for the purpose" by park officers, George Putnam recalled. The relative absence of park workers from the city directory, however, suggests both their transience and their concentration in uptown wards. (Park worker Patrick Carberry, for example, lived in a shanty in the 80s near Eighth Avenue; when health wardens descended on the area to clean up the "pig nuisance," Carberry's wife "defended the rights of poor people in general and her own in particular in a way that would have touched the heart of any philanthropist," the *Times* observed.)[80]

Central Park competed for workers with other construction projects. As the economy picked up in the late spring of 1859, Chief Engineer Grant told Olmsted that "to keep the best" rock foremen, daily wages of "$2.00 will be necessary for the season." Laborers, too, were bargaining up their wages. In early May 1859 workers employed by private contractors on the new reservoir went on strike. At least two gangs and possibly as many as 150 park workers joined the strike, though recruitment was difficult, the *Tribune* reported, because "the whole police force of the Park [was] early distributed over the ground," and "the rules of work preventing any one from conversing with the men were enforced." Olmsted moved quickly to fire the men who joined the reservoir strike and rewarded loyal park workers by raising their pay from $1.00 to $1.10 a day. The board had already authorized a twenty-cent pay raise, but it seems to have taken a strike threat to get even half this amount out of the superintendent. Park workers, however, were unable to retain even this slight gain, and by the following year, laborers' pay rates had fallen back down to the previous ten-cent-an-hour rate.[81]

Although park officials never managed to bring the laborers, artisans, and gardeners wholly in line, the large numbers of dismissals gave credence to new standards of work discipline. In 1859 park officers fired 284 men for ineffi-

IN THE CENTRAL PARK.

DISTINGUISHED FOREIGNER. "My good man—aw—can you diwect me to the Wide—the Wotten Wow—aw—where people wide in your Park!"
LABORER. "Is it the Ride ye're wantin'? Faith, thin, ye're in it now."
Distinguished Foreigner notes down this fresh proof of American barbarity and resolves to devote a Chapter to it in his forthcoming Book on this Country.

In this cartoon a "distinguished foreigner" is shown asking a park laborer for directions to the not-yet-completed equestrian paths.

ciency and 286 for violation or neglect of rules and temporarily suspended another 477 for breaches in discipline from intoxication to "insubordination." In 1860 they fired 11 foremen for inefficiency and 419 laborers or cartmen for breaking rules or not working hard enough. The result, general foreman C. D. Clark reported, was that "men employed on the park will compare favorably with any men I ever knew, and a great deal better than street laborers." Another general foreman, Chester Sufford, who had worked six years as a contractor, agreed that "he had never worked a gang of men so hard on any contract as he had done on the park."[82]

An *Irish News* reporter took a different view of the commissioners' new model of labor discipline, worker productivity, and the benefits of public works. "It is good to see men industriously employed," he observed in May 1859. "Meandering through the two divisions of the park today, while they blasted and sank and dammed and busied themselves in a variety of ways, I mentally hoped they would be in no very great hurry or subject themselves to anything like sun stroke, in order to save a few dollars to the municipal purse. While so many undeserving grubbers are diving into it, it is no sin to wish that the hard-workers should have their honest share of it—laboring as they are for the public and for posterity."[83]

Respecting the men who worked on behalf of the public, the *Irish News* recognized, as many other New Yorkers did not, that the costs of the park's construction could be measured in the toll on workers' health as well as in dollars and cents. As men struggled under the broiling sun to move earth, break granite, and shape the terrain—to create a "natural" landscape—they also struggled to claim a fair share of the resources devoted to building Central Park. They succeeded only at the first task. Meanwhile the sometimes invisible social processes underlying the creation of this landscape became visible as New Yorkers began to get nervous about what the park was costing "the municipal purse." These concerns renewed debate over whether the board and Olmsted were managing construction as efficiently as they claimed and whether new methods (and new managers) would be needed to finish Central Park finally "for the public and posterity."

7

ANDREW GREEN AND
THE MODEL PARK

In April 1859 the *Herald* reported that the work on Central Park was "progressing with commendable rapidity" and optimistically predicted that some drives would be finished in the early summer and the rest by September. The newspaper's earlier criticism of the Greensward plan (the paper had Democratic sympathies) had given way to enthusiastic praise for the new Ramble and Mall.[1]

Despite this press support, park finances worried the commissioners and eroded their confidence in the executive abilities of their architect-in-chief. That same April they asked the legislature to authorize extending the park's northern boundary from 106th to 110th Street and also requested an additional $832,666 for construction. Albany lawmakers granted them only half this amount, stipulating that no plan should be undertaken that exceeded the authorized sum. By July 1859 the commission had spent half of its $2 million construction budget. To complete the park as designed, the board estimated at that time, would require at least $3.6 million—$1.6 million beyond the limit allowed.[2]

Art versus Accounting

As the commissioners launched a multifold investigation into where the money was going at such a rapid rate, they especially scrutinized the design of bridges, estimated to cost more than a half a million dollars. Calvert Vaux and his assistant, the English-born architect Jacob Wrey Mould, planned to use primarily natural materials for the bridges to keep these "architectural" features in harmony with the natural scenery. Vaux had definite preferences about the

In 1862 Victor Prevost photographed Central Park's "builders" on the Willowdell Arch on the East Drive near 67th Street. *From left to right:* Andrew H. Green, George E. Waring (?), Calvert Vaux, Ignaz Pilat, Jacob Wrey Mould, and Frederick Law Olmsted.

kinds of stone to use. He thought marble, for example, was "too white to be agreeable in the country." Granite, used alone, was cold and "expressionless," and brownstone produced a "melancholy, dingy, monotonous, and uninteresting look," though both granite and brownstone might be brought to life when used with brick. Far preferable was the "delicate, luminous gray tint" of weathered bluestone, "unrivaled as a building material" and "far more beautiful than any brownstone, marble or brick."[3]

The park commissioners had approved a number of Vaux's simple and elegant bridge designs, but by the spring of 1859 they were expressing alarm at the cost of the stone. Vaux should no longer use bluestone unless the board explicitly approved it, Commissioner John Butterworth informed Olmsted in June. Marble could be had at one-fourth the cost, he thought, and "unless we take some steps to reduce the common expense of bridges you may be sure that

Calvert Vaux, with the assistance of the English architect Jacob Wrey Mould and the engineers, designed the bridges of Central Park. The designs reflected Vaux's aesthetic preference for natural materials and the limits of the construction budget. *Left to right, top:* Playmates Arch (located below the 65th Street Transverse Road between Sixth and Seventh avenues), Glade Arch (near Fifth and 79th); *bottom:* Glen Span (at Seventh and 102nd), Spur Rock Arch (at Seventh and 61st, torn down in 1934).

the stone bridges will certainly be abandoned." But Butterworth probably preferred marble as much on aesthetic as economic grounds; he persuaded the board to build the Marble Arch at the foot of the Mall in place of a less ostentatious and less expensive bridge proposed by Vaux. Other commissioners also used the debates over the cost of bridges to press for a different aesthetic.

Commissioner Charles Russell disliked Vaux's polychromatic mixing of stones, preferring the consistently formal pallette of the Ecole des Beaux-Arts. He wanted the board to order Vaux to use "stone of one uniform color" on two bridges and to substitute stone for the more prosaic brick on a third.[4]

Commissioner August Belmont believed that for both aesthetic and economic reasons less expensive iron bridges were preferable to bridges of either quarried stone or brick. Although Vaux and other architects (and John Ruskin in England) were defending the "honesty" of stone and brick in comparison to "artificial" building materials, Belmont knew some architects championed cast and wrought iron as "modern" and sophisticated. By contracting out bridges to the iron houses, moreover, the board could eliminate masons' and stonecutters' labor costs. The stonecutters' wage protests probably strengthened Belmont's argument. (Vaux himself had already chosen cast iron for the Bow Bridge over the skating lake, for its light graceful effect in relation to the Lake and Ramble. He and Mould had mastered the ornamental qualities of this artificial material but wished to use it selectively.)[5]

As the board debated Belmont's proposal, new Democratic commissioner Henry Stebbins, a banker, suggested that bridges of different kinds of stone would be educational for parkgoers. The finance committee and the president of the board, Andrew Green, endorsed Stebbins's arguments. They also insisted that "no further purchase of the Nova Scotia [sand]stone be made; its cost delivered at the park is excessive" and enough had already been used on bridges "to present an example." Apparently Vaux won an exception to this new rule for the Bethesda Terrace, for it is faced with "New Brunswick" sandstone richly embellished by Mould's decorative motifs representing the four seasons. The Terrace was the one architectural feature of the park that the designers believed ought to call attention to itself through its magnificence.[6]

Despite Vaux's success in protecting the Terrace from an increasingly cost-conscious board, the principle of "economic expenditure" affected the construction of other bridges. In 1860 the board turned over the remaining stone arches to private contractors and contracted with iron houses for new bridges to span the walks and rides. But the budget cutting also supported Vaux's preference for natural materials as the board approved more rustic (and less expensive) wood and fieldstone bridges in the northern park.[7]

In the summer of 1859 the commissioners began to look more closely at other expenditures. Even Olmsted's friend Charles Elliott, now treasurer, questioned his handling of accounts. When Belmont aggressively challenged Olmsted's managerial competence by introducing a resolution requesting an explanation of "increased cost occasioned by . . . changes" in the Greensward plan, the architect-in-chief responded defensively that the board itself had mandated separating the drives, walks, and rides and introducing bridges—all of which substantially increased the building costs. Olmsted explained that he had added improvements in the Ramble—the Cascade, Spring-Rock Waterfall, and the stone Rustic Arch—and these enhanced its appeal, if also its cost. But new features did not entirely account for the cost overruns. In fact, from the beginning he and Vaux had greatly underestimated the expense of grading and draining the land and of building roads, particularly the high labor costs of moving earth and rock to achieve their open pastoral vistas. Even without the subsequent modifications of the Greensward plan, there had never been a real possibility of building the park within its original $1.5 million construction budget.[8]

Andrew Green and the other practical members of the finance committee suggested eliminating some features and postponing the construction of others.

Calvert Vaux, who thought of the Terrace as the park's drawing room, was especially pleased by its blending of architecture into the natural landscape. Jacob Wrey Mould designed the whimsical motifs of the four seasons which ornamented the bannisters.

They gave priority to "development of the natural features of the ground" and the completion of drives, rides, walks, and the fall planting. They also directed Olmsted to reduce the cost of the bridges and defer construction of the two northern transverse roads, the arboretum ponds, the flower garden, some architectural structures (including an exterior iron fence and gates previously approved by the board), and the drives and rides between 86th and 97th streets. The board also tacitly dropped Vaux and Olmsted's proposal for a music hall east of the Mall and an adjacent palm house and conservatory.[9]

Green Takes Charge

With the commissioners closely watching the balance sheets, pressure on the park officers increased. Olmsted's discouragement and exhaustion in the late summer of 1859 showed in strained personal relations with individual commissioners, particularly that Republican stalwart John Butterworth. Incensed that Olmsted had not hired one of his candidates for a park police position, Butterworth made thinly veiled threats: "Your course in many matters is to me very unsatisfactory," he told Olmsted. "I once *saved your head.* I doubt whether I in so doing served the interest of the Park." After returning from a brief recuperative trip to Saratoga Springs, Olmsted was stricken by fevers. Plagued also by chronic insomnia, he was, as he reported to his father, "thoroughly worn out, used up, fatigued beyond recovery." It was as a respite for just such nervous exhaustion that Olmsted had envisioned Central Park. But the commissioners proposed the more traditional remedy of their class and in late September 1859 advanced five hundred dollars for Olmsted to go abroad for six weeks and "employ the time examining European parks."[10]

Through that difficult summer, Olmsted's strongest supporter on the board was the man he would later blame for all his troubles—President Andrew Green, who repeatedly backed Olmsted, especially on aesthetic issues. "No one but Green knows or will take the trouble to inform himself of the facts bearing on any question of policy sufficiently to argue upon it effectually," Olmsted once observed to a friend. Green, a bachelor, regularly joined the Olmsteds for Sunday dinner to discuss the work's progress.[11]

A New Englander who cherished Milton and enjoyed listening to Protestant hymns, Green shared Olmsted's belief in duty, order, hard work, and efficiency. He was deeply attached to his family's rural Worcester, Massachusetts, homestead (Green Hill) and had embraced Olmsted and Vaux's pastoral aesthetic. Perhaps because Green thought he so fully understood the designers' goals for Central Park, he decided in the fall of 1859 that the only way to see their vision realized was to take charge of the construction himself. When Olmsted sailed for Europe in late September to recuperate, Green persuaded the board to appoint him to a new position, park comptroller, and he preempted Olmsted's superintending responsibilities, effectively ensuring that the architect-in-chief would never again control the building of Central Park.[12]

First as treasurer and then as president, Green, a reform Democrat, had aligned himself with the Republican commissioners in shaping the park board into a new model institution for the administration of public works. He shrewdly negotiated with the other commissioners and local and state politicians while molding his reputation as a gentleman whose honesty placed him entirely above politics.

Trusting neither colleagues nor subordinates to achieve his own rigorous standards of economy, Green now set policy and took personal responsibility for day-to-day park operations. His earlier notes to Olmsted already gave hints of the brusque management style that would leave park officers "quaking in their shoes" when he took over supervision. A flood of letters complaining about the new regime followed Olmsted across the Atlantic. To save money, Green cut wages, laid off engineers, foremen, and assistants—in some cases without reference to seniority rules—and merged the work gangs together. The clerk Alexander Dallas, who considered himself Olmsted's confidential assistant, fretted that his own job would soon be lost in Green's drive to discharge "supernumeraries." Green "means well," the drainage engineer George Waring reported to Olmsted, "but he is so cross and crabbed that all with whom he comes in contact wish him to the devil a dozen times a week." The comptroller was "likely to show up at any part of the park before 9:30 A.M. and before then it

Andrew Haswell Green (1820–1903), who became the president of the park commission in 1860, tried to keep the park's construction within its budget by overseeing every detail.

is 'eyes right.' After he has gone there is a general unbuttoning and 'stand at ease.' "13

Green himself "growled a great deal at the unpopularity attached to him while he [was] obliged to discharge so many," Mary Olmsted wrote her husband. Despite the reduced work force, the comptroller was determined to see the lower park drives opened and as much planting as possible completed before the winter set in. More funds would have to be requested from the state legislature the following spring, and barren hillsides and unfinished roads and bridges would give ammunition to the park board's opponents. The sooner New Yorkers started using the drives and admiring the vistas, the more local support there would be for increased funding.14

"The Central Park Swindle"

The park was once again in the thick of local political scheming in the fall of 1859, and rumors were flying about various Republican commissioners' interests in either running for mayor or seizing the park for party benefit. The uncertain finances—the last appropriation would be exhausted by March—

made the board of commissioners particularly vulnerable to city Democrats' cries of "malfeasance."[15]

When in January 1860 the board asked the state legislature for another $5 million ($2.5 million to complete construction and $2.5 million for maintenance), it faced a storm of protest. The pro-Tammany *Leader* stepped up its vociferous attacks on the "Central Park swindle," charging that the commissioners had abused taxpayers' trust. Prominent Democratic merchants, who had little truck with Tammany politicians, also expressed reservations about the costs. Even the Republican *New York Times* conceded that "the demand for so enormous an amount naturally invites inquiry, and creates the feeling that they are making quite too lavish an expenditure of the public money." The leader of the opposition, Assemblyman F. A. Conckling, warned that the total costs would exceed $13 million: "This is more than the Erie Canal cost originally— more than the Hudson River Railroad cost—more than the cost of any public park in Europe." "To tell the truth," the *Irish News* wrote, "the sum is enough to make a greenhorn stare."[16]

The *Times* rallied to the board's defense, circulating the commissioners' arguments on behalf of increased funding. Central Park was valuable to the city as an employer: 70 percent of the construction cost "has been paid to labor," a *Times* editorial observed, "to those classes of our population who must necessarily expend in New York itself all that they receive." Furthermore, the park stimulated the real estate market, and "a carelessly and cheaply laid out park" would discourage the land speculation that enhanced the tax base and thus paid for the interest on park bonds. The *Leader* had already vigorously condemned the board's policies as an employer; it now greeted with equal contempt the argument that rising land values justified the spending: "It is a real estate speculation carried out at the expense of the laboring and mechanic classes."[17]

Republicans controlled both legislative houses, however, and Democrats therefore had little chance of blocking the new authorization for the park improvement and maintenance funds. But they did win one concession: an investigation into the park's management. More than fifty witnesses—often making conflicting claims—appeared before the state senate investigating committee in the summer of 1860. On one side were disaffected engineers, foremen, and suppliers who had been discharged from the park; on the other were engineers, foremen, and suppliers who would have risked their jobs and lucrative contracts had they said anything against the board. The testimony revealed countless intrigues among commissioners, suppliers, and park workers, as well as difficulties and adjustments in building the park. Areas had been graded and regraded, the lines of roads changed, and a bridge erected on quicksand. Engineers had made erroneous calculations, suppliers were not always reliable, blacksmiths played quoits, the architect-in-chief wrote for the newspapers and pursued other jobs in his "spare time." And party politics continued to run through most of the park's affairs, from general foreman Millard's tavern curse "that he would cut out the heart of every Republican on the park" to the commissioners' use of bribes and strategic appointments to secure their own ends.[18]

In the fall of 1860 the senate committee set aside "trifling and unimportant" testimony and brought in an outside expert to assess the quality of the work. The Swiss engineer Julius Kellersberger reported that the roads were "as perfect as possible," some bridges were "rather stronger than the occasion actually requires," and the "best order and system prevails in the different offices as well as on the ground, and . . . in this respect there is no other public work in the United States to be compared with the Central Park." Taking Olmsted's title literally and overlooking the contributions of Calvert Vaux and the engineers, Kellersberger announced that the park did "as much honor to the taste, refinement and wealth of the metropolis as credit to its designer and executor."[19]

In January 1861 when the committee issued its report to the Republican-dominated senate, it proclaimed the board's administration of the park a "triumphant success." Noting that rising uptown property values offset the interest for improvement bonds, the senators concluded that in forty years New Yorkers would gratefully pay back the principal and that the city had "not the least ground for complaint growing out of the expenditures for the park." The investigating committee absolved the commissioners of charges of "malpractice, dishonesty, or delinquency." Ignoring abundant evidence of patronage and politicking as usual, it credited the park commission with being the engine of reform, and its members with having "steadily set their faces against any political interference in the park." The park was half finished and deserved the full support of the legislature and the common council.[20]

"It was an old story of park making and every other sort of grand undertaking," the *Irish News* observed, anticipating the senate conclusion. "Especially when [it is a] question of the public money—the ultimate expense is always about ten times the original estimate. It is the regular order of things." Central Park would very likely cost $30 million before it was done, the *News* concluded, and in "1960 be a place worth looking at."[21]

Yet there was also a new story behind the senate's endorsement. The park board and its officers had been "guided by a desire to complete the work acceptable to the portion of the public who appreciate the benefits of good management," the committee observed. Appealing to the business values of the city's wealthiest taxpayers, the senate had endorsed the board's administrative model of public policy making removed from a democratic process. The commissioners took their cue from private corporations and established their reputations as a "board of directors" that acted for "the public." By invoking the judgment of an expert and reviewing the elaborate "system of accounts," the senate committee's report satisfied prominent Republican and Democratic business leaders worried about the spiraling expense. Tammany Democrats, however, continued to resent the interference of an outside body in city affairs and denounced the Republican politics that underlay the park board's "reforms."[22]

For park workers the question of accountability to the community revolved less around costs or local political control than around the board's responsibilities as a fair employer. The senate's endorsement of the board's managerial principles did not bode well for workers' efforts to preserve their own standards against Andrew Green's drive for efficiency and economy.

"Greenism"

The week after the senate investigating committee submitted its report in January 1861, Olmsted announced that he wished to resign as architect-in-chief and superintendent. The immediate cause of his resignation threat (and of a second ultimatum issued in March 1861) was his inability to match the estimates for the 1860 construction year with the work done or to render a precise accounting of the year's expenditures. "Much less was accomplished on the park last year than you had intended," he informed the board in March, "and the cost of what was accomplished was much in excess of your estimates." Not only was it "still quite impracticable to prepare a statement in detail of the cost of the work last year," Olmsted reported, but completion "would cost more than the [new] sum which the Commission is pledged not to exceed, by 32%." Olmsted felt obliged to offer his resignation in the face of what he himself called "prima facie evidence either of incompetence or neglect of duty." Yet he denied responsibility for the cost overruns and blamed the lack of necessary support: the comptroller had curtly rejected his pleas for more assistants and the engineers and draftsmen, who worked eleven and a half hours a day or longer, were exhausted. Furthermore, he said in March, the commissioners' continued reliance on patronage had undermined his efforts to maintain an efficient work force.[23]

Olmsted did not expect the board to let him leave. When commissioners asked him to explain, he urged the board to restore the park to his sole control. Olmsted acknowledged that political negotiations with the legislature and common council had "rendered it inexpedient for the Commission to hand over to its Superintendent that entire control in all respects which a commercial body, an independent and self-sustaining corporation . . . would have done . . . for the sake of economy, efficiency and success." But he apparently saw little connection between the board's responsibility for raising taxpayers' money and his own accountability for spending it. Nowhere in his remarks did he step outside the drama of his own "humiliation" to reflect on the political and practical implications of cost overruns for a public commission.[24]

Olmsted tried to impress upon the board his own value, indeed indispensability, as the park's designer. His confident assumption of "the title of artist"

and insistence on his own "natural, spontaneous, individual action of imagination—of *creative fancy*" carried echoes of discussions with his partner. Nonetheless, he repeatedly referred to "my design" and the exercise of a solitary
inspiration. "No one but myself can understand, *at the present time,* the true
value or purport of what is done on the park, of much that needs to be done." It
was the first time he had fully articulated a claim to artistic over administrative
talent, but then, the occasion was not entirely propitious for asserting a genius
for professional management.[25]

Although Olmsted blamed the entire board for interfering with his administration of the park, he singled out Green as his chief obstacle. When Olmsted
returned from his European "cure" in December 1859, he had found that
Andrew Green had become comfortable—to the extent that Green permitted
himself or anyone else to feel comfortable—with his new prerogatives as
comptroller. By January 1860 Green was peppering the architect-in-chief with
a steady barrage of notes demanding information, directing operations, and
warning, "I am afraid your payroll is getting too large." He scrutinized every
bill, large or small, paring away expenses. "Not a dollar, not a cent, is got from
under his paw that is not wet with his blood & sweat," Olmsted later complained
to a friend. His "tenacity" in holding onto money is a hardship for "some poor
fellows who earn the amount of their small bills ten times over in the labor
necessary to overcome his constitutional reluctance to pay."[26]

In August 1860 Olmsted's leg was shattered in a carriage accident; while he
tried to oversee construction from a litter carried by park workers, Andrew
Green once again took charge of day-to-day operations. By December the park
below 79th Street was largely complete. Park laborers had filled the lower pond
with water, finished the arches over the drives, opened another two miles of
walks, and planted seventeen thousand trees and shrubs.[27]

Far from being relieved that the work had gone forward, Olmsted insisted in
his January 1861 resignation letter that his own "mortifying" run-ins with the
comptroller over "picayune details" threatened the artistic integrity of the
Greensward plan. He was reluctant to challenge a "superior officer" directly,
Olmsted told the board's executive committee, but others were warning that
Green "was laying a deep plot to supersede" him. Under the existing "arrangement . . . of the relative and associated duties of myself and Mr. Green, no two
men who have much self-respect could work long together without quarreling."
At the core of the park's mismanagement, Olmsted thought, was this flaw in the
"machinery" of its administration.[28]

Green's own later account confirmed Olmsted's worse fears that the comptroller had planned to "supersede" him. Dictating his reminiscences to his
niece, Green found it unnecessary to mention Olmsted, Vaux, or any other
commissioners or park officers by name. He described himself as the "Executive Officer" of the park board with "complete supervision of the engineers,
landscape architects, gardeners, and the whole retinue of employees, some-

times comprising as many as three thousand men." No less than Olmsted himself, Green did not easily share credit for his accomplishments, but unlike Olmsted, he understood how to manage his personal ambitions in relation to the "practical" conditions of public service.[29]

Within a year of his 1855 election to the New York City School Board, Green had become president. He had risen to the presidency of the park board just as quickly. Only two years older than Olmsted, Green was, even his nephew conceded, "imperious . . . vain . . . parsimonious," but he was "lavish" in his "unrequited work for the benefit of mankind." The seventh child of eleven, at age fifteen he had left Worcester for the New York City mercantile world, where he became a real estate lawyer. He thrived as a Yankee Democrat who believed in both individual initiative and the leadership of the "best men." In a family that produced ministers, doctors, teachers, engineers, and missionaries, Green had internalized a mission of public service, and he mastered the art of intimidation to achieve his ends. Faced with Olmsted's relentless protestations of purity of motive and judgment, Green seems to have relished demonstrating that he was not only a better but a stronger Puritan. Inattention to accounts was a luxury that no man could afford. In Olmsted's eyes, however, Green's motives bordered on sadism—"a systematic small tyranny, measured exactly by the limit of my endurance."[30]

Calvert Vaux, who himself lost no fondness on Green, dismissed Olmsted's posture of "a badly used and injured innocent" at the hands of Green. "I always felt," Vaux informed his partner, "that you were a little insatiable in your ambition and that your theory [of controlling the park] left no room for Green or anybody else." Olmsted's administration had not been "particularly comprehensive, calm, statesmanlike or well founded," Vaux observed, and his "diplomacy" was "very defective & impatient." Olmsted's own program for managing the park as a "machine" had "cut & pared and stifled it down to Green's level" of business management; he should not, therefore, have been surprised when Green took control.[31]

But the Central Park commission (including Green) could not afford to let Olmsted resign. As architect-in-chief he claimed sole credit for the system of "checks and precautions" that (as he reminded the board) the senate investigating committee had especially commended in concluding that Central Park "was the best managed public work in the country." With what Olmsted called "tremendous puff" articles in both the *World* and the *Atlantic Monthly* that spring, he had made himself the park's "representative man" before the public. His resignation over new financial problems might fuel a scandal at the time the board was asking the legislature for yet another appropriation.[32]

But in June 1861, with new appropriations secured, the board in effect decided that it trusted the supervisory skill of its own member, Andrew Green, more than that of Olmsted. So it relieved him of those responsibilities and limited his duties to overseeing the finishing operations and superintending the park keepers. The Civil War spared Olmsted from having to acknowledge this defeat. That month he departed for Washington to serve on the U.S. Sanitary Commission, which oversaw the supplying of the Union Army. Although Olmsted kept in touch, Green and, under him, Vaux (who had been appointed consulting architect in 1859), the gardener Ignaz Pilat, and the engineering corps managed the park's completion.[33]

Green easily consolidated his own power with an autocratic management style that Olmsted disdainfully dubbed "Greenism." He kept track of the minutest detail of expense and—no less than an Andrew Carnegie or John D. Rockefeller—scrutinized the park's affairs with a Calvinist determination. But less attached than Olmsted to the new system of centralized management and more attentive to the actual bottom line, he also returned to the use of contract labor to control costs. Green recognized, as Olmsted did not, that administering the park required meeting the expectations of wealthy taxpayers who, in the end, cared less about reform for the sake of reform than for the sake of saving money.[34]

Green's approach troubled the engineers, who saw their reputations threatened by the park's financial troubles and their authority undermined by the introduction of private contractors. But professionally embarrassed though they were by the discrepancy between their estimates and actual costs, J. H. Pieper and Francis Hawks rejected Olmsted's explanation that the overruns stemmed from "incompetent and inefficient" workers demoralized by the commissioners' use of patronage. The two engineers implicitly indicted both Olmsted's and Green's leadership—the former for frequently "shifting gangs without apparent cause" and changing the plan "in order to produce the desired result" and the latter for "requiring certain portions of the work to be hastily completed under unfavorable circumstances." The solution, Pieper and Hawks agreed, was to adopt a more precise plan of operations, permitting "no alteration in plans" unless "a decided saving in expenditures" was at stake. When Vaux instructed Hawks to make a "slight alteration" in the shape of a meadow, Hawks referred the request to Pieper, who passed it on to Grant before the ten-to-twelve-dollar expense was approved as "within the estimates for work in that vicinity."[35]

Under Green, cost estimates became the ruling concern. Private contractors took charge of the reservoir area and the walls of the transverse roads at 85th and 97th streets, while the engineering corps and blasting gangs moved steadily north, grading and shaping the upper park. Olmsted had already warned that the northern park would need to be built with "a ruder workmanship and method of construction" to stay within the budget. Tightening their procedures to meet Green's standards, the engineers also made subtle changes in design and specifications to save money.[36]

The Viennese landscape gardener Ignaz Pilat took charge of the finishing work. Much to the dismay of the engineers, he tried to adhere to the Greensward plan regardless of cost. He consulted regularly with Vaux and sent copies of his laconic weekly reports to Olmsted. But Pilat was far more knowledgeable than either designer about plants and their scenic arrangement, and he selected and grouped trees, shrubs, and bulbs to suit his own sense of how they could be placed to best advantage. In 1863 Olmsted left the Sanitary Commission to become superintendent of the Mariposa Mining Company in California. Traveling by way of Panama, he sent Pilat an effusive letter of suggestions on how to use native northeastern plants on the Ramble to create the "mysterious" illusion of lush tropical vegetation. Pilat shared the letter with Vaux, and the two were "much entertained" by the proposal to plant such mundane—and to some sensibilities unattractive—plants as skunk cabbage, catbrier, and the like to achieve tropical effects in New York's temperate climate.[37]

The 240,000 trees and shrubs Pilat's men planted between 1861 and 1863 transformed the appearance of Central Park. When in 1863 the French gardener Eugene Baumann evaluated its landscape for Green, he commended the "harmonious connection of various kinds of trees and shrubs . . . which show the skill of the leading hands in this department." Baumann apparently saw little loss from Olmsted's departure: Pilat's landscaping on the west side of the reservoirs, he observed, showed "an improvement . . . which admits of a favorable and advantageous comparison with some of the formerly finished parts; there is more 'Ensemble' in the general arrangement and the planting is more judicious." But even Pilat had to bend to the economic imperative. With visitors pouring in and money running low, "temporary" plantings (which remained for more than a decade) were set out in large areas of the park to give it a finished look.[38]

"Pilat is a gentleman and a trump," Vaux informed his partner, indignant that Olmsted had referred to Pilat as a "docile" worker. In 1865 Vaux sent Olmsted a copy of a note that accompanied a five-hundred-dollar gift to the gardener on behalf of their partnership. "We are well aware that very much has depended on you," Vaux told Pilat, "and that if our design has been virtually carried out, it is your persistent adhesion to its letter, and to its spirit . . . that has ensured the result under circumstances of peculiar embarrassment."[39]

The "circumstances of peculiar embarrassment," of course, referred to Vaux and Olmsted's difficult relations with Andrew Green. When Olmsted departed for Washington, Vaux had stayed on as consulting architect; after April 1862 he represented the firm of Olmsted and Vaux, which had been appointed landscape architects to the board. He repeatedly acknowledged that Green was a "main prop" in realizing the Greensward plan, but Vaux had his own run-ins with "his Comptrollership—just the proper name for his work," as he noted. In the midst of a delirious fever in 1862, Vaux raved to his wife that Green—who was paying a call—should not be permitted near him, nor should his name be mentioned in the sick man's presence. Still, it is a measure of his success in dealing with Green that Vaux and Mould's beloved (and expensive) Bethesda Terrace was executed largely as designed.[40]

If Green conceded that some "extravagance" was legitimate, he remained firmly determined to complete the park within the authorized funding. He successfully blocked a move by local Democrats to use the war as an excuse to shut down operations. Stopping construction, he warned, would create a hardship for the city's working families. But Green himself reduced the number of workers each year, and by 1862 more than a third of them were working under contractors. Like the contractors, Green took advantage of the recession triggered by the wartime interruption of the cotton trade, reducing the daily wages for cartmen from $2.00 to $1.75, and for the stubborn stonecutters from $2.00 to $1.65. In the spring of 1861 the laborers' workday went from nine to ten hours to take advantage of increasing daylight, but their daily wage remained the same, ninety cents. By 1862 park workers were repeatedly petitioning the board to raise wages (which wartime inflation further reduced), and in June the masons working on the park under contract went on strike. Green reluctantly brought other park workers' pay back up to 1860 levels, explaining in his annual report that "demand for men for the army" had "occasioned a general nominal increase in the rate of wages."[41]

The 1863 conscription law that permitted wealthy men to buy their way out of the draft through substitutes outraged working-class families already angry at the economic dislocations of the war. In July, when the draft lottery was scheduled to begin, four days of rioting, arson, looting, and lynching erupted. At least some park workers joined the antidraft demonstration, which began in a gathering at Central Park. "On the first morning of the July riot," the *Times* later reported, "one or two of the gangs of workmen employed on the Central Park left their work, and marched down[town], forcing or inducing the other gangs to leave their work also and follow them, and the whole body then proceeded to take part in the business of murder and rapine then going on in the City, and continued engaging in it during two entire days, furnishing by far the best organized, and, therefore, most dangerous and destructive of the bands." The rioters targeted the houses of prominent unionists and abolitionists as well as institutions associated with the Republican cause. "The mob sent word one night that they were coming to burn the hospital" for union soldiers, which had been set up in the Mount St. Vincent convent buildings in the park, as the daughter of the park's new superintendent, Cornelius Ryan, later recalled. (Ryan, the former general foreman of blasters, may have gotten the post through a boyhood connection in Worcester with Green). Although her father unsuccessfully sought to dissuade "his men joining the rioters," only the presence of the Sisters of Charity (who had returned to work in the hospital) saved the building.[42]

The antidraft demonstration spun out into a race riot and a citywide protest against the economic hardships brought by the war. Rioters identified Republicans not simply with the unfair conscription act but with industrial employers' general indifference to working families' poverty. Andrew Green, of course, was a Democrat, anxious to establish the park board's reputation as a nonpartisan administrative body, aloof from the political turmoil of the era. But his tightening of Olmsted's managerial regime served the interests of the city's wealthiest taxpayers and businessmen, and the park workers understood this deeper level of political antagonism. Working-class New Yorkers were not included in the public to whom the board held itself accountable.

"How Fine It Would Be to Have No Gates"

Under Green's grip, the park moved toward completion. By the end of 1863 the grounds, drives, and walks below 102nd Street had opened to the public; in the next two years, Green turned his attention to the territory between 106th and 110th streets, finally acquired in 1863 after four years of delay. These additional sixty-five acres, which covered the rocky woodland at the northwest corner and a swamp to the northeast, brought the park to its current size of 843 acres. Although much less was done to rearrange the northern end's rugged topography than had been done elsewhere, park workers built a twelve-acre lake called the Harlem Meer on the swamp, carved out and planted the Ravine and Waterfall, and constructed another mile of drive, a mile and a half of walks, and several rustic bridges.[43]

When wartime inflation bested even Green, he approached the state legislature with a request for more money for construction and maintenance—and more power while he was at it. "The public works that have heretofore been carried out on this island, and in the State and nation," he announced, "have been conceived on too limited and narrow a scale." The legislature came through with more money for the park and for new projects, including the improvement of Manhattan Square (the territory between 77th and 81st streets, from Eighth to Ninth Avenue, which was officially added to Central Park in 1864 and later became the site of the American Museum of Natural History) and the widening and planting of Seventh Avenue as a boulevard running from the park to the Harlem River. With Radical Republicans in charge of the legislature, the park board became the model for an expanded program of "civil and institutional reform" that historian James Mohr has described as "Reconstruction at home." As elite New Yorkers flocked to the park drives to display the gains of wartime affluence, wealthy Republicans and Democrats alike credited the Central Park commission with establishing New York City's reputation as cultural capital of the nation.[44]

The question of how to underscore the triumph of Central Park's completion to the parkgoing public provided the occasion for the board's last internal battle. During the early war years, park commissioners departed for the army, diplomatic posts, and European tours. The remaining seven continued to refer most management decisions "to the comptroller with power." But in considering the park's finishing touch—the gates—the commissioners were less ready to submit to Green's aesthetic tastes or austerity. Commissioner Russell promoted his brother-in-law Richard Morris Hunt's designs for four gateways at the southern entrances. In April 1864 the board directed the comptroller to begin their construction.[45]

Hunt, the son of a prosperous lawyer and congressman, had been the first American student at the Ecole des Beaux-Arts in Paris; at thirty-seven, he was just establishing the practice that was to make him New York's most fashionable architect. He now proposed elaborate plazas for the Fifth and Eighth Avenue entrances with iron gates, pedestals and statues, and terraces decorated with fountains. Hunt believed such gates (as well as two slightly less ornate designs for the entrances at Sixth and Seventh) would offer an "elegant and appropriate" transition from city to park. His plans invoked the continental aesthetic of artificial civic display explicitly rejected by the board in choosing the Greensward plan. One admirer suggested that they pointed the way for transforming the park into "one great open air gallery of Art, instead of being, as some dreamers fancy it, a silent sketch of rural landscape caught up and enclosed within the raging tumult of a vast metropolis." But for Vaux (and presumably for the absent Olmsted) such monumental architectural flourishes contradicted the conception of Central Park as a pastoral retreat from the city.[46]

Green (possibly influenced by Vaux) initially disregarded the board's directions to build Hunt's gates and assigned priority to completing the grounds. Although Olmsted and Vaux had resigned as Central Park's landscape architects in May 1863 (after seeing the board adopt their plans for the extension to 110th Street), Vaux informally consulted with Green on park affairs—receiving, as he pointed out to the comptroller, "neither honor nor profit" for this "eleemosynary contribution." In the spring of 1865 Hunt arranged an exhibit of his plans at the Academy of Design to force the issue of building the gates. Vaux responded with a letter to the *Post* accusing the park board of abandoning the prize-winning Greensward design. He intended, he told Olmsted, to convince the public "that we have employed the Commissioners to carry out our plan as long as they behaved themselves and that we now discharge them for misconduct."[47]

Mobilizing support behind the scenes, Vaux successfully used personal and press connections to pressure the commissioners to abandon Hunt's gates. Their continental design, he argued, violated the park's democratic spirit and "buttressed" the pretensions of the "panjandrum." The "imperial style presumes that people wait [and] wait [and] hang around[,] and provision is made for clients, courtiers, subordinates, laqueyes," he suggested to art critic Clarence Cook. "But when the New Yorker enters his park, the great panjandrum

In 1865 Richard Morris Hunt held an exhibition of his designs for the gates of Central Park. Vaux protested that Hunt's elaborate continental style would destroy the park's pastoral effects. The drawings here show plans for statues and a plaza, including a terrace to the Pond, at the Fifth Avenue entrance, and an arcade of statues at the Sixth Avenue pedestrian entrance.

enters exactly at the same moment and in the same suit of clothes." "How fine it would be to have no gates" in a democratic park, "to keep open House and trust all always."[48]

Although the park would not have the gates envisioned by Hunt, it would have an enclosure. The designers disliked the aesthetic of a spiked iron fence promoted by some commissioners who admired continental public grounds such as the Paris Tuileries. An "iron railing," Olmsted quoted Ruskin, "always means thieves outside or Bedlam inside." Conceding at the time of the park's financial crisis that an iron fence was cheaper than stone, Olmsted had urged that it be disguised by a hedge. But by 1863 Vaux had persuaded the board (after "six months of serious trial") to abandon the "cage like suggestion" altogether and build a low stone wall that would permit the eye of the "outsider" to "roam at will" over the park's natural features. At least for the moment, Central Park had been finished as a pastoral landscape.[49]

The press celebrated the artistic triumph of the park and the administrative triumph of the board (a model of "intelligence, integrity, and culture"). Forgotten, for the moment, were the patronage, cost overruns of $4 million, and raw power struggles among city and state officials, commissioners, park officers, and workers. "The construction of the Park has been easily achieved," a committee of the board declared in 1866, "because the industrious population of New York has been wise enough to require it, and rich enough to pay for it." The committee proposed to "extend to each citizen a rightful welcome," by naming the park's four principal entrances for "Artisans," "Artists," "Merchants," and "Scholars," the last class to include editors, statesmen, and lawyers.[50]

Who Built Central Park?

Vaux saw in the praise for Central Park a new public appreciation of the value of landscape architecture. As the controversy over the gates unfolded, he took the high road of artistic principle, successfully recruiting a number of prominent artists and critics to his position, and urged Green to use his formidable power to reinstate Olmsted and himself as the park's landscape architects. With the city economy still booming from war contracts and the Republican-dominated legislature liberally meeting Green's request for more power and money, Vaux informed Olmsted that the reappointment would be the first step to an expansion of their influence. "Who are they to get" to execute the board's new projects (Manhattan Square and Seventh Avenue), Vaux asked rhetorically, "who will the public trust?" His answer was the firm of Olmsted, Vaux & Company. Vaux well understood that their work for the Central Park commission would provide the launching ground for creating parks across the county.[51]

Olmsted was in California superintending the Mariposa gold mines. (The miners met his wage cuts with a strike and the "rumor," as he reported to his employer, that Olmsted had "swindled the laborers on Central Park and had been sent here to play the same game.") Through the early summer of 1865, Vaux sent Olmsted weekly reports of his "campaign" for their reappointment, seeking to entice him back to their practice on new terms of fraternal equality. Vaux admired his partner's artistic abilities, but more important, Olmsted's name had "stood before the public" in relation to Central Park. If he failed to return, Vaux needled him, "the public will naturally say if Olmsted really was the prime mover in the C[entral] P[ark] why is he not ready to go forward in the path that he started in."[52]

In suggesting to Olmsted that their work on Central Park had made them the leaders of a new profession of landscape architects, Vaux hoped to instruct his partner in the principles of republican cooperation he believed essential to the creation of democratic art. Their reunion rested, as far as he was concerned, on a "fair subscription of the power" and "fair work & fair acknowledgment of all our friends labor." Vaux pointedly informed Olmsted that he had unilaterally acknowledged the firm's particular debt to Pilat and Grant, who had helped realize the Greensward plan. In undertaking new projects, Vaux cautioned, they must "go in as artists and keep the art *management* in the shade for a week or month or year or two till we ha[ve] the whole thing done." Olmsted expressed reservations about this approach, protesting, "I don't feel strong on the art side." But he said, "I can do anything with proper assistants or money enough. . . . I can combine means to ends better than most, and I love beautiful landscapes and rural recreations."[53]

When Olmsted and Vaux were reappointed as landscape architects on July 19, 1865, they added new features to enhance the park's attractions and convenience. Vaux (working with Mould) designed the Gothic-style Belvedere Castle on Vista Rock to draw viewers' eyes from the Mall and reward visitors who climbed through the Ramble. He created the Moorish-style Mineral Springs Pavilion at the northwestern edge of the Sheep Meadow. His Ladies Refreshment Salon (later called the Casino) adorned the site east of the Mall originally planned for a concert hall. Borrowing a suggestion first made by Samuel Gustin in his entry for the design competition, the partners created the Dairy to dispense fresh milk and designed the nearby Children's Shelter. At the edge of the southwestern Playground they placed the Boys' Playhouse and designed a smaller playhouse for girls on the other side of the park. As the board's budget expanded Olmsted and Vaux were able to develop new plans for a Conservatory near Fifth Avenue and 72nd Street and a zoo on Manhattan Square.[54]

The building of Central Park ignited enthusiasm for landscaped parks across the country. As Vaux had predicted, Olmsted, Vaux & Company became the nation's leading landscape architecture firm, taking some of Central Park's engineers, architects, gardeners, and foremen on to new projects, including

Brooklyn's Prospect Park and parks in Buffalo, Chicago, and Albany (as well as the grounds of private estates, colleges, and asylums). Impressed by the effect of Central Park on real estate values and the city's reputation for refinement, committees of gentlemen in Philadelphia, Baltimore, Boston, Hartford, Detroit, and other cities now mobilized to create their own "central parks." They sought guidance from the source, requesting copies of the board's reports from Green and inviting Olmsted and Vaux to consult.[55]

Others who had worked on Central Park parlayed the reputations they earned there into new avenues of success. Grant went on to the city public works department and eventually became superintendent of the U.S. Naval Station in Washington, D.C. J. H. Pieper, who had followed Olmsted to the California mines, became the head engineer of the city of San Jose; Montgomery Kellogg served as chief engineer in the New York Department of Public Parks; park superintendent Cornelius Ryan would later become the proprietor of Central Park's two leading restaurants, the Casino and Mount St. Vincent; George Waring became the nation's most noted "sanitary engineer" and took credit for the equally difficult tasks of saving Memphis from yellow fever epidemics and cleaning up New York City's streets. Many of the youthful members of Central Park's engineering corps also found comfortable positions on other public works projects. John Bogart directed the construction of Prospect Park and later served as New York's chief engineer for parks and advised the Rapid Transit Commission. Addison Crittendon Rand, perhaps taking a lesson from the experience of building the 79th Street Transverse Road under Vista Rock, made a fortune inventing new pneumatic rock drills for tunnels and aqueducts. Park engineer Peter Hogan devised the plans for the first deep-sea disposal of New York City's garbage.[56]

The careers of the engineers suggest the extent to which Central Park provided a training ground for public works, which accelerated in the second half of the nineteenth century. But perhaps the park board had its most significant impact in providing a new administrative model for "comprehensive" city planning by executive commissions. From 1865 to 1869, with the blessing of the city's business community, Green steadily expanded the Central Park commission's authority as a planning agency responsible for laying out the streets and public squares of northern Manhattan. Through careful planning, Green argued, the board could introduce order and economy into the city-building process by efficiently arranging utilities and arbitrating among the competing interests of private landowners. In 1868 he suggested that proper planning required coordination beyond the confines of the city, and he envisioned consolidation of parts of Westchester, Kings, Queens, and Richmond counties with Manhattan "under one common municipal government." Almost forty years later, Green's vision would be realized with the adoption of his proposal for "Greater New York."[57]

For more than another century, the commission's administration of Central

After Olmsted and Vaux returned as the park's landscape architects in 1865, they introduced new features. They conceived of the picturesque Dairy (at Seventh Avenue, just south of the 65th Street Transverse), as a comfort station that would offer fresh milk to mothers with children. Vaux and Jacob Wrey Mould designed the Gothic-style Belvedere Castle as a lookout tower and platform on the top of Vista Rock. (Owing to budget constraints, only the right side of the building shown in this drawing was constructed). Vaux's two-tiered boathouse (at the east end of the Lake) also provided park visitors with a waystation from which to contemplate the landscape (and the crowds of boaters). The Casino, located east of the Mall, was originally designed as the Ladies Refreshment Pavilion and rapidly became one of the city's most fashionable restaurants.

The Completed Park: Lithographs such as this made views of Central Park available to a national audience.

Park would be also held up as a model for the nonpartisan management of public cultural institutions. But not all New Yorkers shared this judgment. Even as the individuals who managed Central Park moved on, the political conflicts that had racked the park's construction remained, with far-reaching consequences. The bitterness Tammany Democrats and working-class New Yorkers felt toward the Republican party—and particularly toward its state-appointed commissions—provided the impetus for a restoration of home rule and the return of Democrats to power under the leadership of William Tweed. Setting out to build a public works project infamous for its cost overruns—a courthouse—Boss Tweed used contract labor and paid himself and his cronies a hefty commission. And it was Andrew Green, acting as city comptroller, who added up the accounts that brought the Tweed Ring down.[58]

We know almost nothing about what became of the laborers and artisans who built Central Park. In 1895 the *Herald* could find only one foreman, William Monahan, who had worked on its construction. As time went on, it became even more difficult to remember that the daily judgments, tastes, and skill of ordinary workers helped create the landscape. Men like Monahan had built the park, but it was men like Olmsted—possessed of the skill of literacy— who constructed the park's *history*. Drawing on Olmsted's voluminous letters, Green's annual reports, and the board's extensive minutes, subsequent historical accounts would record that Olmsted, architect-in-chief; Andrew Green, comptroller; and the gentlemen of the board had built Central Park.[59]

But just as different groups of New Yorkers contributed to the building of Central Park, so they crafted different versions of its history. While the gentlemen's account was enshrined in the history books, an alternative version circulated orally in the city's Irish working-class neighborhoods. In 1933 that memory was still alive and was shared by a Bronx "Old Timer" with the readers of the *Daily News*. "I wonder if any of these artists, landscape architects, or [merchant philanthropists] . . . know how the poor of New York built Central Park. When my parents used to take me to the park as a child, my father used to tell us how my grandfather and great uncles had worked on the park job at 50 cents a day. . . . The park area was given to the city in the first place by a few wealthy men to make work for the poor. And it was understood that the poor were to enjoy the park."[60]

As the Old Timer understood, the conflicts embedded in park making and, later, in history making also found expression in clashes over park use. With the drives, paths, and lakes ready to receive visitors, the question remained: Would the "poor people" who had built Central Park also get to enjoy it?

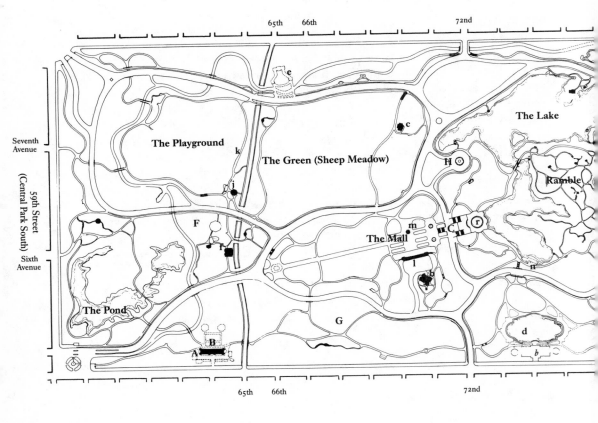

A	Arsenal	
B	Menagerie	
C	Bethesda Terrace	
D	Ladies Pond	
E	East Drive	
F	Children's District	
G	The Dene	
H	Cherry Hill	
I	Loch	
J	Pool	
K	Great Hill	

a	Mount St. Vincent (McGown's Pass Tavern)
b	Casino
c	Mineral Springs Pavilion
d	Conservatory Water
e	Sheepfold
f	Dairy

g	Belvedere Castle
h	Metropolitan Museum of Art
i	American Natural History Museum
j	Carousel
k	Boys' Playhouse
l	Wisteria Arbor
m	Bandshell
n	Boathouse
o	Obelisk
p	Summit Rock
q	Vista Rock
r	Bethesda Fountain
s	Blockhouse
t	Bow Bridge

a	site of Seneca Village
b	site of the proposed Conservatory

Reservoir

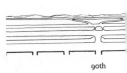

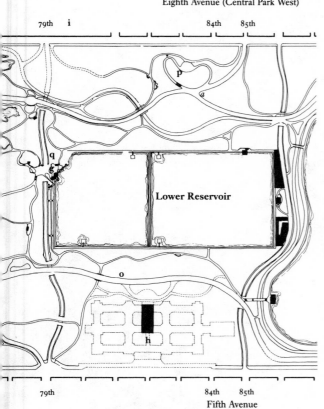

Eighth Avenue (Central Park West)

Map of Central Park, ca. 1870

Lower Reservoir

Fifth Avenue

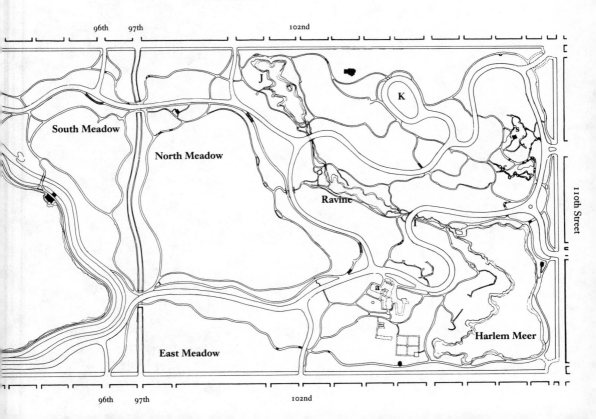

South Meadow

North Meadow

East Meadow

Ravine

Harlem Meer

110th Street

Central Park, The Drive, Currier and Ives, 1862.

III. THE ELITE PARK

8

"THE GREAT RENDEZVOUS
OF THE POLITE WORLD"

On a December Sunday in 1858 about three hundred skaters showed up at the newly frozen, only partially filled Central Park Lake at West 73rd Street. No one cut a ribbon or made a speech, but these venturesome ice skaters may have been the first New Yorkers to play in Central Park. Ten thousand turned up on the following Sunday and perhaps twice as many on Christmas Day. On workdays, however, the more than two thousand laborers still outnumbered the visitors, and the unfinished park sometimes presented difficulties. The stone breakers' noisy chorus competed with the first park concerts, for example, and winter thaws turned ungraveled roads to mud.[1]

The next December, the *Herald* reviewed the park's first year, declaring that "there was never perhaps an institution established for public enjoyment which has grown popular and available so rapidly." Large crowds welcomed each new phenomenon: after the skating pond in the winter of 1858–1859 came the Ramble in June and the first three and a half miles of park drives in November. Every few months, or even weeks, newspapers proclaimed new park attendance records. Fifteen thousand visited the Ramble on a Sunday at the end of July; twenty thousand came on a Sunday in late August; forty thousand enjoyed a particularly clear and sunny mid-October Sunday; fifty thousand skated or watched the "skating carnival" on the park's second Christmas Day. In 1860, 2.5 million people came. Over the decade, attendance more than tripled, growing fifteen times faster than the city's population.[2]

From the start, the *Herald* enthusiastically described the new skating scene, typically noting that the park police had maintained "the best of order through-out the day"—a direct refutation of its own previous editorial anxiety that "the lowest denizens of the city" would drive out "any better dressed man." "Every-thing was thoroughly democratic. Masters Richard and William from Fifth avenue, in their furs, and plain Dick and Bill from avenues nearer the river . . . mingled in joyful unity, forgetting the distinction of home in their enjoyment of a common patrimony—free air and free water."[3]

Ignoring the inequalities of wealth and power inherent in the political process that had created the park, the *Herald* and other newspapers implied that all New Yorkers could discover common values as they gathered in this grand new public space. The park, the press reported as the decade advanced, encompassed "the ragged urchin" and "the millionaire in his richly-robed carriage," "hard-handed labor" and "soft-palmed wealth," "the wife of the downtown merchant" and the "poor beggar woman," and even "the legal swindler" and the "pickpocket." Newspapers also applauded the crowds' good manners.[4]

Yet we should not mistake nineteenth-century journalism for twentieth-century social science (even acknowledging the limitations of the latter). Reports about park use reflected civic boosterism, democratic ideology, and journalistic conventions as well as close observation. These reports could sometimes disguise the more complex and changing social realities of park use in the second half of the nineteenth century. Although reporters and park officials had reason to highlight orderliness, Central Park was never free from the conflicts of the city. Even more important, celebrations of the park's democratic character masked class-specific patterns of use in the 1860s, when wealthy New Yorkers defined the new public park as their own.

The Society Carriage Parade

It is apparent from the extraordinarily thorough visitor counts the gatekeepers maintained for the first thirteen years of the park's operation that the largest and most regular group arrived at Central Park by carriage or horse. Relatively few New Yorkers owned either, but bankers, merchants, landlords, manufacturers, and politicians—the richest 5 percent—did. These were the sort of gentlemen and ladies Anna and Robert Minturn had thought about and consulted with when they put forward the park idea in the first place.[5]

Back in 1850 the *Herald* had bemoaned a deficiency of "fashionable promenades and drives" in the city on the "scale of magnificence that marks European cities." Some opponents of the Jones Wood site had objected to it on the grounds that its limited size precluded an appropriately grand carriage drive. In December 1858 a *Herald* editorial said with relief that when Central Park's roads were completed "our citizens will be in possession, for the first time, of a good drive and ride, both of which have been so long needed." "Every equipage in the city," it explained a few months later, "will be daily directed" to Central Park, "soon to become the permanent and habitual resort of pleasure, pretension and fashion."[6]

Even before the park was finished, wealthy New Yorkers turned out in their carriages. This 1860 drawing by Winslow Homer appeared in *Harper's Weekly* and gave readers an idea of the various carriage styles as well as of the park's popularity.

One of the first Central Park guidebooks (published in 1860) devoted more space to information on how carriage owners and horses could get to the park than on how to get there by public transportation. By 1863 most of the nine miles of carriage drives were finished, and almost two-thirds of the visitors arrived by carriage. The proportion remained above 55 percent for the rest of the decade, in part because carriage owners visited the park so regularly. It would be hard to come up with a more precise marker of mid-nineteenth-century class status than a carriage. Money—lots of it—was the only prerequisite. A large French-style coupé (with the driver's outside seat separate from the passengers' roofed carriage), which the *Herald* predicted would be "a favorite vehicle for driving in the new Central Park, as it is convenient both for seeing and being seen," cost about twelve hundred dollars. Obviously, such a purchase was out of the question for, say, bakers and shoemakers, whose annual incomes averaged around three hundred dollars at midcentury, or for those laborers who had built the park, who earned even less, or even for the park's engineers.[7]

Maintaining horses, stables, harnesses, and especially coachmen cost even more than the carriage outlay itself. And carriage owners needed different vehicles for summer and winter unless they had a calèche, the nineteenth-century version of a convertible. "Not half the poor people in the city," one newspaper protested, "are as well fed and cared for as the horses of our rich nabobs." Park Commissioner August Belmont owned four or five coaches and perhaps a dozen horses; his lavish stables had gaslights and running water at a time when most homes in New York had neither. Even relatively modest turnouts ran up substantial bills. The annual cost in 1878 of operating a two-wheel tandem (touted for its "inexpensiveness") was about fifteen hundred dollars.[8]

When the *Herald* proclaimed the presence of "every class of society" on the carriage drives, it hasted to add, "moneyed society, we mean." In 1863 the editor of the *New York Coach-Maker's Magazine* estimated that carriages constituted 5,000 of a total of 13,500 horse-drawn vehicles in the city. Such a figure indicates that fewer than 3 percent of the city's households maintained private carriages. Since perhaps 3 to 5 percent of New Yorkers accounted for 55 percent of the users of Central Park in the 1860s, park use was apparently only slightly less skewed than wealth distribution in mid-nineteenth-century New York.[9]

The rich were not, of course, the only people to drive. At the street railway stations near the park, hack drivers shouted their offers to "take you all around—see every thing—for a dollar!" Some New Yorkers hired carriages for longer periods at one of the city's many livery stables, which charged a dollar or two per hour—a sum within the reach of the middle class, at least on special occasions. But by far the largest group of ordinary people who regularly rode through the park in elegant equipages were the coachmen.[10]

The new park, then, was both effect and cause of a growing enthusiasm for carriages among the upper classes. That interest had fostered widespread elite support for the park movement. In turn, "the opening of Central Park, with its fine drives," New York journalist Junius Browne wrote in 1869, "has more than anything else given a new interest to fast horses and fine stables. The park is a magnificent place to exhibit horses, and men buy them for the privilege of displaying their good points and high spirit there." The *New York Coach-Maker's Magazine*, whose appearance in 1858 was another sign of the maturity of that local industry, agreed: "Central Park is the life and soul of [New York] carriage making."[11]

The carriage-manufacturing journal concerned itself primarily with the park's impact on business—on the carriage trade—but some observers focused on the park's even greater effect on the other group summoned up by the same phrase, the wealthy buyers of carriages and their accouterments. "Central Park," explained a *Herald* reporter within a year of the opening of the drives, "has already commenced a revolution in New York society that is being felt to its very depths." Visiting the park to chart the revolution, the reporter described the daily display of horses and carriages as a drama, whose "first scene may be said to commence at daylight" with "equestrians and health seekers who go out in their carriages to strengthen mind and body for the day's labor." With their departure the park "appears almost deserted" until two o'clock, "when the equestrians and stylish turnouts make their appearance, and by three P.M. all the favorite drives are alive with carriages of all kinds, and by four P.M. a stranger would think that the whole of New York was out on a grand trotting spree to see which had the fastest pair of horses or the gayest and most costly equipage."[12]

The gatekeepers recorded the daily rhythm of park use in meticulous attendance logs. In the mid-1860s, about half the visitors entered between 3 and 6 P.M.; 4 to 5 P.M. was the most popular carriage-driving hour. In January carriage riding sank with the sun; few rode after 5:00 P.M. Obviously, carriage riding was not tied to the workday clock. New Yorkers whose carriage ritual most commonly peaked between 4 and 5 P.M. but shifted with the seasons had a great deal of control over their leisure time. They were older retired men; middle-aged men wealthy enough to have retired early or powerful enough to set their own hours; young men enjoying their family's affluence; and, most important, women of what Thorstein Veblen would soon call "the leisure class."[13]

Elite New Yorkers established an unwritten set of social rules for park use: who should use the park, for what purpose, and at what time. In *The Mystery of Central Park*, a popular novel of the late nineteenth century, the heroine departs from the behavior expected of a wealthy heiress when she walks in the park "at a hideous hour every morning," shocking her idle rich friends, "who don't think it good form." The carriage of Henriette Seligman, wife of one the city's leading German-Jewish financiers, Stephen Birmingham writes, "always arrived at her door at precisely the same moment each day for her drive through Central Park, and neither the length nor the route of the excursion ever varied." Abby Maria Hall Ward (a banker's widow, who was friendly with the Minturns and whose brother-in-law John Ward signed Robert Minturn's petition of gentlemen and floated some of the Central Park bonds) invariably went in the afternoon, generally at 3:00 or 3:30. One day she headed to the park at 2:00, but as she noted in her diary, "it was too early—not pleasant." No entry appears more regularly in her diary of the mid-1870s than "drove to the park." In one month in fall 1875, for example, she took her carriage to the park on eighteen days. Her absences reveal as much as her presence. Illness, inclement weather, a rheumatic coachman, a lame horse, carpet cleaning, family visits, and summer trips to Saratoga and Newport interrupted her daily park routine. When her daughter-in-law and grandchildren went home after a month's visit that kept her too busy for driving, she promptly picked up a friend and headed for Central Park. She never drove to the park on Sundays.[14]

Newspapers noted the paucity of expensive carriages during the hottest months of the summer and their return to the park in late September and early October. One reported of a Saturday in October 1860 that there were now in the park "more of the fashionable classes of our citizens, whose prancing steeds and gilded carriages have been seen at Saratoga, Newport and other famous resorts during the past summer." Carriage riding as a percentage of park use peaked in October, November, and March, when about three-quarters of the visitors came in carriages. In October 1866 from 5 to 6 P.M., 92 percent came in carriages and another 1 percent on horseback. At such times, Central Park was the playground of New York's upper classes. "In New York," a newspaper noted in 1864, when the fall "season" opened, "there are only two fashionable places of amusement—the Park and the Opera. . . . The Park will be thronged with splendid equipages, the Opera with splendidly dressed ladies and gentlemen. . . . There will be new walks, new trees and new drives at the Park, and new singers, new operas, and new scenery at the Opera. Between the private carriages at the Park and the private boxes at the Opera there will be ample opportunity for display."[15]

Although horseback riders were a relatively small group—fifty to a hundred thousand a year—they too were generally wealthy.[16] Even some of those counted as pedestrians were dropped off and picked up at park entrances by their coachmen. Other wealthy New Yorkers walked to the park in an era when long walks were a common form of exercise and recreation.

At the same time that rich New Yorkers announced themselves and claimed social recognition by riding, driving, and sometimes even walking in Central Park, they also negotiated their place within the social constellation. Owning a carriage and riding in the park established one's membership in the city's upper class. In November 1860 the *Herald* observed that "commodores, lawyers, editors, importers, butchers, shipping merchants, bakers, hotel keepers, bankers, politicians, and aldermen sweep the drives of Central Park every afternoon with their fast teams, whose value ranges from $2,000 to $12,000." "These days," it concluded, "to have money and not own fast horses . . . is to be nobody." Yet, as the *Herald*'s eclectic list of occupations indicates, the moneyed class was diverse, including not only merchants from old Knickerbocker families but also newly wealthy wholesale butchers and even foreign-born politicians. Central Park, as "the great rendezvous of the polite world" (in the *Herald*'s words) served as a unifying institution for this increasingly divided elite. The arriviste New York aristocrat, one commentator said, immediately "buys a lot on Fifth Avenue, puts up a palatial residence . . . sports his gay team in Central Park, carpets his sidewalk, [and] gives two or three parties."[17] On the park drives, wealthy New Yorkers spatially constituted themselves as a class each afternoon.

In the first third of the nineteenth century, a largely New England–born group of merchants such as Minturn and Grinnell had challenged the dominance of old Knickerbocker families like the Beekmans over New York's elite circles; by the 1850s the two groups had intermarried. Yet at the same time and increasingly over the next two decades, waves of newcomers entered the elite. In the thirty years before the opening of the park, the number of New Yorkers worth more than a hundred thousand dollars multiplied seven times, and accumulation accelerated as railroads, finance, and Civil War profiteering swelled the ranks and bank accounts of the upper class. By the late 1860s denunciations and satires of nouveau-riche war profiteers were rife in the city's social commentary; the standard portrait of these "sybarites of shoddy" or "shoddyites," as they were often called (after the cheap goods they sold), invariably took note of their lavish carriages and "striking liveries." Traditional Protestant strictures on leisure and display were easing. "The fortunes of many old families had been vastly increased by Civil War profits," writes one chronicler of New York high society, "and many more young men than ever found no need to labor on Wall Street or anywhere else." James Gordon Bennett, Jr., son of the *Herald*'s founder and publisher came home from Paris in 1861 to serve in the Union navy—on the family yacht. After the war, he became one of the leaders of the city's (and Central Park's) "fast set."[18]

"No society in the world," Junius Browne wrote in 1869, "has more divisions and subdivisions than ours—more ramifications and inter-ramifications,—more circles within circles—more segments and parts of segments." Browne offered five categories to describe "the grand divisions" among the wealthy. In the 1860s and 1870s wealthy German Americans developed their own networks and hierarchies. By the 1890s, as historian David Hammack shows, New York City had at least five relatively distinct social elites: "three consisted of British-American Protestants—those who most valued wealth, ancestry, or cultivation—others consisted of German Christians and German Jews."[19] Probably the sharpest visible divide within upper-class circles was between "old wealth" (cultivation and decorous behavior) and "new wealth" (flaunting of possessions). But "old wealth" in New York was rarely very old, in the European sense at any rate.

The antebellum years in New York City were later remembered as the "Golden Age of Society." Edith Wharton, herself a Jones and Schermerhorn descendant and a child of this world, who later eulogized Minturn's grandson as one of the last of the "American gentlemen," gave her world a classic expression in *The Age of Innocence*. Speaking presumably of the 1830s and 1840s, Mrs. Newland Archer comments in the novel, "When I was a girl, . . . only the people one knew had carriages." The small group of early and mid-nineteenth-century carriage owners that Wharton knew from family connections were among those who had launched the cultural offensive for Central Park in the early 1850s, recognizing, as social arbiter Nathaniel P. Willis put it back in 1844, that "as a metropolis of wealth and fashion, New York has one great deficiency—that of a *driving park*."[20] Now it had remedied that lack.

Robert Minturn died barely six years after the carriage drives opened; within another decade two-thirds of the gentlemen with whom he had hatched the idea of a public park would also be dead. As the generation of merchant princes died off, the older republican ideology of stewardship, including the civic obligation of wealthy families to act as models of moral conduct, also began to fade. Although Abby Ward, who was almost as old as the century, and a few other members of Minturn's social circle could still be found on the drives in the 1870s, the children of merchant princes did not always share their parents' earnest moralism. Robert Minturn, Jr., for example, recalled his father's disapproval of the growing disposition of young people in the 1860s toward "extravagance in dress in the streets of New York."[21]

Unlike such elite institutions as the men's clubs or the boxes at the Academy of Music, Central Park's carriage drives posed no entrance barriers based on family background, source of wealth, or even religion. All one needed was money. The carriage parade marked (and encouraged) the increasing openness of the city's social circles to new wealth. French composer Jacques Offenbach saw this mixture of openness and snobbery as characteristic of a society "where work and the dollar determine the only aristocracy." Visiting the park with a prominent New York gentleman, he noted that his companion "bowed very low to some people," but "barely touched the edge of his hat" to others. Asked about his behavior, the New Yorker explained that the "gentleman I have just greeted so respectfully . . . is worth a million dollars. This other passing now is worth only a hundred thousand. . . . I greet him with less ceremony."[22]

Central Park responded to, and hastened, this redefinition of "society" on the principle of wealth rather than breeding; it "stir[red] up the fashionable world," said the *Herald*, "changing the lines that have so long been in existence and remodeling the aristocratic circles on a new test." Within the open-air social world of Central Park no one exemplified the new style of display more than Park Commissioner Belmont. As early as the 1840s, a youthful Belmont had allied with a circle of younger Knickerbockers to challenge their genteel elders; now in the 1860s he had a grander stage. Every morning before work he drove through the park in a two-seater carriage "painted maroon with a scarlet stripe on the wheels," the coachmen outfitted in "maroon coats with scarlet piping and silver buttons embossed with 'the Belmont crest' . . . and black satin knee breeches with silver buckles." The spectacle impressed even the reserved Abby Ward. After she drove past Belmont in the park one day, she noted in her diary the sight of "his four in hand sleigh, he on the box, scarlet plumes on the horse's head." It was the only time that she ever recorded seeing anyone but a friend.[23]

The extravagance of this "King of Fifth Avenue," as Belmont was called, brought a "continental outlook and culture" to upper-class New York, one historian has observed. But in the 1850s and 1860s, older styles and practices still held considerable sway. The lumbering coaches, staid horses, and modestly garbed servants of what Nathaniel Willis dubbed the "Knickerbocracy" bespoke a "conspicuous modesty" that offset the "conspicuous consumption" of the arrivistes. For a minority even that display was not reserved enough. Many of the newly rich German bankers apparently stuck to walking because they believed carriages were only for "lazy men."[24]

By the 1880s the late afternoon drive in Central Park had become a fixed ritual for the "circles within circles" of elite New Yorkers who took one another's measure.

Women of Leisure, Fashionable and Not So Fashionable

Some wealthy New Yorkers refused to join the carriage parade; others asserted their superiority through critical commentary on the passing scene. "The rich in their carriages," wrote one newspaper reporter, "occupy their thoughts chiefly in criticizing each other's dresses and equipages." George Templeton Strong, who had business and social connections with the Minturn crowd, often joined his wife Ellie in her regular rides through the park. Still, he grumbled about the "broad torrent of vehicular gentility." "The profits of shoddy and petroleum were largely represented. Not a few of the ladies who were driving in the most sumptuous turn-outs, with liveried servants, looked as if they might have been cooks or chambermaids a very few years ago." Where appearances became the standard of social position, there was the disturbing possibility of misinterpretation or even deception. After all, the notorious abortionist Madame Restell, in Paris fashions and dazzling diamonds, drove her magnificent barouche through the park every afternoon. And Josie Woods, operator of the city's most exclusive brothel, owned a luxurious Victoria and employed liveried footmen.[25]

Guidebook authors and newspaper reporters instructed spectators on how to assess the carriage parade correctly. Lest park visitors be taken in by its "brilliant appearance," the moralistic Junius Browne revealed the reality behind the "elaborate tinseling." In one carriage, he found "fleshy, gross, and very showily dressed" women—"the wife and the sister of a contractor who made a fortune during the war by defrauding the government, and who ten years ago played 'friendly games' with marked cards." Just ahead of them, he spotted a carriage of women, who the "newly rich women imagine" to be "leaders of fashion and privately long for an introduction." But the carriage actually "bears a brace of unfortunates whose mode of livelihood is no mystery in Mercer Street," a thoroughfare known for its brothels. The one carriage that reflected "true refinement and breeding" was also subject to misinterpretation, precisely because it was plain, and its "plainly dressed" inhabitants, who "wear no diamonds," were "free from all appearances of affectation."[26]

However misogynistic, the commentary of Strong, Browne, and others recognized that women more than men dominated the carriage parade and shaped its larger social meaning. Gatekeepers did not keep track of the sex of park visitors, but impressionistic accounts often depict women as park "regulars"; drawings and paintings of park carriages also often show more women than men. "Scores of splendid equipages and beautiful women are on view daily in the grand drives," noted a British visitor.[27]

Wealthy women (as Thorstein Veblen would later point out) served as emblems of their husbands' wealth and judges of their own and others' status. In nineteenth-century New York more than in other cities, historian Frederick Jaher observes, women "organized most of the social affairs, appointed the arbiters, and decided who belonged and who received the lion's share of publicity." But despite their social dominion, wealthy women remained economically vulnerable, for men controlled most of the wealth. To secure their economic position, and especially that of their daughters, they were required to take an active part in the marriage market, and here, too, Central Park provided a new and important arena. Clara Jerome, wife of wealthy sportsman Leonard Jerome, felt vastly inferior to Caroline Perry Belmont (the wife of her husband's friend and rival August Belmont) because Caroline could drive "herself at high speed around Central Park," whereas Clara was "unable to handle any reins adroitly." She was "determined," her husband's biographer writes, that "her daughters should be of harder fiber, and she supervised their upbringing in detail," insisting in particular on riding lessons. Perhaps it was this "education" that brought her daughter Jennie to the attention and affections of the ardent English sportsman and horseman, Lord Randolph Churchill. Seeing and being seen in the park was part of the "job" of wealthy women, a way of establishing their position and that of their family and of maintaining their livelihood. Participation in high society required as much energy and acquired some of the

For these women seated along the Wisteria Arbor (east of the Mall near 70th Street) in the 1860s the park offered a new place to socialize beyond the reach of demanding husbands and children.

same characteristics for women as banks and mercantile businesses did for their husbands.[28]

Wealthy women no doubt also found their daily carriage drives a pleasant, even liberating, experience as well, a ritual by which to assert more control over their lives. In the first half of the century, codes of correct conduct had warned young women against appearing in public alone; even their "coming out" took place at home within a family circle of appropriate acquaintances. Movement through the city was tied to a regular series of duties and obligations—church-going, charitable work, visiting friends, and tending sick relatives. After 1859 the Central Park drive (like the shopping district of the Ladies Mile along Broadway from 14th Street to 23rd) offered women a less confined space—and for recreation, not duty. Edith Wharton recalled that after her mother completed "the onerous and endless business of 'calling,'" she would drive to the park and "hunt for violets and hepaticas in the secluded dells of the Ramble."[29]

Women could drive through the park with a friend, a brother, a suitor, or even alone—well, for the wealthiest, not quite alone. A coachman was pretty much obligatory. "When I drove the first pony phaeton ever seen on Fifth Avenue," May King Van Rensselaer recalls of the 1860s, "members of the Union Club, as I passed, shook their heads and feared the young Miss King was rather 'fast.'" A turn-of-the-century carriage-driving etiquette guide permitted women to drive carriages "properly safeguarded and within reasonable limits" but never without a servant: "No woman can 'afford' to keep a horse who cannot also afford a capable and presentable servant to attend her." Similarly, a society woman might ride on the park's bridle paths, with a groom or riding master following discreetly behind.[30]

In the controlled environment of Central Park elite women could enjoy themselves without worrying about the needs of others, and they were "protected" from urban street life. "Good conduct" is "so thoroughly established" in the park, a magazine noted in 1861, "that many ladies walk daily . . . without attendance." Abby Ward encountered the curses of beggars on downtown streets; she met no such unpleasant epithets in the park.[31] Women were, in turn, expected to behave "properly." They could meet friends there, encounter, or at least inspect, people who were richer (or poorer) as well as more (or less) socially established than they, survey the latest fashions, read a book under a willow tree, or just do nothing. In a society anxious to insulate such women from the "insults" of city life, Central Park offered contact with that intensely urban world, while controlling and limiting its terms.

The Carriage Parade and the City

New Yorkers in the park—both men and women—were thus engaging in an internal class dialogue that helped shift the attention of the rich toward wealth (rather than work or family name) as a standard of value and display of that wealth as a claim on esteem. Still, wealth alone was an inherently unstable standard; new wealth continually undermined old. Rich New Yorkers circling the park simultaneously marked the outer boundaries of their class and jockeyed for the best position on the inside.

If Central Park figured prominently in the lives of wealthy New Yorkers, the reverse was also true: the well-to-do were quite central to the park. Particularly in the 1860s the carriage parade became one of the primary frames through which the park was perceived. Junius Browne insisted that it "is open to all and that the poor enjoy it more than the rich," but he devoted only one paragraph in *The Great Metropolis* to "the laborer or mechanic . . . luxuriating in the mere absence of toil," and spent four pages detailing the afternoon carriage parade's "worth and wealth." Newspapers described the "fairy circle of flashing equipages" (sometimes including the names of passengers), even while insisting upon the democratic character of the park. "Probably in no other country would it be possible to permit all classes of persons to commingle as they do here," was a typical newspaper comment from the mid-1860s. But an equally typical newspaper account declared: "London has its Hyde Park, Paris the Bois de Boulogne, where each day the *elite* congregate, where rich and handsome, gay and well dressed *dames du monde* may be seen, gazed at, admired. New York, the capital of the New World, was not to be outdone in that respect by either London or Paris."[32]

What did those outside the elite circles make of this display of luxury and extravagance or the counterdisplay of restraint and refinement? "The hard-working mechanic . . . sees the handsome carriage" and "envies him who has such abundant wealth," Browne concluded, assuming, as did others, that the carriage parade established and legitimated the cultural authority of the rich. Ordinary New Yorkers could purchase a pamphlet, *The Tally-ho*, identifying the colors of each coach (and its drivers) in the annual parade of the Coaching Club up Fifth Avenue to 59th Street, through the park to Mount St. Vincent, and back down Fifth. Yet the new familiarity of the wealthy classes could erode as well as enhance their stature. The crowds that stood on the Terrace—"the best place to view the array of horseflesh and vehicles"—expressed awe at the "display of beauty and fashion" but offered "not a few shrewd criticisms . . . on their appearances," reporters said. Ethel Dana recalls in her memoir of growing up on the Upper East Side that her Irish nurse "expressed strong disapproval when a lady drove by in an open victoria wearing a feathered bonnet and a dress with velvet panels and cascading fringes and flounces," though she respected the "ladies in plain bonnets who were driven in broughams by the coachman only, and pulled by one horse in a handsome but quiet harness."[33]

Spectators, thus, both looked up to the occupants of the carriages and brought them to their own level. One contemporary story depicts two men in Central Park watching *New York Times* editor Henry Raymond and financier and sportsman Leonard Jerome passing by in an expensive carriage. "Reckon I'd like to know what Raymond and Jerome are talking about," one comments. "Just hosses," responds his friend.[34] Similarly, the city's nascent gossip columns simultaneously presented the rich as a breed apart and as people just like everyone else, with the same human problems and tragedies.

Some who walked along the park paths did not feel even this ambivalent admiration, but looked on the rich with indifference, even contempt. An August 1860 account suggests that German immigrant children threw rocks at passing carriages. That same summer, the Tammany Democratic organ, the *Leader*, published a report by "Timothy Dismal," who argued that tensions between the patrons of the carriage drives and the footpaths were a good reason to stay away: "I do not often visit that now famous locality," he wrote, "as I have understood that 'cold shoulder' is the kind of refreshment which humble people are most likely to be furnished with thereabouts. Besides, I cannot afford to hire either riding horses or carriages, and I hear that pedestrians have acquired a bad habit

In the 1860s working-class New Yorkers most often visited the park while serving the rich as nursemaids and coachmen.

of being accidentally run over in that neighborhood." Walt Whitman observed the "oceanic tide of New York's wealth and 'gentility'" in Central Park in May 1879, and found the carriage parade "an impressive, rich, interminable circus on a grand scale, full of action and color," but as he peered through the windows of the richest carriages, he saw "faces almost corpse-like, so ashy and listless." The American rich, he concluded, "are ill at ease, much too conscious . . . , and far from happy . . . there is nothing in them which we who are poor and plain need at all envy."[35]

If the poor did not always envy the rich, they nonetheless got employment from them in a host of service jobs (as coachmen, grooms, and nurses, for example) created to cater to the needs of wealthy parkgoers. Real estate promoters, merchants seeking out-of-town clients, and organizers of the nascent tourist industry benefited even more handsomely from the growing perception of New York as a center of wealth and fashion. "The effect of Central Park in increasing the wealth of New York, by helping to draw to it people of fortune from all parts of the Union, has unquestionably been very great," the *Times* reported at the end of its first full decade of use. It is "fast becoming the chief attraction not only of New-York, but of the whole country," the *Tribune* boasted in 1860. Tourists became one of its most important constituencies, and those who did not visit "viewed" the park in the stereographs, lithographs, and illustrated weeklies that advertised it to a national audience.[36]

Newspapers highlighted the celebrities—from Mary Todd Lincoln to General Santa Anna of Mexico—who toured the park, some suggesting that it could become the nation's leading summer "watering place," combining "rural scenery" with access to the "sights, shows and society of the metropolis." Yet in the 1860s, New York remained primarily a commercial city, and most out-of-town visitors were probably there on business—negotiating loans, placing orders, arranging distribution networks. One "custom maker of gentlemen's wear" published its own guidebook to the park, presumably with visiting businessmen in mind.[37] That the city's most important noncommercial public space attracted these commercial visitors must have pleased those merchants who had predicted that Central Park would promote economic growth.

As New York became the center of both fashion and a fashion industry, the park's symbolic and commercial aspects became closely intertwined. In urging visiting carriage makers "to spend at least one half day in the Park and on Fifth Avenue" and promoting Central Park as "the mistress of carriage fashions in the United States," the *Hub and New York Coachmakers' Magazine* was insisting on the importance of New York manufacturers (and its own publication) to the national industry. The "carriage trade," whether social group or manufacturing business, relied on Central Park to make New York a center of both.[38]

The Middle-Class Park

For every four million New Yorkers who arrived at the park in carriages and on horseback in the 1860s, another three million or so came on foot. Few came from the city's poorest neighborhoods, a sizable number came from the city's upper circles, but most were probably part of a vaguely defined "middling" class, about one-third of the city. Families of independent artisans, young professionals, and shopkeepers made their way to the park by foot or streetcar. They came to skate, stroll through the Ramble, hear the free Saturday afternoon band concerts, picnic when the lawns were open, flirt on a boat ride, promenade down the Mall, feed the swans on the Lake, admire the decorative bridges and the richly ornamented Terrace, and take their children to the zoo that was developing behind the Arsenal. There is little direct evidence of exactly who took part in the park activities. We do know, for example, that a youthful law clerk named Frank Fetherston often walked up to the park from his boarding hotel on Bleecker Street, because he recorded those trips in his diary, but we do not know what he did there.[39] All we know for certain is what was available to visitors on a summer Saturday, for example, or a winter evening or a Sunday.

At 4:30 P.M. on Saturday, July 9, 1859, Harvey B. Dodworth struck up his band for a free concert in the Central Park Ramble. At this inaugural concert four to five thousand people listened to "compositions of the higher and more instructive kind . . . intermingled with what is commonly known as 'popular music,'" according to the *Times*. Three weeks later the band played such diverse selections as a quartet from *Rigoletto*, the "Wedding March" from Mendelssohn's *Midsummer Night's Dream*, a "Teutonic" polka, and "My Love Is Like a Red, Red Rose." For the next quarter century, Dodworth's band would offer about twenty Saturday afternoon band concerts a season to crowds of forty-five thousand or more.[40]

Olmsted had rejected the common council's offer to finance the concerts because he feared that aldermen would attach "embarrassing conditions" to the funding; instead, the park board turned to the safer patronage of "public spirited and generous gentlemen" like themselves. Even when that generosity ran dry, the commissioners kept control out of the hands of local politicians on the common council, with support first from the street railway companies (which profited from the increased use of their lines on Saturdays) and then from the board's own funds.[41]

Retaining financial control of the concerts enabled the board and Olmsted, as he wrote, "to sustain that character in the concerts that I deem essential." Dodworth played an eclectic mix of pieces: "The programme is so constructed," the commissioners explained in 1865, "as to give each class a fair share of its favorite music, without admitting anything not in keeping with the standard of all the surroundings of the Park. . . . The aim is, on the whole, to be a little in advance of the average taste." After the first year the commissioners shifted the concerts from the Ramble to the Mall, thereby allowing for chairs, benches, and formal seating.[42]

The concert crowds responded to the setting with the "quiet and decorum" that the press and the commissioners thought appropriate. After the first concert the *Tribune* reported happily: "We saw no conduct which would have been out of place or inconvenient to the most scrupulous or delicate nerves in the private garden of a gentleman." Parkgoers dressed up for the concerts too. Newspaper accounts regularly described the crowds as including "richly dressed ladies," "elegantly attired gentlemen," and "daintily-attired damsels."[43]

Still, a free outdoor concert could not maintain the formality of an evening at the Academy of Music. Beginning in 1861, the commissioners allowed concertgoers to sit on the grass—not the seating arrangement likely to be used by those in rich attire. In addition, the absence of an admission charge encouraged people to bring along their children, who could not be expected to follow the music with the same "quiet enjoyment" as their parents. When Dodworth

This early (pre-1864) band concert on the Mall apparently drew a heavily female crowd.

played a polka, the *Herald* reported in 1865, children set "at naught the frigid rules of etiquette and the regulations of the Park Commissioners [and] . . . did what many of their elders longed to do—they danced to the music." Free admission and the outdoor setting encouraged another transgression of more formal etiquette: people came and left while the concert was in progress. One newspaper even recommended that Dodworth divide his programs evenly between classical and "light" music so that the admirers of each would "know what time they can roam about without losing their favorite pieces." In 1860 a *New York Times* reporter implicitly compared the park "concert-room" to the Academy of Music, noting, "There is no reservation of front seats, and no distinction of pit and parquette, gallery and dress-circle. . . . The barriers and hedges of society for the time being are let down;—unfortunately also a few of its decencies are forgotten." The reporter complained of "a gentleman in a seedy coat," who blew cigar smoke in his face, Germans with beer on their breath, and people who drummed their fingers or hummed along with the music.[44]

Although the "promiscuous assemblage" of the park concert crowd ruffled the *Times*'s sensibilities, other papers found it "orderly, well-conducted and respectable in the full sense of the word."[45] *Respectable* was a term middle-class New Yorkers used to describe themselves or members of the working classes who behaved, spoke, and dressed as they did. Unskilled and semiskilled immigrant workers—the Irish laborers who built the park, for example—were seldom accorded this label.

Reporters attributed the respectability of concert crowds to the *absence* of the city's lower orders—that is, probably two-thirds or so of the New York population. The *Herald* described the concert crowd as "respectable" just after it noted that the assemblage contained no "'roughs' or loafers." The *Tribune* observed that the concerts "will further establish the remarkable popularity of the Park with a somewhat large class . . . , whose tastes are above grog shops and lager bier gardens but whose pockets are not equal to Newport or Saratoga." Later that same summer, the *Herald* said the concert crowd was "somewhat more pretentious [than] that of the mechanic and laboring classes."[46]

Newspaper reporters did at times spot "hard-fisted mechanics" and "fellows of German persuasion" in those crowds. German immigrants, among them substantial numbers of skilled artisans, brought along a strong musical tradition and were probably the best represented working-class group in the park; German newspapers covered the concerts closely from the start. But most working-class New Yorkers were at their jobs on Saturday afternoons. Even clerks and other office workers had only recently gained a free Saturday half-day. "There was," the *Sun* noted of an 1869 concert, "a goodly quota of clerks who pay weekly dues to the Early Closing Association, and get a free afternoon once a week accordingly." "These young men," it added, "sported their finest hats, their sleekest broadcloth, their thinnest shoes and their broadest grins" in the hopes of winning "recognition" from "the young damsels who have very little to do and a good deal more finery to wear than they can put on at one showing."[47]

More women than men came to the park concerts. Probably the largest number of working-class women were nurses taking their charges for an outing. Some women, no doubt, were the wives of carpenters and blacksmiths who were still at their shops. Most were wives and daughters of shopkeepers and professionals. As with the upper classes, the park, particularly on Saturday afternoon, offered them (especially young, unmarried women) a proper and safe public setting in which to see others and be seen. And if the shopkeeper's daughter or the youthful clerk could not attract attention with an expensive equipage, then fine clothing could provide a ready substitute. As one report noted, the women turned out in "hats and bonnets of every conceivable shape and color."[48]

Carriages appeared in larger-than-usual numbers on concert days, but there was an even greater jump in pedestrian attendance. The wealthy kept themselves literally above the crowd, listening to the music from the comfort of their carriages. "Without the inconvenience of descending," as one guidebook put it, the wealthy "lolled back on their easy cushions" in the carriages, looming over the heads of the rest of the crowd, symbolizing and reinforcing the class hierarchy Central Park was supposed to transcend.[49]

Skating Mania, A "Respectable and Gay Assemblage of Both Sexes"

The opening of the park unleashed what the *Post* called "skating mania," the revival of a sport that had been fading in New York as the growing city swallowed up existing ponds. In the late 1850s and throughout the 1860s ice skating drew enormous crowds—more than 40 percent of the pedestrians in the mid-1860s—to the Lake south of the Ramble. On an average winter day about thirty thousand *additional* people came to skate or to watch others. Some days the crowds were immense—upwards of seventy-five to a hundred thousand people. About 95 percent of all pedestrians entering the park on a typical January day apparently came to skate.[50]

Newspapers celebrated the skating ponds as evidence of American democracy. And to be sure, many more New Yorkers put on skates than mounted carriages. The Central Park Skate Emporium (a private enterprise that capitalized on this public sport) advertised "skates to suit everybody, from 50 cents to $25" in 1859. Skates could also be rented at the park from licensed vendors for as little as ten cents per hour, although a one-dollar deposit was required.[51]

Still, the skating ponds also reflected the social divisions of mid-nineteenth-century New York. Even the relatively modest charges for skate rental were out of the reach of the poorest New Yorkers, as was the expense of getting to the park by public transportation. The *Leader* noted that many people "need warm shoes and stockings before they may enjoy exercise on skates." Time may have established a more substantial barrier than money for working people eager to skate in the park, at least on weekday evenings, when skating drew some of its largest crowds. Travel time to the park and back could amount to as much as two hours—a formidable addition to a typical ten-hour workday. For lower Manhattan residents, a trip to the park on the Third Avenue horse railway (the most popular route) took forty-eight minutes, followed by a ten-to-twenty-minute walk across 71st Street. Hackney coaches were available at the streetcar terminals to avoid what Olmsted called the "long and bleak walk" to the Lake, but fares were exorbitant. By the 1860s, thousands of working families lived within easy walking distance of the park, though most working-class families, especially the Irish, still lived in lower Manhattan.[52]

Working-class adults may have been reluctant to wear poor-quality skates and inexpensive clothing when all those around them had the best equipment money could buy, but working-class children, especially boys, may have been willing to go skating with the cheapest available equipment. Some poor youths (who no doubt also skated) earned money by fastening on the skates of more affluent patrons. When an "overdressed pompous youth" asked the price, the *Post* reported, one boy replied: "Well my price to decent people is three cents, but I'll charge *you* five dollars." When the *Times* said everyone from the "ragged urchin with one broken skate to the *millionaire* in his richly robed carriage," skated on the Lake, it may have been painting an accurate portrait, although misleading in its implications of mixed-class socializing.[53]

Still, unlike the structured and orchestrated space of the drives and paths, the park's lakes were an open terrain—too open for some New Yorkers. Around 1863 the wealthy began to segregate themselves in private skating ponds outside the park. The most prominent of those arenas, the Fifth Avenue Pond, was, the *Herald* said, the "resort of the higher classes who desire to be select in their skating as well as in everything else." As the overdressed and pompous departed, Central Park Lake became less elite and also less socially diverse. By 1867 the *Sun* described the park lakes as accommodating those "who cannot afford to expend the price of admission to private ponds." Like the Saturday concerts, ice skating appears to have attracted predominantly a "middling" crowd of clerks, tradespeople, skilled workers, and their families.[54]

The open-air setting and "the very influence of the exercise" permitted certain departures from parlor manners. "The breathing of highly oxygenated air," explained the *World* in 1870, "causes the blood to flow more rapidly, the spirits to be more buoyant and less inclined to submit to the trammels of society, which . . . must be thrown out before the amusement can be enjoyed to the full." On the untrammeled skating pond, the *World* continued, friends met in ways more flexible than on the street or at the ball. They "can devote as much time as they please to a friend, and enjoy greater freedom of action, can laugh and converse, and thoroughly enjoy life without fear of giving offense to any one." Nevertheless, provision was made to deal with possible offense. "Any person observing any act of indecorum," the official regulations decreed, "may signalize a park-keeper by holding aloft or waving a handkerchief," and skating took place under the watchful eyes of the park police.[55]

Women may have especially enjoyed this sanctioned and controlled break from middle-class conventions of public behavior. Middle-class women had few opportunities for energetic, unrestrained amusement and exercise. Skating provided, the daughter of a clergyman recalled, "a way of showing off" equivalent to "driving spirited horses . . . for men." It was one of the rare activities in which it was acceptable for "respectable women" to display their ankles in public. Moreover, the presence of women on the Lake, the *News* reported in early 1861, "renders the place more attractive to the men, who would not come out in anything like such numbers for the mere sake of individual exercise or to look at one another." Not only did the skating pond bring young men and women together, but it often gathered them in the dark and in close physical proximity. (The regular winter closing time of eight o'clock was extended to midnight in the skating season.) "It is not, indeed, until the dark hours that the

Winslow Homer's *Skating in the Central Park* shows the freer decorum (including women revealing their ankles in public) that prevailed on the skating pond.

fun culminates," one guidebook pointed out, "such hours better suiting, perhaps, the convenience of the lads, and the flirting proclivities of the lassies and lads both." Skating is "essentially a love-making medium, involving such timorous reliance of the trembling novice upon the trusty arm of the bold practitioner, such gallant arrests of tripping steps, such tender cautions against dangers seen and unseen." "Many a young fellow," said another guidebook of the same era, "has lost his heart, and skated himself into matrimony, on the Central Park pond."[56]

Initially, the commissioners set aside a separate Ladies' Pond (an extension of the main lake, west of the drive) to protect women from unwelcome male attention. They could bring male escorts, but unaccompanied men were banned, and the park police saw to it that "perfect order" was maintained. No doubt some women skaters found the male flirting (and catcalling) annoying and preferred to skate with female companions, but most apparently felt comfortable in the mixed environment of the Lake. Before the park opened, a local guide to skating said, "a lady on skates was . . . a rare and novel sight in this vicinity" and would have "outraged . . . feminine propriety," but "now the reverse is the case," and the nonskating woman is "tabooed as 'slow.'" When the *Herald* called the skating scene a "respectable *and* gay assemblage of both sexes," it captured the dual appeal of the lakes (and the park as a whole) for many middle-class men and women.[57]

For the rich the park was but one institution within a seasonal circuit that took them from the opera to summer resorts, but for the families of clerks, young professionals, and independent artisans there were few alternative places to assemble. Pressed by the rising costs of housing and the shrinking space of their homes, middle-class New Yorkers welcomed a beautiful, controlled, and free public space for respectable socializing and amusement.

The People's Day in the Park

Working-class families were largely excluded from Saturday afternoon concerts and wintertime skating because of their six-day workweek and the distance of their homes from the park. On Sunday, however, the most popular day of the week, when the park attracted about one-quarter of its visitors, the carriage riders ceased to dominate. Their numbers dropped by one-quarter; and the crowds of pedestrian parkgoers assumed a somewhat more proletarian character. Even on Sundays, New Yorkers arriving by carriage made up two-fifths of the park's visitors. "Six-day-toilers" and "the men, women, and children of the poorer classes" thronged the park, newspapers said, but the *Herald* noted of one crowd that it was "above the class that gravitates toward the engine house, the grog shop or the political club" and more typical of "the middle classes of our citizens." In fact, working-class families remained vastly underrepresented at Central Park, contributing no more than an eighth of the total annual visitors and a third of Sunday visitors.[58]

One important reason was money; at ten to twelve cents for a round trip by street railway, a family of five would have had to spend fifty to sixty cents, a substantial expenditure for skilled workers. Artisans (the park's own masons and blacksmiths, for example), who earned about three dollars per day by the mid-1860s, probably made up the largest group of working-class New Yorkers to use the park. For unskilled laborers, on the other hand, such transportation costs could represent a third of a day's wage ($1.50 in 1864), a burdensome expenditure.[59]

For workers who lived beyond walking distance, a family visit to Central Park was probably a special outing, perhaps on the most important summer holiday. On the Fourth of July, 1865, a huge crowd of close to a hundred thousand New Yorkers gathered, and "the people reigned supreme," said the *Herald*. It was "the People's Day in the Park," when "many of those present now saw our urban gardens of delight for the first time." The Fourth of July was "the only day in the year on which the working classes can enjoy the liberty of the Common, stretch themselves on the grass and listen to music on the Mall." Newspapers stressed the working-class character and style of these Independence Day crowds, the lively presence of "the artisan, the laborer, the shop girl, the kitchen deities, and the rest of the working classes" and the conspicuous absence of "the elegantly appointed carriages."[60]

German families were in the majority on July 4, 1866. For that day at least they transformed the park. "Here was the rotund Falstaffian form of the father lying under one of the trees near the Mall, calling aloud in stentorian tones for the dozen of young Fatherlanders that formed his family. Before him is a coil of Bologna sausage . . . an odiferous head cheese . . . and a jar of lager flanked with Limburger and pretzels." Dodworth acknowledged the audience with a program "suitable for the occasion and the audience," including the overture to *Dichten und Bauer* and the "Sturmoogel Galop." A few years later the *Tribune* reported, "The placards 'Keep off the grass' and 'Do not touch the flowers' were unheeded" on the Fourth of July, and added, "To judge by the constant devotion to Gambrinus [the mythical inventor of beer], a great many of the visitors were foreigners."[61]

But a single "people's day" in Central Park was a long way from the democratic "people's park" journalists sometimes assumed. Working people were not absent from Central Park in the 1860s, but neither were they represented in anything approaching their percentage of the population. Moreover, different classes tended to use the park on different days of the week, at different times of the year, and in different ways. An elaborate class choreography of use sharply restricted, though it did not eliminate, interclass contact in Central Park. And in any case, two-thirds to three-quarters of the city's residents seldom or never came to the park at all.

Jones Wood and Working-Class Culture

One reason so many stayed away was the difficulty for those with little money, long work hours, few holidays, and many children to get to a park far from the center of the city. But it was also a matter of choice. No workers, as far as we know, left memoirs or diaries expressing their views about Central Park. There are many indications, however, that in the late 1850s and the 1860s working-class New Yorkers—especially immigrants—spent their limited leisure time and money in ways that were not permitted or encouraged in the park.

In the space that had almost become the public park of New York City, the Jones Wood estate, working people discovered a more congenial place to play. The Schermerhorn and Jones families quickly realized that though they had won the battle to keep the grounds in private hands, they had lost the war over uptown development. "The nabobs that enjoyed its cool, sequestered shades," the *Times* had reported, "found the avenues and streets butting them hard, lager bier [sellers] setting up tents on all their outskirts, their orchards and gardens tempting vagrants to break the Sunday and anti-stealing commandments." Seeing the handwriting on the wall, the families leased a portion of their Upper East Side estate for a commercial picnic ground and hotel.[62]

Many ethnic groups—especially Germans—retreated to Jones Wood for summer excursions and festivals, where they could listen and dance to band music, play games of chance, and watch gymnastic performances.

The former Jones family mansion at 71st Street was converted into a hotel and restaurant, and picnic grounds, swings, hobbyhorses, a dance pavilion, quoit grounds, bowling alleys, a billiard saloon, and a shooting range were all provided. Sometimes the new pleasure grounds were open to the "general public," but more often the proprietors rented the facilities as a whole to ethnic, social, athletic, or religious groups, or even to other entrepreneurs, for excursions or festivals. Though the grounds were as distant from downtown Manhattan as Central Park, working-class New Yorkers flocked to them. More than forty such festivals took place at Jones Wood during the summer of 1862.[63]

German societies patronized Jones Wood with particular enthusiasm. By the early 1870s, "German master" John F. Schultheis had taken over the management. "There are benches and tables in the German fashion," noted one contemporary visitor, "where the holiday-makers can sit close to the water; at one side is an immense wooden structure used as a ball-room: another larger building between the entrance and the house [is] used for gymnastic exercises." Even before Schultheis took over, German immigrants had adopted Jones Wood as a space where they could maintain their traditions and ties. They could picnic in family groups, dance to German music, watch gymnastic exhibitions, drink lager beer, and affirm their loyalties to their *Vereine* (the hundreds of social groups popular in Germany).[64] Even in the less constrained atmosphere of Fourth of July celebrations, Germans had no similar opportunities at Central Park.

The 1863 Pfingsten celebration at Jones Wood was typical of dozens of such events in this period. On Monday morning, May 25, a procession of three to four thousand German musical, athletic, and military society members marched up the Bowery and over to the East River, to board a barge or a steamboat for Jones Wood. More than fifty-five thousand other Germans (and some people of other nationalities) came on the Second and Third Avenue street railways to join them. "The amusements of the day," the *World* reported, "consisted of the athletic exercises of the Turn Verein, the singing of the glee clubs, the dancing at the different stands, singing and roaming about under the trees. . . . Above all there was no lack anywhere of lager, and four-horse teams bringing it up continually from the city could hardly keep up with the supply." Even when Jones Wood events were not under specifically German sponsorship, Germans often dominated the scene. The July 1859 Mammoth Musical Festival featured, for a twenty-five-cent admission, an orchestra, fireworks, Tournoure's Circus, magic shows, balloon ascensions, and dancing, as well as offerings by German choral societies. "A visit to the ground," the *Tribune* promised, "will be equivalent to a voyage to Germany, for the very essence of German festal life will be generously displayed."[65]

The Scottish Caledonian Society also held its annual track-and-field games there before large crowds. Irish church groups, temperance societies, and literary associations rented Jones Wood for annual excursions and picnics. On June 23, 1859, St. Mary's Roman Catholic Church celebrated the eve of Corpus Christi with a Jones Wood excursion, at which fifteen thousand or so Irish Catholics enjoyed a brass band, "negro minstrels," a sword swallower, swings, merry-go-rounds, and speeches by prominent local pastors and politicians. "A surprising supply of fiddlers" played for dancing, it was reported, "in a style of rollicking gaiety and hearty good-humor that was eminently characteristic of the 'green sod.'" As was often true of the Irish-sponsored picnics, the event also raised money, in this instance for a new parochial school building.[66]

Under more purely commercial auspices, these gatherings were even more unrestrained. A prizefighting exhibition by the Irish-American boxing champ, John C. Heenan, brought, the *Tribune* typically complained, "thousands of thieves, pickpockets, murderers, pimps, and others of that class of sporting gentry" to Jones Wood. On July 4, 1859, two impresarios attracted ten to twelve thousand people for a festival featuring music, dancing, picnicking, beer drink-

Visitors to Jones Wood—unlike those to Central Park—could picnic on the grass and drink beer.

ing, sword swallowing, hobbyhorses, and swings. The unofficial events garnered as much interest as the official ones, and according to the *Tribune*, "all sorts of tricksters, roamed at large over the ground." A German with a shooting gallery offered two shots for three cents, a Spaniard threw knives and did other tricks, a young fellow took bets on whether anyone could knock a coin off a stick, and members of rival gangs went at each other with fists. A tightrope performance later that summer attracted "lewd women and rowdy men," grumbled the *Tribune*. Of course, decorum is often found in the eye of the beholder. The *Herald*, generally more tolerant of the city's immigrants, thought the day proceeded with "good order."[67]

New York City's working-class families made themselves at home in many other venues besides Jones Wood. Churches, ethnic associations, and male social clubs held excursions and celebrations at a variety of commercial pleasure grounds from Yorkville to Hoboken to Yonkers as well as at their own downtown buildings. Less directly ethnic in character, but still infused with ethnic loyalties, were myriad and interlocking street-based pursuits and institutions: saloons, gambling, prizefighting, fire companies, political clubs, street gangs. Commercial entrepreneurs attracted enthusiastic crowds to the theaters of the Bowery, the dime museums, and the hundreds of German beer gardens.[68]

These institutions collectively constituted New York's diverse and fragmented working-class culture at midcentury. Ethnic associations tended to be much more insular and traditional than the commercial institutions, which crossed ethnic as well as class lines, but both tended to be more family-centered than the largely male street and saloon life. The values of mutuality and reciprocity that the city's German and Irish communities sustained in their use of leisure time to raise money for benevolent organizations obviously did not extend to the market-dominated commercial culture. And whereas members of temperance societies and regular churchgoers tended to favor abstemiousness and greater self-control, partisans of the street scene were inclined to self-indulgence and boisterousness.

Leisure space, and even public space in general, was less a place of regular and coherent class assembly for members of New York's working families than such space was for the wealthy. There were important exceptions, of course. In May 1865, for example, the Workingmen's Union brought fifty thousand people to Jones Wood for an enormous picnic to launch a campaign for the eight-hour day. But the Fenian campaign to win freedom for Ireland by a plan to invade Canada gathered twice as many in the same spot the following year. The Fenian Rally—and innumerable smaller gatherings of Irish Catholic churches and German gymnastic societies—reflected the powerful ethnic accent in most working-class gatherings in these years. The associations that oversaw such leisure activities also incorporated an emerging middle class, often in leadership positions. If elite New Yorkers affirmed their common bonds through the fall carriage parade, working-class New Yorkers divided themselves into separate ethnic communities with their midsummer excursions.[69]

Divided among themselves, working-class New Yorkers also stood outside the public created by the wealthy and the middle class in Central Park. In some cases, working-class New Yorkers distanced themselves in order to maintain ethnic, rather than American, traditions and ties. In other cases, they preferred pursuits that the native-born (and often nativist) Protestant middle class would have disapproved: gambling, heavy drinking, Sunday sports, and prizefighting, for example. Often expressive working-class styles of public behavior departed from bourgeois dictates of restraint and formality. Such preferences and differences help to explain why working families formed such a limited part of Central Park's cultural public in its first decade of operation, why that public achieved neither the unity nor the democracy promised by promoters.

The distinctions between the world of Jones Wood and the world of Central Park were, of course, not absolute, nor was New York's broad and diverse working class completely absent from Central Park. The park's design as a pastoral landscape excluded the attractions of the commercial pleasure garden, but working-class New Yorkers also enjoyed pursuing their amusements in a natural setting. Germans, who tended to spend their leisure time in family groups, were particularly likely to visit the park on Sundays, for example, and the park's appeal seems to have been greatest among workers who were "above the class that gravitates toward the engine house or the political club."[70] If most preferred Jones Wood, it was only partly because of differences in design or even accessiblity. Equally important was who controlled Central Park. If time, money, and cultural preferences influenced whether working-class New Yorkers visited Central Park, the rules set by park officers determined whether they felt welcome to use this grand new public space.

9

"A PARK PROPERLY SO-CALLED"

In 1859 Frederick Law Olmsted reported to the Board of Commissioners of the Central Park an incident that he had found disturbing: "A private carriage containing a gentleman and ladies was observed driving through the narrow walks of the finished ground north of the pond, the wheels often running upon the borders and putting the trees and shrubbery recently planted in much peril." A "policeman hastened to remonstrate with the gentleman," but the offender retorted "angrily that the park belonged to the *public* and he should drive where he pleased in it."[1]

Park policeman were more likely to clash with working-class park visitors than with gentlemen like this one, but the incident illustrates issues that resonated through the history of Central Park. What is proper behavior in a public park? Who decides? Who is the "public" of this public park? New Yorkers would wrestle for generations to come with questions they they confronted for the first time in the late 1850s and the 1860s. Never before had they had such a vast public space, and its organization and management raised novel and difficult questions about the meaning of the "public."

Central Park and Jones Wood were both public parks in the sense that they were open to anyone in the city who chose to visit them, though Jones Wood was privately owned and operated for profit, and Central Park was owned by the city and managed, at least in theory, for the benefit of all New Yorkers. Still, public property was not to be mistaken for common property. As representatives of the "public," government officials—the Central Park commissioners—set rules for permissible use of the park. During its first decade, Andrew Green, Olmsted, and the force of park keepers governed this public space. Some park users ignored or disobeyed various of the rules and regulations, but in the 1860s at least, enforcement brought behavior into conformity with the prescriptions of gentlemen who hoped to instruct the public in manners and values. Central Park was open to the public, but not all behavior was equally welcome there.

Training the "Ignorant" How to Use a Park

Olmsted claimed credit for crafting the park's rules and enforcement procedures; in 1863 he informed Calvert Vaux that the "administration & management of the public introduction to and use of the park" was his "most valuable property" in the entire project. But Olmsted hardly shaped the rules for park use by himself. The board of commissioners had begun to consider park ordinances and policing before Olmsted joined the staff as superintendent. They did ask him to draft the regulations, and the first set of rules seems to have been devised by Olmsted in collaboration with his rival, Chief Engineer Egbert Viele. Olmsted himself held undisputed authority over the park for only a brief time between his appointment as architect-in-chief in May 1858 and Andrew Green's appointment as comptroller in October 1859. He and Vaux resigned as landscape architects in 1863 and they returned in that capacity two years later. Their connection to the park was interrupted again when Tammany Democrats captured the board from 1870 to 1871 but resumed in November 1871. A year later Olmsted and Vaux dissolved their partnership; Olmsted continued on the park in various superintending positions until 1877, and Vaux was a consulting landscape architect for some of this time. Park politics, however, constrained Olmsted's control of the park keepers and other administrative matters.[2]

Olmsted had set the tone for public use of Central Park in the first place back in the 1850s. "A large part of the people of New York," he told the commissioners shortly after he was hired as superintendent, "are ignorant of a park, properly so-called. They will need to be trained to the proper use of it, to be restrained in the abuse of it, and this can be best done gradually, even while the Park is yet in process of construction." From the start, he was determined to "train" the public to understand the difference between this park and other open spaces; he drew a particularly sharp line between public property (as government-owned property) and both unregulated private property and common property. "Visitors to the Park, should be led to feel as soon as possible," he declared, "that wide distinction exists between it and the general suburban country, in which it is the prevalent impression of a certain class that all trees, shrubs, fruit and flowers, are common property."[3]

Olmsted hit on the same theme fifteen months later just as the first ice skaters were venturing onto the frozen lake. The *New York Times* reprinted and expanded on his remarks on the importance of "instructing [people] in the proper use of the park." The "careless stupidity" Olmsted discovered among early park users came from the mistaken notion that a park was like a "wood," with which Americans associated "the idea of perfect liberty." The *Times* agreed

The Park Proper: A promenade along the Lake.

with the need to distinguish parks from what it called "common spaces."
Central Park should not be treated like other public spaces in New York City,
which it believed the municipal government had surrendered to "sharpers and
rowdies": "The treasury, the streets, the wharves, the City Hall, the urinal, the
Court-rooms, 'the [City Hall] Park' have all been left to the care of the elements
and the peculators; so that the mere fact of a piece of ground's belonging to the
public has become very naturally to be considered by the less intelligent
classes . . . a license to commit nuisance on it. . . . Everyone must cease as soon
as possible to associate [Central Park] in his mind with the dirty play-ground in
front of the City Hall or Jones' Wood."[4]

Writing on the aesthetic motive of the Greensward plan in 1859, Olmsted
had explained that the park "should present an aspect of spaciousness and
tranquility . . . thereby affording the most agreeable contrast to the confinement,
bustle, and monotonous street-division of the city. The Park should . . . as far as
practicable, resemble a charming bit of rural landscape, such as, unless produced by art, is never found within the limits of a large town."[5] For Vaux this
aesthetic goal had the intrinsic value of creating a beautiful public space that

could be enjoyed by all citizens, but for Olmsted it incorporated the larger social motive of improving public behavior and assuaging competitive individualism.

In defining the park as an antidote to the strains the city imposed on the "nerves and minds" of its residents, Olmsted (who regularly worked himself into nervous exhaustion) probably had people like himself in mind. Yet he disavowed any class bias in spelling out his social motives. "The primary purpose of the Park," he wrote, "is to provide the best practicable means of healthful recreation for the inhabitants of the city, of all classes," including "the poor and the rich, the young and the old, the vicious and the virtuous." Moreover, when he talked about the need to train the public, he drew his examples of improper park use from the upper and lower classes alike.[6] He was convinced that the only way to protect Central Park as a unified work of landscape art was to keep people from damaging the turf, the plantings, and the drives.

Although Olmsted did not direct his prescriptions for proper park behavior and use at any particular class, his ideas were nonetheless shaped by his own class and culture and by his personal experiences. Rejecting the views of his "cowardly conservative" opponents, for whom class-based cultural divisions were fixed, he believed members of the lower classes should and could acquire "the refinement and taste and the mental & moral capital of gentlemen." The "moral influence" of public parks, like that of public schools and libraries, offered a way for the working classes to acquire that "capital" as a means of cultural improvement. Although Olmsted did not accept the concept of immutable class distinctions, he disliked mobility motivated by materialistic ambition. Common cultural pursuits should reinforce the "simple and sensible social life."[7]

Olmsted's definition of democracy had no room for the sort of grass-roots participation advocated by artisans in the cooperative movement in the 1850s or the Knights of Labor and the populists slightly later in the century. Democracy, he believed, required the leadership of an appointed board of "gentlemen," and he enthusiastically supported the use of such a board to keep the park out of the hands of local Democratic politicians. "Refinement and taste" and "proper" park decorum implicitly excluded the sort of lively amusements and recreations that German and Irish immigrant workers pursued a few blocks east at Jones Wood and on the city streets.

The Sparrow Cops

In 1858 the state-appointed police commission granted policing authority to officers nominated and paid by the park board. Olmsted organized his twenty-four park keepers along paramilitary lines; he insisted on military salutes and

Gatekeepers posted at the entrances helped the park police enforce rules such as the one forbidding the use of drives by commercial vehicles.

clothed his corps in uniforms that the Democratic *Leader* ridiculed as aristocratic imitations of the garb of Windsor Forest's keepers. (Later, the gray-coated park keepers would be nicknamed "sparrow cops," in disparaging reference to the less dangerous beat they walked than those of the blue-coated city police.) By the spring of 1859 he had spelled out an elaborate set of "Rules and Conditions of Service." Each park keeper was required to "carry himself erect" and to "march at a quick step from one part of his beat to another." He was forbidden to "converse with visitors unless first addressed by them"; to use "harsh, exasperating or unnecessary disrespectful language"; to drink "ardent spirits" on the job or to frequent "taverns or tippling houses" off the job. Keepers were to appear "perfectly clean, hair brushed, beard combed . . . , and in full uniform in every particular, cloth clean, brass polished, shoes clean and newly oiled or polished, coat buttoned to the neck and no white collar visible, gloves clean." Soon Olmsted was insisting that the keepers be ready for quizzes on their "ability to direct strangers to different parts of the park."[8]

Following Olmsted's lead, the sparrow cops rigidly policed their domain.

YOUNG NEW-YORK.

Anxious Mother.—"Now, CHARLES, HADN'T YOU BETTER WAIT FOR YOUR UNCLE TO TAKE YOU? —YOU MAY LOSE YOUR WAY IN THE PARK."
Y. N. Y.—"OH! NO, NO!—I DON'T WANT TO BE BOTHERED LOOKING AFTER THE OLD MAN; AND, BESIDES, I'M WELL KNOWN TO THE PARK POLICE!"

This *Vanity Fair* cartoon from 1863 suggests that the park police spent considerable time trying to control the antics of young parkgoers.

Almost immediately after the skating lake opened, one young man who stole a pair of skates was promptly arrested, and the police sought a stiff sentence that would make an example of him. He got thirty days in jail. In the same year, the keepers even picked up a supreme court judge for walking across some freshly planted grass. Though the judge was not prosecuted, strict enforcement of park regulations across class lines shocked some well-to-do New Yorkers. "Persons who have cut or broken shrubs," Olmsted complained, "will hardly ever believe that an officer has not exceeded his duty in arresting them until brought before the magistrate. I have been frequently sent for, in the confident supposition that I would reprove an officer for arresting a man for merely cutting a common branch, or pulling up a root of sassafras."[9] Needless to say, he did not.

But despite their military bearing and their vigilant enforcement of the rules, Olmsted saw the keepers more as teachers than policemen. "The chief duty of the Park Keepers," he wrote, "is by timely instruction, caution and warning to prevent disorderly & unseemly practices upon the Park, and thus as far as practicable to avoid occasions for arrests." Considering the 2 million or so visitors who came to the park in 1859, the 228 arrests that year seem quite modest, and on a per-visitor basis, the 1859 haul was roughly eight times higher than the park arrest rate for the rest of the 1860s.[10] Perhaps Olmsted shifted his keepers away from a rigorous arrest policy because it annoyed elite patrons. Or perhaps the hard line taken in the first year succeeded in "training" visitors in proper park use, and violations diminished. Most likely, both were true.

"Fast Trotting," "Vulgar" Wagons, Gambling, Hawking, and "Indecent Language"

About half the rules focused on proper movement through the park, reflecting the emphasis of the Greensward plan on the visitors' relationship to the scenery. Parkgoers were enjoined to enter only at the specified gateways, to use the paths (not the grass), and not to block the roads with horses or carriages. More than a hundred signs scattered across the park directed the movement of individuals through the landscape and to particular features.[11]

Two other rules on movement affected who would use the park and how. The first concerned speed limits. In an effort to keep out sporting men and trotting matches, the Greensward plan had omitted long, straight drives; nonetheless, some newspapers worried that Central Park might turn into an "aldermanic commons for fast driving." It was a realistic fear. In the 1850s harness racing was the nation's leading spectator sport, according to sports historian Melvin Adelman, and New York City had at least seven trotting tracks. The *Irish News*, reflecting the cross-class nature of the sporting crowd, bemoaned the absence of "a raised, broad carriage and equestrian drive, round the park," a "grand Excelsior Course" that the "great Equestrian Order of New York" could "race and rattle over, to their hearts' content." "Is there any amusement in the world," it asked rhetorically, "which we prefer to . . . the whirling action of a gay nag throwing one mile behind her in three minutes?"[12]

Trotting matches and fast driving did not "stir the blood" of most park commissioners as it did the editors of the *Irish News*. The preliminary rules recommended to the board in September 1859 set the speed limit for carriages at five miles per hour and for horses at six. When the preliminary regulations were reported, one board member, the well-known fancier of fast horses August Belmont, moved to raise the speed limit for carriages to eight miles per hour and to eliminate all speed limits on the bridle paths. The board settled on a compromise of seven miles per hour for carriages and ten for saddle horses.[13]

Belmont had specifically crafted his proposal to "keep the fast-trotting men and other rowdies out" of the park. As his biographer explained, Belmont "liked to race horses on and off the racetracks," but "he did not think the park would be an appropriate setting for anything that might be dangerous to wives and children." Moreover, he was shifting his affections from harness racing to thoroughbred racing, then emerging as the favorite sport of wealthy New Yorkers. He regarded the heterogeneous sporting crowds that gathered to join in (and bet on) street harness races as an inappropriate constituency for Central Park.[14]

Despite speed limits and curved roads, the park initially proved "vastly attractive to the trotters," but soon regular arrests "made generally understood," as the *Atlantic Monthly* reported, "the law and customs of the park . . . restricting speed to a moderate rate." Between 1862 and 1863, speeding arrests dropped by two-thirds. The ban on fast driving was intended to ensure not only safety but also gentlemanly refinement. The *Herald* explained that "the rowdy habit of rapid driving" excluded a man from "the recognized list of gentlemen. . . . Any person thus demeaning himself upon a public fashionable promenade would be as indelibly stamped as ill-bred as if he were to be found running violently up and down a ball room in the midst of the dance."[15] Just as women governed manners within the ballroom, they would also determine what constituted decorum on the park drives.

If the park was like a ball room, not only certain speeds could be judged "vulgar" (as the *Herald* put it) but certain types of vehicles as well. The thousands of commercial wagons owned by cartmen, undertakers, and other tradespeople that filled the city streets were, from the start, barred from the park. Regulations prohibited omnibuses and express wagons, as well as "any cart, dray, wagon, truck, or other vehicle carrying goods, merchandise, manure, soil, or other article." Olmsted's ban was intended to provide a noncommercial alternative to the city streets, but it had class implications. His "business regulation," explained one local newspaper, would prevent the "invasion of the Central Park by improper vehicles and improperly behaved persons" and would thus keep the park from being "deserted by the better classes of our population."[16] At a stroke, Olmsted and the commission stopped butchers and bakers from joining bankers and brokers on the drives.

Trouble broke out almost immediately. Just a few months after the carriage drives opened, Olmsted reported that "frequent altercations take place between gatekeepers and persons endeavoring to enter the park with vehicles which gatekeepers judge should be excluded in obedience to the ordinances." "Some of our wagon-owning citizens," the *Times* noted around the same time, "have been already greatly aggrieved at finding themselves excluded from the 'people's park' by the 'people's policemen,' when they took their families there for a Sunday's drive in the respectable vehicles which do duty during the week in transporting legs of mutton, or cans of milk, or kegs of crackers, or boxes of candles from their shops to the customers' houses." These "sufferers . . . instantly break forth into indignant denunciations of the 'aristocracy,' and impassioned vindications of the 'rights of labor.' "[17]

Perceiving the implicit class bias in the park regulations, the *Leader* sarcastically praised them for setting out "what is *au fait* in a place of public resort" and wondered whether "our democratic citizens" would be "turned out of the enclosure as Adam and Eve were kicked out of the Garden of Eden." In prohibiting gambling, gaming, fortune-telling, hawking, peddling, or any other unlicensed commercial activity, the board had excluded not only the activities many wealthy New Yorkers found disagreeable but the equally disagreeable people who enjoyed them. Not coincidentally, the regulation against "threatening, abusive, or indecent language" followed the rules against peddling and riding in commercial wagons and preceded the rule on gambling and fortune-telling. In the mid-nineteenth century, respectable New Yorkers lumped these activities together as part of a lower-class street scene. Such prohibitions furthered Olmsted's larger aspiration to set the park apart from other urban public spaces, to institute "the most agreeable contrast" to the "bustle" of the city.[18]

Other rules adopted in 1859 insisted on the distinction between the park and the woods or the commons. One regulation explicitly barred visitors from cutting, breaking, or defacing the trees, shrubs, and plants, and another prohibited "persons" from turning cattle, horses, goats, or swine into the park to graze. In effect, officials wanted to ensure that the park would not be "common," in either sense of the word—nonexclusive or low and vulgar.

Olmsted's early efforts to grapple with the problem of controlling public use of Central Park could not entirely anticipate the controversies that would emerge when it opened. Within a year of adopting the original park ordinances, for example, the board added rules forbidding swimming or fishing in the ponds, setting off fireworks, playing musical instruments, displaying any "flag, banner, target or transparency," posting any bills or notices, or parading in military or target company or civic processions.[19]

From Olmsted's perspective, however, the most persistent threat to the park came from any destruction of the turf. The original ordinances did not include the later infamous "keep off the grass" rule, but the first visitors did find placards advising: "For the Present Visitors are Prohibited to Tread on the Grass." The seemingly temporary ban (justified by the newly seeded lawns) became permanent. By fall 1860 the first item on the poster that listed park regulations warned visitors "not to walk upon the grass; (except of the Commons)." Olmsted had decided to ban walking on the meadows but to permit exceptions by labeling some areas either temporarily or permanently as "commons," thus ceding some public right of free access. Park officials allowed Saturday visitors to use the lawns, particularly the twenty-two-acre Green in the center of the park (originally called the Parade and later known as the Sheep Meadow). But as the *News* pointed out in 1860, such park regulations did not permit "the family of the poor artisan," who could only visit on Sunday, to "carry the basket of cheap luxuries, a few apples or peaches, the home made pie and sandwiches . . . and sit and enjoy them under one of the trees of the only rural retreat open to him and his after the confining toils of the week." Olmsted's effort to preserve the lawns interfered as a practical matter with one of his own announced goals for the park: to provide the opportunity for poor families to enjoy as well as contemplate nature.[20]

THE CENTRAL PARK.

A delightful resort for toil-worn New Yorkers.

A *Frank Leslie's* cartoon of 1869 satirizes the rules that prevented parkgoers from walking on the grass.

Challenging and Flouting the Rules

Throughout the 1860s, parkgoers posed new demands and questioned Olmsted's definition of "proper" park behavior and a park "properly so-called." Sometimes these confrontations took on an overtly political cast as groups petitioned the commissioners on behalf of particular interests; other challenges were less direct, simply a disregarding of the rules. Advocates of a quiet, orderly, and decorous park—a park that resisted rather than embraced the variety and spontaneity of the city—generally held the line against such challenges throughout the first decade.

In early December 1858, before the park had even opened to the public, the Knickerbocker, Eagle, and Empire baseball clubs (three of the city's four oldest clubs) urged the park board to provide ball grounds. Over the next eighteen months, another half dozen or so petitions requesting ball fields arrived at the commission offices. Local newspapers backed the ball clubs. Grading "the cricket and baseball ground," noted the *Times*, "has been very properly first attended to, as it will be most beneficial to the public." The *Irish News* wanted the projected "play or cricket ground" to be enlarged by combining it with the nearby Parade. "The cricket field," it declared, "is the next thing to the horse-road in our loving regard."[21]

The expectation that sports fields would be a key attraction of the new park was widespread, and some early guides to the park reinforced it. One depicted on its cover a game of cricket with a crowd of spectators; another promised that baseball and cricket matches could be "comfortably witnessed by ten thousand persons." The guidebook authors had taken their cues from the official plan. Following the competition specifications, the winning Greensward plan had designated three areas as playgrounds: a ten-acre site below 66th Street on the west side of the park (Heckscher Playground after 1926); an area immediately east of the rectangular Lower Reservoir, which became the home of the Metropolitan Museum of Art in the 1880s (roughly 79th to 85th streets, from Fifth to Sixth); and a tract north of the 97th Street Transverse Road in the middle of the park (later the North Meadow). In January 1859, the park board noted that the "numerous applications of clubs of skaters, of baseball and cricket players for accommodation in the Park, indicate that expectations of its influence as a promoter of manly, vigorous out-of-door exercise will be fully realized."[22]

But they were not. The reasons why lay in the transformation of popular sports, particularly baseball, just at the moment the park was being built. In the 1850s New York and other large cities experienced an athletic boom; interest burgeoned in cricket, prizefighting, boating, ice skating, gymnastics, foot racing, horse racing, and especially baseball. "From immemorial time," a sporting newspaper explained in 1860, "base ball has been a school-boy's game." It "was, until recently, considered undignified for men to play. . . . Within five or six years all this has changed; B.B. Clubs outnumber the debating societies almost as much as they surpass them in enthusiasm." In the five years before the Civil War, baseball completely displaced cricket. "From only a dozen clubs in Brooklyn and New York in 1855," writes Melvin Adelman, "the number of organized teams increased eightfold in just three years."[23]

As baseball grew, the social composition of the teams changed. "By the mid-1850s," Adelman says, "baseball in New York City and Brooklyn began to slip from the polite hands of the urban gentleman, becoming a sport for all social classes with the notable exception of unskilled workers." These working- and middle-class players had less access to fields than had their wealthier predecessors, particularly after new construction devoured the open lots on which teams had once played. The Independent Baseball Club explained in petitioning to use Central Park that "their present ground at the corner of 2nd Avenue and 81st street cannot be leased for another season in consequence of the opening of a new street." In 1865 alone the commissioners received "some twenty to thirty applications" for ball fields "from the employees of several manufacturing establishments."[24]

Baseball was attracting not only more players but bigger crowds of fans. As early as 1860 a match between the two leading Brooklyn teams drew more than fourteen thousand spectators. The game ended inconclusively when one team quit in protest over the unruly behavior of the other team's fans, evidence,

Adelman notes, of "the growing rowdyism . . . and especially gambling and partisanship" that was infecting baseball. "Indeed," comments another sports historian, "the revenues from liquor sales and gambling were the engines driving the sports boom of the 1850s."[25]

New Yorkers organized new baseball clubs almost weekly in the late 1850s at the same time that the city swallowed up many of the available playing fields—the "out-lying common[s]," as a sporting paper called them. The ball clubs saw the new park as the answer to their dreams, but Olmsted and the board began to wonder whether their presence might prove, instead, to be a nightmare. In May 1861 the commission rejected the applications of baseball clubs for use of the park. "It is obviously impossible," it explained, to accommodate more than fifty ball clubs with more than fifty members each; "the space is not sufficient." Nor, the board explained in a later annual report, would it be possible "to satisfy the requirements of the numerous cricket, ball, and other adult clubs within the area of the Park, and at the same time preserve in the grounds an appearance that would be satisfactory to the much more numerous class that frequent the Park for the enjoyment of the refined and attractive features of its natural beauties." "The Park," the 1861 annual report had similarly noted, "has attractions to those that visit it, merely as a picture. . . . Whatever defaces or injures this picture makes it less attractive to the great mass of visitors, and should, for the general good, be excluded." Moreover, as the board later said, banning the ball clubs "effectually prevented" "match games and the objectionable features that have been the frequent attendant of these games."[26]

If the park board would not allow baseball and cricket clubs, what was to be done with the playgrounds that had been in the plans from the start? After nine years of intensive discussion, probably under the influence of Andrew Green, a former president of the board of education and now comptroller of the park board, the commissioners restricted the playgrounds to schoolboys who could produce a certificate of good attendance and character from a teacher. And even these exemplary lads found the fields open to them only three days of the week. Working-class youths were largely excluded, since relatively few of them went beyond elementary school in this period.[27]

A year after the commissioners opened the fields to schoolboys, they made a similar arrangement for girls. In 1867 they permitted schoolgirls to play croquet (whose popularity had boomed in the United States after the Civil War) on the lawns three afternoons each week. (Adults were permitted to play on the East Green.) Several contestants in the design competition, aware of the growing interest in physical fitness for women at midcentury, had proposed equipped fields for women's gymnastics, but these suggestions were not pursued by the commissioners, because they feared that equipped fields would detract from the park's scenic beauty.[28] The genteel and restrained game of croquet, whose movable equipment could be stored, fitted better with the designers' conceptions of a natural park. The park would be open to women's recreation, but only

Only schoolboys with a note from their principal were permitted to use the ballfields in the 1860s. But youthful players varied in their decorum—as these contrasting images suggest.

to those genteel and restrained forms of exercise that the park's male managers deemed appropriate. Of course, many "respectable" women probably shared the board's view that men's sports and games impinged on their own enjoyment of the lawns and the drives.

"The most generally attractive features of the Park," the 1863 annual report argued, "are its natural beauties" and "a much larger number of persons derive gratification from the appearance of the lawn well preserved, than . . . [from] the practice of any special amusement that would destroy it." More than the greatest good for the greatest number was at stake. The commissioners and Olmsted as park superintendent were making a *choice* about what they considered to be a "proper park"—a choice with some significant implications for park use. Certain modes of park use were more proper than others. The report conceded, for example, that the "Sicilian and Scotchman are dissimilar" in their habits and traditions and that "individuals, even of the same nationality" have diverse habits and interests. "There is, however, a universality in nature," it maintained, "that affords a field of enjoyment to all observers of her works."[29]

Despite the board's universal claims, such policies favored individual recreation and exercise over group play and games, particularly those of chance, competition, make-believe, and simulation. The park did not prohibit active uses by small informal groups—walking, horseback riding, carriage driving, and skating were all encouraged—but Olmsted and Green regarded those activities as purposeful (they provided exercise) and directed (they moved parkgoers through the landscape). But they avoided undue stimulation or excitement. Emerging park policy also favored visual over multisensual experiences, mental relaxation over physical exertion. One 1860s park report, for example, acknowledged the "pleasure found in walking on a lawn" but said that such pleasure would interfere with the lawn's more important "power to gratify by sight." Another report explained that the park should provide "a succession of views of a rural character," since these are "the natural food and refreshment of the human eye."[30]

Parades, Picnics, and "Places of Entertainment"

The preference for the individual over the group extended well beyond sports. Guidebooks from the 1860s frame the park experience largely as a series of individual encounters with nature.[31] This focus meshed well with Olmsted's notion of the park's contribution to individual moral improvement and "sensible" sociability, though not with the experience of wealthy carriage riders, who were likely to be judging one another's financial rather than moral "capital" and disregarding the scenery.

Even before the park opened the board had moved to block or restrict that group activity (and spectacle) most widely assumed to be part of a public park—

the drills and displays of target and military companies. In 1858 they had reduced the Greensward plan's original provision for a twenty-five-acre Parade. Then, the Parade literally disappeared; when Olmsted reported to the commission on the work done as of January 1859, he referred to the area as "a country green or open common." Soon, official documents and unofficial guidebooks began labeling that site (now only twenty-two acres) the "Green." The expectation of military processions and drills in the park persisted, nonetheless, and Olmsted acknowledged in his 1859 report that the Green "may be used upon special occasions for military displays." Yet when military companies turned up at the board offices in 1859 and 1860, they were briskly told that such activities were "incompatible" with the park's "objects." The sense of incompatibility was no doubt reinforced by the growing association of militia and target companies with the rowdy working-class culture of the saloon, the fire company, and the political clubhouse.[32]

When the park's own keepers formed the Renwick Guard with the intention of setting off on a target excursion outside the park, Olmsted refused to let them wear their park uniforms or to parade "in such a manner as would cause them to be recognized as keepers of the park." Nor would he permit them to use his name as a sponsor. Green was equally negative, concluding that a target excursion "will not elevate the force in the public estimation, and is objectionable on their own account as well as on account of the Park." The "manners of a crowd attending any great muster of militia [are] always . . . particularly antagonistic" to what he had sought in Central Park, Olmsted later observed. Military parades in the park, he declared, would make it "subject to the humor of a multitude as uncontrollable and as dangerous to all that is peculiarly valuable in [Central Park] as a street mob is found to be when it has broken into a private house."[33]

The coming of the Civil War accelerated the pressure to permit military drills in Central Park, but the board continued to resist, defiantly asserting the pastoral quality of the Green by grazing sheep on it. (It was because of the sheep, introduced around 1864, that some began calling it the Sheep Meadow, a name that took hold in the early twentieth century.) But neither board resolutions nor the grazing sheep stopped the First Division of the New York State National Guard, which simply marched onto the Green in April 1864 and began to drill and parade. Another regiment followed. The park keepers stood by helplessly as the troops marched through the gates. Responding to this blatant defiance of park rules—no doubt understandable in the midst of a war—Green in 1865 secured passage of a state law explicitly banning military parades in Central Park. But the issue of whether the park should accommodate parades or other large gatherings persisted.[34]

So did the problem of large picnics. Sometime during the park's first year, officials apparently decided to ban all group picnics. Recalling a recent Methodist Sunday school picnic in the park, the *Times* commented in August 1860

This 1862 lithograph shows the sort of scruffy and disorderly militia company that Green and Olmsted wanted to keep out of Central Park.

that "such scenes are no longer permitted." It conceded that "the mere fact of an orderly and well behaved set of Sunday School scholars going to the park for a day's recreation and taking their lunch with them would, in itself, do no harm or bring disgrace upon the management." Nevertheless, to allow Sunday school picnics would open the door to excursions of "military or fire engine companies," which in turn would "require all the force under [Police] Superintendent Kennedy to keep order and preserve the peace."[35] German singing societies and Irish Catholic churches could not organize an excursion to Central Park like those they enjoyed in Jones Wood.

Some of the most troublesome demands to use the park came from those with something to sell. "Having become the resort of large assemblages of people," the commissioners explained in 1863, "the Park is considered too advantageous a field for advertising to be neglected by those who would force their wants or wares upon the public attention at every turn." Such commercial interest, they believed, posed a threat to the park's integrity: "If all the applications for the erection and maintenance of towers, houses, drinking fountains, telescopes, mineral water fountains, cottages, Aeolian harps, gymnasiums, observatories, weighing-scales, for the sale of eatables, velocipedes, perambulators, Indian work, tobacco, segars, for the privilege of using steam-engines, snow-shoes, ice-boats . . . were granted, they would occupy a large portion of the surface of the Park . . . and give to it the appearance of the grounds of a country fair, or of a militia training-field."[36]

The *Irish News*, however, saw Central Park more as "a hippodrome than a pedestrian pleasure ground," and it urged the opening of "a number of refreshment houses for—anything you please." The commissioners were not prepared to allow "anything you please," but they did realize that a proper bourgeois park should incorporate facilities to accommodate the expectations of respectable parkgoers, who were dining out with increasing frequency in this era. Olmsted himself pointed out that the failure of the park to offer satisfactory eating facilities left patrons to make their own arrangements. Some parkgoers "came supplied with baskets of food and drink" and left the park cluttered with "litter and debris"; others resorted to the fifty "shanty dram shops" and the more than half a dozen "larger establishments" for the sale of liquor that had sprung up near the park by spring 1860. One such place even made "a speciality of selling liquor in pocket flasks, with lunches, to be carried into the park," Olmsted told the board.[37]

The way to defuse the "danger of disorder" posed by these "low dram-shops" was for the park itself to provide food and drink in a regulated setting. By licensing refreshment places, the board could keep people away from the surrounding saloons, control what was sold in the park, and also benefit financially from license fees. Over the next several years, therefore, the commission implemented a policy of controlled commercialism, allowing the sale of refreshments, the rental of ice skates and boats, and a carriage service. In doing so, they tried to ensure that business activities would conform to their notions of order and propriety. Regulations of boat rental, for example, specified the prices, the number of passengers allowed, and even the colors of the boats; the boatmen were required to have "sober habits," to refrain from smoking, to wear a "suitable uniform," and to "be respectful and obliging in their deportment." At the same time, the board rejected dozens of applications for permission to operate other activities, ranging from weighing scales to concert halls. So frequent were the requests that Olmsted developed a form letter telling amusement entrepreneurs that "the Commission does not at present seem to contemplate the establishment of any places of entertainment upon the park the ensuing season."[38]

The Fight over Sunday in the Park

In the 1860s countervailing pressures for park use came to a head in a sharp controversy over Sundays in the park. That confrontation emerged in the context of a larger struggle over how New Yorkers should spend the Christian sabbath. Members of Presbyterian, Dutch Reformed, and Methodist churches urged a quiet, church-centered Sunday. More liberal denominations and "free thinkers" tolerated a wider range of activities, and tens of thousands of European immigrants, particularly Germans, favored even more secular and permissive sabbath pursuits. In April 1857 "leading Christian citizens" organized themselves into the New York Sabbath Committee to fight for the maintenance of existing Sunday blue laws prohibiting commercial activities. Most of its elite leaders—lawyers, merchants, importers, company presidents—were active in the city's missionary and Bible societies.[39]

This sabbatarian revival occurred at the same time as a well-organized *anti*sabbatarian movement gathered force in the city's growing German community. "In the mid-1850s," Stanley Nadel observes in his history of Little Germany, "the most important issue for the masses was neither slavery nor wage slavery but rather the defense of their right to recreation." In September 1859 the antisabbatarian American Society for the Protection of Civil and Religious Liberty applied for permission to hold Sunday music concerts in Central Park; the *Staats-Zeitung* backed the plan, arguing that Sunday concerts would make music in the park available to those workers and shopkeepers who worked on Saturdays. The park board dodged the issue by tabling the motion.[40]

But the matter was not settled. The following summer, when the board considered proposals for boat service in the park, Commissioner Waldo Hutchins, a nativist and a Presbyterian, moved that any license for such services specify that no boats be operated on Sundays. The board narrowly divided on the motion and left the question in abeyance. The Sabbath Committee responded with a pamphlet titled *Our Central Park* and with letters to the newspapers, which charged that the "continental sabbath" was infiltrating the park. New Yorkers might follow Europe in "the art of landscape gardening," but founding "a great Park, after the style of the Bois de Boulogne or the Prater" did not "carry with it the Sunday pastimes of Paris and Vienna." The sabbatarians invoked the slippery slope: "If the bars are once laid down," then it would be only a short time before the park was filled on Sundays with bands, target shooting, horse racing, prizefighting, bullfighting, gambling, fortune-telling, and "thimble-rigging."[41]

Although the Sabbath Committee framed its arguments in terms of morality and the "rights of peaceful, conscientious Christian citizens, and their families, to the quiet enjoyment of an enclosure they may have paid thousands to create," their opponents saw the issue in class terms. "The real object of the 'Sabbath Committee,'" the *Herald* charged, "is but a covert design to shut up the Park entirely on Sundays—to lock the gates and exclude the poor and working classes from all enjoyment within its precincts; to secure it, in short, for the 'respectable' and 'pious' portion of the community exclusively." In effect, the debate turned on the definition of the park's "public," with differing claims made by the "producing classes," who had built the park, and the tax-paying "classes who have contributed most of the money to form it."[42]

In practical terms, the differences between the two sides were never as sharp as their rhetoric. The concrete issues remained whether the park board would allow music, boat rentals, and refreshment sales on Sundays. Perhaps because of the passions aroused, the commissioners avoided all but a few direct votes on these matters. By such evasions, they and Olmsted (even though he called himself a "Sabbath cracker") generally bent to the more politically influential sabbatarians. No music and no boat rentals were permitted on Sundays in the 1860s. Refreshment sales were allowed; beer sales were not. Such decisions hardly closed the park on Sundays, but neither did they make it more appealing or enjoyable for the working families who had only that day on which to visit.[43]

"The Charms of Decency and the Advantages of Order"

As the park commissioners debated what sort of park New York would have, they faced genuinely difficult choices in organizing a public ground in a diverse and democratic society. Their decisions, moreover, did not always follow rigid principle. They resisted commercialism, yet allowed restaurants and boat and carriage rental. They resisted team sports, yet allowed playing fields to be used by schoolchildren. They resisted opening the lawns but allowed people on them on Saturdays. They resisted certain activities but kept the park open on the Christian sabbath. Still, some general patterns emerged. The commission tended to favor quiet, contemplative, non-commercial, and individual or family uses of the park over boisterous and rough sports, fun and games, collectively organized amusements, and large-scale spectacles. They did permit the orchestrated socializing of the carriage parade, the band concerts, and the skating rink, but those activities could be safely organized under "respectable" auspices and posed little threat to the turf. Thus, the interests of wealthy and even middle-class New Yorkers weighed heavily in the park's initial management. Most fundamentally, the commissioners sought to separate the park clearly from the city, to make it a distinct alternative to other urban public spaces.

Policies do not, of course, determine behavior. It is one thing to announce, as Olmsted did, that "the main object" of the park was to "produce a certain influence on the minds of people," and quite another to stop the "moods and habits" of the city at the park gates. The park board never fully enforced the regime of order and decorum it desired: some visitors got drunk, ignored the rules against walking on the grass, flouted the carriage drive speed limits, scrawled or cut "names and obscene words" on benches and walls, and littered the grounds with "broken fruit, and waste of all sorts." Similarly, the city's popular and working-class cultures seeped through the gates as did workers themselves. Working-class youths irritated "respectable" skaters; flask-carrying visitors brought liquor into the park; German families set out picnics on the lawns on Sundays; elderly women sold tea and cakes without licenses.[44] Yet even the strongest challenge to the park's decorum only points up how orderly it was in the 1860s.

In the summer of 1860, a reporter for the *Express* described the edges of the park on a Sunday afternoon. At one spot near the entrance, he found "the hawkers of fruits, ballads, and exhibitions who generally locate on the verge of a populous thoroughfare," near them a Methodist tent featuring gospel singers, religious discussions in both English and German, and missionaries distributing tracts and testaments to the surrounding crowd. "At a short distance from these, numerous motley groups had congregated at the doors and windows of the many liquor stores near the Park, drinking, smoking, lounging, and indulging in all the intoxicating 'beverages' of a gin mill." Sunday liquor laws had little effect on the operations of these saloons. "Judging from their crowded appearance," the reporter noted, "they presented more attractions to many than the park itself." Yet this lively and chaotic scene of hawkers and peddlers, gospel tents and saloons, remained squarely *outside* the park. The commission may not have been able to regulate the periphery, but it did achieve a remarkable degree of control over what went on inside. Even the borders gradually came under its influence. By the fall of 1860 (if not earlier) Olmsted and Green were pressing the police to remove the apple stands from the streets adjacent to the park. By 1867 the board of commissioners had won the right to remove any shanties, booths, or stands from walks bordering the park. The surrounding saloons gradually closed; in 1886 only about eleven of the ten thousand places licensed to sell liquor in Manhattan were on blocks facing the park.[45]

The park's stone walls were a social and cultural as well as physical boundary. What most struck contemporaries about the park in the 1860s was how *different* it seemed from the city, how it presented "the very antipode of the city," as the *Times* put it in 1865. The park's propriety seemed more remarkable to many early observers than its pastoralism. "The admirable order which prevails on the Central Park," said the *Times* in a typical report, "is of itself a moral lesson and encouragement . . . in the midst of the official corruption and general municipal disarray of the times. . . . Give us at Albany, at the City Hall, at the Federal Capital, the same honest energy and discipline which have rule in the affairs of the Park, and it would soon be found that Americans are no more insensible than other people to the charms of decency and the advantages of order."[46]

The *Times*'s celebration of the park as an island of order in a disorderly city, as a model for the rest of society, reflected the paper's hostility to the city's political leadership. But other papers offered similar judgments. In September 1857 the *Herald*, alluding to the possibility that cockfighting, bearbaiting, and other rough sports might take over the park, was concerned that it might become "nothing but a huge bear garden for the lowest denizens of the city." Less than two years later, it found with relief that "orderly, well-conducted, and respectable" crowds refuted "the fallacious arguments of those who asserted that the Park, if ever completed, would be little better than a bear garden." Even James McCabe's 1868 guidebook, *Secrets of the Great City,* with its lurid emphasis on "the vices, the mysteries, miseries, and crimes" of New York, agreed that "there have been no acts of rowdyism or lawlessness within the enclosure, for even the most depraved feel themselves compelled to respect the rules of the place."[47]

The surprisingly low level of arrests that prevailed throughout the 1860s similarly suggests few problems of misuse, misbehavior, and disorder in the park. The commissioners were probably right to boast in 1863 that "of the great numbers that visit the Park, but a very small portion require the hand of authority to check mischievous practices." Sympathetic newspapers attributed the remarkable decorum to the honesty and efficiency of the board and its employees, particularly Olmsted. Olmsted himself suggested that it reflected the tractability of Americans. "The American public," he wrote in his journal, "is one of the easiest in the world to regulate if any body will take the responsibility of regulating it." Others thought nature itself was responsible; the "humanizing influence of beauty" in Central Park, wrote one journal, works "a mysterious spell" to bring "decency and order" out of "licentiousness and confusion."[48]

But these comments missed the most important (and most obvious) reason for the decorum—the dominance of elite parkgoers. Once wealthy carriage drivers learned to obey the speed limits, they seldom ran afoul of park rules or disturbed the lawns, trees, or vistas. "There is little fear that drivers will offend except in the matter of speed," Olmsted told Green in 1860.[49] And given the values they shared with the gentlemen who ran the park, rich New Yorkers who stepped out of their carriages were even less likely to offend against propriety and park rules.

But decorum and order are, after all, culturally and historically defined concepts. When mid-nineteenth-century newspaper editors and public officials talked of them, they meant bourgeois manners. From their perspective, an Irish picnic with drinking, gambling, and dancing was by definition "rowdy" and offensive, and a park that attracted the city's "best" citizens was an orderly park. Although newspaper reporters in the 1860s often celebrated Central Park as both democratic and orderly, it was precisely its lack of "democracy" that made it a park, in Olmsted's words, "properly so-called."

In the 1860s (and after) perceptions of the park were decisively shaped by the class and cultural vantage from which one evaluated it. Nothing illustrated this point better than one of the most triumphant moments in the early history of the park, when in October 1860 half a million people lined Broadway to greet the visiting Prince of Wales. A headline in the local press called it "One of the Wonderful Events of the Age." A distinguished reception committee—including the modest but ubiquitous Robert Minturn—organized an elaborate series of events to demonstrate New York's sophistication to the visiting royalty. The itinerary, of course, included a carriage drive through Central Park, where Andrew Green helped the prince plant an English oak and an American elm. This symbolic validation of the park by European royalty, the *Herald* explained, ensured that "hereafter [it] will be looked upon with still greater favor."[50] No doubt gentlemen like Robert Minturn who had found inspiration for Central Park in their trips to Europe agreed.

Many Irish-American New Yorkers did not. A weekly Irish newspaper praised the Irish-American Sixty-ninth Regiment for refusing to join the celebration. "Would it not be humiliating to them as men, as natives of Ireland, to be arrayed in the presence of a young prince, whose family has never rendered an act of Justice to Ireland?" "If the Americans forget the inhuman atrocities practiced by the great-grandfathers of this royal youth," said another paper, "are the Irish to imitate their example?" Almost twenty years later the pro-Tammany and pro-Irish *Evening Express* still remembered the prince's visit to the park as a disgraceful episode that featured "Green and the Greenswards abjectly holding the roots, while the descendant of George III, shoveled the dirt around them." For the *Express*, "the nobler picture was that of Colonel Corcoran and the Sixty-ninth regiment standing aloof and waiting for the coming war to vindicate their patriotism."[51]

Some park workers may have viewed that scene with the Prince of Wales with equal distaste or irony. The men who had moved 2.5 million cubic yards of stones and earth to create Central Park were lined up to watch Andrew Green, the man who had relentlessly pushed them to work harder, pick up a shovel for the first time to shift a little dirt. Meanwhile, Olmsted, the man who had not always been careful about acknowledging the work of others, complained that the designers had been ignored. "I arranged & superintended all the police arrangements," he wrote to his father, "but neither Vaux or I were taken any notice of."[52]

In the 1860s the "gentlemen's" vision had triumphed, even if not everyone had behaved in a gentlemanly fashion. Central Park, Minturn wrote to Olmsted in 1860, "is acknowledged by everybody to be a complete success and of inestimable benefit to the city."[53] In the 1870s and 1880s, however, the gentlemen who governed Central Park in its first decade would face new challenges. Working-class New Yorkers who had initially stood "aloof" would begin to question the political and cultural boundaries of Minturn's notion of "everybody"—of Central Park's public.

IV. REDEFINING CENTRAL PARK

"The Rough and Ready of New York," 1888.

10

THE "SPOILS OF THE PARK"

At 5:15 P.M. on April 20, 1870, the Board of Commissioners of the Central Park adjourned its final meeting, expressing "apprehension" and "deep concern" about the future. The commissioners entrusted the board's property to Andrew Green, one of two members who would join the new Board of Commissioners of the Department of Public Parks. Two weeks earlier, the Democratic-controlled legislature had approved a new city charter that would dramatically alter the city's subservient relationship to the state. This so-called Tweed charter—a backhanded tribute to Tammany boss William Tweed, whose political skills and timely bribes had secured the restoration of home rule—transferred control of Central Park. Henceforth, the mayor would appoint the park commissioners, and debates over its management would remain in the thick of city politics.[1]

Anti-Tammany editors marked this moment in 1870 as initiating the destruction of the park that had so triumphantly represented the values of elite New Yorkers (and even received the blessing of the Prince of Wales). For the *New York Times* in the 1860s, the park had been the "antipode" of the city and its "official corruption"; now the paper worried that Tweed and his "unclean horde" would take over the park, bringing "the total and irretrievable ruin of a magnificent work of art." By the next year the *Times* was charging that "park administration" under the leadership of Tweed's closest adviser, Peter Sweeny, "has become thoroughly demoralized . . . overthrowing the best and only well-executed work in the City." Subsequent historians have shared this gloomy verdict. With the passage of the Tweed charter, a typical recent account notes, "the shadow that fell on Central Park became dark night."[2]

Popular culture, too, has upheld the link between Tweed's depredations and the park. The 1945 musical *Up in Central Park* (and the 1948 film, with Vincent

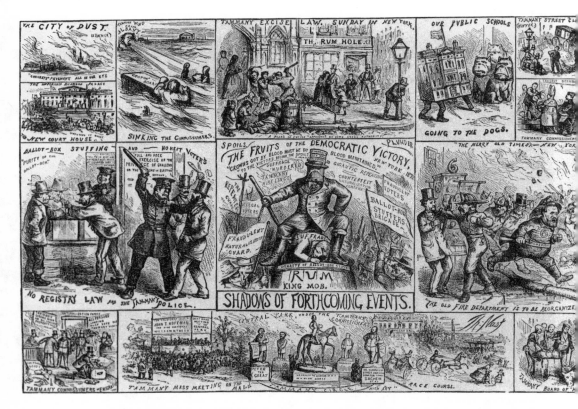

"Shadows of Forthcoming Events": Thomas Nast's 1870 cartoon warned that Democratic control of the city under the new Tweed charter would destroy public institutions. Note in the lower panel Nast's vision of Central Park ruined by statues, political rallies, and a race course.

Price as Boss Tweed) retold the story of political greed and corruption, albeit with a kind of raucous jollity. The romance between the daughter of an Irish ward heeler and a crusading *Times* reporter ends happily with a rousing chorus singing the praises of the "Big Back Yard of the City."[3] But most contemporary (as well as retrospective) accounts agree that the park continued to deteriorate long after Tweed's brief regime ended in 1871.

Such charges found their fullest and most famous expression in 1882 when Frederick Law Olmsted published a pamphlet titled *The Spoils of the Park*. Central Park had taken on a "slovenly and neglected aspect," Olmsted charged, because city politicians and their "ignorant" appointed commissioners had surrendered park service to "that form of tyranny known as influence and advice and that form of bribery known as patronage." City officials had failed to keep the park under the supervision of trained professionals who could protect and fulfill its true purpose as a public work of landscape art and the site of healthful and moral recreation. "In distinct contemptuous repudiation" of the original design, moreover, commissioners had endorsed a new ideal of "cockney villa-gardens," which "bears a relation to natural landscape-gardening, like that which the Swiss peasants of Mrs. Leo Hunter's costume lawn-party bear to the healthy cow-girls of Alpine pastures."[4]

Olmsted provided as evidence twenty-three vignettes in which commissioners bowed to political pressure or park workers violated their public duty. "I don't get any salary for being here," he quoted one commissioner; "it would be a pretty business if I couldn't oblige a friend now and then." As an example of the "tyranny of influence," Olmsted decried proposals for new entrances and roads that would "tell to the advantage of somebody's real estate." And as evidence of park workers' insubordination, Olmsted recalled that the mechanical detectors he had installed to make sure that night watchmen did not sneak off their beats to sleep in park sheds had been smashed "by sledges" within a week.[5]

In attributing the decline primarily to patronage, Olmsted put forth an analysis that influenced the reformers of his generation and also later historians. Yet the tendency to frame park politics—or city politics for that matter—only as a duel between "corrupt" politicians and "public-spirited" citizens obscures the larger issues that shaped the management of Central Park as a public institution, the struggle over who would control the public purse and whose interests would be served by government. In the mid-nineteenth century, wealthy and professional men and women—many of them Republicans—had advocated a wider arena of state action and had experimented with centralized governmental authority. As they expanded public services, new executive commissions, like the one that controlled Central Park from 1857 to 1870, restrained popular sovereignty. But for genteel reformers, this expansion of government also carried a risk. As happened when the Tweed Ring captured Central Park, new city bureaucracies could fall into the "wrong hands" and veer from their advocates' cardinal values of efficiency and taste. In politicians' hands, the resources of an expanded public sector could be used to court the votes of working-class and immigrant New Yorkers.[6]

In looking for managerial solutions to the problems posed by party rule, Olmsted and others tried to imagine a public order insulated from political brokering and from the competitive free-market economy. To Olmsted the original state-appointed Central Park commission had come to represent a model for shielding public administration from politicians; in the same way Olmsted imagined the public space of Central Park as shielding citizens from the tensions of city streets. The park could not embody a pristine civic order, however. The money and labor that maintained it were embedded, after all, in the same conflicting interests that underlay the larger political economy and culture of the city itself.

Moreover, the three groups Olmsted now blamed for the park's decline—politicians, park workers, and landowners—did not agree that "spoils" represented only self-interest. Politicians saw patronage as essential to preserving party loyalty and, hence, the electoral system itself. Park workers who resisted degrading work rules believed that the municipal government that employed them had an obligation to meet the standard of fair wages and hours. And landowners argued that public improvements like Central Park, which bene-fited their property, sustained the city's economic growth.

In the boom years after the Civil War, politicians as unlike as Andrew Green and William Tweed thought the public sector could accommodate these dif-ferent interests. Prosperity inspired confidence in local government's ability to coordinate economic growth, to provide new public institutions, and to support an improved standard of living for more city residents. But in the 1870s, with fiscal crisis and economic depression, the city's manufacturers, bankers, and wealthiest taxpayers rejected this growth-oriented vision of government and attacked the "excesses of democratic politics" as a drain on their own private resources. Reformers who took up the cry of "spoils" regarded Central Park's decline as symptomatic of a larger decay.

In focusing on freeing the park from politicians, Olmsted and others ignored the more fundamental cause of the deterioration of the landscape. Public institutions required public money, and as Commissioner Salem Wales ob-served, Central Park was an "expensive luxury" to maintain.[7] When propertied taxpayers demanded budget cuts, city officials slashed park maintenance funds as well as park workers' wages. The fight over the "spoils" of the park in the 1870s thus rested on the larger issue of who would control public resources.

Cashing in on the Park

Through the Civil War, bankers had collected interest on war bonds in gold, railroad investors had accumulated fortunes from government-subsidized land grants and troop transport, and city manufacturers had gotten rich by supplying the army with uniforms and boots. For working people wartime inflation was a severe burden, from which their living standards did not immediately recover; but in the aggregate, post–Civil War New York City prospered as never before in its history. The gaudy carriage parade in Central Park displayed wealthy New Yorkers' exuberant confidence in the value of public works. Not only had the city matched European capitals by building the park, such public improvements had promoted new levels of economic growth and cultural attainment.

In the expansive context of the Gilded Age, New Yorkers with varying and often deeply antagonistic interests looked to state and local government to support their personal and civic ambitions. Republicans and Democrats quar-reled over which party would control the public sector, but elected representa-tives of both parties endorsed new governmental ventures to protect public health, improve public schools, regulate the labor and housing markets, and build parks, boulevards, and museums. If politicians could work compromises, and if the economic pie continued to expand, it seemed that prosperity could satisfy all appetites—those of landowners, bankers, merchant philanthropists, contractors, and workers.

In December 1865 Andrew Green, as the Central Park commission's comptroller, outlined an ambitious agenda for city planning. The commission had proved itself with the park and was now prepared to manage uptown streets and other public places. In a report to the board, Green described a street plan that would reach along the West Side from 59th Street to Washington Heights, including a principal north-south thoroughfare ("the Boulevard," now Broadway), a "riverside drive" along the top of the Hudson River bluffs, and a new "public pleasure ground" adjacent to the Hudson River. This "riverside park," like Central Park, would spare the city the cost of cutting regular cross streets into the steep and rocky bluffs.[8]

Green, viewing the park board's mission as analogous to that of the 1811 Street Commission that laid out Manhattan's grid, had little doubt that a well-planned city required the overarching intelligence of "a single mind or a single interest"—his own. City businessmen endorsed the expansion of the board's planning authority as a way of countering the chaotic competition of city building. Radical Republican legislators applied the Central Park model of commission government to other city departments, including the fire department and the board of health in 1866. By 1869 state lawmakers had expanded the park commission's authority into the southwestern Westchester district that later became part of the borough of the Bronx.[9]

Green was torn between the satisfaction of controlling vast stretches of the city's public landscape and his habitual commitment to economy, and he distinguished between *planning* for future development and *building* new public works. Property owners would petition and pay assessments for the actual construction of parks and boulevards, he suggested, only when "a compensating use can be made of the[ir] property." Although he was a real estate lawyer himself, Green misjudged the ambitions of uptown landowners, who enthusiastically endorsed (and indeed took credit for securing) the expanded responsibilities of the Central Park commission. Rather than wait for the "compensating use" of their own building projects, landowners urged that new public works begin at once. John McClave, a house carpenter who had become one of the city's most successful real estate operators, spoke for many uptowners when he announced that "he had no faith in buying farms and mapping them out into streets and avenues unless they are contiguous to the grand improvements." "The only way to create an intrinsic value in real estate is to put capital upon it"—especially public capital.[10]

In advocating new public grounds and spacious boulevards, landowners drew on the precedent of Central Park: parks would spare the city (and proprietors) the cost of building streets and would pay for themselves by establishing new elite residential quarters that would expand the city's tax base. In the optimistic climate of a boom economy, few downtown taxpayers protested when state lawmakers, heeding the uptown lobbyists, approved the creation of Riverside and Morningside parks and authorized the boulevard bonds.[11]

With this signal that uptown real estate was ripe for new buyers (and with greenback dollars fanning the flame), many uptown landowners decided to cash in on the promise of Central Park and its radiating "grand drives" as a real estate amenity. After the economic dry spell that reached from the panic of 1857 through 1863, land speculation ignited. Estate administrators and old-time New York families with large tracts jumped into the market and sold off uptown parcels to brokers and smaller investors. On the East Side, James Lenox reaped as much as $3 million by selling lots on the thirty-acre Lenox Hill estate his father had acquired in 1818. In 1868 executors of the Talman estate on the West Side sold two blocks between 66th and 68th streets for $200,000; a month later the southern block alone was resold for $172,000. That same year a block along the southern border of Central Park went for $840,000.[12]

New investors in 1866 were spending $5,000 to $7,000 for lots on uptown cross streets that had brought $400 in 1857. A Fifth Avenue plot facing Central Park that cost $13,000 in 1867 sold for $24,000 the following year. Brokers made fortunes by trading other people's land; between 1857 and 1868, John McClave claimed, he handled $15 million worth of uptown property and earned nearly $1 million in commissions. Other large landowners—the Zabriskie and Jones families, for example—tenaciously clung to their uptown land, expecting yet higher prices once the territory had been fully improved with paved streets, sewers, and gas lines.[13]

Newspapers and Clinton W. Sweet's *Real Estate Record and Building Guide*, closely following the real estate boom, welcomed landowners' efforts to coordinate their interests. In 1866 landowners west of Central Park formed the West Side Association to promote uptown improvements. Among the early members were some of the city's most solid citizens, including the former park commissioner John A. C. Gray and the former mayor Fernando Wood, who, after reaching the nadir of political repute in his support of southern secession, had abandoned politics and returned to the respectable ranks of investors. East Side landowners quickly followed the trend toward coordinating "sectional interests" and formed their own real estate association. These landowners' groups formally disassociated themselves from party politics, but many uptowners and building contractors did identify their interests with Tammany's recapture of city government under Tweed's 1870 charter. If the city controlled its own affairs, including uptown improvements and the further embellishment of Central Park, landowners might overcome Andrew Green's (and hence the park commission's) reluctance to push forward the construction (and not just the planning) of public works.[14]

While uptown landowners cashed in on Central Park and endorsed local Democrats' plans for uptown improvements, city workers made their own claims to a share of the new prosperity. By 1867 park laborers, who had earned as little as ninety cents a day in 1861, recouped the losses of the past decade's inflation and secured a two-dollar daily wage. Skilled construction workers in the private sector made even more substantial gains when they threatened disruptive strikes if contractors did not meet their demands for union work rules and the eight-hour day. At the end of the Civil War, the city's trade unionists also moved toward independent politics, joining the National Labor Union and establishing a statewide Workingmen's Assembly to lobby the legislature for an eight-hour law. Most employers and business groups believed that permitting more leisure time would only subvert discipline among workers. But in 1867 lawmakers from both parties acknowledged the labor movement's militance by passing an eight-hour bill, albeit one that failed to provide for enforcement. In 1870 the law was narrowed to apply to *public* workers alone.[15]

New York City Democrats appealed to their labor constituents with the promise of jobs on an expanded public improvements program as well as with their backing of the eight-hour law. By 1870, one historian has estimated, city government employed one-eighth of the voters.[16] Thus, Tammany Democrats rebuilt their political control of New York City and its administrative departments by means of public works that tacked together a tentative coalition between real estate interests and labor.

Creating an Orderly Park

The Tweed charter gave the new Department of Public Parks jurisdiction over Central Park, all the small parks, and the improvements on the West Side. With Peter Sweeny (the reputed "brains" of the Tweed Ring) at its helm, the new board employed men in numbers that matched those of the early days of Central Park's construction, an average of 1,587 workers in 1870 and 2,970 in 1871. In its first year, the Sweeny board spent more than $600,000 improving the park, and another $340,000 maintaining it.[17]

Some of this money went to complete architectural features inherited from the old commission, including the Carousel, Dairy, Belvedere Castle, Bethesda Terrace, and stables. Funds were allocated to repair walks and drives worn down by heavy use. (Carriage traffic eroded an inch and a half of paving from the drives each year.) Many of the picturesque plantings, which had been placed quickly and temporarily to meet budget constraints and the expectations of the first visitors, were, as Olmsted and Vaux noted, in need of "extensive revision." The new board, however, interpreting in its own way "the principle that distance, expanse, and extent should be constantly aimed at," now directed a rigorous program of planting, pruning, and thinning trees and clearing out "shrubbery that obstructs the view." Even the suspicious *Times* conceded in the summer of 1870 that the new commissioners "seem determined to make some

A substantial portion of the park's budget went to maintaining the carriage drives, which heavy traffic eroded by an inch and a half each year. Sprinkling wagons moistened the gravel surface to keep down dust.

show for the money they spend." But when the Department of Public Parks issued its first annual report, Andrew Green, who had been effectively isolated on the board by the Tammany commissioners, issued a disclaimer. The report, he charged, showed "a singular want of comprehension of the methods, purposes, and designs of the original commission."[18]

The Sweeny board had, in fact, rejected the earlier design in favor of new aesthetic goals for managing Central Park. The new Democratic commissioners, including Robert Dillon (who had urged an "artificial" style at the time of the design competition), envisioned the park as the urbane symbol of the city's cultural accomplishments; they ignored the advice of Olmsted and Vaux, who were dismissed as the park's landscape architects in November 1870. The board's first annual report proudly displayed illustrations of new architectural attractions: menagerie buildings, the interior of the Arsenal fitted up for a museum, plans for a crystal-palace-like conservatory at Fifth Avenue and 74th Street, and the Sheepfold designed by Jacob Wrey Mould (and today incorporated into the Tavern on the Green restaurant).[19]

With respect to the natural landscape, the Sweeny board simply wanted a

THE LARGE CONSERVATORY
Now erecting on
THE CENTRAL PARK.

THE SHEEPFOLD AND BARN.
Now erecting on
THE CENTRAL PARK.

The parks department's lavish 1871 *Annual Report* featured new architectural attractions. Jacob Wrey Mould designed the Sheepfold at the western edge of the Sheep Meadow and 66th Street, which later became the Tavern on the Green restaurant. Construction of the conservatory, planned for the present site of the Conservatory Water (73rd Street and Fifth Avenue), was abandoned after Tweed's fall.

bright, clean, and orderly park that showed the effect of good housekeeping. Responding to criticisms of the park's rusticity, workers straightened paths for convenience, exposed bridges to the parkgoers' view, pruned the low branches of trees to open new vistas, planted shade trees (that blocked old vistas), and brushed moss and leaf mold off the rocks. Gardeners cleared out the "catbriers and tangled weeds" (as they considered the native plants) and created arabesque flower beds with more than thirty-eight thousand bulbs and other flowers in "conspicuous portions of the Park." Whatever distress these interventions caused New Yorkers sympathetic to the aesthetic motives of the original plan, many editors, parkgoers, and adjacent landowners welcomed them as improvements.[20]

During what proved to be a nineteen-month regime, the Sweeny park board broadened its services beyond Central Park and lavished more than a million dollars on small downtown parks, which an editor described as "neglected, repelling, and unpleasant places." At the Battery, Tompkins Square, and City Hall Park, workers repaved walks, repaired benches, and introduced fountains along with flower gardens, music pavilions, and new trees, shrubs, and grass. "It would not be candid to deny or ignore the generally improved conditions of these bright oases," the *Tribune* noted in an editorial accompanying a lengthy survey of the small parks. But reluctant to acknowledge any benefit from Tammany, the editor also cautioned readers not to credit "a robber who throws you pennies . . . out of your own stolen wallet."[21]

Despite the parks department's expansive program, the Tammany administration invested its greatest efforts in the Department of Public Works, headed by Tweed himself. While West Siders complained of delays on *their* public improvements, Tweed ordered street paving, sewers, and gas lines through the Upper East Side and Harlem. In these territories, where a close circle of his supporters had bought land, the sooner streets were built, the sooner and more profitably these speculators could sell. At the end of the century, Tammany politician George Washington Plunkitt dubbed such favors "honest graft." Reformers later spent years trying (unsuccessfully) to add up the extent of the Tweed administration's "dishonest graft"—the "boodle" politicians pocketed or used to bribe the press and other lawmakers. Roughly $20 million, one investigating committee suggested, had come out of the difference between the actual and billed costs of the courthouse and other enterprises; Tweed ring members had spent a portion of this sum on generous printing orders and advertising that persuaded publishers to look the other way. (The lavishly illustrated 427-page parks department report printed by William C. Bryant and Company in January 1871 was typical of such enticements). Members of the Tweed Ring who stole public money or used it for bribes were far from the only beneficiaries of the program of public improvements: the spoils of the pro-growth political coalition had been widely distributed.[22]

City laborers won jobs and the eight-hour day on public works without a cut in their two-dollar wage. Skilled construction workers found steady work as developers followed street improvements and raised more than two thousand buildings a year. Still, workers' incomes, which ranged from five to eight hundred dollars a year, paled in contrast to the spoils of land speculation. By the conservative calculation of the city's assessors, land values increased by $341 million between 1865 and 1871. Uptown landowners and speculators garnered the biggest gains as assessed land values north of 40th Street—even though dramatically undervalued—tripled in that same period. Few doubted that Central Park had spurred the uptown boom.[23]

New York bankers initially welcomed Tammany's massive public works program as they pocketed hefty commissions on municipal bonds. The city debt more than doubled between 1868 and 1870, to $88 million. But investment bankers themselves finally blew the whistle. City department heads—including President Peter Sweeny of the parks department—showed no disposition to confine spending to the appropriated budget, and by the early fall of 1871 bankers had begun to worry that the city would not have enough money to meet interest payments due in November. Following a series of exposés in the *New York Times* in September 1871, leading citizens organized "a tax and investment strike," as the political scientist Martin Shefter describes it. The bankers and merchants formed the bipartisan Executive Committee of Citizens and Taxpayers for Financial Reform of the City to recapture control from Tweed and his followers. "One thousand of New York's largest taxpayers announced that they would withhold their taxes until the municipal government's books were audited," Shefter writes, "and the city's major bankers indicated that they would not extend any loans to municipal government." Led by banker and former Central Park commissioner Henry Stebbins and backed by reform Democrats such as Samuel Tilden, this Committee of Seventy, as it called itself, looked for "the most honest man in the city" to place in the city comptroller's chair. With little difficulty they found Andrew Green.[24]

"Pushing Labor to the Wall"

Andrew Green had gained new powers as the head of the Central Park commission during the late 1860s, only to find himself all but ignored on the Sweeny park board from April 1870 to Tweed's fall in September 1871. But now Green returned to power as city comptroller to put the fiscal house in order. He refused to pay any municipal bills without an audit, an investigation, and in many instances, a court order as well. The "slow wits of the [Tammany] opposition," a reform lawyer informed Samuel Tilden, had sarcastically dubbed Green "Handy Andy" for his relentless tenacity. As city comptroller Green decreed that officials spend no more than the appropriated budget and reduce the $88 million debt. He scrutinized the operations of city departments with the same exactitude that had driven Olmsted from Central Park in the early 1860s. One politician offered Green a glass of wine at a New Year's reception, suggesting that a little imbibing might foster a new spirit of generosity. "On the contrary," Green replied, accepting the glass, "the more wine I drink the tighter I get."[25]

The parks department had to pare its budget and lay off workers, but Green (who also remained a park commissioner until 1873) initially gave it wider latitude than most city agencies. When Sweeny resigned as park commissioner in November, the Committee of Seventy persuaded the mayor to appoint Henry Stebbins, who had served on the old commission from 1859 to 1870, as president of a new park board. The new commissioners reappointed Olmsted and Vaux as landscape architects, endorsed the designers' recommendations for restoring Central Park's picturesque "rusticity," and secured additional improvement funds from the legislature. But when Green decreed that city departments could no longer turn directly to Albany for special bond issues, Olmsted worried that maintenance would suffer because of the priority assigned to accommodating visitors at concerts and skating.[26]

Green's campaign to reduce the debt and operating budget struck at the heart of city politics, particularly the political coalition that had supported Tammany's expansive (and expensive) development program. The only way to rein in the debt was to halt the construction of public works. Although Green advocated comprehensive planning, he found the building of virtually all the planned uptown improvements "premature." West Side landowners, already unhappy that the Tweed administration's projects had favored the East Side, vociferously complained about Green's policy and the higher tax bills when he directed assessors to revalue underassessed uptown land.[27]

Throughout 1872, city workers felt the effects of retrenchment in reduced public employment opportunities and long delays in payment of wages. In May 1872, with the citywide labor movement at its militant peak, "park, pipe and boulevard" workers held a mass meeting to push for prompt payment, wage increases to $2.25 a day, and the organization of a municipal laborers' union. Then in the fall of 1873 the collapse of the railroad bond market triggered a nationwide financial panic. Retrenchment took on new meaning as local manufacturers laid off thousands of workers. Employers, who had already begun to organize themselves to take back the labor movement's gains, further capitalized on the depression by cutting wages and extending hours. In 1874 some strikes to protest wage cuts turned violent. Irish laborers attacked Italians who accepted $1.75 for ten hours.[28]

The real estate market, propped up by inflated greenback dollars, took longer than the labor market to register the effects of Wall Street's crisis. Land speculators' "noiseless panic" initially attracted little attention, the *Real Estate Record* observed, but by November 1874 the Pine Street real estate exchange was "filled with auctioneers and referees enforcing court decrees against those who had defaulted." August Belmont and other mortgage creditors futilely tried to bid up prices to cover the value of their loans to speculators. In 1871 Belmont had extended a $210,000 mortgage for the sale of park-front lots on Eighth Avenue; three years later, no one topped his own lawyers' bid of $160,000 at the foreclosure sale. Belmont, of course, could easily absorb the loss, but one real estate agent estimated that three-quarters of the speculators who had purchased uptown land in 1871 went bankrupt.[29]

By the mid-1870s, economic depression had sundered the political alliance of real estate and labor. Uptown landowners themselves held contradictory interests in the city's fiscal policies: as taxpayers, they welcomed budget cuts that would reduce taxes; as real estate investors, they wanted public improvements. To resolve this contradiction, members of the West Side Association abandoned their earlier tacit support for a large city work force and instead launched a litany of familiar complaints about inefficiency. The city was "paying four times the proper and legitimate cost" of improvements, landowner Simeon Church informed a state senate committee in 1875. To prove his point, Church told the story of a gentleman acquaintance who jumped out of his carriage to strike rock with a hammer alongside a street gang and did more work in fifteen minutes than the workmen would do in an hour. (No one asked if this gentleman could have kept up his furious pace for eight or ten hours.) Complaining that park workers sat around as at "picnic parties," other landowners decried city employment practices as an "outrage upon the rights of property and an outrage on the rights of the men who [did private] contract work" and earned as little as ninety cents for a for ten-hour day.[30]

Tammany aldermen valiantly resisted the calls of employers, reformers, and taxpayers to reduce city wages, extend the work day, and turn public works over to private contractors. Yet, in contrast to politicians' response to the 1857 depression, public officials also rejected unemployed demonstrators' demands for job relief. By the summer of 1875 Mayor William Wickham, a Tammany-affiliated diamond merchant (who had also been a member of the Committee of Seventy) gave in to reformers' pressure and directed department heads to cut city laborers' wages to 20¢ an hour, paying $1.60 for an eight-hour day. The only department to hold out for the $2.00-a-day wage was the Department of Public Parks.[31]

In 1873 a new reform city charter reorganized the parks department by staggering the five-year terms of commissioners appointed by the mayor; an 1874 state law reduced the board to four commissioners. The next year, Mayor Wickham, hoping to appease his restless uptown constituency, appointed to the park board William R. Martin, a lawyer and real estate agent who had served as the West Side Association's first president. Martin passionately advocated continuing public improvements on a massive scale, but unlike other uptown landowners, he also believed in paying public workers at the established "average wage" for eight hour's labor. When Park Commissioner Henry Stebbins moved to cut park laborers' wages, Martin (and Joseph O'Donohue, another Wickham appointee) resisted.[32]

The commissioners' employment policies infuriated wealthy taxpayers and reformers, who regarded subsistence wages for park workers as a form of patronage. In the fall of 1876 a "citizens committee" demanded that the mayor dismiss Commissioners Martin and O'Donohue for violating that "public duty which requires that the Commissioners of the Central Park . . . go into the market and pay fair [market] wages for the classes of labor and no more."

Citizens were "indignant," the lawyer Dorman Eaton announced, that the park commissioners "have paid two dollars a day all the time, when "you can get all the labor you want for 90 cents a day."[33]

The ensuing debate had important consequences for park workers—and all city workers—for the rest of the century. During the campaign for the eight-hour day, the New York labor movement had successfully established the principle that, as an employer, government had an obligation to meet minimum working standards, including a living wage. In the context of the depression, however, private employers charged that such a policy "demoralized" their own exploited workers, and taxpayers complained that it inflated the city budget. Martin and O'Donohue believed that demands that the city observe the rules of labor-market supply and demand represented nothing less than a concerted attack on the laboring classes. "We would rather be found urging the judicious program of public improvements with the result of giving employment to laborers," Martin and O'Donohue said, "than to sit in the parlor of the Union League club, pandering to the prejudices of the wealthy, who want their taxes reduced." Propertied taxpayers were "turning only the sacrificial side of 'public retrenchment' to the laborers, who really, though indirectly, are bearing their full share of the taxes."[34]

Tapping the new vocabulary of class conflict bequeathed by the 1871 Paris Commune, Dorman Eaton denounced O'Donohue and Martin's "communistic scheme of lifting up the lower levels of life in this city to comfort." Such a policy was "opposed to scientific government." But George T. Blair, president of the Workingmen's Assembly, defended Martin's resistance to men "who stand ready and willing to degrade labor as it never before was degraded in the history of the city." If the gentlemen "persist[ed] in pushing labor to the wall," Blair warned, city government would bear a new cost "in the expense of erecting more almshouses and prisons."[35]

Unlike other uptown landowners, Commissioner Martin saw no tension between his advocacy of labor's interest and extensive public improvements. In an attack on Andrew Green's retrenchment policy, Martin argued that continuing public improvements would prime the pump of the city economy, create jobs, and relieve the tax burden by increasing the value of assessed property. Public parks remained the centerpiece of this strategy. Martin repeatedly pointed to the advance in land values surrounding Central Park to urge that the parks' maintenance budget be increased, that Riverside and Morningside parks be built immediately, and that the parks department adopt Olmsted's new parklike street plan for the recently annexed district in the Bronx.[36]

The Patronage Notebook

Debates within the parks department over how to accommodate the strictures of retrenchment—and particularly the battle between Comptroller Green and Commissioner Martin—filled many pages of Olmsted's "patronage note-book," the basis for *The Spoils of the Park*. In scrappy penciled notes, he recorded rumors of political dealings and his own observations of the negotiations of commissioners, politicians, and park workers over appropriations and jobs. His notes recorded Olmsted's frustration at losing personal control over Central Park. Although he was head of the Bureau of Design and Superintendence from 1873 to 1878, park commissioners (divided among themselves) did not heed his advice about design, maintenance, and policing. But beyond his own battles, Olmsted's notes reveal his effort to explain why "the government of our cities is costly and bad, demoralizing, humiliating, and disgraceful." The problem was that politicians ran public institutions the way petty tradesmen ran their businesses, with an eye to personal benefit; no one cared for a larger "public interest." Elected officials catered to the men "least favored by society," who nonetheless expected to be "taken care of."[37]

Just as Olmsted had been horrified in 1857 by a crowd of unemployed workers, so during the 1870s depression he recoiled from the "mob of [job] candidates" who thronged outside the park board's meeting room, "the larger part of whom were of the dirty ruffianly and loafish sort. The large room with all the windows opened was filled with a sickening odor from them." Nor did Olmsted share Commissioner Martin's concern that working families could not live on less than two dollars a day. Olmsted supported wage cuts and turned a sympathetic ear to a masonry contractor who complained that "the course pursued by the city in supporting a large number of lazy men at high wages" prevented him from hiring cheap labor and thus lowering his bids. The contractor indignantly protested that the presidents of two trade unions, including the Stone Masons Society, worked as foremen on Central Park. Olmsted himself complained to the board that park cartmen were allowed "to knock off work at 4:30" in order to have time to return to the stables and untackle and clean their horses before the day's end.[38]

But despite his advocacy of wage cuts and longer workdays, Olmsted's notes are curiously silent about the charges against Commissioners Martin and O'Donohue, whose employment policy he so strongly disapproved. On other issues, Martin had proven himself Olmsted's strongest supporter on the board, professing unfailing admiration for the Greensward plan and endorsing Olmsted's efforts to regain superintendence of the park. No doubt their alliance was encouraged by Martin's brother Howard, Olmsted's personal secretary. The Tammany-affiliated real estate developer and the reform-minded landscape architect also campaigned together for Olmsted's plan to lay out the Riverdale section of the Bronx with curvilinear streets. Opponents saw the Riverdale plan as a needlessly expensive scheme to promote a luxury suburb in a district that might be more economically and flexibly developed for commercial uses and inexpensive housing.[39] Had Olmsted himself embraced the patronage of real estate developers to push his Riverdale plan forward? His patronage notebook does not subject his own motives to the searching criticism he directed at the other beneficiaries of public support.

Redefining the Political Public

At the heart of debates over municipal governance in the 1870s stood the question of the identity and interests of New York's "political public." To men like Olmsted, preoccupied with the issue of "spoils," the relationship between voters and public officials seemed not an expression of popular will but rather a fundamentally corrupt exchange. The party patronage bargain placed public services in the hands of unqualified and incompetent administrators and workers. Olmsted regarded the legitimate "public" (and especially parkgoers) primarily as consumers who had lost the full value of services to which they were entitled and which only men like himself could give them. Other reformers, sharing Olmsted's contempt for party politics, argued instead that propertied taxpayers constituted the legitimate political public because they paid for city government. A taxpayers' revolt, which first appeared during the economic boom of the 1860s, gained steam in virtually every northeastern city during the depression of the 1870s. Although propertied families had themselves been among the strongest advocates of new municipal services—from better schools to parks—many now considered the tax burden of an expanded public sector an imposition arising from the "excesses" of democratic politics.[40]

In 1876 Governor Samuel Tilden tapped this reform sentiment and appointed a twelve-man commission to make recommendations on the governance of cities in New York. The following spring the Tilden Commission issued a report that took off the gloves in the class battle over control of municipal resources. City government, it asserted, should be regarded as a closed municipal corporation. Control of revenues should be restricted to a board of finance elected by property owners and tenants who paid at least $250 in rent—more than half the annual income of the majority of city workers.[41] It was an attempt, in effect, to institutionalize the 1871 coup of the Committee of Seventy—the bankers and merchants who had seized control of city government from the Tweed Ring and appointed Tilden's close friend Andrew Green as their financial officer. The Tilden Commission further recommended that all public works not financed by assessments on adjacent landowners be built only with current tax revenues; in other words, it ruled out new projects that would be financed—as had the construction of Central Park—through bonds.

With this report propertied taxpayers and reformers announced that they were no longer willing to let the representatives of a democratic electorate determine which public goods and services city residents needed. Nor would they contribute to a public sector that provided decent working conditions for city employees. Business would flee the city, one municipal society warned, unless a new system of government checked the power of "those who have everything to gain by voting away the prosperity of others." The reformers did not believe that working people contributed to the city's wealth through their labor and the rents that covered landlords' tax bills. Gone was Calvert Vaux's vision of "true and intelligent republicanism" in which disparities of wealth would be a "comparatively unimportant matter" because all citizens could enjoy the comforts of public institutions—from parks and libraries to public baths and theaters—through which a "man of small means *may* be almost on the same footing as the millionaire." Gone too was the confidence that such public improvements as Central Park both marked and propelled the city's progress. The progrowth coalition of land speculators, contractors, and workers had been repudiated.[42]

The Tilden Commission cast its proposals to dismantle democratic local government in the form of a constitutional amendment to reorganize the administration of municipal corporations. In the fall of 1878 New York City voters rejected the movement by electing Tammany representatives to the state legislature and common council. Nonetheless, bankers and wealthy taxpayers could not be ignored. When Tammany's own "reform" chief, John Kelly, succeeded Green as city comptroller in December 1876, he acknowledged the weight of businessmen's judgments and rigorously pursued retrenchment. As both "reform comptroller" *and* Tammany boss, Kelly made the Department of Public Parks the special target of fiscal and party discipline. In February 1877, at his direction, new Tammany commissioners outvoted William Martin and cut wages to twenty cents an hour, with the provision that park workers would be "permitted" to labor an additional two hours to earn two dollars a day. Kelly also slashed the department's appropriations by 25 percent. Then in the fall of 1877 Kelly informed the board president that he was withholding Frederick Law Olmsted's salary.[43]

There is a certain irony in Kelly's step. In effect, he reduced the codesigner to the status of an ordinary park worker, rigidly applying the same disciplinary rules that Olmsted himself had advocated for public employees. Olmsted, the comptroller charged, had missed work for more than two days—indeed, for nearly a month—to pursue "multifarious employment outside the City of New York" (including the Buffalo and Montreal park systems, on which Olmsted worked during this period). Kelly deliberately ignored Olmsted's growing national reputation. Perhaps he was venting his spleen at Olmsted as the "representative man" of Tammany's harshest gentleman critics at the Union League. But Kelly claimed that Central Park no longer needed the expensive advice of a landscape architect. The office had become a "sinecure," echoed a new Tammany park commissioner, and in the face of budget cuts, the board could better use the money to pay "poor laborers and policemen."[44]

Kelly probably did not anticipate the outcry Olmsted's firing would trigger in the press. Olmsted's well-connected friends mobilized a protest that moved from the parlors of private homes and the lounges of the Century Club and the Union League to the editorial and letters columns of the *Tribune, Post, World,* and *Herald.* However much they might welcome budget cuts and efficient executive authority in principle, reformers did not intend that the burden of retrenchment should fall on one of their own—or on their own park.[45]

Calvert Vaux viewed the protests with mixed feelings. Although he and Olmsted had dissolved their partnership in 1872, Vaux had few doubts that his former partner's dismissal was unfortunate for Central Park. He was nonetheless distressed to see his own contribution once again erased by such men as E. L. Godkin, who wrote in a two-column protest letter to the *Tribune* that it would be no exaggeration to say that Olmsted, "who designed the Park and has for twenty years nearly watched over its execution, holds a leading position among the professors of this art. The credit due to him is heightened by the fact that no other American has worked in the same field with equal success." Vaux felt he had no choice but to correct the record in his own letter to the *Tribune.* Satirically invoking the metaphor of the division of "their joint artistic property" in Central Park first articulated by Olmsted in 1863, Vaux complained that Godkin had assumed the status of "administrator" of a joint estate—the divider, one might say, of the spoils of reputation—and had directed "to F. L. Olmsted, everything; to C. Vaux the cut direct."[46]

Olmsted had gone to Europe in January 1878 to recover his health, and his wife Mary quickly intervened; she directed their son Owen to publish an acknowledgment of Vaux's equal contribution to Central Park's design. She and Vaux met to discuss the matter, but soon found themselves trading insults. Mary Olmsted's attitude, Vaux complained in a letter to Godkin, was "that of a successful buccaneer." She said that "her husband was always a more popular man" and that Vaux had been "utterly dependent on him," particularly on Olmsted's connections to the press. Vaux had a "chivying English disposition," Mary Olmsted complained to her son John, objecting to Vaux's sarcastic allusions to Olmsted's "vagrant disposition" and to his claims that her husband had been very "weak" and "owed everything to [Vaux's] manliness." She could only conclude that her husband's former partner was not driven by legitimate claims of coauthorship but rather was "out of his head with worry that he has no business."[47]

The painful episode impressed upon Vaux "how nearly I was engulfed in oblivion." Nonetheless, leaving the cry of "spoils" to his former partner, Vaux began his own campaign to defend their design, focusing single-mindedly on the "art element" of the park, which represented to him the purest statement of its democratic possibilities. Again and again he would work behind the scenes to mobilize fellow artists and editorial writers into a single-issue lobby to block proposals to alter the plan. Although Vaux relied on an educated public that shared his own tastes, he nonetheless believed that his efforts were serving the larger principle that in a republic all citizens were entitled to enjoy the benefits of society's wealth through public institutions.[48]

The "Secret of Decline and Decay"

The retrenchment of the 1870s took its toll both on the park and on the individuals most closely identified with it. Yet if Olmsted and Vaux found decreasing demand for the talents of public landscape architects, they were spared the worst effects of the depression. Tens of thousands of New York wage earners were unemployed, and some were driven to despair. In August 1875 Andreas Fuchs, a forty-year-old shoemaker, shot himself to death in a secluded part of Central Park, explaining in a note left for his wife and children, "I have no work and do not know what to do." (By 1879 suicides in the park had become so frequent that the police had standing orders to search the shrubbery and out-of-the-way spots each morning for victims.) By 1881 William Martin had left the park board and had lost his real estate fortune and even his private residence to foreclosure. After taking desperate measures of his own, Martin was threatened with disbarment for abusing his fiduciary responsibilities as an estate administrator by "borrowing" the heirs' money.[49]

"Notwithstanding the ruin of some who have unwisely speculated in it," Olmsted reported in January 1878 to a gentleman who wished to know whether Central Park had succeeded, "real estate near the park has continued to increase in substantial value." Olmsted, who had noted the advantages of parks to land values in his addresses to such groups as the Social Science Association, was concerned that the depression not discredit this argument. Despite the "wailing" against "unnecessary and extravagant public works," he maintained, "neither from press, pulpit, nor stump has there yet been the slightest symptom of remorse for the Central Park."[50]

Olmsted spoke too soon. Six months later, the *Real Estate Record*'s publisher Clinton W. Sweet picked up a theme he had first sounded during the panic: Central Park had been such a real estate disaster that it should be cut off below 72nd Street. The park's "original investors," he wrote, "were a body of real estate speculators," who had hoped to increase the value of their land by seeing more than eight hundred acres "ruthlessly, unceremoniously, and thoughtlessly appropriated" into the public domain. For speculators, the park had become "the brilliant but false beacon that has lured to destruction." Denying any "irreverent or iconoclastic spirit," Sweet nonetheless complained that Central Park's maintenance placed an "enormous burden" on taxpayers. If the lower park were sold, the money could pay off the city debt, and parkgoers would "hardly" notice.[51]

No one appears to have taken Sweet's proposal seriously. Yet, in the gray light of the depression, some New Yorkers wondered whether they could indeed afford Central Park. For the next two decades (and really the next century) they would debate how much they were willing to pay in order to maintain it.

The physical deterioration of their preeminent public institution dismayed genteel New Yorkers. Editorials in national journals and letters to local newspapers complained of worn-down carriage drives, muddy paths, overgrown vegetation, unrepaired bridges, and of the taste of the park's new administrators. The carriage parade proceeded apace on weekday afternoons, but the backdrop of landscape art was peeling away. In the late 1860s the city had been spending about $250,000 per year for the maintenance of Central Park. Ten years later it spent $100,000 less on taking care of *all* city parks. Although deflation compensated for some of the 60 percent drop in spending, the responsibility for twenty-three additional parks and squares meant a drastic cut in the money available for maintaining Central Park.[52]

In 1879, as the maintenance budget hit an all-time low, *Harper's Weekly* offered an explanation for Central Park's shabbiness: "The secret of the decline and decay of the Park is that its management is political." And so it was. But by viewing politics solely as a matter of party spoils, the writer overlooked the larger political struggle over public finance that had tarnished Central Park as the unambiguous symbol of elite New Yorkers' political and cultural leadership. When politicians cut the park budget and workers' wages, they were also meeting the demands of what the Tilden Commission had called "the best men."[53]

The gentlemen and gentlewomen who had promoted Central Park in its first thirty years had envisioned a public institution that could transcend the city's economic divisions. For two decades they had pointed to the park as a representation of their own civic achievements and the potential refinement and moral order of a democratic society. As the park's designers conceived it, this was a society that would find harmony and inspiration in a pastoral landscape set apart from the city. The restoration of the park to home rule had challenged this vision and reopened aesthetic debates over whether the park's original design best represented the attainments of a prospering city. In retrospect, the Sweeny board's "betrayal" was closely identified with its preference for an orderly park that featured architecture as well as nature. It was as though in abandoning the mid-nineteenth-century romantic sensibility that regarded nature itself as a repository of virtue, the park's new administrators had laid bare the social fissures that even the most profuse display of nature's bounty could not keep hidden.

Still, the Sweeny board had not ruined Central Park. It had, in fact, lavished money on upkeep, and that was the crux of the problem. Even after Tweed went to jail for his theft and Sweeny retired from politics, the structure of the political system that had supported their regime remained. Working-class New Yorkers would vote for politicians who promised jobs and decent hours and decent pay on public works. And during boom times, propertied New Yorkers would support the generous investment of "public capital" to propel the city's economy. But the policies and taxes that supported higher public wages cut into private profits. "Governments," the Tilden Commission had concluded, are not created for "sentimental purposes." "They are contrivances to furnish protection to the industrious citizen" who wishes "to pursue his private avocations."[54] During the depression, bankers, merchants, industrialists, and landowners mobilized politically to defend their private interests by minimizing their economic contribution to the public sector.

If Central Park was only one of many public institutions that suffered from budget cuts, it was the one nearest to the hearts of the city's most comfortable citizens. Nonetheless, propertied New Yorkers chose to sacrifice its maintenance to the discipline of the marketplace. Because they feared losing control of city government to Tammany politicians and their immigrant working-class supporters, they tried, as the historian C. K. Yearley puts it, "to starve the party by starving the state."[55] Wealthy New Yorkers continued to use the park and to defend the designers' original vision, but they would never again confidently regard it as the symbol of their own standing as the "representative class" of a unified public. The era of Tweed and retrenchment marked a retreat from the optimism with which elite New Yorkers had advocated creating a public park that would accommodate their own desires and needs *and* elevate those citizens below them. They realized that providing working people with, in Olmsted's terms, the "mental & moral capital" of leisure time and space might encroach on their own financial capital. Precisely because Central Park was "public," new groups—park workers seeking a living wage, park officials advocating a different aesthetic, or politicians running the party system—made new claims on its administration. Whatever the problems of patronage, the restoration of home rule had given a voice to new constituencies that would work to open city politics and the park itself to a broader public.

Charles Eliot Norton, one of the most prominent advocates of civil service reform, believed the significance of Olmsted's 1882 pamphlet on spoils reached far beyond the issue of "the preservation of a great and beneficent public work of art [or] the vindication of an honorable reputation." Rather, Norton was convinced that Olmsted addressed the problems of "the very existence of popular civic institutions and administration."[56] Bemoaning the park's "decline," Norton and others like him doubted that a democracy could sustain such public institutions as Central Park. But in the decades that followed, the political currents unleashed by restoring the park to the city continued to transform its character as a popular civic institution. The park that had in the 1860s represented elite accomplishment would become in the 1880s and 1890s a more genuinely democratic public space.

II

RESHAPING PARK POLITICS

In December 1880 Salem H. Wales, a prominent Republican and editor of *Scientific American,* joined the Board of Commissioners of the Department of Public Parks and immediately began campaigning to open its meetings to the public. Wales had heard rumors of raucous closed sessions in which commissioners resorted to throwing inkstands at one another. He hoped that public sessions would restore dignity to the proceedings.[1]

When meetings opened, reporters attended "the sittings of the board in the confident expectation of getting what is called 'a funny item'" for their papers. The four-man board was split into four factions and could not agree on a chair after thirty-one ballots. Debate at the December 18 meeting was so chaotic that Andrew Green (who had been reappointed to the board by anti-Tammany mayor Edward Cooper) quietly lectured the other members on parliamentary procedure. A Tammany commissioner ignored his advice; whereupon Green rose from his chair: "His voice had lost its calm sweetness and rang out like the discordant tongue of a town clock on frosty midnight air." Commissioner Wales responded (with his own lack of decorum): "I think it is unfortunate that [Green] did not marry when he was young. A good woman might have brought out those delicate and tender sentiments that lie dormant in his breast." Bachelors "do not fuse as easily as married men." The meeting broke into laughter.[2]

The appointment of two new commissioners the following year did little to alter the proceedings, which the *World* described "as a state of catalepsy tempered by epigrams." Commissioner William Oliffe was a wealthy druggist who, according to Central Park's superintending gardener, "delight[ed] more in cockfighting than in the beauties of natural sceneries"; the second new member, Charles F. McLean, was widely believed to be the proxy of his former law partner, Andrew Green. Reporters turned even the rare moments of accord into

CENTRAL PARK—THE DANGERS THAT THREATEN IT.—Drawn by Thomas Worth.

Harper's Weekly brought national attention to the political controversies surrounding Central Park. In this 1879 cartoon, Thomas Worth satirizes wrangling commissioners, lazy park workers, overzealous pruners, and vandals attacking John Q. A. Ward's 1866 statue *The Indian Hunter.*

a "funny item," noting, for example, the "softening effect" of the Christmas season: "Mr. McLean did not glare at Mr. Lane with his usual ferocity . . . and Mr. Wales indulged in one or two agreeable quotations from Shakespeare appropriate to the season, and Mr. Oliffe's countenance beamed good will."[3]

Press coverage of the board's antics in 1880 and 1881 revealed a shift in administrative style since the relatively staid days of the original board of gentlemen. Park politics had become part and parcel of city politics. In the same era that Central Park itself was becoming more eclectic, diverse, and open to the city (more *part* of the city), park politics became more contentious, and more open to different views. When the Tweed charter of 1870 restored Central Park to home rule, park commissioners faced the demands of often antagonistic constituencies—politicians, reformers, taxpayers, landowners, and working-class families.

Against a backdrop of class polarization, the issues of money, management, and maintenance remained central in the last quarter of the nineteenth century. Politicians steered clear of dishonest graft, and factionalism limited the park commissioners' use of patronage, but reformers continued to oppose budget increases that might feed party rule, or park workers' families, and instead campaigned to place Central Park in the hands of "disinterested" civil servants. Even professional managers, however, needed the support of special interests to win increased appropriations for maintenance. With real estate development proceeding unevenly along the park's borders, landowners successfully asserted their proprietary interest in this public space and pressed for both repair and modification of its landscape. Workers, meanwhile, faced a continuing drought in the public sector.

In rejecting public workers' claims to fair wages and hours, propertied New Yorkers were in effect rejecting the claims of all working people to conditions that would allow them the leisure and the financial security to enjoy the city's public institutions. But in 1886 the eight-hour movement and Henry George, a self-taught journalist and political visionary who ran for mayor as the United Labor party candidate, challenged this status quo. As he spoke from a flatbed wagon in working-class neighborhoods, George offered a fresh vision of democratic government in which the "revenue from the common property could be applied to the common benefit." "To give all classes leisure, and comfort, and independence, the decencies of life, the opportunities of mental and moral development," George had written in *Progress and Poverty*, "would be like turning water into a desert."[4]

George's campaign marked a turning point in the debate over the workings of democratic public institutions. His campaign, and the labor movement on which it built, disrupted the routine rhetoric that pitted reformers against party politicians. George defended working families' rights to define the issues of democratic politics. Those issues ranged from making government itself a responsible employer to securing the leisure time in which to enjoy the benefits of public parks, playgrounds, and museums. The political mobilization that followed (though it did not win George the mayoralty) had its counterpart in a "cultural mobilization" of sorts, through which ordinary New Yorkers claimed access to Central Park and to new small parks in their own neighborhoods. In the process, they were redefining both the city's "public" and Central Park as a public space.

Looking for "Men Who Understand"

The Republicans and Andrew Green, who dominated the first park commission, had claimed the mantle of disinterested stewardship, but in the three decades after 1870, commissioners—two-thirds of them members of the Democratic party—unapologetically took an active part in local politics. Factions pitted Tammany Democrats against the reform-minded (and frock-coated) "swallowtails" associated with the County Democratic organization. Furthermore, the staggered five-year terms produced new alignments on the board roughly every two or three years and thus limited commissioners' ability to deliver the department's patronage to any one political faction or, for that matter, to set a clear agenda for parks.[5]

The majority of commissioners after 1870 came from comfortable middle-class backgrounds and made their fortunes in real estate, contracting, and law. Elite, Yankee control of the board now gave way as substantial numbers of New York natives and smaller numbers of second-generation Irish and German Americans served as commissioners. This shift alarmed newspaper editorialists, who invoked the standard of the first Central Park board, repeatedly calling for the appointment once again of "citizens of wealth and established reputation, well fitted for the park commission as men of culture." The *World* complained in 1884 that a new member, John D. Crimmins, was "known only as a contractor, which is of itself a palpable disqualification for the place." By contrast, the *Times* hailed Crimmins's successor, the Harvard-educated banker J. Hampden Robb, as a man whose "character, education, and associations are a guarantee for his faithful fulfillment of the duties."[6]

Editors generally endorsed landowners' claims to be represented on the board. In 1881, for example, the first chief engineer of Central Park, Egbert Viele (who had become a Civil War general and then a West Side landowner), campaigned for the position of commissioner by presenting a lengthy evaluation of the park's defects to the West Side Association; his efforts were rewarded with an appointment in 1883. Landowners from the annexed district of the Bronx (where the parks department had charge of building streets as well as parks) also secured a regular seat on the board.[7]

Political fighting handicapped the commissioners' efforts to win more money from the board of estimate, which oversaw city spending. In 1880, for example, when the Republican Salem Wales aligned with a Tammany commissioner in asking the board of estimate for a $400,000 increase over the previous year's appropriation, Andrew Green, a County Democrat, used his own careful audit of department accounts to challenge his colleagues' estimates "by line item." Denouncing their waste and extravagance, Green went so far as to appeal to the cause of the "poor widow taxpayer whom an extra $5 causes to turn away and weep." Following this performance, the board of estimate granted the department $330,000 less than it had requested.[8] Constrained by inadequate appropriations, maintenance of Central Park declined further in the early 1880s, despite the loud complaints of editors and nearby landowners. Rather than face the question of how much money was needed to maintain the park as designed, however, editors demanded professional management.

Although Olmsted and Vaux conceded that there could be "intelligent" differences in aesthetic taste, they had rested their charges of political incompetence on the board's pursuit of policies that subverted the overarching design motive of creating a pastoral landscape within the city. Thus, the designers denounced the Sweeny board's program of tidying up the plantings and introducing features that had the effect of distracting parkgoers' attention from the natural scenic effects. A neat landscape might please visitors who found unkempt nature disconcerting; for the designers, however, such policies only underscored the need to place the management of Central Park, in Vaux's words, "in the hands of men who understand what it is, what the designers intended it to be." Reporters and editors, themselves preoccupied in the late nineteenth century with establishing professional standards for journalism, listened sympathetically to arguments that maintenance should be referred to "experts" in matters of taste and landscape architecture.[9]

Not the least of the problems involved in finding a "professional" park superintendent in the era of reform, however, was deciding what the job entailed. Sensitive to taxpayers' charges that park workers were inefficient and lazy, in 1879 the board appointed as superintendent John Dawson, who had worked as a contractor and could, as the *Times* put it, "handle bodies of men." When Dawson came to blows (literally as well as figuratively) with park workers in the spring of 1880, he was replaced by "Whiskey" John Halloran, a Tammany contractor turned liquor dealer. But it was a measure of Tammany's waning influence over the parks department that Halloran's tenure lasted less than six months.[10]

In August 1881 the board settled on a Welsh carpenter, Aneurin Jones, as the new superintendent. Jones had his own ideas on how best to maintain Central Park. Responding to complaints that the park "was kept in a very slovenly manner"—"vines and weeds have hidden the rocks" and shrubs and trees "straggle at will"—Superintendent Jones readily concluded that his first duty was to oversee extensive pruning and removal of underbrush. "Over a thousand loads of dead wood and rubbish have been cleaned out of Central Park," Jones proudly informed the board shortly after taking office. His show of industry impressed Commissioner Wales, who "admire[d] Jones for making the men do their day's work which pleases the taxpayers."[11]

Meanwhile, Olmsted and Vaux each took up the campaign to bring Central Park back under "professional" superintendence. After the park board abolished his office in January 1878, Olmsted had moved to Boston, where, in partnership with his eldest stepson John, he had begun designing that city's parks. Despite his growing national prominence, he continued to follow politics in the city where he had first made his reputation. When in the fall of 1881 his friends advised him that Superintendent Jones was "mutilating" shrubs in his campaign to permit "the healthful circulation of air," Olmsted wrote his pamphlet on the park's spoils. Controversy heated up when Jones began cutting vistas through trees to provide parkgoers with a view of the Mineral Springs Pavilion and the Third Avenue elevated railroad, a widely admired engineering marvel.[12]

Vaux, too, was lobbying for a professional superintendent who would uphold the naturalistic aesthetic. Although Vaux had other projects—including designing houses for Charles Loring Brace's Children's Aid Society and Samuel Tilden's townhouse and country estate—he "lived to defend the artistic creation of Central Park . . . which expressed his conception of what a people's pleasure ground should be in New York," as an associate would later observe. For more than twenty years, Vaux had urged that the quality of the park's maintenance "should be taken up in the editorial columns and kept before the public." And despite Mary Olmsted's remarks about her husband's stronger press connections, Vaux proved an effective publicist; he drew upon his friends at the Century Club and prodded Olmsted to use his own influence. When the *Tribune* published a lengthy editorial in 1881 advocating Vaux's return to the park as landscape architect, one observer assumed that Vaux had written the piece himself.[13]

More tolerant of "practical" politics than Olmsted, Vaux used his connections with Andrew Green to win reappointment as the park's landscape architect and then insisted that the board give his junior partner, Samuel Parsons, Jr., the unpaid position of superintendent of planting. Vaux later explained to Olmsted that he had intended to train Parsons as their successor. "When I last took the position . . . it was with the expectation of being forced to resign after a time on some quotable issue." As it turned out the resignation came in December 1883, over the board's construction of a new skating house without consulting him. But Vaux had secured for his junior partner "the opportunity to know the park . . . and to make a record on maintenance that could be used in the future."[14]

Parsons, the son and grandson of prominent Queens County nurserymen, had attended the Sheffield Scientific School at Yale. But in 1881 he had little experience with either superintending workers or planting trees. The landscape gardener Jacob Weidenmann complained to Olmsted that Parsons had not "the slightest gift for the art," and even Vaux was not always confident of his student's commitment or talent. Nonetheless, when Olmsted visited New York in 1884, he conceded that, despite all the intrigue over superintendents, "the park was looking better than [he] supposed it would be."[15]

"It was a feather in my cap," Parsons proudly noted in his memoirs, "to have secured such powerful and loyal friends" as Green, Tilden, and William R. Grace, the city's first Catholic mayor. Temporarily losing his position when Egbert Viele became a commissioner, Parsons served as superintendent of Evergreen Cemetery on Long Island, in which Grace owned the controlling stock. With Vaux, Parsons also landscaped Grace's country estate, and in 1885, through Mayor Grace's intervention—patronage—Parsons became Central Park's "professional" superintendent, launching an association with the park that lasted more than two decades. A pragmatist in park politics, Parsons "determined never to resign" over principle.[16]

While Vaux hoped to train Parsons to maintain the aesthetic principles of the Greensward plan, other advocates of administrative reform focused on the issue of patronage raised by Olmsted's spoils pamphlet. State assemblyman Theodore Roosevelt saw an opportunity to launch his own reform career by championing Olmsted's call for placing the park in the hands of an unsalaried board of directors, which would "exercise conservative control" by reviewing the superintendent's policies. A similar determination to establish "professional," "businesslike," or "scientific" government propelled the reform campaign for a civil service law in New York State in 1883. Olmsted's friends Charles Norton and E. L. Godkin read his pamphlet as supporting this cause, though Olmsted denied that this was his purpose. Legislative efforts to reform the park board never went very far, but in 1884 New York lawmakers extended civil service to municipal government by establishing new examination procedures for salaried officers in city departments.[17]

In repeatedly attributing the deterioration of city parks to patronage, Olmsted and other reformers overlooked both the constraints that factionalism placed on the commissioners' use of patronage and the notable continuity and professionalism within the parks department itself. Some officers, including Chief Engineer Montgomery A. Kellogg and Superintendent of Gardening W. L. Fischer, dated their association with Central Park from its initial construction. Others—"Green men"—had joined the park in the early 1860s. Workers, particularly in the police and gardening departments, also received their training through long years on the park. Many longtime employees greeted the civil service regulations with suspicion. When one gardener who had served on the park for twelve years failed the department's own "oral, practical and written" examination in 1882, his superintendent, W. L. Fischer (who had "apprenticed" with the Royal Horticultural Society in London), protested to Commissioner Wales that the examination "was not worth a damn." Nor were the park commissioners happy with civil service procedures. When two park keepers were arrested in 1885 for robbery, Commissioner John Crimmins blamed the civil service board for not having looked into the "character" of men on their list. The board regularly evaded the law by assigning "skilled workers" (who were not covered by civil service regulations) to both the clerical and engineering staffs.[18]

All in all, the new civil service measures had relatively little effect on the management of the park. Just as many workers and managers were skilled "professionals" before 1883, so, too, patronage did not disappear after that date. Moreover, the quality of maintenance depended more on the level of appropriations than on either patronage or professional managers. Mayor Grace initially backed his endorsement of Superintendent Parsons with an increase in the park's maintenance budget for 1886, but when a taxpayers' reform committee launched yet another barrage of criticism against "waste," Grace reduced the next year's budget. Still, the park maintenance budget averaged $348,000 a year from 1885 through 1889, a nearly 40 percent increase over the previous five years. In the end, reformers and politicians had less influence on park policies than New Yorkers who made their voices heard at meetings of the board of estimate. And by the mid-1880s, no group was more vocal and more interested in the park's management than landowners, developers, and the park's new neighbors.[19]

"Attracting Fashionable Residence" along the Park

A pamphlet promoting lots near Central Park in 1865 predicted, "The supply can never be increased, and the demand, when it once sets in, will arise among the class who are able to pay what they want." This logic propelled land speculation around the park in the late 1860s and early 1870s, tripling prices in less than five years. By the time the 1873 panic hit, however, it was clear that builders could not profitably both purchase and improve land held at speculators' inflated prices. When demand for lots dried up and mortgages came due, countless overextended land speculators, including William Martin, lost their shirts along with their lots.[20]

Central Park had "failed as a device for attracting fashionable residence," the *Real Estate Record and Building Guide* observed in 1878; wealthy New Yorkers were "unwilling to [live] opposite a vast open space which presents so dreary and bleak an appearance in winters." Far from appreciating the splendors of nature, fashionable families dreaded the "unwholesome influences emanating from such a large surface of unimproved land" and preferred to have "opposite neighbors to enliven the monotony of daily life." In the late 1860s Edith Wharton's aunt Mary Mason Jones had met such skepticism head-on. Ensconcing herself in the "Marble Row" at Fifth Avenue and 57th Street, she simply waited for "fashion" to discover the neighborhood's cachet and demand building lots on her extensive adjacent landholdings. In 1877 expectations rose when the Lenox Library (designed by Richard Morris Hunt) was built at Fifth and 71st Street. The following year railroad magnate Cornelius Vanderbilt and Standard Oil executive J. A. Bostwick announced plans to build palaces at the park's southeastern corner. By the 1880s merchants, manufacturers, and heirs were commissioning elegant townhouses on the side streets below 72nd Street between Madison and Fifth. Sky-high prices along Fifth Avenue itself limited settlement to the scattered mansions of such "pioneer" families as the sugar-refining Stuarts and the investment-banking Schiffs. Then in the 1890s, with Caroline Schermerhorn Astor leading the way, the tycoons arrived in full force on Fifth Avenue and permanently linked Central Park with "Millionaire's Row."[21]

West Siders gloomily watched the East Side's ascendancy as "*the* fashionable district." In the slow market of the 1870s, some West Side landowners had continued to collect minimal ground rents from shanty dwellers; others had put up cheap wooden flats, stables, and saloons. Large landowners, however, worried that such "low-class" buildings discouraged respectable development. Only by coordinating their efforts through joint investments and restrictive covenants, landowner and Singer Sewing Company executive Edward C. Clark told a meeting of the West Side Association in 1879, could developers establish the neighborhood's "exclusive character" and attract well-to-do families. That same year Clark contracted with architect-builder Henry J. Hardenbergh to construct the nine-story luxury Dakota Apartments, named for its frontier

Millionaire's Row: Fifth Avenue, north from 65th Street in 1898. Richard Morris Hunt designed the mansion in the foreground for Caroline Schermerhorn Astor—*the* Mrs. Astor.

location on the corner of Eighth Avenue and 72nd Street facing the park. Clark believed the Dakota would advertise to other builders, as well as to consumers, the "distinguished pre-eminence" of the neighborhood. To the same end Eighth Avenue was renamed Central Park West in 1883. Clark filled in adjacent side streets with respectable rowhouses, as did other builders on the blocks near the new elevated stations at 72nd and 86th streets.[22]

"It may be objected, perhaps," Clark observed of his proposal for coordinating the West Side's fashionable development, "that no provision has been made for the laboring population." "There is the highest authority for believing that the poor will always be with us," said the man who supplied the sewing machines that drove down thousands of seamstresses' wages, "but it does not follow that the poor will necessarily occupy any part of the West Side plateau." "The poor would be sufficiently with us if they lived in New Jersey or Long Island." Clark joined other West Side landowners in campaigns to "stamp out

The developer Edward Clark hoped that the luxurious Dakota Apartments built at 73rd Street and Central Park West in the 1880s would establish the Upper West Side as a fashionable district. But first the nearby shanties had to go.

the squatters," the saloons, and the shanties, and by the late 1880s the forces of uptown "improvement" could claim victory in that fifty-year war. A few shanties remained, but the *Real Estate Record* denied their very existence by counting any uptown lot occupied by a wooden or a one-story brick building as "vacant."[23]

West Side builders less disdainful than Clark of a working-class housing market, however, erected cheaper "flats" near the park, particularly south of 72nd Street along the elevated tracks on Ninth Avenue and on Tenth Avenue, renamed Columbus and Amsterdam avenues in 1890 to supply the neighborhood with character and tradition. Thus, the Upper West Side slowly formed as a mixed-class neighborhood.[24]

By the end of the century, collecting the spoils from real estate investments near the park required new strategies. In the preceding decades, individual landowners like James Lenox, brokers like John McClave, and developers like

Edward Clark had made fortunes on "Central Park lots," but the era of park entrepreneurs was passing. If the profits from real estate were enormous, so were the risks and the capital requirements of land development. In the 1890s the *Real Estate Record* predicted that "incorporated companies" would soon dominate speculative building, for even "old operators . . . seem to have reached the conclusion that larger capital is now needed . . . than has hitherto been at the command of single individuals." With this "larger capital" in hand a new generation of Manhattan builders followed Clark's lead and turned to luxury and middle-class apartments to tap yet another spring of the park's value to real estate investment. Although middle-class New Yorkers had initially resisted apartment living, the Dakota, the Central Park Apartments (built in 1883 on Central Park South), and other high-rises along the park established the respectability of multifamily dwellings and provided the solution to the problem of high land costs that had plagued development around Central Park.[25]

Modifying the Park Landscape

In 1886 a friend reported to Olmsted that Superintendent Parsons had followed a commissioner's direction to "cut among the screen woods at 68th and 5th Avenue . . . to oblige Mrs. R. L. Stuart whose residence is opposite."[26] As new fashionable neighborhoods formed in the late nineteenth century, individuals and real estate groups lobbied for their own interest in the maintenance and arrangement of the park's landscape.

The drainage problem particularly worried uptown developers. The stagnant lakes bred malaria, reporters charged, warning parents to keep their children away. "Two-thirds of the drainage system," Commissioner Crimmins advised the board of estimate in 1884, "is so imperfect as to be of practically no benefit." The pipes installed twenty-five years earlier by George Waring had been "of very inferior quality and of improper sizes" and were now clogged by tree roots; the concrete pipes William Grant had used to save money on construction had "disintegrated and crumbled away." The lawns and meadows were reverting to swamp, the half-filled lakes were covered with "green scum," and the transverse roads and bridle paths flooded after every rain. To make matters worse, sewers from the park's comfort houses dumped waste into the ponds.[27]

With rumors of malaria threatening the uptown real estate market, adjacent landowners backed the park board's request for special appropriations to dredge the lakes and replace pipes. Parsons and Vaux (who once again returned as landscape architect in 1888) oversaw the filling of the west arm of the Lake at 77th Street—once known as the Ladies' Pond—and redesigned an adjacent bridle path. But by the 1890s, the lakes were stagnant cesspools once more. This time the board turned to asphalt and then concrete bottoms. However pleasing the illusion of a natural landscape, artificial materials were easier to maintain.[28]

The original Greensward plan had enclosed Central Park to create a self-contained pastoral landscape, but the wall and the limited carriage and pedestrian entrances along the east and west borders represented a constant source of irritation for the park's neighbors. When Crimmins, who lived on East 68th Street, became a commissioner, East Side landowners were able to get a new entrance into the park at 67th Street. By the end of the decade, West Siders, who had no entrances between 59th and 72nd streets, were demanding the same accommodation. "It should not be necessary for any of us to walk nearly a half a mile before obtaining access to this great breathing space," the *Real Estate Record* editorialized. "Elderly and invalid people who would use the park," Laura Lyman (who lived on West 63rd Street) informed Mayor Abram Hewitt, were deterred "by reason of the long walk necessary to get there." Responding to such complaints (as well as pressure from the West Side Association) the board arranged for new pedestrian entrances near West 62nd and 66th streets, and also new carriage entrances north of 72nd Street.[29]

The park's neighbors were even more annoyed about their difficulties getting *across* the park. By the early 1880s the four transverse roads had so deteriorated that the one at 85th Street bore virtually all crosstown traffic. Sidewalks had been laid through the narrow and walled sunken roads, but pedestrians were loath to compete with two lanes of wagons and carriages. "How long are the residents of this city in the vicinity of Central Park to suffer?" one East Side householder demanded of the mayor. The park was a "nuisance to those like myself who are separated from friends [on the West Side] by it." While some uptowners crossed the park on the 72nd Street carriage road, developers petitioned for a new surface road across the park. Transit companies also proposed building tracks for horse railways on the transverse roads. Meanwhile, the park's neighbors campaigned to extend the curfew to midnight and to light the paths so that they could walk across the park at night. A local manufacturer and park neighbor had complained to the mayor that the "very desolate looking" and impassable condition of the unlit sidewalk facing Central Park West "creates an unfavorable impression upon those who purpose residing in our section."[30]

Adjacent land developers also pushed park officials to finish landscaping the long-neglected northern end of Central Park, which, the East Harlem Improvement Association complained in 1890, rendered their nearby lots "unmarketable." One such improvement was construction of the Conservatory at 105th Street and Fifth Avenue in 1899. And despite the reservations of Calvert Vaux, the board also approved elaborate entrances at the 110th Street east and west corners. The *Real Estate Record* successfully campaigned for the introduction of flower beds at the park entrances—an aesthetic trend Olmsted denounced.[31]

Neighbors also took offense at "nuisances" tucked out of the path of most

When real estate organizations like the Harlem Improvement Association complained of the neglected condition of the northern park, the board introduced improvements such as bedded flower gardens (shown here at Mount St. Vincent), a trend Olmsted particularly disliked.

park visitors. In 1888 Julia Robinson, who lived on West 65th Street, complained to the mayor about the park's manure heap at Eighth Avenue and 66th Street; the Women's Protective Association launched a campaign to remove it and another (six feet high and fifty by a hundred feet in area) at 78th and Fifth. Superintendent Parsons explained that the manure had been kept at these sites so that livery stables could donate their horses' waste as fertilizer. "Of course it must smell rank now and then," an old park worker explained to a reporter, "but that does not matter much. People around here are used to it, and it's a good saving for the park to get so much fertilizer free." But the park's new affluent neighbors were not "used to it" and refused to tolerate the smells.[32]

Landowners and residents on Fifty Avenue campaigned against other odors and perceived nuisances, repeatedly (and unsuccessfully) urging that the zoo be moved from behind the Arsenal at 64th Street. Commercial proprietors on Ninth Avenue enthusiastically greeted one proposal to rebuild the zoo on the West Side, but residential developers marshaled the West Side Association to defeat this threat to their own exclusivity. The park board told Fifth Avenue residents that it would move the zoo to the North Meadow if they would pay the costs. Although Vaux mobilized editorialists and artists to oppose these proposals, that the zoo stayed at the Arsenal site was as much a tribute to West Siders' resistance and East Siders' parsimony as to the park board's loyalty to the Greensward plan.[33]

The intensified use that accompanied uptown development prompted incremental changes in design. The board widened and straightened drives when carriage traffic led to more accidents. From its first adoption, the plan had been adjusted to accommodate new needs and pressures. As landscape architect, Vaux "fully recognized that changes must come," Parsons observed, "but he also asked that they be made so as to keep whole the essential spirit." Thus, while cooperating with the board to make the park more convenient, Vaux (again in an unintended alliance with landowners) also helped organize protests to block businessmen's proposals to use the park for a world's fair.[34]

Uptown landowners and residents formed an influential constituency. They supported increased appropriations to maintain the park's value as a real estate amenity and demanded new consideration of visitors' convenience. With the backing of these landowners, the department partially reversed the deterioration. But in contrast to the late 1860s, landowners maintained their distance from larger political coalitions. Retrenchment had driven home the message that propertied and working-class New Yorkers had little in common as a public. Whether joining reformers in calling for professional management or urging that the park landscape be modified for their own convenience, propertied New Yorkers wanted to consume parks without having to think about the labor that produced or maintained them.

"We Are All Politicians That Vote"

A basic question confronted New Yorkers in defining their rights and goals as a democratic sovereign body that provided "popular civic institutions" like Central Park. Who had the power to decide how public resources, including land, labor, and tax revenues, should be controlled and allocated? Who, for example, would set the terms of employment for workers who maintained public spaces like Central Park? Like private employers who used their power as proprietors to establish the conditions of work, propertied New Yorkers saw a fundamental threat to their own interests and pocketbooks if the linked sovereignty of workers and voters determined the conditions of public employment. But male city workers employed by a democratic government were, in theory, themselves members of the sovereign public and, hence, their own employers.

Politicians, of course, recognized this paradox and rewarded workers who voted them into office with public jobs. Although thousands of workers accepted the necessity of exchanging political favors for employment, the organized labor movement deeply mistrusted party politics and patronage.[35] Instead, labor leaders sought to hold government accountable as an employer and to advance the interests of all working families by establishing the standards of fair wages and hours in the public sector.

The debates over the administration of Central Park encompassed these questions of how a democratic government should act as an employer. Through the mid-1880s, park workers, like those in other city departments, were on the defensive. Reformers commanded the rhetorical high ground in their attacks on city workers' "inefficiency." But while citizens' committees framed debates over public finance as matters of waste, park workers asserted their rights to decent wages and hours of work. They drew strength from their ties to the larger labor movement, which revived in the early 1880s. Some skilled park workers, the stonemasons, for example, were active labor leaders within their trades. In 1882 the stonemasons and carpenters won a restoration of wage cuts, a concession that the board gradually extended to petitioning plumbers, painters, blacksmiths, and steam engine operators.[36]

These gains did not extend to unskilled laborers, who made up the majority of city employees and roughly 60 percent of the parks department work force. Laborers who petitioned the park board to raise their wages in the early 1880s were as likely to see their requests tabled or, worse, to face a layoff when funds dried up. In July 1881 Mayor Grace had authorized a 10 percent pay raise, to $1.76 a day, but only after securing the consent of the city's leading private employers. Female washroom attendants continued to earn no more than $1.50 for a ten-hour day.[37]

Through the 1880s, most park commissioners identified with the class interests of the city's employers and propertied taxpayers. But John Crimmins, who became president of the board in 1884, had an independent vision of what it meant to open the political process to new groups, particularly Irish Americans. Crimmins had inherited his construction business from his Irish-born father and had extended his wealth through West Side real estate investments and later, through rapid transit projects. He was both a close associate of some of the city's wealthiest capitalists and a sympathetic friend to park workers. A County Democrat, he boldly rejected the pieties of liberal reform. "We are all politicians that vote," he declared. If the parks department was hiring and if a man "was recommended by a politician, all other circumstances being equal, it would not prevent his appointment." Crimmins saw nothing wrong with patronage, but he put ethnic and religious loyalties above party obligation.[38]

Crimmins often ignored aldermen's demands and recruited men for the park from his private contracting business and then rehired them when they were laid off from the park. The department's Irish-American cast under his leadership especially enraged the Vermont-born Rush Hawkins, leader of the Council for Municipal Reform, who wanted to return local government to Yankee rule. Answering charges that "no good New York American boy can get on the Central Park police," Crimmins observed, "I can safely say that the majority of the park-keepers are American born." (He did not add that their parents were often Irish.) Crimmins, a member of the lay board that oversaw the construction of St. Patrick's Cathedral and a generous contributor to Catholic charities, also defended the custom of allowing nuns from Catholic hospitals to collect donations from park workers on pay day. "Those poor men themselves feel a pride in contributing," he observed, "they feel that by those small contributions when they make application to the sisters to take care of them in their hospitals they have some claim on them."[39]

In 1886 when Crimmins found himself the target of yet another investigation into the department's "inefficient" management, he called for a different kind of reform from that which the taxpayers' committees had in mind. If the department's laborers were not efficient and "if a better class of men will not apply to us," it was because "they [could] get 50 to 75 cents a day more on other works." Seasonal layoffs, Crimmins complained, also created "a great injustice and hardship" for the park's unskilled laborers, few of whom could find work for more than 150 days in the year. Still, the park often hired back the same seasonal laborers. "There seems to be something about the public labor, or the public service," Crimmins observed—taking reformers' own sacred phrase— "that attracts men to it, and I am surprised that it should be so."[40]

As both a public and a private employer, Crimmins relied on the conventions of patronage to advance the interests of the Irish-American community and park workers. Still, his paternalism had its limits, and in 1886 those limits were challenged when the city's working classes entered the electoral arena in a new way.

Claiming Membership in the Political Public

Henry George's third-party campaign for mayor altered the balance of class power in New York City and placed labor issues prominently on the political agenda. Backed by the Central Labor Union (organized in 1882), the Knights of Labor, and thousands of nonunion laboring families, George secured one-third of the vote in a three-man race, doing particularly well among the city's

Political demonstrations were banned in Central Park, so the labor movement looked elsewhere to hold its mass rallies, such as this 1882 Labor Day Parade in Union Square, to demand the eight-hour work day.

second-generation German and Irish Americans. Although the campaign itself rested on an interclass alliance, most local political observers read it as a working-class political insurgency.[41]

George had first laid out his political vision in 1879 in *Poverty and Progress*, which argued that the private monopoly of natural resources led to new extremes of wealth and hardship, erratic cycles of boom and bust, and "rotten democracy." By what right did individuals or corporations profit from concentrated landownership when the value of this "common property" arose from the labors of the entire society? The only way to abolish poverty, George wrote, was to tax away the "unearned increment," that is, the increase in land values stemming from the progress of society as a whole. Such a tax would defeat monopoly, open land to independent producers, and improve the bargaining position of all workers. George's advocacy of a single tax on land and his larger vision of social cooperation appealed to middle-class New Yorkers seeking reassurance that the American political economy could move toward harmony. But George's appeal to working-class New Yorkers lay as much in his demands that they be given a full political voice as in his specific economic theories. "The people are the source of political power" in a democracy, he insisted, and "it is time for the great body of the citizens of New York to take some step to . . . demonstrate their powers in a way to make their influence felt in every branch of administration."[42]

The George campaign challenged the different ideas about public resources that had influenced the gentlemen advocates of Central Park in the 1850s, the free-spending Tammany growth coalition in the late 1860s and early 1870s, and the proponents of retrenchment who followed. Rejecting the promotion of public improvements to increase real estate values, George and his followers denounced speculation like that around Central Park. "The enormous value which the presence of a million and a half people gives to the land in this city, properly belongs to the whole community," George declared in his platform, and "it should not go to the enrichment of individuals and corporations, but should be taken in taxation and applied to the improvement and beautifying of our city, to the promotion of the health, comfort, education and recreation of its people." The labor candidate also rejected private philanthropy as a substitute for civic institutions: "We, the people of New York, ought to furnish the institutions ourselves" in order to "do for the equal benefit of all such things as can be better done by organized society than by individuals."[43]

Although George lost the election, he believed his strong showing had "given the powers that be a very sincere respect for the workingmen's vote." His campaign forced Democrats and Republicans to acknowledge working-class New Yorkers as members of the political public and to develop new strategies to absorb the insurgents back into party organizations. The formation of the United Labor party pushed Democrats to reunite for the first time in twenty years under the Tammany banner; they also elaborated the paternalism of men like Crimmins to retain the loyalty of city workers. Republicans, who achieved local power only through the fusion of different reform factions, also regularly courted labor's support by advocating "progressive" programs.[44]

Through the 1880s and 1890s, organized workers tested politicians' commitment through a series of legislative campaigns to strengthen labor laws, including the eight-hour day for public workers. Despite labor's new voice in politics, park employment in any given year continued to reflect the unstable conditions of the larger labor market, union strength outside the park, the attitudes of particular commissioners, and the demands of taxpayers for budget cuts. And the labor movement responded to the pressures of competition by narrowing its vision of who should be included within the political public. From the 1870s, for example, African Americans had unsuccessfully campaigned to be hired as park workers. Seeking to overcome such divisions, George had "solicit[ed] the suffrages of all citizens, rich or poor, white or black, native or foreign born." (George's democratic sentiments did not, however, extend to the Chinese; he supported their exclusion from the United States.) The United Labor party platform had even called for equal pay for equal work "in public employment . . . without distinction of sex." But in the face of mounting economic pressures, the labor movement backed an 1889 eight-hour law that made citizenship a requirement for public employment.[45]

Even with new laws, park workers had to fight to enforce the eight-hour day. In 1889 park gardeners and drivers protested to the mayor when Superintendent Parsons introduced a new system of monthly payment and granted foremen the authority to define the "number of hours to constitute a day's work." Proudly reporting to the park board that the new system had all but eliminated overtime pay, Parsons considered the "permanency" of park workers' employment "sufficient to counterbalance this extra [unpaid] work." He ignored the gardeners' protest that "6 days work is plenty for a hard working man" and continued to permit foremen to require labor on Sunday.[46]

If Parsons believed that security of employment justified extra work without pay, workers believed that long service to the department obligated the city to provide for their health and old age. In 1885 the park keepers had established a fraternal association to allow retiring members a small pension, but the parks department, unlike the metropolitan police, contributed nothing. "What have we to look forward to?" a committee of park police asked the mayor, after detailing injuries from catching runaway carriages and the health risks of "standing nine hours at a time upon the frozen lakes protecting skaters." "Having served the city faithfully for fifteen or twenty, or . . . 25 or 26 years, and getting old, and nearly if not altogether broken in health, we are dismissed from the force, without a dollar and physically unable to earn one."[47]

Crimmins supported the demand for a pension; it was "revolting to [his] sense of justice and humanity" to act as the agent of "public ingratitude" by dismissing "old and disabled men without any means of support." But not until 1892, when Tammany state senator George Washington Plunkitt took up the cause, did park keepers win a pension law. The city's reform groups denounced such "notorious measures" as yet another effort of Tammany politicians to secure the votes of city employees. That park police gained their pension through legislation, however, also revealed the labor movement's power in pressing its own political issues. In 1894, anxious to stave off working-class radicalism in the context of another depression, legislators even applied the eight-hour day and prevailing wage rules to private contractors on public works, as organized workers had been demanding since the days of unemployed demonstrations on the grounds of the unbuilt park. Such a law, of course, flew in the face of sanctified free-market competition and threatened taxpayers' favorite solution for reducing the expense of municipal services; it was declared unconstitutional.[48]

In the end, the labor movement's legislative efforts had mixed consequences for park workers. Although the eight-hour rule was observed in theory, foremen could still demand extra hours without paying overtime. In 1893 a state law restored the two-dollar daily wage park laborers had first won in 1868, but they saw no further increase for nearly a decade. There was a limit to what politicians would do for them. Moreover, the parks department's significance as an employer declined in the late nineteenth century as other city departments expanded. While the parks department stabilized its maintenance work force at roughly four hundred laborers, the street-cleaning department employed more than thirty-five hundred workers (including black and Italian Americans, who continued to be informally excluded from park work). In the late 1890s when the Central Labor Union and Knights of Labor carried street cleaners' demands to the legislature, they won a wage scale at "prevailing rates" and a pension for all sanitation workers. Park laborers did not have the same kind of political influence, and without a pension, they could not afford to retire. By 1916 the Manhattan park commissioner complained, one-third of the maintenance workers were over sixty-one, including forty-four "park veterans" who were over seventy-one.[49]

Still, both in the security of employment and in working conditions, positions on the park compared favorably with other arenas of employment for unskilled workers. The requirement of citizenship for public workers reserved many park jobs for second-generation Irish Americans. By contrast, the Irish immigrants who built and ran the city's privately owned transit system earned substantially less for longer days. And although park workers appear to have preferred stability of employment to militancy, they continued to petition for wage increases. When they finally won the five-dollar day in 1919, however, that wage was worth only three-fifths of what it meant to Henry Ford's auto workers in 1914.[50]

Claiming the Benefits of Municipal Resources

Throughout the late nineteenth century, debates over the "spoils" of city government obscured larger questions. How should a city sharply divided between rich and poor determine its priorities in allocating public resources? Socializing goods and services—from public schools to public parks—was one of the great achievements of nineteenth-century democratic society. Yet a minority of New Yorkers claimed a veto power over the extent of those public benefits because the municipal finance system, relying primarily on real property taxes, made them the heaviest taxpayers.

In the aftermath of the 1870s retrenchment, propertied taxpayers restricted claims on public resources. Between 1876 and 1896, appropriations increased less rapidly than population for education, charities, and asylums—that is, for many basic welfare services. "Such economy is wicked," observed park worker Patrick McCabe, described by a reporter as "an intelligent Irishman" who advocated increasing appropriations for the board of education and board of health as well as for his own department. "These departments affect closely the public—morally, physically, and intellectually. There are other directions in which true economy could and should be practiced. But then what do these fellows that lead a sedentary life downtown know about it?"[51]

Propertied citizens and politicians knew their own priorities lay in building and maintaining the city's infrastructure to accommodate the needs of commerce, real estate investment, and middle-class families seeking a pleasant living environment. The most rapid increase in appropriations between 1886 and 1896 was for public works, street cleaning, and the parks department's street construction in the Bronx. But the downtown business and professional community remained vigilant even on public improvements. In the early 1880s when property owners in the Bronx campaigned for new parks in their district, declaring that New Yorkers "could not have too many pleasure grounds and breathing spaces," downtowners objected that the costs would "cause serious injury to the business interests of the city." The Bronx park advocates won their parks by stressing the benefit of pleasure grounds to property values rather than to people. Once again Central Park provided the prime example of how public policy endorsed the "unearned increment" of land speculation.[52]

Although propertied citizens continued to control the allocation of public resources, the working-class mobilization of the 1880s did have an impact. Politicians now recognized that they could not take the support of labor for granted. Thus, at the same time that Mayor Hewitt opposed the "extravagance" of issuing bonds to purchase park land north of the Harlem River, he conceded that it was the "city's duty to provide at least as many facilities for the poor as it does for the rich." Hewitt (who had only narrowly beaten George six months earlier) surely learned his lesson from his opponent, who had charged that "the children of the rich can go up to Central Park, or out to the country in the summer time; but the children of the poor, for them there is no playground in the city but the streets."[53]

"The lack of such things" as recreational facilities, Hewitt thought, had "made an opportunity for Henry George." The "poor people feel they are denied the commonest necessities of life, and they lend a willing ear to anyone who promises them better things. The only way to meet this case is to remove the cause of discontent." With these concerns in mind Hewitt endorsed an 1887 law authorizing a million-dollar annual appropriation to build small parks in the tenement neighborhoods, many of which had backed the George campaign. In effect, the law finally endorsed the small downtown parks that land reformers and the German press had urged as an alternative to Central Park more than three decades earlier. Middle-class progressives (like those who had supported George) championed such public facilities as a way of overcoming the extreme class antagonisms of the late nineteenth century.[54]

Although such measures acknowledged working people as members of the public, Tammany Democrats, who returned to power in 1888, only selectively endorsed programs that benefited working families. In part, this selectivity

reflected the fears of Democratic voters and politicians that an activist government with a reform agenda would impose restrictions on drinking and other
popular amusements. Although Tammany backed labor laws, it did not carry
through with building small parks in working-class neighborhoods. Despite
the million-dollar annual appropriation, by 1900 only four parks had been created. Tammany answered to demands for working-class recreational resources
through the party rather than the government. Through ward clubhouses (set
up to counter the success of the George campaign in neighborhood organizing),
politicians courted the loyalty of voters with an annual calendar of picnics and
festivals at the existing parks and the commercial pleasure grounds, at which
free beer, ice cream, rides, games, and fireworks were provided by local political
leaders.[55]

Whatever the priorities of politicians and large taxpayers, the city did not
lack the means to pay for public goods and services. Despite repeated depressions, its economy was rapidly expanding, especially in manufacturing and
finance. But whereas property owners generally favored more and better city
services, they opposed financing those services through higher taxes, even
though their tax burden was quite modest by modern standards. Wealthy
families like the Astors particularly benefited from the widespread underassessment of real property, and the underassessment of personal property was far
more serious: in 1890 real estate was assessed at nine times more than personal
property. This imbalance (as well as aggressive evasion) meant that William
Vanderbilt paid taxes on only $500,000 in personal property, although his estate
was valued at $40 million. When assessors tried to tax J. P. Morgan for
$1 million in personal property, the financier appeared before the local tax
board and swore an affidavit claiming that he had "no personal property over
debts other than untaxable assets." In denouncing this tax system with its
"premium on fraud," Henry George had introduced his audiences to a new
term: "'Tax dodgers' they call them."[56]

Rich New Yorkers—corporations as well as individuals—were accumula-
ting fortunes on which they evaded paying local taxes, but even the middle-class
households could not complain about excessive taxes. Between 1886 and 1896
the city tax rate fell, dropping in 1889 (and remaining for seven years) below the
2 percent of assessed value so strenuously advocated by reform-minded taxpayers. "It is perfectly conceivable that, without going too far into 'socialistic'
enterprises, New York might still, with true economy, expend a larger proportion of the people's income in collective undertakings," concluded economist
Edward Dana Durand in his 1898 study of municipal finance.[57]

City officials took advantage of the economic growth to increase per capita
appropriations for city services slightly between 1886 and 1896. Yet, it is some
measure of the tensions produced by immigration, labor militance, and the
widening gap between rich and poor that in 1890 the police department received the largest appropriation in the city, exceeding that for schools, public

works, and the combined allocation for parks, asylums, public health, and street cleaning. (Of course, local politics also explained the generous funding of the police. Tammany had to share parks department patronage with other political factions, but the police department was theirs alone.)[58]

Still, as working-class New Yorkers protested social inequality and its impact on democracy, they did help alter the terms of politics. In the 1870s middle-class New Yorkers had blamed workers for the city's fiscal problems; by the 1890s a new generation of progressive reformers increasingly focused on making corporations and wealthy New Yorkers pay their fair share of taxes. Mounting demand for tax equity and broader public services prompted campaigns to reform the tax system, culminating in 1917 with the adoption of a progressive state income tax in New York.[59]

The turmoil of city politics reshaped park politics in the late nineteenth century. Mobilized by the George campaign, by the labor movement, and more ambiguously by Tammany, working-class New Yorkers, including park workers, won some modest improvements in employment conditions and the distribution of public resources. With Irish Americans such as John Crimmins or German Americans such as George Clausen serving as park commissioners, the city's ethnic communities gained a voice on the board as well as jobs on the park. Landowners, who had been part of park politics from the outset, aggressively reasserted their interests in park management to ensure profitable uptown development. Although cost-conscious reformers campaigned equally hard, their long-term impact was more limited. The park came under professional superintendence, but day-to-day management changed relatively little. Despite the persistence of patronage, park workers enjoyed relatively secure tenures; and despite the cries of "spoils," in the end there is no evidence that they worked "inefficiently."

By the end of the century, it was no longer possible to hold up the park as the "antipode" of the city. The first stage in the transformation of park politics had come in the 1870s when elite New Yorkers embraced fiscal austerity and abandoned their commitment to maintaining a landscaped public park, the next stage in the turbulent 1880s when other groups asserted their claims on the park. But the opening of Central Park to all the city did not take place simply through electoral politics, petitions and letters, or at the meetings of the board of estimate. Instead, democratization occurred informally in the day-to-day use of this and other popular civic institutions. In the late nineteenth century working-class New Yorkers not only joined the political public, they also transformed the cultural public of Central Park. At the same time that the park board opened its meetings, the park itself became more and more open to the public.

12

THE "MANY SIDED, FLUENT, THOROUGHLY AMERICAN" PARK

About a year after Central Park first opened to visitors, the *Irish News* expressed its hope that "no unworthy exclusiveness shall be found operating to diminish the pleasure of the citizens in their ornamental Pleasance." But the paper added philosophically and, as it turned out, prophetically, "At all events, there will be time enough for all parties to have control over it and cherish and beautify it. Nothing here remains long in any one way. . . . We democrats have only to wait our turn."[1]

Within just a decade, new "parties"—Boss Tweed and his followers—had taken control of the park, but they, too, did not remain long. During the last three decades of the nineteenth century, control of Central Park bounced from one political faction to the next. Particularly after the working-class upsurge of the mid-1880s, the definition of who constituted the public expanded; gentlemen could no longer claim a monopoly on moral and mental capital—or on the management of Central Park.

Just as post-1870 park politics could not be separated from conflicting interests in the city, so did park use mirror the changing culture of New York, with which Tweed or any other politician had relatively little to do. The move toward a more eclectic and socially diverse park started even before the Tweed Ring took power in 1870 and continued well after Boss Tweed went to jail. Moreover, the greatest impetus for change came not from the park commissioners but from below, from ordinary New Yorkers, who made their way to the park in growing numbers, transforming the social character of the crowds. In the process, they also introduced new modes of socializing that subverted the genteel decorum of the first decade, making the park more like rest of the city and, in effect, more "public."

Millions More Make the "Journey to Leisure"

The year 1870 represented something of a benchmark in the use of the park. After reaching 7.6 million in 1865, park attendance remained essentially stable for the rest of the decade, but in 1870 attendance began to climb. It rose by 16 percent that year and in 1871 by 26 percent. It leveled off again for the next three years, and after that, the gatekeepers stopped counting. One of the few available sources suggests another 40 percent increase (to 15 million people) over the next two decades or so.[2]

It was becoming easier to get to the park. In 1878 the Sixth Avenue elevated line shortened the "journey to leisure" by cutting twenty minutes off the streetcar trip from lower Manhattan, although initially it also doubled the price. By the end of the decade, visitors had five different horse car lines and three elevated lines to choose from. At the same time, fewer park visitors needed public transportation, for they had moved within walking distance. Every year the center of city population had edged farther uptown, and the "rural districts" had become more and more urban. In the forty years after the opening of the Central Park, Manhattan's uptown population multiplied more than seven times, three times as fast as that of the rest of the city.[3]

But the large jump in visitors occurred *before* the new transportation or the changes in social geography. The park began attracting wholly new constituencies. Only about one-fifth of the 2 million new visitors who came to the park in 1870 and 1871 arrived by carriage; the other four-fifths were pedestrians. The proportion of visitors on Sunday—the only day available to most working-class New Yorkers—increased, and contemporary journalists noted more working people in the park, especially on Sundays. In May 1871 the *Times* paused from its steady criticism of park management to celebrate "bright weather and cheerful scenes" in "Central Park on a May Sunday!" It reported "all kinds of people in the Sunday crowd," but "by far the majority belong to that order which is dignified . . . by manual toil."[4]

By the end of the decade, the newspaper articles on Sunday in the park carried headlines like these: "The People's Pleasure Ground," "The People's Pleasure Day," "The People's Great Playground," and "The Poor's Holiday"—the sort of terms reserved solely for the Fourth of July in the 1860s. "Eighty per cent of the visitors to the park yesterday," a reporter calculated in the spring of 1877, "were workingmen and their families." "It is chiefly the poor," said a typical article from the same period, "who, escaping from the cages in which they have been imprisoned for a week, most enjoy God's holiday on the broad walks and among the flower-fringed rambles of our beautiful Park." German Americans were singled out as the most noticeable group among the park's Sunday visitors.[5]

Unevenly rising real wages (up 50 percent overall between 1870 and 1900) enabled more working-class New Yorkers to afford the streetcars or the elevated, and the eight-hour day gave many skilled workers new leisure time. Despite these gains, Sunday remained the *only* day when most working people could get to the park, some not even then. "The Central Park may do for the rich, or the humble residing within convenient distances," the *Irish Democrat* said bitterly in 1871, but for "poor families" downtown, "the brightness and beauty of the resort are as unattainable as if fifty times further removed." Two decades later in *How the Other Half Lives,* the reformer Jacob Riis noted that in one downtown public school only three of forty-eight boys had ever been to Central Park. And in 1902 an Irish immigrant maid, who lived downtown and supported a family of seven, explained to a reporter why she had never visited Central Park in her thirty years in the city: "I have never seen ten cents for carfare that wasn't needed some other way more—that's why."[6] But if truly equal access remained illusory in an unequal society, working people in general were making more use of the park than in the past.

Easing the "Iron Rules"

As more and more working-class New Yorkers headed for the park on Sundays, some sabbatarian regulations imposed in the 1860s gave way. Boat rentals, once so hotly debated, became a regular feature of park Sundays; so did pony rides and goat carriage rides for children. The Sweeny board of the early 1870s, under constant pressure from religious groups, was still not ready to allow Sunday concerts, but even this taboo disappeared in 1877, when the board began to experiment cautiously, limiting the concerts to after 7 P.M. In 1884 the commissioners finally voted unanimously to permit regular Sunday afternoon concerts. In part, the decision reflected the waning power of sabbatarians in both local politics and the Protestant church. For example, Henry Ward Beecher, still a popular and respected minister despite the charges of adultery leveled against him in a lurid trial nine years before, told a reporter in 1884 that he found "no harm" in a Sunday afternoon park concert as long as park commissioners prevented drinking and rowdyism.[7]

The concert decision also stemmed from the altered politics of the park board and the city. Park boards of the last three decades of the nineteenth century never represented working-class interests or priorities in any direct way, but as appointees of a popularly elected mayor rather than members of a self-perpetuating board, commissioners now responded to local political pressures. In what the *Times* called the "Sunday concert war," some commissioners weighed the consequences of their park policies against electoral votes rather than the prestige of the people on the two sides. Commissioner Egbert Viele, a Democratic party activist, led the fight on the board for Sunday concerts. His impending campaign for Congress no doubt made him particularly sensitive to public opinion. Commissioner John Crimmins supported him on the issue. "As a contractor, I employ large numbers of men. . . . These are some of the people who will be attracted Sundays," since they "have not time" or are "too tired" to attend Saturday concerts. The Central Labor Union and the Clothing Cutters' Union passed resolutions, local cigar factories circulated petitions, and Catholic priests preached sermons for Sunday concerts. German Americans, a growing voting bloc that included Protestants, Catholics, and Jews, mobilized against what they called the "fanatics" and "hypocrites" of the Sabbath Committee. When sixty thousand people showed up for the first Sunday afternoon program, the board was deeply impressed.[8]

The *Times* said the commissioners' vote for the Sunday concerts showed "a proper appreciation of the needs of the general public," but what was really at stake was an expanded definition of "the general public." The *Times* itself contributed to this redefinition as applied to Central Park when its editors sent reporters to Catholic priests and labor leaders for comments. Twenty-five years earlier, when the *Times* had explicitly warned the park commissioners not to heed unnamed and unquoted "vulgar agitators," such voices had been largely ignored in public debates on the nature of the park. Now, the *Times* embraced and promoted the continental Sabbath.[9] In an era of sharp labor conflict, Sunday park concerts had come to seem less threatening to social order than Sunday "idleness" in the corner saloon or radical political agitation. Better Sunday concerts on the Mall than Henry George in City Hall.

The *Staats-Zeitung* reported that working people made up the vast majority of Sunday concert crowds, creating "a completely different picture" from that of the " 'better society . . . in their velvet and silk" who attended the Saturday concerts. There were many working-class women: "Two-thirds of the crowd at Central Park yesterday afternoon wore white dresses," the *World* reported of an 1884 Sunday concert. "There was the usual complement of men in uncomfortable looking clothing, but they were in the microscopic minority. Even the babies outnumbered them three to one and the girls outnumbered the babies in almost as large proportion."[10]

The *Times*—emphasizing the presence of working-class families as well as unaccompanied women—described the first concerts in the park as "a great big labor-union picnic." "The masses who slave from daylight till dark six days in the week" filled the air with the "babel of tongues." The only middle-class New Yorkers the reporter spotted in the throng were "a few eminently respectable men of middle age, who hung on the outer edges of the multitude" and "wished it distinctly understood that they were in no way part or parcel of the crowd." They "were attracted merely by a curiosity to see how the common people behaved." They found, to the surprise of many officials and reporters, that they behaved very well. Twenty years earlier Central Park had been the place to watch the elite on parade; now, at least on a summer Sunday, it was a place to see "how the other half lived."[11]

"Dear me, this is quite as good as going to Coney Island!" a *Herald* reporter

In the 1880s working-class New Yorkers successfully campaigned for band concerts in Central Park on Sundays, their only day of rest.

heard a young woman say as she "emerged hot and rumpled from the crush." A laborer who worked fourteen hours a day in a gashouse said the concert was "the only real pleasurable Sunday I have enjoyed in ten years." He told the *World* that he had "never heard of the Park until of the music, and to-day I have been as happy as a king." After the first month of Sunday afternoon concerts, the *World* wrote that "the crowds have learned more about the Park and instead of remaining as heretofore close to the [bandstand] . . . they scattered all over the great pleasure ground, every seat from the ramble to the reservoir harboring at least one couple."[12]

Families in trade wagons joined the concert crowds on Sundays. By the 1870s gatekeepers no longer vigilantly barred commercial vehicles on Sundays. Newspaper accounts include descriptions of the "modest wagon in which the good man had peddled his wares during the week, and which is now furbished up and gay with the joyous smiles of a happy household." On weekdays, the fashionable carriage parade continued in full force, but on Sundays the "German provision man" out with "his family for a drive in a heavy old wagon" and the "ambitious persons of small means" in hired vehicles took over the carriage drives.[13]

The loosening of Sunday park rules prompted park commissioner Matthew Borden (a distant relative of the infamous Lizzie and the sort of Republican Yankee merchant who might have sat on the original board) to complain that the park was turning into a "circus ground." He sought a Sunday ban on the use of swings, goat rides, sailing boats, and the Carousel. But Borden was now an anomaly on the board. Crimmins allied with his fellow board member and business associate Henry Beekman, a politically active lawyer and real estate man, to defeat his proposal.[14]

While sabbatarians and antisabbatarians fought over use of the park on a particular day of the week, other skirmishes centered on use of particular areas of the park, especially its lawns. The Sweeny board responded to pressure for more space for active sports by opening part of the North Meadow between 97th and 102nd streets to baseball, though it still refused calls to allow working men and youths as well as schoolboys to play the national game. "I do not think it just to our class," the president of a team of "working boys," complained about the policy. Nevertheless, the official ban on adult baseball games remained in place until the 1920s.[15]

Still, resistance to other sports in the park, particularly those that reflected the growing middle-class enthusiasm for competitive games and "strenuous living," weakened. In the 1880s the commissioners began to permit archery, lacrosse, football, and tennis on lawns, roller skating on paths, and bicycling (with some restrictions) on the drives. Tennis, first permitted in 1884 with temporary nets on the South Meadow just below 97th Street on the park's western side (the site of the present-day tennis courts), was particularly popular with both middle- and upper-class New Yorkers. By 1892 there were 125 grass courts in the upper park, though all who used the courts had to get permits.[16]

The longtime concern about the condition of the lawns continued, but the "keep off the grass" regulations aroused constant protest. The newspapers denounced "iron rules" that made the lawns "meadows only in name," "panoramic beauties to be gazed upon but not enjoyed." Even the *New York Times*, which had faithfully supported park regulations in the 1860s, complained in an 1875 editorial: "The rules about not walking upon the grass are now enforced so rigidly that sending children to the Park is rather a punishment for them than a treat."[17]

But the rules were not always enforced so rigidly. A park visitor in 1873 saw "dozens of people in a single place, coolly ignoring the notice, 'Please keep off the grass,'" and particularly on warm Sundays, the huge crowds overflowed the

When tennis became a popular new sport among wealthy and middle-class New Yorkers in the 1880s, the park commission set up courts on the meadows north of the reservoir. The first paved courts were constructed in 1912.

paths onto the lawns. At a Sunday concert attended by sixty thousand people in 1884, the *Times* observed, " 'Please keep off the grass' was unheeded."[18]

In 1875 Olmsted urged that the baseball grounds be closed for the year, but politically minded commissioners refused to go along. Whether schoolboys could continue to use the lawns had "long agitated the deliberations of the Park Commission," the *Herald* explained. Commissioners "who wished to become popular earnestly advocated granting the privilege while those who cared more for the beauty of the Park than for the applause of the people as earnestly resisted the demand."[19]

The vacillation continued throughout the nineteenth century: commissioners loosened restrictions and enforcement, then tightened them again. But the general direction was toward relaxing the originally rigid policy. By the 1880s most of the lawns were designated by a blue pennant with white stars as "common" (or open) on Sunday. Permits were also granted for children's (but not workers') May Day picnics on park meadows. Policies varied, however, by time and place. It took a rather large red sign to explain the rules for use of the Green (Sheep Meadow):

> Whenever the turf of the green is not specifically unfit for use, permission will be given to certified members of the public schools, under 16 years of age, for ball-playing upon it on Saturdays. It will be open for croquet-playing Mondays, Wednesdays, and Fridays for ladies and gentlemen. It will be open to the public in general on Sunday. A red flag on the staff will indicate that the green is closed. A blue flag with white ball that it is open for the ball-players; a white flag with red ball that it is open for the croquet-players; a blue pennant with white stars that it is 'common,' or open to the public in general.[20]

By the 1890s pressure was growing to eliminate the keep-off-the-grass regulations entirely. In 1895 the commission briefly removed most of the signs, only to return them when intensive use made the lawns look "like vacant lots in a tenement house district." Two years later, the president of the park board again "called in or overruled every 'Keep Off the Grass' sign in the city." "This may offend artists and landscape architects," a "philosophical park policeman" observed, "but, after all, it is the way parks should be used."[21]

Still, even under the most liberal regimes, many of the familiar activities of ethnic and working-class picnics were prohibited. In 1895 a British visitor praised park officials for not giving in to "the multitude who cannot dissociate beer and skittles from their conception of bliss." In 1881 park officials did allow a procession from the Società Mazzini, which was headed for the statue of Italian nationalist leader Giuseppe Mazzini (near 67th Street on the park's west side), but on the condition that they "remove the little flags from the horses' heads and lower the flags carried in the carriages." "The lowering of the flags," one member protested, "made the procession not a procession." The next year, the society's members simply decorated the statue quietly and then went off to Wendell's Elm Park at 92nd Street and Ninth Avenue to have "a good time." Most ethnic associations, churches, and trade unions continued to hold their festivals at commercially run picnic grounds such as Elm Park, Jones Wood, and Sulzer's Harlem River Park.[22]

The *Times* may have described the first Sunday afternoon concert as resembling "a great big labor-union picnic," but labor picnics usually included speeches, beer kegs, dancing, sports, and games of chance—none of which were officially permitted in Central Park. Therefore, after the nation's first Labor Day parade in 1882, festivities were scheduled for Elm Park. Some less official labor gatherings do seem to have escaped the notice of Central Park officials. In the 1880s, as cloakmaker Abraham Rosenberg later recalled, garment workers unhappy with piecework rates would stop work for the day and "go off to a picnic to 'Cendele' (Central) Park," where their employers "would know where to look for them."[23]

But Central Park rarely—if ever—served as a space for overt political mobilization. Instead, rallies took place at Tompkins Square (site of the 1874 unemployed demonstrations and the 1877 rally in support of the nationwide railroad strikes), Union Square (gathering spot for the first Labor Day parade), or City Hall Park. In 1886 Henry George took his campaign to the docks, factory yards, elevated stations, commercial picnic grounds, street corners, and Tompkins and Union squares—but not to Central Park. Park officials were, however, willing to provide a forum for presidents, mayors, and other political leaders at ceremonial dedications of statues and museums—political uses of the park that posed no threat.[24]

Rides and Restaurants

The park commissioners resisted many of the commercial enterprises that solicited a place in the park. Nevertheless, some of the barriers against these "intrusions" came down and parkgoers began to encounter new amusements that resembled the attractions of the commercial entertainment world. From the opening of the park, the board had debated how much of the marketplace to allow in. Even before the Sweeny board took power, Andrew Green (whose eye never wandered far from the bottom line) saw franchise fees as a means of raising park maintenance funds. By the end of the 1860s the board was giving out licenses to entrepreneurs to operate boats (sixty cents an hour), carriages (twenty-five cents for a ride around the park), wheelchairs (fifty cents an hour with an attendant), a goat cart on the Mall (ten cents), and a photo house that snapped and sold pictures. Plans for a children's carousel south of the 65th Street Transverse Road were carried to completion under Sweeny.[25]

Both before and after 1870 the park board tended to be more indulgent of commercial attractions in the park if children were the primary beneficiaries. The popular Carousel (ten cents), which was turned by a blind mule and a horse kept in the basement and instructed by one or two stomps on the floor above, boosted park attendance in 1870 and 1871. In 1874 John Lucas was granted permission to operate a donkey ride (ten cents) for children between the Bow Bridge and Vista Rock. The following year, pony rides (ten cents) were added.[26]

The charges for "the go-carts, the ponies, the hobby horses, and the boats," a reporter noted during the depression of the 1870s, "are above a poor man's means. . . . Ten cents is asked a child for a ride . . . , while many of the fathers of the children . . . are glad during the week to get work at 12 cents an hour." Poor children, indeed, were more likely to be the purveyors of commercial goods and services than their consumers. They led the goat carts, for example, and in the 1890s immigrant East Side and Yorkville youths—including future movie mogul William Fox and future U.S. senator Robert F. Wagner—regularly sold candy in the park despite the long-standing ban on peddling and hawking.[27]

Children were both the workers and the customers for goat rides on the Mall.

Commercialization thus reinforced class distinctions among children as among adults.

By the late 1860s officials allowed four permanent refreshment spots in the park: the Casino east of the Mall; a small refreshment stand under the Terrace; Mount St. Vincent (the old convent building, now converted into a restaurant); and the Mineral Springs Pavilion (located at the northwest corner of the Sheep Meadow). In 1871 the Dairy (in the lower park) was completed and temporarily turned into another eating place rather than the milk dispensary the designers had planned as the center of what came to be called the Children's District. In the early 1870s, Mount St. Vincent and the Casino were renovated and expanded, and increasingly served only the park's wealthiest visitors. Both offered easy access for carriages. An 1877 guidebook described Mount St. Vincent as "the focal point where the Drives and Bridle Roads and the Park Carriage Route terminate." This terminus was a favorite stopping point for sleighs, carriages, and riding parties and for Coaching Club excursions headed for upper Manhattan.[28]

Describing Mount St. Vincent's "cozy little parlor, with its rich crimson plush drapings and furniture" and its wealthy patrons, a *Times* reporter observed that "many of the armchairs . . . were occupied by portly gentlemen who own good horses, keep good bank accounts, and who know what real comfort is." Another reporter called it the "favored resort of those who have more greenbacks than brains." Particularly in the evening, it acquired a reputation as a gathering place for the city's male sporting crowd, for rich horse fanciers like

August Belmont and William H. Vanderbilt, as well as Tammany politicians, and "men about town." That reputation grew after 1883 when Mount St. Vincent was rebuilt after a fire and came under the management of Patrick McCann, brother-in-law of Tammany kingpin (and former park dweller) Richard Croker. The Sisters of Charity asked that their name no longer be used in conjunction with a place that had come to seem morally suspect, and it reclaimed its eighteenth-century designation as McGown's Pass Tavern.[29]

The Dairy served ice cream, sandwiches, pastry, ale, porter, and coffee and attracted, the *Times* wrote, people of "more modest desires"—and means. Still, it was far from cheap. A *Herald* reporter protested that the coffee, at ten cents, was double the downtown price, and Bass ale at thirty-five cents was ten cents more than the tariff at the city's bars. Prices and customers varied with the restaurant. According to the *Herald* reporter, "Ice cream from the same freezers" cost fifteen cents at the Dairy and the Terrace, twenty cents at the Casino, and twenty-five cents at Mount St. Vincent.[30]

This market segmentation simply reproduced the restaurant practices of the city. Still, some observers pointed up the contradiction posed by such class-based segregation within a public park. "In this . . . garden of pleasure and recreation for our citizens," West Sider Lloyd T. Seaman told the park commission in 1891, "there have been provided three restaurants—McGown's Pass Tavern, the Casino, and the Dairy—in all of which refreshment is provided for the rich and middle classes, but none for either the poor or the very poor."[31] The two expensive and, hence, exclusive restaurants provided a place for wealthy and middle-class New Yorkers within a park they no longer controlled, a form of class insulation in an increasingly heterogeneous public space.

The availability of lager beer for five cents at the Terrace brought in some visitors (particularly German Americans) who might otherwise have spent their Sunday at a commercial beer garden. And while ten cents for a goat-cart ride probably stretched the pocketbook of an unskilled laboring family, it was not out of the reach of skilled working families, particularly by the 1880s. Moreover, in 1877 the park board's prolabor and Tammany-allied president, William R. Martin, cut the fee on the Carousel from ten cents to five. Even for laboring families, then, a trip to the park with its free zoo and its modestly priced rides was one of the cheapest ways to enjoy commercial entertainment on a special occasion. "A trip to Central Park, with a ride in the goat wagon, was something that came to you on your birthday if you were lucky," Al Smith recalled of his childhood on the Lower East Side in the early 1880s.[32]

The "Relapse into Barbarism"

In October 1872 Olmsted complained to the board that "the park is much misused," compared to the early days, when "a lawless habit was rare among visitors." The villain in this decline was obvious: the Sweeny board, which,

NEW YORK CITY.—THE STUDY OF BOTANY UNDER DIFFICULTIES—A SCENE ON A BY-PATH IN CENTRAL PARK.

The park police were not always successful in enforcing rules against picking ferns and flowers.

"indifferent to the danger," had allowed the park keepers' discipline to lapse. But Olmsted acknowledged a broader cause for the changed behavior of parkgoers. "It was to be expected," he told the board, "as the city should in effect be brought nearer, year by year, to the park, and it thus came to be more easily, familiarly and numerously visited, that the means used for instructing and reminding visitors of their duty would be found less effective."[33]

Olmsted's perception of a loss of manners reflected, in part, the increase in the numbers of working-class visitors, who did not necessarily follow the prescribed codes of bourgeois gentility, and also, in part, the changing behavior of middle-class New Yorkers, who had themselves begun to question "proper" park decorum. Although there is no easy way to untangle the perception of increased disorder or crime from the reality of changing public behavior, newspaper accounts of the late nineteenth century do provide overwhelming evidence of growing concern about improper conduct in the park. Papers that in the 1860s had praised the park's orderliness, now lamented its "relapse into barbarism." News articles complained most frequently about the relatively innocent act of picking flowers or ferns or breaking off branches of lilacs or rhododendrons. Press accounts were often vague or contradictory on the identity of the guilty parties. Sometimes, the culprits seem to have been well-to-

The 1869 dedication of the monument to the German naturalist Alexander von Humboldt. By the 1870s visitors could admire twenty-four statues, most donated by ethnic associations and private benefactors. Olmsted worried that the enormous crowds that turned out for the dedications would trample the landscape.

do—"neatly dressed boys" or "charming young girls." Yet the newspapers also blamed "loafers" or "evil disposed persons." New parkgoers may have seen little wrong in picking flowers in a park. Patrons of uptown barrooms who openly took rhododendrons from the park to decorate their favorite saloons may not have believed that they were violating any laws or ethical standards.[34]

When big crowds gathered, the problems loomed particularly large—at least to Olmsted. On May 15, 1877, a record-breaking crowd turned out to see President Rutherford B. Hayes dedicate a statue to the Knickerbocker poet Fitz-Greene Halleck. The dedication went smoothly, according to press accounts. A school principal, James Herbert Morse, noted in his diary the "picturesque beauty" of the crowd. But Olmsted angrily called it *essentially a mob, lawless and uncontrollable.*" He was outraged not simply by the sight of "women and girls breaking off branches of lilacs" or others "trampling over shrubs and vines" but because the offenders "seemed surprised" when he confronted them with their transgressions. On another occasion, in 1875, Olmsted had been equally distressed to encounter between fifty and two hundred "rude fellows" "beyond the school age" playing ball in the park.[35]

Olmsted did not specify the class of these "rude fellows," but other observers saw rowdy behavior as endemic to the immigrant working class. "The rich as a general thing know how to behave themselves," explained a letter to the *Sun* in 1871, "but unfortunately the poor boys, at least those whom I have seen on the playgrounds, manifest a strong propensity to deviltry and cannot control themselves, being invariably very boisterous and rowdy in their activities." But not only working-class men and boys defied park rules. The *Times* in an 1895 story complained that the "young women were worse than the men"; "their sport" involved tossing around "handkerchief balls" stuffed with grass "obtained by tearing it up by the roots from the lawns."[36]

Some observers were distressed at the growing indifference to official park regulations among both middle- and working-class users. Others were unhappy over transgressions of etiquette enshrined in manners handbooks rather than the park rule book. In mid-1873 Jan Vier wrote a series of letters to the *Tribune* warning of an "increased tendency to disorder" in the park. "A couple near an open, frequented walk" had particularly offended Vier when he saw them "caressing each other under an umbrella in a way fit only for strict privacy." Vier's condemnation rested on bourgeois standards of conduct that proscribed displays of intimacy and affection. Yet those standards no longer governed public behavior as strictly as they once had. Indeed, Vier could be accused of violating a basic rule of etiquette. The "essence of true politeness," said *The Illustrated Manners Book,* is "in the homely maxim, 'MIND YOUR OWN BUSINESS.' "[37]

Courting had long been a part of the park scene, but nineteenth-century observers noted with increasing frequency that the park had become a "trysting place" for "young people who work in the factories and shops." One contributor to the *Herald*'s "complaint book" thought "scandalous and objectionable conduct" in Central Park (of a sort "not fit to be mentioned in the *Herald* or any other respectable journal") reflected poorly on "the influence of a Christian City." A less puritanical letter writer, however, saw nothing very shocking about courting in the park; the young couples who "belong to the working classes . . . have no homes in which to make love, so they are compelled to make a public exhibition of themselves."[38]

Working-class couples valued the freedom that the park offered from the watchful eyes of parents. One report on an early Sunday concert observed that a mechanic's sixteen-year-old daughter and her friend from the upstairs tenement had "at the first opportunity slip[ped] away to mingle in the crowd and pick up more congenial companions from the male friends they [were] . . . sure to find." Nor was the appeal of Central Park as a place of assignation confined to mechanics' daughters. In *The Custom of the Country,* Edith Wharton located an illicit meeting of a social-climbing young woman in the Wisteria Arbor. "The habit of meeting young men in sequestered spots was not unknown to her," Wharton wrote. Young middle- and upper-class women, who were expected to have chaperones in other settings, could meet suitors much more freely in the "protected" park.[39]

But where women found freedom, some male observers sensed danger. Vier denounced the "horrible indecencies perpetrated after nightfall" in the park: "Many a servant maid and shop girl comes in virtuous and goes away ruined, for it is notorious that the Park is now more than ever a favorite and fruitful resort for the pimp and seducer." Curious about the validity of such charges, Joseph Pulitzer's *World* assigned its crack female reporter to investigate. Elizabeth Cochrane (who wrote as Nellie Bly) had made a speciality of going undercover to expose iniquities of big city life. She had revealed the cruel treatment of women prisoners and of sweatshop workers. Her most famous exploit was her 1889 besting of the "around-the-world-in-eighty-days" record of Jules Verne's fictional hero Phineas Fogg. In the summer of 1888 Cochrane disguised herself as a "country girl" to uncover what she called "the infamy of the park"—the wiles of a wicked stable foreman who drove a carriage through the park daily, picking up women and enticing them into prostitution.[40]

The sensational *National Police Gazette* also wrote luridly of the "perils of the park," which included "murderous attacks upon the chastity of pure-minded young females"—apparently a reference to men exposing themselves. The *Police Gazette* was especially distressed that this "crime of a most revolting nature has left its ordinary haunts in some of the streets and byways of the city and established its headquarters in Central Park."[41]

The fragmentary police records of the period bear out to some extent the *Gazette*'s alarm over new sexual behavior and assaults in the park. In the 1860s crimes relating to "decency," or sexuality, did not even rate a separate listing in the park arrest statistics, although a few such arrests may have been counted among the "other offenses." By the late 1870s and the 1880s, "indecent exposure," "indecent conduct," "indecent assault," "crime against nature," "cohabiting," "sodomy," "attempted rape," and "rape" all appeared in the arrest classification scheme. Still, the arrest levels for such crimes were considerably lower than the sensational coverage would suggest. They accounted for fewer than 6 percent of arrests in all city parks between 1879 and 1886; in those same years, only one man was arrested for rape in a city park.[42]

Prostitution, illicit sexuality, and violence against women were far from unusual in late nineteenth-century New York, but as far as we can tell, the demimonde flourished in downtown streets, saloons, and brothels, not in uptown parks. And—as is true today—women faced as much danger from assault by their husbands and others in their homes as by strangers in the parks. Perhaps Central Park's only attempted murder in the 1880s was Bertram Rodway's shooting of his estranged wife in the bushes near the southwestern Playground.[43]

If "public" threats in the park were less grave than newspaper reports implied, why was there so much talk about peril? Was Central Park "no longer a safe place for women and children"? Editors expected Central Park, unlike the city, to be free of crime. Moreover, journalists recognized the public fascination

"Perils of the Park": In 1878 the *Police Gazette* published the lurid warning that visitors were no longer safe in Central Park.

with the seeming paradox of urban dangers lurking in a pastoral pleasure ground. In 1872 when an out-of-town-visitor became the first person murdered in the course of a robbery in the park, the *Times* mourned that "murder has actually stained the turf of that green fairy land." The *Police Gazette* similarly headlined its first article on the "perils of the park": "How Our Beautiful City Resort Is Polluted by Foul Tidings in Human Form."[44]

But the intense focus in these accounts on the dangers faced by women and the language used to express those fears lead one to suspect that the concern was as much *about* women as *for* them. Reporters and editors may have been reflecting a deeper anxiety about changing relations between the sexes. In the early 1870s, when public fears about women's safety in the parks were particularly strong, feminists were strongly pressing their demands for equality. The feminist newspapers *Revolution* and *Woodhull and Claffin's Weekly* (both published in New York City) raised the banner of equal rights for women and also challenged traditional male prerogatives in their advocacy of "free love," by which they meant equality for women and men in sexual relations.[45] In the context of this sharp challenge to the traditional gender hierarchy, talk about "protecting" women may be understood as insistence that women were not, in fact, equal, that they were dependent on men for their well-being and their physical safety.

Newspaper accounts repeatedly and paternalistically pointed to women as vulnerable when they were *alone*. "It is now disagreeable," observed an 1872 *Times* editorial, for "women to enter the Park in the daytime unaccompanied by a man." Six years later, a local judge explained that "ruffians" never "insult respectable females" *except* "when they are unprotected. They know too well the consequences of such an act if discovered by a male friend or escort."[46]

Such comments may have exaggerated the danger, but they did accurately reflect a growing tendency of women to visit the park without male companions. Women were increasingly taking the reins of park carriages themselves and leaving even the coachman at home. And small groups of women could be found riding horses together in the early morning without an accompanying "riding master." By 1891 a local carriage industry journal was grumbling about "the somewhat dangerous nature of the driving of women in Central Park" in terms that prefigured later complaints about women car drivers.[47]

The bicycle craze of the late 1880s and the 1890s most dramatically expanded the ability of women to propel themselves independently through the park. Marie E. Ward, who had ridden the carriage drives with her grandmother Abby Hall Ward back in the 1870s, announced in *Bicycling for Ladies* (1896) that "the bicycle supplies . . . a new pleasure—the pleasure of going where one wills, because one wills. . . . Riding the wheel, our own powers are revealed to us. . . . You have conquered a new world, and exultingly you take possession of it." Women cyclists could transform themselves from the driven to the drivers,

In the 1890s the "new woman" could pursue sports like tennis and bicycling in the park. "The bicycle supplies . . . a new pleasure," Marie E. Ward declared, "the pleasure of going where one wills, because one wills."

particularly if they donned "sensible" costumes that gave them greater freedom of movement. To Annie Nathan Meyer, a feminist (and also an antisuffragist), a "wheel-woman" (whose face was "crimson with exertion . . . . her suit . . . about as unbecoming as genius could make it") made a much more appealing figure than a fashion-conscious woman in a park carriage ("perfectly gowned" with cheeks "as smooth as cream . . . *can make them*"). Meyer recalled the "exhilaration" and "the sensation of rapturous freedom" of having been the first woman to use the park tennis courts in the mid-1880s. But she objected that the freer mixing of men and women in sports in the park of the 1890s was simply reinforcing older patterns. She lamented the loss of an earlier sense of noncomformity. "Now that society applauds the 'out-of-door girl,' that delicious sense of overtopping the rest of the world, of looking down upon the unhappy, conventional ones is gone."[48]

On occasion, the question of single-sex recreation sparked controversy. When the croquet fields temporarily closed in 1877, women apparently were divided over whether men should be allowed when the fields reopened. One woman urged "girls who love the game" to "compel" the park commissioners "to return to us what long possession has made us consider our right." Other New Yorkers believed that women and men should be able to play together. The croquet fields reopened to men as well as women, and the segregation of facilities by sex within the park gradually gave way to new patterns of mixed socializing. By 1891 the tennis tournaments included ladies-singles but also mixed-doubles competitions.[49]

As new patterns of behavior and use became possible, some women demanded access to park facilities and a number also wrote to the mayor to protest "nuisances" in the park, from manure piles to unlighted paths. Without the right to vote, they could not fully claim their rights as members of the political public, but through their clubs and civic associations they participated in debates over park policy. Still, it would take almost a century for the prophecy of the women's rights activist who clashed with the board in 1893 to be fulfilled. "The day was coming," she said, "when women would have their rights, and when women would sit on the park board."[50]

"Tramps and Other Unpleasant People"

Whatever uneasiness assertive and independent women generated in using the park in the late nineteenth century, most New York men accepted (indeed welcomed) their presence. Similarly, while some may have complained that working-class visitors did not know how to "behave themselves," working-class New Yorkers became a familiar part of the park's public in these years. But that public, though expanded, had its outer boundaries.

For many parkgoers the arrival of the nineteenth-century equivalent of "street people"—tramps and homeless women—marked decline rather than "opening up." Reports of "tramps" in the park increased markedly in the mid-1870s, when the depression threw thousands out of work (and indeed, the word came into currency as a disparaging description of men without jobs or homes). At least some of the unemployed found the park a pleasant place to sleep, to pass the day, or perhaps even to do some panhandling. "Tramps," *New York by Sunlight and Gaslight* noted in 1882, treat Central Park as "a favorite lodging-place . . . in warm weather."[51]

Some New Yorkers without homes claimed the park as a place to live; others without jobs claimed it as a place to earn money on their own. Driving through the park in April 1887 one parkgoer "saw as many as 15 to 20 men, women and

This montage, "The Tramp Nuisance: Birds of Passage and Their Roosts in the City Parks," appeared in the *New York Daily Graphic* in 1888.

boys, digging dandelions." The police pursued the culprits, but some continued to eke out a living by selling dandelion greens to vegetable dealers for ten cents a quart. (Like so many park rules, this one was enforced selectively. Ethel Dana, daughter of a well-to-do Episcopal clergyman, often picked dandelions in the park without police interference.)[52]

Many middle-class parkgoers found contact with the homeless and the jobless disturbing. "Tramps and other unpleasant people," the *Tribune* commented with disdain in May 1877, have "quit their Winter quarters for the benches in the Park. These persons are often an annoyance and prevent much enjoyment in the secluded walks. Ladies and children hesitate to venture into the Ramble without escorts." Contrary to the *Tribune's* implication, most unemployed men who were spending their days in the park did not insult women or molest children. The article contains a detail that reveals much about the true nature of the threat. With some puzzlement, the reporter observed that nannies "are the only ones who seem to be perfectly at ease and never timid" when facing the "tramps." Perhaps it was because these women also came from a similar class background. Poor women themselves, moreover, constituted about one-fifth of parkgoers arrested for vagrancy.[53]

Some commentators more frankly acknowledged what was at stake in the growing heterogeneity of the city's public spaces. Finding park seats and benches occupied by "ragged and vicious tramps" or people of "a class just above begging and vagabondage," who "smoke their rank pipes" and "eject their filthy tobacco-juice," *Appleton's Journal* recommended the immediate removal of "the free seats" and the substitution of "chairs at a small charge, after the custom generally adopted in Europe." *Appleton's* allowed that the "idea of perfect democracy in our public places is no doubt very fine in theory," but "true democracy has its limitations—it does not give any one the privilege to be as filthy as he pleases, as disgusting in his habits as he likes, or as worthless as he chooses." The park is for "that large, respectable mass of people," who are prepared to treat it as "a sort of public parlor" and "not for vagabonds—a class who have no rights that anybody is called upon to consider or respect."[54]

This effort to define "vagabonds" as outside the park's proper cultural public in effect paralleled the Tilden Commission's attempt two years later to define propertyless New Yorkers as outside the political public altogether. Neither succeeded in narrowing the public. Yet the park board did instruct its police force to maintain limitations on what *Appleton's* called "perfect democracy." Later in the century, park police continued to use their arrest powers to exclude certain kinds of people and prohibit certain kinds of behavior as unacceptable in the park. Acknowledging the "necessity" of "police regulations and police men," park police captain Henry Koster reasoned that "civilization has not yet invented a patent to make homogeneous the inclination, manners and action of an incongruous people."[55]

By the late 1880s park police were apparently arresting five times as many people as they had in the 1860s. Few of those arrests involved crimes against people (e.g., assault) or against property (e.g., robbery or picking pockets). In 1886 more than 90 percent targeted some form of improper behavior, primarily disorderly conduct, drunkenness, vagrancy, or violations of park ordinances. Park regulations in the early 1870s permitted the police to remove "filthy or offensive persons"—a provision that no one had thought necessary when the park first opened. Improper conduct had been the basis of most park arrests in the 1860s as well, but neither drunkenness nor vagrancy had rated a separate arrest classification then, and "fast driving" accounted for almost half of all arrests. Twenty years later, the comparable category ("reckless driving") made up less than 3 percent of park arrests. Park crime, like park use, had moved down the social scale, with the city's poorest and least respectable citizens (tramps and prostitutes, for example) most likely to encounter police harassment.[56]

The growing level of arrests as well as heightened alarm in the press about various forms of park misbehavior (from courting to sleeping on benches) should not lead us to think that crime or disorder overran Central Park. "Tramps" were ubiquitous in the depression-shrouded New York of the late nineteenth century, but there were probably fewer in Central Park than elsewhere in the city. Similarly, Olmsted was shocked to find "prostitutes . . . seeking their prey without hindrance" in "the most secluded and sylvan districts" of the park, but they plied their trade with a great deal less harassment by the police on downtown streets. The park remained a much more orderly and serene public place than the city streets, the commercial pleasure grounds, or the downtown squares. "You cannot anywhere get away from the misery of life" in New York City, William Dean Howells wrote in his 1896 essay "Glimpses of Central Park." Still, he would rather "walk in the pathways of the Park than in the streets of the city, for the contrasts there are not so frequent, if they are glaring still."[57]

Pluralism in Bronze

The Central Park landscape began to display new material evidence of heterogeneity as well. The entrants in the original design competition for the park—though not the winners Vaux and Olmsted—had recognized the appeal within the natural landscape of statues, a common feature of the city's pleasure gardens and European parks.[58] But as new groups brought eclectic tastes to the park, some New Yorkers mobilized to block the proliferating statuary, which they believed undercut the designers' goals in creating a pastoral park.

The pressure for statuary came primarily from below, from organized ethnic groups seeking concrete public recognition in bronze and stone of great men (and only men) from their countries of origin. Indeed, more than half of the fifteen statues of individuals erected in the park in the nineteenth century were financed and promoted by ethnic associations: Johann Schiller, Alexander von Humboldt, and Ludwig van Beethoven by German Americans; Walter Scott and Robert Burns by Scottish Americans; Giuseppe Mazzini by Italian Americans; Thomas Moore by Irish Americans; and Albert Thorvaldsen (a sculptor) by Danish Americans. The choice of these mostly cultural figures is revealing: immigrant New Yorkers were emphasizing their status as "cultivated" people by honoring leading cultural (not political or military) figures in the city's most "cultivated" space. And as if to underline the message, the sponsoring associations invariably chose the sculptor from their own ethnic group: Gustav Blaeser for Humboldt; Giovanni Turini for Mazzini; Dennis Sheahan for Moore; Sir John Steel for Burns and Scott. Park rules might not permit formal ethnic gatherings, but the dedications of these statues sometimes turned into ad hoc ethnic festivals.[59]

In at least one case, park statuary sparked conflict and competition between ethnic groups. With the four hundredth anniversary of Columbus's voyage approaching, Italian and Spanish Americans each asked for the prime location of the Fifth Avenue and 59th Street entrance to the park to celebrate *their* national hero. The park board rejected both proposals and offered the Italians Eighth Avenue and 59th, and the Spanish Americans an isolated site at the southern end of Mount Morris Park at Fifth Avenue and 120th Street instead. Editor Carlo Barsotti raised money from Italian Americans through his paper, *Il Progresso*, to pay for the thirteen-foot-high statue (sculpted by Italian Gaetano Russo) on its towering twenty-six-foot granite column. A crowd of ten thousand gathered on Columbus Day 1892 for the dedication, and Columbus Circle soon became what the *Times* called "a sort of Mecca," where "troops" of "swarthy sons of the Sunny South wander about the bit of marble, looking it over with the deepest interest."[60]

Spanish Americans were disgruntled at being offered a "second class place." They turned it down and abandoned their project. Two years later the elite New-York Genealogical and Biographical Society unveiled its own statue of Columbus at the south end of the Central Park Mall. (The tribute to the "discoverer" of America—like the statue *The Pilgrim* erected in the park by the New England Society in 1885—could be seen as an "ethnic" assertion by native-stock Americans who felt beleaguered in a city more and more dominated by immigrants.) By the 1930s, however, the statue on the Mall had become the site for the *Dia de la Raza* (Day of the Spanish Race) ceremonies organized by Spanish-speaking Harlemites, most of them from Puerto Rico.[61]

The city's immigrant groups were not the only ones to push for statues in the park, nor were the statues only of individuals. Sculptures honored Daniel Webster, Alexander Hamilton, and the fifty-eight members of the Seventh Regiment killed in the Civil War. And in 1871 the nation's telegraph operators presented a larger-than-life bronze of Samuel F. B. Morse. Four years earlier

Guidebooks directed park visitors to novelties like the Obelisk, brought from Egypt by William Vanderbilt and shown here being placed on a knoll west of the Metropolitan Museum of Art in 1881. "To gaze at the Obelisk was regarded as a far greater treat by the majority of park visitors than to watch the wondrous developments of nature," the *Herald* declared.

Morse and others had given the park Auguste Cain's sculpture *Tigress and Cubs.* Other private donors placed sculptures with "natural" themes—*Eagles and Prey* and *The Indian Hunter*—at sites in the park; these particularly appealed to parkgoers who thought that decorations should reinforce the distinction between the park and the city.

Commissioners let private donors take the initiative for almost all the statuary. Vaux and Mould's 1862 proposal for twenty-six statues of leading Americans at the Terrace—the park's most formal space—fell victim to cost overruns. When the Terrace was finished in 1873, it included only a fountain, with classical stone vases at the north end of the Mall. The life-size neoclassical bronze angel in the middle of the fountain was the only sculpture commissioned as part of the initial park design. Some critics thought the *Angel of the Waters* was too expensive (at sixty-three thousand dollars) or unsightly (it reminded them of a "servant girl executing a polka"). Even more criticism centered on the selection of the sculptor, Emma Stebbins, a sister of park board president Henry G. Stebbins, to produce the work. In retrospect, one might speculate that some of the criticism also stemmed from awarding such an important commission to a woman—the first time this had been done in New York.[62]

Olmsted and Vaux hoped to restrict statues, such as this 1870 monument to Shakespeare by John Q. A. Ward, to the Mall and the entrance gates.

As sculpture gradually filled the park, immigrants came to pay homage to their cultural heroes, and guidebooks devoted considerable space to detailing each work and its location. The guidebooks (and newspapers) paid particular attention to the park's most spectacular piece, a seventy-one-foot-high obelisk snatched from Egypt over the objections of both Egyptians and Europeans and transported to America at William H. Vanderbilt's expense. It was erected behind the Metropolitan Museum of Art in 1881, where its ancient heritage (ca. 1461 B.C.) and "strange" hieroglyphic markings made it "one of the chief attractions of the grounds," in the words of one guidebook. Cultivated New Yorkers saw the appropriation of such a great monument of classical civilization as further testimony to their city's stature as "the metropolis of the Western World."[63]

In 1873 the park board acted to restrict commemorative sculpture to the

Mall and the entrance gates and to require prior review of artistic merit by a committee made up of the presidents of the Metropolitan Museum of Art, the National Academy of Design, and the American Institute of Architects. Expert arbiters of taste and culture, the commissioners insisted, should control the ornamentation of the park. But the review committee was only advisory. It could not stem the pressure to commemorate immensely popular figures, nor did it approve sculptures of a quality everyone could endorse. The original park board had accepted only five of the twenty statues offered by donors. But ten more were added in the 1870s, and by the mid-1890s, there were twenty-four pieces. In 1897 the charter that incorporated the five boroughs into Greater New York established the Art Commission of the City of New York to govern the placement of works of art on city property; it was to be controlled by representatives of the art world—experts—not the public park board.[64]

The City Park

The immigrant and working-class crowds who came to Central Park in growing numbers in the last two decades of the century asserted their right to enjoy the park in their own way. "The Sunday excursionist," a *Herald* reporter suggested in 1881, "is not in quest of quiet pleasures, as a rule: it is a sensation that he or she is looking for. To gaze at the obelisk was regarded as a far greater treat by the majority of the Park visitors than to watch the wondrous developments of nature as set forth in tree or shrub." In 1883, to the outrage of *Harper's Weekly*, one park commissioner even maintained that "the people don't care about country in the park." "The Mall, Terrace, and all the favorite promenades were as crowded as Broadway on a gala day," the *Herald* noted in a typical Sunday report, observing in another, "Every seat, every arbor, every nook was occupied, and the music of human voices and laughter drowned and silenced the precocious chirping and whistling of insects and birds. In these crowded centres the illusion of country was completely lost."[65]

Olmsted bemoaned and fought the loss of the "illusion of country" that had formed the heart of the park's original aesthetic. In 1874 he persuaded the board to refuse permission "for any exhibition, show, or entertainment on the Central Park" that would charge a fee. But the commissioners' decision to use limited funds to keep up the popular concerts and skating rather than the natural landscape frustrated Olmsted. "I tell you," he wrote to a journalist in 1874, "that I think the park is going to the devil and have grave doubt whether the undertakings to provide a *rural* recreation ground upon such a site in the midst of a city like this was not a mistake, was not doomed to failure because of the general ignorance of the conditions of success and the impossibility of getting proper care taken of it."[66]

Yet the natural features of the park did not disappear, despite the new

Central Park Mall, 1902: On Sundays the park became another crowded urban space.

crowds and new uses. Each spring, the grass turned green, trees leafed out, and the shrubs bloomed. And throughout the year, thousands, perhaps millions, came to observe nature, to wander through the Ramble, to enjoy the vistas. In the 1870s and 1880s, school principal James Herbert Morse regularly walked in the park, writing poems in his head, noting "signs . . . of the coming season of flowers," observing the "birds flitting and fluttering" in the shrubbery, and praising an open field surrounded by trees as a "fine broad amphitheatre for the reverberation of sound." At almost the same moment that Olmsted was writing *The Spoils of the Park,* Morse was enjoying the park according to the designers' intentions. "After three weeks of hard work and dissipation, parties, theaters, dinners, and clubs," Morse wrote in his diary in March 1881, "I am in the park, alone, with a joyous spring sunshine pounding down upon the world." A British visitor in the mid-1890s similarly found the park filled with "the open spaces, the varied outlines, the graceful curves which Nature everywhere supplies . . . . and large expanses of grass, the greenest which I saw in the States."[67]

But Morse saw more than natural beauty in his rambles through the park: panhandlers approached him for pennies, children ran across the lawns, his own children fed the animals at the menagerie, men sat on the lawns smoking pipes and reading scandal papers, and an elderly woman in a "shabby grey shawl" and with "ill-shod feet" picked dandelions to sell. And he partook of the new "urban" institutions that the park offered; on December 18, 1888, when the Metropolitan Museum of Art opened its first wing on park land, Morse

While many New Yorkers enthusiastically greeted new Central Park attractions like the zoo, statues, rides, and restaurants, others continued simply to enjoy contemplating nature.

participated in the ceremonies as a member of the Mendelssohn Glee Club, whose concert included an ode, "Of Glorious Birth Was Art," which Morse himself had written especially for the occasion.[68]

Morse experienced Central Park not as an insulated "rural recreation ground" but as a city park that encompassed a wide range of people, sensations, and activities. As the social and physical landscapes changed, the park was becoming what Vaux had called a "many sided, fluent" public institution. And the contrasting groups of parkgoers, from dandelion pickers to lovers of art, and their contrasting ways of using the park mirrored the contradictions of the city itself.

The Eclectic Park

The eclecticism of the park resided not simply in the diversity of the crowds and their activities but also in the ability of people to interpret the same experiences in *different* ways. One day (probably in the early 1890s), Annie Nathan Meyer rode through the park, looking at the Sheep Meadow and thinking about the "calming touch, the healing power that seems to reach out from these scenes." Then she turned to look at the other women in her carriage: "Have they seen the sheep, I wonder? One of the ladies opposite to me did bend forward, I remember, but merely to see a cape that was more elegant than hers flash by in a noiseless victoria."[69]

Olmsted had worked to create a park for men like James Morse and women like Annie Nathan Meyer, not for the old woman gathering dandelions or the young woman surveying the latest fashions. But the effort to impose a unitary vision of the park proper, to insist that the "best use" lay in appreciating the natural scenery, remained illusory. As time went on, crowds of parkgoers and the experience of parkgoing became even more eclectic. It was not an experience of democratic social mixing, however. Rich and poor New Yorkers may have shared the "public" space of the park, but their differing circumstances structured how they used it.

The bon ton might drive on the East Drive of Central Park on a fall afternoon or stop at Mount St. Vincent after a sleigh ride. But they were less likely to join the sweaty crowd squeezed together on the Mall for the free Sunday afternoon concert. Even in 1871 a *Times* reporter noted how park visitors "quickly disperse in various directions. The boys to the ball-ground, the ladies to the lawns and seats around the music-stand, . . . the country visitors to the menagerie, and the nurses and babies to the Mall and goat carriages."[70]

Two decades later, a *Sun* reporter viewed this choreography in sharper ethnic and class terms when he observed that the area around the Dairy and the Carousel was "a side to the Central Park distinct from the victorias, the cabs, and the carriage ways. . . . This part of the Park might be called the poor people's end of Central Park, or the foreign quarter." The reporter speculated that immigrant parkgoers "get their ideas from the pleasure grounds of German cities, where the classes separate and frequent their respective parts of the park or pleasure ground." Another article in the same issue acknowledged that Americans also "separated" out by class; it berated wealthy New York women for their ignorance of the park, since "their enjoyment of it is confined to the East Drive between four and six in the afternoon. Within five minutes of six the high-backed victorias . . . quickly disappear." Although the carriage parade had always been concentrated in a limited period of time, it was now also concentrated in a limited stretch of the park, as wealthy New Yorkers turned the East Drive (near Fifth Avenue) into the American equivalent of Hyde Park's "Rotten Row," the drive that attracted the richest Londoners with their carriages. About the preference for the East Drive Commissioner Henry Beekman commented, "I do not know why the East Drive should be so crowded, while the West Drive is comparatively free, except that the former happens at present to be the more fashionable."[71]

One way parkgoers responded to the growing heterogeneity was to draw

Well-to-do German-Jewish New Yorkers turned the Mineral Springs Pavilion at the northwestern end of the Sheep Meadow into a local replica of "Kissingen, Carlsbad, and other European waterplaces," the *Times* reported.

their own boundaries through patterns of use. Such self-segregation had a temporal as well as a spatial dimension: fashionable women on the East Drive on weekday afternoons, gentlemen's riding clubs on the bridle paths on weekday mornings, working-class families at the menagerie on Sunday afternoons, sporting men at McGown's Pass Tavern in the evenings. Some spots attracted quite specific groups. In the 1890s most of the early morning patrons of Vaux's Moorish-style Mineral Springs Pavilion were well-to-do gentile and Jewish German Americans—including leading ministers, bankers, lawyers, and brewers—who lived in upper Manhattan. A *Times* reporter found it reminiscent "of Kissingen, Carlsbad, and other European waterplaces."[72]

There were demarcations by sex and age, as well. Children delighted in the zoo, Carousel, boats, swings, baseball fields, and pony and goat rides.[73] On weekdays in the spring and fall, nurses and governesses accompanied the children of wealthy New Yorkers to the park; on summer weekends, working-class parents brought their own children. On the pony and goat rides, rich and poor children met as customers and workers, not as playmates. Young men— schoolboys and "rude fellows"—held sway at the southwest Playground or the Sheep Meadow. Women favored the concerts and the croquet fields as well as the Children's District; and they tended to avoid certain implicitly "male" park spaces. "Respectable" women stayed away from McGown's Pass Tavern, for example, when the sporting crowd gathered there.

Women and men also formed themselves into special interest groups in their use of the park. Tennis players, bicyclists, and model-boat racers were all park constituencies. Although some such interests—tennis, for example—often had particular class inflections, others transcended conventional lines of division. The social reformer Henry George and the socialite Julie Grinnell Van Rensselaer Cruger may have had little else in common, but both enjoyed biking in Central Park. Even nature lovers were now becoming a specialized group that could no longer be assumed to include all visitors. Thus, in the 1890s the parks department gave out permits for those who wanted to collect autumn leaves in Central Park. "Yesterday," the *Times* reported in October 1898, "the autumnal tints attracted a large number of the lovers of nature who are regarded by the Park officers and attendants as a class by themselves."[74]

Even as the "classes" of users segregated themselves, using the park in their own ways, individuals could not help but rub shoulders. Immigrant working-class couples from the East Side tenement houses, the *Sun* reporter observed, routinely entered the park at the Fifth Avenue entrance and would "walk along the driveway and watch the people in carriages."[75] As they, in turn, were watched.

Some found what Henry James would later call the "polyglot" park and its "polyglot" visitors unsettling. A snobbish character in Israel Zangwill's early twentieth-century play *The Melting Pot* derided the park as having "no taste," only "modern sculpture and menageries!" *Munsey's Magazine* observed disapprovingly in 1895 that because of Central Park's popularity and accessibility, "some New Yorkers" had come to see it as "rather a commonplace picnic spot for the use of the masses, and, except in a carriage or astride a fine horse, to be avoided." But others appreciated, even celebrated, the pastiche, the mixing of disparate peoples and features. For them, Central Park resembled that quintessentially urban and eclectic theatrical form, the variety show or "vaudeville," as it came to be known in the 1880s. A "great charm of Central Park," wrote J. Crawford Hamilton in *Munsey's Magazine,* "is the marvelous variety of its scenery and embellishments," including the crowds. The Mall, said Hamilton, noting the plethora of "monuments of foreigners" and the "imported music discoursed by a band principally composed of imported musicians," was the "headquarters" of "cosmopolitanism."[76]

William Dean Howells also liked the cosmopolitan Mall, but other prominent literary figures, editors E. L. Godkin and George Curtis (both longtime associates of Olmsted) among them, increasingly viewed the immigrant working class as a threat to civilization, particularly in the aftermath of Henry George's mayoral campaign. Almost at the same moment that Olmsted was fleeing the city's machine politics and settling in the Boston suburbs, Howells was making the reverse migration, from Boston to Manhattan. And it was the urban and eclectic park—the Mall filled with "mostly foreigners"—more than Olmsted's pastoral park that intrigued him. "For me," he wrote of the immigrant crowd, "they all unite to form a spectacle I never cease to marvel at, with a perpetual hunger of conjecture as to what they really think of one another."[77]

We can only conjecture as well. In the late nineteenth century, most New Yorkers of foreign birth or recent immigrant stock spent their social lives within insular ethnic communities, and the barriers and conflicts between those communities remained substantial. In 1870 religious and ethnic tensions culminated in the Elm Park Riot, which started in the commercial pleasure ground at 92nd Street and Ninth Avenue but spilled over into Central Park, apparently drawing park workers into the melee. What seems to have been the park's first murder occurred when a crowd of Protestant Irish "Orangemen" shot and stabbed William Kane as he walked through the park on his way home from work. (They mistakenly believed that he was one of a group of Irish Catholics who had attacked them earlier.) In the 1890s the Columbus statue became a magnet not only for Italian Americans but also for anti-Italian vandals, who threw mud at it.[78]

Ethnic clashes were apparently an exception rather than a rule within Central Park. Perhaps most remarkably, African Americans, who (as the *New York Freeman,* a black newspaper, noted) "find it most unpleasant to visit a majority of resorts in New York and New Jersey," were apparently accepted as regular users of the park in the late nineteenth century. References to black parkgoers are scarce in the papers and other sources, in part because African Americans were only about 1.5 percent of the city's population in those years. White and black New Yorkers mixed in the park most often as employers and employed: coachmen and nurses were often black. But newspapers did occasionally remark on black visitors, usually describing them with the same reportorial conventions used for immigrants, though perhaps with some added condescension directed at their dress. One report noted a "colored lady" who "dazed the spectators with her paradisiacal outfit." Another commented on the "smart looking colored women with marvelously decorated male companions." Black-owned newspapers occasionally reported on the concerts, encouraged youngsters to get permits for baseball and picnics in the park, and noted prominent visitors "out driving" on the carriage roads.[79] This degree of racial integration in Central Park, however limited, is noteworthy, given the rise of Jim Crow laws in public spaces in the South in this period and ongoing de facto segregation in the North.

Some New Yorkers seem to have experienced the park as a place to transcend some of the boundaries that otherwise divided them. Standing in crowds at the zoo or amid the throng waiting for Sunday concerts, they may have seen themselves as part of a broader cosmopolitan public. The young German American who stopped to admire the statue of the Scottish poet Burns could

break free, in a small way, from the ethnic insularity that so strongly characterized urban life in this period. The 1884 concert crowd that cheered for *both* the
Catholic "Ave Maria" and the Protestant "Nearer, My God to Thee" revealed a
degree of mutual tolerance, if not appreciation, that would have been surprising
a decade earlier.[80] Young Hungarians and Poles who chose to spend their
Sunday at Central Park rather than Tompkins Square (located within their own
Lower East Side neighborhood) may have been crossing part of the social
divide. Having joined the heterogeneous throng at the park, they might more
easily join the heterogeneous crowd parading for the eight-hour day or cheering
Henry George.

Not everyone, of course, used the park in what Howells called "the spirit of
fraternity and equality."[81] Park use reinforced as well as dissolved social divisions. But out of the tensions and conflicts that accompanied the opening of the
park to new users and new uses came a broader definition of the public. In
claiming access to the park, in pressing for new policies in its governance, and in
themselves contributing to the park's attractions, working-class New Yorkers in
particular transformed the genteel (and, in practice, exclusive) Central Park of
the 1860s into the eclectic (and common) Central Park of the 1890s.

Like the city, the park had become multivocal, incorporating different
people, different experiences, and different meanings. The triumph of Vaux
and Olmsted's design had been to turn a swampy and rocky "wasteland" into a
beautifully composed pastoral landscape. The triumph of the New Yorkers who
visited the park was to remake it in a way that realized the democratic implications of Vaux's vision of it as a "many sided, fluent, thoroughly American high
art work."

13

A PUBLIC MENAGERIE AND
TWO PRIVATE MUSEUMS

In March 1856 financier August Belmont wrote from the Hague to his father-in-law, Commodore Matthew Perry, about the new park proposed for Manhattan. Three years earlier, Perry had opened Japanese ports to American ships, and Belmont had been dispatched by President Franklin Pierce to the Netherlands to negotiate the opening of Dutch ports in the East Indies. Now the two men were thinking about opening uptown Manhattan to elite residential development. Just as they looked to the national government to facilitate private trade ventures, so too they saw new opportunities for private initiative in the city's provision of a public park. "Your project of buying and building on the Central Park seems a very good one," Belmont told the commodore. But if the park was to protect such investment and attract "nice neighbors," it would have to be properly managed. Thus, two years before he joined the park board himself, Belmont was already speculating on what rules would be necessary to "keep the fast trotting men and other rowdies" out of Central Park and its surrounding neighborhoods.[1]

Belmont's speculations to his father-in-law went beyond the question of how public officials should manage the park in the best interests of adjacent landowners to a new kind of private initiative: the creation of a private zoological and botanical garden within the public Central Park. If the city set aside thirty or forty acres, Belmont suggested, a state-chartered private company headed by "a few of our spirited citizens," might take control of the property and open a zoo, "only to subscribers." "A great many much smaller places than New York, such as Brussels, Antwerp, etc. have similar establishments without any aid of Government," Belmont noted, "and they have succeed[ed] very well." How much greater the chances for success if the city provided the land.[2]

Belmont's vision of a private zoo and botanical garden was not realized.

Instead, the Central Park Menagerie developed under public auspices and with a much more emphatically popular appeal than the exclusive institution Belmont had imagined. But two other important institutions emerged within Central Park in the last third of the nineteenth century that much more closely matched Belmont's model of private and elite control of public cultural institutions—the American Museum of Natural History on the West Side at 77th Street (in Manhattan Square, which had been annexed to Central Park in 1864) and the Metropolitan Museum of Art in the park facing Fifth Avenue near 81st Street. Although taxpayers provided the land and funds to build the museums, a private board of trustees controlled their management and use.

The divergent paths marked out by the zoo and the museums reflected the park's own changing relationship to its publics. In the 1860s when the zoo emerged on an ad hoc basis, the park's political public was composed of gentlemen like those on the original board and its cultural public was dominated by the gentlemen and gentlewomen of the carriage parade. By the 1870s and 1880s, as the two museums took shape and the zoo acquired its popular audience, the political and cultural publics were broader and more divided. The museums' elite founders viewed this democratization as a threat to their prerogatives and mission as patrons of art and science—particularly because they believed that party politics and popular crowds might undermine the cultural authority of their own institutions. Museum trustees accepted the need to deal with politicians to secure public funds, but they resisted opening their institutions to the same inclusively defined public that now infused the park. Their resistance was only partly successful. Dependence on public money ultimately forced the museum trustees to yield to the demands of working-class New Yorkers for greater access, particularly on Sundays.

The stake that new groups had developed in the park—and their definition of it as a common space—became most evident when a coalition united across party, class, and ethnic lines to block the introduction of a fourth cultural institution, a racetrack. A broadly constituted public defense of the park, rather than Belmont's private initiative, succeeded in keeping the "fast trotting men" out of Central Park.

The "Poor Man's Monkeys"

The Greensward plan did not provide for a zoo, although other design competitors had favored the idea. In 1859 August Belmont, now back from Europe and on the park board, persuaded the commissioners to look into the operation of English and European zoological and botanical gardens. That year's annual report called for a zoo to be run by a private group that would pay rent and charge admission. Shortly after the beginning of the new year, some of the city's wealthiest gentlemen—including Belmont and four of the original signers of the Minturn petition for a park (as well as Frederick Law Olmsted)—organized the American Zoological and Botanical Society to plan the zoo. Within another few months, the state legislature authorized the board to set apart up to sixty acres in Central Park for a zoological and botanical garden to be run by the new society.[3]

As had been true of the initial movement to create a public park, prominent New York gentlemen impressed by European models led the way. Although no American cities had zoos at this time, many of the founders of the American Zoological and Botanical Society had probably visited the Jardin des Plantes in Paris and the London Zoological Garden. And like early advocates of the park, these gentlemen saw a zoological garden as a way to establish New York as "the acknowledged seat of wealth and moral power."[4]

Just as some advocates viewed Central Park as the future rendezvous of the polite world, so some enthusiasts imagined a zoological garden as a place for their socializing—particularly if it were organized, as Belmont had urged, with special privileges for subscribers. The private society's projected zoo would be open to the public but closed to the general public on Sundays. (London's Zoological Garden admitted only subscribers on Sunday, "the fashionable day" to visit.) The *Herald* warned that "such class regulations" "in favor of the wealthy few" would not be tolerated in republican America, and the *Irish News* similarly declared the plan to restrict the zoo on Sundays "absurd" and "un-American."[5]

Some early elite advocates also envisioned the zoo as a more republican institution that would educate ordinary citizens. Thus, the comptroller, Andrew Green, who had begun his career of public service as a school commissioner, repeatedly stressed the park's educational mission. In 1862 the board's annual report picked up on this theme, arguing that a zoo would serve as an auxiliary to the "great free educational system" of the city itself.[6]

The board acknowledged that a display of wild animals would have yet another appeal: "that such an establishment is demanded, both for *popular amusement* and instruction, there can be no question."[7] Most New Yorkers, who had never visited European capitals, had seen wild animals only in the traveling "menageries" (a term that generally connoted a less scientific enterprise than a "zoological garden"), which had been coming to the city since the early part of the century, or to the permanent menageries that had been a feature of New York's popular entertainment in New York at least since the 1830s.

The *Irish News*, one of the most enthusiastic promoters of a zoo, summoned up the alternative appeal of the menagerie when it described the zoo as "a wilderness peopled with all sorts of *fera natura*—lions, tigers, elephants and jaguars—monkeys chattering in a row to please the nurses and children, and huge black bears performing gymnastic exercise on long poles to keep the cramp out of their legs." *Frank Leslie's Illustrated Newspaper,* speaking for its middle-class readers, offered a similar vision; it made fun of the exclusive, elite vision of a zoological garden and declared: "We want some camels, an elephant or two, a deep-chested lion, and plenty of quaint bears, and funny monkeys—but bears especially—in the Central Park."[8]

When the zoological society's plans foundered during the Civil War, the state legislature authorized the park commission to establish a zoo under its own auspices in 1864. Olmsted had recommended in 1860 that the board set aside the relatively level land east of the rectangular Lower Reservoir (between 73rd and 86th streets along Fifth) that Viele had once envisioned as a parade ground and the Greensward plan had designated for a playground. But by 1864 Olmsted and Vaux were insistently opposed to a zoo in the main body of the park, and they drew up a plan to put one at Manhattan Square (the tract of land between 77th and 81st streets and Eighth and Ninth avenues, later the site of the American Museum of Natural History), which the 1864 legislation annexed to Central Park. Delays in grading the surrounding streets slowed progress, and at the end of 1869, only preliminary excavations and a portion of the foundation wall were completed.[9]

As park officials argued about management, location, and organization, a zoo had actually emerged under their noses. Almost from the opening, people had been making gifts to the board, including a strange assortment of historical relics (shells fired at Fort Sumter, for example), art works (a large collection of plaster casts from the late sculptor Thomas Crawford, which were ultimately displayed in the old Mount St. Vincent Chapel), and especially live animals. Olmsted recalled later that most of the first animals received were "pets of children who had died" or left town. If true, New York children kept a rather weird collection of pets in the 1860s, since among the animals presented to the park were a deer, a goose, an alligator, a peacock, a porcupine, a pelican, a prairie wolf, a silver gray fox, and a boa constrictor. By the summer of 1863, the board had set up a wire-enclosed space near the Mall for some of these animals. There, a disabled Civil War veteran looked after five or six deer, three bald eagles, two yellow-tufted cockatoos, an antlered buck, a raccoon, and three monkeys.[10]

Mounting donations—more than 250 animals arrived in 1864 and 1865 alone—gradually built the zoo. In 1865 General William T. Sherman contributed three African Cape buffaloes he had picked up in his march through Georgia. That same year, the commissioners placed the collection in more permanent quarters at the Arsenal. In warm weather larger animals—for example, Sherman's buffaloes—grazed out behind the Arsenal, tied to a willow tree. In 1868 the park authorities fenced in an area east of the Lower Reservoir (the present site of the Metropolitan Museum) for a deer park. Despite continuing complaints about the need for better quarters, the zoo emerged as one of the park's most popular attractions, especially after an 1865 fire destroyed the "happy family" animal exhibit run by America's best-known entertainment impresario, P. T. Barnum, at his American Museum. Such upper-class New

Yorkers as George Templeton Strong griped that it "amount[ed] to little" and was arranged "without any system" but conceded that it received "much attention from visitors."[11]

With the ascension of the Sweeny park board in 1870, the zoo received even more attention from park administrators. A few months after taking office, the new commissioners turned over the Arsenal interior to park offices and a burgeoning natural history collection and moved the animals into five newly constructed buildings in the Arsenal yard. The parks department then began to buy animals rather than just take whatever was left at its doorstep. Commissioner Henry Hilton, reported the *Times* in July 1871, "has purchased eight well-trained 'low comedian' monkeys." These "comical 'Darwinian links' will occupy two splendid cages." Even Olmsted, who had very little good to say about the accomplishments of the Sweeny board, admitted that the new zoo buildings were "the best of the class on the continent."[12]

Although the Sweeny commissioners did not record their motives for renovating and expanding the zoo, such attractions (and the jobs created by the new construction) were popular among the constituents who had swept the Democrats into office. Meanwhile, the Tammany board proposed shifting the permanent site of the zoo from Manhattan Square to the North Meadow. Olmsted and Vaux denounced the idea as a "fatal mistake" that would destroy "the only broad space of quiet rural ground on the island which has been left undisturbed by artificial objects," but the board had little sympathy for the designers' vision of a pastoral park. For the next three decades designers and politicians would debate zoo sites (Olmsted later counted twelve different unsuccessful proposals), and meanwhile visitors streamed in to visit the "temporary" menagerie.[13]

The renovation of the menagerie and the Arsenal museum in 1870 (and the opening of the Carousel) together provide the best explanation for the dramatic jump in park attendance around that time. In 1869 about one-quarter of the park's pedestrian visitors came into the park through the Fifth Avenue gates nearest the zoo; just two years later close to half were entering there. By 1873, according to the menagerie director William Conklin, the zoo attracted more than two and a half million visitors, about one-quarter of all those who came to the park. And by 1888 Conklin claimed that "nine out of every ten persons who enter the Park by the lower entrances wend their way to the menagerie." The zoo was particularly popular on Sundays, when working-class New Yorkers, especially children, flocked to see the exotic animals.[14] It brought new crowds to the park precisely because it was one of the few *free* attractions to which working-class families could bring their children.

As a popular cultural institution, the zoo subverted the genteel conception of Central Park as an arena of bourgeois (and primarily adult) decorum and order. Critics derided the "ill-assorted" menagerie, claiming that it attracted a "rabble of curiosity seekers" and was "useless" for education. The line between the zoo

Menagerie, Central Park

In 1870 the Sweeny park board built permanent quarters for the zoo west of the Arsenal.

and commercially organized amusement centers was increasingly blurred as the visitors and animals shuttled back and forth between them. Barnum developed an especially close relationship with the zoo, for in the cold months of the year, he and other circus operators quartered their animals there. In turn, Barnum used the zoo's collection as a resource for his commercial operations. When he needed an eagle for his Centennial Show, he borrowed one from the Central Park.[15]

Popular newspapers also had a reciprocal relationship with the zoo. They provided unusually detailed coverage of the animals in order to sell newspapers and entertain their readers. Readers would turn out to look at the new kangaroos or see how much "Murphy, the Hippo" had grown. On November 9, 1874, the *Herald* devoted its entire front page to a story that described in grisly detail an escape of the animals. The sensational hoax threw many New Yorkers into a panic. Even the *Herald*'s war correspondent showed up at the zoo with two big navy revolvers, ready to fight the rampaging animals. The response showed how centrally the zoo had come to figure in the popular imagination.[16]

Monkeys held a particular fascination for crowds in an era in which Darwin's theories were being popularized. The menagerie's peak as a center of popular amusement probably came in the mid-1880s after it acquired a chimpanzee brought back from Africa by the American consul to Liberia. Overflow crowds packed the Monkey House to get a look at the first chimp exhibited in

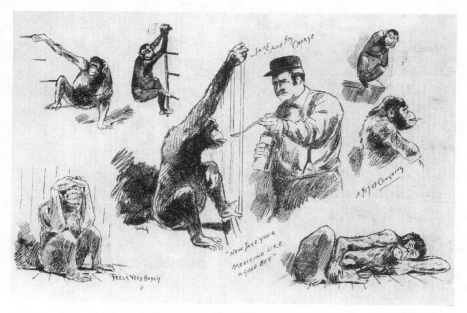

"The Late Mr. Crowley of Central Park in His Last Illness": New York newspapers closely followed the life and death of the first chimpanzee exhibited in the United States, who was also the park's most famous celebrity.

the United States. Former president Ulysses S. Grant and dozens of photographers and artists showed up. Controversy flared over whether the name given to the chimp—Mike Crowley—was an insult to the Irish, and Irish-American organizations sent protest delegations to the parks department. When "Mr. Crowley" took ill, the zoo had to issue regular bulletins about his condition, which were printed daily in the newspapers. Letters poured in offering sympathy and popular health remedies. Faith healers showed up to pray for the chimp, and prohibitionists protested against the use of ardent spirits as a cure. After he recovered, a paperback book (price: thirty cents) recounted the chimp's life and times.[17]

Such a popular sensation could not escape the notice of the aging Barnum, who desperately wanted the chimp as a leading attraction of his Greatest Show on Earth. When the park board rejected his initial bid of five thousand dollars, he offered to throw in the largest elephant in his collection, which he valued at ten thousand. "All these propositions being declined," Mr. Crowley's biographer reported, "the great showman departed, with some vexation on his usually cheerful features."[18]

That the zoo had a bigger drawing card than Barnum no doubt pleased park officials, but for Olmsted such popular attractions had nothing to do with the Greensward plan. Asked by the board in 1890 to review the still-controversial question of the best location for the zoo, Olmsted readily conceded that there was no "portion of the Park that is more crowded, or in which the people, and

In 1873 more than 2.5 million people (roughly one-fourth of all parkgoers) visited the Central Park Menagerie.

especially the children find more amusement." But "the leading purpose of the Park is not the amusement of the People," particularly the sort of amusement provided by a menagerie, a theater, a "Punch and Judy performance," or a "negro minstrel show." Quite the contrary, the "proper and only justifying purpose of so large a park" was to provide "great numbers of people living in a compactly built town . . . with an opportunity to get quickly out of the scenery of buildings, streets and yards into scenery to be formed with a view of supplying a refreshing contrast with it."[19]

By 1890 Olmsted's objection to the menagerie reflected his increasingly adamant insistence that Central Park should provide natural scenery and little else. Most New Yorkers who joined Olmsted in his opposition, however, wanted the zoo moved because it was the wrong zoo in the wrong spot rather than because they saw a fundamental incompatibility between parks and zoos. One chorus of complaint came from wealthy Fifth Avenue residents who were offended by the smell of the animals and the demeanor of the crowds the zoo attracted. West Siders similarly objected to a proposal to relocate the zoo on their side of the park. Another group of menagerie critics found it too much like a "Punch and Judy" show, as Olmsted had put it, and not sufficiently emblematic of New York's metropolitan stature and refinement. The zoo, complained the *Post* in 1883, "has long disgraced the city and the park" with its "mangy and uncultivated beasts."[20]

For such critics, the problem lay with the zoo's public management. "Four Park Commissioners," said the *Tribune* in 1883, "could not buy a pelican or kangaroo without a wrangle." (The *Times* agreed. Two years earlier it had likened the board's sessions to the antics of the animals.) The *Tribune* contrasted the "sleepless vigilance" of the "independent" trustees of the park's two museums with the "dickering and bickering of Aldermen and small politicians" who oversaw the zoo. To make it "an object of genuine civic pride," the *Tribune* urged, the zoo should be turned over to "private enterprise, generosity, business tact and watchfulness"—albeit supported by "municipal aid." [21]

From the mid-1880s, Andrew Green sought state authorization to create a private zoological society that would be provided with city park land in the Bronx. The bill met repeated defeats, because zoogoers perceived it (correctly) as an underhanded means of destroying the popular Central Park Menagerie. But in the late 1880s and early 1890s New Yorkers who wanted a "true" zoological garden rather than a Barnumesque menagerie and those who just wanted the zoo out of Central Park joined together to support a plan for a private zoo.[22]

In the early 1890s Green's efforts gained the support of a group of wealthy and prominent big-game hunters and sportsmen (Theodore Roosevelt among them), many of whom were members of the Boone and Crockett Club. They backed the idea of a new zoological *park*, not in Central Park, to preserve and display large wild animals in settings approximating their native habitats. The Central Park Menagerie, with its cramped cages and nine acres of ground, could not accommodate such a vision. The coalition of Green and the Boone and Crockett Club, whose members were well connected in Republican party circles, won state approval in 1895 for a new Bronx zoo. It chartered the private New York Zoological Society and gave it control of public resources—city land as well as municipal funds—to create the new zoo. The New York Zoological Park in the Bronx represented an alternative model for organizing the city's cultural and scientific institutions. Even more than the original park board, the managers of the zoological society were to be insulated from public political pressure. But such was the political and popular support for the Central Park Menagerie that the bill for the Bronx zoo had to be altered to protect the park zoo as well.[23]

As even the New York Zoological Society's official historian concedes, there was "a certain lack of candor" among its incorporators. Although the bill did not eliminate the Central Park Menagerie, society members expected the Bronx zoo's "accommodations would be so overwhelmingly superior that the menagerie's out-of-doors animals, at least, would be transferred to its keeping." When it came time to raise money for the new zoo, the private society appealed particularly to people "whose property would be greatly benefited by the opening of our zoo and the consequent . . . absorption of the existing menagerie." Despite these continual threats, the "poor man's monkeys," as they came to be called, remained in Central Park. At every attempt to abolish the zoo, park official Samuel Parsons said later, "a cry went up from the aldermen who represented the great east side that the rights of the people were being invaded."[24]

August Belmont and the gentlemen who had formed the private zoological and botanical society in 1860 had favored placing such an institution in private hands. But when their own effort to establish a private zoo failed, the legislature formally recognized the ad hoc menagerie and invested control in the park commissioners. As the zoo became one of Central Park's most popular attractions, public officials found their authority limited by parkgoers themselves. Acting through politicians to prevent the removal of the menagerie, ordinary New Yorkers defined it as an essential feature of their public park. The Central Park Menagerie thus remained a fully public institution, paid for by taxpayers and managed by public officials.

A Museum "Without Any Humbug"

The two other major cultural institutions that developed in Central Park and helped redefine its relation to the city, the American Museum of Natural History and the Metropolitan Museum of Art, did follow the model of Belmont's private society. Private control of public resources made those institutions less immediately responsive to the public.

Despite the specifications for an exhibition hall in the design competition, the Greensward plan gave only passing mention to the idea of a park-based museum. Olmsted and Vaux thought the Arsenal, which had been inherited on the park grounds, was "a very unattractive structure" but noted that it had "a great deal of room in a form that adapts it very well to the purposes of a museum." Eight months later, when Olmsted reported on the progress of park construction, the idea of a museum did not rate even this brief mention, though he did note that space had been reserved for a zoological garden and an astronomical observatory. For one thing museums were expensive. By 1859 as construction costs started to run over the original estimates, the board had dropped a projected music hall and conservatory. Moreover, Vaux and Olmsted had never been enthusiastic about placing conspicuous structures in the park, and their reluctance would develop into a strong principle over the next two decades. "Buildings," declared the Greensward plan, "are scarcely a necessary part of a park."[25]

Although Andrew Green endorsed this vision of a pastoral park, he also believed the park should be a center of educational, scientific, and cultural activity. Other entrants in the design competition had proposed a wide range of museums to display, for example, art, rocks, and dinosaur bones. And the upper classes, who dominated the first park board, showed growing interest in the creation of cultural institutions, especially after the war. From many of the same motives that had fostered the creation of the park, and also the zoo—civic boosterism, display of elite cultivation, promotion of education and moral improvement—wealthy New Yorkers were devoting considerable energy to the creation of museums, libraries, and observatories. They thought of Central Park as a logical location in part because it offered available land in a crowded city with high real estate prices. But even more important, they associated the cultural program of the park with the cultural agenda of museums and similar institutions, which the commissioners now invited to locate there. "Institutions of this nature are desirable," the 1859 annual report concluded, "and would be fitly placed on the park."[26]

The frugal Green worried about the costs of establishing and maintaining such institutions, however. Although the park board "would probably be authorized to provide a suitable structure," the annual report noted, "it would be better to leave them to the care of private hands, or of associations." Such a model for cultural institutions would follow the long-standing precedent of the city's cultural and benevolent organizations and even the first school system, run by the *private* Public School Society. Although Green had championed and served on the board of the new *public* school system in the 1850s, he saw museums in a different light.[27]

Private associations quickly responded to the board's invitation, proposing the zoological and botanical garden, an astronomical observatory, and a museum of science and art. The Civil War disrupted all these plans, although the science and art museum advocated by the New-York Historical Society came close to realization. In 1862 the society won legislative approval to use the Arsenal and its surrounding grounds for a "Museum of Antiquities and Science, and a Gallery of Art." It hired architect Richard Morris Hunt to design a massive Renaissance-style building for the museum, a copy of the Louvre's extension on which Hunt worked just after his student days at the Ecole des Beaux-Arts. But the board and Olmsted and Vaux evidently found Hunt's building too imperial for the site. Vaux, after all, had just finished campaigning against Hunt's similarly grandiose gates for the park's southern entrances. The board pressed the society to shift the museum to the area facing Fifth Avenue between 81st and 84th streets—the site that had been recommended for the zoo in 1860.[28]

The historical society came up short in its campaign to raise the "private munificence" to finance the "Museum of History, Antiquities, and Art in the Central Park," possibly because of the very social exclusivity that had given the society its great prominence in the city. A few years later, the society turned down the chance to join with the incorporators of the Metropolitan Museum of Art because, as of one of the society's leading members put it, "some of the sponsors of the Metropolitan Museum were not gentlemen."[29] The city's new philanthropists were men who had either made or multiplied great fortunes during the Civil War-induced boom; they now saw cultural display as one way to legitimate their newly acquired wealth and power. That boom and the consequent emergence of new great fortunes provided a crucial context for the appearance of the American Museum of Natural History and the Metropolitan Museum of Art.

In 1860 Albert Bickmore, who was to become the founder of the natural history museum, went to Cambridge to study under pioneer naturalist Louis Agassiz, who had recently organized the Museum of Comparative Zoology at Harvard. The ambitious young scientist soon began to dream of establishing his own natural history museum in the "city of our greatest wealth." In 1867 war-enriched New Yorkers greeted Bickmore's plan with enthusiasm. A committee of nineteen—among them a glass importer, Theodore Roosevelt (the future president's father); a corporate lawyer, Joseph H. Choate; a financier, J. Pierpont Morgan; a department store magnate, A. T. Stewart; and at least six bankers—signed on. Some, like Roosevelt, were amateur naturalists, but most acted out of local "patriotism," convinced, in the words of John D. Wolfe, a retired merchant and first president of the museum, that such a museum "would be a good thing for the city to have." Bickmore shrewdly played to this sentiment when he persuaded the organizing committee to adopt the name *American* Museum of Natural History to signify that the new institution would have the same stature in the United States as the British Museum had in England.[30]

As with the creation of Central Park itself, this notion that a natural history museum would reinforce New York's claim to metropolitan stature and cultivation also reinforced the claims of the city's elite to the status of a metropolitan gentry. The museum scheme especially appealed to those whose wealth was recently acquired or expanded, among them A. T. Stewart (whose army and navy contracts netted him nearly $2 million a year during the Civil War), steamship operator Marshall O. Roberts (another Civil War profiteer who made almost $3 million chartering and selling steamers), and Robert L. Stuart (a sugar refiner who had expanded his father's candy business into a vast enterprise). Once the museum got under way, its ability to impart social credibility and status attracted financial supporters. Museum officials organized spring and fall receptions, attended by subscribers—"the *élite* of the city," according to the *Times*. "The fashionable world thus became partially involved in the maintenance of the Museum," minerals curator Louis P. Gratcap later explained, "not

The receptions held by trustees of the American Museum of Natural History for its members became part of the fashionable social season.

so much because it cared for the purposes of the Museum itself as because it was the right thing, Autumn and Spring, to attend its receptions."[31]

The museum's members and trustees, who aspired to recognition as public patrons, defined their mission broadly. The trustees rejected Agassiz's idea that the museum should primarily serve scientists and specialists. They instead endorsed Green's vision of the museum as an adjunct and "aid to the great educational system of the city." An 1869 *Times* editorial, noting the lack of "sufficient supply" of "skilled young men in all mechanical arts," urged a science museum to "train our young men for these new professions" and to provide for "the culture and good habits of the masses."[32]

Looming over the effort to launch the new museum was the smiling face of the city's most famous museum operator, P. T. Barnum. From its opening in 1841, Barnum's American Museum had included natural objects among its eclectic displays and shows; his cabinets of specimens helped legitimate his less edifying entertainments—Tom Thumb and the Fejee Mermaid, for example— offered elsewhere in the building. Even if New York's leading citizens had no particular quarrel with Barnum's presentation of natural history, they did not endorse his general approach to popular culture. Less than a year before the new philanthropists decided to call their institution the *American Museum* of

Natural History, Barnum's own American Museum had burned to the ground (for the second and final time). In the aftermath, the *Times* had asked hopefully, "Why cannot we now have a great popular Museum in New-York without any humbug?" The *Herald* from a similar perspective had two years earlier called for the creation of a national museum within Central Park that would be "commensurate with the wealth and tastes of the city." Defining a museum as "a library of facts, in which the public can . . . attain knowledge," the *Herald* explicitly counterposed a "museum" to a "show," which might be got up by "museum mongers."[33]

The commission's invitation to cultural institutions to locate in the park reinforced the trustees' campaign to wrest the very definition of *museum* from the man the *Herald* called the "charlatan general of showmen."[34] Barnum's American Museum, on the corner of Broadway and Ann Street, had been in the heart of the city's commercial district. The philanthropists' American Museum in Central Park would be in the heart of the city's most cultivated space and close to the genteel residential district Belmont and others envisioned. There, the founders would lift the museum (both the institution and the word) from the world of the streets to the world of the park.

The founders, at the same time, redefined the museum as a "public" rather than a "private" institution. A *Herald* editorial had objected to Barnum's museum: "Private efforts for the mere purposes of profit can never accomplish anything in the right direction." "Private individuals may get up a show, but a museum, to be of any sterling value, must be a public institution." Although the natural history museum's founders owed their fortunes to "the mere purposes of profit," they agreed that a proper museum would have to be public in the dual senses of noncommercial and "open to all." At the same time, they had no intention of making it public in the further sense of being democratically controlled and administered. Moreover, the organizers (many of whom were Republicans) were opposed to big-*D* Democratic control as well as small-*d* democracy. This would be "their" museum, and they were determined to keep it out of the hands of "greedy, corrupt, and treacherous" politicians. (Republican lawyer Joseph Choate, a founder of both the art and the natural history museums, once suggested that the solution to Irish home rule was for the Irish to go home and rule Ireland, since they had proved so adept at ruling New York City.)[35] The museum founders resisted public *control* as they courted public sanction and resources.

From the earliest days of the Republic, state legislatures had granted charters to incorporate benevolent and cultural associations, thereby permitting them to act as independent economic entities. Thus, in a political culture distrustful of governmental power, state governments delegated responsibility to private associations for providing particular public services. In the 1820s New York's municipal government also contributed money and space to a coalition of patrician cultural organizations (including the New-York Historical

Society, the Academy of Fine Arts, and the Lyceum of Natural History), which then formed the New York Institution of Learned and Scientific Establishments. But in 1830, historian Thomas Bender notes, the common council withdrew public financial support when mechanics protested against "subsidizing the culture of the elite." Private benevolent associations (for example, the asylums and the House of Refuge) continued to receive public money, but promotion of the arts and sciences remained a private enterprise.[36]

The trustees of the natural history museum differed from their patrician predecessors in self-consciously asserting a public mission that would reach beyond elite circles. Thus, they turned to the legislature not only for a charter but for public money and facilities. In effect, the museum was organized as a hybrid institution, and it would be a model for many future cultural establishments in the city, under private control but public in their relative openness, nonprofit motives, and use of city and state resources.

In arriving at this arrangement, the museum trustees had built upon and modified the model of Central Park itself as a public institution. The park's creation had marked a major departure from the older method of organizing cultural institutions through private incorporation. Because land was taken through eminent domain and partly paid for with tax dollars, the park became an entirely public institution, created at a moment of optimistic support for expanding government responsibilities. In the 1850s the private Public School Society also fully surrendered its control over schools to the public board of education.[37] Yet the legislature's appointment of the original commission also signaled the limits on such experiments. The first board was a self-perpetuating body: the commissioners nominated their own successors. Even so, their internal partisan fights (as well as repeated conflicts with the common council over money and policy) probably reinforced the museum trustees' distaste for the model of a public commission and their determination to insulate their institution from public control and, hence, from politics.

As park comptroller, Andrew Green worked out much of the legal mechanism for this new hybrid of a "public" cultural institution controlled by a private board of directors. By 1868, having successfully secured a maintenance budget for the park, Green confidently lobbied for a law authorizing the city to subsidize museums within Central Park by erecting buildings and paying maintenance bills. The park board would oversee the general arrangements, but management would remain entirely in the private hands of "intelligent citizens[,] men of leisure & scientific men." Green, of course, saw no conflict of interest in his own service on the boards of both the public park and the public-private American Museum of Natural History.[38]

But the trustees had to work with politicians to secure a charter. "Why, this is just like getting a railroad charter through," a railroad executive told Bickmore. "Here, I will give you a letter of introduction to Mr. Tilden, who is the greatest railroad lawyer of our day. He is interested in libraries, he will probably be interested in your museum." Tilden, in turn, dispatched Bickmore to Boss William Tweed with another letter of introduction. "Well, well, what can I do for Mr. Tilden?" Tweed asked Bickmore. "Senator," he replied, "I hope you will agree with . . . [the museum's organizers], that to found such a grand institution as they have in mind, it is proper and necessary for them to have a charter, creating them a body corporate by a special act of the Legislature." "All right my young friend, I will see your bill safely through," Tweed assured Bickmore, thrusting the charter "into his capacious outside pocket," as the naturalist later recalled. Under Tweed's watchful eye, the legislature chartered the natural history museum and authorized the park board to establish a gallery of art and a meteorological and astronomical observatory. The museum's founders did not want to cede control to "treacherous" politicians, but they were not averse to getting their help. As one irreverent historian points out, Tweed deserves to be known as a father of the museum as much as any of its more illustrious founders.[39]

Bickmore now raised funds from wealthy citizens to buy a collection. The museum had started to amass a mix of artifacts (mounted birds and reptiles in alcohol, for example), which the park board agreed to display in the Arsenal. In the spring of 1870 the old park commission went out of business, but the new one proved an equally enthusiastic partner to the museum.[40]

The Sweeny board's support for the natural history museum did not extend to Green's other cherished educational project in Central Park, a spectacular "Paleozoic Museum" on the west side at 63rd Street. By 1870 the board had already spent thirty thousand dollars excavating a site for a Crystal Palace–like structure of cast iron and glass to house sculptor Benjamin Waterhouse Hawkins's life-size models of dinosaurs. At the same time that Commissioner Henry Hilton directed park workers to give the Arsenal a fresh coat of gray paint and construct elaborate display cases, he also dispatched workers to invade Hawkins's studio, where they smashed the dinosaur models and buried the pieces. Whether the demise of the dinosaur museum came in retaliation for Hawkins's public criticism of the Sweeny board or out of concern about its possible effects on Tweed Ring real estate speculation or, most likely, as revenge against Tammany's staunch political foe Andrew Green, the board's preemptive action probably only confirmed the natural history museum trustees' distrust of the ability of public officials to run cultural institutions.[41]

Although its new building in Manhattan Square (officially part of Central Park) would not be ready until 1877, the natural history museum attracted sizable crowds to its temporary quarters. By 1876 more than a million people visited the Arsenal museum each year, close to 10 percent of all park visitors.[42]

The trustees had lofty goals about education and uplift, but they tended, as businessmen, to measure success in quantitative terms, "by the number of people who come," as Superintendent Bickmore complained. As a result, founders who had rejected Barnum's style, now found themselves looking for

PALAEOZOIC MUSEUM.
SHOWING THE REHABILITATED FORMS OF ANCIENT ANIMAL LIFE IN AMERICA.
NOW BEING CONSTRUCTED IN CENTRAL PARK.

The last annual report of the original park commission included drawings for a Paleozoic museum, which would have displayed Benjamin Waterhouse Hawkins's models of dinosaurs. The Sweeny park board abandoned the project.

the sorts of novelties and curiosities the great showman had used to bring in crowds. On the museum's first collecting trip to Europe trustee William Blodgett brought back "a life-sized mounted exhibit of a lion attacking an Arab on a camel," explaining that "it will add greatly to the popular interest of the museum and aid us in getting subscriptions." Blodgett urged the museum to seek out the new and unusual: "We must sprinkle our wholesome bread with a little sugar." If the bankers and businessmen on the board had trouble maintaining the line between popular entertainment and education, visitors could hardly be blamed for treating the natural history museum as another variant on Barnum's American Museum, particularly considering its location in the midst of the park menagerie. Noting the "astonishing number of stuffed and mounted birds, serpents, mammals, fishes, insects, and other curious skeletons," an 1871 guide to the city recommended the newly opened museum as "one of the most attractive centers for the naturalist, the antiquarian, or the curious, on the entire island."[43]

The new museum building—a red-brick Victorian Gothic structure designed by Calvert Vaux and Jacob Wrey Mould—opened on Manhattan Square on December 22, 1877. "The next day after our grandly successful opening," Bickmore later wrote, "we experienced the depressing effect of our spacious exhibition halls nearly deserted." With the elevated railway still only reaching to 59th Street and Ninth Avenue, the new museum was "too far from the settled part of the city" to attract "the casual visitor," according to the superintendent. Especially damaging was the loss of the spillover crowds from the more popular park menagerie around the Arsenal. In the 1880s Bickmore aggressively linked the museum to the public school system, developing teachers and school-children as an important constituency. Retired railroad executive and merchant banker Morris K. Jesup, who became president in 1881, pushed the curators to develop more popular and accessible exhibits.[44]

Even so, the popularization of the museum proceeded slowly. In the mid-1880s, for example, curators took the birds off their mahogany stands and mounted them in groups amid reproductions of their nests. But not until 1900 did the curator in charge of displaying shells add common names to the Latin ones on the labels. As late as 1886 attendance was less than one-sixth what it had been at the Arsenal.[45]

Converting "Railroad Shares" into Old Masters

Just weeks before the opening of the natural history museum at the Arsenal on April 27, 1871, the trustees had been in Albany lobbying for their more elaborate and more permanent quarters. Allying with the promoters of the fledgling Metropolitan Museum of Art, they sought legislative authority for a million-dollar municipal bond issue to construct both museums within the park. Once again, the trustees turned to Boss Tweed for help, and he secured public financing. Clearing the sites and constructing the buildings (both of which were designed with the expectation of future expansion) took several years. In 1880, three years after the natural history museum, the Metropolitan Museum of Art opened a matching building, also designed by Vaux and Mould, almost directly across the park.[46]

Several men served on the boards of both museums, and their histories had been intertwined from the outset. Less than a year after the campaign for a natural history museum was launched, the Metropolitan had its formal start at a meeting at the elite Union League Club. Presiding at the 1869 meeting, William Cullen Bryant, whom most educated New Yorkers took as the exemplar of culture, hit on many of the same themes of metropolitan destiny, civic responsibility, and moral uplift that motivated the natural history museum's founders as well as, of course, the gentlemen who first advocated the park. At the dedication of the Victorian Gothic building on the park eleven years later, museum leader Joseph Choate similarly invoked a mission of diffusing "knowl-edge of art in its higher forms of beauty" in order to "humanize, to educate and refine a practical and laborious people."[47]

THE MUSEUM. CENTRAL PARK.

Calvert Vaux and Jacob Wrey Mould thought that their Ruskinian gothic design for the Metropolitan Museum of Art would blend with the park's natural landscape. But some observers complained that the building looked like a cross between a train station and a packing house.

Yet in practice the Met's trustees tended to view this mission somewhat ambivalently—much more so than the natural history museum's founders. The trustees closed the doors to the public on Sundays, and they courted the rich by holding private receptions for paid members. Curators and trustees also assiduously cultivated the city's wealthy art collectors, who took up Choate's challenge to "convert pork into porcelain, grain and produce into priceless pottery, the rude ores of commerce into sculptured marble, and railroad shares and mining stocks . . . into the glorified canvas of the world's masters." Noting its reputation for snobbishness, the *Tribune* in 1880 charged that the Met was "an exclusive social toy."[48]

That perception spread in the 1880s following a scandal. Leading art critics and most New York newspapers charged the museum director, Louis P. di Cesnola, with misrepresenting the authenticity of objects in the Cypriot collection he had sold to the museum. (The anti-Semitism he displayed in answering charges from a Jewish art dealer received much less criticism.) A long and sensational trial seemed to vindicate him, but the trustees themselves felt besieged. "Public service in this country does not reward us," one of the trustees wrote Cesnola after the trial. Even a sympathetic historian of the museum notes a "cooling of the trustees' democratic and educational fervor" in the last decades of the century. They abolished their art classes for artisans and shifted from collecting copies and casts to acquiring original Old Masters, emphasizing, as art historian Michele Bogart argues, the idea of "true art" as "an autonomous object of rarefied appreciation, detached from any obligation to express common social values." By the 1890s trustees viewed the terms of their lease from the city—the use of the buildings in exchange for free admission of the public—as an imposition that deprived them of admission fees that could purchase new art works.[49]

The trustees' fastidiousness about the manners of their visitors matched their growing mistrust of cultural democracy. Museum guards scrutinized the dress of visitors; cracked down on those who whistled, took photographs, spat tobacco juice on the floor, or talked loudly; and charged a fee for the mandatory checking of canes, umbrellas, and lunch baskets. When Mark Twain was told that he had to leave his cane in the cloakroom, he quipped loudly: "Leave my cane! Leave my cane! Then how do you expect me to poke holes through the oil paintings." After the museum barred a plumber wearing overalls, a local newspaper headlined: "Sober Workman Has to Leave Art Galleries: Art for the Well Dressed: Sensitive and Refined Plumber Affronted." Cesnola was unrepentant: "We do not want, nor will we permit a person who has been digging in a filthy sewer or working among grease and oil to come in here, and, by offensive odors emitted from the dirt on their apparel, make the surroundings uncomfortable for others."[50]

Closed on the Sabbath

Tensions over how New Yorkers should behave inside the museums were small compared to the much larger conflict over when they should be allowed to enter. Complaints about closing the natural history museum on Sundays emerged even before the new building at Manhattan Square opened in 1877. "I should like to know," asked a letter writer to the *Herald* earlier that year, "why it is that the Museum at Central Park is kept closed on Sundays as if to exclude the working classes, the real payers of all burdens. Are we really living in a democratic city where a place maintained with public funds is solely for the benefit of the wealthy part of the community?"[51]

When the newly opened Met followed the same sabbatarian policy, questions increased. In 1881 ten thousand German New Yorkers petitioned for Sunday opening; three years later, the Clothing Cutters' Union coupled its resolution in support of Sunday concerts with a plea that the "doors of the museums and art galleries [be] thrown open to the public on Sundays." When the crowds showed up for the first Sunday afternoon concerts in 1884, the pressure to open the museums mounted. Working-class demands for public access grew louder along with growing class unrest marked locally by the Henry George campaign. In early 1886, 120 labor organizations representing more than fifty thousand workers petitioned the two museums to open their doors on

THE METROPOLITAN MUSEUM.

Cartoons like this one in *Puck* attacked the hardheartedness of the sabbatarian trustees of the Met for closing their museum on Sundays and so shutting out the city's working people.

Sundays to "the working people [who] have to contribute the larger share toward the maintenance of these public institutions."[52]

Both museum boards were filled with conservative Presbyterians, and the trustees of the two museums greeted these protests with a combination of disdain and incomprehension. The *Herald* called the natural history museum "practically a Presbyterian Chapel." Robert L. Stuart, president of the museum from 1872 to 1881, was a staunch Presbyterian who gave more than a million dollars to church-related causes. His successor, Morris Jesup, was also the president of the New York City Mission and Tract Society and the American Sunday School Union and a founder of the Presbyterian Hospital and the Brick Presbyterian Church. Similarly, the first president of the Met's board was John Taylor Johnston, a Presbyterian who made his fortune in railroads. His father was such a stickler for sabbath rules that he declined to meet the pope on a visit to Rome because the audience had been scheduled for Sunday. The father of William C. Prime, vice president of the board (and its most active officer in the 1880s), was a Presbyterian minister, and he himself gained his interest in art from biblical studies.[53] For such men, sabbath observance was a matter of deep

principle. The museum could hardly serve its mission of educating and uplift-
ing the working classes by violating the Christian sabbath.

At the annual meeting in February 1886, President Johnston warned board
members that the "erroneous idea has gained some currency that *your* Museum
is a public institution." It was the two museums' obligation to a particular and
narrow public—the "educated, intelligent people," as one Met trustee called
them, who took out annual subscriptions and donated natural history specimens
and works of art—that fueled their bitter opposition to Sunday opening. Jesup
told the board of estimate in October 1885 that private donors provided three-
quarters of his museum's revenue: "The very large majority of these subscriptions have come from those who desire that the Lord's Day be observed and
protected."[54]

Yet for all these vigorous assertions of the private character of the two
museums, they were heavily indebted to the public purse. The city, after all, had
provided valuable land, constructed the buildings, and from 1873 onward
contributed to their annual maintenance. The shift in the composition of the
political public—the emergence of Irish and Germans as massive voting
blocs—had forced the park board to liberalize its sabbath rules; it had less
immediate impact on the museum trustees. But the two museums wanted the
city to provide more money for upkeep and new buildings. The common
council could withhold such funds in retaliation for the unpopular sabbath
policy. In the early 1880s Catholic mayor William R. Grace steadfastly blocked
city expenditures for a new wing for the natural history museum. Catholic
voters, an Irish Catholic correspondent told Jesup, saw the Sunday closing as
"just one more bit of Protestant meanness." And in 1885 the park board, the
board of aldermen, and the board of estimate threatened to cut off maintenance
funds if the museums did not open on Sundays. Two years later new mayor
Abram Hewitt, a staunch Protestant who had suffered politically for enforcing
the Sunday closing laws, told Jesup that "he personally doubted if either
Museum would ever again be granted public funds for any purpose" unless they
opened on Sunday. In 1889 only legal technicalities prevented the next mayor,
Hugh Grant, and the board of estimate from making the $400,000 appropria-
tion authorized by the legislature for a second Met wing contingent on Sunday
opening.[55]

When the city offered additional funds if the museums would open *either* in
the evenings or on Sunday, the trustees chose evenings. Both museums expected large bequests from the estate of Robert L. Stuart, and they worried
(rightly it turned out) that his widow would cancel the gifts if they yielded on the
Sunday opening. Jesup, the "life and soul of opposition" to sabbath opening,
was similarly a major benefactor of the natural history museum.[56]

In 1891 Lower East Side Jews, who kept their own sabbath on Saturday,
provided fifty thousand of the eighty thousand signatures on petitions drawn up
by settlement house workers. Faced with these petitions as well as growing

support among wealthy New Yorkers, a vigorous outcry from the press, and a bill in the legislature to compel Sunday opening, the Met finally yielded. The American Museum of Natural History held out for another year and then gave in as well to what the *Times* called "popular opinion unmistakably expressed."[57]

The battle over Sunday opening showed the ambiguous status of private institutions within a public park. New Yorkers who demanded access to the museums along with Sunday concerts in the park did not distinguish between the two kinds of institutions. And dependence on public money made the museum vulnerable to political pressure, although the public continued to have very little say in their management. As with the park in which the museums were located, the gentlemen founders were only partially successful in imposing their own cultural vision. That goal became even more elusive when they finally opened their doors on Sunday. Attendance at the natural history museum jumped by 50 percent: three-quarters of *all* visitors came on Sundays. The change in the attendance pattern at the art museum was less dramatic but substantial: about one-third of its visitors came on Sundays. But some of the museums' wealthiest supporters walked out of the newly opened doors; within six months, about 115 of the Met's 1,850 or so paying members quit.[58]

The Met's trustees bemoaned the loss of "the sympathy and favor of an important portion of the public," but they had gained the interest of a much larger (if less "important") portion of the public. The ten thousand people who showed up on the first Sunday, the *Sun* reported, were "distinctively a New York crowd" and "for the most part . . . people who had never seen a museum before . . . workers of all nationalities and trades." Reporters, curious about the new museumgoers, followed them around and noted some distinctive patterns. A party of fifteen Italians, "evidently from the lace-making country," according to the *Sun,* examined a case of antique Italian lace "minutely, and the women made frequent exclamations of delight." The men who were attracted to the armory and knights, by contrast, were "quite distinct. They had large, hard hands, and there were traces of oil on their fingers that spoke of the engine, the lathe, or the forge. The skill of the early forgers of iron seemed to be particularly fascinating, for there was a large crowd around the alcove all afternoon." Visitors gathered in large groups around the oil and watercolor paintings. Pictures of a "devotional nature" attracted particular attention.[59]

Despite the interest in religious art, the museum's new visitors did not treat the art museum as a sacred space. The convention of reverential public silence in palaces of culture did not seem to prevail. Many visitors brought babies, who cried loudly. "It was a good-natured crowd," explained the *Sun* reporter; "it talked freely and confidingly with itself, and told of its personal enjoyments and troubles." The conversations were loud enough for reporters to overhear what was being said about the paintings: " 'So that is Joan of Arc, the lady soldier! My, how brave she must have been!' ' "The dying poacher"—how cruel to kill a man for shooting a few birds and hares!' "[60]

This distinctive style and aesthetics of museumgoing could also be glimpsed at the natural history museum, which finally opened on Sundays in October 1892. Large numbers of "laboring men and women" admired particular artifacts—diamonds, ostrich feathers, and monkeys, according to one reporter. But here the contrast between Sunday and weekday crowds was perhaps less dramatic, since the natural history museum had already made efforts to accommodate and attract a more popular audience.[61]

Civic Grandeur in the Pastoral Park

The two museums were now able to win greater support from elected public officials, who had held them at arm's length while the buildings remained shuttered on Sundays. Between 1890 and 1901 the city's maintenance appropriation for the Met multiplied six times. By the end of the century the balance of power had shifted between the publicly controlled park and the privately controlled museums. In the museums' first two decades, the park board had provided their buildings and set the level of public contribution to maintenance. Now, a reform mayor, William L. Strong, appointed park commissioners with close ties to the museums and even gave museum officials a veto over his selections. "No appointments will be made to the Park Department *that will not be agreeable to our Museums*," Jesup, the president of the natural history museum, told the Met's president in 1895.[62]

In the 1890s the natural history museum enjoyed a particularly cozy relationship with one of the city's premiere political insiders—George Washington Plunkitt, the Tammany politician who had been born in Seneca Village, literally a stone's throw from the museum. The museum hired Plunkitt supporters, and he, in turn, worked in Albany and in City Hall to increase maintenance and building appropriations for the museum. Plunkitt persuaded the legislature to appropriate almost $5 million for expansion in the 1890s, enabling the museum to add five new wings and complete the south facade. The trustees realized, as Jesup put it, that they "could work with the Irish politicians more easily than with the so-called honest Yankees of twenty-five years ago." Ironically, the museum suffered from the reform movement that weakened Plunkitt's power in the early twentieth century. "Those d-mned reformers are going to ruin us all," Plunkitt wrote Bickmore in 1903, explaining his inability to get a museum-building bill through the state legislature.[63]

At the art museum, the trustees pointed to Sunday crowds to win public funds for a major expansion. The Met had already opened two new wings in 1888 and 1894, designed by two close associates of the museum who had added classical motifs to Vaux and Mould's original Victorian Gothic design. In 1895 the state and city authorized another one million dollars for a Fifth Avenue wing.[64]

As both museums expanded, new architectural styles and structures suggested a changing conception of their relationship to the park. The new wings visually asserted the distinction between these cultural institutions and the park. Yet, at the same time that the museums were severing their historical ties to the park, they were reshaping the park's identity. As powerful urban attractions, the museums undermined the definition of the park as a pastoral landscape. The new packages in which these attractions were wrapped returned to the aesthetic of artificial civic display that had lost out to romantic naturalism when the Greensward design was selected back in 1858.

Facing 77th Street and designed in the ponderous rusticated Romanesque style popularized by H. L. Richardson, the new west wing of the natural history museum (opened in 1889) overshadowed Vaux and Mould's simple Victorian structure. The trustees of the Metropolitan even more decidedly abandoned an older generation's Ruskinian taste, embracing a neoclassical architectural statement of civic grandeur. Richard Morris Hunt, the man responsible for altering the Met's spatial and aesthetic relationship to the park, had been trying for years to leave his imprint on the park. He had been foiled first in his proposal for gates at the southern entrances and then in his design for the historical society at the Arsenal. A trustee of the Metropolitan, Hunt had been passed over as the architect for that museum's first building in 1871 and for its first two additions. Indeed, the closest Hunt got to the park was to design the Lenox Library across the street at 70th Street and Fifth.[65]

Vaux and Mould's simple red-brick and granite design for the Met looked nothing like the French Renaissance buildings that Hunt had designed for the Lenox Library and sketched for the historical society a few years earlier. The Met's first architects, who shared Ruskin's admiration for the early Gothic buildings of Venice and worked under severe budget constraints in the mid-1870s, designed a modest building, opening onto the park. In contrast to Hunt's awesome vision of grand civic architecture, Vaux and Mould wanted their museum to blend in with the natural landscape, which for Vaux represented the pinnacle of art. The first building's distinguishing feature was a gallery skylight that placed the art works in natural light. But when the Met first opened, some critics thought it looked like "a cross between a cotton press and pork-packing establishment with the interior of a railroad station."[66]

When Hunt won the commission for the Met's Fifth Avenue wing in 1895, he set a new tone by designing a massive Beaux-Arts structure on the building's east side, reorienting it away from the park and toward Fifth Avenue. In 1906 McKim, Mead, and White extended Hunt's civic monument until classical grandeur largely enveloped the museum's original brick building. (Today, the remaining west facade of the Vaux and Mould structure can be glimpsed only from inside the Lehman Wing.) Just as conspicuous consumption had triumphed over modesty on the carriage drives, so did the architecture of display and grandeur triumph over the romantic Victorian architecture of restraint and moralism.[67]

Richard Morris Hunt's design for a new wing of the Met, opened in 1902, reoriented the museum toward Fifth Avenue and marked the triumph of the Beaux-Arts style over Victorian romanticism.

The construction of Hunt's building brought to a close a half century of conflict over what would occupy the seven-block tract east of the Lower Reservoir (between 79th and 86th streets and Fifth and Sixth). Competing plans for the site—Viele's parade ground, the Greensward plan's playground, the zoological garden, Hunt's museum for the New-York Historical Society, Vaux and Mould's museum building—remind us that us that the different visions of the park evident in the original design competition (the aesthetics of the commercial pleasure ground, of romantic naturalism, and of artificial civic display) remained in contention. And by the last decade of the nineteenth century, the museums, zoo, Carousel, statuary, and restaurants brought all three aesthetic traditions into play on the park. Even as the Met's new classical wings invoked civic order through monumental display, other attractions captured the diverting appeal of the commercial pleasure ground.

The park's aging designers themselves remained committed to the unity of their romantic conception of a pastoral landscape. As the parks department's landscape architect, Vaux acknowledged the political process that governed changes in the park and made concessions to new features—from widened drives to new play facilities. Olmsted was more rigid and denounced all "amusements" or facilities that detracted from the pastoral scenic effects. By

1890 he called the decision to allocate space in the park for the art museum "an act now generally regretted."[68]

From the perspective of parkgoers, the zoo, museums, and other attractions reinforced the park's definition as a "many sided, fluent" public space that could accommodate a variety of tastes and needs. Contained within slices of land at the edges of the park, the museums and zoo did not destroy the broad expanse of nature; they existed alongside the scenic vistas. The crowds that moved easily from the carriage parade to the Carousel, from the Ramble to the goat-cart rides, from Mr. Crowley's cage at the menagerie to Rosa Bonheur's painting of the horse fair at the Met, rejected Olmsted's unitary definition of Central Park as "*a place of rural recreation*" and the museum trustees' program for elevating public taste. Some parkgoers enjoyed contemplating nature, others sought cultural refinement at the Met, and still others preferred the lively entertainment of the zoo. But moving among these attractions, many New Yorkers also discovered richly interwoven possibilities for enjoying the park they helped shape.

"Assert Your Rights in the Park"

As the broadened "cultural public" made its presence felt on the Mall, in the museums, and at the menagerie, it also—but much less often—made its presence felt in park politics. In the 1880s and early 1890s working-class park users petitioned and pressured their political representatives to gain access to museums and park concerts on their primary day of leisure. But the mobilization of the "public" did not always follow simple class lines. Particularly in the 1890s the overt class politics of the George campaign gave way to new progressive coalitions that addressed the continuing question of what sort of public space Central Park was to be and what institutions it should include.

On March 17, 1892, the state legislature authorized the construction of a seventy-foot-wide "public drive" for fast trotting horses on the west side of Central Park. The next morning the park board directed the department's engineer to stake out the new "racetrack" (as its opponents soon dubbed it) or "driveway for light wagons" (as supporters called it) and requested funds from the city. George Washington Plunkitt had sponsored the bill; it had the backing of Tammany "sporting men" and wealthy horse fanciers, including a publisher, Robert Bonner; a railroad baron, Frederick W. Vanderbilt; and a financier, Russell Sage. Mayor Hugh Grant, himself a trotting aficionado, exemplified the sporting style that aligned Tammany politicos, wealthy transit magnates, and Irish and German workers around a shared love of drink, gambling, and fine horseflesh.[69]

The proposal prompted howls of outrage from Protestant moralists and reformers. Earnest young men, including the lawyer Richard Welling, the drug company heir William Jay Schieffelin, and his cousin John Jay Chapman,

THIS MAY BE THE CENTRAL PARK OF THE FUTURE.

Some opponents of the speedway, such as the *World*, argued that horseracing would transform Central Park into a "sporting park," with circuses, prizefights, and other disorderly amusements.

mobilized opposition against the plan through the City Reform Club. These prominent men had a deep-seated hatred for Tammany. Yet the opposition to the racetrack also galvanized New Yorkers who had in the past been the object rather than the subject of "reform."

When Welling and the Reform Club began a petition drive and issued a call for a mass meeting at Cooper Union, they were surprised at the "overwhelming response." Just one week yielded fifteen thousand signatures on petitions and $150,000 in contributions. All the city's newspapers—with the exception of the *Herald*—denounced the racetrack scheme as an "unmitigated outrage," to quote but one of them. Delegates of such disparate groups as the Stock Exchange and the Amalgamated Society of Joiners and Carpenters, the New-York Historical Society and the United Building Trades, the Young Men and Young Women's Club of Forsyth Street (on the immigrant Lower East Side) and the uptown real estate men of the West Side Association—all shared the speaker's platform at the Cooper Union protest rally. On behalf of its sixty-five thousand members ("all voters"), James P. Archibald of the Central Labor Union denounced this "infringement upon the liberty of the masses." "If this steal is permitted, where can we go to escape the filthy conditions of our streets, choking the air with dust-laden germs of disease? . . . We are the ones, whose tenement homes are a mockery to human existence, who most need Central Park, and more if we could get it."[70]

In the 1850s at least some working-class New Yorkers had wanted a trotting track within the new park. But because the racetrack would displace existing uses and even more because it was presented under elite auspices, few workers now spoke out on its behalf. Instead, a call for a meeting of East Siders (whose organizers included Jewish journalist Abraham Cahan and settlement house worker and future park commissioner Charles Stover) attacked the speedway as "class legislation" that would allow a "few wealthy people to appropriate . . . the entire western side of the park." Noting that Lower East Side residents had "fought hard" the previous spring for the opening of the art museum on Sunday, the group urged them once again to "assert your rights in the park." Middle-class opponents charged that wealthy New Yorkers were monopolizing an area of the park, just as John D. Rockefeller, a trotting enthusiast behind the scheme, was monopolizing the oil industry. But they worried even more about "roughs and toughs," who would turn the park into a "race course, and the gambling iniquities, which constitute the chief attraction of those who frequent race-courses."[71]

Real estate men, mobilized in such groups as the West End Association, worried that the racing crowd would menace private property. "Along Eighth avenue facing the park," the *World* reported, "property owners are beginning to be alarmed at the effect . . . on valuations in the neighborhood. . . . All the unimproved property in the neighborhood is held at a high figure, because of the sylvan quietness of the park, which the race-track would destroy." Others argued that it would ruin the park's naturalistic design. William Stiles, editor of *Garden and Forest,* telegraphed Olmsted to get him to weigh in with a statement calling the speedway "unjust and immoral." At the Cooper Union meeting, Stiles said that the racetrack would interfere with the purpose of a park—to provide "rural recreation" in a "broad natural way." "I tried to get in a little high doctrine on what you have told me is the essential value of parks," he reported back to the aging Olmsted.[72]

Faced with this storm of protests, Tammany Hall quickly backed down. The politicians had misread public sentiment. Although wealthy and influential men such as Rockefeller and Bonner supported the racetrack, it was never a project of the upper classes as the museums or the park had been. And although Plunkitt, Grant, and other Tammany leaders found the speedway either appealing or inoffensive, their view was not shared by other Democratic party stalwarts. Three days after the Cooper Union meeting, Plunkitt announced, "I bow to public opinion," and he introduced a bill repealing his original racetrack legislation.[73]

Like Olmsted, Calvert Vaux must have been gratified to observe this public mobilization to defend the pastoral park as designed, but he paid a personal price for his strong dissent from the park commissioners' projects. Two days before the racetrack bill was introduced (and not entirely coincidentally), the Tammany-linked commissioners of accounts launched an investigation of the department's "old guard" employees, including Vaux and Parsons. Observers described Vaux's clumsy testimony as nothing short of a "humiliation." When the landscape architect acknowledged that he did not know the botanical names of park plants, the commissioners recommended that he be fired for "incompetency." Vaux, already suffering from shingles, plunged into a deep depression. But when in 1894 the park commissioners started to build a new Harlem speedway without consulting Vaux, he was at the center of another massive protest. He maintained that such a project required the advice of a professional designer and that the speedway should accommodate "the people" with an adjacent public walkway along the Harlem River. This second controversy over the design and use of public space sustained the antiracetrack coalition and helped link it to a wider political battle.[74]

"The uprising against the proposal to ruin the Park by the establishment of a race track will not have fulfilled its whole or its best function if it merely prevents this atrocity," the *Times* had announced in 1892. It prodded the "organizations of the protestants" to continue as an anti-Tammany "citizens' municipal party." The proposal was prophetic. Fueled by vice and police scandals and a crushing depression, an anti-Tammany reform coalition solidified over the next two years. In 1894 businessman reformer William L. Strong defeated racetrack advocate Hugh Grant for mayor. The alliance of businessmen, reformers, trade unionists, Lower East Siders, artists, and landscape architects forged in the crusade against the Central Park speedway briefly captured City Hall.[75]

The political public that stopped the racetrack and elected Strong was never homogeneous or fully unified. Like the cultural public that crowded the Mall on a spring Sunday, it included people of diverse backgrounds, cultures, and views. By 1896 the Strong coalition had fallen apart, unable to accommodate conflicting demands for both increased public services and increased governmental economy, for enforcing Sunday closing laws and allowing German Americans to enjoy the continental Sunday, for meeting city workers' demands for better hours and wages and retaining the support of employers and larger taxpayers— the same issues that had always divided New Yorkers in their claims on Central Park as a public institution. A broad spectrum of New Yorkers—a "public" of sorts—had been able to agree that they did not want a racetrack for wealthy men, their audiences, or gamblers in Central Park, but agreement on other issues of park policy would never be so easily achieved. Trade unionists such as Archibald, who focused on issues of equity and access, did not share the same vision of the park as the real estate men, middle-class reformers, or advocates of the naturalistic landscape.

Such differences widened in the next century, as the city grew and social and cultural divisions multiplied. As more and more New Yorkers asserted their stake in the park (their membership in its cultural and political public), the debate over what it meant to use and operate a public park became more difficult to resolve.

The Great City Checkerboard

V. THE NINETEENTH-CENTURY PARK IN THE TWENTIETH-CENTURY CITY

14

THE FRAGMENTED PARK

At nine o'clock on the morning of November 21, 1895, a dock worker discovered Calvert Vaux's body floating in Gravesend Bay, Brooklyn. Vaux, then seventy-one, had left his son's Bensonhurst house for a late-afternoon walk two days before. When he failed to return, his alarmed children notified the police and the newspapers. The parks department's landscape architect had weathered his humiliating battles with Tammany politicians over the Central Park racetrack and Harlem Speedway. He was, his son told reporters, "on most friendly terms with the new park commissioners" appointed by the reform mayor, William Strong. But when he finished feverishly designing a section of the Bronx Park in August, "he was almost in a state of collapse."[1]

"If I can only manage to live until 1898," Vaux's daughter recalled her father saying, "my plans for the improvement of Central Park will be completed, and I won't have to worry about any other work. Three years more and I'll be satisfied." But Vaux, who had been deeply depressed since his wife Mary's death in a carriage accident three years earlier, suffered from shingles and was in failing health. Neighbors reported that he had become melancholy and told them "he did not believe he would live to see the completion" of his work. "Probably no one will ever know," a *Tribune* article observed, "whether Mr. Vaux accidentally fell into the water," as his family believed, "or committed suicide, as the police suspected.[2]

Vaux's former partner, Frederick Law Olmsted, now seventy-three, was not well enough to be told the news. His own life had been filled with accidents, recurring illness, and long bouts of insomnia, and he now suffered from episodes of senility. His family waited for a more lucid interlude, and three months later they told him of Vaux's death. In 1898 he entered McLean Asylum in Waverly, Massachusetts, where he lived for five years in a cottage on grounds that he had designed. ("They didn't carry out my plan, confound them!" he grumbled). In August 1903, at age eighty-one, he died.[3]

The death of Olmsted's old antagonist Andrew H. Green came a few months later. In the early afternoon of November 13, 1903, Cornelius Williams, a forty-three-year-old janitor, accosted Green as he entered the house at 91 Park Avenue where he lived with his nephew and nieces. "Mr. Green why did you back that woman to slander me?" Williams demanded. "Go away from me. I do not know you," Green responded and turned to enter the vestibule. Williams pulled out a .38-caliber revolver and shot Green five times.[4]

The killer had mistaken Green, an eighty-three-year-old bachelor, for the lover of a woman Williams believed had spread false rumors about him. Front-page headlines reported the sensational murder, and editorialists eulogized Green as "the father of Greater New York" and "the creator of Central Park." All the competing candidates for that honor—William Cullen Bryant, Andrew Jackson Downing, Robert Bowne and Anna Mary Minturn, Fernando Wood, Calvert Vaux, and Frederick Law Olmsted—were now dead, exactly fifty years after the Central Park bill had passed the state legislature. (The only man who had gone to court to defend his rights to that title, Egbert Viele, had died quietly at age seventy-seven at his Riverside Drive home the year before. A believer in the afterlife, he had had a buzzer installed in his sarcophagus in case he revived.)[5]

By the time the park's founding generation passed away, the political, aesthetic, and cultural unity they valued had already fragmented. In the last third of the nineteenth century, management slipped from the genteel hands of the state-appointed Board of Commissioners of the Central Park to Democratic city politicians. Alternative principles of design, rejected in the original competition of 1858, had now reasserted themselves. Richard Morris Hunt's Beaux-Arts Metropolitan Museum of Art had introduced the continental aesthetic of civic display that had been rebuffed in the 1850s and 1860s. Meanwhile, the piecemeal addition of restaurants, statues, children's rides, and a popular zoo had brought the park closer to an eclectic pleasure ground. And in formal and informal ways, working-class New Yorkers had declared their membership in the park's political and cultural publics and transformed the elite park of the 1860s.

Preserving a unified conception of the park and its public would be even more difficult in the twentieth century. If the city had changed dramatically over the park's first fifty years, the pace now accelerated. Political consolidation and the rise of the boroughs, uptown Manhattan settlement, the competing attractions of commercial amusements and public playgrounds, introduction of new modes of transportation—all these altered the park's relationship to its neighborhoods and the city as a whole. The physical landscape remained fixed by the contours and motives of Olmsted and Vaux's pastoral Greensward plan, despite dizzying change in the surrounding city. But even this aesthetic unity was fractured as skyscrapers on the borders reframed the nineteenth-century park's relation to the twentieth-century metropolis.

"Buildings above the Leafless Trees"

In Robert Nathan's 1940 novel *Portrait of Jennie* an artist, Eben Adams, walks slowly home through Central Park on a cold winter evening. As he heads down "the long, deserted corridor of the Mall," the "city sounds" appear "muted and far away, they seemed to come from another time, from somewhere in the past." In the shadows, he spots a little girl playing hopscotch. As the novel and its romance develops, Adams learns that the girl, Jennie, is from the past, from the turn of the century.[6]

Nathan's choice of the park as the setting for this brush with the past was no accident. What other space in New York had changed so little since the nineteenth century? Where else would the presence of old Manhattan be so strong? In 1947 when David O. Selznick made the film version of *Portrait of Jennie*, he shot turn-of-the-century New York in Central Park rather than on a Hollywood sound stage. Two decades later Jack Finney's novel of time travel to the 1880s, *Time and Again*, also used Central Park as the place where his protagonist could slip back into the nineteenth century.[7]

In a city legendary for rapid change, Central Park was, and is, remarkably resistant to visual alteration. And in no period, perhaps, did it change less than in the three decades after the deaths of its creators. If, as Viele had anticipated, he had awakened in the early 1930s in his sarcophagus (and found his buzzer working), he would have had little difficulty finding his way around the park. Nor would he have noticed many features not remembered from the 1890s. If the park's designers had accompanied Viele on this ghostly walk, they would have found the terrain reassuringly familiar—until they looked to the borders. There, the poet Sara Teasdale suggested in 1917 in "Central Park at Dusk," they would have encountered a new and startling kind of beauty:

> Buildings above the leafless trees
> > Loom high as castles in a dream,
> While one by one the lamps come out
> To thread the twilight with a gleam.[8]

Nothing transformed Central Park's visual relationship to the city so dramatically as the new skyline; even as early as 1892, guidebooks pointed out the "handsome hotels and flats [that] line the street" on the park's west side, and photographers captured the new frame as "Byron" did in his famous 1895 winter photograph *Skating in Central Park*, showing the luxurious Dakota Apartments at West 73rd and the six-hundred-room Hotel Majestic a block south,

These skyscrapers and hotels at the southeastern corner created new vistas that highlighted rather than hid the park's relation to the city.

looming over the tiny figures skating in the park. Describing the recently opened Majestic in 1895 as "a massive fairy vision before the rambler through Central Park," the *Illustrated American* suggested that such views offered park visitors a new aesthetic pleasure.[9]

In the 1890s Caroline Schermerhorn Astor, whose family had played such a central role in the park's early history, had chosen 65th Street and Fifth Avenue for her dazzling $300,000 mansion (designed by Richard Morris Hunt). The presence of *the* Mrs. Astor had validated the avenue's social prestige, and real estate prices had skyrocketed; by 1900 spectacular mansions lined the park up to the Metropolitan Museum at 82nd. In 1902 August Belmont II bought the corner lot on 81st Street and Fifth Avenue, intending to join the elite residential enclave his father had envisioned more than forty years before. Then the aging Andrew Carnegie—seeking "the park and sunshine"—pushed Millionaire's Row into the 90s. In 1906 Carnegie's former partner (and current rival) Henry Clay Frick arrived in New York and spent $2.5 million to buy the Lenox Library property on 70th Street, then replaced it with a Florentine palazzo that he hoped would make Carnegie's home "look like a miner's shack."[10]

By 1914, when the Fricks moved in, the neighborhood was already declining—but only if a shift from the palaces of multimillionaires to the apartments of millionaires could be seen as decline. In 1910 the Century Holding Company had purchased Belmont's still-vacant lot and hired McKim, Mead, and White to design an apartment house at 998 Fifth Avenue that would entice tycoons to move from their mansions. In the next two decades, dozens of luxury apartment buildings went up on Fifth and, particularly after World War I, on Park Avenue as well. Even the city's richest families found the price of a Fifth Avenue lot daunting, and their new apartments often had more rooms than a standard townhouse. Douglas Elliman, the rental agent for 998 Fifth, later recalled that when it was built, 90 percent of high society lived in private houses; twenty years later 90 percent lived in apartments. After World War I, an almost solid ring of towering hotels and apartment buildings rose to surround the park, culminating on the West Side in 1931 with the opening of the art deco Century Apartments (between 62nd and 63rd streets) with their distinctive twin towers.[11]

The new buildings created a new constituency of park users who never passed through the gates. Apartment dwellers and hotel guests gazed at the landscape from on high. The emergence of this distinctly passive and *urban* mode of using the park was not, however, lost on real estate agents or wealthy New Yorkers. In 1926 when steel magnate Elbert H. Gary sold his Fifth Avenue mansion for replacement by an apartment house in which he intended to live, he stressed that he would command as much of the park's space and air from his apartment as from his mansion—more, in fact, if he rented a ten- or twelve-story apartment. The *Times* agreed: Central Park was contributing to the "vogue of the multiple-family dwelling," since "along the periphery of the park one might build up into the air and multiply by four or five times the number of residents profiting by this greatest of front yards." Real estate ads for Fifth Avenue and Central Park West apartments now prominently touted their "permanent view of beautiful Central Park" and their "unrivaled view of woodland, greensward and lake." Ironically, the park's very success as a pastoral real estate amenity threatened its rural character.[12]

To Olmsted's son, Frederick, Jr., who followed his father into landscape architecture, the skyline seemed "inherently ugly, restless, and distressing," and he felt that it destroyed the unity and serenity of the park's romantic design. But what could be done about it? Some people urged drastic height restrictions for new skyscrapers, others suggested thickening the park's boundary plantings

Joseph Pulitzer, publisher of the *World*, tried to outdo William Randolph Hearst by donating the Pulitzer Fountain at the park's southeast corner, designed in a more restrained, classical style than the flamboyant *Maine* Monument. This view looks up Fifth Avenue.

to try to "obscure the skyline created by the new buildings." But those critics who saw the naturalistic aesthetic as old-fashioned suggested that now that the "visible frame" had become "hopelessly un-rural and insistently architectural," the design of Central Park itself should be allowed to become more "frankly urban." While architects and landscape architects debated the aesthetic implications of the skyline, thousands of parkgoers welcomed the towers as navigational aids in negotiating the park's wandering paths.[13]

Even before the tall buildings had registered their full impact, adherents of formal urban design had seen an opportunity to recast the park's visual relationship to the city by introducing architectural features that would acknowledge and embrace the modern city. In his will Joseph Pulitzer, publisher of the *World*, bequeathed fifty thousand dollars to build a grand fountain just outside the park's southeast corner at 59th and Fifth to resemble "those of the Place de la Concorde." The firm of Carrère and Hastings, working in the Beaux-Arts tradition, designed a formal pedestrian plaza and fountain as a grand entrance to the park—just the sort of thing Vaux had bitterly resisted when Richard Hunt proposed ornate gates in 1863. Three blocks to the west, the other principal southern entrance, at Columbus Circle, also received a new monument in the second decade of the twentieth century. Not coincidentally, the sponsor was William Randolph Hearst, publisher of the *Journal and American* and Pulitzer's longtime rival. On Memorial Day 1913 Hearst joined city officials in dedicating the *Maine* Monument to the Spanish-American War his paper's yellow journalism had done so much to promote. Although the Columbus Circle site had not been his first choice, it had some advantages: not only was it one of the most prominent spots in the city, but a monumental entrance would enhance Hearst's real estate holdings nearby.[14]

Pulitzer knew of plans for the *Maine* Monument before his death, historian Michele Bogart points out, and sought "to meet his archcompetitor Hearst on equal ground" by choosing the Plaza site for his own fountain. The restrained and elegant style of the Pulitzer Fountain was a deliberate counterpoint to the much more animated and flamboyant *Maine* Monument.[15] Despite the contrasting styles and sponsorships, the Plaza and Columbus Circle finally provided the metropolis with the sort of grand urban entryways into the rural park that had been rejected fifty years earlier.

A Fragmented Political Public

On January 1, 1898, New York City became Greater New York. A single and singular piece of state legislation multiplied the area of the city five times and increased its population by two-thirds, expanding it past Manhattan Island and the Bronx (which had been annexed in two stages in 1874 and 1895) to incorporate Brooklyn, Staten Island, and Queens. With close to three and a half million people, New York became the second largest city in the world after

Columbus Circle, 1920: New automobile traffic flowed around the Columbus Statue, dedicated in 1892, and the *Maine* Monument, donated by the publisher William Randolph Hearst in 1913 (*upper left*).

London. The huge leap was, of course, artificial: the creation of Greater New York did not add people, it simply altered political boundaries. But consolidation did inaugurate another sustained period of rapid population growth: the old New York had more than doubled in the previous forty years; the new New York doubled again in the next forty years.[16]

The consolidation altered the political administration of Central Park. Under the 1897 charter, the mayor appointed a three-person park board, one member representing the Bronx, another Brooklyn and Queens, and the third, the president, representing Manhattan and Staten Island. The Board of Commissioners of the Department of Parks gave out contracts, established general rules, and hired citywide officials, but it did not, as before, set day-to-day policy. Each commissioner had relatively sovereign control over the parks in his boroughs, though all three operated under the thumb of the mayor. An 1895 law incorporated into the new charter gave the mayor power to fire department heads without the permission of the governor—overturning a state law of the 1870s intended to protect Andrew Green's rule as comptroller.[17]

Each new mayor, rewarding political friends and courting the votes of new constituencies, chose three new commissioners. More than half of those who served between 1898 and 1934 (when the system changed again) were active political partisans, three-quarters of them Democrats. As in the late nineteenth century, most were well-to-do lawyers, contractors, or real estate operators, but a labor leader and a settlement house worker also served as Manhattan commissioner. About two-thirds were of Irish or German descent. Few, if any, were the sort of "gentlemen of taste" who had dominated the original Central Park commission. Indeed, newspaper editorials and reform and business groups continued to agitate for replacing the mayor's appointees with a nonpartisan board of citizens on the model of the museums and that first park board.[18]

If park commissioners had to look over their shoulders to get the mayor's approval, they also had to contend with other municipal officials. In the first decade of the new century, the mayor's power was partially counterbalanced by the parks department's landscape architect, then Samuel Parsons, the only surviving link to the founding generation. As a result of the mobilization of artists and architects during battles over the Central Park racetrack, Harlem Speedway, and expansion of the natural history museum, Parsons's office had gained new authority. The 1897 charter mandated that the park board obtain the landscape architect's assent to any significant design changes. The ten members of the New York Art Commission, which the 1897 charter empowered to review works of art to be located on city property, also scrutinized the board's actions on statues and monuments. After 1901 artistic additions to the park, as well as the entire park budget, also needed the approval of the powerful board of estimate, which comprised the five borough presidents, the mayor, the comptroller, and the president of the board of aldermen.[19]

The park board had never had financial autonomy, but it had controlled the policing of the terrain. In 1898 the sparrow cops merged into the new Metropolitan Police. Park commissioners could no longer decide how many policemen would patrol the parks or how they would enforce park rules. Even the rules to be enforced were no longer determined by the board alone. After 1901 the board of aldermen had to concur in any change in park ordinances—another decrease in the commissioners' sovereignty and increase in the influence of elected officials.[20]

Even as the commissioners faced new limitations on their power within city government, they had to listen to the increasingly loud voices of park advocates outside city government. As in the nineteenth century, newspaper editors and publishers scrutinized and often protested new policies. In some cases, editors' interest in parks, particularly Central Park, seems to have been disproportionate to other local issues, perhaps because Central Park had the same sort of status as a citywide civic institution that they sought for their newspapers.

In the years after 1896, when Adolph Ochs took control of the *New York Times* and turned it into the nation's preeminent newspaper, it also became the leading local voice of opinion on Central Park. In a single month in 1909, for example, the *Times* published twenty-nine editorials opposing a plan to locate a new National Academy of Design building in the park. "Sometimes the editors of the *New York Times* seem to think they invented the idea of Central Park," Arthur Hays Sulzberger, Ochs's son-in-law and the paper's future publisher, observed wryly in the 1920s. Sulzberger's wife, Iphigene Ochs Sulzberger, was one of the leading park activists of the period; they lived only a few steps away, on East 80th near the Metropolitan.[21] Other papers also took a proprietary interest in the park. In a three-month period in 1924, for example, the *Daily News*, the city's leading tabloid with a million readers (most of them working-class New Yorkers), ran twenty-two editorials about Central Park even though it generally carried only one or two editorials each day on any subject.

Twentieth-century park officials faced, in addition, a regular barrage of criticism from a growing number of lobbying groups. Civic associations, women's clubs, city beautification and planning societies, and real estate and trade organizations as well as groups specifically interested in playgrounds and parks regularly addressed park questions. In their growing outspokenness, the press and pressure groups were symbiotically connected. Newspapers with a strong viewpoint like the *Times* helped to create "public opinion" on particular issues by seeking out comments from leaders of what became a "park lobby." And park lobbyists, in turn, mobilized press connections to pressure city officials. People like Iphigene Sulzberger, with a foot in each camp, played important intermediary roles. "I believe that the *Times* might take up the matter," she reassured an activist worried about a change in the park.[22]

Even the original Central Park commission had always faced external pressures. Now these had multiplied, especially when commissioners tried to make any dramatic shift from prior policy. And in a few instances, commissioners faced not only the criticism of the press, of elected officials, lobbyists, and organized artists, but of ordinary New Yorkers, who mobilized—even rioted—to defend their rights to free public space.

"The Hired Chair Outrage"

In June 1901 the Manhattan park commissioner, George C. Clausen, licensed Oscar Spate to rent chairs in city parks for a nickel each. The practice was common in Europe, but it met immediate protests in New York. In downtown Madison Square Park, tensions ran high. "The parks are free to the public," shouted one elderly man as rental agent Thomas Tully yanked him from his seat for refusing to pay. Yelling "Kill him" and "Break the chairs on his head," an angry crowd of a thousand men and boys chased Tully from the park.

A few days later, three thousand people gathered in another spontaneous protest. Some just sat down on the green chairs and refused to pay the fee; others kicked the chairs to pieces or threw them under the wheels of passing wagons. Police arrested eleven people.[23]

Three hundred rental seats were placed in Central Park, and parkgoers there joined in the boycotts and civil disobedience. "When the Sunday morning crowd from the lower part of the City got to the park," the *Sun* reported, "they made straight for the chairs, sat down and told the attendants they would not pay." The police called it "Chair Sunday." People jeered Spate's agents and the few patrons who paid for seats in the shadiest spots. Some broke the wooden chairs or cut out the cane seats with knives.[24]

Commissioner Clausen, a wealthy German-American businessman (who had previously encountered public fury when he served on the park board during the 1894 Harlem Speedway controversy), quickly backed off, and after the second Madison Square Park riot, revoked Spate's chair license. Clausen even offered to purchase the chairs personally and donate them to the city. The *Journal and Advertiser*, which had led the crusade against the "hired chair outrage," sponsored a rally that drew twenty thousand people to Madison Square Park to celebrate the victory with speeches, songs, and fireworks. The happy resolution masked deeper—and continuing—tensions over how the city's public parks should be managed and for whose benefit in an era when the parks' public expanded and fragmented. As an appointed city official, Clausen answered only to Tammany mayor Robert A. Van Wyck; yet when he reversed course, he said that he was responding to pressure from "the great public of New York."[25]

The "great organs of public opinion"—Clausen's phrase for the newspapers—had fanned the protest. Hearst's *Journal,* for example, did more than publicize the chair controversy; its editorials urged readers to write to Clausen himself (suggesting that they tell him that "his conduct would disgrace a microcephalic marsupial"); the *Journal*'s lawyers defended those arrested for refusing to pay the chair rental fee; and its editors cabled Tammany boss Richard Croker in England to ask him to intervene with Clausen. Without waiting for orders from their boss, other city officials quickly deserted Clausen when the *Tribune* and other papers suggested Tammany would be held accountable for the chair rental scheme in the upcoming mayoral election. After the first Madison Square brawl, for example, the police commissioner refused to let his men enforce the chair rental plan.[26]

If the newspapers helped orchestrate the protest, the greatest pressure to end chair rentals came from the direct action of large numbers of New Yorkers, recent Jewish and Italian immigrants prominent among them, who deeply resented the encroachment on their rights. "I will not pay five cents for what I have always had free. . . . This is a public park," explained Abraham Cohen when he was arrested for refusing to pay. But other New Yorkers defended the

PAY! PAY!! PAY!!!

In 1901 editorial cartoons protested park commissioner George Clausen's plan to license Oscar Spate to charge a nickel for seats in the park.

chair scheme precisely because it did allow for distinctions within the public, because it offered "self-respecting" people, as one letter writer to the *Times* put it, an alternative to "the ordeal of sitting next to unclean, often drunken, and generally foul-mouthed loafers" on park benches.[27] Should the city's parks be for the "self-respecting" people who considered five cents a reasonable price for a private seat in the shade or for Abraham Cohen, Dominick Lovelli, and Terry McGovern—all of whom indignantly refused to pay?

"The Empire of the Nickel"

New Yorkers violently protested paying a nickel for seats in their free public parks, but they more willingly paid a nickel as the entry price to a new world of entertainment that was booming in the early twentieth century. The commercial leisure revolution displaced Central Park as "central" in the recreational world of many New Yorkers. Of course, commercially operated pleasure grounds— for example, Jones Wood (which remained open until an 1894 fire)—had coexisted with Central Park from the outset. But in the late nineteenth and early twentieth centuries New Yorkers had gained more time and money to spend on leisure. Between 1900 and 1940 the average work week (nationally) dropped from fifty-six to forty-one hours, and real wages almost doubled.[28] As a consequence, numerous leisure entrepreneurs emerged to take advantage of the new market.

Nothing symbolized this rise of commercial leisure more than Coney Island's ascendancy over Central Park as the city's most popular leisure space. In 1880 Coney Island claimed 4.5 million annual visitors, considerably fewer than Central Park, but on hot summer days the crowds at the seaside resort rivaled

Dreamland at Twilight, Coney Island, 1905: The lights, colors, and thrills of commercial amusement parks in the early twentieth century competed with Central Park.

those at the much more accessible public park. In the 1890s summer Sunday crowds at Coney Island were double those at the park; when temperatures surpassed a hundred degrees in the summer of 1894, the *Herald* counted a hundred thousand at Coney Island and found Central Park "almost deserted."[29]

Like Jones Wood, Coney Island—especially its working-class West Brighton Beach section—offered a range of amusements Central Park did not allow. With its "dime museums, beer saloons, shooting galleries, bowling alleys, chowder booths, concert saloons, cheap restaurants and electric lights," a *Herald* reporter commented in 1884, West Brighton Beach "bears a great resemblance to the Bowery, especially as one meets the same class of people—workingmen and their families, young clerks and saleswomen—the toiling dwellers in crowded tenements." The opening of three spectacular amusement parks—Steeplechase Park, Luna Park, and Dreamland—at the turn of the century made Coney Island, historian John Kasson has said, "the unofficial capital of the new mass culture." The new entrepreneurs successfully courted middle-class in addition to working-class crowds. With the opening of the subway and the honky-tonk boardwalk in the 1920s, it became known as the "empire of the nickel."[30]

Coney Island was far from the only example of the new commercial leisure. The city's first nickelodeon opened around 1906; just two years later the Manhattan *Business Directory* listed 123 movie theaters. By 1912 a sociology graduate student at Columbia found movie houses more popular than churches, clubs, theaters, dance halls, poolrooms, and even saloons among workingmen. In the 1920s movie audiences and movie theaters grew even larger. Radio City Music Hall opened in December 1932; with sixty-two hundred seats it was the largest indoor theater in the world. The new Madison Square Garden, which opened in 1925, could seat as many as twenty thousand people for boxing, hockey, basketball, rides, ice skating, and bike races—and Communist party rallies and society horse shows. The new Polo Grounds, opened in 1912, could accommodate sixty thousand fans for baseball and football. The Yankees, who initially shared the Polo Grounds with the Giants, were so successful by 1923 that they could fill a new baseball stadium, the nation's largest, with seventy-five thousand people.[31]

Access to leisure was still structured by income. Middle- and upper-class New Yorkers, for example, filled the ringside seats at Madison Square Garden, the box seats at Yankee Stadium, and the loge seats at Radio City Music Hall, and "stepped out" to the more exclusive entertainment spots—the lobster palace restaurants of the 1890s and the 1900s, the cabarets of the 1910s, and the nightclubs of the 1920s and 1930s—that working-class New Yorkers only entered as waiters. To state the obvious: the commercial leisure world demanded cash as its price of admission, and disposable cash for such things remained quite limited. When the young sociologist Robert Coit Chapin surveyed working-class living standards in New York in 1907, he discovered that families spent on average less than $8.50 per year for recreation. Living standards improved for families of skilled workers in the relative prosperity of the 1920s (and deteriorated drastically in the hard times of the 1930s). Even in the twenties, however, the families of many poor and unskilled laborers stood outside or on the margins of the commercial leisure world.[32]

With commercial recreation sorting out the public by the price of admission, hundreds of thousands of New Yorkers depended on free parks for space to play. Overall, New York's working-class families had about as much leisure time and money as working-class families around the country, but access to recreational space presented particular difficulties in the densely populated city. The replacement of slow-moving horses by fast-moving cars and trucks made many city streets unavailable or unsafe for play, and rising land values had squeezed out many uptown pleasure gardens. Even after the expansion in public parks and playgrounds in the early twentieth century, New York—in part because the city was so crowded and land was so expensive—lagged well behind other major cities. Among the nation's thirty-seven largest cities, New York ranked thirty-sixth in per capita park space in the late 1920s. A 1928 survey of outdoor recreation facilities concluded that Manhattan had only about half the public recreation space it needed.[33]

"Around the World in Search of Fairyland"

The shortage of public space in Manhattan increased the demands placed on Central Park in the twentieth century, especially since new generations did not go to the park just to enjoy its beautiful natural landscape. More and more visitors came to Central Park hoping to play, to be entertained, to see something—a show or spectacle—just as those who could afford it did at Coney Island or the movie house. And park administrators, politicians, and reformers all sought to meet these expectations, to demonstrate that the city's grandest public park had kept pace with the times.

Musical offerings were expanded. Although park concerts fluctuated with available public (and, increasingly, private) funds, summer band concerts were generally offered twice weekly around the turn of the century and three times weekly after 1910, when the parks department built a new bandstand at McGown's Pass. In 1914 an orchestra performed with the United German Chorus; in 1915 community singing became a popular event, and the massive "song and light" festival of 1917 brought fifty thousand people to hear the one thousand voices of the New York Community Chorus. The spectacular lighting effects reminded one reporter of a "child's conception of fairyland."[34]

Around the same time that the song and light festivals began using the vibrant display techniques of consumer culture to transform the park into a city spectacle, the new Conservatory, which had opened in 1899 at 105th Street and Fifth Avenue, turned nature itself into a spectacle of sorts. Its exhibits, like those of the menagerie, attracted huge crowds; in 1901 more than 1.4 million people came to see the fall chrysanthemum display, which, like the Easter flower show, became an annual park event in the early twentieth century.[35]

The 1897 city charter had more firmly implanted the two museums within the park and within the parks department by stipulating the city's commitment to constructing and maintaining new museum buildings. Both museums now expanded. The Metropolitan Museum of Art had extended Hunt's classical facade to the north and south, and now began to fill in wing after wing behind it. The American Museum of Natural History, which had enlarged its vast Romanesque building to the west and north at the end of the nineteenth century, made smaller additions in 1908, 1924, 1926, and 1933. Then in the midthirties, its Roosevelt Memorial building on Central Park West between 78th and 80th streets transformed the facade facing Central Park into a Beaux-Arts reflection of the Metropolitan. By the 1920s the two museums were drawing more than a million annual visitors, double the attendance at the beginning of the century.[36]

SONG AND LIGHT FESTIVAL
Central Park, September, 1916

In sponsoring new events like this 1916 song and light festival, the parks department brought some of the attractions of commercial culture into the park.

The expanding museums (as well as other museums and libraries that the parks department maintained) added a new burden to the department budget. In 1915 it contributed almost five times what it was spending on playgrounds to the upkeep of these quasi-public institutions. By 1927 the park's two museums were receiving more than $830,000 annually from the city—twenty-seven times their appropriation forty years earlier. Considering the political clout of their trustees, park commissioners had little choice but to support museum maintenance, even though they were given little voice in museum management.[37]

The Central Park zoo, which attracted three million visitors in 1902, continued to outdraw both museums even after the much larger Bronx Zoo opened in 1899. At the turn of the century, the menagerie director John W. Smith reported that "Italian laborers—as many as twenty together—not finding work in the early morning, come to the menagerie with their shovels under their arms and spend an hour or two looking at the animals." In the 1890s Lower East Side Jews who relied on Mount Sinai Hospital (at 67th Street, two blocks from the park) often stopped at the nearby zoo on the way to or from the clinics. "The only thing that interested Jews in Central Park was the zoo," the *Jewish Daily*

The Central Park Conservatory's annual flower shows turned nature itself into a display.

Forward said. "They were afraid to venture farther into the park lest they get lost." Proposals to remove the zoo from Central Park met with strong resistance in uptown working- and middle-class districts. In 1909, for example, a Yorkville settlement house worker reported that the children from her neighborhood were writing letters to oppose replacing the zoo with a building for the National Academy of Design. "You should hear the boys and girls talk about the animals," she told a reporter. "They can tell you what each one of them likes, and how he eats it."[38]

Nonetheless the zoo received only one-fifth as much city money as either of the privately controlled museums, both of which also had substantial financial resources of their own. As a result, it began to show signs of deterioration. By 1920 attendance was declining and park commissioner Francis Gallatin drew public attention to the dilapidation by warning that rust had so corroded the bars of the cages that lions might escape.[39]

Park visitors who came to see flower displays at the Conservatory or monkeys at the zoo arrived largely as individuals, couples, or families. But in the early twentieth century, park events also began to attract more *groups* of New Yorkers—something park rules had previously forbidden or discouraged. The May Day picnics for children, which had begun in the 1870s, grew dramatically in size and number. Religious, ethnic, and civic organizations arranged annual gatherings that brought as many as two hundred thousand children to the park.[40]

Tammany Hall quickly got into the act, and among uptown Democratic leaders, Central Park became a popular spring venue for "bread and circuses."

The People's Park: Abandoning the old rules that forbade group picnics in the park, Tammany politicians sponsored annual festivals for their constituents, such as this May Day party in 1907.

In 1904, for example, James J. Hagan, leader of the Nineteenth Assembly District, organized a May picnic for thirteen thousand West Side children, with "Irish," "German," "Italian," and "colored" May kings and queens leading the procession to the park; Tammany district captains handed out box lunches and dished out five hundred gallons of ice cream. In the afternoon, boys of the Young Amsterdams and the St. Matthew's parish club played baseball. In the 1920s the Thomas Farley Association (named for the leader of the cement layers' union, a Yorkville politician) marched, ten to twenty thousand strong, every year on Central Park in what the *New York Times* called "a Coxey's Army in its variety of political supporters and future voters." (Farley later achieved notoriety for telling Judge Samuel Seabury's investigation of political corruption that his personal wealth came from a "wonderful" "tin box"—later immortalized in Jerry Bock's musical *Fiorello!*—in which he saved almost $400,000 in six years even though his salary was only $15,000. Asked by the judge to explain why a police raid found a number of well-known gamblers standing around a crap table in Farley's clubhouse, the politician had a ready answer: "The members that was there was busy packing baseball bats, skipping ropes, and rubber balls, because our May Day party took place the next day.")[41]

Not to be outclassed by Tammany politicos, progressive reformers organized civic pageants and patriotic festivals that might build community solidarity and instill American values in new immigrants. As the largest and most prominent public space in the city, Central Park presented itself as the logical site for

JAPANESE DANCERS AT CENTRAL PARK PAGEANT "IN SEARCH OF FAIRYLAND," REPRESENTING THE "FAR EAST."

The Reformer's Park: "Around the World in Search of Fairyland," 1912. Leaders of the progressive playground movement, assisted by city businessmen, organized civic pageants like this one on the Sheep Meadow, in which children from playgrounds around the city dressed in foreign costumes and performed folk dances.

efforts to forge a new civic culture. The parks department welcomed and helped orchestrate mass participatory events. In 1911 the girls branch of the Public Schools Athletic League sponsored a Folk Dancing Fête on the Sheep Meadow in which ten thousand school girls frolicked before a crowd of many thousand spectators, including the mayor and other civic dignitaries. The following year, the department's own bureau of recreation organized an "Around the World in Search of Fairyland" pageant, bringing five thousand children in "old world" costumes to Central Park from the city's dispersed playgrounds to perform before a crowd of thirty thousand. Some park preservationists grumbled that "great gatherings or boisterous games" had no place in a "great work of landscape art," but massive athletic, patriotic, and historical pageants and festivals became a regular feature of the park in the 1910s and 1920s.[42]

Still, sharp limits persisted on the types of gatherings permissible in Central Park. Political events were out—unless, of course, they supported the status quo. Park officials allowed patriotic celebrations of the Fourth of July and Evacuation Day (commemorating the departure of British soldiers from the city in 1783) or farewell salutes to troops going overseas, but they briskly rejected protests against the executions of Sacco and Vanzetti. The single exception to the ban on political meetings came in 1914, when the progressive administration of Mayor John Purroy Mitchel agreed to permit a women's suffrage meeting on the Mall. But two years later, when the National Woman Suffrage Association planned a tableau and concert, park commissioner George Cabot Ward refused them permission to use the same space because they would be presenting "political propaganda."[43]

Commercial events were also barred from the park. The city rejected pageant impresario Percy Mackaye's community masque to celebrate the Shakespeare tercentenary because he would have charged admission. But even progressives, who criticized the vulgar excesses of "cheap amusements," made use of the techniques of commercial culture in organizing their pageants and festivals. In a controlled way they sought to infuse the color, excitement, and novelty of the city's commercial institutions into their pageants and festivals. "Around the World in Search of Fairyland" in 1912 was based on a play performed at the Hippodrome, and leading theatrical promoters (the Shuberts) and mass merchandisers (including Macy's and Gimbels) provided props, costumes, transportation, and funds. New York Edison illuminated the Sheep Meadow with ten thousand red, white, and blue lights, creating a colorful fantasy environment that departed sharply from the Protestant restraint of the park's founding generation.[44]

Playgrounds and Country Clubs

Alongside the competing attractions of movies, sports, and commercial spectacles in the early twentieth century, the dramatic expansion of the citywide park system decentered Central Park. After consolidation, Central Park constituted only about one-eighth of city parkland. In addition to thirty-eight hundred acres set aside for parks in the annexed district of the Bronx in the 1880s, the consolidation of Greater New York incorporated another fifteen hundred acres, including Forest Park, Queens, and Prospect Park, Brooklyn (also designed by Vaux and Olmsted).[45] Although Central Park retained its symbolic centrality for editors and lobbyists, it no longer set the standard for the design and use of public recreation space. The nineteenth-century conception of parks as works of landscape art now took second place in the minds of many New Yorkers to their value as places for play. As the park system expanded, the parks and playground movement, led by progressive reformers, pushed for new organized facilities and supervised play programs for children within the city's public spaces. Here too Central Park stood on the margins of the new developments.

As was true of so many progressive efforts, recreational reformers initially focused their attention on children. Drawing on new theories of child psychology, progressives saw play as essential to human development. "The boy without a playground," the playground movement warned, "is the father to the man without a job." But to encourage the skills and values necessary to cope with modern society, play needed structure, supervision, and especially equipment.[46]

In New York, as elsewhere in the country, playgrounds had appeared first under private auspices, but in the early twentieth century the board of education and then the parks department began to take charge. In 1910 the settlement house worker Charles B. Stover became Manhattan's park commissioner; he implemented the program of the playground movement by establishing thirty new public playgrounds—ranging from sand gardens for toddlers to swings, seesaws, and slides for children and fully equipped athletic fields for older boys. Stover set up a separate bureau of recreation within the parks department to initiate programs for organized and supervised play. Playground clubs, inter-park baseball leagues, girls' folk dance festivals, and citywide pageants proliferated. By the mid-1920s, New York had ninety-three park playgrounds, almost half of them in Manhattan. Those in Manhattan were less than an acre in size, on average, but expensive to run, absorbing 9 percent of the department's total budget in one year.[47]

The development of recreation programs also altered the composition of the park labor force: more than half the play supervisors hired in 1910 were women; by 1916 women, employed as clerks and cleaners as well as playground attendants, were almost one-tenth of the department's work force. Each play supervisor organized the sex-segregated activities of a hundred to three hundred children—for girls, roller skating, pantomime, and rope jumping; for boys, baseball and basketball; and for each group, the "passive work," as the superintendents called it, of basketry and carpentry.[48]

Although most progressive reformers regarded playing fields, field houses, and gymnastic equipment as essential park features, before the 1920s, the playground movement had only a limited physical impact on Central Park. In the 1890s reformers had successfully introduced a small sand garden in the shadow of Umpire Rock on the southwest Playground. By 1912 play supervisors ran five summer programs for children in the park, but without equipment. In the spirit of the playground movement, park officials did now permit a number of competitive sports—including soccer, field hockey, and football, as well as the traditional baseball and croquet—on the meadows. Commissioners made only tentative gestures, however, toward building new facilities. Commissioner Stover, for example, paved—first with gravel and then with clay—the temporary lawn tennis courts that had been set up on the South Meadow (south of the 97th Street Transverse Road) in the 1880s. By 1914 ten thousand people were taking out permits to play tennis there or on two other spots in the park. Still, as late as the 1920s, only about 9 percent of the park's terrain was devoted to playfields or special programed events.[49]

The introduction of paved tennis courts and, in the outer-borough parks,

Although progressive reformers in the Public School Athletic League were not successful in their campaign for ball fields in the park, they did hold exhibitions there. Ten thousand schoolboys participated in this 1913 demonstration of fitness.

golf courses reveals the influence of another recreational institution that had begun to spread through suburban America beginning in the 1890s—country clubs. Unlike the new equipped public playgrounds and playfields, golf and country clubs, of course, also created a new privileged access to recreational space. Most of the New York clubs were outside city limits. In the early 1920s the sixty-seven private clubs of just Nassau and Westchester counties covered about as much land as *all* the public parks and playgrounds of New York City, and the 52,000 golf and country club members in the greater New York region enjoyed the use of 21,000 acres of private land, about 2.5 people for each acre. The 6 million residents of New York City, by contrast, had access to 9,400 acres of public park land—about 640 people for each acre.[50]

In the early twentieth century, working-class New Yorkers scorned the exclusivity of country clubs. Provoked to sarcasm by Commissioner Clausen's chair rental scheme, for example, the Central Federated Union suggested that since golf "has taken such a fascinating hold upon the hearts of our best citizens," the commissioners might as well turn the parks themselves into golf links and surround them with high fences so the wealthy would not be "inconvenienced by the gaze of the common people." But the clubs' modern sports facilities also created a new standard by which to judge the offerings of public parks. In 1910 a citywide committee advocated building a stone tennis house in Central Park "in the style of a country club." Such innovations were most readily added to public parks in the outer boroughs. By 1928 the parks department had introduced four golf courses to the park system, but not until two year's later did Central Park's tennis house finally get built.[51]

Jungle Gyms and Society Orchestras

Only gradually did the nineteenth-century park began to accommodate the new expectations of the twentieth-century city. The skyline placed the park in a new frame, but the landscape itself remained relatively unchanged. The bright lights and colors of commercial culture appeared in pageants, but Coney Island, not Central Park, was the empire of the nickel. Even the progressive reformers, who reshaped recreation throughout the city, made only a modest imprint on Central Park. But in the 1920s two new features, a playground and a nightclub, in many ways epitomized its adjustment to modern recreation and new competing class constituencies.

The Heckscher Playground at 61st Street and Seventh Avenue, added only in 1926, became the sole equipped playground within the park. It was bitterly opposed by several real estate and civic groups, including the League of Women Voters and the Federation of Women's Clubs. The Central Park West and Columbus Avenue Association, which represented West Side property owners, argued that "Central Park was designed as a park where people could go and rest and walk and drive and that it was intended to be maintained with grass and trees." But the area at 61st and Seventh Avenue was designated as a playground in the original Greensward plan of 1858 and had long been in use for children's play and sports. In a political climate sympathetic to the reformers' playground movement, philanthropist August Heckscher used his personal prestige to persuade park officials to ignore the opposition and accept his gift of an equipped playground, 4.5 acres, including swings, merry-go-rounds, spiral slides, jungle gyms, a field house, and a wading pool just south of Umpire Rock.[52]

The Heckscher Playground proved instantly popular, although not with the park's closest and wealthiest neighbors. On one day in July, some urban planners tracked the arrival and departure of each child as well as his or her address. Of the twenty-two hundred children who came to the playground that day, only *three* were from the entire forty-two block East Side area from Fifth to Park Avenue and from 59th to 80th Street, and only slightly more were from the equivalent blocks along the west side of the park. Though the residents of the park's "Gold Coasts" apparently spurned the new playground, children who lived in the less affluent, slightly more distant neighborhoods surrounding the

In 1926 August Heckscher donated the park's first equipped playground. The site at 61st Street and Seventh Avenue had long been used for children's play.

park had come to the Heckscher Playground in great numbers. Unlike most urban playgrounds, which drew children from the nearest blocks, Heckscher Playground attracted 90 percent of its children from more than a quarter of a mile away. More residents of a single block in working-class Yorkville, three-quarters of a mile away, used the Heckscher Playground than residents of the wealthy eastern perimeter.[53]

Despite the relative class segregation, the children and their mothers apparently accepted a noteworthy degree of racial integration at the playground. In addition to white children from adjoining and more distant neighborhoods, the children of San Juan Hill, a largely black and poor district in the west 60s, seem to have made heavy use of the it. Twenty years earlier, when Robert Chapin had studied working-class recreation, he had found only one black family who mentioned going to parks. By contrast, almost three-quarters of the Bohemian and Austrian households as well as about one-third of the native-born and German and one-half of the Russian (Jewish) households said they used public parks.[54]

The relative absence of African Americans from the parks in the first decade of the century may have reflected white New Yorkers' hostility in a period when the black population was growing rapidly. In 1900 racial tensions between Irish

Historic Pageant, Central Park. "O! That Watermelon." under the direction of the Bureau of Recreation.

Although some playground programs in the park were racially integrated, black children still encountered racial stereotypes as in this pageant scene of the American South.

and black residents of the Tenderloin district (around West 34th Street) had erupted into a riot in which large numbers of African Americans were beaten by white mobs and police officers. A decade later Mary Ovington, a social reformer who lived for a time in the San Juan Hill neighborhood and helped found the NAACP, reported watching an Irish boy throw sticks and shout "nigger" at a group of black kindergarteners who were walking to Central Park. Two years later the parks department annual report noted that four black girls had joined a recreation program in a West Side Manhattan park: "This is given special mention because of the changing attitude of the neighborhood in allowing children through the streets to this park without molestation, which never happened in former years."[55]

In the 1920s black New Yorkers were probably still made to feel uncomfortable in many of the city's parks, but the rise of a cohesive community in Harlem had given them new political influence. With their votes, black families could also more confidently assert their membership in the city's public, winning some modest recreation facilities in their neighborhoods and taking advantage of new features in Central Park such as the Heckscher Playground.[56]

The concentration of working-class children at the Heckscher Playground reflected the ongoing class segmentation of the park's user public in the late 1920s—a period in which the gap between rich and poor was growing. The presence of Fifth Avenue adults in the Casino restaurant on the east side of the Mall near 70th Street further dramatized this pattern. The Casino had "never been noted for catering to the poor," the *Times* dryly observed in 1929, but that year the restaurant became even more exclusive when it was transformed into a nightclub for New York high society.[57]

It was, in effect, a gift from former song writer Jimmy Walker, elected mayor in 1926, to his friend Sidney Solomon, who had been in the hotel business and won Beau James's affection by introducing him to his tailor. Walker had asked Solomon if there was anything he could do for him in return. As a matter of fact, Solomon replied, "I'd like to take over the old Casino in Central Park and make it an outstanding restaurant." City lawyers evicted the Casino's prior licensed operator in February 1929. To oversee his enterprise, Solomon promptly appointed a board of governors comprising prominent New York business and social leaders, including socialite William K. Vanderbilt, realtor A. E. Lefcourt, investment bankers Robert Lehman and Jules S. Bache, and two theatrical magnates, Adolph Zukor and Florenz Ziegfeld. Heading the board was Anthony Drexel Biddle, Jr., millionaire scion of the socially prominent Philadelphia clan and a friend of the mayor's. "We feel," Biddle explained, "that New York needs a dining place around which the cultured life of the city can rotate. . . . It will give Central Park a touch of the life and color that has been lacking for a number of years." Even before the Casino had opened, former mayor John F. Hylan charged that it represented "a new seizure by royalty of the city property." Biddle responded disingenuously: "All we wanted to do is something for the public."[58]

Solomon changed the exterior of Vaux's original brick and stone building very little, but he recruited the Vienna-born designer Joseph Urban to redesign the interior in modernist style. The Casino would have a tulip pavilion, an orange terrace, a silver conservatory, and a spectacular black-glass ballroom. Walker and his mistress, Betty Compton, both reviewed Urban's sketches before Solomon spent the approximately $500,000 it took to carry out the renovations. There would be tables for six hundred patrons and parking for three hundred cars.[59]

More than two thousand people sought an opening night invitation to what was being touted as "the most beautiful and elegant restaurant in the world." Liveried footmen met the "brilliant throng" from "New York's distinguished and wealthy families" at the door. "Inside," the *Times* reported, "the guests came under the influence of Mr. Urban's rhythms of maroon and green." In Urban's black-glass ballroom, they danced to the music of Emil Coleman's society orchestra, while a yet-unknown Eddie Duchin played one of the two

After the Viennese designer Joseph Urban renovated the interior of the Central Park Casino in 1929, it became one of the city's swankest nightclubs. Robert Moses had the Casino demolished in 1935, shortly after this picture was taken.

grand pianos. The maître d'hôtel was René Black, known as the "Master of Forty Sauces," and guests dined on a special French menu prepared by the former chef to banker Louis Rothschild. The following night Jimmy Walker and Betty Compton showed up to hear the orchestra strike up Walker's own tune, "Will You Love Me in December?" The fashionable carriage crowd, which had faded from the park in the previous few decades, had now reappeared in full splendor inside the Casino.[60]

On opening night, June 4, 1929, "a good deal of cynical talk was bandied about" among the crowd who watched the socialites arrive. In the fall mayoral campaign Fiorello La Guardia attacked Walker for leasing the "whoopee joint" in the park to his close friends for a ridiculously low rent—friends who, in turn, obtained some of their financing from gangster Arnold Rothstein (the man who reputedly fixed the 1919 World Series). The stock market crashed that same fall and federal prohibition agents raided the Casino. The elegant playground of the rich had become a symbol of decadence and corruption.[61]

"Dementia Automobilia"

As Central Park confronted the modern age, the most "frankly urban" intrusion—the automobile—penetrated its interior, transforming both the illusion of a pastoral retreat and the experience of parkgoing forever. When the first motorists applied for permission to drive horseless carriages in the park, commissioners said no, pointing to the existing problems of carriage and bicycle traffic and accidents. In 1899 the Automobile Club of America challenged the ban on cars by dispatching drivers into the park to get arrested. After a judge ruled that automobiles were "pleasure carriages" and thus allowed by park rules, officials relented and issued the first permit for driving an "electric automobile runabout" in Central Park. A week later, motorists persuaded Commissioner Clausen, an avid horse lover, to try the "experiment" of taking a spin through the park. When the car broke down, Clausen walked home.[62]

In the first decade of the twentieth-century, the new motorcars, often driven by chauffeurs, skirmished with carriages, often driven by coachmen, for control of the park drives. Equestrians, pedestrians, and carriage riders alike complained that the foul-smelling, noisy cars frightened horses, disrupted the decorum of the carriage parade, and ruined their own retreat to nature. The chains that automobilists placed on their wheels to improve traction, moreover, tore up the drives' gravel paving. When park officials oiled the drives to keep down dust, the carriage riders warned that their horses had difficulty maintaining a firm footing on the oil-slick surfaces. Park police tried valiantly, but in vain, to enforce the eight-mile-an-hour speed limit and to stop cars that had chains and the worst-smelling vehicles at the gates. In 1906 three people died in what may have been the park's first fatal auto crash.[63]

Carriage riders urged motorists to go to the "country" for their drives and leave the rural park to those who could less readily escape the city, but the tide was running in favor of the automobile. In 1909 the president of the Carriage Builders' National Association told the annual meeting that the onrush of "dementia automobilia" meant that it was time "to sing the swan song of the high-grade carriage builder." By 1911 motorcar showrooms had displaced the carriage trade from the strip of Broadway running up to the park from 42nd Street, and it became known as "Automobile Row"; car salesmen used the park's hills to demonstrate performance. In 1912 the parks department began asphalting the carriage drives to make them more suitable for high-speed automobiles. A few years later, the speed limit for cars in the park was doubled to fifteen miles per hour. "In the roads of the Park, as on all other roads," a *Harper's* writer noted in 1914, cars "are now accepted as something that has naturally happened and belongs in every scene."[64]

World War I marked the final demise of the carriage parade. Wealthy automobile owners did not find the park as appealing as had carriage drivers: "In older days, when horses still hauled or carried us, [the carriage drive] . . .

was about as far as carriage people had time to go of an afternoon. Now that the motor-car is the prevailing vehicle, the Park seems smaller." New York society no longer assembled daily on the park drives to pay their respects to one another. Not only were more and more wealthy families adopting the car as a new status symbol, the telephone made it easier for the "circles within circles" to arrange their visiting without relying on the spontaneous encounters of the promenade. Wealthy women were as likely to do their visiting at department store tearooms or to drive their cars to exclusive country clubs as to turn out in the park.[65]

In the 1920s, with the middle class now adopting the automobile, general street traffic overflowed into the park; four out of five cars on its drives were simply "passing through" by the shortest possible route. Cars threatened the safety of parkgoers and even of the park itself: in 1922 cars crashed into two hundred park lampposts. In 1929 urban planners counted eight thousand cars on the drive north of the Sheep Meadow in a six-hour period and warned of the danger to pedestrians who tried to cross the forty- to sixty-foot-wide park drives "with no 'isles of safety' for the pedestrians at the crossings."[66]

By the mid-1920s planners and letter writers to the newspapers were continually calling for a ban on automobiles in the park. Short of such drastic intervention, some thought that the solution to the "car menace" lay in slowing down motorists by making the park's drives more winding. Others proposed instead to straighten and widen the old carriage roads to speed up the traffic. Planners urged widening the transverse roads, and also Fifth and Eighth avenues, to absorb park traffic and called for reducing the park's speed limit, now twenty miles an hour (and mostly ignored). "Central Park was laid out as a restful recreation area," state senator Nathan Straus, Jr., said in 1924 when urging that cars be banned, "not as a thoroughfare for mechanical transportation." But by 1932 the automobile was firmly entrenched in city life, and park administrators installed in the park those most prosaic and mechanical of city features, traffic lights.[67]

Commuters, Tourists, Park Neighbors, and Enthusiasts

The automobile, together with the subways (first opened in 1904), altered Central Park's relationship to the larger city by both bringing people in and carrying them away. Although Greater New York was growing and social commentators tended to associate the city with crowding and congestion, Manhattan's population dropped after 1910. Between 1905 and 1930 even the density of population on the Lower East Side fell by half. The literally millions of people living in the outer boroughs were much less likely to see the park as "central" to their lives than had nineteenth-century Manhattanites. Still, Central Park remained a citywide park. More than two million people from the outer boroughs and the surrounding suburbs entered Manhattan to work each day.[68] Some commuters visited the park at lunch or after work; some kept horses at nearby stables and went riding before work every morning; some drove their cars through the park to lower Manhattan from their homes in Westchester County. Even New Yorkers who lived and worked in the outer boroughs traveled to the park for special occasions (the free concerts on the Mall) or attractions (the zoo and the Metropolitan Museum).

If time, distance, and neighborhood facilities deterred many people from leaving Brooklyn, Queens, or the Bronx, new institutions also attracted them to the vicinity of Central Park. By the 1930s, major religious centers (Temple Emanu-El, the Ethical Culture Society, and First Church of Christ, Scientist); social clubs (the Knickerbocker, Harmonie, and New York Athletic clubs); museums (the Frick Collection and the Museum of the City of New York); and hospitals (Flower and Mount Sinai) lined Central Park, east and west, and brought people from the city's periphery to the park's borders, if not inside.

People also came to Central Park from more distant parts of the nation and the world after mass tourism took off in New York in the 1890s. By 1910 New York daily accommodated between one and two hundred thousand visitors who neither lived nor worked there. An increasing number of those visitors stayed right on the edge of the park in seven major hotels, among them the Sherry-Netherland, Pierre, and Essex House, that opened between 1927 and 1931 along Central Park South. They advertised spectacular views of the park as one of their major attractions. Newspaper columns promoted other attractions in the park: Broadway "chorus girls and leading ladies of the stage are there rollerskating" on the Mall, and George M. Cohan could be found taking daily walks at the reservoir. ("Katharine Cornell trots around.") "I walk around everyday," Cohan told a columnist, "and have a nodding acquaintance with the mob that strolls there. That's my Broadway today."[69]

As the park moved into the tourist spotlight, it also finally achieved the spatial centrality for Manhattan's two million residents that park promoters had envisioned back in the 1850s. When construction began on the park, only 10 percent of the city's residents lived north of 40th Street. Three-quarters of a century later, in 1930, 70 percent of all Manhattanites lived in Upper Manhattan. The million or so people who lived within just a mile of the park exceeded the population of all but a handful of major cities.[70]

When Central Park first opened in 1859, native-born, Irish, and German Americans dominated the city; eighty years later, ethnic communities included East European Jews, Italians, Poles, Puerto Ricans, Hungarians, Swedes, Norwegians, Greeks, and Chinese. And by that time Jews (almost 30 percent of the city's population) and Italians had outstripped the Irish and Germans as the city's largest ethnic minorities. In those same years, the African-American population multiplied thirty times.[71] These different ethnic and racial groups helped make up the million people who lived in the dozen or more distinct *and* changing neighborhoods that surrounded the park in the first four decades of the twentieth century.

During the building boom of the 1880s, developers north of the park began the physical transformation of Harlem into a neighborhood of shaded streets, ample elevator apartments, and spacious brownstones, which initially attracted upper-middle-class New Yorkers, especially successful Germans. Yet the full expanse of Harlem (defined as covering most of the area north of 96th Street and east of Eighth Avenue) was never quite as genteel as the Harlem Chamber of Commerce liked to boast in the early part of the twentieth century. By the 1890s poor Italian immigrants filled five-story tenements in the area east of Third Avenue and between 105th and 125th streets. East Harlem would soon become the largest Italian-American settlement in the United States. By 1910 about a hundred thousand first- and second-generation East European Jews had become the leading ethnic group in the section of Harlem that ran south of 125th Street and west of Third Avenue.[72]

By the second decade of the twentieth century Harlem was once again reconstituting itself. Real estate speculators, who had overbuilt, scrambled to fill empty apartments by renting to black New Yorkers who paid higher rents than white tenants for the same space. Harlem's black population, which increased from fewer than twelve hundred families in 1902 to about fifty thousand people by 1914, more than tripled again by 1930. As black migrants from the South and the West Indies settled in Harlem following World War I, white families, particularly Jews, migrated to outer boroughs.[73]

In those same years, Puerto Ricans also started to arrive in Harlem in large numbers. In 1916 fifty Puerto Rican families lived in what was to become "El Barrio" (between 110th and 117th streets along Park Avenue); a decade later, as many as sixty thousand people from the United States protectorate had settled in two neighborhoods—East Harlem and South Central Harlem—directly bordering Central Park.[74]

In 1939 the *WPA Guide to New York* spoke of "The Harlems" as plural and defined three sections: an Italian section along the East River; a Spanish settlement north and east of Central Park; and "Negro Harlem," largely north of 125th Street. These ethnic boundaries were never absolute. Starting in the 1930s, for example, black settlement extended south toward Central Park and 110th; by 1940 African Americans made up almost 90 percent of the fifty thousand people who lived in what could be called "Central Park North," the twenty-four blocks north of the park and south of 118th Street.[75] Perhaps half a million people lived in these Harlem neighborhoods, and most of them were poor.

The extraordinary wealth of the park's other well-known neighbor, Fifth Avenue, underscored Harlem's overwhelming poverty. The lower Fifth Avenue district facing the park (between 63rd and 77th to Third Avenue) contained the most expensive apartments in the city. In 1940 its residents paid seven and a half times as much in rent as East Harlemites, who lived just thirty blocks to the north, and 44 percent of all employed people in the district were servants. Some Fifth Avenue families employed enormous staffs. The family of four of National City Bank president Charles E. Mitchell, who lived along the park at Fifth and 74th Street, was, for example, served by a housekeeper, a butler, two footmen, two parlor maids, a personal maid, a valet, a houseman, two laundresses, a cook, an assistant cook, two kitchen maids, and a governess.[76]

In the park's heterogeneous adjacent neighborhoods on the east and west were a vast number of people who fell somewhere in between the rich of Fifth Avenue and the poor of Harlem. In the predominantly German and Central European neighborhoods of Yorkville, east of Lexington in the 80s, three-quarters of the household heads worked in craft, factory, service, or clerical jobs. Heads of native-born, Irish, and Jewish households who lived in apartments on the park's west side were twice as likely to work as professionals, managers, or proprietors. Although some real estate agents touted Central Park West as more fashionable than Fifth Avenue, the upper-middle-class families in West Side apartments between 62nd and 74th streets paid less than half as much rent as families in the East Side district directly across the park.[77]

By the 1930s, then, the million or so people who lived within a mile of the park included almost the entire range of the city's population: the families of Yankee bankers, Puerto Rican garment workers, Jewish dentists, German shop clerks, Italian laborers, Irish firefighters, and African-American laundresses as well as the Irish cooks, Scottish nurses, and German governesses living in the households of the rich. Although these people lived in close proximity to one another, upper Manhattan was no melting pot. Distinct ethnic communities within these sometimes heterogeneous neighborhoods had their own churches, clubs, political organizations, and their own ways of enjoying Central Park. Still, the park offered a common ground, and many, if not most, of the park's neighbors made some sort of claim on it. Immigrant families began picnicking on the North Meadow, for example, and youths played ball there. Other claims were asserted and recognized through the political system, as when neighbors lobbied for new entrances or gained a new band shell at McGown's Pass. Given the vast range of peoples and needs represented in Upper Manhattan, the claims of the park's neighbors often conflicted, for instance, the repeated fights over the Central Park Zoo. Neighbors, moreover, formed only one set of constituents for the park.

Other groups of parkgoers gathered themselves into specialized constituencies based on hobbies or common interests. The growing prominence of these specialized user groups—of birdwatchers, horseback riders, tennis players, nature lovers, model-boat sailors, roller-skaters—was part of a larger process through which the park's cultural public was fragmenting. Bird watching, for example, first attracted a regular set of enthusiasts in the 1890s. More generally, the "back to nature" movement of the early twentieth century increased the number of people who came to the park "to get away from it all." But even the enjoyment of nature could represent contradictory needs and interests in Central Park. Some people fished in the lakes in order to supplement low wages; others fished for sport. In 1906 the Anglers' Club persuaded park officials to build an exclusive, padlocked dock for their fishing on the Harlem Meer. When thousands of people turned out for their annual fly-casting competition, the nineteenth-century ideal of *rus in urbe* gave way to "urbe in rus" spectacles.[78]

Despite the crowds, existing social divisions did not disappear. Black children were accepted at the Heckscher Playground, but their parents were not welcome at the Casino. Some lines of division were invisible to many parkgoers. Historian George Chauncey has documented, for instance, that in the early twentieth century Central Park became "renowned within the gay world both as a social center and as a cruising ground." Most nongay observers were unaware of the principal pickup spots—the benches near Columbus Circle and along the quarter-mile walk from the southeastern corner of the park at 59th and Fifth to the Mall.[79]

Lines of division by gender substantially weakened in the twentieth century as the free mixing of women and men, so prominent at Coney Island, infused Central Park as well. The Public School Athletic League did separate the games and sports of girls and boys, but some women insisted on equal participation. In 1909 eighteen-year-old Ellen O'Connor defied police arrest in violating the rule that still limited ball playing to boys under sixteen. Unchaperoned women had become regular riders on the park's bridle paths, and young women and men played tennis together—the park sport that enjoyed the greatest increase in popularity in the early twentieth century.[80]

The park had always been a place for young men and women to meet, and not always decorously. In 1905 Morris Friedlander, running for the goal line during the Harlem football championship, crashed into Bertha Persky, one of the hundreds of spectators. The collision in Central Park later led to marriage. Of course, women found some breaches of decorum unpleasant or frightening: in the first ten months of 1929, police arrested 335 men for annoying women in Central Park. (In the park's most famous sexual harassment case, two decades earlier, police arrested opera singer Enrico Caruso for annoying women at the zoo.) Guardians of public morality also worried about "fast" men and women getting together in the park. One summer evening in 1920, an undercover investigator for the Committee of Fourteen (the city's major antivice society) "scouted around" the "dark sections" of Central Park and noted "couples laying on grass, or sitting on benches, kissing and hugging each other."[81]

A study of the leisure activities of teenage girls from Italian East Harlem in the early 1930s came up with the finding that girls classified as "questionable" or "delinquent" were much more likely to spend time in Central Park or Thomas Jefferson Park (at 111th Street along the East River) than those who had no trouble with authorities. What had been conceived, in part, as a space

Observing the "polyglot" crowd in 1905, Henry James wrote: "The park has to have something for everybody since everyone arrives famished; it has to multiply itself to extravagance."

dedicated to moral uplift had now been transformed into a place to avoid close moral scrutiny. For these young women, the park offered an escape from the strict supervision of the Italian home. "From many sources," noted the study's author, "it was learned that the walks and the visits to the parks and museums were usually with the hope of meeting a boy, or when one already had a 'boy friend' the definite aim was to meet him at a regular rendezvous."[82] Although their parents disapproved, the park offered these girls a way out of the insular world of Italian East Harlem and into the culture of the modern city.

"The Fruit of the Foreign Tree"

Henry James, who visited Central Park when he returned to New York in 1905 after three decades in Europe, observed that "the alien" had taken "possession" of the park. He conceded that the immigrant-filled park showed "New York at its best" and provided some reassurance about the "social question," but he seems to have found it difficult to share this public space with the "polyglot Hebraic crowd of pedestrians" and "the common element" from the "dense Italian neighborhoods." "Central Park," he wrote in *The American Scene*, "showed the fruit of the foreign tree as shaken down there with a force that smothered everything else." "Do we not feel ourselves feeding, half the time, from the ladle, as greasy as he [the immigrant] chooses to leave it for us," James asked. The park, he concluded, was "overly overdone by the 'run' on its resources. . . . It has had to have something for everybody, since everybody arrives famished; it has had to multiply itself to extravagance, to pathetic little efforts of exaggeration and deception."[83]

The immigrants themselves viewed matters differently. "The commissioner of parks wants to preserve the flowers," the *Forward* observed in 1910; "the Jewish mothers want to preserve the health of their children." Pauline Newman, who immigrated from Lithuania in 1901, recalled that at age eight she had gone to work in the Triangle Shirtwaist Factory. "Conditions were dreadful in those days. . . . But despite that, we had good times. In summer we'd go to Central Park and watch the moon arise." "Oh my God, what a treat it was to go to Central Park," Adriana Valenti similarly remembered. "This is heaven," thought Yetta Adelman of her gatherings with "the people from the Old Country" in the park on Sundays. Valenti recalls that before her mother took the family to the park, she would make sure "they were all buttoned, and . . . looked presentable" and "would lecture" them, "Don't pick the flowers, the flowers are for beauty."[84]

Yet one letter writer to the *Times* in 1914 felt besieged; he reported that on a spring Sunday, he had noted "the thousands of 'just as good as anybody' people swarming upon the tender grass, breaking through the choice shrubbery and scattering their millions of waste papers far and wide." "It seems," he concluded, "as though the city is persistently 'casting pearls before swine.'" A *Times* reporter similarly complained after a summer Sunday in 1913 that the northern end of the park, the area most accessible to surrounding Jewish and Italian neighborhoods, looked like "a cheap picnic ground or the old Bowery or Coney Island because of the litter scattered about."[85]

By the 1920s, with the parks department more readily giving out licenses to food vendors and less readily enforcing regulations against those who operated without licenses, twenty or more refreshment booths offered many of the same treats found along the Coney Island boardwalk—hot dogs, candied apples, soft drinks, chewing gum, and "twenty varieties of wrapped tidbits." This "active push-cart concession," complained one park official in the 1930s, featured "unkempt, bad-mannered, and often downright dirty servitors," who brought with them what Olmsted called "customs suitable to paved streets or commons." Annie Nathan Meyer, who had been going to the park for more than three decades and understood Olmsted's vision better than most, wrote a letter to the *Times* in 1928 to complain that peddlers, "instead of remaining quietly near or under their umbrellas, have begun to shout their wares. To sit anywhere near one of these stands is to imagine one is near the entrance of a circus."[86]

May Day, 1905: New programs, crowds, and vendors in the park increased the problem of litter.

While Meyer thought the peddlers a "public nuisance" for the noise they produced, others faulted them for the litter they generated. In 1927 Manhattan park commissioner Walter Herrick banned the sale of peanuts from Central Park to stem the rising tide of peanut shells. (There was a brief episode of peanut bootlegging in response.) The cause of the mounting piles of trash was the growing habit of consuming food in public and the increasing use of disposable materials for wrapping and eating it. Nineteenth-century picnickers had been much more likely to bring their own silverware, glasses, ceramic plates, and cloth napkins than their twentieth-century counterparts.[87]

Contemporaries, however, blamed the litter on the arrival in the park of large numbers of "new immigrants" from eastern and southern Europe who lived in uptown Manhattan. The department's 1916 annual report, for example, complained that "we still have in our midst elements of our population who appear to be entirely ignorant of the fact that liberty means the opportunity to give the other fellow the same chance you enjoy yourself" and who "wantonly destroy park features and litter the park areas." A few years later, Commissioner Francis Gallatin explained to a *Times* reporter: "Here you have the matter of birth. I am a New Yorker and the feeling of responsibility for my city is instinctive. Not one man in four now living here was born here. The great majority bring in different ideas from elsewhere."[88]

To tame what a *Times* reporter in 1919 called the "park bench Bolshevik,"

Peanut vendors faced periodic crack-downs from park officials worried about litter.

newspaper editorials and park officials demanded tighter enforcement of park regulations and the posting of more signs. When Brooklyn officials complained that visitors were turning Prospect Park "into a garbage pail," the police arrested more than a hundred Jewish immigrants, and many were sentenced to a night in jail and a ten-dollar fine. Manhattan magistrates were more lenient, but the periodic litter crackdowns in Central Park also targeted recent immigrants. In 1926 the Republican Women's Neighborhood Association of 110 East 60th Street began its list of suggestions for "beautifying" Central Park with the recommendation that the city erect antilittering signs in Italian and Yiddish as well as English, for "thousands of people visit the park before they speak English or become citizens." (The frequent distribution of foreign-language antilittering handbills, of course, added another layer to the lawn debris.)[89]

Park officials and lobbyists rather imprecisely tended to lump immigrants who dropped peanut shells on the ground or picked flowers with people who maliciously smashed benches or defaced other park property, calling them all "vandals." The term captured the feeling of many native-born New Yorkers that barbarians—uncivilized foreigners who were not seen as part of the "pub-lic"—had overrun the park in the early twentieth century.[90]

Amid all the talk of trash and vandalism, the press pronounced that the park had reached "the most dangerous crisis" in its history. But as had been true in the nineteenth century, the quality of maintenance revealed as much about taxpayers' priorities and willingness to confront new demands on the public sector as about parkgoers' changing manners. In the 1910s and early 1920s the city was spending fewer dollars on a park that was used more and more intensively. Contemporary observers put annual attendance at twenty to thirty million, which would have made these decades the most active period of use in the park's history.[91]

By the 1920s automobile traffic was taking a much heavier toll on the drives than the carriages ever had, and no doubt the air pollution spewed out by the cars and by factories and coal-burning heating systems also took a toll on the trees and shrubs. Warmer winters, which limited the number of days when the ice froze, and changes in local fashion meant that ice skaters were no longer a major portion of park visitors—and ice was the most easily renewable landscape resource. At the same time, loosened park regulations and enforcement prac-tices were subjecting the lawns, a less easily renewable resource, to more intensive use. Further, new patterns of use required modernizing the infra-structure—adding modern plumbing and sewers for comfort stations and elec-tric lights on the paths at night.[92]

These demands on parks department resources increased in a period of declining budgets. When the outbreak of World War I in 1914 prompted European creditors to call in their loans, New York faced a fiscal crisis; the Federal Reserve Board and private investment bankers dictated a new regime of financial stringency. Between 1913 and 1919, spending on Manhattan parks (in real dollars) dropped by half; not until the late 1920s would park appropriations return to the levels reached in the early 1910s. Whereas in the nineteenth century the park budget had overwhelmingly gone to Central Park, moreover, by 1916 only about 7 percent of the department budget was spent there, less than went to the maintenance of the American Museum of Natural History.[93] Indeed, the department was spending less on the park than it had fifty years earlier, though use was far more extensive.

Under budget constraints—and the force of nature itself—parts of the landscape deteriorated. Periodic droughts damaged the grass, topsoil eroded, and photographs show that most of the tall, vigorous elms that lined the Mall in the 1890s had died by the 1920s. The particularly severe winter of 1917–1918 killed off large numbers of other trees as well as most of the thirty thousand rhododendrons Mrs. Russell Sage had given to the park a decade earlier. Despite the problems of nature, "lack of appropriated money," the *World* noted in 1920 (around the low point in park spending for the entire twentieth cen-tury), was "the root of park evils of decay."[94] Central Park was expensive to maintain, and the parks department was not spending nearly enough money to maintain it properly. When spending finally began to rise after 1920 under Mayor Hylan, most of the money went first to higher wages to redress the losses of wartime inflation.

Still, the park never decayed as badly as critics said it did. In 1927 when the parks department hired Herman W. Merkel, superintendent of the Westchester County Park Commission, to survey its condition in preparation for a million-dollar rehabilitation, his report did document numerous instances of deterioration: the appearance of the Ramble and the northern park was "disreputable," and there was an "appalling number of wholly or partially dead trees," which gave the park "a neglected and unkempt appearance." But his overall conclusions were measured. "In general," Merkel wrote, "the condition of Central Park is fairly good." He labeled "much of the criticism which has appeared in the public press" as "unjust" and argued that despite "over-use" Central Park "today contains an infinite amount of charming vistas, of splendid greensward and magnificent trees."[95] Merkel's survey reminds us that for all its urban characteristics and woes, the park still remained pastoral.

Yet by the 1920s Central Park had changed, not through dramatic alteration of its design but through incremental accommodation of the larger city. The early decades of the twentieth century placed new pressures on the landscape and introduced new groups of users. Had the ghosts of the nineteenth-century park observed immigrant children thronging the zoo, peanut vendors on the paths, cars speeding down the drives, elegantly dressed society folk arriving at the Casino, litter left on the lawns by picnickers, and apartment houses and hotels towering over all, they would have been unlikely to describe it as a "refreshing" and "spaciously natural" contrast to the "compactly built town."[96] New Yorkers had exchanged the romantic landscape that celebrated the universal qualities of nature for an urban park that encompassed most of the tensions, contradictions, and possibilities of the city itself.

Sometimes, the mixing caused strains. Just as Italian parents were uneasy about their daughters' visiting in the park with people from outside their community, so some nativists were unhappy that they had to share the park with immigrants. "Central Park on Saturdays and Sundays," wrote a letter writer to the *Evening Mail* in 1917, "is filled to overflowing with the tribe of Israel," who left not even "a few feet of ground for us poor Americans." But others viewed the variety of activities and crowds more indulgently. After a tour through the park on a Sunday in 1928, a *Times* reporter concluded that "it is difficult to feel sympathy for the New Yorker who remembers with a sigh the good old days when Central Park was the fashionable promenade of the town, . . . when there was plenty of room to sit down without having popcorn spilled in one's lap, and when nobody walked on the grass. For here are a lot of tired people who have nowhere else to go. If this be the 'popular demoralization' expected and feared, one hopes that New York will make the most of it. It is their park."[97]

15

WILL THEY EVER DRAIN THE RESERVOIR? MODERNIZING THE PARK

In January 1910 newly elected mayor William J. Gaynor appointed Charles B. Stover as Manhattan park commissioner and president of the board. The now middle-aged settlement house worker was a somewhat unconventional choice. Stover's "luminous eyes" and contagious smile concealed a fierce anger at "the slightest injustice," said Henry Moskowitz, who had grown up in a tenement across Forsyth Street from Stover's home. With a single-minded intensity, Stover had thrown himself into campaigns for municipal ownership of transit lines, tenement district playgrounds, and other causes that captivated progressive young people of his generation. The dark back room of his apartment was cluttered with stacks of daily newspapers, which Stover read obsessively. He worked late into the night in a narrow front room, rarely stopping for regular meals, his intense eighteen-hour workdays alternating with "tortured moods when all his life seemed in vain." Doctors today would no doubt describe him as manic-depressive.[1]

Stover had been born in 1861 to the family of a Pennsylvania country storekeeper, and after graduation from Lafayette College and Union Theological Seminary, he had preached Presbyterianism to cowboys in the Dakotas and studied theology in Berlin. Then in the 1880s Stover moved to New York's immigrant Lower East Side, where he was to spend the rest of his life.[2]

Parks and playgrounds had been one of Stover's passions since his arrival in New York City. Mary Simkhovitch, a settlement house veteran, recalled that at the earliest meetings of the Lower East Side Recreation Society, "his blue eyes [were] brightly fixed on the playgrounds, his hopes envisioned. He had a somewhat fanatical manner, uneasy but determined." Stover helped found the New York Society for Parks and Playgrounds, which set up the city's first (temporary) playground in 1891; and as the energizing force behind the Outdoor Recreation League, he created New York's first permanent playgrounds

Progressive reformer Charles Stover dedicates one of the many playgrounds opened during his term as park commissioner, July 19, 1912.

and persuaded the city to take responsibility for them. He ardently opposed the Central Park racetrack and the museums' Sunday closing policy, collecting thousands of museum petition signatures on the Lower East Side with the help of an army of immigrant youngsters like Moskowitz.[3]

Stover, now in the mainstream as park commissioner, in 1910 established the first bureau of recreation, launched plans to boost the number of city-run playgrounds, added more tennis courts and band concerts, and suggested that Central Park, and the smaller parks, as well, might offer a variant of Hyde Park's free speech corner.[4] But within six months of taking office, he clashed with the parks department's longtime landscape architect, Samuel Parsons, and that was his ultimate undoing.

The park board fired Parsons in 1911 ostensibly for promoting the interests of a New Jersey soil supplier and perhaps over policy differences. In response, angry editorials (written by Parsons's many newspaper friends) criticized Stover's efforts to "popularize" Central Park, probably helping to bring about the bizarre end to Stover's term as park commissioner. On October 15, 1913, Stover went out to lunch and did not return to work or home. Two weeks later he sent in a letter of resignation in an unmarked envelope. When he finally turned up on the Lower East Side in late January, he explained laconically that he had been traveling through the South making an "exhaustive study of parks and other municipal conditions." He conceded later that the sharp newspaper attacks had thrown him into despondency.[5]

Stover was never quite the dangerous radical that his critics claimed. True,

A summer Saturday afternoon in the People's Playground, 1910. As Central Park's new immigrant neighbors "swarmed over the lawns," park attendance reached its all-time high in the early decades of the twentieth century.

he believed that Central Park needed to respond to new social conditions. "At the northern end of the Park an immense population has grown up, which is using the Park more and more," he told a reporter. "We must accommodate these people. . . . It is all very well to quote the views of the landscape architects, who laid the Park out, but they lived in 1860 and we are in 1910." Still, he was not insensitive to the park's natural features; he opposed one plan for an elaborate recreation center and swimming pool on the North Meadow. He suggested instead putting the pool on a "new" piece of park land—the thirty-five-acre rectangular Lower Reservoir (between 79th and 86th), which was no longer needed for the city's water supply. (For almost a decade, former park commissioner John Crimmins had been proposing that the same reservoir be roofed over to create an exhibition palace and a recreation space for children.) But in 1910 the Water Department was not ready to surrender the Lower Reservoir to park officials.[6]

In 1912 advancing work on the new Catskill water system revived the talk, and Stover came forward with a new proposal, one that reflected another preoccupation of his generation of reformers. This time Stover responded to the changing physical rather than social needs of the city, although he, like most progressives, regarded the two as intricately related. Noting the growing traffic along Central Park West, he suggested a complicated scheme to move the trolley tracks to the center of the avenue and sink the road in front of the American Museum of Natural History. "Over the depressed street," he explained to a reporter, "there should be some connection between the facade of the natural history museum and the park—a majestic bridge or something similar—over which not only pedestrians but pleasure vehicles coming from the Park might travel." The majestic bridge would then continue through the park to the Metropolitan Museum, which would be turned around, in effect, to face the natural history museum. The Lower Reservoir, which lay in the intervening space, would be transformed into a formal garden. "If that is done," Stover declared, "New York can have the grandest setting for its museums of any city in the world."[7]

Stover's museum parkway drew upon widely disseminated ideas about creating the "City Beautiful" through formal, monumental, classically styled civic structures and spaces. City Beautiful advocates dreamed of bringing order to a seemingly chaotic city by means of wide, tree-lined boulevards and grand civic centers. A new generation of city planners followed Andrew Green, as well as Olmsted and Vaux, in placing parks at the center of a system of boulevards and parkways, but unlike Green, they preferred diagonal avenues to the existing Manhattan street grid, which they dismissed as monotonous and inefficient. And unlike the park's designers, they wanted to integrate Central Park visually with the city.[8]

One such architect, Ernest Flagg, had suggested in 1904 that New York sell off most of Central Park as an obsolete "suburban pleasure ground" and use the proceeds to construct a ten-mile-long version of the Champs Elysées that would bisect Manhattan. On an equally grand scale, an advocate of the "Geometric Park Movement" proposed that Central Park be transformed into a "huge formal park"—the city's "acropolis," its crown and center—to "integrate its plan with the city plan." "Why," he asked, "should a public garden in an unusually unrustic city be contrived out of billowy meadows, rocky hills, labyrinthine lakes, and tufted shrubberies . . . the amalgam of a Herefordshire sheepwalk and the location for a movie version of 'Hiawatha'?" Disclaiming the designers' rationale about the restorative power of nature, such enthusiasts believed that a more formal park linked into a formal cityscape would aesthetically and, hence, socially unify an otherwise fragmented city.[9]

Stover's first suggestion for the Lower Reservoir site had featured the playground movement's definition of the park as an active recreation space, but his museum parkway plan featured architectural enhancement to promote civic order and ceremony. These latter inclinations led him to support the Pulitzer plan for a Place de la Concorde at the southeastern corner, an unsuccessful scheme to relocate Richard Hunt's Beaux-Arts Lenox Library to the site of the Arsenal, and proposals to straighten the park's paths in order to provide long vistas and direct routes.[10]

"We all have the sentiment of preservation of beautiful things," Stover said, "so when a suggestion is made like that of mine for connecting the museums by means of a plaza or boulevard, it is sure to outrage the feelings of conservatives." A few days after his plan appeared in the newspapers, William B. Van Ingen, a landscape artist and vigilant defender of the park's pastoral design, wrote to the *Times* opposing any departures from the original plan. "Why," he asked, "not inquire what Messrs. Olmsted and Vaux would have suggested had the 35 acres now occupied by the receiving reservoir been available for park purposes?" His answer, quoting Vaux, was that they would have recommended landscaping it so as to "make a definite meadow-like impression on the eye." A week or so later, Van Ingen told the American Society of Landscape Architects that any park plans should strictly follow the letters of Vaux and Olmsted he had recently uncovered in the parks department offices. "Not a tree should be moved or a statue erected without bearing in mind that the original designers knew exactly why that tree stood where it did and why that statue was in place on any particular site." Just as Charles F. McKim had gone back to the original plans when asked to renovate the White House, those who made any changes in Central Park must conform to the "original" Olmsted and Vaux plan.[11]

The three positions marked out in 1910 and 1912 by advocates of the progressive or recreational park, the City Beautiful or civic park, and the Olmstedian or naturalistic park each brought interventions over the next two decades—the Heckscher Playground, the Pulitzer Fountain, and the rehabilitation of the landscape according to the Merkel proposal. But the debate over the Lower Reservoir site in the park's center went literally to the heart of its design. Battle lines and coalitions shifted over the years, and some progressives such as Stover stood in more than one camp. Still, the three positions roughly sketched out the differing visions of how the nineteenth-century park should respond to the twentieth-century city.

A Great Civic Monument or a Great "Atrocity"?

In 1917, to commemorate the completion of the hundred-million-dollar Catskill water system, the Catskill Aqueduct Celebration Committee decided to erect a *civic* monument. They chose the Lower Reservoir in Central Park as the best site and selected a designer who shared their desire to bring a formal European accent into the city's most pastoral place.

Thomas Hastings, the leading heir to the Beaux-Arts style of architecture that Richard Morris Hunt had promoted in the nineteenth century, was, like Hunt, one of the leading "society" architects of his day with a long list of country estates and Fifth Avenue mansions to his credit. Hastings had been born into New York's upper class, the offspring of a prominent Anglo-Dutch family, grandson of the composer of the hymn "Rock of Ages," and son of the president of Union Theological Seminary (Stover's own alma mater). Hastings and his partner John M. Carrère received their first big commission from Henry M. Flagler of Standard Oil, one of his father's parishioners. Today, the two are best remembered for their grand Beaux-Arts New York Public Library.[12] The partners had already made their mark on the park's southeastern corner with their design for the Pulitzer Fountain, completed in 1916. A few years earlier, Hastings had tried to put a Beaux-Arts imprint on the interior of the park when he unsuccessfully proposed that Hunt's Lenox Library building be moved from 70th Street and Fifth Avenue to the site of the Arsenal. In 1917 the Catskill Aqueduct Celebration Committee (appointed by the young progressive mayor John Purroy Mitchel) offered him a chance to bring his architectural style into the very center of the park by designing a monument to replace the rectangular Lower Reservoir.

Hastings sketched a vast sunken garden, flanked at the south by an amphitheater of turf terraces, seating twenty thousand people and descending to a central music pavilion. North of the amphitheater would be an equally vast lagoon surmounted by Frederick MacMonnies's monumental fountain of "Columbia seated on a Barge of State with Fame at the prow sounding the trumpet and Father Time steering at the helm," a recasting in bronze of a fountain that was an architectural highlight of the World's Columbian Exposition held in Chicago in 1893. An eighty-foot jet of water in the Upper Reservoir would furnish "the central feature of the entire scheme."[13]

"In every city of Europe," Hastings explained in a letter to the landscape architect Frederick Law Olmsted, Jr., "one finds the Public Squares, the Garden and the Park, and these important features are indispensable in the growth of the city." New York had only parks and public squares; "it has no recreation garden which should be architecturally designed and in the heart of the city." The Lower Reservoir, Hastings argued, finally gave New York the opportunity to create a "civic" or "municipal garden" that would rank with London's Kensington Gardens or Paris's Luxembourg Garden and Tuileries. "In the happier days before the war, these were the very things that Americans went to Europe to see."[14]

Hastings's French schooling and his continental references linked him to earlier advocates of a more formal park, from Robert Dillon to Richard Morris Hunt. Yet, the amphitheater would provide space for the sort of large-scale civic pageants and festivals promoted by progressive reformers, and the MacMonnies fountain would symbolically connect the plan to the City Beautiful movement. George McAneny, the chair of the Catskill committee, provided an even

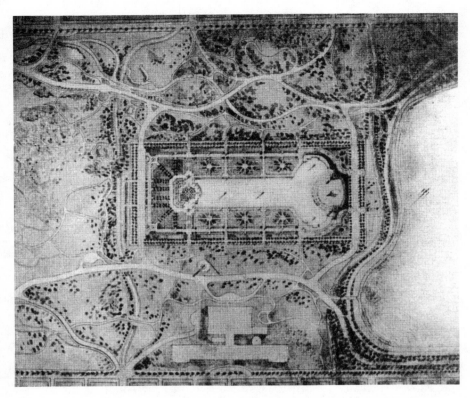

Thomas Hastings's 1917 plan for a Catskill monument on the site of the Lower Reservoir shows the influence of Beaux-Arts design ideas. Note the formal sunken gardens on either side of the lagoon and the music pavilion at the south end.

more direct link. As president of the City Club and the board of aldermen, he had drawn deeply on City Beautiful ideas in his efforts to bring city planning to New York.[15]

Other local figures also influenced Hastings's plan, none more so than Henry Fairfield Osborn, the socially prominent paleontologist and director of the American Museum of Natural History. Osborn's father was a railroad president; his brother, William, a leading corporate lawyer and president of the Metropolitan Museum of Art; and their uncle, J. P. Morgan, a major benefactor of both museums. Henry first glimpsed the possibilities of connecting his museum with his brother's when Crimmins proposed roofing over the Lower Reservoir in 1910. Until his death in 1935 he advocated an "intermuseum promenade" with the same energy and tenacity he applied to expanding his museum and lengthening his résumé. (It eventually exceeded one thousand items.) The promenade, he believed, would greatly increase attendance by improving access from the East Side and would enhance the stature of the

The "intermuseum promenade" promoted by Henry Fairfield Osborn would have linked his American Museum of Natural History with the Met across the park.

natural history museum by giving it a grand entrance onto the city's premiere public space. Osborn apparently persuaded Hastings to modify his 1917 plan to provide "a wide terraced driveway" that would supply "a much-needed connection" between the two museums. Addressing Osborn as "My dear Champs Elysées," Hastings invited him to look at the finished drawing for the Catskill monument, since "there is so much of you in it."[16]

Like Hastings, Osborn looked to Europe, where "art buildings form an integral part of the Park system." He complained to *Times* editor John H. Finley of the difficulty of supplying city politicians with "the intelligence and artistic spirit which only come to men like you and myself who have traveled all over the world." And like earlier generations of gentlemen who had been to Europe, he argued that any plans would have to be "on a scale worthy of . . . the Great Empire City."[17]

Van Ingen, Olmsted and Vaux's champion, disagreed. Citing chapter and verse from his growing collection of Central Park books and documents and taking a dig at Hastings's role as architect of the New York Public Library, he charged that "to build in Central Park a formalized, architectural sunken garden would be as great an atrocity against the rural motif of the landscaping as it would be to put a gothic steeple or Moorish arch on the public library building." The *Times,* although it had already turned itself into the house organ of park preservationists, did not join Van Ingen's assault on the Catskill monument. The reason, probably, was the auspices of the Hastings plan: the progressive Mitchel administration and the Catskill celebration committee. The *Times* strongly supported Mitchel's election, and besides, McAneny, the chairman of the Catskill committee, had recently left his post as president of the board of aldermen to become a business executive for the *Times.* [18]

Hastings's proposal for a formal plaza on the reservoir site was also opposed by more populist advocates of a recreation-oriented park. Brooklyn alderman Alexander S. Drescher, who had been elected on a platform that urged increased municipal provisions for recreation, called on the city to "dedicate that vast area to play, not to scenery." "The people demand parks dedicated to use and equipped for use." Uptown alderman Thomas Farley (whose May Day picnics brought thousands of his constituents to the park) agreed: "It is about . . . time that the grand facilities of Central Park be used for direct benefits and practical conveniences of the masses." No doubt the support for the monument by Mitchel and the progressives fueled the opposition of Farley and other Tammany politicos. Still, their rhetoric revealed a perception that class inequality flourished in the operation of Central Park. A Bronx alderman, for example, charged that Hastings's plan would benefit "the nabobs and dandies who would like to disport themselves in a summer garden to the exclusion of the masses of people." Prodding the city to build a swimming pool and a beach on the reservoir site, Patrick J. Conway, president of the Irish-American Athletic Club, denounced the "high mucky-mucks wanting to build a flower garden in Central Park." The *Evening Mail,* the only newspaper to oppose the monument, collected and publicized such charges as part of its crusade to substitute a swimming pool and playground for what it regarded as a "mere plaything of the rich."[19]

America's entry into the war diverted the city's attention from Central Park. In 1917 park commissioner George Cabot Ward, a City Beautiful sympathizer and supporter of the Catskill monument, joined the American forces in France as an aviator.[20] Between November and February, Manhattan had five different park commissioners. Then, Democrat John F. Hylan defeated reform mayor Mitchel in the fall 1918 elections. With Mitchel's progressive fusion coalition out of office, the coalition behind the sunken garden in Central Park also collapsed.

Mitchel's death in an air force training accident eight months later opened a different possibility for a grand monument on the reservoir site. Hastings dusted off his Catskill plans and proposed a section, with some modifications, as a memorial to Mitchel. Once again the proposal foundered, in part because the water department insisted that it still needed the Lower Reservoir as a reserve. But such a massive tribute to a fusion mayor, even one martyred in war, probably never had much of a chance anyway with the city now solidly back under Democratic control.[21]

"It is so hopeless to ever accomplish anything in the City of New York in the way of an improvement, because of so much contention and disagreement upon things, that it is really disheartening," Hastings wrote Olmsted, Jr., in a last-ditch effort to win his support. Hastings brightened, however, at the prospect of an impending trip to Europe: "It will be good to see London, Paris and Rome, where they still do things even though ours is considered the most modern and growing of cities." "If Fate could have granted him one wish," a memoir published soon after his death noted, "doubtless it would have been for the power to do for Manhattan what the Napoleons did for Paris."[22]

But Hastings's dream of being New York's Baron Haussmann proved elusive in a democratic polity in which political power was highly fragmented. Back in 1900 the *Herald* had conducted a forum titled "How Can New York Be Made the City Beautiful?" The one participant from outside the city, a Danish sociologist, Niels Gron, had challenged the premises underlying the newspaper's question. "All this talk of beautifying New York seems strange to me," Gron commented. "We expect of her power and magnificence, but not beauty. If a European came over here and found New York was beautiful in the same way as the European cities he knew, he would be very much disappointed. I do not see how you can make New York beautiful in that way, with the laws and the democratic spirit that you have here." "The kind of beauty that makes Paris charming" had come chiefly from "the efforts of Napoleon, a despot."[23] Gron's basic insight had eluded the park's nineteenth-century designers and those who sought to redesign it in the early twentieth century: there was no easy way to maintain (or reshape) the park as an aesthetically unified landscape (either pastoral or formal) in the midst of a city driven by powerful democratic energies as well as market forces.

"More Parks for the People"

In 1922 after a committee appointed by Mayor Hylan to select a World War I memorial rejected the sixty-seven designs submitted in an open competition, it invited Hastings, who had done the temporary victory arch welcoming home the troops, to propose a design. The architect pulled out his Catskill monument plans for the third time and made two key changes: to replace the MacMonnies fountain with a 150-foot-long "Arch of Freedom," incorporating allegorical and historical sculptures representing the war, and to add a recreational center

In 1923 Hastings transformed his Catskill monument into a World War I memorial, retaining the lagoon but adding allegorical and historical sculptures.

complete with a twenty-acre swimming pool, running tracks, and playgrounds. In effect, Hastings merged into a single package the recreational and City Beautiful approaches to the Lower Reservoir site that had often competed with each other for the past decade.[24]

The changes deftly answered the politically damaging charges that the Catskill plan had favored "the classes" rather than "the masses." Henry Osborn, for one, found that logic compelling in his unending quest for the intermuseum promenade. When some people criticized the recreational features of Hastings's plan, Osborn told him to hold firm: "It was as a playground for younger children that I first secured the attention of the Board of Estimate to this thirty-one acre park space." As Osborn and Hastings understood, the inclusion of recreational facilities expanded the coalition they were trying to forge around their joint project.[25]

Hylan, whose committee endorsed Hastings's design, had been elected mayor in 1917 and reelected four years later. An urban populist of sorts, he rhetorically invoked the claims of the common folk against the special interests. He began as a railroad worker, attended night school, became an obscure Brooklyn judge, and then leapt to the mayor's office through the patronage of William Randolph Hearst, who encouraged his championship of municipal ownership of subways and the five-cent fare. By the 1920s Hylan's urban populism was in the mainstream of New York City Democratic politics. In the late nineteenth century, city Democrats had generally associated activist government with Protestant and Republican moral reformers who wanted to regulate saloons and other aspects of working-class life. Democrats might favor public works to provide jobs and promote real estate, but they generally took a laissez-faire approach to government. Republican Seth Low, elected as a fusion mayor in 1901, had spent four times as much on municipal parks, buildings, and schools in two years as his predecessor, Tammany Democrat Robert Van Wyck, did in four years. But the election of reformers, the consolidation of Greater New York, and the arrival of millions of new immigrants from southern and eastern Europe had gradually convinced Tammany Democrats to broaden their base beyond its traditional Irish core.[26]

Charles F. Murphy, who captured control of Tammany Hall in 1902, realized that support for a strong and positive government that might intervene on behalf of working-class New Yorkers would win Democrats the support of newer Jewish and Italian immigrants, most of whom had less visceral distrust of an active state than did the Irish. One of the people Murphy learned this strategy from was Hearst, who had supported unions, government regulation of corporations, and municipal ownership of subways and utilities in his own unsuccessful runs for mayor in 1905 and 1909. Under Murphy, Tammany took note of Hearst's strong support among skilled working-class, lower-level white-collar, and foreign-stock voters and moved toward support of an activist state and city government—an emerging welfare-state politics that was variously labeled "urban populism," "urban progressivism," or more generally "urban liberalism." Al Smith, a product of Murphy's machine, was to ride this rising tide of urban liberalism into the governorship and the 1928 presidential campaign.[27]

Progressivism became New York's common political coin in the second decade of the twentieth century. Both Tammany politicians and anti-Tammany candidates such as Mitchel advocated new and improved city services. But as would be true for later liberal administrations, paying for these services remained a problem. In 1913 Mitchel won the votes of both native-stock elites and foreign-stock workingmen by promising an honest and efficient government providing new services at a low price. Mitchel's cost consciousness was reinforced by the fiscal crisis of 1914–1915 and his ties to big business. Although this conservative economic policy contributed to his defeat in 1917, "efficiency" remained the other side of the progressive coin.[28]

The conservative wing of the progressive movement advocated closely supervised playgrounds as part of a program of reducing juvenile delinquency and molding immigrant children into orderly and adaptable American citizens. But progressives committed to social justice, including park commissioner Stover, regarded open spaces as basic necessities for tenement dwellers' health and safety. Stover believed such public spaces would remedy social inequalities and build new forms of community solidarity. Whatever their politics, most progressives shared an overarching faith in the possibility of fostering social harmony by modifying the city's physical environment.[29]

The few social investigators who asked working-class immigrants themselves found support for the progressives' program of increased public recreational facilities. "Have more bath houses and playgrounds and more parks," an eighteen-year-old Italian printer had told sociologist George Bevans. "More recreation centers and open places in this large city of ours, wherein the workingman could derive more outdoor exercise, which is an absolute necessity to a man confined indoors during the day (at labor)," said a twenty-nine-year-old Irish electrician. Canvassing the Lower East Side for views about a new neighborhood park, Stover found that "as one man they do want a playground and gymnasium in Seward Park in addition to 'lawns and shrubberies.'"[30]

After he became park commissioner in 1910, Stover was criticized for allowing too many sports and games in Central Park. "They accuse me of trying to destroy the parks," he replied, "whereas I am trying to improve them and make them more *useful* to the public." Like many working-class New Yorkers, on whose behalf he acted, Stover embraced a pragmatic and eclectic view of Central Park, reflected in his willingness to recommend a giant swimming pool and a Beaux-Arts intermuseum promenade and in his support for the Lenox Library, clay tennis courts, free speech for suffragists, orchestra concerts, children's play festivals, the Pulitzer Fountain and the *Maine* Monument, an entomological school in the Swedish schoolhouse, and paved roads for cars— all of which enraged his critics and fueled the charges that he was "popularizing" the park. But his efforts won the support of the settlement house movement and of organized labor, though working-class New Yorkers themselves more often mobilized in this period not to demand new facilities but to win access to those others had or to defend their prerogatives to free public space. In 1909, for example, the Central Federated Union circulated petitions against the plan to allow the National Academy of Design to erect another museum in the park. "It is necessary for the welfare of the people in the congested portions of the island," declared patternmaker Arnold B. MacStay, "that all the park spaces we have should be jealously guarded."[31]

Working-class families also encouraged and endorsed new progressive recreation programs through their use of the park. Thus, when Stover observed hundreds of Harlem residents enjoying Central Park's lawns, he concluded that the city must recognize this new constituency in order to channel their claims on public facilities constructively: "If we are to control the people who swarm in on us . . . we must provide proper accommodation for them."[32] The continual proposals for sports arenas, playgrounds, and swimming pools in Central Park, which appeared throughout the 1910s and the 1920s and were incorporated into the war memorial, positively acknowledged this (literally) grass-roots pressure. Unlike progressive reformers who touted the instrumental value of organized play in training good citizens, working-class families sought public facilities that would meet their own needs for recreation and socializing. Still, working-class New Yorkers never organized their own distinctive park or playground movement. After all, divided as they were by ethnicity, race, religion, occupation, politics, and neighborhood, they rarely, if ever, in these years spoke with a united voice on any question, and they gave more attention to winning recreational time (the eight-hour day) than to demanding recreational space.

By the 1920s the reformers' campaigns for parks and playgrounds had moved into the mainstream of city politics. A generation of New Yorkers had grown up with supervised playgrounds and athletic programs as part of their public school education. When a young reformer, Robert Moses, proposed a massive park-building program for the State of New York in 1923, an initially skeptical Governor Al Smith soon changed his mind. One of his backers told an Albany reporter that "supporting parks meant that the Governor would be helping the lower- and middle-class people, and thereby winning their support, and that the intellectuals would be for him because they saw parks as part of the new pattern of social progress. . . . And besides, 'parks' was a word like 'motherhood.' It was just something nobody could be against." The same logic prevailed within the city as well. In the 1920s the parks department's operating budget for Manhattan more than doubled. Just as an expansive economy in the 1850s had created a favorable climate for building the city's first large park, so the boom economy of the 1920s fostered growth of the park system.[33]

The populist newspapers of the 1920s promoted the expansion of recreational facilities to serve their working-class readers. The *Daily News*, founded in 1919 by onetime socialist Joseph Medill Patterson, was especially ardent about parks. In 1924 the *News* made "More Parks for the People" the sixth plank on "The *Daily News* Platform for New York," which appeared each day on its editorial page. It joined other planks that emphasized the paper's populist orientation: "A Seat for Every Child in the Public Schools"; "A 5-Cent Fare and Better Service"; and "Improved Traffic Conditions on the Streets." What is particularly striking to contemporary ears is that the *News* coupled its calls for a more activist and humane government with a recognition that "THIS WILL MEAN MORE TAXES."[34]

In the 1920s and early 1930s the *News* focused on the Lower Reservoir as an easy way to help fulfill its call for more parks. "Here we have thirty-four acres plus of the most valuable land in the world," read one typical editorial. "It is going to such absolute waste that the public can't even get a good look at close range." Beginning in 1922 and through the early 1930s the *News* offered a series of different proposals for the reservoir site: the park war memorial; an underground parking garage covered with "playgrounds, a mall, park landscape"; a "subterranean playground" with "park land" on top; a municipal swimming pool; half playground, half park; and ball fields and playgrounds.[35]

To dramatize its 1928 call for transforming the Lower Reservoir into a vast swimming pool, the paper staged a series of publicity stunts. The editors arranged for four cast members from a Ziegfeld show to go canoeing there, for Mille Gade Corson ("the first mother to swim the English channel") to take a dip; and then for a famous deep-sea diver to scout the bottom. It also sent its "inquiring photographer" to Central Park West and 110th Street to ask, "Are you in favor of making the lower reservoir of Central Park a large playground for children, or do you prefer to see it made into a beautiful spot to be used as a playground only on special occasions?" Not surprisingly, all interviewed wanted the playground. Six months later, the inquiring photographer was back in the park to ask young people from uptown working-class districts and governesses and nurses employed uptown about the Lower Reservoir. Nineteen-year-old John Falquero's response was typical: "I'd like to see the city make the reservoir all over into baseball fields, football fields, soccer fields, swimming pools, and cinder tracks. We should also have club houses where we can dress and take showers."[36]

The class edge to the *News*'s rhetoric sharpened as the city and nation slid into depression. "Wealthy people who live along the rim of Central Park," it complained in 1930, "want the park kept as a sort of beautiful back yard in which their children can play, attended by their governesses or tutors. And they don't want a lot of young roughnecks from beyond the park's borderland coming into the park and making loud, unrefined and joyful noises." "We do not want to raise the class issue in this matter," it added unconvincingly. "But that is the way the thing stacks up."[37]

As for the war memorial, the political support for it turned into a liability. As it became overidentified as a *political* project, it lost support as a *civic* monument. As "Hylan's Monument," it drew the fire of all Hylan's opponents in a period when he was facing growing opposition from both progressives and Tammany Democrats. The opposition to the war memorial mounted, moreover, because the mayor had proposed a second—and still more controversial—project for Central Park at the same time: a six-acre music and art center in the southwestern corner, a sort of 1920s version of Lincoln Center. When critics attacked the art center for taking park land, Hylan linked the two projects, arguing that the addition of reservoir space would make up for the land lost to the art center. Despite the opposition, the board of estimate gave preliminary approval to the memorial on three different occasions.[38] But an intense campaign waged against it by a coalition of park "preservationists" won out in the end.

Crusaders for Central Park

In December 1925 the Central Park Association was incorporated to promote "the preservation and rehabilitation of Central Park in accordance with its original design as the greatest single work of art in the city of New York." The organizers of the group had just played a crucial role in quashing the war memorial. They won a reversal of the board of estimate's endorsement and put off further consideration until the new Jimmy Walker administration took office in January 1926, effectively killing any chance of passage.[39]

Some of the same people—lawyer Richard Welling among them—had been battling what they called park "encroachments" since the racetrack furor of 1892. Others joined the park preservation cause during the skirmishes over the National Academy of Design in 1909, the Lenox Library in 1912, the proposal for a sports stadium in the upper park in 1913, and a Safety Museum in the Arsenal in 1919; some had signed on with an array of local groups concerned with parks and playgrounds. The Central Park Association was a spin-off from a prior organization, the Parks Conservation Association, and in three years it would merge with the Parks and Playgrounds Association and the Battery Park Association to form the Park Association of New York City.[40]

The preservationists who enlisted in the park "crusade" and made up the association's board of directors were primarily landscape architects, like Harold Caparn, who viewed the preservation of Central Park as a matter of professional pride or ideology; leaders of real estate and business groups, like William J. Pedrick of the Fifth Avenue Association, who wanted maintenance of the park's landscape to preserve land values; and finally, a heterogeneous group of park activists and preservationists, including lawyers Richard Welling and George Battle, who defended Central Park out of personal passion more than from economic self-interest.[41]

The new group drew some of its support from the American Society of Landscape Architects (ASLA) founded by ten men and one woman in 1899. Among the eleven present had been John Charles Olmsted and Frederick Law Olmsted, Jr., stepson and son of the park's codesigner; Downing Vaux, son of the park's other codesigner; Samuel Parsons, Jr., Vaux's last partner; and Warren H. Manning, who had worked with the Olmsted firm in Boston. All had professional as well as personal attachments to Central Park, and by identifying themselves with it, they also hoped to win public recognition and support for their fledging profession. "It was felt," ASLA leader Rollin Saltus explained to Olmsted, Jr., in 1912 "that the Society might increase its dignity of position and influence, by taking a more prominent part in public questions." The New York chapter sought to "make our influence felt," for one thing, by opposing the proposals to move the Lenox Library into Central Park. It was a fight that revealed the landscape architects' professional conflicts with architects, particularly Thomas Hastings, whom they accused of wanting to give "architectural treatment" to the entire park system.[42]

Five years later, when Hastings was promoting his Catskill monument for the Lower Reservoir, he acknowledged to Olmsted, Jr., that "perhaps the profession of landscape architects think I may be butting in on them." His solution was to seek "the collaboration of a thoroughly good man in your profession," even though "there will be little work for him," since "the problem is quite an architectural one." Hastings's perfunctory professional courtesy won him few friends. The man he chose to work with, Charles Downing Lay, onetime landscape architect to the park board, said privately that Hastings "has little respect for our profession." Lay's "collaborationism" (as well as his statement that there was "no inherent sanctity in any park design") earned him the enmity of ASLA leader Rollin Saltus, who branded him a "an out and out L.A. [landscape architect] Bolshevic" for being willing to work "with people like Mr. Hastings who it seems to me would go to h[ell] gladly if he could have a free hand at various parks etc. first."[43]

Olmsted, Jr., played a pivotal role in mobilizing landscape architects to defend the pastoral design. Not only did his name link him to the park's creation, but in the early twentieth century he was emerging as one of the most prominent figures in landscape architecture—president of the ASLA, organizer of the first professional training program at Harvard, designer of numerous city plans, private residences, and public parks. He had served with Hastings on the National Commission of Fine Arts, which carried out the McMillan Commission's City Beautiful plan for Washington, D.C., which he himself had helped devise. But as he explained in a 1927 letter to New York landscape architect Ferruccio Vitale, "My attitude toward matters relating to Central Park differs from my attitude toward almost any other problem of landscape architecture. I feel about Central Park certain obligations, certain motives, which influence me little or not at all in regard to any other professional problems." One was his personal obligation to "my own father, who was also my master and preceptor in our art," but there was also a larger professional obligation. "Like many of our fellow landscape architects, I feel that Central Park, as the most famous and the earliest of our great public parks in this country . . . has a peculiar and really national importance to our art and our profession; and that the protection of its artistic integrity and its functional success has a correspondingly national importance for us as artists and professional men."[44]

Such powerful "obligations" help to explain why Olmsted and other landscape architects, not necessarily conservative in their professional practice, did take a profoundly conservative stance on Central Park. In a 1926 report for the Central Park Association, Olmsted, Jr., acknowledged that the park faced changed conditions, particularly automobile traffic and the surrounding skyscrapers, but denied that these were grounds for any "radical change of design." He insisted upon his father's dictum that the "controlling purpose of Central Park [was] to provide . . . a quality . . . completely in contrast with normal urban conditions." Central Park was "a great work of art" even if not necessarily "the particular kind of artistic endeavor to which any succeeding generation would turn on its own initiative. One does not burn up a Titian or a Rembrandt because he feels more fully in sympathy with the work of John Sargent."[45]

If Olmsted, Jr., saw his father as a Rembrandt, he was less generous toward his father's partner, Vaux, whose role in designing the park was increasingly obscured in the 1920s. Projecting the professional rivalries of his own era backward in time, Olmsted, Jr., implicitly contrasted his father's work as the park's "landscape architect" to that of Vaux as its "architect." (He ignored—or overlooked—the old letter that showed that Vaux had worked hard to persuade a skeptical Olmsted that "landscape architecture" would best describe their joint work in designing parks.) Pronouncing the landscape design "beautiful" and "timeless," Olmsted, Jr., dismissed Vaux and Mould's buildings for the park as "mechanical and impoverished." Nevertheless, even this "unskillful" architecture "fits into place in the landscape of the park" better than more recent park structures, although they were "more skillful in their execution." Olmsted's rather backhanded defense of the original park buildings was a response to a call to replace them "with more modern and sightly structures."[46]

The proposal appeared in a report issued by the Fifth Avenue Association shortly before Olmsted's own plan for the Central Park Association.[47] The Fifth Avenue Association's longtime general manager Colonel William J. Pedrick had been one of the founding directors of the Central Park Association, but his group did not entirely share the park association's and the landscape architects' view that the park was sacred terrain. Nonetheless, the Fifth Avenue Association and other similar real estate and merchant groups were to play a key part in the preservationist coalition of the 1920s and 1930s. Pedrick served on the CPA board, and so did leaders of the Broadway Association, the New York Junior Board of Trade, and the New York Real Estate Board. These groups (as well as the Central Park West and Columbus Avenue Association, later more active on park questions) advocated preservation in order to promote the business and real estate holdings of their members.

The reemergence of a real estate–based park lobby in the 1920s coincided with the land boom around the park, as luxury apartments arose along its eastern and western flanks, and hotels along the south. Apartment developers and hotel managers who had attracted tenants and guests with the promise of the park as an elegant front yard now had a powerful interest in ensuring that the city keep that yard well tended. The rising land values of "Fifth Avenue and other adjacent streets," the president of the Real Estate Board explained in the early 1930s, "have been based in large measure on the attractiveness of the outlook. Naturally any objectionable development affecting the view or bringing noises would be detrimental to private property."[48] For the merchants and bankers who sat on the Fifth Avenue Association's board, the status and reputation of the park as an elegant public space was intimately tied to the status and reputation of "their" street as the most elegant public thoroughfare in the city.

Property owners and merchants along Fifth had organized their association in 1907 in fear that garment factories (and especially garment workers) were lowering the tone of the city's most exclusive street. With the passage of the nation's first zoning legislation in 1916, they successfully excluded all manufacturing from the luxury shopping district. In subsequent decades, the association drove out beggars, loiterers, and peddlers and got rid of gaudy signs and loud noise in order "to buttress," in the words of the group's official history, "the dignity" (and high real estate values) "to which the thoroughfare has laid claim for a century and a half." By the 1920s, as the association began to extend its concerns farther uptown, it also began to worry about whether the park's deterioration might not be a threat to the intangible "dignity" of Fifth Avenue.[49]

Such worries led it to fight the war memorial on the reservoir site, which it feared would bring the sorts of crowds that had threatened to ruin lower Fifth, and along with them, "the cheap, the tawdry, the raucous, the ephemeral." Although the Fifth Avenue Association opposed park "encroachments" (the word itself had its local resonance from the fight of real estate men against "nuisances"), they were more actively interested in promoting stricter treatment of "vandals" and litterers and in gaining physical restoration of the park. Indeed, the association's political influence probably weighed heavily in the city's 1927 decision to appropriate a million dollars for the park's rehabilitation.[50]

The emphasis on improvement more than artistic restoration exacerbated tensions between the Fifth Avenue Association and the Central Park Association, which focused on preserving the park as a work of landscape art. The Fifth Avenue group wanted better management, more workers to maintain the landscape, more police to enforce the rules, and they pressed for "eliminating the present pushcarts in favor of small and goodlooking booths." After Pedrick compared the Central Park Association's "talk of landscaping or other gloriously indefinite plans" to his own "hard-headed thinking" about maintenance, equipment, and supplies, he quit the CPA board.[51]

The CPA also quarreled with another group of prominent New Yorkers who concerned themselves with Central Park in the 1920s, the city planners who had joined together to develop a regional plan for New York with funding from the Russell Sage Foundation. The planners' emphasis on developing a comprehensive plan for future growth made them immediately suspect in the eyes of the Central Park Association, which accused them of being more "interested in replanning Central Park" than "in preserving and restoring it." The preservationists also feared that leading planners such as housing reformer Robert De Forest (who had also been a City Beautiful advocate) were working for the war memorial and the intermuseum promenade. According to Richard Welling, De Forest had joined Osborn and Hastings: "They want a big plaza, war memorial, series of masonry columns and everything else out of touch with Olmsted's original plan and they are so rich and highminded that they are going to be very hard to resist," he wrote to a friend.[52]

Welling's comment about his "rich and highminded" opponents reveals the feuds within the upper class. Welling's opposition to the intermuseum promenade, for example, put him in the opposite camp from his boyhood friend

Henry Osborn, director of the American Museum of Natural History. "It is . . . too sad for words," Welling wrote, "that I should be in the group opposing you." Osborn and Welling remained on warm terms, but Osborn did not retain similar ties to all of his preservationist opponents. His letters, for example, scolded Nathan Straus, Jr., the offspring of the wealthy retailing family, who served as president of the Park Association of New York City (which replaced the CPA in 1928). Apparently seeing a conspiracy of the city's German-Jewish elite against his museum promenade, Osborn continually identified as his most stubborn opponents Straus and the *Times*, published by the German-Jewish Ochs and Sulzberger families. "The opposition to this self-evident promenade plan," he wrote in the early 1930s, "has in recent years been headed by Mr. Straus [and] warmly supported both in the news columns and editorials of the NEW YORK TIMES, largely I believe, through unconscious racial sympathy."[53]

Though wealthy New Yorkers divided on the question of the park's future, many became preservationists who had strong feelings for the park, in part because they used it regularly—riding their horses, walking their dogs, skating on the ponds, watching the birds, driving their cars to work. The landscape artist William Van Ingen, perhaps the most ardent preservationist of the period, often went to the park to paint. As a young boy in the 1860s, Welling was required by his father to ride a horse there every afternoon because he was "a trifle undersized and nervous." In his seventies, Welling (by then quite self-confident as well as six feet, four inches tall) continued to ride on the same bridle paths. Both Welling and Van Ingen were born the year the park opened and had literally aged along with it. Three out of four of the CPA board members were over fifty years old when the association was organized. No doubt they felt some nostalgia for the less built-up and less cosmopolitan city and park of their youth. The poet Arthur Guiterman explained in his "Open Letter to the Park Commissioner" that as boys "We loved our Park; we love it now as men." He pleaded with his readers to "save, unmarred, the Park our boyhood knew."[54]

Iphigene Ochs Sulzberger, who had lived a few doors west of the park as a child, recalled that "unquestionably, the high point of my week was Sunday, when my father stayed home and took me to Central Park." Later, as a Barnard College student in the prewar years, she developed an interest in philanthropic work (volunteering at the Henry Street Settlement House and the Cedar Knolls School for disturbed children) and in journalism. But her publisher father decreed that a newspaper room was no place for women, least of all his daughter. Instead, her husband, Arthur Hays Sulzberger, whom she married in 1917, went to work at the *Times* while she raised their four children. She gradually returned to her educational and civic interests, joining the park association in 1928 and taking over its presidency in 1934 from Nathan Straus, Jr., who had grown up across 72nd Street from her.[55]

Sulzberger's leadership symbolized the emergence of women as leading park activists, a reflection of the increasingly visible role of women in civic organizations in the 1920s. Anna Minturn was not even invited to sign the petition for the park that she had been the first to advocate; now women composed almost one-quarter of the Central Park Association board. Some, including Jeanette Hodgdon, Annie Matthews, and Mary Simkhovitch, were also active in women's civic organizations, among them the Women's Municipal League, the Women's City Club, the League of Women Voters, and the Women's Trade Union League. Others, now that women were enfranchised, played leading roles in the political parties. Mabel Parsons, the daughter of landscape architect Samuel Parsons, was active in Republican politics, and Belle Moskowitz, a close adviser of Al Smith. Her husband, Henry, whom she met through settlement house work, had been a youthful campaigner for Sunday museum openings.[56]

Sulzberger and Straus were part of the city's German-Jewish elite. When they were young, many "Our Crowd" families lived just south of the park around Fifth Avenue and sent their children (supervised by private tutors or servants) to the park to play. As the century progressed, increasing numbers of wealthy German Jews moved to the east and west sides of the park. Sulzberger, after she married, continued to live across from the park. Such residential patterns partially explain why prominent German Jews became leaders of the preservationist cause, but there may have been a cultural explanation as well: perhaps they identified with a traditional "Yankee" aesthetic as part of their own strategy of assimilation. If that was the case, they achieved a success of sorts in 1930 when the *Daily News* attacked "Straus' class" as "Brahmins."[57]

Welling's preference for the naturalistic Greensward plan no doubt reflected his own cultural traditionalism; he disliked modern art and music. He had been a shy youth, even as a Harvard student. "It was long walks through the scenic New England countryside," his biographer notes, "which provided much-needed respite from his innermost insecurities." Many years later, he could still speak about the "whole conception (almost mystical) of a serene landscape with shade and foliage." In contrast to his friend Osborn, who proposed a gregarious urban promenade, Welling saw the park as a solitary, contemplative experience. At one point, he proposed turning around the benches: "Instead of facing the sun's glare on a shining walk with perhaps a tramp staring at you on the bench opposite, one is better placed to drink in the quiet and serenity, and it might help educate some of our extroverts and movie fans who inevitably think of a park as so much unused space."[58]

Central Park's preservationists were also part of a larger movement in the late nineteenth and early twentieth centuries to preserve the landscapes and buildings of a "simpler" American past. Some wanted to enshrine the artifacts of an Anglo-Saxon "heritage" threatened by new immigrants, others embraced the structures and landscapes of the past as antidotes to the alienation produced by industrial society, contrasting the authenticity of skilled craft work to the interchangeability of mass-produced goods and the sincerity of nature to the vulgar commercialism of the city streets. The American Scenic and Historic Preservation Society, founded by Andrew Green in 1895, took a leading role in this wider movement and joined ardently in the specific battles to protect Central Park.[59]

Preservationists and the Gospel of Olmsted

Many preservationists and many leading landscape architects considered Central Park sacred space, but not sacred as the founding generation would have meant, implying moral, spiritual, or religious values that distinguished it from the profane. This was a more secular concept, denoting "specialness," and Welling may have adopted it earlier than most. During the battle over the racetrack in 1892, he had a giant map prepared with pictures of "ferris wheels, side shows, sight seeing boats and other Coney Island extravaganzas that were from time to time seriously proposed for the park." For years afterwards, he took his map around to the city high schools where he "preached park sacredness."[60]

Welling's notion seems to have been, at the time, more the exception than the rule. The racetrack, for example, was largely fought as a land grab by rich sporting men and politicians. Many people remembered and approved incremental changes in the park's design from the addition of the zoo and new entrances to the realignment of drives and bridle paths. By around 1910, however, more voices identified the park as sacred ground. And twenty years later this notion had become accepted gospel, so much so that an ardent bird watcher could complain to Welling in 1930 of what he called "idolatry of Olmsted"—"repeated arguments I hear year after year whenever Central Park is mentioned, that we cannot and must not change one iota of the Olmsted scheme of things."[61]

By that time the gospel had been spread and published in what the CPA called "our park Bible, our constitution," the authoritative texts that outlined the original design and the principle of Vaux and Olmsted. Van Ingen had begun to collect documents about park history in the early 1890s; by the 1910s he had the largest extant collection of books on the park. In a vast number of articles, letters to newspaper editors, interviews with reporters, and talks to civic groups, he mobilized his impressive command of park board minutes, early newspaper articles, and the writings of Olmsted and Vaux to pronounce on what the park's "original designers" had "intended." By 1922 his fame as an authority on the park led Albert S. Bard, a leader of the Municipal Art Society (and subsequently of the Central Park Association as well), to approach the Russell Sage Foundation about supporting the publication of a book by Van Ingen on the park. The Sage Foundation was sympathetic but soon discovered that Olmsted,

Jr., was already planning to publish four or five volumes of his father's "professional papers."[62]

Olmsted's work on his father's papers fulfilled both familial and professional obligations. He was documenting the history not only of his father and his firm but of his profession. In 1912 he published the first fragment of his father's autobiography in *Landscape Architecture*, the ASLA journal edited by Henry V. Hubbard, his former student at Harvard and future partner. Eight years later Olmsted turned the editorial work on the papers over to Theodora Kimball, Harvard's landscape architecture and city planning librarian and coauthor with Hubbard of the standard professional text in landscape design. (In 1924 Kimball and Hubbard would marry and close this tight circle of professional relationships.)[63] Olmsted obviously intended that his father's papers would serve as one of the canonical texts for the nascent field of landscape architecture, precisely the same status he envisioned for Central Park.

The discovery of the Olmsted publishing project complicated matters for the Municipal Art Society. The group decided to abandon Van Ingen and seek financial support, instead, for a modified version of one of the volumes that Olmsted, Jr., and Theodora Kimball were already editing, which would focus exclusively on Central Park. With the intervention of the wealthy architect and print collector I. N. Phelps Stokes, who had also taken an early interest in the park's history and had rescued and restored Vaux's original drawing of the Greensward plan around 1910, they secured a four-thousand-dollar grant from the Sage Foundation. (Despite his avid interest in the park, Stokes did not note in his extensive local histories that his wife's grandparents, Anna and Robert Bowne Minturn, had played such a crucial part in its creation.) The first volume of the *Professional Papers of Frederick Law Olmsted, Senior* appeared in 1922, in time for the centennial of his birth; but the second volume on Central Park was not published until early 1928.[64]

One significant side effect of the way the project was carried out received no public comment at the time. The Central Park "bible" that preservationists had sought for the past two decades appeared as the "professional papers" of only *one* of the park's two designers. It was also edited by the son of that one designer in collaboration with the wife of that son's professional partner. To be sure, Vaux's sons cooperated with Olmsted, Jr., and Kimball by sending copies of letters they found among their father's papers. Recognizing the delicacy of the collaboration, the editors acknowledged Vaux in the first paragraph, but readers could hardly be faulted if they came away from the book talking about "the Olmsted plan." Not only had Olmsted, Jr., and Kimball selected fragments of letters from Vaux that supported Olmsted's image as the park's—and indeed American landscape architecture's—founding figure, they also silently edited out the tensions of the Central Park collaboration. Kimball recommended, for example, that they had "better not publish" a poignant letter from Vaux explaining the disappointment he felt upon first realizing that Olmsted did not truly believe that their respective contributions were equal and had failed to represent them as such.[65]

Planting the Seeds for the "Great Lawn"

The Olmsted and Kimball volume appeared at a triumphant moment for the preservationists; its subtitle, *Central Park as a Work of Art and as a Great Municipal Enterprise,* nicely summarized their view of the park's past and present. The inauguration of Jimmy Walker in January 1926 brought in a mayor avowedly friendly to the expansion of the park system and the preservationists' goals. In just two years, his administration spent $10 million to add twenty-three hundred acres of park land to the park system—more space than had been developed in the previous fifteen years. In 1930 Walker launched an even more ambitious $30 million effort to provide play space in crowded areas, although the increasingly severe depression as well as corruption and poor management left most of that program uncompleted. Using the tactic of delays, Walker killed off the Hylan-Hastings war memorial for the reservoir site. He also supplied the million-dollar appropriation for rehabilitating Central Park that its friends had been urging for years.[66] Thanks to this capital appropriation as well as a higher operating budget for the parks department, Central Park looked better in 1930 than it had in many years.

At least initially, the Great Depression actually improved the park's condition. New York City's privately funded Emergency Work Bureau saw the parks and playgrounds as one of the easiest places to employ relief workers. By December 1930, sixty-four hundred new workers were engaged in a general cleanup of the city's parks. "The unemployed put to work" in Central Park, the *Times* noted in May 1931, "may not have been born gardeners, but having had gardening thrust upon them they have, under intelligent guidance, accomplished much." The park "does look unusually beautiful this spring." Walker further pleased preservationists by firing Park Commissioner Francis Gallatin, a holdover from the Hylan administration, who the preservationists feared had been too close to their bête noire Tom Hastings. They applauded his replacement, Walter Herrick, as a "good . . . friend of Central Park."[67]

An even greater triumph from the preservationists' perspective came on the long-debated matter of the Lower Reservoir. For a moment in the late 1920s, when the *Daily News* pressed for swimming pools, sports fields, or playgrounds, and Osborn renewed his frenetic lobbying for a promenade, it looked as though the city would fill the reservoir site with a combination of play space and scenic effects. But in June 1930 the city adopted a plan drawn up by the New York chapter of the ASLA for converting the drained land almost entirely into an "oval meadow" or "Great Lawn for Play," as their plan called it—the design that both landscape architects and preservationists had long urged as most faithful to the original plan. As a concession to recreationists, the plan included two small play areas for young children, "entirely enclosed with foliage so that they need not detract from the park-like aspect of the remainder of the treatment." As a gesture to the advocates of a formal aesthetic, the landscape architects ringed the meadow with an oval walk and introduced a small alley of trees at its northern end. The plan also proposed a new lake at the southern end of the lawn.[68] After two decades of wrangling, preservationists and landscape architects had seemingly triumphed both over populist and progressive advocates of recreational facilities and over City Beautiful proponents of memorials and grand promenades.

If the preservationists had been asked to explain their apparent victory, they would, no doubt, have argued that they represented the wishes of the "public." But however one defines that term, a park referendum would probably have chosen one of the populist proposals the *News* had put forward. The preservationists' success stemmed in part from an extremely able lobbying campaign by the Central Park Association and its successor, the Park Association of New York City. William B. Roulstone, the CPA's general counsel, and Nathan Straus, president of the PANYC, were masters of the sort of pressure-group politics that was gradually displacing (or at least complementing) party politics as the way to assert influence. At the same time, both men also had traditional party ties. Straus, who had been elected to the state senate with Tammany support, was extraordinarily well connected in two of the city's most powerful groups—Tammany Hall and the German-Jewish elite. Roulstone and other park activists forged close ties to Walker, praising his park record and backing him for reelection in 1929. Straus even endorsed Walker's transformation of the Casino into a high society night spot.[69]

The park groups also had paid directors with talents or backgrounds in the arts of public relations and promotion. It did not hurt that the owners of the city's most influential paper, the *New York Times*, took an almost proprietary interest in the park. Publisher Adolph Ochs apparently played a behind-the-scenes role in the organization of the Central Park Association, and his daughter, Iphigene Sulzberger, was emerging as a leading park protector. Many more New Yorkers read the *Daily News*, but *Times* readers were much more likely to turn up at board of estimate hearings or to write letters to aldermen.[70]

The larger political and economic configuration of the late 1920s, too, helped the preservationist cause. The extremely rapid development of Fifth Avenue and Central Park West for luxury apartments had created a new constituency of wealthy and influential residents and real estate investors with a powerful interest in the rehabilitation and preservation of the park as a dignified public space that would attract the well-to-do and support high rents. Jimmy Walker may have been a Tammany mayor, but he spent many late evenings in the elegant and lavish Casino nightclub.[71]

Finally, the preservationists triumphed, because they opposed change.

"If 'Improvement' Plans Had Gobbled Central Park": Richard Welling's map, first used in the 1892 fight against the racetrack, was widely circulated in different versions by preservationists.

Since the 1890s changes in the park had been largely incremental: the museums got bigger, new entrances were opened and paths introduced, the Casino was renovated and expanded, rules were loosened, tennis courts paved, new sports permitted, speed limits increased, statues added, and more peddlers licensed. The cumulative effect was large, but most of the steps had been small. Large-scale changes faced much harder sledding; given the fragmentation of the park's user and political publics, it was exceedingly difficult to build a coalition behind any significant design modification. The shifting coalitions of *opponents* were invariably more powerful. Change, moreover, cost money. Even small property owners from the outer boroughs sometimes joined with large Manhattan realtors against massive park construction projects that might increase taxes.[72]

Welling had pioneered the strategy of presenting maps showing the end result "If 'Improvement' Plans Had Gobbled Central Park." It was a brilliant propaganda device; different variations on these maps appeared over and over again in subsequent years, and so did long lists of proposed changes to the park. These lists and maps exemplified the preservationists' "domino theory": if one of these changes had been (or was now) implemented, the whole park would turn into Coney Island.[73]

By equating trivial and serious proposals for change, the maps tended to dismiss any alternative vision of the park as unworthy of consideration. The lists and maps reinforced the sense that the park was continually under siege. Certainly the number of proposals for altering the park—for adding museums, monuments, playgrounds, and sports facilities—had multiplied after 1900. The park's constituencies were expanding, while the public spaces that might satisfy their demands were diminishing.

Still, the maps could just as easily have carried a quite different message: the degree to which the park had proved immune to schemes for change. For the preservationists' lists of proposed incursions simply documented that between the late 1880s and the early 1930s virtually every major proposal for altering the park or adding new structures had met defeat—in part because of the same social and political fragmentation that had stimulated the variety of proposals in the first place. In the early twentieth century, as its cultural public dramatically expanded, New Yorkers made new and sometimes incompatible claims on the park. Their demands (mobilized through new lobbying groups and the press as well as through party politics) further fractured the park's political public and made it extremely difficult to reconcile these competing claims. The significant lesson to be drawn from the maps (and from the thirty-year fight over the reservoir) was not that the park was vulnerable to change but that changes were so hard to achieve.

16

ROBERT MOSES AND A NEW DEAL

When, on January 23, 1930, a city worker turned a valve to drain the Lower Reservoir in Central Park, there was little fanfare, only a brief flurry of interest in the local legend that a giant salmon lived in its deep end. Three months later the American Society of Landscape Architects presented its plan to transform the site into a "Great Lawn." It received lavish praise, and Commissioner Walter Herrick quickly adopted it.[1]

"Forgotten Man's Gulch"

Those who looked closely, however, saw some ominous signs. The *Daily News* refused to join the celebration, denouncing the ASLA plan as an "attempt to run away with the people's land and save it for the wealthy only." It threatened to "incite or pay groups of kids to enter on the restricted 'Great Lawn for Play' and do some real playing." "This city's poor people must be given some kind of square deal, or in time this city's poor people will make trouble." New York's poor people were already making trouble—but over the absence of jobs. On March 6, 1930, the deepening depression brought tens of thousands of unemployed New Yorkers to Union Square for a massive Communist party–led demonstration that culminated in brutal police beatings of the protesters. The same conditions that spilled blood in Union Square stymied the ASLA's plan for the Lower Reservoir. With construction around the city slowly grinding to a stop, the contractor hired to raze the reservoir walls and fill in the cavernous hole couldn't find the rock and soil to finish the job. Even if he had, the city, teetering on the edge of bankruptcy, suspended plans for landscaping of the Great Lawn along with other city improvements.[2]

Almost immediately after the reservoir was drained, homeless men discovered a large, empty tunnel beneath it. By the following winter, they had fixed up what they wryly dubbed the "Little Casino" with tables, chairs, chintz curtains, and red lanterns. Six men spent the cold winter nights playing cards and sleeping in the tunnel until a passing patrolman overheard an argument and arrested them for vagrancy. The police broke up their improvised home with axes.[3]

The *Times* described the men rousted from "Central Park's almost sacred precincts" as "hoboes"—the term (along with "bums") they used to describe job-shirking transients. But as unemployment spread, the newspapers started to concede that not everyone without a job or a home was a hobo. When in the summer of 1931 police arrested twenty-two men for sleeping in the park, the men told Yorkville magistrate Maurice H. Gottlieb that they were out-of-towners looking for work. The judge agreed that they were "not ordinary bums," suspended their sentences, and even gave them two dollars each out of his own pocket. Magistrate Gottlieb took an indulgent view of men who had treated the public park as if it were a "common" resource in the midst of an economic crisis deep enough to prompt many Americans to question the sanctity of private property rights. As the depression worsened in the early 1930s, such sympathy spread. In 1933 Robert Nathan published a romantic novel, *One More Spring*, about a bankrupt antiques dealer, an unemployed violinist, and a prostitute who spend a harsh depression winter living in a laborer's shed in Central Park.[4] (By the time the film version appeared two years later, Al Jolson had already made *Hallelujah I'm a Bum*, a lighthearted musical about men living in the park.) Nathan no doubt read the local papers and knew that by the winter of 1931 at least nine and perhaps as many as forty jobless men had taken up residence in shacks left behind by the workers who had begun filling in the Lower Reservoir site.

Others had also begun to construct homes in the park. When police arrested seven such men, another Yorkville magistrate dismissed the charges and allowed them to go back to their improvised digs. The *Times* reporter who visited the men painted a much more charitable portrait than had been given in previous accounts of "tramps" and "vagrants" in the park. He described his guide to the colony as "sincere" and "affable" and emphasized the small domestic comforts in the shack the park dweller shared with two other men: wall bunks, a bed, two large chairs, a homemade stove, three dishes, two ornamented water pitchers, and bits of carpet on the floor.[5]

The colony grew in 1932. (Almost precisely a century before, that same area, then known as York Hill, had been the home of another community of poor New Yorkers.) By September 1932 seventeen completed houses sat on the reservoir site, and four more were under construction. Ramshackle huts sat beside more substantial structures. Three unemployed bricklayers had used abandoned building materials to erect a twenty-foot-high brick structure with a

Central Park Hooverville, 1932: Temporary shelters were built by unemployed men on the site of the Lower Reservoir.

roof of inlaid tile, variously known in the squatter community as "The Manor," "Rockside Inn," and "Custer's Last Stand." It included a fireplace, carpets, chairs, three beds, reading lamps, and curtained windows. "It was quite home-like," wrote the *Evening Journal* in a typical report. Colonists called another of the huts "Radio City," because it was the only shack with a radio and therefore served as the settlement's entertainment center.[6]

The squatters themselves offered entertainment to the increasingly large crowds who came to see the park's latest attraction. One man played the flute and collected coins from passersby. Ralph Redfield, an unemployed vaudeville tightwire walker who lived with several others in an abandoned water main, set up a wire and did daily shows. Even New Yorkers who just read in the newspapers about the community, which residents and reporters dubbed "Hoover Valley," "Shanty Village," "Shack Town," "Squatter's Village," and "Forgotten Man's Gulch," probably enjoyed the stories as a diversion from their own depression woes.[7]

"The Manor," as it was dubbed by other park squatters, was home to three bricklayers, who constructed it with abandoned materials.

Despite the light, almost romantic press coverage of the squatters, they were a symbol of a serious local and national problem. More than 1.2 million Americans were homeless the winter of 1932–1933. At least two thousand homeless New Yorkers preferred life in the city's more than twenty different squatter villages to that of the overcrowded and tightly regulated missions and municipal lodging houses. "These queer communities," a *Times* reporter wrote of the Hoovervilles, "look, frankly, like the resorts of tramps. But most of the men who people them are masters of trades and proud of their skill. Some are professional men, college trained." City authorities were periodically "urged by indignant citizens of standing to run the campers out." Such complaints by property owners along Fifth Avenue may have been the reason for some arrests and a health department investigation at the reservoir Hooverville in the fall of 1932. But the squatters remained relatively unmolested. The post office delivered mail. And even the mayor declared, "I cannot see that the camps constitute a nuisance or menace to health."[8]

"An Undesirable Element" Playing Ball on "The Great Lawn"

Most Fifth Avenue residents did not share the mayor's benign view of the squatters. The Park Association of New York City was apparently besieged with letters and phone calls inquiring about the long delay in the "improvement" of the reservoir site. In April 1933 association president Nathan Straus, Jr., urged the parks department to hire unemployed men to carry out the stalled ASLA plan. Manhattan commissioner Herrick responded that they lacked the necessary fill dirt, and the money to pay for any fill, or even the trucks to carry the fill to the site. In the midst of this dispute, the city got a new park commissioner. The new mayor John P. O'Brien (Jimmy Walker had resigned amid corruption charges) replaced Herrick with John Sheehy, an uptown Tammany district leader.[9]

At first, O'Brien and Sheehy seemed responsive to the preservationists. The city came up with the fill from excavations at DeWitt Clinton Park, trucks from the sanitation department, and relief workers from the welfare department. The *Times*, the landscape architects, and the park association warmly praised officials for *finally* getting the project under way. But the euphoria quickly turned into a feeling of betrayal. The preservationists now realized that Commissioner Sheehy was interested in the sort of recreational uses of the land that the *Daily News* had been promoting for the past five or six years. As dump trucks filled up the reservoir and the squatters bemoaned the end of their community, Sheehy announced that he would turn the tract into playgrounds and athletic fields, with a wading pool, running tracks, broad jump pits, and five or six baseball diamonds. On May 13 Sheehy inaugurated the first ball field before an audience of newsreel cameras and several hundred spectators. Even before the official opening, boys began to play on improvised diamonds.[10]

"From the point of view of the designers," an ASLA leader told the *Times*, the athletic facilities "are out of place in Central Park." Straus denounced Sheehy's "ignorance" and called the plans "the beginning of the end of Central Park." The *Times* quoted Olmsted ("whose memory the city should ever hold green") on the "main purpose of the park" as the provision "of natural, verdant and sylvan scenery for the refreshment of town-strained men, women and children." The park association, with behind-the-scenes leadership from Iphigene Sulzberger, lined up dozens of civic and artistic groups against the ball fields: from the Municipal Art Society to the Women's City Club, from the National Society of Beaux-Arts Architects to the City Garden Club.[11]

Even more potent opposition came from the real estate operators, whose organizations weighed in with a greater force and uniformity than they had ever mobilized before on a park question. The collapse of the real estate boom of the 1920s had made the realtors particularly sensitive to "grave injury to property values in the neighborhood of Central Park." The ball fields, according to the rental agent for several Central Park West buildings, threatened "to destroy the fine character of the park. . . . Already parts of the reservoir are being used for baseball, and have drawn an undesirable element from other parts of the city which have caused considerable annoyance. . . . The outlook from the adjacent buildings is less pleasant, and a pleasant and quiet spot such as was intended is being turned into a noisy open space." Real estate agents and property owners

This cartoon in Hearst's *Evening Journal* supported ball fields on the Lower Reservoir site. Wealthy Fifth Avenue residents, who could leave the city for the summer, should let poorer children play ball in the park.

on the east and west sides of the park agreed that playing fields were "detrimental to the character of the park and the sections surrounding Central Park." Residents of buildings overlooking the park wrote dozens of letters.[12]

Central Park's "other" neighbors, the residents of the more distant and less affluent uptown districts, lined up behind Sheehy, who had himself grown up in Harlem and Yorkville. The Yorkville Civic Council, the Yorkville Division of the Irish American Unified Society, the Lenox Hill Neighborhood Association, the Yorkville Recreation Association, the Uptown Chamber of Commerce, the Washington Heights Playground Conference, Posts 263 and 712 of the American Legion, the Washington Public School Athletic League, and the Labor

Commissioner Moses adopted the naturalistic plan for the Lower Reservoir drawn up by the American Society for Landscape Architecture. It included some concessions to recreational uses in the two playgrounds at the northern edge. Note the new Belvedere Lake at the south end.

Sports Union all endorsed Sheehy's playground plan. A less formal group of sixty-six women, presumably from the working-class neighborhoods of York-ville and the West Side, simply signed their endorsement as the "Mothers of Heckscher Playground."[13]

The class gap between the Fifth Avenue Association and the "Mothers of Heckscher Playground" was obvious to most New Yorkers. If anyone managed to miss the lines that were being drawn in this latest battle, the *News* reminded them with almost daily editorials. "By and large," explained a characteristic one, "the opponents of the Sheehy plan for the lower reservoir are the wealthy property holders and residents along Fifth Ave. between 59th and 110th Sts. . . . Why? We attribute it to fear of the poor; hatred of the sight of underprivileged people." *News* editorial cartoons made the same point: in one, a well-dressed man and woman in chauffeured limousine drive by children playing in the park; the woman comments: "Omigawd, Henry, what's Central Park coming to? The little brats act as though they owned the place."[14]

The *News*'s "Voice of the People" letters column carried the same message of class resentment. A representative letter declared: "God bless Park Commissioner Sheehy for telling the googoos where to get off, and going ahead with his plans to put playgrounds and ball fields in the Central Park lower reservoir site." The issue had touched a sensitive nerve at a moment of deep class division in the city. A Bronx "Old Timer" drew on family history to remind New Yorkers, especially "artists, landscape architects, [and] . . . Nathan Strausites," that "the poor of New York City built Central Park." The battle was not, however, fought purely on class lines. Well-to-do Gustavus Kirby, a Community Council leader and an old friend of Richard Welling's, had long advocated more play facilities in the parks, including Central Park. At a 1927 meeting of the City Club, he and Welling debated turning the Lower Reservoir into a playground, Kirby defending "the advantages of a parklike setting to playgrounds," Welling countering that facilities for children's "rough play" would come at the expense of "the park needs of the rest of the population."[15]

Welling saw parks and playgrounds as "eternal enemies," but in this view he was more absolutist than a number of his colleagues. Many preservationists staunchly supported playgrounds in other parts of the city. The Parks and Playgrounds Association, a predecessor of Straus's park association, for example, had operated its own playgrounds in the 1910s and 1920s. In relation to Central Park, the distinction between preservationists and recreationists hinged on questions of priority and propriety. Preservationists, who believed the protection of Central Park was more pressing than the creation of new playgrounds, thought equipped play facilities were fine but not if they were in Central Park. "I may properly say," Electus Litchfield declared in the midst of the reservoir battle, "that the Municipal Art Society has consistently taken the position that this very desirable playground space should be provided elsewhere and not in Central Park."[16]

The *News* responded sarcastically: "We wish to ask Mr. Litchfield, where, in God's name, is 'elsewhere' in the borough of Manhattan? There is no 'elsewhere' for Manhattan young people." It hinted that "elsewhere" really meant that rich people wanted poor people to stay out of their neighborhood—and Central Park was their neighborhood. Real estate interests opposed to the ball fields may well have conceded as much, but most preservationists sincerely believed the fields would damage the historic Greensward plan. When challenged by the *News*, the Park Association of New York City put together a list of alternative sites for ball fields in Manhattan. But the high cost of Manhattan real estate limited the alternatives, and the expansion of the park system initiated under Mayor Walker had centered on the outer boroughs. Straus acknowledged, "I can't pull playgrounds for Manhattan out of my hat."[17]

The massive mobilization on both sides of the issue once again brought a standoff. The mayor and the park commissioner held a series of sometimes raucous hearings. In mid-June 1933 an apparent compromise was reached.

Sheehy agreed that the ball fields would be only temporary and that the site would be landscaped as a meadow as soon as the money was available. Yet the reporting of the compromise leaves doubt. The *Times* headline said, "Sheehy Agrees to Landscape Reservoir Area" and also that the Great Lawn "*might well be utilized* for supervised play." The *News* headline of the same day said, "Kids Come First, Lawns Later in Park Compromise," and the article reported that "when the landscaping is completed a large oval meadow in the center *would be utilized* by boys and girls up to 18 for any conceivable form of recreation," including "baseball on grass diamonds with movable backstops."[18]

The reservoir question remained as stalemated as it had been for the past thirty years. "Self-appointed park defenders," the *News* complained, "oppose every scheme for increased public use and enjoyment of the park. . . . We suppose this will go on until, sometime when there is more money available than there is now, some powerful public official with courage and political sense will blast these societies out of existence and modernize the park." The *News* was not the first combatant to suggest a park strongman as the answer to the park's problems. Henry Fairfield Osborn had argued in 1927 that the regeneration of Central Park required a "Mussolini," and a friend of Welling's had written in 1930 hoping that then-commissioner Herrick might be a "Moses" to lead them out of the park wilderness.[19] Central Park would soon have both.

"A New Deal" for Central Park

In the midst of the 1933 spring flare-up over the Sheehy ball fields, aspiring mayoral candidate Fiorello La Guardia declared his opposition to "putting all this hodge-podge in Central Park." The *News* found it "rather shocking . . . for a man with Major La Guardia's liberal record" to oppose the ball fields but attributed the statement to his effort to get support from "assorted thou-shall-nots" in his quest for the nomination of the City Fusion party—a coalition of Republicans and "good government" reformers ("googoos" in the derisive term of their opponents).[20]

La Guardia may have been sincere in his conviction that "there is no more place for a playground in a park than there would be a park in a playground," but it was also true that some of the most ardent opponents of the ball fields were among those whose support La Guardia needed if he was to win the fusion nomination. Welling and his friend Billy Schieffelin, for example, circulated in the good-government organizations whose backing was to prove critical to La Guardia; and Nathan Straus, Jr., was precisely the sort of wealthy clean-government Democrat who would be key to a fusion victory. The fusionists first offered the nomination to Straus, who said no, then turned to La Guardia.[21]

One man with strong connections in these same good-government circles supported La Guardia's bid even though he desperately wanted the fusion nomination for himself. At forty-five, Robert Moses, a Republican, had won an international reputation by his dramatic expansion of New York State's park system under Democratic governor Al Smith. His greatest triumph had come with the opening of the Jones Beach State Park in August 1929, the most lavishly praised public works project of the decade, heralded for its vast expanse of beaches, its enormous parking lots, its tastefully designed bathhouses and restaurants, its workers' neat sailor uniforms, and its scrupulously clean boardwalk. A writer described the difference between Jones Beach and Coney Island, which it had displaced as New York's most famous seaside resort: "There are no concessions, no booths, no bawling hot-dog vendors. You won't see any weight-guessers or three-throws-for-a-dime-and-win-a-dolly alleys or blaring funhouses. For almost the first time in the history of public beaches, this beach is conceived as a spot for recreation, not amusement stimulated by honky-tonk."[22]

La Guardia admired Moses' accomplishments as a park builder and knew that the hero of Jones Beach was the man he wanted to work magic on New York City's parks. Whether or not he offered Moses the job as the price of his endorsement, this was exactly the sort of "nonpartisan" expert La Guardia had promised to bring into city government; Moses, moreover, had valuable ties to ex-governor Al Smith. And to top it off, Moses knew how to get the federal dollars the bankrupt city needed if it was to build anything at all.

La Guardia was prepared to pay the stiff price necessary to get Moses. "I told the Mayor," Moses later recalled, "that I was not interested in taking the city job unless I had unified power over all the city parks and, even then, only as part of unified control of the whole metropolitan system of parks and parkway development." Not only was Moses to be appointed parks commissioner of the entire city, not only was that office to be expanded to include power over parkways, not only was Moses to receive control of two "authorities" with power to build local bridges and roads (the Triborough Bridge Authority and the Marine Park Authority), but also he would be permitted to retain his four different state jobs concerned with parks and roads. The first bill La Guardia submitted to the state legislature, drafted by Moses, consolidated the borough-based park system, gave the commissioner vast new powers, *and* arranged for him to hold the multiple city and state posts.[23]

When he took office in January 1934, along with La Guardia, Moses moved with incredible speed to transform the city's park system. One small matter on his desk was the long-festering issue of the Lower Reservoir. Uncharacteristically, Moses delayed a few months before announcing his plan, which in its basic outline looked very much like the old ASLA design, down to the large oval meadow. Moses had made a few small changes, expanding the two playgrounds and setting aside space on the edge of the Great Lawn for adult recreations, such as croquet, lawn bowls, and shuffleboard. (The last was a Moses favorite; he had also installed this shipboard game at Jones Beach.) But by and large, Moses was endorsing the earlier plan to turn the reservoir site into a scenic meadow. He had many reasons to do so. La Guardia had endorsed the ASLA plan several months earlier. Also, a chief aide of Moses, Gilmore D. Clarke, had been director of design for the committee that drew up that plan in 1930. Perhaps most important, Iphigene Sulzberger supported the proposal. She had led the fight against the Sheehy ball fields and had just become president of the park association, a position she would keep until 1950. Her father, Adolph Ochs, was, of course, proprietor of the most important newspaper in the city, the *New York Times,* whose good will Moses worked hard to cultivate. The *News* protested that Moses had "knuckle[d] under to Iphigene Ochs Sulzberger (daughter of Adolph Ochs), the landscape architects and wealthy residents of Fifth Avenue in the matter of the Lower Reservoir site in Central Park."[24]

Moses now set a vast number of laborers, most of them paid by federal relief programs, to work on the reservoir site. By the summer of 1934, he had opened one of the two playgrounds; two years later, the Great Lawn was essentially completed.[25] The landscape architects and the preservationists had finally won the long battle of the reservoir. Ultimately they would discover that they had also lost the war.

Moses had close ties to many park preservationists. He had emerged from the reform world that Welling and Schieffelin inhabited, and he socialized in the same elite German-Jewish circles as Sulzberger and Straus. Like many of the preservationists, Moses was a progressive who believed that a healthful environment could influence social behavior. His allegiance to "good government" and faith in the rule of experts endeared him to members of the park association, who longed to see the management of public space insulated from politics. Most preservationists now assumed that Central Park had been placed in the hands of an individual who shared their sentimental attachment to the park of their youth. They were wrong. Moses, as it became clear, had little interest in the natural qualities of parks, nor did he see Central Park as a special kind of park. A product of the progressive playground movement, Moses viewed all parks as places for active, wholesome play, for ball fields, tennis courts, swimming pools, and playgrounds; he believed in recreation, not conservation. For him, Central Park was "essentially a playground," Moses explained on more than one occasion. His views resembled those of Charles Stover, a veteran of the city's settlement houses, as, indeed, was Moses' own mother. Moses embraced another side of the progressive legacy, too—its deep commitment to order, economy, and efficiency, a commitment that had marked Mayor Mitchel's administration and the Bureau of Municipal Research, where Moses had first gained his familiarity with city politics and finances in the 1910s.[26] These dual legacies guided Moses as he began to transform Central Park into a fair approximation of the model of the progressive park.

Reviewing Moses' first year in office, the *New York Times Magazine* declared that "Central Park also has a new deal." It pointed to "the brand-new brick-

Central Park Zoo, Opening Day, December 2, 1934: Robert Moses used federal relief funds to renovate the entire park, including the popular zoo.

and-concrete zoo" that replaced the "hideous old wooden sheds," the "swank restaurant and cafe [Tavern on the Green] now housed in the shined-up sheepfold buildings," "the garden plaza enclosed by the new zoo," "the refurbished State Arsenal," the extensive "plowing, seeding, planting, and replanting," and the new athletic fields on the North Meadow that gave the "grass effect of a big-college football field or the polo field of a country club." A *Times* editorial the next day enthused that Moses "has not only kept his promises. He has exceeded them." In his first year in office Moses employed thirty to sixty thousand park workers in the city as a whole. In the next seven years, he would oversee a 50 percent growth in city park land (from 14,500 to 22,500 acres), a tripling of playgrounds (from 119 to 424), and a thirtyfold increase in swimming facilities. By the following summer, he was supervising twenty-six hundred Works Progress Administration workers in a $2 million renovation of Central Park.[27] Not since the park was first constructed had so many worked there, and not since that earlier era had it undergone so many changes in such a short period, decisively shaping the park New Yorkers use today.

By the time Moses was finished, he had substantially enlarged the recreational facilities to provide "leisure de luxe," as a newspaper headline put it. In 1934, after seventy-five years, Central Park still had only a single playground, the Heckscher Playground in the southwest part of the park. In just three more years, it had twenty-two, including seventeen (twenty by 1941) "marginal playgrounds" dotted along the park's outer rim—each equipped with slides, swings, jungle gyms, playhouses, and sandboxes and circled by benches for mothers and nurses.[28]

Moses replaced the old Casino, located just east of the Mall, with the Rumsey Playground, put a play area for adults (with a skating track as well as clay and turf croquet and, of course, shuffleboard courts) on the Great Hill at West 106th Street, reconstructed the Heckscher Playground, and built the two playgrounds planned for the Great Lawn. His force of relief workers constructed a new model-boat house at the Conservatory Water, reconstructed the bridle paths, and added a field house and formal baseball diamonds to the North Meadow (around 98th Street), where informal ball playing had been going on for many years.[29]

By the end of the 1930s, the park's thirty-one-person recreational staff was overseeing a crowded schedule of folk dancing, kite flying, Ping-Pong, softball, baseball, football, field hockey, horseshoe pitching, shuffleboard, volleyball, lawn bowling, tennis, croquet, and ice and roller skating, as well as myriad festivals, carnivals, and tournaments. They organized contests in everything from amateur photography to model airplanes to jacks playing. Stover's parks department had concentrated on providing facilities and programming for children; Moses' saw the needs of older children and adults as also part of public responsibility. With the new marginal playgrounds limited to small children, the playground in the northeast corner of the Great Lawn was reserved for older children, and the Great Hill was set aside for adults. In the 1920s, it seems, the restriction limiting the ball fields to those under sixteen had been dropped; now, access was expanded further as Moses added new fields.[30]

The marginal playgrounds had concrete surfaces—anathema to the partisans of a naturalistic park—but Moses argued that the hard surface was much easier and cheaper to maintain. The preservationists avoided loud objections because Moses was doing so much to clean up the park and because he was the sort of "nonpartisan" commissioner they had sought for so long. The *Times* editors admitted that they were as "reluctant as all lovers of this great park to permit" the playgrounds to "trespass upon its attractive domain of 'rural scen-

In the 1930s Moses placed twenty equipped playgrounds, like this one at Fifth Avenue and 100th Street, on the park's borders.

ery,'" but "Central Park has been so well treated by the present administration—a model of care—that the public can have no anxiety that there may be admitted anything within its borders that works an abomination."[31]

The progressive emphasis on efficiency and order was as characteristic of Moses' regime as his insistence on active play facilities. Park workers blocked off the Cave in the Ramble, tore down the expensive-to-maintain glass Conservatory, filled in the northern end of the Pond at 63rd Street, opened new entrances, and realigned and straightened roads and ripped down the Marble Arch to accommodate cars better. (Under Moses, the auto in the park became "naturalized" and an unquestioned feature of the landscape.) The parks department standardized the designs of fences, wastebaskets, and benches, thus ensuring that fewer craft workers would be needed to produce these accessories and making repair or replacement of broken equipment easier. Observers noted that the new wire wastebaskets were "light enough for Park employees to handle, too unwieldy to steal, and too openly constructed to retain swill." The combination of concrete supports and wooden seats on the benches provided an admirable "blend of comfort and immovability."[32]

Andrew Green, and even Olmsted, might have admired Moses' rational program for reducing park maintenance costs, but surely Vaux would have protested the lack of respect for the ornamental work of artists and artisans who had extended Central Park's naturalistic aesthetic through the detailing of iron lampposts and stone bridges. Moses did not revere the spontaneity of nature. He opted instead for a principle of neatness, and his push for order, efficiency, and lower costs also doomed some of the most colorful features of the eclectic park. After taking office, Moses had indicated, "I believe it is the function of the parks to provide recreation, as distinguished from amusement," and he soon cracked down on unlicensed peddlers, who had had little trouble in the 1920s and even when arrested had found the charges dismissed by Tammany magistrates. Moses won effective control over the police for the first time since the demise of the sparrow cops, and park police now arrested many unlicensed vendors; those who lacked the cash to pay fines went to jail. Moses also canceled licenses and replaced the miscellaneous pushcarts (from "converted baby carriages to vehicles resembling the creations of Rube Goldberg," as a parks department employee put it) with four unobtrusive food stands and a fleet of "twenty modern brightly painted service wagons." Uniformed employees of the Union News and Terminal Operating Companies, which won the franchise, sold soda, popcorn, candy, and cigarettes—but no hot dogs.[33]

The strict regulation of peddlers was part of a general policy of tighter enforcement of park rules, particularly those forbidding littering and walking on the lawns, and by the late 1930s, police were again arresting homeless men found sleeping in the park. The most notorious case of rigid enforcement of regulations was the two-dollar fine imposed on Fela Biro, the Polish immigrant mother of two-year-old John Reed Biro who had been digging in the park. She could not pay the fine, and she and her baby spent four hours in jail. Moses justified the arrest by observing that Biro was "an actress and a Communist [who] seems to believe in a liberal amount of self-expression and opposition to authority."[34]

The push for order and cleanliness, the emphasis on "wholesome" recreational programs and facilities, the standardization of refreshment stands, the repainting of all parks department equipment in the new official color (café au lait), and the introduction of employee uniforms (including the nautical theme of yachting-style caps) were all evidence that Moses was out to replicate his first great success in park building and to "Jones Beachify" Central Park.[35] Even more direct reminders of Moses' middle-class seaside paradise came in the events surrounding the opening of the Tavern on the Green restaurant and the closing of the Casino.

Moses, the WPA, and Federal Money

Moses had many reasons to shut the Casino. La Guardia had long denounced it as a symbol of Tammany corruption, and his view was shared by reformers and local newspapers. Even the *News*, though not viscerally hostile to the Democratic organization, saw the low rent paid by the "high hat hut" as an example of "robbery at the people's expense." And Moses had a personal grudge: Jimmy Walker, once a protégé of Al Smith's, had politically betrayed and humiliated the ex-governor who had started Moses on his political career. The Casino was Walker's "place." Moses "never said it straight out," recalled the city corporation counsel, "but everyone around him knew why he was doing it—he wanted to get back at Walker for what Walker had done to Governor Smith. God, he wanted to get Walker!"[36]

Moses had to go to court to break the ten-year lease that Sidney Solomon held on the Casino. The court agreed with Moses that Solomon had a "revocable license"; in the process, it affirmed Moses' right to hold all of the "several offices he now occupies." When it became clear that Moses intended not only to close the Casino but to rip it down and replace it with a playground, he faced another lawsuit, and again he won, the court affirming the far-reaching powers granted to him under the 1934 park reorganization. Although no one noticed when the bill was passed, it turned out that the commissioner no longer needed the approval of the landscape architect for changes in the park. "As one lawsuit after another is decided in his favor," the *Times* commented of Moses' victory, "he is rapidly becoming *de jure* the sovereign that he has long been *de facto.*"[37]

Moses explained that "none of the general public can afford to eat in a place like the Central Park Casino. Such a restaurant does not belong in a public park." When the case got to court, Solomon's lawyers were eager to question Moses on precisely what sort of restaurant he thought *did* belong in a public park and who, in fact, was the general public. One of their strategies was to focus on the new Tavern on the Green restaurant, which Moses had created in the old Sheepfold (just west of the Sheep Meadow at 66th Street) almost immediately after coming to power. (The sheep were exiled to Prospect Park.) Cross-examining Moses on the witness stand, Solomon's lawyer pointed out the expensive wines, $1.75 steaks, and 25¢ pots of coffee on the Tavern's menu. But Moses argued that it met his criteria of a popularly priced restaurant, where the "general public can get what it wants."[38]

In part, Moses was right. Compared to the Casino, the Tavern on the Green was a "moderate priced tavern." It had no cover charge and offered cups of coffee and glasses of beer for a dime as well as full dinners for $1.50. Dinner at the Casino could run to $10 or considerably more, counting the exorbitant setup charge for White Rock soda to mix with the bootleg liquor patrons brought with them. Coffee cost 40¢. The Tavern could not, however, really be called popularly priced at a time when the nickel cup of coffee was still common and $1.50 represented about half the daily wage of the men who had transformed the Sheepfold into the Tavern on the Green. As at Jones Beach, Moses had taken something that had been an exclusive privilege of the rich and made it available to the middle class but not to the "masses."[39] Socialite Tony Biddle's definition of the Casino's society clientele as "the public" had set off five years of contention; Moses' equally arbitrary assertion that the Tavern on the Green served the "general public" met little challenge.

Moses did face complaints from preservationists about his plans to tear down the Casino, not because he was destroying a historic structure—Calvert Vaux's Victorian refreshment salon—but because he proposed to install another playground "almost directly in the center of Central Park and adjacent to the Mall," a spot better suited to adult "quiet and relaxation." "Playgrounds for small children," Iphigene Sulzberger wrote on behalf of the park association, "should be situated on the margins of large parks, or, better still, in small neighborhood parks." Moses dismissed her objections, imperiously reminding her that the preservationists had won the reservoir battle: "You can't win every argument as to restful park spaces for adults." A few days later, Moses' wife, Mary, patched up the squabble at a New Year's Eve party in Adolph Lewinsohn's Fifth Avenue mansion (a short walk south of the Sulzberger home): "You know Iphigene's a good friend. . . . Now you tell her you're sorry and you kiss her." Sulzberger made her own apology public two days later, releasing a letter reiterating her objections to the playground but disavowing any desire to "quarrel" with Moses. "You come close to our ideal of what a Park Commissioner should be and we have no desire to be associated, even for a moment, with those who have attempted . . . to hinder you in your plans."[40]

Moses seemed to be just about everyone's "ideal" park commissioner. Newspapers, organizations, and individuals who for years had been squabbling over Central Park now joined in a chorus of praise: the News as well as the Times, the Community Council (supporters of the reservoir playgrounds) and the Regional Plan Association as well as the park association and the Municipal Art Society, playground advocate Gustavus Kirby as well as preservationist Welling.[41]

There were even signs that the Olmstedian orthodoxy, formulated in the 1910s and 1920s and codified with the publication of Olmsted's professional papers, was in for some reformation. Paul B. Schumm, a member of the ASLA and a parks department employee, writing in 1937 in Landscape Architecture, praised both the original Greensward plan and the changes to it undertaken by his boss. Olmsted had sought to screen out the city, believing that "the sight of

Park association president Iphigene Ochs Sulzberger presents an award to her friend Park Commissioner Robert Moses, 1935.

adjoining buildings would suddenly check the imagination, interfering fatally with the desired effect," but "the hardened New Yorker who has grown up with his city . . . can enjoy the Park in his own way and does not feel the loss of virtues which he never knew and never learned to value." Schumm acknowledged that "it was no part of Olmsted's intention to provide special facilities for active recreation," but maintained that this view could no longer be easily justified when "the surrounding city is so solidly built up that scarcely a plot of open ground remains for blocks around." Restoration of the park meant adherence not to the historic plan but to "that ideal of essential public service" that he associated with Olmsted. Flexibility, not sanctity, was Schumm's park creed: "Nowhere have the aspects of the physical environment and the terms of social life altered more completely than in New York City between Olmsted's day and ours. We have seen how little the details of the physical form of the original Olmsted Park actually remain. These have changed inevitably with the times but the fundamental conception remains, and the best tribute to the founder's genius which we can now pay will consist in adapting its physical expression as intelligently and as completely as possible to the inevitable new conditions."[42]

In effect, Schumm was honoring Moses, as well as Olmsted, as a central figure in the park's history. This configuration was made even more explicit in a three-part "Profile" of Central Park by Eugene Kinkead and Russell Maloney in the *New Yorker* a few years later. The second installment of that series was illustrated by a drawing of two busts surrounded by a border of birds, squirrels, and trees; the heroic-looking figures inside the border were Olmsted and Moses. "New York," said the last piece, "will never outgrow Central Park provided a man like Frederick Law Olmsted, the designer of the Park and its first superintendent, or Robert Moses happens along once in a hundred years or so." There was no room for Calvert Vaux in the drawing. Perhaps the cruelest irony was that the series ended with a long quotation from Olmsted protesting that his love for parks bespoke *"no regard for Art or fame or money."* It was taken, though the authors did not mention this, from a long, self-justifying letter Olmsted had written to Vaux in 1863 in response to his complaint that Olmsted's friends were giving him the sole credit for the park's design.[43]

But soon "idolatry" of Moses came to supplant even idolatry of Olmsted. In retrospect the seemingly universal praise for Moses in the later 1930s appears remarkable. Why did people with such sharply contrasting visions of Central Park come to celebrate him? One reason was Moses' brilliant cultivation of the press. The *Times,* which had sharply attacked so many park commissioners, only gently chided Moses for policies it didn't like. Another reason was that Moses' vast arrogation of power gave him the ability to get things done without having to wait for issues to be resolved in public debate. He had to clear nothing with a landscape architect, the other members of a park board, the board of aldermen, the board of estimate, or even the mayor. "No law, no regulation, no budget stops Bob Moses in his appointed task," La Guardia explained. He referred to his other appointees as "my commissioners," but Moses as "our parks commissioner." Moses even managed to disregard most of the rules of the federal agencies that were supplying the money for his park projects.[44]

Almost paradoxically, Moses' ability to disregard the ordinary rules of politics also accounted for his success. What some might have seen as dictatorial behavior, good-government groups and park preservationists saw only as the sort of nonpartisan, nonpolitical park administration that they had been looking for ever since the demise of the original Central Park commission. Although Richard Welling was unhappy over Moses' redesign of the zoo, he praised the commissioner for his nonpartisanship, a cause Welling had been championing even longer than he had been defending Central Park. He reported with delight an exchange in which Moses had rebuffed the effort of Tammanyite James Farley (Franklin Roosevelt's postmaster general) to assign the party faithful to work in the parks. "I am entirely opposed to appointments for partisan reasons," Moses had declared. It was one of the few moments since the 1860s when the city's reform-minded elites—claiming an authority based on education, expertise, wealth, and "Yankee" values—could see in the leadership of the city parks a reflection of themselves. To Iphigene Sulzberger, for example, Sheehy seemed a crude "political hack" with no feeling for Central Park, but Bob Moses appeared to be both "a man of vision" and the sort of person you might invite over for breakfast on New Year's Day.[45]

The legend persisted that the park had been dominated by political corruption throughout its history. Moses, like Olmsted before him, had painted himself as a white knight who would save the parks from spoilsmen. "When you see 'Up in Central Park,' " he told a meeting of the park association in reference to the musical that was helping to revitalize that legend, "you must realize how far we have come from the days of Boss Tweed."[46] Moses overlooked the mid-nineteenth-century partisan politics through which the Republicans had seized control of the park, and he glossed over the dependence of his own "nonpartisan" regime on the dollars and blessing of a Democratic administration in Washington that had added parks to the national political agenda. Yet, to add another paradox, despite his seeming disdain for the conventional rules of politics, Moses was accommodating popular sentiment more fully than any earlier park commissioner. Suddenly, the city's working-class communities had full entry into a recreational world previously reserved for the middle and upper classes. Access to recreation was undergoing its most dramatic "democratization" of the past hundred years. Ironically, it was brought about by the most autocratic regime in the park's history.

But the real reason Moses was able to do so much was federal money. Money had always set the limits of what was possible. In the 1850s cost overruns had forced the scaling back of the original Greensward plan; in the 1870s retrenchment in city finances had reduced park maintenance; in the 1910s fiscal crisis had curtailed maintenance and policing. In the subsequent decades funding limits had required a hard choice: either the city could maintain and rehabilitate Central Park or it could build and operate small playgrounds around the city.[47] It could not easily do both. The dispute over the Sheehy ball fields could have been easily finessed if the city had been in a position to build athletic fields someplace else, but the Lower Reservoir was the cheapest and most available site.

Now New York was receiving more than its share of the newly flowing federal dollars, in part because La Guardia enjoyed good relations with Franklin Roosevelt's New Deal administration—good enough to smooth over the problems caused by the president's hatred for Moses, which went back to old fights in New York State. But Moses also assisted the city in extracting money from Washington. Whenever Congress appropriated money for a New Deal program, he was ready with the carefully prepared blueprints, specifications, and topographical surveys that the emerging federal bureaucracies required. Theda Skocpol and other scholars have argued that an underdeveloped "state capacity"—that is, the information and bureaucracy to manage large-scale government programs—prevented federal, state, and local governments of the

Relief workers from the WPA and other federal agencies repaired basic features of the park including the transverse roads.

1930s from fully undertaking vast new projects. If so, Moses' parks department was an exception.[48]

Moses also took advantage of the New Deal's ideological commitment to expanding public recreational facilities. Harold Ickes, secretary of the Department of Interior and head of the Public Works Administration, hoped to implement the progressive program of revitalizing democracy by building community institutions such as recreation centers and playgrounds. Other New Dealers, influenced by economist Simon Patten, believed that public facilities for organized play helped introduce Americans to a new ethic of consumption by encouraging the pursuit of pleasure beyond the confines of the industrial workplace. Harry Hopkins, who headed the Works Progress Administration, joined with other "proto-Keynesian" New Dealers in arguing that mass consumption and spending would offer the best solutions to the nation's economic problems.[49] New York City was an ideal workshop for such ideas.

With the launching of the WPA in 1935 La Guardia won special state-level status for New York City and a direct link between the city and the new federal agency. Just one day after La Guardia asked the parks department to propose projects for WPA funding, Moses sent over an enormous eight-foot-high pile of plans for work totaling $50 million. As a result of his foresight and readiness, more than four-fifths of the first $19 million the WPA spent in the entire country went to New York City. By 1936 more than seventy thousand WPA workers were employed on the city's park projects. In the first two years of the WPA $113 million was spent for parks and recreation in New York—more than two and a half times as much as any other New York City department received. After 1937 Moses' arrogant refusal to submit to federal regulations led to sharp cutbacks in his WPA work force; yet even in these years, between 1937 and 1942, almost one-fifth of the city's WPA construction workers were employed on park projects.[50]

Moses had more money for construction and maintenance than any previous New York park commissioner. With the depression conditions, he could hire unusually well qualified workers at rock-bottom wages. These circumstances enabled him to satisfy demands that had previously seemed contradictory. Preservationists and real estate people got a rehabilitated park that was even better maintained than it had been in the late 1920s. Wealthy Upper East Side horseback riders wrote in to say that the bridle paths had never been "so well constructed, so serviceable and beautiful as at the present time." Yorkville mothers now had a wide selection of playgrounds for their children to play in; so did mothers all over the city. And the unemployed appreciated his ability to create jobs. Moses hired thousands of laborers and skilled construction workers, and in just his first ten days in office he put six hundred engineers, architects, and landscape architects on the payroll.[51]

The money, which came largely from federal work relief budgets, was necessarily temporary. After the WPA was gone, how were the new parks and playgrounds to be maintained? Given the proportion of the city budget that New Yorkers appeared willing to devote to parks and recreation, Moses not only built the city's park system; he overbuilt it. Moses was aware of the problem of long-term support. He repeatedly admonished city officials, "We cannot build these things without running up the bill for personnel, maintenance, and operations." His 1939 report, *Six Years of Park Progress*, pointed out that while the city's recreational facilities themselves had tripled, his budget had increased only 25 percent. As a result, "facilities less than six years old have already begun to deteriorate due to inadequate maintenance." But he kept on expanding his recreational empire all the same. "That's the next generation's problem," he told Iphigene Sulzberger.[52]

Ultimately, too, the price of power would have to be paid. The checks and balances built into the park system and the fragmentation of New York politics had stalemated proposals for major alterations to Central Park in the past, yet had allowed for incremental changes that had accommodated many popular demands. With essentially no limits now on what Moses could do, New Yorkers had little voice in deciding how their public parks would be maintained and how the system should grow. "Work relief has rid us of the slow and cumbersome but democratic procedures," complained a letter writer to the *Times* in 1936. "All that is considered is project desirability from a social and engineering standpoint, suitability for relief labor, the relationship of the cost of materials and equipment for hire to the estimated requirements for labor."[53] Preservationists who had welcomed shifting the parks from the more democratic arena of politics to the purview of an expert manager would find that without any democratic controls Moses could, and did, ignore their claims.

If the park's political public had been reduced to a single individual, its cultural public—its users—now became Moses' "average public." An average, however, is not always fully inclusive. For example, black neighborhoods did receive more new recreational facilities under the federal programs, but they did not approach an equitable share of the new parks. In a discussion of the causes of the 1935 Harlem riot, the president of the board of aldermen pointed to the "totally inadequate" recreational facilities. Of the 255 playgrounds Moses built in the 1930s, only one was in Harlem. Moreover, like many of his contemporaries, Moses thought public recreational facilities should be racially segregated, and he had the power to implement his prejudices. According to Robert Caro, by employing only white lifeguards and attendants, Moses ensured that black and Puerto Rican Harlemites felt unwelcome in the Thomas Jefferson Park swimming pool in heavily Italian East Harlem. Further, because he believed that African Americans "don't like cold water," he kept the pool unheated. "Well, you know how RM felt about colored people," a Moses aide explained to Caro. Such feelings may explain why the northern part of Central Park, the area most accessible to Harlem residents, received little attention from Moses' parks department for seven years. Soon after the United States entered the war, even that belated rehabilitation was abandoned. Only in 1947—twelve years into the Moses regime—did the Harlem Meer fully reopen.[54]

Nor did Moses perceive park workers as full members of his general public. He considered the WPA workers whose labor he relied on "bums, jailbirds and riffraff." He set the terms of employment and repeatedly clashed with federal officials over control of relief workers. He refused, for example, to allow park supervisors to respond to any charges workers brought before the WPA Labor Appeals Board. When the WPA reinstated workers his office had discharged with claims that they were loafers, strikers, or agitators, they had to work elsewhere in the city. Moses would not reemploy them. Moses and his tough foremen (the "ramrods" he hired from private construction firms) drove park workers with a relentlessness Andrew Green would have envied. Civil Works Administration workers, often without adequate warm clothes, labored through the severe winter of 1934 (the mean temperature for that February was 11.5 degrees) with no letup. In 1936 when seventy WPA workers refused to shovel snow on the Mall during a sleet storm, park officials fired them. The hundreds of newly hired architects and engineers faced similar pressure, but in more

In 1942 bench sitters enjoy a quiet Sunday in front of the zoo restaurant built by Moses.

comfortable circumstances. When plans needed to be completed, Moses expected them to work through the night—with perhaps a few quick naps on the cots set up in the corridors of the Arsenal.[55]

The deeper problem was that Moses had sympathy for ordinary people only in the abstract. Frances Perkins was later to say that he "doesn't love the people. . . . He loves the public, but not as people. The public is just *the* public. It's a great amorphous mass to him; it needs to be bathed, it needs to be aired, it needs recreation, but not for personal reasons—just to make it a better public."[56] Whereas in the middle and late nineteenth century, genteel reformers like Olmsted had sought to create a public in their own image, in the early and mid-twentieth century progressive reformers like Moses claimed a new kind of authority as professionally trained experts who would manage the public according to abstract principles of efficiency and rationality.

Yet, as always, the ordinary people, the public, proved more vibrant and diverse than the park's visionaries—whether Olmsted in the nineteenth century or Moses in the twentieth—allowed for. Central Park resisted any attempts to make it into what two observers called "a prissy outdoor Y.M.C.A." It remained "the sort of place where anything can happen," where someone might ride a mule on the bridle path or two middle-aged men might go swimming in the seal pool.[57]

Moreover, whatever the elitist sources and implications of Moses' technocratic progressivism, the impulse for vastly expanded recreational facilities also came from the bottom up. The New Deal–era programs responded to the belief—expressed in the petition campaigns for Sunday concerts and museum openings, the 1901 chair riot, and the thirty-year battle over the Lower Reservoir—that city residents had a "right" to the public provision of space and recreational resources. That idea took even firmer root in the 1930s. In March 1937 when Moses padlocked 142 playgrounds in one of his many conflicts with WPA officials and Mayor La Guardia, West Side mothers and children staged a sitdown strike and took control of "their" playground, and in other parts of the city, mothers circulated petitions. Such actions reflected what Judith Davidson in her study of federal support of recreation identifies as a growing conviction in the 1930s that recreation was "a civic right for all rather than . . . a special privilege for the rich or charity for the poor."[58]

Moses' autocratic rule of the park system would last another two decades. But even he could not suppress the growing claims of park users (and park workers as well) on the city's public resources and open spaces. Moreover, the passing of the Moses era in the 1960s would bring even greater contention over the control and use of Central Park and other public parks. For the next fifty years, the politics of the park would remain as tightly embedded in the politics of the city as it was when James Beekman first introduced legislation to create a large public park.

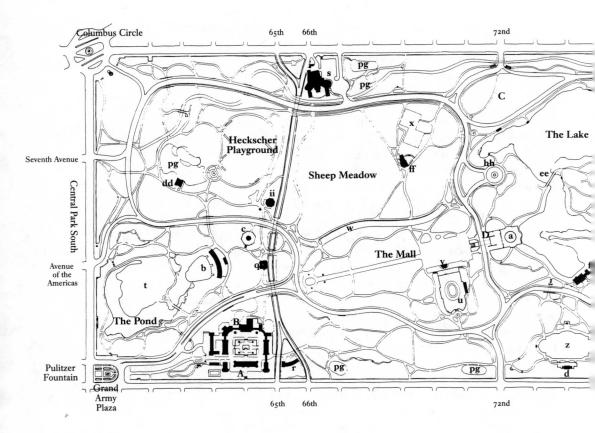

The Lake

C

Heckscher Playground

Sheep Meadow

Seventh Avenue

pg

dd

ii

hh

ee

ff

x

Central Park South

c

w

The Mall

D   a

Avenue of the Americas

b

q

v

t

u

y

The Pond

B

z

Pulitzer Fountain

A

r

pg

pg

d

Grand Army Plaza

90th

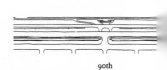

pg

A	Arsenal	**o**	Harlem Meer Boat House
B	Zoo	**p**	Tennis Courts
C	Strawberry Fields	**q**	Dairy
D	Bethesda Terrace	**r**	Lehman Children's Zoo
E	Loch	**s**	Tavern on the Green
F	Pool	**t**	Hallet Nature Sanctuary
G	Great Hill	**u**	Rumsey Playfield
		v	Naumburg Bandshell
a	Bethesda Fountain	**w**	Former Drive (volley ball, roller skating)
b	Wollman Rink	**x**	Bowling and Croquet Greens
c	Chess and Checkers House	**y**	Central Park Police Precinct
d	Kerbs Model Boathouse	**z**	Conservatory Water
e	Tennis House	**aa**	Swedish Cottage
f	Loeb Boathouse	**bb**	Shakespeare Garden
g	Belvedere Castle	**cc**	North Meadow Center (basketball)
h	Delacorte Theater	**dd**	Puppet House
i	Metropolitan Museum of Art	**ee**	Bow Bridge
j	American Museum of Natural History	**ff**	Mineral Springs (refreshment stand)
k	Obelisk	**gg**	Blockhouse
l	Belvedere Lake (Turtle Pond)	**hh**	Cherry Hill
m	Lasker Pool-Rink	**ii**	Carousel
n	Conservatory Garden	**pg**	playground

90th

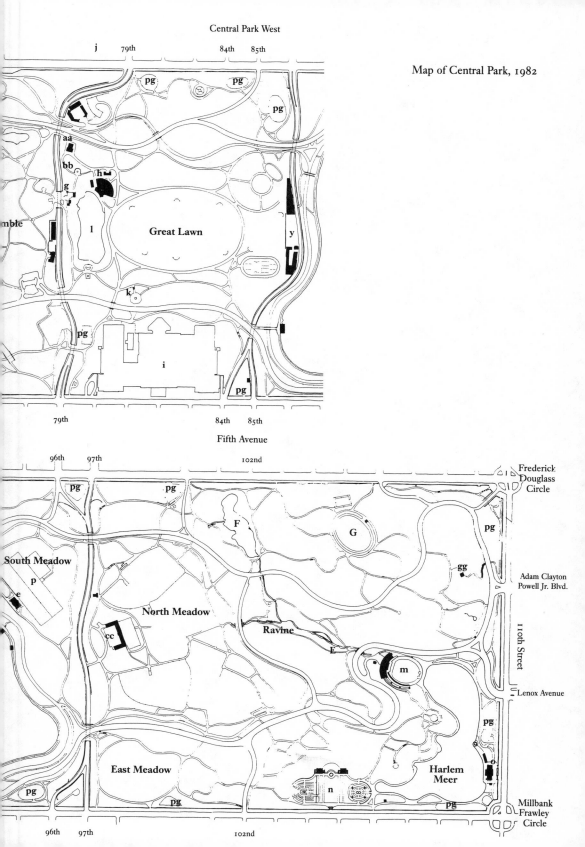

Map of Central Park, 1982

VI. THE PAST FIFTY YEARS

17

SCENES FROM A PARK, 1941–1980

In the early spring of 1950 an errant baseball narrowly missed the head of Iphigene Ochs Sulzberger. The ball had come from the Great Lawn of Central Park, the site she and other preservationists had fought so hard to turn into a pastoral meadow. Walking across the park, she was "shocked" to discover that the parks department had just installed several permanent baseball backstops on the Great Lawn. "I suppose it is too late to do anything about this," she wrote in a letter of complaint to her friend Bob Moses, then in his seventeenth year as park commissioner (just as she was in her seventeenth year as president of the Park Association of New York City). She proposed, nonetheless, that a fence might prevent injuries to passersby. She also advised Moses to see that the playground in the northwest corner of the Great Lawn was paved—"it is now nothing but a sea of mud under the children's play apparatus."[1]

Moses' reply was friendly, ending with the hope that he and his wife, Mary, would soon get together with Iphigene and her husband, Arthur (publisher of the *New York Times* since the death in 1935 of Iphigene's father). But in private Moses noted scornfully to an assistant: "You can see from this that the park association has ceased to be of any use to us or anyone else." He replied to Sulzberger more carefully, explaining that "the demand for active recreation facilities, particularly ballfields, has increased to such an extent that we must, within reason, use all available space." He was under pressure from "Bill Hearst" and "his boys on the Journal American" to "permit full use by the public at all times in the summer of all lawn and landscaped areas." As for the muddy playground, Moses said it had been constructed under the WPA at a time when "the idea of even a small area of pavement in Central Park was anathema to a great many people, particularly to members of your association."[2]

Visitors to the Great Lawn in 1950 could see the full fabric of Moses' vision of Central Park as a place of baseball backstops, asphalt, and efficiency. If they had returned again three decades later, they could have glimpsed the unraveling of Moses' vision. On June 12, 1982, three-quarters of a million people packed themselves onto the Great Lawn to denounce the nuclear arms race and to urge a freeze on the production of nuclear weapons. Some said it was the largest single protest demonstration in American history. Moses, who had been dead scarcely a year, would have detested both the demonstrators' politics and their use of Central Park for any political purpose. Thirty-five years earlier he refused to allow a "monster citizens rally" in support of rent and price controls to gather on the Mall. Only musical and patriotic events were permitted in the park.[3]

In the four decades between the end of the Great Depression and the nuclear freeze demonstration, the park opened up in dramatic ways: recreational facilities expanded and oppositional political demonstrations found a place in the park for the first time in its history. Yet the social tensions that accompanied economic and social changes in postwar New York also entered the city's leading public space and required New Yorkers once again to re-negotiate the meaning of the city's cultural and political publics.

After World War II, the United States emerged as the dominant power in the world economy, and New York established itself as the center of international capitalism, the headquarters of dozens of national and multinational corporations and banks. Immediately following the war, the city's economy expanded, as new, although often less well paid, service positions replaced the old industrial jobs. At the same time new groups of workers in the city—telephone, hospital, and government employees—successfully unionized. But after the economy reached its postwar peak in 1969, it went into a severe recession that ended only in 1977. In that period, New York lost one-sixth of its jobs in manufacturing and trade. By 1986 only 11 percent of New Yorkers worked in manufacturing jobs compared to about one-third at the end of the war. Corporate offices disappeared as well: one-third of the *Fortune* 500 firms headquartered in New York in 1974 had departed by 1981. By 1979 New York City, for many years substantially more affluent (in the aggregate) than the rest of the United States, had family income levels 16 percent below the national average. While poverty decreased nationally in the 1960s and 1970s, the number of poor New Yorkers increased.[4]

The city's overall economic decline and the collapse of its industrial economy, where immigrants had traditionally found jobs, proved particularly devastating for the most recent arrivals in New York. In the 1940s, 1950s, and 1960s, the largest number of the in-migrants came from Puerto Rico and the American South. Between 1940 and 1970 the city's total population increased by only 6 percent, but its black population more than tripled and its Puerto Rican population multiplied ten times. By 1980 two-fifths of all New Yorkers were African American or of Hispanic descent; one-third lived in poverty.[5]

The 1965 immigration reform sparked another demographic shift. Particularly after 1975 tens of thousands of immigrants from the Caribbean,

Central America, Hong Kong, China, Korea, the Philippines, Pakistan, India, and elsewhere settled in New York. The census category "Spanish origin" was no longer a synonym for Puerto Rican; by 1980 only 60 percent of the city's Latinos were from Puerto Rico. By the mid-1980s some scholars estimated that, counting undocumented aliens, the foreign-born had reached 40 percent of the city's population—as high as it was in 1910, in the heyday of what we think of as the "immigrant city."[6]

This dramatic remaking of New York's economy, and of its capitalist and working classes, once again raised the question of how different New Yorkers would define the political public (the public with the power to make decisions about the allocation of municipal resources) and the cultural public (the public permitted and encouraged to use those resources). Whereas in the mid-nineteenth century New York merchants had worried about the behavior of "rowdy" Irish laborers in the park, and in the early twentieth century native-born middle-class New Yorkers had fretted over the litter left behind by Italian and Jewish immigrants, in the middle and late twentieth century many white, middle-class New Yorkers, some themselves descendants of immigrants, associated the park and young black and Puerto Rican men with crime and fear. Despite the similarities to earlier class and ethnic conflicts, Americans' disavowal of the language of class in the cold-war years meant that many New Yorkers interpreted enduring class tensions largely through the constricted frame of "race relations."

By 1980 New Yorkers had reached a partial, sometimes tense accommodation with the new social realities. At least in Central Park, they learned to share the park with people of different social backgrounds, sometimes uneasily, sometimes quite easily. While the park's cultural public gradually embraced new groups and greater diversity, the politics of its administration followed the uneven course of politics at large. In the 1950s park users and park workers challenged the previously unquestioned authority of Robert Moses over every aspect of park administration. In the new urban liberalism of the 1960s unprecedented uses of the park were permitted; new forms of "community control" began to influence the use of public facilities. But the fiscal crisis of the 1970s provoked a questioning of such experiments and sharply undercut the city's commitment to public services—the maintenance of public parks among them.

By highlighting a series of episodes drawn from each decade, 1940 to 1980, the following pages sketch the changing views of New Yorkers about the organization, maintenance, and use of their most important public space.

"Terror" in Central Park?

On November 1, 1941, Jerome Dore, age twelve, fatally stabbed James O'Connell, fifteen, on the edge of Central Park at 99th Street and Fifth

Avenue.[7] No one disagreed that the youth's death was a tragedy, that the crime was wrong, and that the young assailant and his accomplices were residents of Harlem. What was much more controversial—and more revealing—was the way the press reported the incident and the way different groups of New Yorkers interpreted it.

The tabloids first emphasized the personal tragedy of the murder, then assigned broad social and racial implications to it. The *Daily News* said that the O'Connell boy—"a brilliant student and highly devout"—and his brother had been on the way home from confession at St. Cecelia's Church when "three colored boys" chased them and stabbed James to get "what few pennies he may have had." Newspapers quickly shifted to a more ominous story of a park "crime wave" instigated by black and Puerto Rican New Yorkers at the park's northern border. "Man Found Choked in Another Park Murder," headlined the tabloid *Daily Mirror* two days after the O'Connell funeral. "Police Act to End Terror in Central Park," the *News*, its competitor, screamed in a story that talked of "roving bands of knife-carrying colored youths" and "the terrorism of rape, robbery and murder in the park." The *New York Times* was only a bit more restrained. Page-one headlines declared: "Crime Outbreak in Harlem," "Youths Running Wild," and "Boy Hoodlums Called the Chief Offenders in Wave of Terror, Especially in Parks."[8]

The black newspapers viewed the O'Connell death and its aftermath in another light. In a front-page editorial two weeks after the murder, the *Amsterdam Star-News* described it as routine: "Some juvenile delinquents in the lower Harlem area" had "ganged up on a white boy or boys, and in the ensuing brawl one white boy was stabbed to death." In the same issue the president of the Manhattan Council of the National Negro Congress, thinking perhaps of the fights between Italian and black youths in Harlem in the late 1930s, called it a "tragic incident" growing out of "one of those juvenile affrays so common to regions that fringe the ghetto."[9]

African-American newspapers did not deny the existence of crime. "We know there is crime in Harlem!" said a *Star-News* editorial, pointing out that it had itself been criticized for overemphasizing crime in the black community. But the *Star-News* and the city's other major black newspaper, the *New York Age*, were deeply concerned about how the city's "mighty and influential white press" was using the incident for "the foulest, most slanderous, inaccurate and biased reporting of which yellow journalism is capable." The O'Connell murder, the *Star-News* charged, "was the kick-off for an all-out attack on Harlem by several daily newspapers whose editors invented a 'Crime Wave in Harlem,' which, in fact, does not exist." The editors reserved their sharpest accusations for the "plutocratic *New York Times*," whose "vast network of communication" made it "aware that the fatal stabbing of James O'Connell was not the first act of violence to occur in the Harlem area, and that his death cannot be truthfully described as a crime wave. Yet nothing has been said and nothing has been done by that newspaper about other disturbances in which Negroes were victims."[10]

The Central Park "crime wave" was, in fact, wildly exaggerated. Some widely reported cases of robberies and muggings (a term just coming into common use) evaporated on closer examination; most of the arrests, which invariably targeted black or Puerto Rican youths, were for less serious infractions. Disputes over the causes of crime and claims that it had a racial dimension would echo through the pages of New York newspapers over the next half century. Beginning in the 1930s and particularly in the postwar decades, journalists used any incidents occurring in Central Park as a powerful symbol for urban crime in general. Although this reporting exaggerated the problem, even incomplete and not entirely reliable evidence leaves little doubt that crime, particularly against persons and property, had indeed increased dramatically in Central Park and throughout the city since the park opened. Most park "crime" in the late nineteenth century—and, it appears, in the early twentieth century as well—involved violations of park ordinances (by, for example, "fast driving" or picking flowers) or of sanctioned norms of public behavior (by littering or appearing intoxicated in public). The number of arrests had gone up; in the 1860s felony arrests averaged about seven per year; by the 1880s they had probably quadrupled. Even so, felonies for *all* the city's parks in that decade were sixty-one per year, probably half or fewer of these in Central Park. One hundred years later, felonies in Central Park had increased almost thirtyfold, averaging close to nine hundred a year from 1979 to 1986. Serious crimes in Central Park in 1980 alone probably exceeded all felony arrests for the entire nineteenth century.[11]

Such comparisons should not be pushed too far, given significant changes in the reporting, gathering, and classifying of crime statistics as well as the growth of population throughout the city, particularly, on the park's borders. After all, people had been worrying about safety, particularly at night, almost since the park opened. In 1862 the park board had believed that "the closing of the Park at night is of such obvious propriety, that it requires no argument for its justification." A decade later Olmsted warned, "I recommend no woman to stroll in the Park" after dark, "and I answer for no man's safety in it from bullies, garroters, or highway robbers after dusk." In 1907 a visitor from New Hampshire scrawled on the back of a postcard of the Mall: "Bad place to be after dark." And in 1929 a British visitor said that walking in London's Hyde Park at night might land you in police court, but wandering through Central Park could put you in the morgue.[12]

The British visitor's perceptions had a firmer basis in 1979 than in either 1879 or 1929. Over the eight years from 1879 to 1886, the police recorded only two homicide arrests for *all* the city parks, but in the eight years from 1979 to 1986, thirty-five murders took place in Central Park alone. Yet murder in the park was always rare when compared with the rest of the city. In the 28th police precinct, directly north of the park, murders in the 1970s and 1980s were more than eighteen times as frequent as in the park, and even in the affluent district along the lower Fifth Avenue border, murders were three times as common. The rate of other felonies in the park was even lower than murders. Such figures support the protestations of park and police officials that Central Park did not and does not deserve a reputation as "a fearful menace," as one television commentator has called it. But if the park was, as officials never tired of reminding people, one of New York's "safest" police precincts, many people believed otherwise.[13]

People heard about crime in the park more consistently than crime in the streets in their newspapers and news magazines, on the radio, and on television. In 1973 the *Times*, a newspaper not noted for crime reporting, covered 3 of the 4 murders that occurred in the park but only about one-fifth of the 1,676 murders in the rest of the city.[14] That all three commercial television networks had their national headquarters within a short walk of Central Park further added to the publicity. In the 1960s when Johnny Carson made jokes about crime in Central Park a national pastime, he was speaking from a studio fewer than ten blocks away. Central Park was, in effect, the local park for the national media. And more than that, it served as a convenient national symbol for urban ills. News stories and jokes about crime in Central Park played well to a national audience because they reconfirmed a familiar "reality" for people living outside the city who would have not as readily paid attention to a story about crime in Tompkins Square or Van Cortlandt Park or on East 120th Street.

Like the old story of "man bites dog," crime in the park violated conventions, in this case pastoral conventions, making it news. "Crime in Central Park is usually exaggerated," the captain of the park police precinct commented in 1959. "It shocks people like crime in heaven." Journalists covered crime in the park for more than its shock value: a large number of rich and important, hence newsworthy, people lived at the park's doorstep, and if these people turned out to be crime victims, that was news. There is a long list of Central Park "celebrity" crime victims—John F. Kennedy, Jr., figure-skating champion Dick Button, Manhattan borough president Andrew Stein, Episcopal bishop Paul Moore, United Nations delegates from Nepal, Cyprus, France, and the Soviet Union. When the Soviet diplomat was mugged, park commissioner August Heckscher called it an "isolated" incident, but added wryly: "It's the first time they got a Russian."[15]

Central Park crime victims were also more newsworthy because they were more likely to be similar in background—meaning white and middle class—to the people who reported for the major newspapers and networks. In part, this well-known class and racial bias in crime coverage explains some of the attention focused on the two most publicized cases of Central Park crime—the murder of Jennifer Levin by Robert Chambers, Jr. (labeled the "preppy murder" by the press) in 1986 and the rape and near-fatal beating of a twenty-eight-

Local and national media reinforced the association of Central Park with crime through such headlines as this one from May 1989.

It was the ultimate urban nightmare. On a cool spring night a 28-year-old investment banker was out for her nightly jog in the park when as many as a dozen teenagers came out of the darkness. She could not escape—there were too many of them. They beat her savagely, raped her and left her for dead, their last casualty in a series of pack attacks that night. As their victim struggled for life, one of the suspects allegedly told police, "It was fun." Here is the story of a crime that shocked the nation—and roused a city to fury.

year-old investment banker, referred to anonymously in the press as the "Central Park jogger," by a gang of "wilding" teenagers from Harlem in 1989. As many critics of the coverage of the jogger case pointed out, equally brutal rapes in nearby Harlem are routinely ignored or downplayed by the media. Even within the park, not all crimes are equal. The vicious gang rapes of two homeless women in Central Park in 1984 had received only passing press attention.[16]

The complaints from black New Yorkers about the reporting of the jogger case echoed those made almost fifty years earlier by black newspapers about the 1941 "crime wave." They point us to the most controversial dimension of the reporting of park crime—the degree to which race enters into such stories. Crimes in which whites are the victims of nonwhite assailants invariably receive considerably more coverage than those in which African Americans or Puerto Ricans are the victims, even though they are considerably more likely to be crime victims than white New Yorkers.[17] Central Park, as one of the great interracial and interclass meeting grounds of New York, has received particularly close scrutiny as an arena for interpreting "race relations" through the prism of interracial crime.

The newspaper practice of placing park crime stories in a racial frame began before World War II as African Americans increasingly settled on the park's northern borders. In the postwar era newspapers and local television evening news shows played with particular intensity to white New Yorkers' anxieties about their changing city. Thousands of migrants from the South and Puerto Rico had transformed the Upper West Side, East Harlem, and Morningside Heights, while the East Side and Central Harlem had changed relatively little—the former still remaining almost entirely white, and the latter entirely black and Puerto Rican.[18]

Puerto Ricans arrived in particularly large numbers in the early 1950s, though at a slower rate than the massive influxes of eastern and southern European immigrants a half century before. Between 1950 and 1955, the Puerto Rican population of New York doubled, and two neighborhoods that adjoined the park—East Harlem and the Upper West Side—were especially popular destinations. In East Harlem, El Barrio had expanded through the district that had once housed large numbers of Jews and Italians. But the tensions were greater on the West Side, where the new Puerto Rican residents shared the neighborhood with a middle- and upper-middle-class white population. Affluent white residents filled the apartments along Central Park West, West End Avenue, and Riverside Drive; poor and working-class Puerto Ricans lived in the formerly Irish-occupied apartments on side streets.[19]

The departure from the city of more than one million middle-class white residents in the 1950s and 1960s (encouraged and subsidized by federal highway building, housing, and home-loan policies that favored suburban development) and the arrival of a comparable number of working-class black and Puerto Rican migrants reshaped many cities.[20] Yet New York's "inner city" (by this time including most of Manhattan) retained a much more substantial white middle- and upper-class population than others. In the 1950s and 1960s, on the West Side of Manhattan as well as in Central Park, New Yorkers of differing class, racial, and ethnic backgrounds lived together in close proximity.

As was true in earlier generations, some middle- and upper-class New Yorkers panicked. One Upper West Sider compared the arrival of Puerto Ricans in his neighborhood to "an invasion of red ants." In 1953 when the journalist Theodore H. White and his family returned to New York after five years in Europe, friends warned him that the West Side was "changing" and "in transition," phrases he recognized as meaning "that blacks and Puerto Ricans were moving in." He rented a three-bedroom apartment on the corner of 84th Street and Central Park West. "From his window," White wrote in the third person, "there was the vista of Central Park, the most splendid of all central-city parks anywhere in the world. . . . But down in the street, the microcosm of life he observed frightened him." His wife worried about her journeys to the nearby delicatessen, and "his children were not safe going to play in Central Park just below the window of his apartment house." Within a year, the Whites fled to the "other side of the park, on the safe white East Side"—"the perfumed stockade," as he called it.[21]

Others stayed to face what White called the "problem" of "two kinds of cultures contesting in the pressure of closed city apartment blocks" and (he

Father and daughter at the Central
Park Zoo.

might have added) an open city park. The yawning cultural gap between the two
groups could be seen in a letter of complaint that one Central Park West
resident sent to Robert Moses in 1955. "Young Puerto Ricans swing from the
sturdy healthy branches like monkeys," she told the park commissioner. Echo-
ing the language and the advice of those who had objected to the Jewish and
Italian immigrants in the early twentieth century, she proposed "a heavy fine for
destroying shrubbery—some stringent method to curb these people who are
not yet aware of the privilege of American citizenship and how it is to be
respected."[22] (The letter writer was herself apparently unaware that Puerto
Ricans are born to U.S. citizenship.)

Mutual distrust and intolerance did not always follow the color line featured
by the contemporary press or even the class line once emphasized by nineteenth-century newspapers. Dominant usage among whites tended to lump
together all African Americans and Puerto Ricans as "minorities" or "non-

As New York began to develop a Puerto Rican community, migrants like the Rodriguez family sought out fresh air and sunshine in the park.

whites," with the further assumption that all were poor. Yet among the black residents of the Upper West Side and Harlem were the families of doctors, lawyers, and ministers, long resident in the North, along with working-class and poor families recently arrived from the American South and the Caribbean. And black and Puerto Rican New Yorkers did not see themselves in the same "nonwhite" category; they jostled over housing, jobs, and "turf."[23]

In *Family Installments: Memories of Growing Up Hispanic,* Edward Rivera captures the mutual suspicion between African Americans and Puerto Ricans in 1950s New York in his description of a youthful Sunday morning outing in Central Park. He and a friend began the day by watching members of the Puerto Rican Baseball League play on the North Meadow, then headed northwest toward the Huddlestone Arch in search of girls and adventure. "The stream dipped and disappeared under a rise of large, jagged rocks which formed a natural bridge to the 'black' part of the park," Rivera writes. "People got killed there, I'd heard, women raped. . . . People from our side of the park, from our neighborhood, stayed away from that section. It was strictly for blacks. I seldom ventured there, never on my own." His disinclination to play "In Black Turf," as he titles the chapter, was reinforced when a group of black teenagers advised him to "stick to your side of the park."[24]

Class, racial, and ethnic tensions were not the only ones to find their way into the park in the 1940s, 1950s, and 1960s. Gay New Yorkers were newly seen as a danger after the war. Central Park had been a gathering place for gay men since at least the turn of the century. In the 1920s they called the open lawn at the northern end of the Ramble the "Fruited Plain." During the 1930s Cole Porter entertained friends at parties with song lyrics alluding to gay men in the park: "Picture Central Park—without a sailor, Picture Mister Lord, minus Mister Taylor." But few others commented on the gay presence in the park in those years. After all, most gay New Yorkers then took some pains to conceal their presence.[25]

During and after World War II, gay men seem to have cruised more openly. But the important change was not so much in the way gay men acted as in how they were perceived. A panic over sex crimes in the late 1940s and early 1950s helped displace the earlier stereotype of the effeminate "queer" as an object of ridicule with a new stereotype of the homosexual as a dangerous psychopath, a menace to young boys. In that atmosphere, gays faced increased surveillance and persecution, and arrests of men for homosexual activity skyrocketed in the late 1940s. In these postwar years, some of the local and national press prominently featured gays—invariably described as "perverts" or "misfits"—in their catalogs of the "dangers" of Central Park. "The Park has become not only a stalking ground for young predators and rapists," wrote Central Park West resident Marya Mannes in the *Reporter* in 1960. "It is a point of assignation for homosexuals, and I need go no further than my own window to see the figure of a man waiting behind a tree and later joined by another man, who walks with him under the heavy shadows of leaves and out of sight."[26]

For Mannes, as for others, such casual park meetings were another sign that "more violence and more perversity" were entering the park. In 1955 Robert Moses proposed transforming the Ramble into a recreational center for senior citizens, in part, apparently, because the Ramble was considered a gathering place for "anti-social persons." Joseph Lyford, who lived on the Upper West Side in the early 1960s, found that many black and Puerto Rican mothers lumped gays with addicts, prostitutes, and alcoholics in discussing their concerns about their children's safety: "One hears frequent stories about children being accosted in washrooms of movie theatres or in Central Park." Actually, gay park users were much more likely to be crime victims than victimizers; thugs, who knew that gay men frequented the park at night and that they were reluctant to go to the police because of a fear of public exposure, preyed on them in the Ramble.[27]

Fears about crime in Central Park seem to have reached a fever pitch by the late 1950s, *before* crime in the park began its steepest climb. Complaints about the dangers were commonplace in these years. In 1961 Ogden Nash even wrote a poem about them:

> If you should happen after dark
> To find yourself in Central Park,
> Ignore the paths that beckon you
> And hurry, hurry to the zoo,
> And creep into the tiger's lair.
> Frankly you'll be safer there.

Television commentator Barry Gray put matters more ominously: "If you value your life . . . [and] if you don't want to be killed or robbed or mugged—keep clear of Central Park, especially after nightfall." He told TV viewers in 1959 that "Central Park is a happy hunting ground taken over by the dope-happy hoodlum, the homosexual, the exhibitionist, the potential murderer. They're there all the time, on the benches, on the grass, lurking behind the trees and bushes. The park is one great open-air cesspool." Yet despite this rhetoric, between 1955 and 1964 there were no murders in the park.[28]

During the late 1960s and the early 1970s (when it peaked), crime in the park did increase dramatically in both absolute and relative terms. Between 1960 and 1970, felonies multiplied nineteen times, four times as fast as crime in the rest of the city. Park felonies as a proportion of citywide felonies were at their highest level in 1970 and then declined over the subsequent two decades.[29]

One might have expected the sharp increases in park crime in the 1960s to have further heightened the hysteria, but as far as we can tell from press discussions, fears actually seem to have diminished while crime itself was getting worse. The increase, in fact, may have been an indirect consequence of decreased fear; as more people went to the park in the late 1960s, crime went up. When the park association surveyed New Yorkers in 1963 about their attitudes toward parks, they found "fear" was "the overriding thought in most people's minds about parks in New York City: People who live in New York City *are afraid to use* their parks." Yet, a decade later—after Central Park's crime rate had risen eightfold—a telephone survey of 650 New Yorkers (mostly Manhattanites) found that only 16 percent avoided the park because of concerns about their safety.[30]

In the end, the story of crime in the park over the past half century is as much the story of perceptions as of realities, of fears as much as criminal acts. Murders, rapes, robberies, always serious, did become more common, particularly during the 1960s and 1970s. Yet even at the worst, the problem of crime in Central Park always paled in comparison with the larger problem of crime in the city. But perception and fear were especially important in relation to park crime because many city dwellers tend to view any unfamiliar urban terrain—spaces filled with people different from themselves or outside their own neighborhoods and workplaces—as threatening.

Thus, in order for New Yorkers to perceive Central Park as safe, they had to learn to share the city's most important public space with people of different classes and backgrounds. Only gradually and unevenly did they learn this difficult lesson in the postwar years. It meant, in effect, rethinking—and opening up—the meaning of the park's cultural public. Many New Yorkers apparently came to view Central Park as relatively safe as they grew more comfortable with people of different backgrounds and came to accept that black and Puerto Rican teenagers or gay men, as such, were not intruders there.

This cultural change took place within the context of a shifting organization of the park's political public. At the same time that New Yorkers redefined the boundaries of acceptable park use and park users, they also redefined (more than once, in fact) the contours of park management and control. That process of rethinking who should set park policy began in the 1950s, as some New Yorkers began to challenge the man who had been the uncontested lord of the city parks since the depths of the Great Depression.

The Mothers Defeat Moses

On Wednesday, April 18, 1956, every newspaper in New York ran a photo of a crowd of mothers, children, and baby carriages blocking a bulldozer on a grassy knoll just inside the wall of Central Park at West 67th Street. "Central Park Mothers Vanquish Bulldozer Set to Raze Play Area" read the *New York Times* headline for a story that explained how "embattled mothers" had won the first round in a struggle to keep the autocratic park commissioner Robert Moses from constructing an eighty-car parking lot for the Tavern on the Green restaurant. This tiny (0.4 acre) play space meant a great deal to the West Side mothers massed in front of the bulldozers.[31]

Over on the other side of the park, nannies cared for children of the rich. Close observers could notice a hierarchy among the East Side nannies; at the 77th Street and Fifth Avenue playground, Tom Wolfe wrote, the English and French nannies ranked highest. "The poor Negro nannies," he quotes a (presumably invented) socialite as saying, "just have to sit off by themselves." The only person "lower than the Negro nannies," she continues, "is a mother who brings her own baby into the 77th Street playground. I mean it! At least the Negro nanny has probably been hired by a reasonably good family. But a mother who has to bring her own baby into the playground is absolutely *nothing!*" Except, of course, on Wednesdays, on the nannies' day off; then East Side mothers took over the playground.[32]

The mostly middle-class West Side mothers brought their own children to the park. In the 1950s few middle-class mothers held paid jobs and even fewer fathers watched the children. And in the heyday of the "baby boom"—the birth rate would reach its postwar peak in 1957—there were plenty of children to watch. (Women coming of age in the 1950s had an average of 3.2 children, a one-third increase over the norm twenty years earlier.)[33]

For the urban mothers of the West Side, therefore, any threat to their play space was a threat indeed. The knoll Moses had designated as the site of a new parking lot was right next to one of the fenced-in perimeter playgrounds he had added to the park in the 1930s. Only children under eight could play there. On a row of benches to the east of the playground, the mothers sat and chatted with one another as they watched younger children on the swings and slides of the playground and their older children romping on the nearby grass. "You know," one of the mothers explained, "at that time in your life, your life centers around your children. We *lived* in that little spot in the park. We took our kids twice a day. . . . That little spot in the park was really the center of our neighborhood. . . . You know, in a city like New York, a spot like that is really precious."[34]

The mothers had learned of the threat to their little patch of greenery two days before, when one discovered the parking lot blueprints an engineer had carelessly left on the ground when he went off to lunch. Almost immediately the mothers wrote up a petition. By Friday they were rallying in front of the Tavern on the Green. Moses promised a quick reply to their petition, but his reply turned out to be a bulldozer. Early Tuesday morning it arrived, and the mothers, with babies in tow, stood in front of it.[35]

The newspapers began to call it "The Battle of Central Park." The mothers turned back parks department bulldozers on two more days, but six days later, on April 24, a crew sneaked in at 1:30 A.M., and before daylight, they had surrounded the play area with a snow fence and had begun bulldozing the trees.[36]

The papers screamed outrage, and so did ordinary citizens. On just one day four thousand letters of protest were piled on Mayor Robert Wagner's desk. The clamor grew louder as the papers turned a spotlight on the cozy financial deal enjoyed by the Tavern on the Green's concessionaire and on the high prices the restaurant charged. Reporters noted the chauffeur-driven Cadillacs parked outside, the society orchestras inside, and dinner tabs of more than twenty dollars for two. Moses found himself defending a restaurant that hardly welcomed the "general public." (In desperation, Moses and his men even turned to the Olmstedian legacy, for which they ordinarily had little use. A parks department aide was dispatched to the New-York Historical Society to look up what Olmsted and Vaux had to say about restaurants in the park; back from the historical trenches, the aide reported that "quite a number of people have been consulting the Olmsted Central Park material during the last few weeks," and he admitted, "I believe that the other side will find more usable quotes than we will in this present situation.")[37]

Three months and a court battle later, Moses surrendered and restored the play space intact. As Moses' biographer Robert Caro explains, his defeat in the Battle of Central Park was a turning point in his previously unblemished career:

Mothers and Bulldozers, 1956: Dramatic photos such as this helped to galvanize opposition to Robert Moses' plan for a parking lot near the Tavern on the Green restaurant.

"Tuesday, April 24, 1956, the day that Robert Moses sent his troops into Central Park, was Robert Moses' black Tuesday. For on it, he lost his most cherished asset: his reputation."[38] The West Side mothers had not meant to topple Robert Moses; they simply wanted a say in the fate of their park space. Still, their actions initiated a gradual expansion of the park's political public to include a more diverse range of contentious groups.

Since the early 1930s Moses had been able to impose his will on the park with little fear of serious opposition. Only an occasional dissent was heard. One came in 1951 when the social and architectural critic Lewis Mumford denounced in the *New Yorker* "the remaking of Central Park," which had been "going on, sometimes ruthlessly, for the last twenty years." Mumford believed that "the worst taste of suburbia" and an inclination toward "firm, man-made boundaries—iron fences, concrete curbs, heavy wooden boundaries," and "dull buildings and prisonlike enclosures" had blighted the park. But his was a lone voice. The park association and the *New York Times* continued to side with Moses.[39]

Moses had made his most dramatic imprint on Central Park in the 1930s.

Private philanthropy enabled Moses to keep building in the park after relief funds had dried up. In 1949 Kate Wollman donated money for a skating rink at Sixth Avenue and 63rd Street, where popular rock concerts also were held in the 1970s.

Using his command of relief workers and federal money, he had steered the park toward providing active recreational facilities and had rationalized design and operations to make for cheaper and more efficient maintenance. He continued to introduce organized play space after World War II, as Iphigene Sulzberger found out when she walked across the Great Lawn in 1950. But the park received less attention from Moses in the last two decades of his twenty-six-year rule as commissioner. He became preoccupied with grander enterprises, constructing new highways, bridges, tunnels, housing projects, and hydroelectric dams. Moses liked to build, and the big money in the postwar era was for roads, urban renewal, and power projects rather than parks. He had substantially less to spend on parks in the 1940s and 1950s than in the era of work relief projects. Each year Moses had campaigned for more funds, while park appropriations grew only slowly, and even declined as a percentage of the total city budget.[40]

Still, Moses had managed to keep building in Central Park by turning from the public to the private purse. The park, after all, sat in the middle of one of the largest concentrations of personal wealth in the world. Moses persuaded

In the era of the baby boom, facilities like the Carousel and the skating rink attracted families to the park.

wealthy foundations and the individuals in the townhouses and luxury apartments along the park's eastern flank to support new park facilities. He suggested that donors might attach their names to the new buildings their money made possible. Kate Wollman, daughter of a wealthy stockbroker, for example, contributed $600,000 in 1949 to build the ice-skating rink that Moses had first proposed in 1945, and it was called the Wollman Rink.[41]

In the 1950s other donations replaced the old wooden boathouse at 72nd Street, the frame model-boat house at the Conservatory Water, and the burned-out Carousel with the new brick Loeb and Kerbs boathouses and the Friedsam Carousel. Private largess provided the Levy and Osborne playgrounds; the Chess and Checkers House at 64th Street, just west of the Dairy, given anonymously by the financier Bernard Baruch; and almost half the money for the Delacorte Theater (the home of free Shakespeare performances, located just southwest of the Great Lawn). But the gift with the most dramatic impact on the park's landscape—the massive Lasker swimming pool and ice-skating rink at the southwestern end of the Harlem Meer in the northern park—came in 1962 to Moses' successor, though no doubt Moses had approved. One nostalgic counterman at the old boathouse muttered, "Phil-an-thro-pists!

Nothing is safe from them," but most New Yorkers welcomed the private gifts to the public parks. In the 1950s Wollman Rink attracted about 300,000 people a year and another 150,000 rode the Friedsam Carousel. Even when fears about park safety were at their worst in the late 1950s and early 1960s, millions of New Yorkers continued to use the park regularly.[42]

The only other Moses park project to spark serious opposition was the Lasker Senior Citizen Center, an indoor-outdoor recreation complex planned to cover fourteen acres of the Ramble. In a 1955 preview of the playground battle to come, a determined group of bird watchers held off the encroaching concrete. But in this case, the Florina Lasker Foundation, which offered the gift, and not Moses, backed away in the face of the negative publicity.[43]

The pressure of the West Side mothers and the bird watchers in 1955 and 1956 was gradually expanding control over the park beyond the authority of the one man who had governed it for the past two decades. At around the same time, another determined group—the park workers—brought a new measure of democracy to the autocratic parks department. Moses had forged a mutually beneficial alliance with the building trades unions on behalf of his massive construction projects, but he had little use for unions, or for most workers for that matter. He and his lieutenants often insisted on seventy-two-hour work-weeks (with no overtime pay). When it rained, outdoor workers were sent home without pay. He ran the parks department like a military operation, requiring unquestioning compliance with his rigid rules and using spies to report infractions of discipline. And then there was the uniform: the green visored cap, long-sleeved green shirt, black tie, jacket with a maple-leaf patch, and polished brown shoes. Park workers, even those hauling trash and debris, had to wear the full regalia. In unannounced inspections, park officials would demand to "see your socks." If they were not green, workers found themselves before a disciplinary board for being "out of uniform."[44]

Park workers were among the most eager recruits in the early 1950s organizing drive of District Council 37 of the American Federation of State, County, and Municipal Employees. The result was Local 924, dominated by blue-collar workers (mostly Irish and Italian Americans) from the parks department. It was soon "the largest and most influential local" in DC 37, as union historians point out. Moses, who had long obstructed collective bargaining, refused to talk to the union, but in 1953 Robert Wagner, Jr., was elected mayor. His father had sponsored the federal legislation that recognized labor's right to collective bargaining. Indeed the Wagner Act had been crucial to the New Deal upsurge in unionization and the political activism that established the claims of industrial workers to membership in the political public. Eager to demonstrate his own prolabor credentials, Mayor Wagner promptly issued an executive order that, in principle at least, gave collective bargaining rights to public workers. The order had little immediate effect on Robert Moses, who saw himself as independent of any directives from the mayor's office. But Jerry Wurf of DC 37 and the park workers of Local 924 changed his mind. Wurf had proved remarkably success-

"Bob Moses' Zoo," 1955: Park workers protest Moses' resistance to their unionization.

ful in signing up park laborers and recreation workers. The union won their loyalty with its attacks on Moses' rule and its effective adversarial role in testifying at disciplinary hearings and the salary appeals board. Still, only a successful confrontation could gain the workers real bargaining rights, and state law forbade public employee strikes and mandated the dismissal of striking workers.[45]

The union decided, therefore, on a one-day job action. On November 3, 1955, more than two thousand park workers ignored their usual assignments and assembled at the Central Park Arsenal, each requesting a day's leave of absence. The workers picketed with signs denouncing Moses' refusal to comply with Mayor Wagner's labor-relations code. In a photograph the newspapers found irresistible, the park workers created an emblematic picture, mounting a steel cage labeled "Bob Moses' Zoo," on a flatbed truck with several uniformed park workers behind the bars. Under the cage appeared the "animals'" identification:

SPECIES:	Park Worker
HABITAT:	New York City Parks
CHARACTERISTICS:	Resembles Normal American Worker BUT

- HAS NO COLLECTIVE BARGAINING
- HAS NO GRIEVANCE MACHINERY
- HAS NO DIGNITY ON THE JOB
- WORKS FOR ABSENTEE OWNER

Pressed by Mayor Wagner and the bad publicity, Moses reluctantly agreed to a union election, the first ever granted by a city department. In early 1956, DC 37 won an overwhelming victory, with all but a handful of park workers selecting it as their representative. The victory over Moses, as Jewel and Bernard Bellush write in their history of DC 37, was "a turning point" for the union, establishing its stature among city workers and convincing them that unionization could succeed. When DC 37 undertook its first full-scale strike five years later, park workers (specifically the zoo keepers, who brought their monkeys and pythons to the picket line) led the way. Years later when the union newspaper, the *Public Employee Press*, told the story of the rise of DC 37 in New York, the headline trumpeted: "Who Built This Union? Robert Moses!"[46]

For nearly a century New Yorkers who used Central Park had given little recognition to the workers who produced it. It had taken the labor upsurge of the 1880s and participation in the Henry George campaign for workers to win some limited influence in politics; now, with union recognition, organized workers became a major force in city politics, full members of the political public. Their interests would have to be considered in future decisions about the management of Central Park.

The victories of the park workers, like that of the park mothers and the bird watchers, signaled the beginning of the end of Moses' dominion. "His imperial majesty, Robert Moses," Wurf had told cheering park workers, would now be forced to operate the parks department "on the same basis as any other" city agency. Moses was far from powerless after 1956, but he had lost what Caro calls his "aura of invincibility." His schemes for more bricks and concrete in Central Park, earlier easily achieved, now met more opposition. The two-story glassed-in cafe he solicited from grocery chain heir Huntington Hartford for the park's southeastern corner met sharp criticism and was never built.[47]

Perhaps Moses' most publicized defeat in Central Park came in 1959 in the fight over free Shakespeare in the park, which Joseph Papp began in 1957. Moses' zealous aide Stuart Constable had developed a deep dislike for Papp, in large part because of the producer's radical political associations and his combative testimony before the House Committee on Un-American Activities. Moses actually liked the idea of free Shakespeare in the park, but he stood behind Constable in his insistence that Papp reimburse the parks department for maintenance costs. Papp could do so only if he charged admission. In a reprise of the battles over unionization and the Tavern parking lot, negative publicity forced Moses to back down a third time. Free Shakespeare continued in the park.[48]

Moses did not. In May 1960 he resigned his park post to begin planning the 1964 New York World's Fair. True, his replacement, Newbold Morris, a devout admirer of Moses, consulted him before making any big decisions. (Morris was the first person to be described as having been "born with a silver foot in his mouth"—a tag that expressed the popular view of him as wealthy and ineffectual.) Although Morris enthusiastically promoted the extensive calendar of recreational programs Moses had introduced in Central Park—from fall harvest dances to top-spinning contests—the era of Moses' rule over the city's parks was coming to a close.[49]

Muste at the Mall and Freaks at the Fountain

On March 26, 1966, ten thousand people gathered on Central Park Mall to hear the Reverend A. J. Muste, the eighty-one-year-old pacifist leader, and other speakers in a three-hour rally to protest the war in Vietnam. The rally culminated in a march of more than twenty thousand demonstrators down Fifth Avenue. That 1966 protest turned out to be an important moment in American opposition to the Vietnam War. The day also marked an important moment in the history of Central Park. It was the first oppositional political event held there since the 1914 women's suffrage meeting and only the second in the park's entire history.[50]

Oddly, no one seems to have paid much attention to the decisive change in park policy. Five months earlier, when city officials went to court to block demonstrators seeking to use the park for a similar antiwar rally, park commissioner Morris had explained that no "political" rallies were allowed in Central Park, only commemorative rallies like those of the Steuben Society or patriotic rallies like those on Citizenship ("I Am an American") Day. True, in 1945 Harry Truman had given a foreign-policy address before one million people gathered on the Sheep Meadow. But Morris did not consider that a "political" event. In 1965 the courts upheld the commissioner's right to deny the permit to the antiwar protesters, but now the parks department itself reversed its policy and permitted Muste's antiwar demonstration. There were reasons. Apparently, the police pushed for an easing of the restriction because they wanted to avoid a repetition of the massive traffic jam resulting from the huge rally on 69th Street between Lexington and Park avenues that followed the court's earlier denial.[51]

Another reason was the growing political force of the antiwar "movement" (now becoming an appropriate description). Between October 1965 and March 1966, the number prepared to march against the war more than doubled. Those same five months had also seen a dramatic transformation in Central Park's management, and the new regime was more willing to listen to antiwar protesters. Just a couple of weeks after the October 1966 antiwar protest, silk-stocking liberal John V. Lindsay swept into office as a "reform" mayor, the first Republican mayor of the city since Fiorello La Guardia. Lindsay's choice for park commissioner, Thomas P. F. Hoving, a curator at the Cloisters, the medieval branch of the Metropolitan Museum of Art, turned out to be one of his most important appointments.

Park Commissioner Thomas Hoving at Cedar Hill "Paint-In," May 15, 1966.

Like his two immediate predecessors, Hoving came from a wealthy family: his father was the chairman of Tiffany's and his mother was the daughter of a wealthy real estate broker. Also like them, he was a Republican, although he and Morris stood on the liberal side of their party, whereas Moses by the 1960s leaned toward the conservative wing. All three were products of prep schools and the Ivy League, although Hoving was a Princeton man in contrast to his Yalie predecessors. But Hoving was quite literally of a different generation from Moses and Morris, just thirty-four years old when he moved from his office at the Cloisters to the Central Park Arsenal. And he chose aides even younger than himself, including Henry Stern (a future park commissioner) as executive director. Hailing a "New Era for Parks," the *Times*'s architecture critic, Ada Louise Huxtable, proclaimed that the "Young Turks have taken over the Arsenal."[52] Although Hoving was in office for barely a year before moving on to direct the Metropolitan Museum, the impact of his regime was at least as dramatic as Moses' own extraordinary first year in office.

Dramatic, but a good deal less concrete. In his first year, Moses had opened forty new playgrounds and began work on twenty more (of the six hundred fifty added during his tenure). Hoving built twelve new "vest-pocket" parks and renovated several playgrounds. But if Moses was the city's greatest park builder, Hoving was its greatest park promoter. In just one year, his staff filled fifty-two scrapbooks with clippings chronicling his exploits in office. Hoving's "happenings" attracted thousands to Central Park to fly kites, celebrate Halloween, observe a meteor shower, throw paint on 105 yards of canvas, and compete in a "Central Park au Go-Go" dance concert. The season's first band concert had attracted five hundred people in 1965; thirty-five thousand came in 1966 for Hoving's Gay Nineties party.[53]

"Build Your Own Castle" Happening, October 23, 1966: Note Belvedere Castle in background.

Hoving's detractors pointed to serious maintenance problems and staff shortages and joked that his middle initials, P. F., stood for "Publicity Forever." Park workers, for their part, charged that Hoving ignored seniority rules and contract provisions and failed to fill vacancies. Victor Gotbaum, executive director of DC 37, which by now represented most of the city's park workers, called Hoving "an intelligent and personable young man [who] doesn't know what the hell is going on with the working men and women in the Department of Parks." Park preservationist Robert Makla protested Hoving's lack of respect for grass and trees, but he admitted that the commissioner's "achievement was the great awakening of the public to the word 'parks.' It was a stupendous achievement."[54]

Hoving's most lasting impact on Central Park arose from an experiment in the summer of 1966, when he closed the park's roads to cars on summer Sundays. The policy gradually expanded to embrace other days and other times of the year. Perhaps no action better symbolized the contrast to Moses, who was legendary for his devotion to the automobile—even though he never drove himself. Moses had realigned park drives, added a number of parking lots, and increased the acreage of paved walks and drives by one-third.[55]

Hoving and his young assistants offered an alternative to what they called the

Bicycling in the Park: Commissioner Thomas Hoving's Sunday road closings brought thousands of bicyclists into the park and dramatized the shift from the pro-automobile policies of Moses.

"conformity" and "chain-link fence" mentality of the Moses era. Moses, of course, had little use for the "hippie happenings" and derided his successor as a "recreational leftist." But remarkably and suddenly, Moses' formidable reputation seemed to crumble. Almost overnight, his once-celebrated playgrounds were "junk" compared to the exciting "Adventure Playgrounds" that young architects such as Paul Friedberg and Richard Dattner were adding to Central Park and other public spaces. Almost overnight, Moses had become "The Maintenance Man," who had worried only about costs.[56]

When Hoving took office he appointed the architectural historian Henry Hope Reed to the new unsalaried post of curator of Central Park. Hoving, who had come to admire Olmsted (though not apparently Vaux, whom he barely mentioned) from his Princeton art history classes, wanted a curator who would care for the park as "an artistic entity" like a "a painting or sculpture." In Reed he had found a fierce and knowledgeable guardian of the Olmstedian *and* Vauxian tradition, and of tradition in general. Reed, an ardent advocate of classical architecture, had once described modern architecture, along with the Great Depression and Prohibition, as the "three greatest disasters to hit New York." He had also been one of the few public critics of the changes that Moses brought to Central Park.[57]

But Hoving's changes also displeased Reed. In October 1966 he sent Hoving a memo blasting his beloved happenings as "grotesque travesties" and "desecrations of Central Park." Their promoters, Reed suggested, had never "heard of Olmsted and Vaux" or even glanced "at the history of American landscape architecture"; otherwise, they would "not desecrate one of the finest American examples of public art." Hoving dismissed Reed's criticisms as "none of his business," scrawling "Crap!" across the top of the memo. Reed eventually made his complaints public and became a gadfly to Hoving and his successor, August Heckscher. And a small number of influential New Yorkers came to believe that Hoving had strayed too far from Reed's view that "what makes the park is the landscape, the green lawns, leafy vistas, and mirrors of water."[58]

August Heckscher, who took over as park commissioner in March 1967, was even more firmly committed to Hoving's version of the eclectic pleasure garden, in contrast to Reed's pastoral park or Moses' progressive, recreational park. Although eighteen years older than Hoving, Heckscher (the grandson of the philanthropist who provided the park's first playground and yet another Yale alumnus) warmly welcomed the young people who had responded most enthusiastically to Hoving's innovations at Central Park. In an earlier position as director of the Twentieth Century Fund, he had sponsored discussions of encounter groups and new forms of communal organization, and he wrote a sympathetic series of lectures on the New Left and the youth movement, "More News from Nowhere—Notes on a New Utopia."[59]

Soon after he took office, Heckscher relates in his memoirs, a delegation of "flower children"—"perhaps the weirdest in dress and speech ever to have entered the fortresslike tower of the Arsenal"—demanded a permit for an Easter "love-in" on the Sheep Meadow. Heckscher responded that "it seemed contradictory to want a bureaucrat's blessing" to hold such an unbureaucratic event. Instead, he said, in effect: "Come in. . . . Central Park is open to all; the Sheep Meadow is a natural gathering place, and as long as you do not flagrantly offend taste or break the laws no one will disturb you."[60]

The hippies—and many others—took Heckscher up on his extraordinary invitation. To be sure, even a sterner and less accepting public official could not have held back the new generation of young people (perhaps the children of the West Side mothers who had fought Moses for play space) intent on breaking down the rules that defined proper behavior in public spaces. In the nineteenth century guardians of morality had frowned at couples "caressing each other under an umbrella"; in the 1960s couples occasionally made love on the Sheep Meadow—without any umbrellas to signal a desire for privacy. Whereas in the 1950s Moses had enforced rules against wearing bathing suits or even halter tops and shorts shorter than midthigh, some park visitors now stripped off everything. Even more shocking to conventional sensibilities was that some of the public displays of affection were not by heterosexual couples. Just one year after the 1969 Stonewall riots that launched the modern lesbian and gay liberation movement, thousands of lesbians and gays marched from Greenwich Village to Central Park to hold a "gay-in" on the Sheep Meadow.[61]

Part of the point of the "love-ins" and "be-ins" and "fat-ins" that filled the park was to challenge playfully the conventions of "appropriate" public behavior.[62] Bethesda Fountain became particularly popular with crowds who gathered to flaunt their sexuality, play guitars, smoke marijuana, and hurl Frisbees. For the first time in its history the park offered a gathering place both for political radicals like the antiwar demonstrators and for cultural radicals. A park originally designed to exemplify the city's official culture now opened its gates to powerful alternative and oppositional "countercultures."

The Bethesda Fountain "scene" attracted young African Americans from Harlem and Puerto Ricans from El Barrio as well as the white hippies. The new enthusiasm for bicycling probably also encouraged gradual desegregation within the park, as bicyclists rode through the sections of the northern park that white New Yorkers had generally left to African Americans and Puerto Ricans. Although sharp racial tensions remained, tolerance was an integral feature of the youth culture of the period. And young black and Latino New Yorkers, imbued with the ethos of civil rights and "Black Power," were no longer prepared to accept the older racial lines that had confined them to particular neighborhoods or sections of Central Park.[63]

Whereas increased racial mixing had frightened New Yorkers away from the park in the 1950s, now it accompanied an expansion of park use. Press coverage probably exaggerated the degree to which park use went up in the late 1960s, for the mass events staged by Hoving and Heckscher, the hippies, and the closing of the park to cars were newsworthy in a way that the ordinary visits of millions of New Yorkers to the zoo, the playgrounds, the ball fields, and the Wollman Rink in the 1950s were not.

Still, the late 1960s did swell park attendance, particularly on weekends. And the crowds and excitement promoted Heckscher's own goals of reclaiming the "public sphere" (which he preferred to 1950s-style "domestic pleasures") and encouraging a "freer and happier use of the parks." A *Times* reporter visiting the park on the last summer weekend in 1968 observed "uncounted thousands of New Yorkers" as they "whirred by on bicycles, cantered their horses on the dusty bridle path, raced down the cracked asphalt on skateboards, . . . tossed footballs, kicked soccer balls, sidearmed frisby discs, played tennis, fished, sailed model boats, rowed real ones, danced, sang, ate picnic lunches, bought pizzas, visited the zoo, waved balloons, barked at their children and played with their dogs, flirted, necked, and watched one another doing all these things." Around Bethesda Fountain, "the liveliest [area] in the park," a Caribbean band played as legal and illegal vendors worked the crowd.[64]

In past decades the eclectic energies of the streets had spilled over into the park *despite* the best efforts of city officials. Now, those same officials deliberately encouraged and even invited acrobats, jugglers, peripatetic musicians, bike racers, marionette shows, Latin music groups, and displays of handicrafts and "kinetic art." Rigid rules were either abandoned or not enforced. On the city beaches, Heckscher literally took an axe to the old signs that spelled out forbidden acts with a giant "NO." The new signs simply said: "ENJOY." In

Central Park he abolished the rules requiring men to wear shirts and artists to have permits to sketch. He also made it much easier for people to get permits to take fashion photographs, to play music, or to put on a show. In response to criticism, Heckscher explained that whereas Moses thinks of parks "as a place to keep off the grass" and Reed thinks of parks "as places where history was enacted a hundred years ago," "I think of parks as a place for people."[65]

Although much of the new energy and excitement came from a loosely constituted counterculture, the results were not necessarily unsettling to the status quo. Newspaper headlines celebrating "Central Park's New Era: Fun for Everyone" fit nicely with Lindsay's efforts to package New York as "fun city" and himself as the exemplar of a new, youthful, shirt-sleeved urban liberalism that could solve the problems of the cities and the nation.[66] The "new" Central Park was also good business for two of the city's largest industries: fashion and tourism.

The *Times* fashion page described Bethesda Fountain as "a proving grounds of avant-garde fashions." "The styles you see here will be populating the country in six months," a fashion designer told a reporter. Just as in the 1860s carriage designers went to the park to see the latest in carriage fashions, so in the 1960s clothing designers and buyers went to the park to see the latest combinations of floppy hats, pink capes, round European sunglasses, sheepskin vests, and bell-bottom jeans. Out-of-towners, who only recently had been warned to stay away from Central Park, showed up to see what all the excitement was about. "There aren't many people like this in Alabama," two young women from Birmingham explained to a reporter. At the same time that Central Park's crime rate was rising dramatically, the news media decided that fear no longer stalked the park. A *Newsweek* article celebrating "Freak Fountain" as the "craziest, gayest, gathering place in the city," noted that only "four years ago it was just another part of a park that had a reputation for muggings."[67]

Not everyone was as enthusiastic as the *Newsweek* reporters. As opposition to the war in Vietnam heated up, more conservative New Yorkers viewed the shaggy young people with growing disgust. Bronx Republican leader Paul Fino attacked Lindsay for giving "the city's punks, vietniks and banana-sniffers, flag burning rights in Central Park." Certain other New Yorkers—particularly wealthy residents of Fifth Avenue and Central Park West—viewed the new park users as untidy and "unattractive." At least some residents of the expensive Dakota Apartments, Stephen Birmingham writes, considered "the new egalitarianism of Central Park . . . a perversion of democracy," which had brought "all the wrong people" to "*their* Park." Euphoric after one park festival, Heckscher found himself berated by an elderly woman: "Commissioner, how could you ever do such a thing—encouraging all these *ruffians* to come into the park!"[68]

Even Heckscher began to have some second thoughts as young people became less "mellow" and more aggressively political in the late 1960s. In

Antiwar demonstrations like this one in 1967 on the Sheep Meadow made the park a center of political protest.

effect, the counterculture had become more counter than Heckscher or Hoving had envisioned. The Youth International Party or "Yippies," a politicized hippie group formed in 1968, chose Central Park as one of their gathering places. "Every year," the *Village Voice* commented of the now-annual Easter Sunday Be-In, "it gets a little larger, slightly more exaggerated, a bit further out, a mite more bizarre, and altogether hairier than the year before." The organizers of the 1967 Easter Love-In had presented to Commissioner Heckscher a gift of multicolored Easter eggs. The 1969 replay gave him only headaches. One young man was hospitalized after he stripped off his clothes and leapt into a bonfire that had been built in the middle of the Sheep Meadow with fences, tree branches, and police barricades. Earlier in the day some celebrants who had congregated at "Hippie Hill" (the outcropping of rock in the southeast corner of the Sheep Meadow) fought with police, shouting "grab the pigs" after officers attempted to arrest a man who threw rocks at them. (The counterculture also infected some police; in 1971 one park patrolman was arrested for growing marijuana behind the police stable.) Contrasting the "innocence and joy" of 1967 with the "senseless, destructive movement" of 1969, Heckscher complained that the hippies "had no respect for the park, or for nature, or even for themselves."[69]

On April 15, 1967, the Sheep Meadow served as a staging area for more than a hundred thousand demonstrators who were to march behind Martin Luther King and Benjamin Spock to the United Nations in the largest antiwar protest to date. The demonstrators damaged grass and shrubs—though perhaps not as much as did the presidential helicopters that began using the Sheep Meadow as a landing pad around this time—and violated park rules by carrying banners and selling literature. And they offended conservative New Yorkers by burning draft cards and an American flag and chanting: "Hey, Hey, L.B.J., How Many Kids Did You Kill Today."[70] Over the past century Central Park had been a place where presidents—from to Rutherford B. Hayes to Harry Truman—had received warm welcomes. Now, it served as a staging ground for those seeking to topple a president, a public space for overt political protest.

Heckscher (although a civil libertarian and an opponent of the war) tried to ban such gatherings as interfering with "the enjoyment of the people in the park," but he was overruled by Mayor Lindsay, who was perhaps worried about retaining the support of the growing antiwar movement as well as accommodating the need of the police for large spaces that would permit effective crowd control. A year later, Lindsay's Urban Action Task Force, presumably with a nervous eye toward a repetition of the 1964 riot in Harlem, permitted a Poor People's Rally on the Sheep Meadow, the same space Heckscher had previously promised for a Girl Scout Jamboree. "The basic problem," he wrote the mayor, "is: who has jurisdiction over parks and who is empowered to make determination as to park use?"[71]

How did one weigh the competing claims of the Poor People's movement and the Girl Scouts to use Central Park? And who should do the weighing? "This responsibility clearly lies with the Commissioner of Parks, and I do not intend to give it up," Heckscher told Lindsay. But city officials (including Heckscher) were now prepared to listen to new and unconventional voices—hippies, antiwar protesters, welfare rights organizers—in deciding park policy. When Heckscher spoke about considering the "public benefit" of proposed uses of the park, he was embracing a much broader concept of the public than had any previous park commissioner.[72]

Culturally and politically New Yorkers claimed Central Park as a space of free expression and democratic dissent. Some believed such new uses violated the park's definition as a place of relaxation and play, but others considered the park an important arena in which to engage the city's public in vital debate. But as the conflict between the Girl Scouts and the Poor People's movement revealed, Heckscher and the rest of the Lindsay administration had not worked out a systematic way to choose among conflicting claims. The late 1960s saw both centralization and decentralization in the parks department's decision making. On the one hand, the department was now merged into a "super-agency" that oversaw cultural affairs as well as parks and recreation. On the other hand, the Lindsay administration experimented with decentralization. The city had established community planning boards in the early 1950s, but they remained largely dormant over the next two decades. Then in 1969 the boards won expanded responsibilities, including oversight of changes in parks and land use. Lindsay and his aides also set up neighborhood task forces, neighborhood city halls, and neighborhood action programs as other ways of bringing decision making closer to ordinary New Yorkers.[73]

In the final analysis, political scientist Ira Katznelson argues, these experiments did much more to contain and redirect the discontent that swept through the city in the late 1960s than to democratize local government. Moreover, Central Park posed particular problems for a program of decentralization; it touched several different neighborhoods (and five different community boards), but it also served as a gathering place for the whole city. These strong and competing claims put considerable pressure on even a commissioner like Heckscher, who was avowedly sympathetic to expanded use of the park and decentralized decision making. "Sometimes, I confess," Heckscher wrote later, "I envied the parks commissioner of old, who could dispose of things around his empire with a more or less free hand. . . . With me, everything seemed to be alive. Touch a tree or a fence, and a whole community would be aroused."[74]

The problem in relation to Central Park was that the "whole community" included those who wanted to preserve the park as a repository of nineteenth-century design and manners and those who wanted to turn it into a headquarters of political or cultural revolution. Heckscher gradually came to see the need to say no, to set limits on uses and users. Yet, even in retrospect, he insisted that "to [have] put tidiness as the first or only consideration" would have ignored "the big things that were happening" and "seemed a betrayal of the city's best hope." "The wear and tear on the grass, or even the inevitable litter waiting to be picked up, seemed a small price to pay" for the excitement that had infused the Sheep Meadow and other park spaces.[75]

Some New Yorkers—particularly the small but growing number who had signed up with the Friends of Central Park, a preservation group Henry Hope Reed and others had organized in 1966—were not so sure. They worried that the parks department was spending too much money on happenings and festivals and not enough on maintaining the grass, the shrubs, and the trees. In the 1970s, those concerns would grow when it became clear that the city no longer had any money.[76]

In the 1970s the San Juan Festival and other ethnic gatherings found a place in Central Park.

Hard Times and Hard Choices

On June 22, 1975, thousands of Puerto Rican families gathered in Central Park for the San Juan Festival, a religious and communal celebration of the feast day of St. John the Baptist, the patron saint of Puerto Rico. This was first time the festival had been held in the park instead of on Randall's Island. Organizers proclaimed it a great success, but park officials complained that the celebrants left behind piles of garbage and the remnants of illegal barbecue fires. Estimating that the cleanup would cost at least eight thousand dollars, Park Commissioner Edwin Weisl, Jr. (appointed in 1974 by Mayor Abraham Beame) decreed that the festival's organizers would forfeit the three-thousand-dollar security bond they had posted.[77]

"Any Monday people say it is a mess in Central Park," protested the Reverend Joaquim Beaumont, director of the Spanish Apostolate for the Archdiocese of New York. "As a matter of fact, when we started the festival, we had to clean the mall area." Charging that Commissioner Weisl "wants to use the

Puerto Rican community as scapegoats," the festival's executive committee pointed out that organizers had spent three hours cleaning the area with "our bare hands," because the parks department had not provided any cleaning "instruments or tools." When Weisl boosted the amount of the security bond required for a Puerto Rican festival planned for August, Victor M. Sorrentini, head of the festival committee, complained that Puerto Ricans were being unfairly singled out by the parks department: "We have the same right to use the park as anybody else and to celebrate our festivals as any other group." The August 1975 festival won praise for its careful cleanup efforts. And the organizers of the 1976 San Juan Festival hired a private sanitation company to help clear the park.[78] But the flap over the festivals reflected deeper tensions facing Central Park in the mid-1970s.

One problem was the cumulative result of the "opening up" that had begun under Hoving and Heckscher. Mayor Lindsay's park commissioners had invited everyone into the park. Now city officials worried that people had taken the invitation too seriously, that, like Sorrentini, they saw use of the park as a "right." Indeed, in this era of increased rights consciousness, Commissioner Weisl sought legal guidance on his authority to deny the use of the park for rallies and demonstrations. Weisl's reservations went beyond the political rallies that had also bothered his predecessors to question all large organized gatherings. By contrast Hoving and Heckscher had welcomed the previously banned ethnic festivals as well as the giant concerts that had become more frequent and more diverse. Hundreds of thousands now were gathering each summer on the Sheep Meadow to hear well-publicized concerts by the Metropolitan Opera and popular performers such as Barbra Streisand. Rock concerts found a regular home at the Wollman Rink. Yet Weisl felt "these massive events" deprived "the public of part of the use of the park" and "do more destruction than you can imagine." "We have grave doubts that this is a proper use of the park," he announced in the aftermath of the San Juan Festival controversy.[79] Weisl was, in effect, reasserting Olmsted's old distinction between a "park, properly so called," and a "common"—a distinction that had begun to lapse in the late 1960s.

And although Weisl did not say so, he apparently thought that *some* groups did not use the park properly. The conflicts over the San Juan and other Puerto Rican festivals suggest that some of the tensions grew out of Puerto Rican New Yorkers' movement literally from the margins to the center of the park. In the 1950s and early 1960s, Puerto Ricans had mostly congregated in the northern section of the park, especially around the North Meadow ball fields. Even in the mid-1970s, writer and editor Ted Solotaroff described how "old folks and little children as well as friends and wives and girlfriends" gathered there in the style of a "neighborhood outing." The baseball "game itself is a communal occasion," he wrote, with "players and spectators wrapped in the same exuberant mood, kicking up their heels in the one area of cold, stony *Nueva York,* beyond the barrio, where they feel at home."[80]

By the midseventies Puerto Rican New Yorkers were beginning to make themselves at home in other areas of the park. African-American and Puerto Rican youths were apparently mixing more comfortably than they had in the 1950s. By the midseventies, with the hippies mostly gone from the Bethesda Terrace and the fountain cafe shut down, Puerto Rican and black youth shaped their own fountain scene, especially early on summer evenings. In 1976 Solotaroff wrote with fascination of the hillside west of the Terrace with its salsa music and Latin dancing as well as dice playing and marijuana selling. Other observers continued to complain as Puerto Rican festivals began to appear at the Mall along with barbecuing, gambling, and liquor sales. White, middle-class parkgoers were even more disturbed by the drugs, the bongos, and the "boom boxes" young people brought with them to the park. And they blamed the black and Latino teenagers for the evident disrepair in the area—the fountain had dried up and turned into a litter basket; graffiti marked the Terrace walls.[81]

But young people had neither turned off the water nor stopped the maintenance of the Terrace. Whereas complaints about the conditions of Central Park in the 1970s often focused on the ostensible results of cultural changes (the "excesses" of the 1960s or "unruly" teenagers who ignored authority), the park's fundamental problems were economic. Park Commissioner Salem Wales had said almost a century earlier that Central Park was an "expensive luxury" to maintain; in the 1970s, as in the 1870s, its maintenance cost more than many taxpayers wanted to spend.

The trouble over the 1975 San Juan Festival thus reflected more than just tensions over accepting new events and people in the park's most prominent spaces. Money was also involved. On the surface, it did not look like much money. Recall that Weisl estimated the cleanup cost for the San Juan Festival at eight thousand dollars. The city had spent much larger sums in the late 1960s and early 1970s to organize and clean up after innumerable happenings, be-ins, and Sheep Meadow concerts. But in 1975 the city was broke. In March bankers closed the credit markets to the city, and for the rest of the year New York teetered on the edge of bankruptcy. The day before the festival the city had announced layoffs of 575 welfare recipients who worked half-time for the parks department. And just five days after the festival, the city fired 19,000 municipal workers (including 831 park workers) in a single day.[82]

The fiscal crisis of the 1970s hit the parks particularly hard. As in earlier crises, bankers and businessmen took charge of city finances and imposed a regime of belt tightening, and the federal government, which had financed the vast expansion of urban public services in the 1960s, was no longer as sympathetic to the problems of people in cities. The *Daily News* headlined (in 144-

point type) a story about the White House's initial rejection of New York City's appeal for help in the fiscal crisis: "Ford to City: Drop Dead."[83]

Poor New Yorkers suffered the most; between 1974 and 1981 the city froze its basic welfare grant, even as the cost of living increased by 68 percent. More generally, consumers of municipal services—from schools and hospitals to streets and parks—took on "the heaviest burdens of retrenchment," in the words of political scientist Martin Shefter. "The middle class is increasingly seeking its recreation outside the city limits," *Times* reporter Anna Quindlen noted in an assessment of how the fiscal crisis was affecting the parks. Meanwhile, "the poor complain that because the parks have increasingly become their oases, the parks are no longer taken care of."[84]

It was, indeed, difficult to defend parks against the competing claims of hospitals and schools and fire and police protection, and the parks department now had little clout at City Hall, in part because of political feuding and rapid turnover at the top. Between 1974 and 1980 the department's appropriation dropped by more than $40 million, a 60 percent cut in real dollars. Even by the early 1970s the number of full-time permanent park workers had dropped from their late 1960s peak of almost 6,100 to about 4,800. Between 1974 and 1979, the department lost another 2,200 workers, although temporary workers provided through the federal Comprehensive Employment and Training Act program made up some of the gap. In the aftermath of the fiscal crisis, the summer work force—crucial to a seasonal agency like parks—dropped from 6,000 to fewer than 2,700. The loss of more than half of the permanent and seasonal work force and of a significant portion of the budget for supplies, maintenance equipment, and trash baskets devastated the park system. Between 1974–1975 and 1975–1976, the department's capital budget, the money used for major rehabilitation projects, dropped from $24 million to $5 million. Asked whether his budget had any "fat" left, Park Commissioner Martin Lang retorted: "We have taken off the fat and we are into muscle and bones."[85]

A *Times* reporter who toured the city's parks in May 1977 found them "in an advanced state of deterioration." More than five hundred parks and playgrounds received only weekly cleaning from mobile task forces. In the absence of regular maintenance, supervision, or policing, many parks and playgrounds suffered vandalism and were filled with piles of garbage. Even after the city's financial plight eased three years later, the parks continued to decay. A later three-part *Times* investigation of the park system described it as "a dirty, unkempt, vandalized shadow of its former self. . . . Perhaps no other municipal facilities have suffered so much in recent years." By 1982 a state study estimated that the city's parks had almost $3 billion in deferred maintenance needs. Although Central Park did not approach the virtual abandonment that some city parks suffered in the late 1970s, its maintenance funds were slashed as well. The Sheep Meadow turned into a dust bowl; vandalism closed Belvedere Castle; beer cans filled the Pond, and graffiti marred Bethesda Terrace.[86]

Harlem Meer Boat House: Vandalism and inadequate maintenance funds led to deterioration throughout the park by the early 1980s.

Central Park also confronted some problems not faced by the other city parks. It had already taken a beating as use increased in the late 1960s and early 1970s. The large gatherings and special events of those years required particularly heavy maintenance. But this intensified use coincided with a decision to focus park spending on programs rather than maintenance or capital improvements. By the final year of the Lindsay administration in 1973, the board of estimate responded to Commissioner Richard Clurman's request and gave preliminary approval to a $7 million appropriation as the first stage in a ten-year, $55 million rehabilitation of the park. A few weeks later, Abe Beame was sworn in as mayor, and the former city comptroller from Brooklyn sought to distance himself from what he called Lindsay's "Manhattanitis." The massive appropriation for rehabilitation of Central Park offered a convenient symbol of that Manhattan-centeredness. Beame promptly acted to halve the Central Park funding and use the other half of the money for major parks in the other four boroughs.[87]

Then in early 1975 the fiscal crisis hit. The rehabilitation projects that had survived the initial round of cuts were mostly put on hold.[88] Maintenance levels slipped further and vandalism worsened. But with bankers insisting on fiscal austerity and the federal government evincing suspicion of cities, those hoping to reverse the park's decline would have to look elsewhere for the money. Out of the fiscal crisis came a powerful challenge to the opening up of the park as well as to the definition of Central Park as a public space, owned, financed, and managed by local government on behalf of all city residents.

18

"WHOSE PARK IS IT ANYWAY?"

On February 25, 1981, Park Commissioner Gordon J. Davis issued an extraordinary report—107 pages (plus 28 attachments)—simply to reject a request for use of Central Park. But this was no ordinary request. The Bulgarian-born artist Christo had asked for a two-week permit to install in the park more than eleven thousand apricot-colored fabric banners suspended from fifteen-foot-high prefabricated metal frames. The panels of Christo's *Gates*, as he called them, would reach about five or six feet above the ground and stretch through twenty-five miles of park paths. Even in a mild breeze the banners would wave horizontally and touch the next gate nine feet away. Like Christo's other dramatic works of public art—his twenty-four-mile-long *Running Fence* in California and his million-square-foot wrapping of the Sydney, Australia, harbor—*Gates* would be complicated and expensive, costing his backers $5 million. Commissioner Davis pointed out in his report that the dramatic art exhibit would produce "the largest, most comprehensive physical and visual alteration of Central Park since completion of its construction in 1873."[1]

The writer Brendan Gill called the exhaustive report "the finest government document I've ever read." It was not surprising, considering Davis's erudition and background. In appointing Davis as commissioner in 1978, Mayor Edward Koch had returned to the tradition of placing the park in the hands of Ivy League graduates. Davis was an alumnus of Williams, had done graduate work in planning and political science at Columbia, and had received a law degree from Harvard. Moreover, he came from a distinguished and well-connected family. His father, a professor of education at the University of Chicago, was the first black scholar to win tenure at a leading university.[2]

Davis had reviewed the request with great care. Christo, after all, was a major artist, and Davis was a public official in the art capital of the nation.

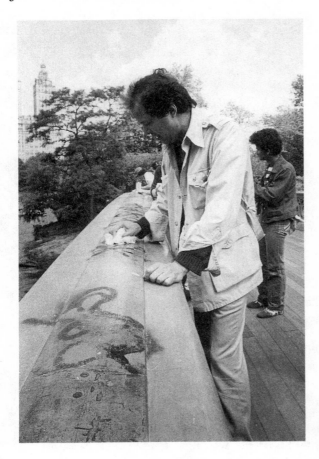

Park Commissioner Davis removes graffiti from the Bow Bridge as part of the park's cleanup in the early 1980s.

Furthermore, he saw this as a chance to offer a well-publicized rebuke to the policy, begun under Thomas Hoving, of "opening up Central Park to 'the people' by permitting a wide variety of events and special functions." Rather than directly criticize Hoving, however, Davis, who had first entered city government under Lindsay, charged that Hoving's "originally well-thought out effort had been allowed to grow into an unattended Frankenstein." Subsequent park administrators had abdicated "meaningful day-to-day responsibility for managing the park" and had ceased to ask, "What is an appropriate park use?" It was "clear," Davis said, "that there must be and are limits" to the use of Central Park. He had no intention of returning to the "anachronistic" policies of the past, which "treated the Park much like a museum." Still, Central Park was a landscape that needed protection from well-intentioned artists as well as an indiscriminate public.[3]

Davis's decision was strongly supported by well-organized Central Park advocates. At the time Christo's request was being considered, these advocates won an even more fundamental and historic change in the administration of the park, which moved crucial aspects of financing and administration from the public to the private sector, that is, to the newly formed Central Park Conservancy. It was a realignment as significant as the two earlier great transformations in the park's administrative structure—the Tweed charter of 1870 and the citywide consolidation of the park system under Robert Moses in 1934. In the 1980s—and for the foreseeable future—control of Central Park was shifted to a "partnership" between the public and private sector.

"A Board of Trustees" for Central Park

In December 1980, when Mayor Koch officially announced the formation of the Central Park Conservancy, the brief article covering the announcement appeared on page 100 of the Sunday *Times*. The board, described primarily as a fund-raising body, comprised thirty private citizens (most of them executives of leading corporations headquartered in New York, such as Revlon and Bristol-Myers, or leading financial institutions, such as Morgan Stanley and Manufacturers Hanover Bank) and six "public" trustees—three mayoral appointees and three city officials serving ex officio. (Iphigene Sulzberger would serve as honorary chair until her death in 1990.) Koch picked philanthropist and retired corporate executive William S. Beinecke as the board chairman; he, in turn, had selected the private board members. After this, they would choose their own replacements.[4]

Beinecke lived along Fifth Avenue in the 70s; his grandfather had owned the Plaza Hotel at the park's southeast entrance just across from the Pulitzer Fountain. As he explained it, the conservancy's goals were "to assist in the physical restoration of the park and to bring about improvements in its maintenance and security." But as the *Times* acknowledged, there was a broader mandate; the conservancy "would, in effect, constitute a board of trustees," on the model of a museum or orchestra board. It would raise money, the *Times* pointed out in an approving editorial, and also serve as "a continuing society of protectors," offering "the judgment and taste without which new investment would make Central Park worse, not better."[5]

The idea of governing Central Park through a board of trustees went back more than a century. After the demise of the Central Park commission, the old "board of gentlemen" of the 1860s, there were repeated calls for a similar independent board, which faded only in the heyday of the Moses administration in the 1930s to 1950s. The physical deterioration of the park in the 1970s revived them. In 1974 a privately funded report on Central Park by a team led by a Columbia Business School professor, E. S. Savas, recommended the establishment of a "Central Park Board of Guardians."[6]

The political and economic climate of the 1970s paved the way. In the fiscal crisis officials began to turn to private money to maintain public services, and this tactic of expediency intersected with the program of neo-conservatives and neo-liberals who doubted the ability of government to provide a full array of city services, or even the desirability of such provisions. Questioning the efficiency and legitimacy of government as a way to meet "public" needs had begun even before the 1970s. As many white, middle-class families abandoned cities and as governmental policies and corporate practices encouraged private solutions to public problems, the urban public sector was coming to be defined, historian George Lipsitz argues, as the "resource of last resort, intended only for those who cannot afford to do better on their own."[7]

The fiscal crisis provided the occasion for New York's most powerful banking and business interests—as in the 1870s—to impose new limits on the public sector and on the definition of necessary public services. The Emergency Financial Control Board, composed of city and state officials and corporate leaders, now received extraordinary powers over the municipal budget (of the sort once given to Andrew Green) and insisted, for example, on increases in subway fares and an end to the century-long tradition of free tuition at the city university. The long-term erosion of the city's tax base made it difficult for city residents to resist these mandated cutbacks. Nor were city businesses and property owners prepared to pay higher taxes. At the same time, federal support for cities declined: between 1976 and 1985 the federal share of New York City's budget dropped from 22 to 15 percent. All these factors undermined the expanded definition of government's responsibilities to its citizens that had been gained through decades of struggle.[8] Central Park, which had once served as a monument to a more activist state and an expansive vision of the public good, was now to provide a testing ground for an experiment in narrowing the public sector.

"Public-private partnerships," "load shedding," and "user fees" emerged as key catchphrases in the parks department in the aftermath of the fiscal crisis. "Unable to meet its awesome responsibilities," the *Times* explained in 1980, "New York City's Department of Parks and Recreation is moving toward turning over large chunks of its domain to private groups and corporations." It noted that the city had already shifted zoos, skating rinks, and parking lots to private operators and hoped to do the same with golf courses. A ten-year recovery plan drawn up by consultants in 1980, moreover, recommended that the parks department move toward coordination and oversight of projects that would actually be operated by private groups and concessionaires.[9] A key financial saving in such contracting out of recreational and maintenance services would come in reduced wages and benefits, thus eroding the major gains that unionized park workers had won in the postwar years.

One dramatic symbol of this transference of public responsibilities to the private sector was the increased use of tax abatements and other incentives in the 1980s to encourage private developers to build parks and plazas. The newly created "public spaces" in New York have most often proved to be plazas, arcades, interior atriums, and festival marketplaces attached to office and condominium towers. "These new and privately owned public spaces," architectural critic Paul Goldberger writes, "have become an artificial substitute for a true public realm. And they have not come free: not only do these spaces and others like them represent the relinquishing of the traditional role of government as the provider of the public realm, they were created only as a result of generous zoning deals by which New York City allowed large buildings to be even larger than they would have been otherwise: a small public gesture in exchange for a vast private benefit." A plaque on the plaza beneath one midtown corporate headquarters summarized the new approach: "PUBLIC SPACE, Owned and Maintained by AT&T."[10]

Although the city's existing park system never moved as far toward privatization as some businessmen and conservative politicians hoped, the new emphasis left a dramatic imprint on Central Park. In the last season before the department closed the Wollman ice-skating rink for renovations in 1980, the city transferred its operation to a private entrepreneur. This "load shedding" proceeded even further when municipal efforts to rebuild the rink collapsed after six years of delays and mistakes, and the city turned over construction to real estate developer Donald Trump, who also operated the new rink when it reopened in 1986. Reporter Wayne Barrett's subsequent account of the rink story indicates that city officials led Trump to the Canadian consultants whose advice made possible the quick and successful renovation. But at the time, conservative ideologues and journalists (and especially Trump himself) cited his rebuilding of the rink in just three and a half months and his subsequent profitable operation of it as further evidence of the superiority of uninhibited private entrepreneurs to "incompetent" and "bureaucratic" public agencies.[11]

The park zoo followed a different path, although along lines marked out almost a century earlier when the private, nonprofit New York Zoological Society created the Bronx Zoo. At the height of the fiscal crisis in the mid-1970s proposals were floated either to close the city-operated zoos in Flushing Meadow, Prospect, and Central parks altogether or to transfer them to the zoological society. In the face of cutbacks Commissioner Davis realized that the parks department would not be able to undertake badly needed renovations and handed the rebuilding and management of the Central Park Zoo to the New York Zoological Society, but this version of load shedding left a great deal of the load on the city's shoulders. The cost of constructing a new zoo had been estimated at $8.3 million in 1980; the final price tag read $35 million, and the city paid almost two-thirds of the money. That the society and the largest private donor insisted on a state-of-the-art facility contributed to the cost overruns. Despite the generosity of private philanthropists, the "public" wound up paying twice—in taxes for the construction costs and in the $1.00 (soon rising to $2.50) admission charge for adults visiting the previously free zoo. The new design was widely praised, but the admission fee closed off—for the first time—a section of the park to casual strollers. The plans of August Belmont and the American Zoological and Botanical Society to create a privately operated zoo in Central Park were finally fulfilled a century and a quarter after they were first proposed.[12]

The development of the Central Park Conservancy paralleled these other experiments, although the specific arrangements of its private-public partnership were more complex. The conservancy did not gain the same direct and contractual control of the park that Donald Trump had over the skating rink or the zoological society had over the zoo. Instead, in an unusual power-sharing arrangement, a Central Park administrator was to serve as the chief executive officer of both the park and the conservancy. The administrator would be appointed (or fired) by the mayor and would report to the park commissioner but would be paid by the conservancy. The conservancy thus had a de facto veto over appointments. In the course of the 1980s, when it came to pay a large number of other bills as well, the conservancy's say over park operations grew stronger. By 1990 the conservancy was supplying half the annual operating budget, half the funds for capital improvements, nearly half the 234-person staff, and almost all the recreational programming.[13]

"Rebuilding Central Park"

In 1979 Gordon Davis had appointed as Central Park administrator Elizabeth Barlow Rogers, a park activist and the author of books and articles on parks and on Olmsted. Four years earlier she had organized schoolchildren to do maintenance and horticultural work in the park. Appalled at its condition, she began to raise private money and to organize adult (as well as child) volunteers for the park. "New York can no longer afford its parks; not even Central Park," she declared in a 1976 article urging private solutions. Davis asked Rogers to raise money privately for her own salary as administrator. In 1980 this arrangement was formalized with the creation of the conservancy, which replaced Rogers's own Central Park Task Force and also another private fund-raising group, the Central Park Community Fund.[14]

As Central Park administrator throughout the 1980s (and beyond), Rogers joined Calvert Vaux, Frederick Law Olmsted, Andrew Green, and Robert Moses as one of the five most influential figures in the park's history. She herself identified most strongly with Olmsted, at times referring to him as "Saint Olmsted." Although Rogers also acknowledged Moses' legacy, a reporter noted, "She speaks reverentially about the designs of Olmsted, more grudgingly about those of Moses."[15]

Rogers's devotion to Olmsted reflected, in part, her own training in art history at Wellesley and in city planning at Yale. Unlike some early twentieth-

In 1979 Mayor Ed Koch appointed Elizabeth Barlow Rogers to the new post of Central Park administrator. She helped the conservancy raise tens of millions of dollars in private funds for restoration.

century park preservationists, she had not grown up near the park. Indeed, her first visit to New York from her native Texas did not come until 1950, when she was fourteen; she and her mother stayed at the Plaza Hotel and never walked across the street into Central Park. But after Rogers moved to New York in 1964, she developed a passionate devotion to the parks of her adopted city—an interest she explored in her first book, *The Forests and Wetlands of New York City*, and in her work with the Parks Council, the successor to the Park Association of New York. A *Times* reporter described her as "not the archetypical public servant" but possessing the "tastes and social graces more frequently associated with Park Avenue than with City Hall." She proved unusually adept at raising enormous sums of money for the park and in administering those funds to impress her own vision on it. In effect, Rogers managed to couple Olmsted and Vaux's pastoral vision with a bit of the realpolitik associated with Robert Moses or Andrew Green. On the one hand, she insisted that "the park is foremost a work of landscape art and I'm not prepared to accept that it's anything else." "Our purpose is to sustain the ingenious designs of Olmsted." On the other hand, she invariably denied any interest in taking "the park back to the 19th century." "It has to be responsive to people's current needs," she told a reporter.[16]

Rogers's deep admiration both reflected and fostered the remarkable revival of interest in Olmsted beginning in the early 1970s. In 1972 Rogers collaborated on *Frederick Law Olmsted's New York*, the catalog for an influential exhibit at the Whitney Museum (which included Calvert Vaux's original Central Park drawings). In the early 1970s a flood of similar books and exhibits appeared, celebrating Olmsted as a landscape architect and a social philosopher. In 1966 Henry Hope Reed complained that Olmsted was "not a household name"; six years later it was in the households of many well-educated New Yorkers. The Olmsted boom had grown partly out of the accidental conjunction of the sesquicentennial of his birth in 1972 with a rising ecological consciousness that suddenly burst on the scene with Earth Day in 1970. Environmentalists adopted Olmsted as a founding father of their movement. It was also a consequence of a heightened interest in historic preservation that burgeoned in the late 1960s and early 1970s. In 1974 Central Park became the first scenic landmark designated by the New York City Landmarks Preservation Commission.[17]

Whatever the mix of reasons, this enthusiasm for Olmsted has had a profound impact. "Olmstedianism," in effect, became the governing ideology of the Central Park Conservancy just as it had been for the park preservationists of the 1920s and 1930s. "A necessary first step in creating the Conservancy," Rogers wrote, "was the acceptance of the Park as its original creators saw it—a scenic retreat, a peaceful space that would act as an antidote to urban stress."[18] Thus, the keynote of the 1980s would be the effort to *restore* the historic landscape and to reverse (or at least arrest) the changes that Moses, Hoving, Heckscher, and the fiscal crisis had brought.

Starting in 1982, Rogers oversaw a talented team of landscape architects who undertook an exhaustive three-year survey of all aspects of the park—from soil conditions to traffic patterns. From this came a master plan, *Rebuilding Central Park*, that envisioned spending $150 million for a "systematic and coherent renovation" over a ten- to fifteen-year period. "Much of the planning and design that have resulted in a commitment of both city and private funding for capital projects—including [the] management and restoration plan—have been initiated by the Conservancy," the published report explained. By the end of its first decade, the Central Park Conservancy had raised more than $65 million for this public-private venture.[19]

The master restoration plan took the Greensward plan "whenever possible, as a reference and guide." There was widespread agreement about the need to reverse the deterioration of the 1970s, although a literal restoration was not possible. The final restoration plan dropped, for example, the recommendations of an earlier draft that called for phasing out some of the twenty-five ball fields, relocating or eliminating some of the playgrounds, and removing "hard-surface activities such as tennis, basketball and baseball . . . to locations outside the park."[20] Such features served too broad a constituency to be eliminated.

Under Davis, the parks department had already begun some restoration. By the end of the 1980s, with the infusion of conservancy money, Central Park looked startlingly different from its appearance just a decade earlier: visitors stretched out on a lush, green Sheep Meadow, now guarded by a fence and by rules against loud noises and active sports; schoolchildren learned about the environment in a graffiti-free Belvedere Castle; skaters glided across the new (Trump-operated) ice-skating rink; tourists picked up information about the park's past and present at a refurbished Dairy; fashion photographers posed their models against the backdrop of a lovingly restored Bethesda Terrace; wedding couples took their vows in a replanted Conservatory Garden; New Yorkers who could afford it dined on the terrace of the renovated Loeb Boathouse. The one important new addition was, appropriately, a landscape project, Strawberry Fields, a parcel of land near the West 72nd Street entrance, landscaped as a memorial to John Lennon with funds provided by his widow, Yoko Ono.[21]

The conservancy generally emphasized restoration and landscaping, but despite her deep commitment to the park's Olmstedian legacy, Rogers was criticized by the Friends of Central Park, a preservationist group founded by Henry Hope Reed and others in the late 1960s. These landscape purists advocated "keeping Central Park as it was originally designed—woodlands, meadows, forests, and streams—rather than as a setting for more buildings, monuments, permanent athletic fields, and assorted fantasies dreamed up by determined philanthropists anxious to have their names embedded everlastingly in concrete." Instead of spending money on building a new tennis house, a new skating rink, or a new restaurant at the Harlem Meer, they urged the parks department to devote its funds to labor-intensive "hand maintenance" of the grounds or to "removing the miles of asphalt walks from the parks which are a permanent reminder of the city streets."[22]

Much as Rogers might personally sympathize with the designers' goal of creating "rural scenery in an urban context" and offering "pleasurable and soothing relief from building," she also recognized that "the park has to accommodate different kinds of class use." "Generally we have learned to swallow a lot," she explained to a reporter of her acceptance of such further additions to the Metropolitan Museum of Art as the Temple of Dendur and the American Wing in the late 1970s and early 1980s.[23] Other features added to the park over the years—the ice-skating rinks, the zoo, the Delacorte Theater, the ball fields, and the playgrounds—had bequeathed a social legacy Rogers and the conservancy could not easily ignore.

The conservancy provided the shaping hand for the dramatic restoration, but it did not act alone. Commissioner Davis had good relations with City Hall and was adept at managing park finances as New York staggered out of the fiscal crisis of the 1970s. The parks department was able to retain the workers who would have been lost when the Reagan administration ended the Comprehensive Education and Training Act program; by 1981 it was able to do some new hiring. Davis's successor, Henry Stern (a former councilman, a close friend of Mayor Koch's, and a creative publicist for the parks department somewhat in the mold of Thomas Hoving, under whom he had served), was able to do more after his appointment in 1983. During his six years as park commissioner, a thousand workers were hired and the department's share of the total city budget actually increased modestly—though both remained below pre-fiscal crisis levels. The conservancy had put millions into Central Park's rehabilitation, but the city actually paid for about three-quarters of the capital improvements.[24]

By the late 1980s newspaper editorials and magazines were celebrating the park's "season of rebirth" under the conservancy's aegis. Movies and advertisements implicitly carried the same message. In the 1970s Central Park had provided a setting for jokes about muggings in such films as *Where's Poppa.* By the late 1980s it was a backdrop for films about urban affluence and elegance— *When Harry Met Sally, Wall Street,* and *Crimes and Misdemeanors.* Glossy advertisements for multimillion-dollar apartments in Trump Parc on Central Park South promised: "Central Park. It's not just a view. It's your front yard."[25]

Whose Estate? Whose Front Yard?

If Central Park was lucky in its park commissioners in the 1980s, from the perspective of the conservancy it was even luckier in the economic climate, which brightened for business after the gloom of the previous decade. Real estate prices, which slowly began rising in the mid-1970s, took off in 1984 after a brief pause in the early 1980s. And starting in the late 1970s, personal income grew in New York City, even as it was declining nationally. The 1980s economic boom, like most others in the city's history, was distributed unequally; yet its very unevenness may have economically benefited the park, since wealthy Manhattanites—and especially people and property around the park—were among the greatest beneficiaries of the good times. Prominent individuals (financier Henry R. Kravis and broker Richard Gilder, philanthropists and longtime park supporters Lucy Moses and Iphigene Sulzberger), foundations (the DeWitt Wallace–Reader's Digest Fund and the Arthur Ross Foundation), and corporations (Corporate Property Investors, Time Warner, Tropicana Products, and the Trump Organization) each contributed more than $200,000 (and in some cases considerably more) in the late 1980s to the conservancy, an organization they identified with the city's future.[26]

Billions of dollars look down upon Central Park. Along the eastern border— the "world's best address," as *Town & Country* magazine calls it—live some of the nation's leading investment bankers, publishers, media stars, moneyed families, and corporate executives. And the southern edge includes the offices of leading corporations such as Paramount and General Motors as well as some of the most expensive hotels in the world. In the financial boom of the 1980s the

"Pookie adores it here. She can see the Central Park Zoo from her bedroom."

Even *Town & County* magazine, where this cartoon appeared, could poke fun at the proprietary claims on the view made by the park's wealthy neighbors.

already costly real estate along the park's southern, eastern, and western peripheries soared in price. In 1988 Trump bought the elegant Plaza Hotel at 59th and Fifth for $390 million; he had made more than $100 million transforming the Barbizon-Plaza Hotel and an adjoining building on Central Park South into the Trump Parc condominiums, each selling for as much as $4 million. A view of the park had become more valuable than actual use of it. Trump hired a firm called Holes, Incorporated, to replace the Barbizon's small windows with giant picture windows. "Those openings alone were immensely valuable," Trump writes in *The Art of the Deal*, "because a great view is worth a small fortune."[27]

The Central Park Conservancy tapped the prosperity of the park's neighbors, especially on its east and south sides. In 1986 it created the Central Park Perimeter Association specifically to raise money from residents of the surrounding blocks to enhance the park's borders. Fifth Avenue residents who paid $14 million for a fifteen-room apartment overlooking the park could surely afford to contribute to its rehabilitation. After all, as one wealthy park neighbor wryly commented, "Central Park is our only estate where I didn't have to hire a hundred gardeners."[28]

Although the park's wealthiest neighbors were along Fifth and Central Park South, the real estate boom wrapped itself around the park. Central Park West, once largely the home of the middle class, now housed New Yorkers who had previously confined themselves to the East Side. The price of a cooperative apartment at the Beresford (Central Park West between 81st and 82nd streets, just two blocks from where Theodore White rented a nine-room apartment for three hundred dollars per month in 1953), jumped from $110,000 to $1.1

As part of the new public-private partnership the Central Park Conservancy contributed millions to the park's restoration. Shown here (*left to right*): Elizabeth Rogers, Park Commissioner Henry Stern, Mayor Ed Koch, and members of the conservancy board: James H. Evans, Henry R. Kravis, and Laurance Rockefeller.

million between 1971 and 1981. By the mid-1980s, speculators began buying Harlem property, particularly on the blocks closest to Central Park. "We have not hit the crisis of people being pushed out yet," commented the president of the Harlem Urban Development Corporation in 1986. "But we are on the cutting edge of it on 110th Street."[29]

To be sure, the park continued to straddle enormous variations in wealth and social composition. In 1980 per-capita incomes at the southeast edge of the park were about fifteen times as high as at its northeast border; residents of surrounding blocks were either virtually all black or virtually all white.[30] But Theodore White's "perfumed stockade" now encompassed three of the four sides. The neighborhoods immediately surrounding the park had come closer to approximating the sort of high-income residential enclave envisioned by the gentlemen speculators in the 1850s than at any other time in Central Park's history.

As had been true in the 1860s, the prophecies of speculators proved too optimistic. The collapse of the real estate market in the 1990s (like the equivalent collapse in the 1870s) awoke developers from their dreams of an entirely gentrified upper Manhattan. Still, Central Park's wealthy neighbors continued to take a proprietary interest in "their" public park, while its poor neighbors worried about being displaced. The abandonment of housing in the 1970s had reduced the number of poor and working-class New Yorkers who lived in the neighborhoods surrounding the park. The population of Harlem dropped by more than half between 1950 and 1980. And by 1980 the per-capita income of residents of blocks bordering Central Park was about two and a quarter times the average for the city. Gentrification in the 1980s only accelerated this trend.[31]

As the city's changing political economy began to alter the social composition of the park's borders, it affected one of the basic conditions of democratic access to a public space. Whether partial displacement of poor New Yorkers from the surrounding neighborhoods has brought about their partial displacement from the park itself is difficult to determine. Compared with a hundred years earlier, the time and expense of getting to the park are much less of a barrier, and thousands of poor and working-class New Yorkers still live within walking distance. Nevertheless, a 1989 visitor survey showed that the proportion of parkgoers who were black or Hispanic had dropped from two-fifths to one-quarter over the previous seven years. The authors attribute the change to "the closing of the Harlem Meer and construction in the Upper Park." Whether this assessment is correct and the change turns out to be temporary will not be clear, therefore, until the completion of the long-delayed rehabilitation of the northern park.[32]

The issue of democratic access to the park has also been raised by the increasing number of homeless New Yorkers. Poor people—from the "squatters" of the 1850s to the "tramps" of the 1870s and 1890s to the Hooverville residents of the 1930s—have always turned to the park land for shelter. Scattered reports from the postwar years indicate the continuing presence of at least small numbers of homeless people in the park. A study by sociologists William Kornblum and Terry Williams estimated that in the fall of 1982 the park had about twenty-five residents. Just seven years later, the park's homeless population was more than a hundred (and perhaps three times that during the summer). Park users were identifying "homelessness" as the aspect of Central Park that most bothered them.[33]

The growing visibility of homeless people in Central Park posed in the starkest terms the contradiction between Americans' commitment to democratic public space and their acquiescence in vast disparities of wealth and power. By 1988 Commissioner Stern began to talk of the need to evict the hundreds of homeless people from the city's parks. "Parks are a refuge, not an asylum," he told a reporter. In March 1989 Stern issued a new set of regulations that outlawed loitering, begging, and lying on benches and allowed the parks department to confiscate any belongings left untended for more than two hours. The rules provoked a storm of protest from homeless New Yorkers and their advocates, who said that the regulations singled out homeless people, who could easily be charged with "loitering" or who might need to put aside their possessions while they enjoyed the park. Such rules, indeed, might have discouraged homeless people from entering the parks at all.[34]

Faced with charges that the rules were "mean spirited" and "misguided," Stern backed down. Further eviction efforts tended to be concentrated in downtown parks such as Tompkins Square, at 10th Street and Avenue A, where large numbers of homeless people had set up camp. At least in theory, Commissioner Stern accepted the principle that (in his words) "you don't have to be in the Social Register or even the telephone book to use a city park."[35]

Closing the Gates?

As the growing presence of homeless people in Central Park reveals, the economic climate that permitted restoration has also introduced new conditions—displacement and homelessness—affecting democratic access. Although less dramatic than Stern's effort to limit the access of one part of the public, other restrictions on park use have been introduced. Davis's rejection of Christo's proposal signaled the new direction of park policy. It was, after all, precisely the sort of project that Hoving or Heckscher would have enthusiastically embraced—a "happening" or a celebration of life in the city. But preservationists thought the landscape could no longer support activities or crowds that hurt the soil and plantings.

Even before the Christo report and the formation of the conservancy, Davis had begun to pull back from the "open park" policies of the Hoving-Heckscher era. In 1978, for example, Davis decided that the Taste of the Big Apple food festival, which had previously drawn enormous crowds to sample the cuisine of dozens of New York restaurants, could no longer use the Mall, and he imposed a temporary moratorium on free popular music concerts. The closing of the Wollman Rink in 1980 for rehabilitation also ended the rock concerts that had long been held there. Nevertheless, Davis did allow a variety of free music at a variety of spots: jazz concerts at the Naumburg Bandshell and the Dairy, Latin music groups at the Conservatory Garden, and Elton John and Simon and Garfunkel on the Great Lawn.[36]

Under Davis's successor, Henry Stern, the mass pop concerts disappeared entirely after rowdy behavior followed a July 1983 Diana Ross concert. The city decided that organizers of large pop concerts (unlike the equally large but more decorously received New York Philharmonic and Metropolitan Opera concerts) would have to pay all police and cleanup costs and make a $100,000 contribution to the parks department. In the next eight years, no concert producers met the city's demands. In 1986 the department also adopted new regulations for the use of the Naumburg Bandshell on the Mall. They required concert organizers to use the department's own sound system and sound technician as a way of "respecting the peace and quiet of nearby residents." Three years later the U.S. Supreme Court upheld the noise regulations against a challenge from Rock against Racism, the promoter of an annual park concert.[37]

By the mid-1980s permit rules were revised to "discourage or rule out" from the Mall hard rock and disco concerts, commercial or promotional events, any events likely to draw more than twenty-five hundred people, and all political rallies. The first draft of the conservancy's management and restoration plan proposed to continue symphony and opera concerts on the Great Lawn but recommended that "art 'happenings,' mass concerts and large political rallies . . . should be forbidden." Political realities apparently prevented rigid implementation of these new policies. The conservancy's final published master plan, for example, more cautiously recommended that "efforts should be made to limit gatherings to a maximum of 100,000 people" on the Great Lawn.[38]

Despite the new restrictions, music did not disappear from the park. In the late 1980s and early 1990s, the conservancy-sponsored Summerstage, an eclectic series of music, dance, and performance art concerts, continued the long tradition of free music.[39] Also, a newer tradition (dating from the 1960s, but advocated by park contestant Susan Parish a century earlier) of impromptu and unorganized musical performances scattered through the park remained a regular and popular Sunday feature.

In addition, a limited number of large events—particularly those organized by groups with assertive or powerful political constituencies—also continued to be held in the park: an antinuclear rally in 1982, an antiapartheid rally in 1986, a Gay Pride rally in 1989, Earth Day in 1990, and the annual San Juan Festival. Rogers might complain that the Catholic "Church has, in effect, appropriated the park for its two biggest feast days—St. Paddy's and San Juan"; but the boss of commissioners Davis and Stern, Mayor Koch, recognized the political clout of the church and of the Puerto Rican community and turned up to salute the San Juan Festival. Even so, in 1990 the festival was shifted back to Randall's Island, and the parks department refused a permit for a Gay and Lesbian Pride rally in Central Park (offering Union Square instead). The activist group ACT-UP, defying the ban, held a rally in the park before joining the larger demonstration downtown.[40]

Although the Central Park Conservancy committed itself to a version of Olmsted and Vaux's naturalistic vision as a matter of first principles, park users sometimes challenged that vision. Partisans of particular park activities—joggers, bird watchers, dog walkers, horse riders, model-boat racers, softball and tennis players—worried about how the proposed improvements would affect their own uses of the park. In the spring of 1981 the conservancy cleared some trees in the Ramble to restore original sight lines in the Olmsted-Vaux design and introduce more light, whereupon bird watchers, concerned that the tree cutting and other contemplated changes would destroy the Ramble as an unusually rich habitat for birds, gathered three thousand signatures on a petition protesting "the mass destruction of mature and irreplaceable trees." In hearings before the landmarks commission the conservancy prevailed, but it also proceeded cautiously, hoping not to antagonize the bird watchers.[41]

Controversies over rehabilitation plans have raised larger questions about whom the park should serve and who should have the power to decide its future. "Whose Park Is It Anyway?" asked a 1982 *New York Times Magazine* article reporting on the bird-watching controversy. Some park advocates worried that it was becoming the conservancy's park and that public priorities were being set by a private group and private money. "There's the feeling that it's money that's driving some of the projects," said Barbara J. Fife, an assistant to then–Manhattan borough president David N. Dinkins and a former head of the Parks Council. "Even when it's private money, it's public property." Migdalia Paris, a representative of the state senator from East Harlem, warned a hearing on park security in 1989 that private fund raising could result in "obstacles to the use of the park by the less affluent." "If people are asked to contribute financial support to security measures," she maintained, "the department risks that their interests will dictate policy."[42]

Park Commissioner Stern candidly admitted the conservancy's powerful role in setting the park's agenda. In 1987 some tennis players opposed a new tennis house, for which the conservancy had raised $2.5 million. "I want it," Stern explained, "because the Conservancy—the people who are spearheading the renewal of the park—want it. I don't want to make the yes or no decision which will antagonize the Conservancy or the community. The Conservancy was founded to raise private money for public goals. If elected officials are opposed, what can we do?"[43]

In 1989 the conservancy set up the Citizens Task Force on the Use and Security of Central Park in the wake of the highly publicized brutal gang rape of a woman jogger. The task force initially recommended converting a section of the North Meadow ball fields into "an area of green meadow for flexible programming," returning it to something closer to the original Greensward plan by removing the permanent backstops and baselines. The most regular users—little leagues and Hispanic teams—protested this proposal to turn the North Meadow back into a "meadow." "Flexible Fields," Marsha Hurst, co-director of the Harlem–West Side Senior League, told the task force, "will not serve the needs of children and youth in organized baseball leagues." Speaking on behalf of the Hispanic leagues, Migdalia Paris echoed these sentiments. She urged the parks department to add spectator stands and lights and to allow more vendors selling foods favored by Hispanic parkgoers.[44]

The hearings demonstrated that New Yorkers have thought long and hard about what they want and need in a public park. "Central Park belongs to all New Yorkers, but it holds a special place for the communities on its borders," observed Marsha Hurst. New Yorkers' vision of the park as a community recreational facility differed from the Central Park Conservancy's emphasis on following the spirit of the Greensward design. Or New Yorkers offered different

The Central Park Conservancy and the National Basketball Association sponsored basketball clinics at the North Meadow in the summer of 1991.

interpretations of that spirit: "Basketball was not invented when the park was designed," state assemblyman Edward Sullivan testified; "I am sure Olmsted would have put in basketball courts had he known about basketball." Whatever Olmsted might have thought about basketball, the conservancy responded to such opinions by securing a contribution from the National Basketball Association to install courts at the North Meadow in 1990 and arranging for professional players to conduct classes for neighborhood teenagers. (The conservancy reconciled the push for basketball with its own opposition to paving more of the park by using an already asphalted area for the half courts.)[45]

Disputes about park use raise the question of the composition of the "political public" underlying the park. Who should decide the park's future? Has the private conservancy acquired too much power in decisions about this public space? To be sure, the conservancy is far from autonomous. Even if commissioners are wary of offending the park's most generous benefactor, they can act as a check on its actions. A variety of public bodies—the five community planning boards adjacent to the park, the Art Commission of the City of New York, the Landmarks Preservation Commission, the city council—have oversight over some of the conservancy's decisions.[46] And of course, aroused public opinion limits what can be done in Central Park. The parks department dropped the plan for the new tennis house in the face of such protests, and the security task force dropped its call for flexible fields, although the idea still appeals to many preservationists.

In the 1970s and 1980s, the community planning boards gained increased influence over park policy, and public hearings gave well-organized groups like the tennis players an opportunity to mobilize opposition to plans. Rogers sometimes found the degree of public oversight frustrating: "My work is under scrutiny all the time because it's so public. But what we shouldn't do is let the process take over and kill the project." And Commissioner Stern worried that "so many levels of review" made it too easy for proposals to be "derailed." "In recent years," he told a forum called "Current Issues Facing Central Park" in November 1989, "the balance has shifted from . . . Robert Moses and his absolute domination of the city to a climate in which it is very difficult to accomplish public improvement or park improvement if there is any significant local constituency that opposes it."[47]

When they are consulted, the park's users and neighbors express strong opinions about how the park should be managed. "I think it vital that recommendations come from the players . . . rather than having an idea imposed without any kind of thought," one tennis player said in a typical comment at the task force hearing. "We must insure," said one local spokesperson, that the proposed new restaurant at the Harlem Meer Boathouse include "free public use of a fair amount" of the tables and seats. A representative of Community Board 11, more generally, urged that park plans be reviewed "at the embryo stages, as opposed to having a plan that was discussed and worked out and then presented to us."[48]

The 1980s and early 1990s brought conflict over who should govern the park, although some of the most vexing political issues remain hypothetical: What if a new mayor or park commissioner wants to appoint a new administrator? What if a new mayor or park commissioner decides to return the park to the greater openness of the Hoving-Heckscher era? What if a new city administration insists on adding more and more recreational facilities to the park? Would the conservancy pick up its half of the park budget and go home? What if economic hard times reduce private donations to the conservancy? What if the city's economy and social geography shift in a way that makes the park less attractive for corporate and personal philanthropy? Such questions have remained unanswered (and largely unasked) as the park has moved into the last decade of the twentieth century.

The city's renewed fiscal crisis has made a reconsideration of the new governing arrangements even more unlikely; it has also introduced new tensions into the public-private partnership. In 1991 Mayor David Dinkins sharply cut the parks department's budget.[49] Faced with a reduced work force in Central Park, the conservancy reluctantly picked up some of the slack, increasing its share of the maintenance budget from 50 to 60 percent. Added responsibilities for both maintenance and programming have made it harder for the conservancy to pursue its goal of restoring the park.

The fiscal crisis also exposed other problems in applying Central Park's public-private partnership to the larger park system. Confronted with criticism of the conservancy's tendency to focus on projects for which gifts are available, Dinkins's new parks commissioner, Betsy Gotbaum (the first woman to hold that post, former associate of a venture-capital firm, and wife of the former head of the union that represents park workers) responded defensively. "It irritates me when people criticize the Conservancy as elitist and privatizing," she told a reporter. "It's made it possible for more people to enjoy the park. I only wish I had more Conservancies for big and mid-sized parks." In fact, she did; in 1989 Commissioner Henry Stern had set up the City Parks Foundation to raise private money for parks around the city. But, as Stern explains, Gotbaum, who had experience in fund raising as well as elite social connections through her family (her father was once the head of the J. Walter Thompson advertising agency), "gave it wings" and made it "fashionable." The new fiscal crisis has increased public reliance on this private philanthropy not simply for restoring and enhancing public spaces but for maintaining them as well. After a successful benefit premiere of Woody Allen's *Alice* that raised $400,000, she commented: "Now I'll be able to buy garbage bags this summer." But some park activists worried, as a reporter noted, that "City Hall is using the new commissioner's money out of the private sector as an excuse to pare away further." And in the absence of adequate private money to compensate for budget cuts, parks and playgrounds have begun to show some of the signs of neglect that marred them in the late 1970s.[50]

Although other cities have taken the Central Park Conservancy as a model for how public-private partnerships can sustain public parks, the obvious benefits of private funding have tended to submerge discussion of other implications of this trend. The conservancy's extraordinary fund-raising success rests in part on Central Park's status as a cultural and artistic treasure. The conservancy has convinced New Yorkers that the park deserves the same financial support as the city's museums, libraries, and symphony orchestras. Yet many wealthy New Yorkers have contributed to the conservancy's efforts because they use the park themselves or because its restoration benefits their business or real estate interests. "In the real estate field," explains one such benefactor, "it's just smart business for us to try and improve the quality of life in the city where we have our major holdings."[51] Of course, the park's rich neighbors and generous benefactors think about more than the direct effect of a well-tended park on the value of their apartments or their corporate towers. Like the gentlemen merchants of the 1850s who first promoted the park, they have a larger cultural and economic investment in promoting and ensuring the world-class stature of a park in the heart of a world-class city. And whatever the motives of those who have given money for rehabilitation (and many have derived no direct benefit at all), the gifts improved the park for all who used it.

The limitations of privatization can be seen most clearly by considering Central Park in relation to the rest of the park system. The creation of Central

Park stimulated the building of public parks throughout the region that would become Greater New York. Yet these parks are unlikely to follow the new model for private fund raising with as much success. Even Brooklyn's Prospect Park—another "historic" park designed by Vaux and Olmsted and considered by some a finer work of landscape design—could raise only about one-twentieth of the $20 million that the Central Park Conservancy was able to collect annually by 1990. Parks in poor areas of the Bronx and Queens have even less hope of raising substantial amounts. Public money for maintaining these parks has been cut, and the City Parks Foundation has not come close to the conservancy's great success with private donors.[52]

What was gained in the 1980s, then, was a very tangible improvement in the physical condition of Central Park. What was lost was a very intangible—but still real—sense of commitment to the public provision of recreational resources for *all* New Yorkers.

In 1991 Commissioner Gotbaum assisted the City Parks Foundation's fund raising by allowing large-scale events in Central Park in exchange for a contribution to the foundation (as well as a commitment to cover police and cleanup costs). A concert before 750,000 on the Great Lawn by singer Paul Simon—the first such event since Diana Ross performed in 1983—seemingly marked a departure from the more restrictive policies implemented in the 1980s. But the $250,000 that Time Warner, the concert's sponsor, donated to the foundation may have looked appealing in a time of fiscal austerity.[53]

By permitting the use of Central Park for fund raising, Commissioner Gotbaum was, in a sense, redistributing the park's unique advantages in attracting private funds. Yet such a policy was also in conflict with the conservancy's priorities of managing the park to protect the Greensward plan and the natural landscape. And although the Simon concert benefited the city's parks, it benefited the corporate sponsors even more. Such efforts, moreover, will never compensate for the vast gap between the conservancy's ability to tap private wealth and the ability of the other city parks. Finally, the new direction in fund raising in effect places a price tag on the use of public space. Just a few weeks after the Simon concert, the Christian evangelist Billy Graham held a rally on the same Great Lawn, attracting a crowd of 250,000 people, including Mayor Dinkins. Like Simon, Graham agreed to pay all expenses ($200,000) and make a charitable contribution.[54] The well-funded Graham organization thus had access to the city's most impressive public space—access that most groups would not be able to afford. Still others—say, an organization opposed to prayer in the schools—might find themselves barred by rules limiting "political" demonstrations.

"The Most Democratic Space in America?"

The fiscal crises of the 1970s and the 1990s have challenged the democratic commitment, built during the previous century and a quarter, to provide public space and public recreation for all. Nevertheless, in the 1980s at least a variety of commentators—using terms reminiscent of the 1860s—continued to celebrate Central Park as "the most popular and democratic space in America" or as "the one truly democratic space in the city." "For years it has been and today continues to be socially and racially integrated, notwithstanding patterns of caste and class stratification and polarization throughout society as a whole," Park Commissioner Gordon Davis wrote in 1981. "Of all its great achievements and features, there is none more profound or dramatically moving than the social democracy of this public space." "One of the geniuses of the park is that, to experience it, people have to desegregate," he told a reporter. "You don't get people coming to you based on sociological groups but on common concerns, about crime or jogging, or what the 110th Street Boathouse should look like. Blacks don't think of themselves as blacks in the park but as, say, bicyclists, and their alliances are with other bicyclists."[55]

But as has been true throughout the park's history, many parkgoers choreograph their use either to avoid unpleasant interactions or because they do not feel welcome in all parts of the park. After the rape of the Central Park jogger, more women hesitated to enter the park after dark. Young people have found it especially difficult to claim full access to such park facilities as ball fields or tennis courts, which require knowledge of the system of permits. Despite increased racial integration within the park, Puerto Rican and black working-class New Yorkers remain concentrated in the northern section, and white upper- and middle-class New Yorkers are overrepresented in the southern section.[56]

Still, Orde Coombs, a *New York Magazine* reporter, agreed with Davis that Central Park was "the single most democratic space in the city." Profiling two Puerto Rican teenagers from East Harlem and the Lower East Side who came to the park on a summer Sunday, Coombs said they had come "to reclaim the only piece of real estate they will ever love. For them, Central Park is a refuge from the slums, the only place in mid-Manhattan where the dispossessed can be at ease without coming under the withering glances of the wealthy." Coombs located the park's democratic character in its openness to the dispossessed; newspaper columnist Sidney Schanberg found it in the provision of "one of the few settings" where New Yorkers come together "not in quest of pluralist perfection but of existing together in respect." For Schanberg the city "at its human best" could be found in a softball game that matched teams of black and white New Yorkers against each other. Although the teams disputed constantly, "they have respect for each other's desire and skills. There may not be love or integration, but there is comprehension."[57]

Openness. Respect. Comprehension. On a warm spring afternoon one can fine many such symbols of these basic preconditions of cultural democracy in the park. Almost forty years ago, James Baldwin, in *Go Tell It on the Mountain*, described the visit of the novel's protagonist, John Grimes, from his home in

Harlem to Central Park on his fourteenth birthday. He climbed up the Ramble, "his favorite hill," and felt an "exultation and sense of power" as he viewed the park and city around him. "And still, on the summit of that hill he paused. He remembered the people he had seen in that city, whose eyes held no love for him . . . and how he was a stranger there." As he dashed down the hill, John "nearly knocked down an old white man with a white beard, who was walking very slowly and leaning on his cane. They both stopped, astonished, and looked at one another. John struggled to catch his breath and apologize, but the old man smiled. John smiled back. It was as though he and the old man had between them a great secret; and the old man moved on."[58]

The park continues to be a space of acknowledgment for people who have, at times, been "strangers" in the city. On June 24, 1989, a visitor to the Great Lawn could join a Gay Pride rally celebrating the twentieth anniversary of the Stonewall riots or, in the summer of 1988, inspect sections of the AIDS quilt displayed on the lawn. Park rules would have barred such mass gatherings before the mid-1960s. And even as late as the 1970s the police periodically swept through and arrested large numbers of gay men in the park. But now, gay New Yorkers—though still facing the threat of violence in the park as elsewhere—can exuberantly claim a place in this public park.[59]

Moments of mutual respect as well as public celebration and sharing do not, of course, erase the deep and divisive problems of the city. Poverty, crime, and bigotry stalked New York City in the 1980s, and such problems do not stop at the gates of the park. At times the reciprocal tolerance of parkgoers has been badly strained. Black and Puerto Rican teenagers sometimes feel that white parkgoers view them all as potential muggers. And older parkgoers sometimes feel that loud music from boom boxes is a deliberate effort to interfere with their enjoyment of the park. Still, on a warm summer day in Central Park, it is possible to glimpse the city "at its human best" and to think more about the possibilities than the limitations of a democratic public space. The park offers opportunities for preexisting communities (rooted, for example, in ethnic ties) to maintain themselves as well as for people to create new user-based friendships (rooted, for instance, in a passion for running, birds, dogs, chess, model boats, or disco roller skating). At the same time, it provides the chance for people who simply stroll through to place themselves within a much larger "imagined community" of ordinary people equally entitled to enjoy the benefits of public resources.[60] The park is a space to see people of varied backgrounds not as sociological categories (blacks and whites or women and men, for example) but as human beings. The creation of such an "imagined community," in which differences are respected and the equal rights of access affirmed, constitutes one precondition for a more democratic and humane society. Those who share a common space may come to share a common vision of the future.

New Yorkers have forged this conception of "common property" through a struggle older than the park itself, over how to define its public and over what a

Disco roller skating, west of the Mall, is a popular Sunday activity for skaters and spectators.

park should be. The gentlemen who created Central Park in the 1850s had a constricted definition of the public that featured themselves as the "representative" or best public. Generally, they shared Frederick Law Olmsted's view that a "park, properly so-called," needed to be artistically designed and managed as a pastoral landscape set apart from the city. Yet the creation of the park under public and democratic auspices opened up the possibility of alternative notions of the public and the park. Whether or not Calvert Vaux would have celebrated the result, the park was gradually redefined as a "many sided, fluent, thoroughly American high art work."

Over time the idea of the park and its public grew more inclusive, particularly in response to pressure from below. Through formal protests (petitions for Sunday concerts or demonstrations against fees for renting park chairs) and informal use patterns, ordinary New Yorkers transformed the gentlemen's conception of the park and its public. These changes did not proceed evenly or always in a straight line. Moses expanded the recreational facilities but also regulated use more tightly, cracking down on vendors and vagrants. His regime was in turn challenged by a new generation of parkgoers, who transformed Central Park into a place for political dissent and cultural experimentation.

When the park was first created, it represented—at least potentially—a socialization of public resources for the good of all citizens. But over the next

With increased concern about health and fitness in the 1970s and 1980s, jogging at the reservoir became a popular pursuit.

140 years New Yorkers had to struggle to achieve its democratic possibilities. In the 1870s and 1880s, for example, they took control of the park back from the state-appointed board of gentlemen and inserted it into city politics, and park workers demanded working conditions that would permit them to join the public in enjoying the city's preeminent leisure space. New Yorkers have often been reluctant to spend sufficient funds for adequate maintenance or wages. The New Deal, however, brought a dramatic infusion of federal money and an increased sense that citizens had a "right" to recreational facilities and public space. And postwar unionization gave city workers better pay and a greater say over their conditions of employment.

Fiscal crisis, however, shook New Yorkers' confidence in their ability as a public to provide and maintain open spaces. So they pulled back and turned to private corporations and real estate developers to provide new public spaces and to private philanthropy to support Central Park. The Central Park Conservancy helped restore the park, enriched its offerings, and also recommended new regulations. Control of the park is now divided between a self-perpetuating board of private (and wealthy) citizens and the city's park commissioner.

The systems that had governed since the 1870s were far from perfect, and the conservancy (like the boards of the art and the natural history museums in the 1880s) responds to pressure from ordinary citizens and elected officials. Nevertheless, the sovereign public has surrendered its commitment to provide free, well-maintained public spaces and has lost a measure of control over its most important public space. Exactly how much New Yorkers have lost in the bargain that restored Central Park for them remains unclear—and debatable—as the twentieth century draws toward a close.

It is also unclear whether the public access that was achieved over time will be sustained in the future. In the 1860s the park was distant from the homes of most working-class New Yorkers, who, in any case, preferred open spaces better suited to their recreational habits. In the late nineteenth and early twentieth centuries, ordinary New Yorkers often lived within walking distance of the park, and they worked fewer hours. They claimed Central Park as their own. In the late twentieth century, the park remains a refuge for the city's poorest residents, but fewer working-class families can afford to live on its borders.

A more serious threat to equal access is raised, however, by the very success achieved by Central Park. Its magnificent rehabilitation throws into sharp relief the much less adequately maintained public spaces in other parts of the city. Is New York moving toward a system in which private fund raising will support superior public facilities in more affluent (and symbolically central) sections of the city, while allowing the general commitment to a "right" to recreational facilities and public space to lapse elsewhere in the metropolis? In the 1850s the *Staats-Zeitung* had asked for "many smaller parks in different parts of the city," instead of a "mammoth park" that would be used only by "the heirs of the Upper Tendoms." Dispersed and well-maintained public spaces are an essential part of any commitment to social and cultural democracy in the nation's largest city.

At the start of the 1990s the future of our public parks—and indeed of the public sector, in general—looks grim. At both local and national levels politicians talk about the need to "downsize" government, to reverse the historic expansion of public services. In a climate where public hospitals, public schools, and public housing are threatened, the claims of public parks and recreation are particularly difficult to advance. In the fiscal crisis of the early 1990s, the New York City departments of parks and cultural affairs (which supports museums, zoos, and libraries) have faced the largest cuts, losing almost 30 percent of their budgets. To those—like us—who argue that parks *as well as* schools, hospitals, and housing are an essential part of a decent and humane city, many local politicians and civic leaders reply that they simply cannot raise taxes any more or businesses will flee. Such arguments are reminiscent of those of the conservative downtown merchants who in 1851 viewed the creation of a grand public park as "humbug." Their suggestion that "if downtown people wish to rusticate, they can find Elysian Fields [in Hoboken] within half the distance" is echoed today in claims that the "private sector" can adequately provide all needs.

But if history teaches us anything it is the contingency of particular historical moments, the possibility that change can come from new and unexpected directions. After all, New Yorkers began building the nation's greatest public park in the midst of a severe depression in the mid-nineteenth century, and they won a dramatic democratization of recreational resources during the worst depression in the nation's history. There are alternative visions of the urban future that challenge the pessimism of those who argue that cities must do less for their citizens. Like the more expansive coalition that won the day for Central Park in the 1850s and like the coalition that Henry George forged in the mid-1880s, some people would argue that the future greatness of New York lies in a livable environment (rather than a low tax rate) that will attract and maintain a healthy economy and culture. "To give all classes leisure, and comfort, and independence, the decencies of life, the opportunities of mental and moral development," George declared more than a century ago, "would be like turning water into a desert."

The fiscal crisis and recession of the early 1990s has already prompted a rethinking of how to fund, create, and administer adequate and accessible public spaces. New coalitions of park activists, environmentalists, and public officials are proposing regional park districts to overcome the barriers between cities and suburbs, decentralized administration to make parks more responsive to their constituencies, and new strategies of funding—including increased federal and state support as well as private philanthropy. But such initiatives can succeed only with the support of a wider public, with, as Calvert Vaux put it, recognition "of the possibilities that are within all classes" and the "genuine life blood" of public participation.

Thus, the challenge of preserving democratic public space within an inegalitarian society remains. To exclude poor New Yorkers from public spaces, to rely solely on private agencies to support and manage public institutions, to fail to ensure that all New Yorkers have access to adequate public spaces and recreational facilities, to settle for cultural democracy without political and economic democracy—all jeopardize the democratic public possibilities New Yorkers have struggled to realize since the founding of Central Park. The greatness of Central Park has more to do with these democratic possibilities than with the artful arrangement of trees, shrubs, bridges, paths, and lawns. In the early 1990s, as in the early 1980s, Central Park is still "the most democratic space" in New York, if not in the United States. For Central Park to remain genuinely a "public" park—in all the senses of that term—New Yorkers must continue to struggle toward that goal both in the park and in the city in which it is inextricably embedded.

Note on Citations

The following notes list all the sources on which we have relied for direct evidence, although not all the primary and secondary sources that we have consulted during our research. Because the Frederick Law Olmsted Papers are available in two different forms (on microfilm and in manuscript boxes) and because they are reasonably well indexed, we have not cited specific reels or boxes. We have similarly not cited box numbers for the Olmsted Associates Papers, although almost all the material relating to Central Park is in Container 502. All the manuscript collections cited as being in NYPL are from Rare Books and Manuscript Division, The New York Public Library, Astor, Lenox and Tilden Foundations. For the Beekman, Morgan, and Mayor's Papers, we have provided citations in the format: Box:Folder, e.g., 88:24 MP is Box 88, Folder 24 in the Mayor's Papers.

In order to analyze the backgrounds of different actors in the park story, we have located biographical evidence on hundreds of different individuals. To save space, we have not indicated the specific source of most this information, but it can be found in standard biographical sources, including the *DAB*, the *NCAB*, *New York Times* obituaries, and city directories. The citations for the New York State Senate and Assembly *Journals* and *Documents* are noted by legislative session. Because the place of publication for most of the books and reports cited is New York, we have only noted the place of publication where it is other than New York City.

Abbreviations Used in Notes

INDIVIDUALS AND INSTITUTIONS

AHG	Andrew Haswell Green
AMNH	American Museum of Natural History, New York
BCCP	Board of Commissioners of the Central Park
CPA	Central Park Association
CP Cons.	Central Park Conservancy
CV	Calvert Vaux
FLO	Frederick Law Olmsted
FLO, Jr.	Frederick Law Olmsted, Jr
JO	John Olmsted
JWB	James W. Beekman
MMA	Metropolitan Museum of Art

NEWSPAPERS, MAGAZINES, AND JOURNALS

Am. S-N	*Amsterdam Star-News*
CA	*Commercial Advertiser*
C&E	*New York Morning Courier and New York Enquirer*
Disp.	*Dispatch*
FL	*Frank Leslie's Illustrated Newspaper*
Her.	*New York Herald*
H-T	*New York Herald-Tribune*
HM	*Harper's New Monthly Magazine* and *Harper's Magazine*
HW	*Harper's Weekly*
Ir. Am.	*Irish American*

Ir. N	*Irish News*
Jour.	*Journal and Advertiser,* which later became *Evening Journal*
JC	*Journal of Commerce*
LA	*Landscape Architecture*
Leader	*New York Leader*
Mail	*Evening Mail*
News	*New York Daily News*
NY Mag.	*New York Magazine*
NYer	*New Yorker*
NYHSQ	*New-York Historical Society Quarterly*
NYT	*New York Times*
Post	*New York Evening Post*
RERBG	*Real Estate Record and Building Guide*
S-Z	*New Yorker Staats-Zeitung*
Spirit	*Spirit of the Times*
Trib.	*New York Tribune*
VV	*Village Voice*
W-T	*World-Telegram*

ARCHIVES AND MANUSCRIPT COLLECTIONS

CP Arsenal	Central Park Arsenal
FH Mss.	Francis Hawks Papers, NYPL
FLO Mss.	Frederick Law Olmsted Papers, Manuscript Division, Library of Congress, Washington, D.C.
JWB Mss.	James W. Beekman Papers, New-York Historical Society, New York
LC	Library of Congress, Washington, D.C.
MARC	Municipal Archives and Record Center, New York
NYCC	Office of the New York County Clerk, New York
MP	Mayor's Papers, MARC
NYHS	New-York Historical Society, New York
NYPL	New York Public Library, Astor, Lenox and Tilden Foundations, New York
OA Mss.	Olmsted Associates Papers, Library of Congress, Washington, D.C.
RC	Register of Conveyances, New York County, Hall of Records, City of New York
RW Mss.	Richard Welling Papers, NYPL

FREQUENTLY CITED BOOKS AND DOCUMENTS

AJ	*New York State Assembly Journal* (Albany, 1851–71).
ASHPS, *AR* [1——]	American Scenic and Historic Preservation Society, *Annual Report, 1—— of the American Scenic and Historic Preservation Society* (Albany, 1896–).

Ass. *Docs.*   *Documents* of the New York State Assembly (Albany, 1849–77).

BA *Docs.*   New York City Board of Aldermen, *Documents* (New York, 1849–75).

BA *Proc.*   New York City Board of Aldermen, *Proceedings* (New York, 1849–71).

BAA *Proc.*   New York City Board of Assistant Aldermen, *Proceedings and Documents* (New York, 1849–53).

BCCP *Min.*   New York City, Board of Commissioners of the Central Park, *Minutes of the Proceedings of the Board of Commissioners of the Central Park* (New York, 1858–69), including documents.

BCCP   New York City, Board of Commissioners of the Central Park, *Annual Report*
AR [18—]

BDPP *Min.*   Board of Commissioners of the Department of Public Parks, *Minutes* (New York, 1871–98). Minutes were issued by Department of Public Parks between 1870 and 1898, but published volumes are not available for every year.

BDPP   Board of Commissioners of the Department of Public Parks, *Annual Report*
AR [187–]   [for the years ending May 1, 1871, May 1, 1872, Dec. 31, 1873] (New York, 1871–74). Between 1874 and 1898, there were no separately published annual reports, although some quarterly reports were included in the *City Record.*.

DAB   *Dictionary of American Biography* (New York, 1928–1988), 20 vols. and 8 supplements.

FLOP   *The Papers of Frederick Law Olmsted* (Baltimore, 1977–90). Five volumes have been issued so far: Vol. 1: Charles Capen McLaughlin, ed., and Charles E. Beveridge, assoc. ed., *The Formative Years, 1822–1852;* Vol. 2: McLaughlin and Beveridge, eds., and David Schuyler, asst. ed., *Slavery and the South, 1852–1857;* Vol. 3: Beveridge and Schuyler, eds., *Creating Central Park, 1857–1861;* Vol. 4: Jane Turner Censer, ed., *Defending the Union: The Civil War and the U.S. Sanitary Commission, 1861–1863;* Vol. 5: Victoria Post Ranney, ed., Gerard J. Rauluk, assoc. ed., and Carolyn F. Hamilton, asst. ed., *The California Frontier, 1863–1865.*

FYLA   Frederick Law Olmsted, Jr., and Theodora Kimball, eds., *Forty Years of Landscape Architecture: Central Park* (1928; rpt. Cambridge, Mass., 1973).

GP   Frederick Law Olmsted and Calvert Vaux, "Description of a Plan for the Improvement of Central Park: 'Greensward,'" *FLOP* 3:162–77.

NCAB   *National Cyclopedia of American Biography* (Clifton, N.J., 1984), which includes the permanent series volumes 1–62.

Pks. Dpt.   Department of Parks, *Annual Report of the Department of Parks of the City of*
AR [1—]   *New York for the Year 1——* (New York, 1898–1934). After 1916, the reports issued by the individual boroughs were published separately, but the Borough of Manhattan Parks Department reports are cited in this same form.

Pks. Dpt.   Department of Parks, *Minutes* (New York, 1898–1933).
Min.

Rebuilding   Elizabeth Barlow Rogers et al., *Rebuilding Central Park: A Management and*
CP   *Restoration Plan* (Cambridge, Mass., 1987).

Rebuilding   *Rebuilding Central Park: A Management and Restoration Plan: Draft Edition*
CP: Draft   (New York, 1985).

Sen. *Docs.*	*Documents* of the New York State Senate (Albany, 1850–51).
SJ	*New York State Senate Journal* (Albany, 1849–54).
SP	Frederick Law Olmsted, *Spoils of the Park: With a Few Leaves from the Deep-Laden Note-Books of "A Wholly Unpractical Man,"* rpt. in *FYLA*, 117–54.
Strong, *Diary*	Allan Nevins and Milton Halsey Thomas, eds., *The Diary of George Templeton Strong*, 4 vols. (New York, 1952).

OTHER ABBREVIATIONS

AR	*Annual Report*
B	Box
F	Folder
LB	Letterbook

Notes

Introduction

1. Donald Knowler, *The Falconer of Central Park* (1984), 9–10; Eugene Kinkead, *Central Park, 1857–1995: The Birth, Decline, and Renewal of a National Treasure* (1990), 175; Elliot Willensky and Norval White, *AIA Guide to New York City* (1988), 336.

2. Walt Whitman, "Specimen Days" (May 16 to 22, 1879), in *Complete Prose Works* (Philadelphia, 1892), 135.

3. William Dean Howells, "Glimpses of New York," in *Impressions and Experiences* (1896; rpt. Freeport, N.Y., 1972), 231–32; Herbert and Dorothy Fields, *Up in Central Park* (1945); Gerome Ragni and James Rado, *Hair: The American Tribal Love-Rock Musical* (1969); E. B. White, *Stuart Little* (1945), 35–46.

4. Edith Wharton, *The Custom of the Country* (1913; rpt. 1981); Robert Nathan, *Portrait of Jennie* (1940); Lyrics from Vernon Duke's "Autumn in New York"; J. D. Salinger, *The Catcher in the Rye* (1951; rpt. 1963), 189–91; Isaac Bashevis Singer, "Neighbors," in *The Collected Stories of Isaac Bashevis Singer* (1982), 599.

5. Marianne Moore, Introduction to *Central Park Country: A Tune Within Us*, ed. David Brower (1968), 19. See "The Painter's Park," portfolio accompanying Walter Karp, "The Central Park," *American Heritage* 32 (Apr.–May 1981): 81–97. The National Museum of American Art's computerized "Inventory of American Painting" includes 200 images of Central Park—most of them landscapes.

6. Ruth Orkin, *A World through My Window* (1978); Nellie Bly [Elizabeth Cochrane], *The Mystery of Central Park* (1889); Carson quoted in August Heckscher, *Alive in the City: Memoir of an Ex-Commissioner* (1974), 236; Robert Lowell, "Central Park" (1963), in *New York: An Illustrated Anthology*, comp. Michael Marqusee (Topsfield, Mass., 1988), 156.

7. The literature on Olmsted is vast. For his writings, see *FLOP; FYLA;* Albert Fein, ed., *Landscape into Cityscape: Frederick Law Olmsted's Plans for a Greater New York City* (Ithaca, 1968); S. B. Sutton, ed., *Civilizing American Cities: A Selection of Frederick Law Olmsted's Writings on City Landscapes* (Cambridge, Mass., 1971). For Olmsted and the South, Dana F. White and Victor A. Kramer, *Olmsted South: Old South Critic, New South Planner* (Westport, Conn., 1979). Major biographies are Laura Wood Roper, *FLO: A Biography of Frederick Law Olmsted* (Baltimore, 1973); Melvin Kalfus, *Frederick Law Olmsted: The Passion of a Public Artist* (1990); Elizabeth Stevenson, *Park Maker: A Life of Frederick Law Olmsted* (1977). Among the most helpful discussions of Olmsted's artistic vision are David Schuyler, *The New Urban Landscape: The Redefinition of City Form in Nineteenth-Century America* (Baltimore, 1986), 59–195; Charles E. Beveridge, "Frederick

Law Olmsted's Theory of Landscape Design," *Nineteenth Century* 3 (Summer 1977): 38–43, and Introduction to *FLOP* 3:1–48; essays in *Art of the Olmsted Landscape*, ed. Bruce Kelly et al. (1981); Elizabeth Barlow [Rogers] and William Alex, *Frederick Law Olmsted's New York* (1972); Henry Hope Reed and Sophia Duckworth, *Central Park: A History and a Guide* (1967; rpt. 1972); Cynthia Zaitzevsky, *Frederick Law Olmsted and the Boston Park System* (Cambridge, Mass., 1982). For different interpretations of Olmsted's social vision, see, e.g., Thomas Bender, *Toward an Urban Vision: Ideas and Institutions in Nineteenth Century America* (Lexington, Ky., 1975), 159–87; Geoffrey Blodgett, "Frederick Law Olmsted: Landscape Architecture as Conservative Reform," *Journal of American History* 62 (Mar. 1976): 869–89; Albert Fein, *Frederick Law Olmsted and the American Environmental Tradition* (1972). Only a few works have been devoted specifically to the park's history; see Edward Hagaman Hall, "Central Park in the City of New York," ASHPS *16AR* [1911]; *FYLA;* Reed and Duckworth, *Central Park;* Ian R. Stewart, "Central Park, 1851–1871: Urbanization and Environmental Planning in New York City" (Ph.D. diss., Cornell University, 1973); M. M. Graff, *Central Park, Prospect Park: A New Perspective* (1985); Kinkead, *Central Park.* Important forthcoming books by Peter Buckley and David Scobey explore Olmsted and Central Park within the context of nineteenth-century social and cultural history.

8. *Oxford English Dictionary* (1971), s.v. "park"; Raymond Williams, *The Country and the City* (1973), 122, 124, 125.

9. Norman T. Newton, *Design on the Land: The Development of Landscape Architecture* (Cambridge, Mass., 1971), 20. For a history of urban parks, see also George F. Chadwick, *The Park and the Town* (1966).

10. John Brinckerhoff Jackson, "The Origins of Parks," in *Discovering the Vernacular Landscape* (New Haven, 1984), 127–30.

11. Edward Hagaman Hall, "An Historical Sketch of City Hall Park," ASHPS *15AR* [1910], 385–424.

12. For a cogent discussion of property rights, see C. B. Macpherson, *Property: Mainstream and Critical Positions* (Toronto, 1978), 4–6.

1. The Gentleman from Europe and the Idea of a Great Park

1. John Punnett Peters, ed., *Annals of St. Michael's: Being the History of St. Michael's Protestant Episcopal Church, for One Hundred Years, 1807–1907* (1907), 104 (quot.), 123; Charles H. Haswell, *Reminiscences of an Octogenarian of the City of New York* (1897), 465–66; Allan Nevins, *The Evening Post: A Century of Journalism* (1922), 193–96; *Post*, July 3, 1844. The tradition of crediting Downing began relatively early, perhaps because of his untimely death in 1852. See, for example, Edward Hagaman Hall, "Central Park in the City of New York," ASHPS *16AR* [1911], 449; *A Guide to the Central Park* (1860), 10–11; Clarence C. Cook, *A Description of the New York Central Park* (1869), 16–17. But in the late 19th century, many others were put forward as the "father" of Central Park. See, for example, *NYT*, Sept. 22, 1871, Oct. 10, 1894, crediting Andrew Green; *NYT*, June 3, 1874 (Samuel Ruggles); Matthew Hale Smith, *Sunshine and Shadow in New York* (Hartford, 1868), 356 (John A. Kennedy).

2. *JC*, June 24, 1851; *Her.*, Feb. 3, 1854. See also *Trib.*, Feb. 1, 1854.

3. Robert Bowne Minturn, Jr., *Memoir of Robert Bowne Minturn* (1871), 65–146.

4. Lyman Horace Weeks, ed., *The Prominent Families of New York* (1898), 406.

5. *JC*, June 24, 1851.

6. Ibid.; *Post*, June 13, 1851.

7. Charles A. Beard, "Some Aspects of Regional Planning," *American Political Science Review* 20 (May 1926): 276–77, 279.

8. On size and cost, see *FYLA*, 54; Edward Dana Durand, *The Finances of New York City* (1898), 100, 147, 326, 379; BDPP *Min.*, doc. 64 (Mar. 5, 1875), 4, 6–20.

9. *Post*, May 7, 1851. The Kingsland address is reprinted in *FYLA*, 24–26, but with the wrong date. We have found no evidence to support the contention of *FYLA*, 24, and other accounts, that the park was advocated in the fall 1850 mayoral campaign. The *Post*, July 6, 1850, did report rumors of a proposal for the city to acquire land for a park.

10. BA *Docs.*, 17, pt. 1, no. 1 (Jan. 1, 1850): 12–13. For the dates of opening of squares, see I. N. Phelps Stokes, *Iconography of Manhattan Island, 1498–1909*, 6 vols. (1915–28; rpt. 1967), 3:968–72.

11. *Post*, Aug. 5, 1850, June 7, 1851; *Her.,* July 15, 1850. See also *Trib.*, June 13, 1851. On the decline of downtown public spaces, see *Her.*, Nov. 2, 1848; *Trib.*, Nov. 22, 1848; and for comparison to European spaces, William Cullen Bryant letter from London, June 24, 1845, in *Letters of a Traveler* (1851), 168–70. See also *Trib.*, June 8, 1847; *Post*, July 6, 1850.

12. *Post*, July 3, 1844, July 6, Aug. 5, 1850; *Trib.*, June 8, 1847; William Schermerhorn to JWB, Nov. 26, Dec. 12, 1850, 25:4, JWB Mss. On Kingsland, see *NYT*, Oct. 15, 1878; on Whig politics, Daniel Walker Howe, *The Political Culture of the American Whigs* (Chicago, 1979).

13. *FYLA*, 25; BA *Proc.*, 42: 543–46 (June 3, 1851); BAA *Proc.*, 42: 522 (June 4, 1851). The aldermen's vote was 14–4; the assistants were unanimous.

14. *Trib.*, June 13, 1851; *C&E*, June 18, 1851. See also *Trib.*, June 8, 1847; Hopper Striker Mott, "Jones Wood," in *Valentine's Manual of the City of New York, 1917–1918*, ed. Henry Collins Brown (1917), 140–59; "Jones Wood," *Central Park Gazette and Guide for Present and Future Reference* (July 17, 1875), 1.

15. Stokes, *Iconography*, 6:108–9; Henry Croswell Tuttle, *Abstracts of Farm Titles in the City of New York, between 39th and 75th Streets, East of the Common Lands . . .* (1877), 287–314. Peter Schermerhorn and General James Jones controlled land beyond their shares as trustees for other family members. See also Richard Schermerhorn, Jr., *Schermerhorn Genealogy and Family Chronicles* (1914); Gene Schermerhorn, *Letters to Phil: Memories of a New York Boyhood, 1848–56* (1982).

16. *Post*, July 3, 1844; BA *Proc.*, 42: 545; *SJ* 74: 689, 710. Even if the owners had been willing to sell, the city would have had to get authorization from the legislature to alter the 1811 street plan as well as to fund the purchase through tax or bond revenues.

17. Robert Minturn to JWB, June 21, 1851, 25:10, JWB Mss.; *Trib.*, July 7, 1851; Moses Beach, *The Wealth and Biography of the Wealthy Citizens of the City of New York* (1855).

18. For biographies and connections among these gentlemen, see Beach, *Wealthy Citizens;* Edward K. Spann, *The New Metropolis: New York City, 1840–1857* (1981), 207–15; Robert Greenhalgh Albion, *The Rise of New York Port, 1815–1860* (1939); Minturn, *Memoir; NYT*, Nov. 27, 1877; *DAB; NCAB;* and *NYT* obituaries. Other petitioners were John Anthon, John Bridge, Stewart Brown, Henry Cary, Henry Chauncey, W. W. DeForest, George Griswold, W. F. Havemeyer, John Hicks, S. S. Howland, D. S. Kennedy, Mortimer Livingston, Charles Marshall, Matthew Morgan, George Newbold, John Palmer, Paul Spofford, and William C. Wetmore.

19. *AJ* 74: 1646–47.

20. Ira Rosenwaike, *Population History of New York City* (Syracuse, 1972), 42. For optimism about the city's growth, see, e.g., *Post*, July 27, Aug. 14, 1850; on wealth distribution, Edward Pessen, *Riches, Class, and Power before the Civil War* (Lexington, Mass., 1973), 33–35; on mortality, Spann, *New Metropolis*, 135–36, 431. For building survey to 30th Street, *Trib.*, Oct. 31, 1850; *Her.*, July 14, 1851.

21. On reform, labor, and nativism, see Spann, *New Metropolis*, 50–52, 270–78, 289–91; Carroll Smith Rosenberg, *Religion and the Rise of the American City: The New York City Mission Movement, 1812–1870* (Ithaca, 1971); Christine Stansell, *City of Women: Sex and Class in New York, 1789–1860* (1986), 63–75; Sean Wilentz, *Chants Democratic: New York City and the Rise of the American Working Class, 1788–1850* (1984), 266–69, 315–24.

22. BA *Proc.*, 42: 544; Elizabeth Blackmar, *Manhattan for Rent, 1785–1850* (Ithaca, 1989), 151–58.

23. *Trib.*, June 13, 1851; *Post*, May 7, 1851.

24. Alexis de Tocqueville, *Democracy in America*, ed. J. P. Mayer (Garden City, N.Y., 1969), 454, and passim; George W. Curtis, "Editor's Easy Chair," *HM* (June 1855): 125; Spann, *New Metropolis*, 165; *NYT*, June 23, 1853. See also Schuyler, *New Urban Landscape*, 63–66.

25. Tocqueville, *Democracy in America*, 237; *Trib.*, June 8, 1847.

26. *CA*, June 5, July 31, 1851. See also *Trib.*, July 8, 1851. On concerns over "suburban" flight, see Kenneth T. Jackson, *Crabgrass Frontier: The Suburbanization of the United States* (1985), 29–30; Spann, *New Metropolis*, chap. 8.

27. *Trib.*, June 13, 1851 (advantaged pecuniarily). For health arguments, see, e.g., Bryant, *Letters of a Traveler*, 169; *Post*, June 7, 13, 1851; *Her.*, July 15, 1850, June 5, 1851; *CA*, June 5, 1851;

C&E, July 24, 1851; *Disp.*, May 11, 1851. On English parks as "lungs," see George F. Chadwick, *The Park and the Town: Public Landscapes in the Nineteenth and Twentieth Centuries* (1966), 42, 50–52; and for American invocations, David Schuyler, *The New Urban Landscape: The Redefinition of City Form in Nineteenth-Century America* (Baltimore, 1986), 60–61. On New York's health problems, see John Duffy, *A History of Public Health in New York City, 1625–1866* (1968), 515–70; Richard B. Stott, *Workers in the Metropolis: Class, Ethnicity, and Youth in Antebellum New York City* (Ithaca, 1990), 181–86; John Griscom, *The Sanitary Condition of the Laboring Population of New York* (1845); BA *Docs.*, 48, pt. 1, no. 23 (Feb. 1, 1851): 347–469.

28. *Post*, May 7, 1851; *C&E*, July 24, 1851. See also *Trib.*, July 8, 1851; *Post*, June 13, 1851; *Illustrated News*, June 11, 1853.

29. *Post*, July 10, 1851; Andrew Jackson Downing, "A Talk about Public Parks and Gardens" (1848), in *Rural Essays* (1855), 143. On antebellum health reform for women, see Catharine Beecher, *A Treatise on Domestic Economy* (Boston, 1841); William Leach, *True Love and Perfect Union: The Feminist Reform of Sex and Society* (1980), 19–37, 66–72; Martha Verbrugge, *Able-Bodied Womanhood: Personal Health and Social Change in Nineteenth-Century Boston* (1988), 11–80.

30. For editorials arguing that only government could withstand the force of private development, see *CA*, June 5, 1851; *Her.*, June 6, 1851; *Sun*, July 14, 1851. On excursions, see, e.g., *Her.*, July 4, 1850; *JC*, June 11, July 19, 1851.

31. On Astor Place riots and cultural bifurcation, see Peter George Buckley, "To the Opera House: Culture and Society in New York City, 1820–1860" (Ph.D. diss., State University of New York, Stony Brook, 1984); Spann, *New Metropolis*, 235–41; on the labor movement, Wilentz, *Chants Democratic*, 363–72; Iver Bernstein, *The New York City Draft Riots: Their Significance for American Society and Politics in the Age of the Civil War* (1990), 78–98; on working-class culture, Stansell, *City of Women* (1986), 63–75, 193–216; Robert Ernst, *Immigrant Life in New York City, 1825–1863* (1949), 135–49; Stott, *Workers in the Metropolis*, 212–76.

32. Strong, *Diary*, 2:149; Minturn, *Memoir*, 43–44. On older customs of patronage and charity, see Amy Bridges, *A City in the Republic: Antebellum New York and the Origins of Machine Politics* (Ithaca, 1987), 72–73, 79–81; on the AICP, Spann, *New Metropolis*, 83–91; Bernstein, *New York City Draft Riots*, 177–84; Roy Lubove, "The New York Association for Improving the Condition of the Poor: The Formative Years," *NYHSQ* 43 (July 1959): 307–27; Rosenberg, *Religion and the Rise of the City*, 245–73.

33. *Post*, June 13, 1851; *CA*, June 29, 1853. Such arguments became more common in the press in 1853 than two years earlier, perhaps in response to the mobilized labor movement. Prior to 1853, Andrew Jackson Downing fully laid out the argument that parks would improve ordinary citizens in his *Horticulturalist* essays, reprinted in *Rural Essays*: "A Talk about Public Parks and Gardens" (Oct. 1848), 138–46, and "The New York Park" (Aug. 1851), 147–53.

34. *Trib.*, June 22, 28, 1853, and see Aug. 8, 1851 (reprinting Downing), Feb. 11, 1854. On Greeley's politics, see Bernstein, *New York City Draft Riots*, 169–71, 180–81; Howe, *Political Culture of American Whigs*, 187, 191–95.

35. Allen Churchill, *The Upper Crust: An Informal History of New York's Highest Society* (Englewood Cliffs, N.J., 1970), 43; *NYT*, Dec. 28, 1886; Minturn, *Memoir*, 53. On women's philanthropy, see also Rosenberg, *Religion and the Rise of the City*; Nancy Hewitt, *Women's Activism and Social Change: Rochester, New York, 1822–1872* (Ithaca, 1984); Lori Ginzberg, *Women and the Work of Benevolence: Morality, Politics, and Class in the Nineteenth-Century United States* (New Haven, 1990); and on elite residential enclaves, Buckley, "To the Opera House," 221–45.

36. *Post*, July 10, 1851. On promenade, see Blackmar, *Manhattan for Rent*, 145–46; Daniel M. Bluestone, "From Promenade to Park: The Gregarious Origins of Brooklyn's Park Movement," *American Quarterly* 39 (Winter 1987): 529–50.

37. *Post*, July 10, 1851; Churchill, *Upper Crust*, 45.

38. *Her.*, July 15, 1850, June 5, 1851. See similar complaints in *Trib.*, July 8, 1851; Curtis, "Editor's Easy Chair," 125.

39. Downing, "A Talk about Public Parks," *Rural Essays*, 143; Buckley, "To the Opera House," 199–201, 228–29, 240–45; Karen Halttunen, *Confidence Men and Painted Ladies: A Study of Middle-Class Culture in America, 1830–1870* (New Haven, 1982) 59–73.

40. Downing, "Public Cemeteries and Public Gardens," *Rural Essays*, 155–56; Minturn, *Memoir*, 51–52. On New York Horticultural Society (formed 1852), see *NYT*, Dec. 6, 1853; on its

lobbying for park, *SJ* 76: 593; George W. Curtis to JWB, Apr. 4, 1853, LB 3, JWB Mss. See also *JC*, July 2, 1851. On the cemetery movement, see also Schuyler, *New Urban Landscape*, 37–56; Ian R. Stewart, "Central Park, 1851–1871: Urbanization and Environmental Planning in New York City" (Ph.D. diss., Cornell University., 1973), 84–89; Stanley French, "The Cemetery as Cultural Institution: The Establishment of Mount Auburn and the 'Rural' Cemetery Movement," *American Quarterly* 26 (Mar. 1974): 37–59; Blanche Linden-Ward, *Silent City on a Hill: Landscapes of Memory and Boston's Mount Auburn Cemetery* (Columbus, Ohio, 1989); Donald Simon, "Greenwood Cemetery and the American Park Movement," in *Essays in the History of New York City: A Memorial to Sidney Pomerantz*, ed. Irwin Yellowitz (Port Washington, N.Y., 1978), 61–77. On horticulture, see also Tamara Plakins Thornton, "The Moral Dimensions of Horticulture in Antebellum America," *New England Quarterly* 57 (Mar. 1984): 3–24; Alexander Von Hoffman, "The Origins of Urban Public Landscapes in Nineteenth-Century America," unpub. paper, 1989, copy in possession of authors; Daniel Bluestone, *Constructing Chicago* (New Haven, 1991), chap. 2.

41. David Tomlinson, "William Cullen Bryant," in *Antebellum Writers in New York and the South*, ed. Joel Meyerson (Detroit, 1979), 37–38; Parke Godwin, *A Biography of William Cullen Bryant*, 2 vols. (1893), 1:322, 334–35, 2:342; Spann, *New Metropolis*, 165; Edmund T. Delaney, *New York's Turtle Bay Old and New* (Barre, Mass., 1965), 11 (Fuller).

42. "Downing, A Talk about Public Parks," and "Hints to Rural Improvers," in *Rural Essays*, 142, 116–17; *A Treatise on the Theory and Practice of Landscape Gardening Adapted to North America* (1859 ed.; rpt. 1967), 2–3, 18, 23. See also George B. Tatum, "Andrew Jackson Downing: Arbiter of American Taste, 1815–1852" (Ph.D. diss., Princeton University, 1950).

43. *CA*, June 6, 1851, also printed in *Rural Essays*, 546–57; Downing, "A Talk about Public Parks," 143. Cf. "The New York Park," 147–53.

44. Norman T. Newton, *Design on the Land: The Development of Landscape Architecture* (Cambridge, Mass., 1971), 263. See also Neil Harris, *The Artist in American Society: The Formative Years, 1790–1860* (1966), 211–16.

45. *JC*, June 5, 1851.

46. *Trib.*, July 12, 1851. See also *JC*, June 24, 1851; *S-Z*, July 11, 1851.

47. Philip L. White, *The Beekmans of New York in Commerce and Politics* (1956), 554–623; *JC*, June 21, 1851. For Beekman's landholdings, see Tuttle, *Abstract of Farm Titles*, 124–39, 227–45. On his attachment to his country estate, see Nathaniel Hawthorne to JWB, Apr. 9, 1853, LB 3, JWB Mss.

48. Spann, *New Metropolis*, 429; Durand, *Finances*, 25–31, 65, 372. On uptown landholding patterns, see Chapter 3.

49. On benefit assessments, see Stephen Diamond, "The Death and Transformation of Benefit Taxation: Special Assessments in Nineteenth-Century America," *Journal of Legal Studies* 2 (1983): 201–40; Victor Rosewater, *Special Assessments: A Study in Municipal Finance* (1898), 29–34; Blackmar, *Manhattan for Rent*, 161–69. For rise in assessments, Durand, *Finances*, 58–59, 372. For antiassessment movement, see their newspaper, *Municipal Gazette*, started Mar. 11, 1841.

50. Peter A. H. Jackson to JWB, Jan. 1850, 25:4, JWB Mss.; BA *Proc.*, 42: 14, 280, 336, 568. Beekman also advocated the opening of Second Avenue, which his neighbors the Schermerhorn and Jones families opposed; see J. Beekman Fish to JWB, Feb. 3, 1850, 3:10, JWB Mss. For antiassessment petitions to legislature (signed by gentlemen on both sides of the park movement), see *Municipal Gazette*, Mar. 22, 1841, p. 9, Apr. 7, 1842, p. 104, Nov. 17, 1843, pp. 145–47. On opening avenues uptown which spurred this opposition, see BA *Proc.*, 47, pt. 2: 385–88. For Beekman's role, see, e.g., Francis Bacon to JWB, Apr. 8, 1851, 25:10, M. Hopper Mott to JWB, Feb. 11, 1850, and E. H. Hudson to JWB, Feb. 19, 1850, 10:3, Luther Bradish to JWB, Feb. 25, 1850, 20:2, JWB Mss.

51. *Post*, July 20, 1851; S. P. Moulton to JWB, Aug. 11, 1849, 5:7, JWB Mss.; Mott to JWB, Feb. 11, 1850. See also *Post*, Aug. 14, 1850; Horace Greeley to JWB, Aug. 8, 1849, 5:7, JWB Mss.

52. On covenants, see Richard Amerman to JWB, Feb. 12, 1850, 10:2, K. Miller to JWB, Mar. 3, 1852, LB 2, on complaints to butchers, Butchers Melting Association to JWB, July 6, 1853, LB 3, all in JWB Mss. On settlement near Beekman's land, see Delaney, *New York's Turtle Bay*, 17.

53. *JC*, June 28, 1851. See also Blackmar, *Manhattan for Rent*, 162–68.

54. *JC*, Oct. 14, 1853. For English precedents, see Chadwick, *Park and Town*, 29–32, 68–89. For Dooley's ties to JWB, see William B. Rockwell to JWB, Mar. 10, 1851, 25:8; George Jacques to JWB, Jan. 3, 9, 1851, 25:4, JWB Mss. Dooley owned four lots between 51st and 52nd Street: Ward 19 Tax Book, 1851, MARC; and Block Index to Reindexed Conveyance, Block 1346, NYCC, New York.

55. Minturn to JWB, June 23, 1851, and cf. Rufus Prime to JWB, June 23, 1851, noting similar objections of Stephen Whitney, both in 25:10, JWB Mss. On difficulties in the assembly, see letters from Minturn and Henry Davies to JWB, both June 21, 1851, 25:10, JWB Mss. For Churchill's landholdings, see Tuttle, *Abstracts of Land Titles*, 269–70; for Crumbie, Block Index, 1419–21, 1440; and for other landowners, Wards 12 and 19 Tax Books, 1851, MARC.

56. Gerard Hallock to JWB, June 24, 1851, 25:10, JWB Mss.

57. *JC*, June 5, 16, 1851; *Post*, June 19, 1851; *S-Z*, June 20, 1851. We thank Marion Deshmukh for help with this and other German translations.

2.   "Give Us a Park . . . Central or Sidelong . . . A Real Park, A Large Park"

1. *JC*, June 28, 1851.

2. BA *Proc.*, 42: 546.

3. *JC*, June 5, 13, 1851.

4. Gerard Hallock to JWB, June 24, 1851, 25:10, JWB Mss.; *JC*, June 13, 14, 16 (quot.), 17, 21, 1851. Cf. letters to *C&E*, June 17, 1851, and *Her.*, June 23, 1851. For answers to these complaints, see, e.g., *Post*, June 13, 1851; *CA*, June 24, 1851; *C&E*, June 26, 1851.

5. *C&E*, June 17, 1851. On bill to tax nonresidents, see Henry Hart to JWB, Feb. 23, 1850, 10:2, JWB Mss.; James Kelly to Edwin Morgan, Jan. 9, 1850, 7:11, Henry Davies to Morgan, Mar. 15, 1850, 4:16; Edwin Morgan Papers, New York State Library, Albany; on tax policy, Edward Dana Durand, *The Finances of New York City* (1898), 190–95; C. K. Yearley, *The Money Machines: The Breakdown and Reform of Governmental and Party Finance in the North, 1860–1920* (Albany, 1970), 6–7, 38–45.

6. *AJ* 74: 1548, 1549, 1560–61, 1607–8, 1646–47, 1685–86; *SJ* 74: 957–58; and for Jones Wood law, BA *Docs.*, 24, no. 5 (Jan. 19, 1857), 81–87; *Sun*, July 14, 1851.

7. *JC*, July 24, 3, 1851; *Post*, June 25, 1851; *JC*, June 28, 1851 (Shaw-Dean exchange). For other alternatives, see, e.g., *JC*, June 20, July 2, Aug. 10, 12, 1851; *Trib.*, July 8, 1851; *Her.*, June 24, 1851. Shaw and Dean had cooperated on winning appropriations for the new reservoir to serve uptown needs. See, e.g., BA *Proc.*, 38: 653; BA *Docs.*, 17, pt. 2, no. 37 (June 8, 1850): 691–96. Dean had probably already selected the site between 86th and 96th streets, from Fifth to Seventh avenues, although it was not formally announced until the *Report of the Croton Aqueduct Department Made to the Common Council, Dec. 31, 1851* (1852), 18–20. The reservoir boundaries were later made curvilinear: BCCP *Min.*, May 7, 13, 1857.

8. BA *Proc.*, 42: 547.

9. *JC*, June 24, 1851; *Trib.*, July 12, 1851; *Disp.*, Aug. 10, 17, 1851; *Subterranean*, July 26, 1845. Walsh was incensed that no taxes were paid on the private park. See also George Bancroft speech (*Post*, Jan. 26, 1853) to the Mechanics Institute endorsing Jones Wood from an equal-rights perspective, and Edward K. Spann, *The New Metropolis: New York City, 1840–1857* (1981), 233.

10. *Trib.*, July 25, 1851; *S-Z.*, Aug. 1, 1851. On the Industrial Congress, see Iver Bernstein, *The New York City Draft Riots: Their Significance for American Society and Politics in the Age of the Civil War* (1990), 85–91; Sean Wilentz, *Chants Democratic: New York City and the Rise of the American Working Class, 1788–1850* (1984), 363–72.

11. *S-Z*, Apr. 21, 1854, Apr. 1, 1853.

12. *S-Z*, July 16, 1853; Apr. 21, 1854. For another exchange on decentralized parks, see *CA*, June 24, 1851; *Her.*, June 24, 1851. On support for public schools, see Wilentz, *Chants Democratic*, 188, 203, 207, 208.

13. BAA *Proc.*, 34: 134–39, 184–85, doc. 3 (July 12, 1849), 64 (ornament), 65–78, and doc. 4 (July 12, 1849): 63–86; *C&E*, June 13, 1851. See also *Her.*, Nov. 8, 1850; Spann, *New Metropolis*,

162–63; *Trib.*, Nov. 22, 1848.

14. For editorials and merchants' letters on Battery, see *C&E*, June 11, 13, 14, 17, 1851; *JC*, June 6, 7, 10, 13, 14, 16, 26, July 4, 1851; *CA*, June 5, 16, 1851; *Her.*, June 6, 1851.

15. BA *Proc.*, 42: 653; BA *Docs.*, 18, pt. 2, no. 44 (June 2, 1851): 773–74; *Trib.*, Aug. 7, 1851; *Disp.*, Aug. 10, 1851. The aldermen were concurring in the Battery resolution passed two years earlier by the board of assistant aldermen. For typical editorials, see *CA*, June 5, 1851; *Her.*, June 6, 1851; *Trib.*, Aug. 7, 1851; *Disp.*, Aug. 10, 1851. See also *Trib.*, July 4, 1851; *Sun*, Aug. 8, 1851.

16. BA *Proc.*, 43: 29–31 (veto), 32–33, 98–99; *S-Z*, Aug. 8, 1851; *Post, Trib.*, Sept. 3, 1851 (special committee). For the political maneuvering over the Battery and Jones Wood, see also *CA*, Aug. 6, Sept. 11, 1851; *Sun, Her.*, Aug. 8, 1851; *Trib.*, Aug. 6, 7, 15, Sept. 11, 1851; *JC*, Aug. 13, 1851; *Post*, Sept. 11, 1851; *Disp.*, Sept. 14, 1851; BA *Proc.*, 43: 342, 350. Just as the expansion was completed in the mid-1850s, part of the Battery was converted into the Castle Garden Emigrant Depot, and the park was allowed to deteriorate: *Her.*, Apr. 5, 1860; *NYT*, May 24, 1891.

17. *CA*, Dec. 2, 1851. The court case revolved in part around suspicious irregularities in the legislature's passage of the Jones Wood bill. See *CA*, Sept. 29, Oct. 7, 13, 21, 1851, Dec. 13, 1851; *Post*, Oct. 20, 1851; *Trib.*, Oct. 6, 13, 1851; *Her.*, Dec. 4, 1851.

18. BA *Docs.*, 18, pt. 2, no. 83 (Jan. 2, 1852): 1471–72 (quots.), and 1459–88, passim. Dodge had joined with Henry Shaw in temporarily blocking proceedings on Jones Wood; Britton had opposed Jones Wood from the first. The third member of the special committee, Ward 19 alderman William A. Dooley, chaired the committee first recommending the Jones Wood site and did not sign the report. In 1868 Matthew Hale Smith suggested that the proposal for the central site originated out of a feud between an "alderman" (presumably Dodge) and a "senator from New York" (presumably Beekman). As a way of defeating the Jones Wood plan, Dodge took up a suggestion made to him by John A. Kennedy of the central site: Matthew Hale Smith, *Sunshine and Shadow in New York* (Hartford, 1868), 356–57. In his 1870 speech "Public Parks and the Enlargement of Towns," Olmsted (possibly drawing on Smith's account) similarly suggested that Central Park originated with "a private grudge of one of the city aldermen": *Civilizing American Cities: A Selection of Frederick Law Olmsted's Writings on City Landscapes*, ed. S. B. Sutton (Cambridge, Mass., 1971), 85–86. See also Olmsted, "Passages in the Life of an Unpractical Man," *FLOP*, 3:84, 91–92.

19. BA *Docs.*, 18, no. 83: 1465–66, 1468, and passim.

20. Ibid., 1473–74, 1487.

21. On efforts to work out compromises in an amended Jones Wood bill, see Henry Davies to JWB, Jan. 13, 22, 24, Feb. 6, 1852, James Crumbie to JWB, Jan. 29 (quot.), Mar. 17, 1852, LB 1, JWB Mss.; Edwin Morgan to James Jones, Feb. 2, 1852, Morgan to Henry Hilton, Feb. 5, 1852, B 62, LB 2, Morgan Papers. For other efforts at compromise, see Crumbie to JWB, Jan. 29, 1852, Rufus Prime to JWB, Jan. 28, 1852, LB 1, Crumbie to JWB, Mar. 17, 1852, LB 2, JWB Mss.

22. Morgan to Robert Minturn, Apr. 1, 1852, and see Morgan to George B. Butler, Mar. 25, 1852, Morgan to Ambrose C. Kingsland, Apr. 1, 1852, B 62, LB 2, Morgan Papers. On Morgan's economic and political interests, see James A. Rawley, *Edwin D. Morgan, 1811–1883: Merchant in Politics* (1955), 3–44. For the common council resolution, see BA *Proc.*, 45: 299–300, 439–40, 572–73; BAA *Proc.*, 45: 247, 287–88. Mayor Kingsland tried unsuccessfully to veto the resolution. See also *CA*, Feb. 17, Mar. 16, 19, 1852; David Valentine, City Clerk, to Morgan, Mar. 1852, 44:4, Morgan Papers. Popular Democratic politician Mike Walsh submitted a petition opposing any "mammoth" uptown park: *SJ* 75: 215. For bill's movement through senate, see *SJ* 75: 88, 171, 215, 340, 344, 370, 382, 479, 562.

23. For charges of speculation, see James Hogg to JWB, July 6, 1853, LB 3, JWB Mss.; *NYT*, June 21, 1853.

24. Morgan to Hamilton Fish, July 11, 1853, Fish Papers, LC; *Her.*, June 24, 1851; on landholding, Wards 12, 19, 20, 22 Tax Books, 1851–53, MARC. On May 1, 1851, David Britton bought the lots from city for $3,200. In October of the following year, *after* his committee had recommended that a park be built on this spot, Joseph Britton purchased the land (for the original price) from David Britton—presumably his brother. Just four months later Joseph Britton resold the lots for two and one-half times what he had paid. But the largest gain came from increasing real estate values not "insider" knowledge. RC 586:550; 589:581; 615:116; 627:77, NYCC. On

McGown property, see Henry Croswell Tuttle, *Abstracts of Farm Titles in the City of New York, East Side between 75th and 120 Streets* (1878), 370–401; Ward 12 Tax Books, 1851–53.

25. Timothy Churchill to JWB, June 21, 1853. On "Forty Thieves," see Spann, *New Metropolis*, 297–305; and on laying pipe, Amy Bridges, *A City in the Republic: Antebellum New York and the Origins of Machine Politics* (Ithaca, 1987), 132.

26. Petition, June 11, 1853, JWB Mss.; Morgan to Gerrit Striker, May 30, June 1, 17, 1853, B 62, LB 3, Morgan Papers; BA *Proc.*, 47: 581–82; *CA*, *Trib.*, June 10, 1853; *SJ* 76: 869–70; *Trib.*, Oct. 31, 1850 (residential park). Apparently Nicholas Dean and supporters of the new reservoir also lobbied against Jones Wood and implicitly for the central site: Morgan to Nicholas Dean, May 30, 1853, Morgan to Abraham Van Schaick, May 31, 1853, B 62, LB 3, Morgan Papers. See also James Hogg to JWB, June 3, 1853, LB 3, JWB Mss.

27. Daniel Tiemann to JWB, Feb. 23, 1852, LB 2, JWB Mss.; *Sun*, Oct. 5, 1855; Smith, *Sunshine and Shadow*, 356–57.

28. Petition headed by James H. Banker, May 1853, JWB Mss.; *JC*, July 7, 1853; Petition, May 24, 1853, JWB Mss. Of the 51 signers of the Banker petition, 42 came from the elite, including 28 merchants. For Astor's opposition to Jones Wood, see *SJ* 76: 747; Hogg to JWB, Henry Raymond to JWB, both June 23, 1853, LB 3, JWB Mss. Elite support for the "middle park" also crossed party lines. Thus, another pro–Central Park petition included both Whig banker Shepherd Knapp and Democratic banker John Cisco: Petition, June 11, 1853, JWB Mss. See also *SJ* 76: 841 for Knapp petition against Jones Wood, and 795 for petition opposing Jones Wood headed by Richard M. Blatchford. Familial tragedies and illness may have removed Robert Minturn from active participation in the park battle in 1852 and 1853: Robert Bowne Minturn, Jr., *Memoir of Robert Bowne Minturn* (1871), 149–53; Strong, *Diary*, 2:139, 149.

29. Petition, May 1853; Petition, June 11, 1853.

30. Strong, *Diary*, 2:87; William C. Schermerhorn to JWB, Dec. 18, 1853, 2:9, JWB Mss.; Petition, May 1853. The engagement of Caroline Schermerhorn to William Astor in June 1853 may have brought Astor into the opposition to Jones Wood: Strong, *Diary*, 2:126.

31. *AJ* 76: 575, 796, 844; *Albany Argus*, Apr. 4, 1853; Crumbie to JWB, Apr. 1852 (on Gale), 2:9, JWB Mss.; *JC*, May 24, 1853. For charges of bribing the clerk, see Affidavit of Henry Hilton, *NYT*, Dec. 2, 1853. See also Crumbie to JWB, Apr. 4, 1853, LB 3, JWB Mss.; Morgan to James Jones, Apr. 1, 4, 1853, B 62, LB 3, Morgan Papers. For senate, see *SJ* 76: 476, 480, 561, 594; and majority and minority reports of the State Senate Select Committee reprinted in BA *Docs.*, 24, no. 5 (Jan. 19, 1857): 165–92. See also Hogg to JWB, June 3, 6, 1853, John Torrey to Hogg, May 31, 1853, J. A. Perry to William Schermerhorn, June 4, 1853, Henry Hilton to JWB, June 7, 1853, LB 3, JWB Mss.

32. Cooley quoted in *CA*, July 2, 1853; Thomas Suffern to JWB, June 4, 1853, LB 3, JWB Mss. See also Cooley's minority report in BA *Docs.*, 24, no. 5, 178–80. On Hoboken riot, see, e.g., *Trib.*, *JC*, May 27, 1851; Hogg to JWB, July 6, 1853, LB 3, JWB Mss. For echoes of Cooley's fears, see *NYT*, July 5, 1853; *JC*, July 7, 1853.

33. Hogg to JWB, June 27, 1853. For other examples of lobbying tactics, see Hogg to JWB, June 3, 23, 30, July 6, 1853, Churchill to JWB, June 6, 21, July 11, 13, 1853, LB 3, JWB Mss.

34. For press support in 1853, see, e.g., *Trib.*, June 22, 28, 1853; *Post*, July 2, 22, 1853; *NYT*, June 21, 23, 24, 30, 1853; *Disp.*, June 27, Aug. 17, 1853; *Her.*, June 11, 24, July 1, 1853; *CA*, May 25, June 29, July 2, 1853. The *Times*, *Post*, and *Tribune* supported taking land for both parks; the *Herald* supported Central Park. The *Commercial Advertiser* favored Jones Wood but began to waver after Cooley's minority report. Surviving petitions are in JWB Mss. See also *SJ* 76: 593, 703, 723, 741, 742, 747, 822, 841, 857–58, 865; Morgan to Henry Hilton, May 27, 1853, Morgan to Striker, June 17, 1853, B 62, LB 3, Morgan Papers; *Her.*, June 11, 1853; *NYT*, June 24, 1853.

35. *JC*, July 7, 1853; *Trib.*, Jan. 30, 1854. See also *Trib.*, May 24, 1853.

36. *Sun*, July 14, 1851; *CA*, June 29, 1853. The *Sun* was never enthusiastic about the park. In 1856 its editor charged that the movement had been motivated by speculative interests and that the city would benefit more from "snug little parks" across the island: *Sun*, Feb. 1, 12, 1856.

37. *Her.*, *CA*, June 22, 1853; James Hogg to JWB, June 24, 27, 1853, LB 3, JWB Mss.

38. *SJ* 76: 866; *Her*, June 22, 1853; *JC*, June 24, 1853. On final votes, see *SJ* 76: 1097–98; *AJ* 76: 1693. On Morgan's sentiments toward assessments, see Hogg to JWB, June 30, 1853.

39. *Albany Evening Journal*, July 22, 1853; JWB to James Roosevelt, Dec. 2, 1853, 10:2, JWB

Mss. (personal attack); *SJ* 76: 1099, 1103–5, 1112; *AJ* 76: 1698–99, 1707, 1708–9. Cooley made similar charges in BA *Docs.*, 24, no. 5, 166. Daniel Sickles gives his version of legislative maneuvering in "The Founders of Central Park, in New York," typescript, reel 5, Daniel E. Sickles Papers, LC.

40. *JC* (quot.), *CA*, July 22, 1853. The senate's official proceedings conveyed the same impression: *SJ* 76: 1097.

41. *NYT*, Jan 9, 1854 (Roosevelt decision). For arguments in the case, see *NYT*, Nov. 29, Dec. 2, 3, 1853; *Her.*, Dec. 3, 5, 1853.

42. Churchill to JWB, Jan. 11, 1854, 2:7, JWB Mss. Some continued to support Jones Wood in 1854, but after the Roosevelt decision and after Beekman left the state senate they had little chance of success.

43. Spann, *New Metropolis*, 329–35, 429; Bridges, *City in the Republic*, 137–38.

44. *Her.*, Jan. 4, 31, Feb. 3 (Harsen) 1854; *JC*, Jan. 14, 27, 1854. For another large landowner's reservations, see James Lenox to E. Merriam, July 29, Aug. 2, 1853, Lenox Papers, NYPL.

45. *Her.*, Jan. 31, 1854; *Trib.*, Feb. 1, 1854; *Post*, Jan. 31, Feb. 3, 1854; *CA*, Feb. 4, 1854.

46. *Disp.*, Feb. 5, 1854; *Her.*, Feb. 3, 1854; *JC*, Feb. 7, 1854.

47. *NYT*, June 30, 1853. See also *S-Z*, July 16, 1853, Apr. 21, 1854. See similar letter to the editor of the *Weekly Budget*, June 4, 1853.

48. Majority and minority reports of the Committee on Lands and Places, BA, *Docs.*, 24, no. 5: 119, 127. See also *JC*, Mar. 28, Apr. 4, 6, 1854; *Her.*, *Post*, Apr. 4, 1854.

49. On depression, see, e.g., *Her.*, Jan. 4, 12, 18, 26, 1855; *Trib.*, Jan. 6, 10, 11, 1855; *JC*, Jan. 6, 10, 17, 1855.

50. *Trib.*, Mar. 9, 15, 24 (veto), 1855; *Her.*, Mar. 9, 1855.

51. Leonard Chalmers, "Fernando Wood and Tammany Hall: The First Phase," *NYHSQ* 52 (Oct. 1968): 380 (quot.), 379–85; Clarence C. Cook, *A Description of the New York Central Park* (1869), 23. On Wood's self-presentation as a reform candidate, see Bridges, *City in the Republic*, 127, 139; Mayor's Address, *Her.*, Jan. 2, 1855. See also Samuel Augustus Pleasants, *Fernando Wood of New York* (1948). The mayor's veto was something of a preemptive strike since the board of councilmen had not yet passed the cutback measure.

52. M. R. Werner, *Tammany Hall* (1928), 85; *Trib.*, June 15, 1860.

53. Bridges, *City in the Republic*, 139; Spann, *New Metropolis*, 371–72; *Her.*, Jan. 8, 9, 1855 (Germans); *Trib.*, Mar. 24, 1855 (veto message). On Wood and immigrant vote, see *Disp.*, Oct. 22, 1854; Bridges, *City in the Republic*, 101.

54. *Trib.*, Oct. 3, 1903, Mar. 24, 1855. See also *RERBG*, Apr. 3, 1875.

3. Private to Public Property

1. James Beekman, "Points for Mr. Hogg," 1853, 10:2, JWB Mss.

2. For ward characteristics, see New York State, *Census* (1855); William Boyd, *Boyd's New York City Tax Book* (1857), viii. The population of the uptown wards went from 11,652 in 1840 to 28,916 in 1850 and to 117,935 in 1860; see U.S. Bureau of the Census, decennial censuses. On uptown neighborhoods, see Hopper Striker Mott, *The New York of Yesterday: A Descriptive Narrative of Old Bloomingdale* (1908), 1–27; Edward K. Spann, *The New Metropolis: New York City, 1840–1857* (1981), 107; Edward Ruggles, *A Picture of New York* (1846), 22–23; Humphrey Phelps, *Phelps' New York City Guide* (1854), 81–82.

3. New York State Manuscript Census for 1855 (original in Bureau of Old Records and Condemnation Records of New York County; microfilm available from Church of Jesus Christ of Latter-Day Saints in Salt Lake City)—hereafter NYS 1855 Census Mss.

4. Estimate based on NYS 1855 Census Mss.; this figure is slightly misleading since the upper wards included some very large institutions—e.g., the Ward's Island Emigrant Refuge and Hospital—located on islands in the East River.

5. Spann, *New Metropolis*, 108–9, 189; Patrick Joseph Dooley, *Fifty Years in Yorkville, 1866–1916; or, Annals of the Parish of St. Ignatius Loyola and St. Lawrence O'Toole* (1917), 1–9; John Punnett Peters, ed., *Annals of St. Michael's: Being the History of St. Michael's Protestant Episcopal Church, for One Hundred Years, 1807–1907* (1907), 81–84. On West Side transportation, see

Peters, 124–25; M. Christine Boyer, *Manhattan Manners: Architecture and Style, 1850–1900* (1985), 193.

6. Peters, *Annals of St. Michael's*, 4–6, 81, 249; Horace Greeley to JWB, Aug. 8, 1849, 7:7, JWB Mss. See also Charles L. Rosenberg, *The Cholera Years: The United States in 1832, 1849, and 1866* (Chicago, 1962), 113–14; John Duffy, *A History of Public Health in New York City, 1625–1866* (1968), 385; Hendrik Hartog, "Pigs and Positivism," *University of Wisconsin Law Review* 4 (1985): 899–935.

7. *Sun*, Oct. 5, 1855; *Her.*, Feb. 2, 1854; Daniel Tiemann to JWB, Feb. 23, 1852, LB 2, JWB Mss. Two 19th-century accounts move directly from talking about the social composition of the park-site residents to the decision to build the park there: Matthew Hale Smith, *Sunshine and Shadow in New York* (Hartford, 1868), 356; Peters, *Annals of St. Michael's*, 123. Quotation on "garden, villa" is from the Archibald Watt petitions in vols. 3, 5, Central Park Condemnation Records, Bureau of Old Records and Condemnation Records of New York County. These records include seven volumes of petitions to the commission, most of the damage and assessment maps drawn up by the commission, and the list of park assessments. The records are hereafter cited as CP Cond. Mss. For the petitions, a volume number is also provided.

8. Phelps, *Phelps' Guide*, 81–82; *NYT*, Mar. 5, 1856; *Post*, May 31, 1856. See also *NYT*, July 25, Aug. 5, 1856, Aug. 19, 1866; *Her.*, Sept. 9, 1857, Aug. 20, 1860; *Trib.*, May 28, 1856; *Leader*, Jan. 11, 1862; "Description of the Central Park," Jan. 1859, BCCP *2AR* [1858], reprinted in *FLOP* 3:205. The following discussion employs the term *park dwellers*, an anachronism we cannot avoid when we speak of people who lived in the area that later became Central Park.

9. Egbert Viele, "Topography of New-York and Its Park System," in *The Memorial History of the City of New York*, ed. James Grant Wilson, 5 vols. (1893), 4:556–57. In 1911 Edward Hagaman Hall reworked Viele in describing the park of the early 1850s as "the refuge of a population of about 5,000 souls . . . a sort of no-man's land, occupied by squatters living in the most abject manner": "Central Park in the City of New York," ASHPS *16AR* [1911], 440. For other accounts of the park dwellers (most of them ultimately relying on Viele or Hall), see Eugene Kinkead and Russell Maloney, "Central Park II: 'A Nasty Place,'" *NYer*, Sept. 20, 1941, 35; Ian R. Stewart, "Central Park, 1851–1871: Urbanization and Environmental Planning in New York City" (Ph.D. diss., Cornell University, 1973), 137, 140; Daniel Van Pelt, *Leslie's History of Greater New York*, 3 vols. (1898), 1:386; Helen Campbell, *Darkness and Daylight; or, Lights and Shadows of New York Life* (Hartford, 1891), 411; "Shantytown," *Edison Monthly* (Apr. 1920): 107; Henry Hope Reed and Sophia Duckworth, *Central Park: A History and Guide* (1967; rpt. 1972), 17, 19; Smith, *Sunshine and Shadow*, 356; *Sun*, Apr. 12, 1935. Some of the accounts also make use of Peters, *Annals of St. Michael's*. One recent exception is Peter Salwen, *Upper West Side Story: A History and Guide* (1989), 46–77, who wonders, "How degenerate was it, really?"

10. Peters, *Annals of St. Michael's*, 92. Only two park residents—Peter Amory, a broker, and Dr. Alfred Wagstaff—had the sort of high-status occupations typical among the biggest uptown landlords. The quantitative generalizations about the park dwellers are based on NYS 1855 Census Mss.; 1850 U.S. Census Mss., National Archives; Parish Records, 1847–74, All Angels' Episcopal Church (hereafter All Angels' Mss.); CP Cond. Mss. (especially the condemnation maps); Wards 12, 19, 22 Tax Books, MARC; Grantor and Grantee Indexes, property conveyances, NYCC; list of people who rented park land back from the city, as published in *Disp.*, June 1, 1856, and in BA *Docs.*, 23, no. 25 (May 16, 1856), 4–24; city directories. Although none of these individual sources provides an adequate picture of the residents of the park land, they can be linked together to develop a tentative list of 316 households in the mid-1850s. With information on the size of about two-thirds of those households, we estimated a total population of around 1,600, not including the 200 girls boarding at the Mount St. Vincent School. Of course, these are just estimates. On the one hand, our reliance on multiple and incomplete sources may have resulted in counting some people who had left by 1855. On the other hand, people who were particularly poor or transient may not have been picked up by any of the sources we consulted.

11. The source of the name Seneca Village is unknown. Although Indian trails went through the park site and Indians and others may have done some hunting there, the nearest Indian settlement seems to have been the 17th-century headquarters of Sachem Rechewac, who lived in what later became Yorkville: Reginald P. Bolton, *Indian Life of Long Ago in the City of New York* (1934), 10; Bolton, *Washington Heights: Its Eventful Past* (1924), 2–18.

12. Information is not available on the race of the remaining 26 purchasers, but it seems likely that they were all black. See Whitehead in Grantor Index and RC, 191:445, 447; 197:344, 346, 348, 350; 207:93; 226:211; 231:144; 252:233; 288:289; quotation from George Walker, "The Afro-American in New York City, 1827–1860" (Ph.D. diss., Columbia University, 1975), 127. On church leaders, see Christopher Rush, *A Short Account of the Rise and Progress of the African Methodist Episcopal Church in America* (1843).

13. Denis Tilden Lynch, *"Boss" Tweed: The Story of a Grim Generation* (1927), 14–15; Peters, *Annals of St. Michael's,* 29–30, 40–41, 248. The first year in which the Ward 12 Tax Books list the Seneca Village landowners is 1829, but the tax listings for Upper Manhattan before that date do not seem to cover relatively small holdings. Hall, "Central Park," 434, lists Matthews as the owner of 4.75 acres of land on the receiving reservoir site. But BA *Docs.,* 4, no. 10 (Jan. 1–June 30, 1839): app., indicates that the land was owned by Tums Van Brunt.

14. Number of houses based on annual listings in Ward 12 Tax Books. Matthews's connection to African Union can be found in 1850 U.S. Census Mss. and African Union petition, CP Cond. Mss., vol. 5. Hall, "Central Park," 444, writes that the black community "crowded west" in 1838. For epithet, see *NYT,* July 9, 1856.

15. On Plunkitt, see *NYT,* July 7, Nov. 20, 1924; William L. Riordon, *Plunkitt of Tammany Hall* (1905; rpt. 1963), vii, xvii, xxiv; 1850 U.S. Census Mss.; on Croker, Lothrop Stoddard, *Master of Manhattan: The Life of Richard Croker* (1931), 16–20.

16. Peters, *Annals of St. Michael's,* 445–46.

17. Some of these links are necessarily tentative. On mobility rates, see Peter Knights, "Population Turnover, Persistence, and Residential Mobility in Boston, 1830–60," in *Nineteenth-Century Cities: Essays in the New Urban History,* ed. Stephan Thernstrom and Richard Sennett (New Haven, 1969), 262; Stephan Thernstrom, *The Other Bostonians: Poverty and Progress in the American Metropolis, 1880–1970* (Cambridge, Mass., 1973), 220–61; James Horton, "Shades of Color: The Mulatto in Three Antebellum Northern Communities," *Afro-Americans in New York Life and History* 8 (July 1984): 41–42.

18. Based on land records and NYS 1855 Census Mss.

19. These family reconstructions are based on manuscript records of All Angels' Church; 1850 U.S. Census Mss.; NYS 1855 Census Mss.; and land records.

20. John Wallace to BCCP, May 2, 1859, FLO Mss. See similarly Francis Brown et al. to BCCP, May 12, 1859, FLO Mss.; BCCP *Min.,* Nov. 2, 1857, Dec. 23, 1858. On shanties, see Citizens' Association of New York, *Sanitary Conditions of New York* (1866; rpt. 1970), 300. On dwelling sizes, CP Cond. Mss. See also Elizabeth Blackmar, *Manhattan for Rent, 1785–1850* (Ithaca, 1989), 205–10.

21. On black workers, see Rhoda G. Freeman, "The Free Negro in New York City before the Civil War" (Ph.D. diss., Columbia University, 1966), 291.

22. Jeanne Boydston, "To Earn Her Daily Bread: Housework and Antebellum Working-Class Subsistence," *Radical History Review,* no. 36 (Apr. 1986): 15–16; Christine Stansell, *City of Women: Sex and Class in New York, 1789–1860* (1986), 50–51.

23. Viele, "Topography," 556–57; James D. McCabe, Jr., *New York by Sunlight and Gaslight* (Philadelphia, 1882), 442–43; Peters, *Annals of St. Michael's,* 92.

24. On black property holdings, see Leonard P. Curry, *The Free Black in Urban America, 1800–1850: The Shadow of the Dream* (Chicago, 1981), 41, 287; Freeman, "Free Negro," 84, 276–78. The census may not have accurately recorded black property ownership. But whatever the actual figures, the higher level of ownership in Seneca Village still stands. On Marshall, see Maritcha Rémond Lyons, "Memories of Yesterdays: All of Which I Saw and Part of Which I Was, an Autobiography," typescript in Schomberg Center for Research in Black Culture, NYPL.

25. The 1855 figures for Seneca Village and the rest of the city are not strictly comparable, because we used multiple sources (census, park condemnation records, land records) to compute property ownership in Seneca Village but based citywide and uptown levels solely on the 1855 census.

26. Harry J. Carman, *The Street Surface Railway Franchises of New York City* (1919), 13; Rush, *Short Account,* 26; African Union petition, CP Cond. Mss., vol. 5. Rush's book, published in 1843, makes no mention of a branch of AME Zion at Seneca Village, nor does another survey of churches published in 1846: Jonathan Greenleaf, *A History of the Churches of All Denominations in*

the City of New York from the Settlement to the Year 1846 (1846). According to Freeman, "Free Negro," 386, the Seneca branch was called AMZ Branch Church Militant by 1854. On African Union, see Greenleaf, 329. On school, see Freeman, 342, and the call for improved schools, originally published in the *Anglo-African* in July 1859 and reprinted in Herbert Aptheker, ed., *A Documentary History of the Negro People in the United States*, 3 vols. (1968), 1:398–402.

27. The development of All Angels' is chronicled in All Angels' Mss. and Peters, *Annals of St. Michael's*.

28. On segregated pews, see Freeman, "Free Negro," 380. Attendance figures for All Angels' and African Union come from the NYS 1855 Census Mss.; the census takers apparently missed AME Zion, but the attendance for that church was given in *Trib.*, Aug. 5, 1853, which also suggests that the congregation preceded the erection of the church building.

29. On black voting, see Leo H. Hirsch, Jr., "The Negro and New York, 1783 to 1863," *Journal of Negro History* 16 (Oct. 1931): 420; New York State, *Census 1845*, 29; Curry, *Free Black*, 218; Walker, "Afro-American," 140. On Gloucester, Seaman, and Ray, see David E. Swift, *Black Prophets of Justice: Activist Clergy before the Civil War* (Baton Rouge, 1989), chaps. 5, 6, 7, and passim; Earl Ofari, *"Let Your Motto Be Resistance": The Life and Thought of Henry Highland Garnet* (Boston, 1972), 90, 93; Aptheker, *Documentary History*, 1:198, 398–401; Walker, "Afro-American," 167, 198; Freeman, "Free Negro," 84, 139.

30. *JC*, Mar. 27, 1855; Dooley, *Fifty Years in Yorkville*, 12–16. Father C. E. Hoefner was kind enough to check baptismal records at St. Ignatius Loyola for the names of Irish-Catholic park dwellers; several names turned up in the records for the 1850s, but it was impossible to confirm these linkages.

31. NYS 1855 Census Mss. On piggeries, see *NYT*, July 9, 1856; *JC*, June 28, 1856; *Post*, June 10, 1856, Dec. 1, 1857. On restrictions downtown, see Duffy, *History of Public Health*, 385–86; Hartog, "Pigs and Positivism," 903–5, 921–24; Rosenberg, *Cholera Years*, 113–14.

32. Hesser petition, CP Cond. Mss., vol. 4; NYS 1855 Census Mss. (agricultural listings).

33. Testimony of Catherine Coggery, CP Cond. Mss., vol. 7.

34. On northwest corner, see Hall, "Central Park," 397–432; Elizabeth Barlow [Rogers], *The Central Park Book* (1977), 126–31; *Rebuilding CP*, 90–95; Stephen Jenkins, *The Old Boston Post Road* (1913), 105, 110–13; Richard J. Koke, "Milestones along the Old Highways of New York City," *NYHSQ* 34 (July 1950): 165–89. The area of the park containing the fortifications was above 106th Street and was not added to the park until 1863. On Mount St. Vincent, see Marie de Lourdes Walsh, *The History of the Sisters of Charity of New York, 1809–1859*, 3 vols. (1960), 1:137–46, 154–57; Edward Hagaman Hall, *McGown's Pass and Vicinity* (1905); Hall, "Central Park," 431–32; NYS 1855 Census Mss.; Sisters of Charity petition, CP Cond. Mss., vols. 2, 3. See also typed and hand-written notes from Archives, Mount St. Vincent, Bronx, New York, which were kindly provided by the archivist, Sister Anne Courtney.

35. Under separate legislation, the Arsenal, with the surrounding land, was sold by the state to the city in 1856; Hall, "Central Park," 437–38.

36. NYS 1855 Census Mss. (industrial listings). On bone boiling, see Duffy, *History of Public Health*, 377, 380–81.

37. *JC*, June 28, 1856, emphasis added. For boxing match, see *JC*, *NYT*, Mar. 27, 1855; for dance houses, *Trib.*, Aug. 5, 1856; on theft, e.g., *Post*, May 31, 1856. For indication that park dwellers were allowed to remove some of their belongings, see BA *Docs.*, 23, no. 25 (May 16, 1856): 2–3. See Boydston, "To Earn Her Daily Bread," 15–16, on scavenging shading into theft. On *shebeens*, see Roy Rosenzweig, *Eight Hours for What We Will: Workers and Leisure in an Industrial City, 1870–1920* (1983), 41, 61.

38. CP Cond. Mss., vol. 7. On limited returns from upper Manhattan land, see Gouverneur Wilkins petition, vol. 5, CP Cond. Mss.

39. *Sun*, May 6, 1857. We have identified only seven households located on land whose owners were unknown, but the sources are incomplete. Still, such land constituted only about 5% of the total park acreage. Squatters may also have taken up residence on land owned by the city and the large tract held by Archibald Watt. One of the 1855 census takers noted that his "property is lying mostly to Commons and is occupied by squatters to a great extent." Nevertheless, it seems unlikely that the number of true squatters ever exceeded the number of property owners.

40. *Post*, Sept. 20, 1853. See also *CA*, Sept. 20, 1853; *NYT*, Oct. 3, 1853.

41. *Trib.*, Jan. 10, 1856; *NYT*, Oct. 3, 1853. See also *Her.*, Nov. 18, 1853. For landowner petitions for particular commissioners, see CP Cond. Mss., vol. 1.

42. These figures probably understate the concentration of ownership, since holdings listed under several names were sometimes part of a large family tract. The information on landownership in the park was gathered primarily from the (incomplete) damage maps in the CP Cond. Mss. For the missing blocks, we used the 1855 Wards 12, 19, 22 Tax Books, MARC. We have calculated 12 lots per acre, which seems consistent with figures given in contemporary documents but not with current measures of acres, which would be closer to 17 lots per acre.

43. For transactions, see Block Index to Reindexed Conveyance, Block 1111, NYCC (hereafter Block Index, 1111). Since the index accumulates all land transactions, some of those listed may be leases or mortgages rather than sales. On uptown property, see Henry Croswell Tuttle, *Abstracts of Farm Titles in the City of New York, between 39th and 75th Streets, East of the Common Lands . . .* (1877); *Abstracts . . . East Side, between 75th and 120th Streets . . .* (1878), 265–94 (on McGown); *Abstracts . . . between 39th and 73rd Streets, West of the Common Lands . . .* (1881), 546–73 (on Dyckman).

44. See Block Index, 1383–86, NYCC; James Lenox to E. Merriam, Aug. 2, 1853, Misc. papers, NYHS; *NCAB*; Boyer, *Manhattan Manners*, 170–71; Henry Stevens, *Recollections of Mr. James Lenox of New York and the Formation of His Library* (London, 1886), 3–4; Arthur B. Maurice, *Fifth Avenue* (1918), 305–6.

45. Watt petition, vol. 5. On Watt's landholdings, see the Grantee Index, NYCC; RC, 232:4, 6, 412, 414, 418, 230:555, 238:203, 205; Tuttle, *Abstracts . . . East Side, between 75th and 120th Streets*, 277–78.

46. Watt petition, vol. 5; *Report of the Croton Aqueduct Department Made to the Common Council, Dec. 31, 1851* (1852), 21. For Harsen, see Block Index, 1111. The Amory sales were not exclusively within Central Park as was true of the 25 sales by the Talmans in 1852. See the Grantor Index, NYCC.

47. Most private colonial grants of uptown land had extended north along both rivers. In 1686 and 1730, royal charters gave the remaining unappropriated property—a central column of largely nonarable land between the future Third and Seventh avenues—to the municipal corporation of New York. See George Black, *The History of Municipal Ownership of Land on Manhattan Island, to . . . 1844* (1897), 38–40. On common land sales, Spann, *New Metropolis*, 50, 161.

48. Only two of the dozens of people who bought park lots from the city in the early 1850s held more than 25 lots. Two-thirds of those who purchased park land at the two city sales in 1852 could be loosely classified as small-business people; fewer than one-third of those who owned more than 20 lots of park land could be similarly categorized. Occupations of landowners were obtained from relevant city directories and, in some cases, the NYS 1855 Census Mss.

49. *Trib.*, Jan. 31, 1856.

50. *Sun*, Oct. 5, 9, 1855; *NYT*, Aug. 10, 1853. The assessed area was actually only to midway between Second and Third and Tenth and Eleventh avenues and narrowed to just Fifth to Eighth below 42nd and above 116th streets.

51. *Sun*, Oct. 9, 1855; Watt petitions, vols. 3, 5. See also Wilkins petition, CP Cond. Mss., vol. 5. Calculations from CP Cond. Mss.

52. Peter Doremus petition, vol. 5, Daniel Farnshaw petition, vol. 3, CP Cond. Mss.

53. Watt petitions.

54. *NYT*, Dec. 22, 1852; BA *Docs.*, 18, no. 28 (Feb. 5, 1851): 574–76. Evidence on buyers from block indexes and city directories.

55. Thomas Shepard petition, vol. 4, and see Diederick Knubel petition, vol. 3, William Mulligan petition, vol. 2, Philip Maas petition, vol. 4, CP Cond. Mss.

56. C. P. Ludwig Sheff petition, ibid., vol. 5. See also petitions from William Matthews, George Moller, Charles Oberlander, Joseph Murray, William Pease, Hammersly Roff, and A. V. Barbaree.

57. Jupiter Hesser petition, ibid., vol. 4.

58. In part, the commission followed existing marketplace judgments about land value rather than simply imposing their own. One crucial determinant of park assessment rates was the level at which land was already assessed for tax purposes. Assessing some of the facing lots around 72nd Street at the maximum allowed by law, the commission then apparently gradually reduced assessments on lands progressively farther east, west, or north. Yet the park assessments did not

simply follow existing tax assessments. Values assessed for tax purposes, which apparently were affected by location, topography, level of development, and the idiosyncrasies of ward assessors, varied a great deal more than the park assessments, which were based primarily on proximity to the park. See, e.g., Ward 19 Tax Books; CP Cond. Mss.

59. *Trib.*, Jan. 10, 22, 30, 31, Feb. 1, 2, 6, 1856; *Her.*, Jan. 10, Feb. 3, 6, 1856; *JC*, Feb. 5, 6, 1856; *Disp.*, Jan. 13, 27, 1856; *Sun*, Feb. 6, 1856; "In the Matter of the Application of the Mayor . . . Relative to the Opening and Laying Out of a Public Space," in BA *Docs.*, 24, no. 5 (Jan. 19, 1857): 103–11; Hall, "Central Park," 461. See also Strong, *Diary*, 2:251. Daniel E. Sickles later claimed that he had played a key role in getting the governor to appoint his friend Judge Harris, because the local judges were hostile to approving the report. "The Founder of Central Park, in New York," typescript, reel 5, Daniel E. Sickles Papers, LC.

60. *Annual Report of the Comptroller of the City of New York* [1857] (1857), 25; *JC*, Apr. 10, 1856; BA *Docs.*, 23, no. 19 (Apr. 14, 1856): 1–6; *NYT*, Apr. 1, 3, 1857; *JC*, Jan. 10, 1857.

61. The deeds for most of Watt's land within the park indicate only that he paid "$1 and considerations." The price of $200–$300 per acre comes from the deeds on his land to the east of the park. Since the records of payments to Watts for park land have not been located, we have extrapolated from the $213,660 listed as due to his daughter (Mary Pinckney) in a comptroller's report (*Annual Report of the Comptroller, Year 1857*, 100). This figure was then divided by 576 and 600—the two figures we have for Watt's total number of park lots. Extrapolating from changing tax rates and assessed values and from one sample deed, we can estimate Watt's total tax bill for 27 years at about $27.84 per lot and his interest charges at around $1.78 per lot.

62. *Trib.*, Feb. 2, 1856; Edward Roberts petition, CP Cond. Mss., vol. 2; Grantor and Grantee Indexes.

63. Between 1855 and 1858, the assessed value of the Fifth Avenue lots on 80th to 81st streets rose by about $500 and that of the lots facing 80th Street by only about $50. The 1855 tax assessment at Fifth Avenue would have had to be at least $516 given the park assessment of $258; the 1858 assessment was $1,000. The tax assessments on some of the lots facing 80th and 81st streets did not increase at all. The lots were undeveloped in both years.

64. CP Cond. Mss.; *Sun*, Oct. 5, 1855. For Lenox's worth, see Edward Pessen, *Riches, Class, and Power before the Civil War* (Lexington, Mass., 1973), 22; *Boyd's New York City Tax-Book* (1857), 118.

65. *Sun*, Jan. 12, 1857; Ward 19 Tax Books.

66. *Sun*, Aug. 9, 1856; *NYT*, Apr. 20, 1857 (ad); *Her.*, Feb. 15, 1856, Feb. 14, 1858 (fancy prices); agent quoted in Eugene Moehring, *Public Works and Patterns of Urban Real Estate Growth in Manhattan, 1835–1894* (1981), 286. On real estate prices, see, e.g., "Clinton," *The Value of Real Estate in the City of New York* (collection of newspaper articles from 1858 to 1860), 2–3, 16; *History of Real Estate, Building, and Architecture in New York* (1898), 156.

67. James Sanders to JWB, May 9, 1856, JWB Mss.

68. *Trib.*, Aug. 4, 5, 1853. On Rush, see Freeman, "Free Negro," 380, 384; Swift, *Black Prophets*, 14, 260–61, 314–15.

69. Peters, *Annals of St. Michael's*, 177–80, 396. Attempts to trace Seneca Village residents in the 1860 census manuscripts and city directories were unsuccessful. A local history published in 1914 suggests that a black settlement located near 54th Street and Ninth Avenue "is composed of the remnants and progeny of the Negro colony called 'Seneca Village.'" But there is no other evidence of this connection: Otto G. Cartwright, *The Middle West Side: A Historical Sketch* (1914), 50.

70. *Her.*, Aug. 11, 1871; "Paddy's Walk," *NYer*, Jan. 10, 1959, 24.

71. Hirsch, "The Negro," 436–38; Albon P. Man, Jr., "Labor Competition and the New York City Draft Riots," *Journal of Negro History* 36 (Oct. 1951): 404; Iver Bernstein, *The New York City Draft Riots: Their Significance for American Society and Politics in the Age of the Civil War* (1990), 119–23; Blackmar, *Manhattan for Rent*, 172–80.

72. Walsh, *Sisters of Charity*, 1:154–55, 181–94, 198–99; typed and handwritten notes from Mount St. Vincent Archives; Hall, *McGown's Pass*, 44–45; Mary Denis Maher, *To Bind up the Wounds: Catholic Sister Nurses in the U.S. Civil War* (1989), 74, 112, 115.

73. Peters, *Annals of St. Michael's*, 141, 323–24; Citizens' Association, *Sanitary Conditions*, 300–310, 240; *Trib.*, Aug. 9, 1859; Stewart, "Central Park," 140; Hesser petition.

74. *JC*, May 30, June 28, 1856; *Trib.*, Aug. 5, 1856.

75. *Post*, June 10, 1856; *NYT*, July 9, 1856. Many secondary sources report that the police were called in to evict the park dwellers, but we could not find any indication of this police action in the contemporary press. These accounts may rest on a subsequent confusion between the eviction of the park dwellers in 1857 and raids two years later by the sanitary inspector and the police on the piggeries along the park's western boundary. At least four of the piggery operators driven out were former park residents. See *Her.*, July 30, Sept. 5, 1859; *Trib.*, Aug. 9, 1859; *NYT*, Aug. 9, 1859.

4. The Design Competition

1. BCCP *Min.*, Oct. 13, 1857; *FYLA*, 40–41. The descriptions accompanying the entries were printed for an exhibition in BCCP, *Description of Plans for the Improvement of Central Park* (1858). A copy on microfilm at NYPL apparently belonged to Robert Dillon and identifies some contestants; pages for plan 12, however, appear after plan 16. A bound copy is at the NYHS.

2. Eugene Moehring, *Public Works and Patterns of Urban Real Estate Growth in Manhattan, 1835–1894* (1981), 41–42; *Acts of the Legislature and Ordinances of the Common Council in Relation to the Introduction, Supply and Use of Croton Water, from 1833 to 1861* (1861), 33–41; *JC*, Mar. 6, 1856.

3. On relationship of state and local authorities, see *Constitution of the State of New York* (Albany, 1846), article VI; also L. Ray Gunn, *The Decline of Authority: Public Economic Policy and Political Development in New York State, 1800–1860* (Ithaca, 1988), 184–97. On the 1856 bill, see *JC*, Mar. 6, 1856, Apr. 12, 1856; *Her.*, June 16, 1856. The assembly refused to pass an amended senate bill that named the commissioners: *SJ* 79: 423, 465–66, 479, 489, 490; *AJ* 79: 754, 859. On the fragmentation of the two-party system and local factionalism, see David Potter, *The Impending Crisis, 1848–1861* (1976), 244–65; DeAlva Alexander, *Political History of the State of New York*, 2 vols. (1909), 2:190–94; Thomas J. Curran, "Seward and the Know-Nothings, *NYHSQ* 51 (Apr. 1968): 141–59; Jerome Mushkat, *Tammany: The Evolution of a Political Machine, 1789–1865* (Syracuse, 1971), chaps. 10–12; and for city politics, Amy Bridges, *A City in the Republic: Antebellum New York and the Origins of Machine Politics* (Ithaca, 1987), 127, 137–39; Edward K. Spann, *The New Metropolis: New York City, 1840–1857* (1981), chaps. 13–14; Leonard Chalmers, "Fernando Wood and Tammany Hall: The First Phase," *NYHSQ* 52 (Oct. 1968): 382–85.

4. On formation of commission, see *Post*, May 15, 1856; *Her.*, June 13, 1856; BA *Docs.*, 24, no. 5 (Jan. 19, 1857): 136; on the board of consultants, *NYT*, *Post*, May 27, 1856; *JC*, June 3, 1856; *Sun*, Dec. 13, 1856; BA *Docs.*, 24, no. 5: 8–9. The consulting board also included James Phalen, Charles Dana, and Charles F. Briggs. For Wood's hirings, see BA *Proc.*, 64: 403–13.

5. For praise for consulting board, see *NYT*, May 27, 1856; *NYT*, *Sun*, July 9, 1856. The *Herald*, June 11, 13, 1856, was more skeptical. For the corporation counsel's maneuvers, see *Sun*, July 9, 14, 25, 1856; *Disp.*, July 20, 1856; *Post*, July 21, 1856; *NYT*, July 12, 22, 25, 1856. The reform-minded Democratic comptroller, Azariah Flagg, also prevented Wood's board from using the rents collected from park dwellers until they moved: *Her.*, Aug. 1, 1856; *NYT*, Aug. 5, 1856; *Post*, Aug. 5, 6, 9, 1856; *Disp.*, Aug. 24, 1856; BA *Proc.*, 64: 405–6. For editors' retreat, see, e.g., *NYT*, Aug. 8, 1856; *Sun*, Dec. 10, 1856.

6. *Trib.*, *JC*, Apr. 30, 1856. On 1856 election, see Mushkat, *Tammany*, 296–99; Chalmers, "Fernando Wood and Tammany," 392–96. On ideology of Republican party, see Eric Foner, *Free Soil, Free Labor, Free Men: The Ideology of the Republican Party before the Civil War* (1970).

7. Abram Wakeman to Thurlow Weed, Mar. 12, 1856, Thurlow Weed Papers, University of Rochester; Ass. *Docs.*, 80, no. 131 (Mar. 2, 1857): 2. For legislative maneuvers, see *SJ* 80: 34, 45, 802, 859–60, 901, 966, 982, 1026; *AJ* 80: 163, 528, 953, 960, 1057, 1086, 1442–43, 1483–84. Daniel Sickles suggests that he drafted the original bill for the 1856 session, although much of the horsetrading he describes appears to have taken place in 1857; "The Founders of Central Park, in New York," typescript, reel 5, Daniel E. Sickles Papers, LC. For Republican party patronage and other "reform" laws, see *NYT*, Apr. 14, 18, 20, 29, 1857; *JC*, Jan. 28, Mar. 28, Apr. 13, 1857.

8. *NCAB* (Cooley); *NYT*, Nov. 27, 1872 (Dillon); *NYT*, July 6, 1889 (Hogg); James Hogg to Weed, n.d. [1857], Weed Papers; Ass. *Docs.*, 80, no. 131: 2.

9. *NYT*, Jan. 26, 1885 (Fields); George Alexander Mazaraki, "The Public Career of Andrew Haswell Green" (Ph.D. diss., New York University, 1966), 8–24.

10. *NYT,* Mar. 7, 1873 (Butterworth); *NYT,* Jan 22, 1884 (Russell); Lyman Horace Weeks, ed., *The Prominent Families of New York* (New York, 1898), 242 (Gray); *Appleton's Cyclopedia of American Biography,* 6 vols. (1886), 5:723–24 (Strong). Hutchins returned to the Democratic ranks following the Civil War; see *NYT,* Feb. 9, 1891. On Elliott, see *NCAB,* and FLO to Charles Loring Brace, July 26, 1852, *FLOP* 1:383.

11. On Minturn, *NYT,* Jan. 10, 1866. Grinnell (*NYT,* Nov. 25, 1881) replaced Elliott: BCCP *Min.,* Apr. 19, 1860. In the spring of 1858, Democratic banker August Belmont (*NYT,* Nov. 25, 1890) replaced Cooley: BCCP *Min.,* Mar. 16, 1858. The following year, the Republican lawyer Richard M. Blatchford (*NYT,* Sept. 5, 1875) replaced Hogg, and the Democratic banker Henry Stebbins (*NYT,* Dec. 11, 1881) replaced Dillon: BCCP *Min.,* Apr. 21, 1859.

12. *NYT,* Apr. 14, 20, 1857. See also *Ir. N,* Feb. 12, 1857; and on commission government, Bridges, *City in the Republic,* 126–31; Spann, *New Metropolis,* 386–94; James C. Mohr, *The Radical Republicans and Reform in New York during Reconstruction* (Ithaca, 1973), 21–60, 90–114.

13. *NYT,* Apr. 29, 1857; BCCP *Min.,* Apr. 30, May 7, 9, 1857. Andrew Green was elected treasurer: Ibid., June 16, 1857.

14. *Post,* May 7, June 13, 1851; *CA,* June 6, 1851; BA *Docs.* 18, pt. 2, no. 83 (Jan. 2, 1852): 1475; *JC,* June 28, 1851.

15. *Her.,* June 15, 1856; *Trib.,* June 28, 1853. See also *NYT,* June 4, 1857.

16. *Ir. N,* Jan. 29, 1859. See also *Disp.,* May 11, 1851, June 8, 1856.

17. *JC,* June 5, 1856; *Sun,* June 6, 1857; *FYLA,* 554; and BA *Docs.,* 24, no. 5. On Viele, see *FLOP* 3:69–71.

18. BA *Docs.,* 24, no. 5: 5, 37, and features outlined, 39–40.

19. Ibid., 36–40.

20. For responses to Viele plan, see *NYT,* July 9, 1856; *Sun,* July 6, 9, 1856; *Post,* Jan. 20, 1857. On expectations for professional designer, see *Trib.,* Feb. 9, 1856; *NYT,* July 9, 1856. On Viele's manners, see, e.g., Charles Elliott to Edwin D. Morgan, Aug. 1861, 6:3, Edwin Morgan Papers, New York State Library, Albany. On proposal for competition, see BCCP *Min.,* June 16, July 7, 13, 18, Sept. 11, Oct. 13, 1857, and doc. 8 (Sept. 11, 1857). Architects and landscape gardeners sought to enhance the status of their professions through design competitions. See, e.g., the proposal for a contest of the landscape gardeners in R. M. Copeland and H. W. S. Cleveland, *A Few Words on the Central Park, July 1, 1856* (Boston, 1856), NYHS.

21. CV, Memorandum, Nov. 1894, CV Papers, NYPL. On Gray's house, see Vaux, *Villas and Cottages: A Series of Designs Prepared for Execution in the United States* (1857; 2d ed., 1864; rpt. 1970), 323–25. The board passed a resolution (BCCP *Min.,* Aug. 18, 1857) thanking Vaux for a copy of *Villas and Cottages.*

22. Transcript of CV Court Testimony, Mar. 1864, FLO Mss. On Viele's suit, see also the trial transcript and FLO to CV, Mar. 25, 1864, reprinted in *FYLA,* 554–62.

23. BA *Docs.,* 24, no. 5, 41–42; CV Testimony, Mar. 1864; *HW,* Nov. 28, 1857.

24. *Trib.,* Feb. 27, 1856.

25. Elizabeth Blackmar, *Manhattan for Rent, 1785–1850* (Ithaca, 1989), 94–99, 106.

26. *Trib.,* June 22, 28, 1853, Feb. 11, 1854.

27. John Brinckerhoff Jackson, "The Origins of Parks," in *Discovering the Vernacular Landscape* (New Haven, 1984), 127–30; Thomas M. Garrett, "A History of Pleasure Gardens in New York City, 1700–1865" (Ph.D. diss., New York University, 1978), 606, 612–13, 615, 620–21. Vauxhall and Niblo's gardens gave way to midtown development in the 1850s: *JC,* Jan. 23, 1854; *Her.,* Mar. 24, 1855. For descriptions of Elysian Fields and other pleasure grounds, see, e.g., *Disp.,* May 11, July 7, 1851; *Her.,* Sept. 1, 1857; *Post,* Sept. 1, 2, 1857; *FL,* Sept. 12, 1857; *Ir. N,* Jan. 29, 1859.

28. *Trib.,* Feb. 27, 1856.

29. Andrew Jackson Downing, *A Treatise on the Theory and Practice of Landscape Gardening Adapted to North America* (1859 ed.; rpt. 1967), 46, 54. See also Roger B. Stein, *John Ruskin and Aesthetic Thought in America, 1840–1900* (Cambridge, Mass., 1967), 2–31; Neil Harris, *The Artist in American Society: The Formative Years, 1790–1860* (1966), chaps. 7–8; David Schuyler, *The New Urban Landscape: The Redefinition of City Form in Nineteenth-Century America* (Baltimore, 1986), 41–46; James Early, *Romanticism and American Architecture* (1965), 54–71. On trends in Europe, George F. Chadwick, *The Park and the Town* (1966), 21–36; Norman T. Newton, *Design on the Land: The Development of Landscape Architecture* (Cambridge, Mass., 1971), 114–46.

30. *Trib.*, Feb. 27, 1856, June 21, 1853.

31. *Trib.*, Feb. 27, 1856. On Bois de Boulogne, see Chadwick, *Park and Town*, 153–56; Newton, *Design on the Land*, 241–45.

32. Schuyler, *New Urban Landscape*, 84. On Crystal Palace, see M. Christine Boyer, *Manhattan Manners: Architecture and Style, 1850–1900* (1985), 63–67; on Cooper Union, see Thomas Bender, *New York Intellect: A History of Intellectual Life in New York City, from 1750 to the Beginnings of Our Own Time* (Baltimore, 1987), 114–15. See also *JC*, June 28, 1851; Robert Dillon's argument as corporation counsel on behalf of taking the land (*Her.*, Feb. 3, 1856); and claim of Henry Shaw (*JC*, June 28, 1851) that a "public park would derive most of its charm from *its utility*. That which is useful interests us."

33. See, e.g., *Her.*, Feb. 3, 1856, June 15, 1856. See also Daniel M. Bluestone, "From Promenade to Park: The Gregarious Origins of Brooklyn's Park Movement," *American Quarterly* 39 (Winter 1987): 529–50.

34. On pastoral landscapes as an antidote to materialism, see Raymond Williams, *The Country and the City* (1973), 120–52. On American romantics, Perry Miller, "Nature and the National Ego," in *Errand into the Wilderness* (1956; rpt. 1964), 204–16.

35. On Protestant mistrust of ritual and fashion, see, e.g., Vaux, *Villas and Cottages*, 28, 34–35; Karen Halttunen, *Confidence Men and Painted Ladies: A Study of Middle-Class Culture in America, 1830–1870* (New Haven, 1982), 155–63, 182. For artists' exposure to European styles, see Harris, *The Artist in American Society*, 287–98. On Haussmann, see David H. Pinkney, *Napoleon III and the Rebuilding of Paris* (Princeton, 1958).

36. *Ir. Am.*, May 2, 1857; *Zeitung und Herold*, June 21, 1856; *Disp.*, June 29, 1856; *Ir. N*, Jan. 29, 1859. Although *Frank Leslie's Illustrated Weekly*, Sept. 12, 1857, suggested inviting Joseph Paxton to design Central Park, it, too, clearly envisioned a popular pleasure ground.

37. *FYLA*, 41–42.

38. J. Lachaume, plan 5, *Description of Plans*. Viele resubmitted his plan for the Wood commission, BA *Docs.*, 24, no. 5; the winning plan 33 by Olmsted and Vaux is at the parks department headquarters at the Arsenal; George Waring's plan 29 is at NYHS. Part of the portfolio of contestant Roswell Graves can be found at the NYHS.

Plans Submitted in the Design Competition

Plan No.	Name	From	Position on park
1	Richard Dolben*	Alleghany City, Pa.	
2	Anon. (Pyramid)	NA	
3	William Rogers*	Cleveland	
4	John Rink	New York	gardener
5	J. Lachaume*	Yonkers, N.Y.	
6	John B. Deutsch*	Tarrytown, N.Y.	
7	Adam Gigrich*	New York	
8	H. Noury*	France	
9	Augustus Fitch*	New York	
10	W. L. Fischer	New York	gardening foreman
11	Augustus Hepp, Charles Vogel*	New York	gardener, engineer
12	Pliny Miles, William Davidson*	NA	
13	Anon. ("Ars longa, vita brevis est")	NA	
14	Anon.	NA	
15	Anon. ("Rusticus")	Boston	
16	Susan Parish	New York	
17	Charles Follen	Boston	
18	Lewis Masquerier*	Long Island	
19	Anon. ("Sigma")	NA	
21	Anon. ("Hope")	NA	
22	Charles Graham, J.A. Bagley	New York	surveyors
23	Arthur Hughes	New York	
24	Charles Lyon	Tarrytown, N.Y.	

25	Roswell Graves	New York	engineer
26	Howard Daniels	New York	
27	Lachland McIntosh, Michael Miller	New York	property clerk, dispersing clerk
28	Egbert Viele	New York	engineer
29	George Waring	New York	superintendent of drainage
30	Samuel Gustin	New York	superintendent of gardeners
31	H. Hoffman, C. Wehle*	New York	engineers
32	James Warner	New York	
33	Frederick Law Olmsted, Calvert Vaux	New York	superintendent
34	Ignaz Pilat**	New York	gardening foreman
35	William Benque, Charles Ravolle**		

*signed
**unofficial entry

Authors of unsigned entries were identified on the copy of the descriptions at the NYPL, which apparently belonged to Commissioner Dillon; names (although generally not assigned to particular plans) can also be found in the payroll accounts that the board of commissioners submitted in their annual report to the common council. We have been able to link all but five authors (Robert Morris Copeland, R. W. Copeland, William Gunman, Edward Poller, Henry Hammond) to specific plans. Plans 13, 14, 19, and 21 are still anonymous, and plan 15, "Rusticus," was apparently by one of the Copelands. See also I. N. P. Stokes, *Iconography of Manhattan Island*, 6 vols. (1915–28; rpt. 1967), 5:1875–76.

39. Plans 18, 8.

40. On extending northern border, see BCCP *Min.*, Jan. 26, 1858; and *NYT*, Jan. 7, 14, 1858; *Trib.*, Jan. 12, 1858; *Post*, Jan. 27, 1858; and plans 9, 22, and 27.

41. For different interpretations of the competition, see Schuyler, *New Urban Landscape*, 83–84; Peter George Buckley, "To the Opera House: Culture and Society in New York City, 1820–1860" (Ph.D. diss., State University of New York, Stony Brook, 1984), 607–20.

42. On reservoirs, see plans 25, 17, 26, 5, 33. For examples of Downing's influence in discussion of plantings, see plans 3 and 23. On treatment of water, see, e.g., plans 22 (quot.), 23, 26. On picturesque effects, see, e.g., plans 10 (rocks), 12, 15; on Vista Rock: plans 1, 5, 11, 33. For further discussion of Downing's influence, see Elizabeth Barlow [Rogers] and William Alex, *Frederick Law Olmsted's New York* (1972), 10–16; George Tatum, "The Beautiful and the Picturesque," *American Quarterly* 3 (Spring 1951): 36–51.

43. Plans 10 (gardening foreman), 9 (keepers' lodges), 5 (columns), 6 (decorative statues), 6 (visitors on foot), 22 (Arsenal ruins).

44. For crystal palaces, see, e.g., plans 11, 15, 16, 17, 19, 23, 32. For column of water, plan 7; fresco mural, 20; arcade for busts, 11. For triumphal arches, see, e.g., plan 6, 8, 13, 21, and the "magnificent portal" of plan 31.

45. For "practical knowledge," see, e.g., plans 3, 4, 12 (Grand School), 24 (theme garden), 35. For labyrinths and zoos, see, e.g., plans 7, 8, 19, 25.

46. Plans 1, 4, 13, 22, 29.

47. For shaded arcades, plan 11; Masquerier, plan 18. Noury, plan 8, was the only designer to present a parade in the imperial rather than the republican civic tradition.

48. On baseball, see plans 22 (quot.) and 32; playgrounds or skating ponds for women, plans 23, 26, 29; bathhouses, plan 12; children, plan 7, 30; rowdies, plan 23.

49. On racing, plans 19, 30, 35; equestrian paths, plans 12, 17, 32; curvilinear roads, plan 33.

50. Plan 16; BCCP *Min.*, Sept. 9, Nov. 4, 1858. Information on Parish comes from the obituary of her sister-in-law, who had the same name: *NYT*, Feb. 16, 1916, *NCAB* for John Delafield; John K. Porter, *Parish Will Case in the Court of Appeals* (Albany, 1862).

51. BCCP *Min.*, Dec. 18, 29, 1857. Although it appears from the minutes that the resolution to invite representatives from the two parks was amended simply to purchase plans and documents, the *Times*, Mar. 23, 1858, reported that the board had extended invitations. On European parks, see Chadwick, *Park and Town*, 58–72, 153–56; Newton, *Design on the Land*, 225–32, 241–45.

52. Charles Follen to *Post*, May 6, 1858. Plans 5, 8, 11, 13, 16, 20, 22, 25, 30, 31, 32, and 33 included portfolios; plans 15, 16, 30, and 31 provided clay or plaster models.

53. BCCP, *Min.*, Apr. 28, 1858.

54. On Daniels, see Schuyler, *New Urban Landscape*, 110–14. For reception of the decision, see *Post*, Apr. 29, 1858; *NYT*, Apr. 30, 1858; *Her.*, May 1, 1858, and discussion in Chapter 5.

55. *NYT*, Mar. 23, 1858. Apparently the rule on anonymity was not understood by all the contestants; although the *Post*, Jan. 8, 1858, sought to clarify it, 11 of the 33 official entries were signed. The *Post* published descriptions of 17 of the plans prior to the decision: Apr. 15, 17, 19, 24, 26, 1857. The *Tribune* apparently charged that this breach would influence the outcome: *Post*, Apr. 19, 1858. Follen, plan 17, referred to complaints in the Boston *Daily Advertiser* in his letter to the *Post*, May 6, 1858. The anonymous author of plan 21 complained of Viele's map.

56. "Passages in the Life of a Practical Man," and FLO to JO, Oct. 9, 1857, both in *FLOP* 3:85–87, 104; CV, Memorandum, Nov. 1894.

57. Gustin was the only horticulturalist to testify on behalf of the central park during the 1853 senate committee hearings, which may explain the intense opposition of Commissioner James Hogg, a former Jones Wood advocate, to his later appointment as the park's gardening superintendent; see BCCP *Min.*, Aug. 4, Sept. 2, 8, 11, 23, 1857. On Gustin's support from Democratic aldermen, see John Butterworth to FLO, May 20, June 16, 1858, FLO Mss. On Miller's relationship to Commissioner Strong, see CV to FLO, Jan. 30, 1864 (identifying Miller as Strong's nephew), and Viele testimony in *FYLA*, 556 (identifying Miller as a son-in-law). For reviews of the exhibition of plans, see *NYT*, May 13, 1858; *Horticulturalist* 8 (July 1858): 23. The Miller and McIntosh plan was not among those the *Post* described in advance of the decision (Apr. 19, 1858).

58. BCCP *Min.*, Apr. 28, 1858. See also *FLOP* 3:26–27.

59. BCCP *Min.*, Apr. 28, 1858; *Her.*, May 1, 1858, and letter in *Post*, denying charge of politics, May 1, 1858. See also letter from Commissioner Fields in *Her.*, May 22, 1858, charging the Republican commissioners had caucused to decide the outcome prior to the meeting.

5. The Greensward Plan and Its Creators

1. *Post*, May 6, 1858.

2. James Marston Fitch, "Design and Designer: Nineteenth-Century Innovation," in *Art of the Olmsted Landscape*, ed. Bruce Kelly et al. (1981), 75. Although Bruce Kelly acknowledges in his own essay, "Art of the Olmsted Landscape," that Olmsted did little designing, he concludes that "Olmsted has become a generic term, symbolizing the team of men" with whom he worked (67, 70). The erasure of Vaux's contribution became most entrenched when Frederick Law Olmsted, Jr., and Theodora Kimball published Olmsted's "professional papers" (among them joint reports of Olmsted and Vaux) in 1928; see *FYLA* and Chapter 15. For other discussions of the collaboration that assign preeminence to Olmsted, see, e.g., S. B. Sutton, ed., *Civilizing American Cities: A Selection of Frederick Law Olmsted's Writings on City Landscapes* (Cambridge, Mass., 1971), 1, 7–9; Albert Fein, ed., *Landscape into Cityscape: Frederick Law Olmsted's Plans for a Greater New York City* (Ithaca, 1968), 44–78; Elizabeth Barlow [Rogers] and William Alex, *Frederick Law Olmsted's New York* (1972); Susanna S. Zetzel, "The Garden in the Machine: The Construction of Nature in Olmsted's Central Park," *Prospects: An Annual of American Cultural Studies* 14 (1989): 291–339. For more balanced discussions of the collaboration, see *FLOP* 3:136–37; Laura Wood Roper, *FLO: A Biography of Frederick Law Olmsted* (Baltimore, 1973), 138.

3. BCCP *Min.*, May 17, 1858; FLO to CV, Nov. 26, 1863, CV to FLO, Jan. 18, 1864, June 3, 1865, *FLOP* 5:152, 179, 388.

4. CV to FLO, Feb. 5, 1864, *FLOP* 5:183.

5. "Calvert Vaux: Designer of Parks," *Parks International* 1 (Sept. 1920): 138–43; Frank Kowsky, *The Architecture of Frederick Clarke Withers and the Progress of the Gothic Revival in America* (Middletown, Conn., 1980), 21, and 161 n. 12. See also John David Sigle, "Calvert Vaux: An American Architect" (M.A. thesis, University of Virginia, 1967); *DAB*; *FLOP* 3:63–68; David W. Matzdor, "Calvert Vaux, 1824–1895" (thesis, School of Architecture, London, 1977). On Downing's recruitment, see CV to Marshall Wilder, July 18, 1852, Smith Mss., vol. 14, Library Company of Philadelphia, on deposit at the Historical Society of Pennsylvania, Philadelphia. See also Frank Kowsky's forthcoming study of Vaux's architecture.

6. Kowsky, *Architecture of Withers*, 21, 23–25, 28–31; Calvert Vaux, *Villas and Cottages: A Series*

of Designs Prepared for Execution in the United States (1857; 2d ed., 1864; rpt. 1970); Vaux, "Should a Republic Encourage the Arts?" *Horticulturalist* 7 (Feb. 1852): 73–77; Vaux, "American Architecture," *Horticulturalist* 8 (Apr. 1853): 168–72. See also CV to Wilder, July 18, 1852.

7. See, e.g., CV to FLO, Apr. 29, 1864, CV to Mary Olmsted Nov. 9, 1864, FLO Mss.; Vaux, *Villas and Cottages*, 36–37; on Vaux's work habits, Mabel Parsons, ed., *Memories of Samuel Parsons* (1926), 4 (quot.); FLO to JO, Aug. 17, 1864, *FLOP* 5:246.

8. Vaux, *Villas and Cottages*, 41, 51, and passim.

9. Ibid. On American romantics and art, see Perry Miller, "Nature and the National Ego," in *Errand into the Wilderness* (1956; rpt. 1964), 204–16; F. O. Matthiessen, *American Renaissance: Art and Expression in the Age of Emerson and Whitman* (1941), 44–55, 132–52, 157–66; Neil Harris, *The Artist in American Society: The Formative Years, 1790–1860* (1966), 199–216. On Ruskin, see Roger B. Stein, *John Ruskin and Aesthetic Thought in America, 1840–1900* (Cambridge, Mass., 1967), 2–31; and the essays in John D. Rosenberg, ed., *The Genius of John Ruskin* (Boston, 1979); and Clive Wilmer, ed., *Unto This Last and Other Writings by John Ruskin* (1985).

10. Vaux, *Villas and Cottages*, xiii, 30, 40, 66, 185 (price); CV to FLO, June 3, 1865, May 12, 1865, *FLOP* 5:386–87, 363.

11. CV to FLO, June 3, May 22, 1865, *FLOP* 5:387, 377. For identification with Downing, see CV to Wilder, July 18, 1852.

12. Roper, *FLO*, 10–65; *FLOP* 1:4–14, 77–80, 83–85, 2:73–75. See also Melvin Kalfus, *Frederick Law Olmsted: The Passion of a Public Artist* (1990); Elizabeth Stevenson, *Park Maker: A Life of Frederick Law Olmsted* (1977).

13. FLO to Frederick Kingsbury, June 12, 1846, FLO to John Hull Olmsted, June 23, 1845, FLO to Charles Brace, June 22, 1845, *FLOP* 1:243, 219, 215. For the context of rural improvements, see Clarence Danhoff, *Change in Agriculture: The Northern United States, 1820–1970* (Cambridge, Mass., 1969), 1–22, 49–72; Tamara Plakins Thornton, "Between Generations: Boston Agricultural Reform and the Aging of New England, 1815–1830," *New England Quarterly* 59 (June 1986): 189–211; and Alexander Von Hoffman, "The Origins of Public Landscapes in Nineteenth Century America," unpub. paper, copy in the possession of authors.

14. FLO to John H. Olmsted, Feb. 10, 1849, "Autobiographical Fragment B," both in *FLOP* 1:324, 117–18; Olmsted, "The People's Park at Birkenhead, Near Liverpool," *Horticulturalist* 6 (May 1851): 224–28; "A Note on the True Soldat Labourer Pear," *Horticulturalist* 7 (Jan. 1852): 14–15; "Apple Orchards in England," *Horticulturalist* 7 (Dec. 1852): 549–52; "Appeal to the Citizens of Staten Island," *FLOP* 1:331–34.

15. JO to FLO, June 8, 1847. Strong quoted in Roper, *FLO*, 219, and see 51–52.

16. FLO to JO, Dec. 9, 1855, *FLOP* 2:376; Olmsted, *Walks and Talks of an American Farmer in England* (1852; 2d ed., 1859, rpt. Ann Arbor, 1967), 61. See also Roper, *FLO*, 86–123; *FLOP* 2:1–39; and Olmsted, *Seaboard Slave States* (1856); *A Journey through Texas; or, a Saddle-Trip on the Southwestern Frontier* (1857); *A Journey in the Back Country* (1860).

17. "Passages in the Life of an Unpractical Man," and FLO to BCCP, Aug. 12, 1857, both in *FLOP* 3:85–86, 76.

18. Petition to BCCP, Sept. 1859; Parke Godwin to AHG, Aug. 21, 1857, FLO Mss.; FLO to John Hull Olmsted, Sept. 11, 1857 (soliciting and definition of position), FLO to JO, Oct. 9, 1857, *FLOP* 3:79–80, 104.

19. CV, Memorandum, Nov. 1894, CV Papers, NYPL; CV to FLO, Jan. 18, 1864, May 22, 1865, *FLOP* 5:177, 376.

20. FLO to CV, Nov. 26, 1863, FLO to JO, Jan. 14, 1858, *FLOP* 5:151, 148, 146, 3:114. On marriage, *FLOP*, 3:59–63.

21. CV Testimony in the March 1864 Viele case, sent to Olmsted Apr. 25, 1864, FLO Mss. See also *FYLA*, 43 and CV Memo, Nov. 1894.

22. On Olmsted's lack of interest in plans on paper, see CV to FLO, May 12, 1865, FLO to CV, June 8, 1865, *FLOP* 5:362, 390. Vaux's Greensward drawings are at the Municipal Archives. On Olmsted's horticultural talents, see CV to Henry W. Bellows, Feb. 25, 1864, FLO Mss. For his early thoughts on planting Central Park, see FLO to BCCP, Oct. 16, 1857, *FLOP* 3:106–11; and for his plans for an arboretum in it, GP 162–77.

23. CV Testimony, Mar. 1864; Vaux, *Villas and Cottages*, 27. For Olmsted's admiration of landscape art, see, e.g., *Walks and Talks*, 52–56, 59, 61.

24. Vaux, *Villas and Cottages*, 27–28, 63–64; Olmsted, "Public Parks and the Enlargement of Towns," in *Civilizing American Cities*, 96.

25. GP 119–24. For other discussions of the plan's aesthetic principles, see Charles E. Beveridge, "Frederick Law Olmsted's Theory of Landscape Design," *Nineteenth Century* 3 (Summer 1977): 38–43; David Schuyler, *The New Urban Landscape: The Redefinition of City Form in Nineteenth-Century America* (Baltimore, 1986), 85–95; Barlow and Alex, *Olmsted's New York*, 5–25. For a perceptive cultural reading of the Greensward "text," see Peter George Buckley, "To the Opera House: Culture and Society in New York City, 1820–1860" (Ph.D. diss., State University of New York, Stony Brook, 1984), 605–20.

26. GP 121–22; Susan Parish, plan 16, Pliny Miles and William Davidson, plan 12, both in BCCP, *Description of the Plans for the Improvement of Central Park* (1858), NYPL; *Sun*, Apr. 27, 1857. On the transverse roads, see also *FLOP* 3:180 n. 14.

27. CV to Clarence Cook, June 6, 1865, and CV Testimony, Mar. 1864, both in FLO Mss.

28. GP 125–26.

29. GP 129; CV to Cook, June 6, 1865. Today the Terrace is called the Bethesda Terrace. The name comes from the fountain sculpture—installed in 1873—*The Angel of the Waters*, a biblical reference to an angel who brought healing powers to the pool of Bethesda in Jerusalem. The English architect Jacob Wrey Mould assisted Vaux in preparing the Terrace plans and designed the rich ornamentation. In claiming credit for its "conception," Vaux referred to its placement in relation to the Promenade and Lake.

30. Olmsted, "Park," *New American Cyclopaedia* (1861), rpt. in *FLOP* 3:355; Vaux, *Villas and Cottages*, 42–43, 125–26; CV to Cook, June 6, 1865.

31. FLO to Ignaz Pilat, Sept. 26, 1863, *FLOP* 5:85; GP 130. See also "Description of Central Park, BCCP 2AR [1858], rpt. in *FLOP* 3:215.

32. FLO to Paul Dana, Mar. 12, 1891, OA Mss.; GP 152–61. As park superintendent, Olmsted had already taken up the question of proper drainage; see FLO to BCCP, Oct. 6, 1857, *FLOP* 3:94–101. On requirements of domestic convenience, see Vaux, *Villas and Cottages*, 56–57.

33. GP 127, 151.

34. CV to Cook, June 6, 1865.

35. CV to FLO, June 3, 1865, *FLOP* 5:385; Vaux, *Villas and Cottages*, 49–50, 30.

36. Vaux, *Villas and Cottages*, 28.

37. Ibid., 38. See also John Ruskin, "The Art of the Gothic" (1853), in *Unto This Last*, 91, 92–95, 101–4, 106–9.

38. Kowsky, *Architecture of Withers*, 161 n. 12, citing article in *American Builder* 1 (Dec. 1868), which Kowsky attributes to Clarence Cook; Vaux, *Villas and Cottages*, 248. For Vaux and AIA, see Henry H. Saylor, *American Institute of Architects: The First One Hundred Years* (Washington, D.C., 1957), 32.

39. FLO to Brace, Dec. 1, 1854, FLO to *NYT*, Jan. 12, 1855, *FLOP* 2:234, 244. Olmsted had previously sounded the theme of his responsibility as a gentleman toward the "ignoble vulgus" when he envisioned himself as a country squire: FLO to Kingsbury, June 12, 1846, *FLOP* 1:243. At the same time, he was self-conscious about his father's efforts to train him as a gentleman with dancing and drawing lessons: Roper, *FLO*, 42; FLO to John Hull Olmsted, Mar. 11, 1846, FLO Mss., and June 23, 1845, *FLOP* 1:219. For other interpretations of Olmsted's political and social views, see Geoffrey Blodgett, "Frederick Law Olmsted: Landscape Architecture as Conservative Reform," *Journal of American History* 62 (Mar. 1976): 869–89; Robert Lewis, "Frontier and Civilization in the Thought of Frederick Law Olmsted," *American Quarterly* 29 (Fall 1977): 388–96; Thomas Bender, *Toward an Urban Vision: Ideas and Institutions of Nineteenth Century America* (Lexington, Ky., 1975), 164–87, and *New York Intellect: A History of Intellectual Life in New York City, from 1750 to the Beginnings of Our Own Time* (Baltimore, 1987), 194–203; Buckley, "To the Opera House," 621–40; Kalfus, *Frederick Law Olmsted*, passim.

40. FLO to *NYT*, Jan. 12, 1855, FLO to Brace, Dec. 1, 1854, *FLOP* 2:243, 234, 245.

41. FLO to Brace, Dec. 1, 1854, FLO to *NYT*, Jan. 12, 1855, *FLOP* 2:235, 244. Cf. *Trib.*, Jan 30, 1854.

42. FLO to *NYT*, Feb. 13, 1854, FLO to Brace, Dec. 1, 1854, both in *FLOP* 2:257, 265, 236. Olmsted believed that the abolition of slavery was unconstitutional but that northerners could work toward gradual abolition by disproving southern charges that the free-labor system degraded

all workers, black as well as white. At the same time, in commending the "combination" of the work force on plantations, he suggested that the relation of "the master to the negro" could be understood as one of "stewardship": ibid., 263–64, 257, 261. For Olmsted's later reflections on gentlemen's responsibility to promote "civilization" against "barbarism," see his unpublished ms. titled by the editors of his papers "Notes on the Pioneer Condition," *FLOP* 5:744–45 and 577–763, passim.

43. CV to Cook, June 6, 1865; Vaux, *Villas and Cottages*, 31, 41 (public debate).

44. Olmsted, "Public Parks and the Enlargement of Towns," 96; FLO to CV, Nov. 26, 1863, *FLOP* 5:153.

45. CV to FLO, Oct. 19, 1863, FLO to CV, Nov. 26, 1863, *FLOP* 5:114–15, 153–54.

46. FLO to CV, Nov. 26, 1863, *FLOP* 5:153–54.

47. CV to FLO, Jan. 18, 1864, *FLOP* 5:177, 179, 180–81.

48. CV to FLO, Jan. 18, 1864, May 22, 1865, *FLOP* 5:177–78, 377.

49. BCCP *Min.*, May 17, 1858; FLO to BCCP, May 10, 1858, FLO to CV, Nov. 26, 1863, CV to FLO, Jan. 18, 1864, June 3, May 22, 1865, *FLOP* 3:191–92, 5:154, 177–79, 387, 377. For Vaux, who thought of his "profession" in the older sense of a calling, Olmsted's position resembled that of an untrained journeyman who performed the craftwork of those who had been regularly apprenticed. Olmsted felt "architect" was an inappropriate description of his position but not because the title obscured the design partnership: FLO to CV, Nov. 26, 1863, *FLOP* 5:147, 149–50.

50. CV to FLO, Jan. 18, 1864, July 21, 1865, FLO to CV, Nov. 26, 1863, *FLOP* 5:180, 178, 404–5, 146–47, 154.

51. *Horticulturalist* 8 (July 1858): 22–23; *Crayon* 5 (July 1858): 210; *Her.*, May 1, 1858; *FL*, May 15, 1858; *C&E*, *Post*, *NYT*, Apr. 30, 1858. See also *Post*, Apr. 26, 1858.

52. *Post*, May 4, 10, 1858, doc. 2 (May 10, 1858), rpt. in *FYLA*, 233–36; GP 154; BCCP *Min.*, doc. 3 (May 17, 1858).

53. GP 126–27; BCCP doc. 2 (1858), *FYLA*, 234; Anon., plan 13, BCCP, *Description of Plans*.

54. On militia companies, see Amy Bridges, *A City in the Republic: Antebellum New York and the Origins of Machine Politics* (Ithaca, 1987), 76–77; Richard B. Stott, *Workers in the Metropolis: Class, Ethnicity, and Youth in Antebellum New York City* (Ithaca, 1990), 228–31; Michael McGerr, *The Decline of Popular Politics: The American North, 1865–1928* (1986), 24.

55. BCCP *Min.*, May 17, 18, 24, 27, 1858. On Dillon, see *Her.*, Nov. 27, 1872. When, as corporation counsel, Dillon had defended the commissioner's awards for park land, he had eloquently invoked the model of Hyde Park, focusing on its artificial rather than pastoral features: *Her.*, Feb. 3, 1856. The *Post*, May 26, 1858, and *Times*, May 27, 1858, printed the Dillon proposals.

56. On Belmont, see *NYT*, Nov. 25, 1890; David Black, *The King of Fifth Avenue: The Fortunes of August Belmont* (1981); and on appointment, BCCP *Min.*, Mar. 16, 1858.

57. *NYT*, June 7, 1858. For Olmsted's report, see BCCP *Min.*, doc. 5 (May 31, 1858), rpt. in *FLOP* 3:193–97. Five Republican commissioners defended the board's procedures: *NYT*, *Post*, June 10, 1858, to which Dillon and Belmont responded, *NYT*, June 11, 1858. See also BCCP *Min.*, May 31, June 3, 8, 1858.

58. *NYT*, June 7, 1858. See also BCCP *Min.*, May 24, 1858; *NYT*, May 27, 1858.

59. *NYT*, June 7, 1858; cf. GP 129–31; FLO to BCCP, May 31, 1858, *FLOP*, 3:129–30, 196.

60. FLO to BCCP, May 31, 1858, *FLOP* 3:195; *Post*, June 10, 1858. The *Times* (June 11, 1858) complained that it was ungentlemanly for commissioners to air their grievances in public; the *Herald* (June 2, 5, 7, 11, 1858) defended Dillon and Belmont and attacked the partisan politics of the board's majority.

61. *Trib.*, June 18, 1858; and see *Trib.*, May 31, June 9, 18, 1858; *Post*, June 3, 4, 11, 28, 1858.

62. *Trib.*, May 31, 1858; *Her.*, May 31, June 2, 3, 5, 11, 22, 1858; BCCP *Min.*, May 17, 1858. On the aldermen's response, see *Her.*, May 31, 1858; BCCP, *Min.*, June 17, Aug. 19, 1858. The editors of the Olmsted papers suggest that on May 27, when Green requested that Olmsted report on the feasibility of separating ways, he had discussed the matter with Olmsted, who was already preparing his May 31 report; in that report, however, Olmsted was far from enthusiastic about the proposal. See *FLOP* 3:24–25, 195–96. For celebration of the park's separate ways, see, e.g., George F. Chadwick, *The Park and the Town* (1966), 185–86.

63. BCCP doc. 11 (Sept. 9, 1858), excerpted in *FYLA*, 378. On Prospect Park, see Barlow and

Alex, *Olmsted's New York*, 32–37; Schuyler, *New Urban Landscape*, 115–25; *FLOP* 6 (forthcoming).

64. Vaux, *Villas and Cottages*, 31; CV to Cook, June 6, 1865; FLO to Richard Grant White, June 3, 16, 1858, FLO to Parke Godwin, Aug. 1, 1858, *FLOP* 3:197–201. For White's editorial, see *C&E*, May 31, 1858. Olmsted came under personal attack for inexperience from the *Herald* in particular, May 23, 31, 1858; the *Times* rallied to his defense, May 29, 1858. Ironically, Olmsted recognized the obligation of architects to modify a plan to suit the client when he advised his father, Aug. 17, 1864, on what to expect in hiring an architect to build a church: *FLOP* 5:243, 247.

65. CV to FLO, May 22, July 31, 1865, *FLOP* 5:376, 419.

66. CV to FLO, July 6, 1865, July 31, 1865, *FLOP* 5:402, 419. See also CV to FLO, May 20, 1865, *FLOP*, 373–74.

67. FLO to JO, Jan. 14, 1858, *FLOP* 3:113.

68. CV to FLO, May 22, July 8, 1865, FLO to CV, Aug. 1, 1865, *FLOP* 5:377, 404, 420. See also FLO to CV, Mar. 12, 1865, 324.

6. Building for "the Public and Posterity"

1. CV to Clarence Cook, June 6, 1865, FLO Mss.

2. BCCP, *6AR* [1862], 6–7. For plantings, see BCCP, *5AR* [1861], 7; *9AR* [1865], 134; *10AR* [1866], 18. On gunpowder used at Gettysburg, see Joseph L. Harsh, "Dear Abe," *Centre View*, Feb. 2, 1989.

3. Quoted in Charles E. Beveridge, "Introduction," *FLOP* 3:15.

4. FLO to Charles Brace, Dec. 8, 1860, *FLOP* 3:286; *Her.*, Nov. 7 (signs), 18, 1857; *NYT*, Nov. 3, 1857. See also *Sun*, Nov. 19, 20, 1857.

5. BCCP *Min.*, doc. 4 (June 2, 1857). On the demonstration, see *Sun*, *NYT*, May 13, 1857. See also *JC*, *Ir. N*, May 13, 1857; *Sun*, May 19, 1857.

6. The aldermen ignored the request for funding until the Court of Appeals upheld the Metropolitan Police Act: *Post*, July 2, 1857. On their resistance, see *JC*, May 5, 13, 1857; *Sun*, May 19, June 4, 1857; *NYT*, June 4, 1857. On open meetings, see BCCP *Min.*, Aug. 24, Sept. 2, 23, Nov. 17, 1857; on hiring, ibid., June 12, July 28, Aug. 8, Sept. 11, 23, 30, 1857; James Hogg to *Trib.*, Dec. 11, 1857 (quot.); Viele testimony before common council, *Her.*, *Sun*, Nov. 10, 1857; "Passages in the Life of an Unpractical Man," *FLOP* 3:89. On appropriations, see BCCP *Min.*, doc. 7 (Sept. 1, 1857); *Post*, Aug. 13, 25, 1857. The *Post*, Aug. 12, 1857, announced that ground had been broken to build the park.

7. *NYT*, Oct. 8, 1857. On panic, see also *Sun*, Sept. 12, 1857; *Post*, Sept. 16, 1857; *Her.*, Oct. 1, 1857; *NYT*, Oct. 7, 1858. On board's difficulties selling bonds and decision to lay off workers, see BCCP *Min.*, Sept. 30, Oct. 2, 6, 1857; *Post*, Oct. 6, 10, 1857; *C&E*, Oct. 7, 1857; on Mayor Wood's request, *NYT*, Oct. 23, 1857; BCCP *Min.*, Oct. 30, 1857. The aldermen appropriated money a week after Wood's address: *C&E*, Oct. 30, 1857; *Post*, Oct. 31, 1857. On councilmen's resistance, see *Her.*, Nov. 8, 1857; on debates over using public works for relief, e.g., *Her.*, Oct. 4, 23, 1857; *Ir. N*, Oct. 17, 1857; *C&E*, Oct. 23, 1857; *Post*, Oct. 23, Nov. 11, 13, 1857; Iver Bernstein, *The New York City Draft Riots: Their Significance for American Society and Politics in the Age of Civil War* (1990), 138–42.

8. *Sun*, Nov. 6, 1857 (right); *Her.*, Nov. 7 (McGuire), 10 (Bowles), 11, 1857. See also *Her.*, Nov. 3, 1857; *C&E*, Nov. 3, 4, 7, 1857; *Sun*, Nov. 7, 10, 1857; *NYT*, Nov. 3, 1857; *Ir. Am.*, Nov. 14, 1857.

9. Bernstein, *New York City Draft Riots*, 89–91, 98–100; Carl N. Degler, "Labor in the Economy and Politics of New York City, 1850–1860" (Ph.D. diss., Columbia University, 1952) 142–97; Amy Bridges, *A City in the Republic: Antebellum New York and the Origins of Machine Politics* (Ithaca, 1987), 103–24, 140–44.

10. For vote, see *Her.*, Nov. 10, 1857; *Sun*, Nov. 11, 1857; *NYT*, Nov. 11, 1857 (quot.); on struggle over jobs, see *Post*, Nov. 20, 1857 (bribes); *Her.*, Nov. 15, 16; *Sun*, Nov. 11–13, 17, 19, 20; *NYT*, Nov. 17, 1857.

11. *Sun*, Nov. 20, 1857; *Her.*, Nov. 18, 25, 26, 1857.

12. *Trib.*, Dec. 11, 1857. Other commissioners sought to censure Hogg for his blatant violation of the board's nonpartisan stance: BCCP *Min.*, Dec. 15, 1857. Wood's supporters on the common council launched an investigation of the board's use of patronage (*NYT*, *Her.*, *Trib.*, Dec. 8, 1857),

but despite workers' complaints, the aldermen decided not to obstruct the park board lest it appear that "since the election the Common Council did not care for the poor": *Trib.*, Dec. 19, 1857; and testimony, *NYT, Her., CA*, Dec. 11, 13, 1857.

13. For initial uncertainty on whether to use contract or day labor, see, e.g., BCCP *Min.*, June 23, 1857, and doc. no. 5 (July 7, 1857).

14. Eugene Moehring, *Public Works and Patterns of Urban Real Estate Growth in Manhattan, 1835–1894* (1981), 37–39, 245–46; Daniel Hovey Calhoun, *The American Civil Engineer: Origins and Conflict* (Cambridge, Mass., 1960), 13–14, 59–77, 145. For opposition to contracting, see Degler, "Labor in the Economy and Politics," 147, citing *Her.*, July 7, 1850; Jean Hurley, "The Irish Immigrant in the Early Labor Movement" (M.A. thesis, Columbia University, 1989), 102–4, 112–13; Sean Wilentz, *Chants Democratic: New York City and the Rise of the American Working Class, 1788–1850* (1984), 232, 333. See also Robert Ernst, *Immigrant Life in New York City, 1825–1863* (1949), 105–6; Catherine Tobin, "Lowly Muscular Diggers: Irish Canal Workers in Nineteenth-Century America" (Ph.D. diss., University of Notre Dame, 1987).

15. Moehring, *Public Works*, 71–81, 259–63. For a typical complaint, see *JC*, Apr. 19, 1854.

16. "Passages in the Life," *FLOP* 3:87, 90; BCCP *Min.*, Nov. 10, 1857. See also FLO to John Hull Olmsted, Sept. 11, 1857, *FLOP* 3:79.

17. "Passages in the Life," *FLOP* 3:90; Olmsted, Report to BCCP, *Her.*, Nov. 25, 1857. See also *NYT*, Dec. 5, 1857; *Trib.*, Dec. 14, 1857. Despite Olmsted's "policy" of not permitting politics on the park, German workingmen complained that foremen watched the polls to see how they voted: *Her.*, Nov. 26, 1857. On intrigues over Viele and Olmsted, see FLO to JO, Oct. 9, 1857, *FLOP* 3:104; and BCCP *Min.*, Sept. 23, Nov. 10, 17, Dec. 8, 1857.

18. Robert Dillon, "Minority Report for Special Committee on Contract," BCCP *Min.*, doc. 9 (June 17, 1858), reprinted in *NYT*, Aug. 26, 1858. See also *Trib.*, Jan. 31, 1856; *Her.*, Sept. 5, 1858.

19. John A. C. Gray and Charles Elliott, "Majority Report for the Special Committee on Contract," BCCP *Min.*, doc. 8 (June 17, 1858), reprinted in *NYT*, Aug. 26, 1858.

20. Bernstein, *New York City Draft Riots*, 172–76. See also *NYT*, Aug. 26, 1858; *Trib.*, Dec. 10, 1858.

21. FLO to BCCP, doc. 7 (May 17, 1858), rpt. in *FYLA*, 294, 293; FLO to JO, Jan. 14, 1858, *FLOP* 3:113.

22. Andrew Green, elected president of the board on May 10, 1858, mediated the dispute. See BCCP *Min.*, doc. 10 (July 15, 1858).

23. James Hogg to FLO, June 21, 1858, B. F. Crane to FLO, Apr. 27, 1860; Charles Elliott to FLO, June 6, 1859, and see, e.g., Crane to FLO, May 4, 1859, Edwin Morgan to Richard Blatchford, Mar. 16, 1860, Richard Kelly to Thomas Fields, May 5, 1860, all in FLO Mss.

24. Elliott to FLO, Apr. 29, 1859, Strong to FLO, Mar. 22, 1858, FLO Mss.; George Haven Putnam, *Memoirs of My Youth, 1844–1865* (1914), 87. See also, e.g., Charles Russell to FLO, May 2, 1829, John Butterworth to FLO, May 16, 1859, Gray to FLO, Apr. 26, 1858, FLO Mss.

25. FLO to BCCP, Mar. 28, 1861, *FLOP* 3:335.

26. John Culyer to Francis Hawks, Nov. 17, 1859 (corps), FH Mss.; Calhoun, *American Civil Engineer*, 47–53, 59–61, 70–73, 182–99. See also Raymond H. Merritt, *Engineering in American Society* (Lexington, Ky., 1969), 8, 10.

27. FLO to JO, Jan. 14, Feb. 2, 1858, *FLOP* 3:113, 115; *Her.*, May 23 (quot.), 31, 1858; FLO to BCCP, May 17, 1858, *FYLA*, 293. Upon hearing of Olmsted's appointment, his father had urged him to "be particularly careful in your accounts": JO to FLO, Sept. 27, 1857, FLO Mss.

28. Report of Special Committee, BCCP *Min.*, doc. 2 (July 21, 1859): 4; Calhoun, *American Civil Engineer*, 74, 54–45 (on Jervis's method); *NYT*, Oct. 12, 1896 (Grant). The engineers are named in the payrolls included in the board's annual reports to the common council: BA *Docs.* [1858–1870], January or February of each year. Our generalizations about the social backgrounds of the engineers come from obituaries in the *Times* and engineering journals as well as from the *DAB*.

29. *NYT*, Apr. 20, 1898; FLO to BCCP, Jan. 22, 1861, *FLOP* 3:302. On Pieper, see also Eugene T. Sawyer, *History of Santa Clara County, California* (Los Angeles, 1922), 412; on Hawks, FH Mss.; on Bogart, *NYT*, Apr. 25, 1920.

30. Engineers hired by Viele also appear as contractors and surveyors in the comptroller's

annual reports to the common council: BA *Docs.*; *Answer of A. W. Craven, Chief Engineer of the Croton Aqueduct to Charges Made by Fernando Wood* (1860), 41.

31. See, e.g., William H. Grant, "Instruction to Engineers," July 13, 1858, Memorandum to Assistant Engineers, July 14, 1858, Dec. 12, 1858, "Instruction to Assistants as to Mechanical Works," May 14, 1859, Grant to J. H. Pieper, Sept. 6, 1860, all in FH Mss. On Clark and Ryan, see testimony before senate committee, *Her.*, Nov. 24, 1860; on Ryan, see also *NYT,* Apr. 5, 1882.

32. CV to FLO, July 8, 1865, *FLOP* 5:404; Grant to FLO, May 2, 1860, FLO Mss.; Culyer to Hawks, May 22, 1861, FH Mss.

33. On Grant's favoritism, see George Waring to FLO, Nov. 17, 1859, FLO Mss. The engineers' anxieties are evident in the letters and memos of the FH Mss. and in Grant's letters to FLO, FLO Mss.

34. BA *Docs.*, 27, no. 6 (Jan. 30, 1860): 21; BA *Docs.*, 28, pt. 1, no. 6 (Jan. 31, 1861): 3.

35. See surveying reports in BA *Docs.*, 24, no. 5 (Jan. 19, 1857): 46–76, 52–53, 59, 69–70.

36. Ibid., 26–35, 74 (quot.).

37. Ibid., 49, and 46–76 passim; Olmsted, "Parks" (1861), *FLOP* 3:355.

38. *Post*, Sept. 9, 1857; *NYT,* Sept. 7, 1857. See also Viele to BCCP, *Min.*, doc. 9 (Sept. 23, 1857).

39. FLO to BCCP, Oct. 6, 1857, *FLOP* 3:96. Olmsted later issued handbills titled "What to Do in Case of Sunstroke," June 26, 1859, Central Park Scrapbook, MARC [hereafter cited as CP Scrapbook].

40. *Her.*, Nov. 25, 1857; "Description of the Central Park," Jan. 1859, BCCP *2AR* [1858], rpt. in *FLOP* 3:212; *Trib.*, Dec. 14, 1857. See also *Post*, Dec. 1, 1857.

41. FLO to BCCP, Jan. 22, 1861, *FLOP* 3:314; FLO testimony, *Trib.*, Dec. 14, 1857; FLO to Brace, Dec. 8, 1860, *FLOP* 3:286. On absentee rules, see *Her.*, Nov. 24, 1857; *NYT,* Sept. 3, 1859; on customary absenteeism, Moehring, *Public Works*, 243–44.

42. BA *Docs.*, 24, no. 5: 12; FLO to BCCP, Oct. 6, 1857, *FLOP* 3:95. See also George Waring's report in "Report of Committee on Draining and Sewerage," BCCP *Min.*, Doc. no 12 (Oct. 30, 1857); Viele to BCCP, ibid., doc. 16 (Mar. 16, 1858).

43. On Waring, see *DAB* and *NYT,* Oct. 30, 1898; on laying drains, BCCP *2AR* [1858], 79–82. Waring was appointed in August 1857; by winter, however, he had come under attack for not following orders, and in June the board abolished his position along with Viele's. See BCCP *Min.*, Aug. 4, Dec. 8, 1857, Jan. 5, May 17, 1858. Olmsted reappointed Waring as drainage engineer: ibid., doc. 6 (June 17, 1858).

44. *Post*, Nov. 17, 1858; BCCP *3AR* [1859], 55; *Trib.*, Dec. 1, 1858. See also *NYT,* Dec. 11, 1858.

45. Waring to FLO, n.d. [1859], Grant to FLO, June 16, 1859, FLO Mss.; Grant to Hawks, July 13, 1861, FH Mss. See also Waring to FLO, June 6, 1859, Grant to FLO, June 18, 1859, "Drain Tiles Laid on Lower Park from 59th to 86th Street" (with notes on broken tiles), and Map of Drained Area, Dec. 22, 1861, showing area to be redrained, all in FLO Mss. On later problems, see John Crimmins to Board of Estimate, Dec. 20, 1884, 85:11, MP; and Chapter 11.

46. "Description of the Central Park," *FLOP* 3:213–14. On grading Promenade, see also *Her.*, June 22, 1858; *NYT,* Nov. 11, 1858.

47. "Special Rules for Blasting," Handbill, CP Scrapbook; *NYT,* Sept. 3, 1859; Grant, "Instructions to Assistant Engineers," Nov. 25, 1858, Grant to Hawks, Jan. 26, Feb. 23, 1859, both in FH Mss; BCCP *Min.*, Oct. 21, 1858 (Flynn); *Ir. N,* Oct. 8, 1859; BCCP *9AR* [1865], 134 (5 deaths); FLO to BCCP, May 1860, FLO Mss. ($50); BA *Docs.*, 27, pt. 1, no. 6 (Jan. 30, 1860): 21 (imprudence). For other deaths, see BCCP *Min.*, Apr. 5, 19, 1860, June 6, 1862. Under common law, as construed by American judges, the commission was not liable for work-related injuries; workers were assumed to have accepted the risk when they took the job. The blasting rules were elaborated when private contractors took over constructing the park in the vicinity of the reservoir; see Grant to Montgomery Kellogg, Sept. 5, 1861, "Time Table, Central Park," Oct. 7, 1861, both in FH Mss.

48. BCCP *Min.*, May 5, 1859; Grant to Hawks, Nov. 25, 1858, FH Mss. See also testimony of foreman Thomas Geary, *Her.*, Nov. 24, 1860.

49. Grant to Hawks, Nov. 25, 1858. On grading problems, see, e.g., Pieper to Hawks, June 15, July 7, Aug. 23, 1859; Hawks to Pieper, June 8, 1860, Grant to Hawks, Nov. 25, 1858, Kellogg to

Hawks, June 15, 1860, FH Mss.; testimony before Senate committee, *World*, June 27, 29, 1860, *Her.*, June 30, 1860.

50. William Grant, *Roads and Walks of Central Park* (1864); BCCP *2AR* [1858], 6.

51. Grant, *Roads and Walks*, 9–17.

52. Ibid., 20–21; *NYT*, June 3, 10, 1859.

53. On transverse roads, see *Trib.*, *Her.*, May 31, 1858; BCCP *Min.*, May 24, 1858; FLO to BCCP, Jan. 22, 1861, *FLOP* 3:312–13. On Pieper's problem-solving method, see, e.g., Pieper to Mr. Bettes, Jan 12, 1859, Pieper to Hawks, July 9, 14, 15, 28, Aug. 23, 29, Oct. 26, 27, Nov. 12, Dec. 10, 1859, FH Mss.; Pieper to FLO, Aug. 17, 1859, Grant to FLO, Aug. 31, 1859, FLO Mss.

54. For unexpected problems, see testimony of John Bogart and William Grant, *Her.*, June 30, 1860; and of Philip Keyes, *World*, June 27, 1860 (quicksand); and notes from Pieper to Hawks in FH Mss.

55. Grant, Memorandum, Apr. 18, 1860, FH Mss.

56.. Report of Special Committee, BCCP *Min.*, doc. 2 (July 21, 1859): 2; John Butterworth to FLO, Apr. 2, 21, 1859, FLO Mss.; *Trib.*, Aug. 28, 1859 (opening). See also Kellogg to FLO, Aug. 25, 1859, FLO Mss. To save costs, the board turned the northern two transverse roads over to contractors: BCCP *Min.*, Apr. 5, 19, 26, May 3, 1860, and doc. 1 (May 3, 1860).

57. FLO to John L. Wilson, n.d. [ca. Jan. 1860], FLO Mss.; Grant, *Roads and Walks*, 18. See also Montgomery Kellogg to FLO, Apr. 16, 1859, Grant to FLO, June 1, July 15, 1859, FLO Mss.

58. Strong, *Diary*, 3:454.

59. BCCP *Min.*, doc. 2 (1859): 5; Grant to Hawks, Nov. 25, 1858; Grant, "Driving and Riding on New and Unfinished Roads," Oct. 17, 1859, FH Mss. On Olmsted's efforts to permit subcontracting of carts, see two handbills, Mar. 15, 1859, and "To the Owners of Teams and Carts Employed on the Park," Apr. 18, 1859, CP Scrapbook; BCCP *Min.*, Dec. 9, 1858, May 26, 1859.

60. Grant to FLO, May 12, 1859, FLO Mss.; *Her.*, *World*, June 27, 1860. On new rules, see *Trib.*, June 26, 1860.

61. *Her.*, June 30, 1860; cf. *Answer of A. W. Craven*, 31–34. See also handbill, Mar. 21, 1859, warning laborers that removal of articles from the park would be prosecuted as larceny, and handbill titled "Caution! Visitors and Workmen Take Notice," threatening heavy fines or imprisonment for removing stakes, boards, or "any rubbish," CP Scrapbook.

62. BCCP *Min.*, doc. 2 (1859): 5. On stonecutters, see Wilentz, *Chants Democratic*, 133–34.

63. On wage policy, see BCCP *Min.*, Oct. 7, 1858, Mar. 17, May 19, 1859, and doc. 2 (1859): 5; Stonecutters to FLO, May 19, 1859, FLO Mss. See also Grant to FLO, May 12, 1859, FLO Mss.; BCCP *Min.*, Mar. 5, Aug. 18, 1859. For stonecutters' stint, see testimony in *Her.*, *World*, Nov. 11, 1860.

64. M. M. Graff, *Central Park, Prospect Park: A New Perspective* (1985), 49 (quot.), 46–48, 54–55. Pilat was assisted by the German-born gardener W. L. Fischer who in later years claimed that he had taken charge of the planting while Pilat oversaw the shaping of the ground. See W. L. Fischer to FLO, Dec. 31, 1882, Jan. 5, 1882, FLO to E. Smith Lane, Mar. 4, 1882, FLO Mss.

65. *Post*, Sept. 9, 1857; Hawks to Grant, Mar. 1, 1861, Grant, Memorandum to Assistant Engineers, July 15, 1861, both in FH Mss.

66. Pieper to Hawks, July 11, 1861, FH Mss.

67. Sen. *Docs.*, 84, no. 18 (Jan. 25, 1861): 23; FLO to Brace, Dec. 8, 1860, *FLOP* 3:286; *Leader*, Mar. 26, 1859 (reservoir workers). See also Moehring, *Public Works*, 246–51.

68. *Her.*, Nov. 26, 1857; "Rights of Men Employed," handbill with note added, Sept. 25, 1858, CP Scrapbook. For rules see also *NYT*, Sept. 3, 1859; "Rights of Men Employed," *FLOP* 3:296–97.

69. *Trib.*, June 27, 1860; *Her.*, June 30, 1860.

70. "Belltower Signals and Order of Role Call," handbill, CP Scrapbook; *NYT*, Sept. 3, 1859; Grant to Hawks, Nov. 25, 1858.

71. FLO to BCCP, Mar. 29, 1861, *FLOP* 3:334. For attendance procedures, see Sen. *Docs.*, 84, no. 18: 24–34. Grant found that his engineers also neglected record keeping: see, e.g., Grant to Engineers, Aug. 19, 1859 (threatening to withhold pay for failure to file reports), "Order as to Checking Time Books and Daily Reports," May 29, 1861, both in FH Mss.

72. *Leader*, Mar. 27, 1858.

73. *NYT*, Apr. 15, 1858; *Leader*, Mar. 27, 1858. On patronage of Italian workers, see Russell to

FLO, May 2, 1859, Butterworth to FLO, May 16, 1859, FLO Mss.; BCCP *Min.*, Apr. 6, 12, 1858; on head of police, Gray, Fields, Hogg, and Strong to FLO, Feb. 16, 1859, Gray to FLO, Feb. 21, 1859, Hogg to FLO, June 21, 1858, FLO Mss. See also *Leader*, June 16, 1860; *Her.*, June 27, 1860.

74. On Irish immigrants and construction jobs, see Moehring, *Public Works*, 262–63; Ernst, *Immigrant Life*, 5–7, 69–70, 73–75, 216; Richard B. Stott, *Workers in the Metropolis: Class, Ethnicity, and Youth in Antebellum New York City* (Ithaca, 1990), 72–84, 102–3, 120–21. Of 52 surnames taken from the payrolls in the park board's annual report to the common council, 13 could be characterized as Irish.

75. *Ir. N*, Aug. 28, Sept. 4, 1858.

76. On tensions between black and Irish workers, see Ernst, *Immigrant Life*, 105, 153, 173; Bernstein, *New York City Draft Riots*, 119–23; on "Black Republicans," *JC*, May 16, 1856; on women employees, payrolls in the board's annual report to the aldermen.

77. Crane to FLO, Apr. 20, 1859, Hunt to FLO, Apr. 8, 1859, FLO Mss.; BA *Docs.*, 28, no. 6 (Jan. 30, 1861): 3 (on promotions). See also "Rules with Regard to Applications for Employment on the Central Park," handbill, CP Scrapbook.

78. FLO, Memorandum, n.d. [ca. Feb. 1860], FLO Mss.; *FYLA*, 533–34; FLO to BCCP, Mar. 10, 1860 (rehiring), FLO Mss.; *NYT*, Nov. 8, 1858 (Central America). On fall layoffs and wage cuts, see, e.g., *NYT*, Nov. 11, 1858; *Ir. N*, Feb. 12, Sept. 17, 1859; *Trib.*, Sept. 7, 1859. Payroll vouchers submitted to the board of aldermen with BCCP annual reports show wives and daughters collecting wages.

79. BA *Docs.*, 28, no. 6: 3; Jeanne Boydston, *Home and Work: Housework, Wages, and the Ideology of Labor in the Early Republic* (1990), 135 ($600); *World*, June 27, 1860 (moonlighting). On Sunday work, see BCCP *Min.*, Nov. 4, 1858, and cf. change of wording from resolution, Oct. 21, 1858. Workers averaged 260 days the next year: BCCP *5AR* [1861], 7. For wage rates, 1857–66, see BCCP *10AR* [1866], 13.

80. Putnam, *Memoirs*, 87–88; *NYT*, Aug. 9, 1859. A sample of 75 names traced in the city directories and 1860 census showed workers widely distributed: 14 above 40th Street, 35 between Houston and 40th Street, 26 below Houston Street. For laboring families' living standards, see Boydston, *Home and Work*, 120–41; Stott, *Workers in the Metropolis*, 162–90.

81. Grant to FLO, Mar. 5, 1859, FLO Mss.; *Trib.*, May 3, 1859. On pay raises, see also Kellogg to FLO, Mar. 18, Apr. 1, 1859, FLO Mss.; BCCP *Min.*, Apr. 21, May 5 1859. On 1860 rates, see FLO to BCCP, n.d. [ca. May 1860], FLO Mss.; cf. BCCP *10AR* [1866], 13, which gives lower pay rates.

82. BA *Docs.*, 27, no. 6: 21; 28, no. 6: 3 (dismissals); *Her.*, Nov. 24, 1860 (Sufford and Clark). See also foremen's testimony, *Her.*, June 26, 1860.

83. *Ir. N*, May 7, 1859.

7. Andrew Green and the Model Park

1. *Her.*, Apr. 17, 1859, and cf. Sept. 5, 1858. See also *Her.*, Apr. 21, 1859; *NYT*, Apr. 26, 1859.

2. F. A. Conckling to *Her.*, July 1, 1860, citing 1859 law; Report of the Finance Committee and President, BCCP *Min.*, doc. 2 (July 21, 1859; printed Sept. 1, 1859): 4, 8.

3. BCCP *Min.*, Apr. 21, May 9, 12, 1859; Calvert Vaux, *Villas and Cottages: A Series of Designs Prepared for Execution in the United States* (1857; 2d ed. 1864; rpt. 1970), 228, 81, 307. For other efforts to account for and save costs, see BCCP *Min.*, June 2, 16, 24, July 7, 11, 21, Aug. 4, 18, Sept. 9, 15, 1859. For the final design of bridges see Henry Hope Reed, Robert M. McGee, and Esther Mipaas, *Bridges of Central Park* (1990).

4. John Butterworth to FLO, June 17, 1859, FLO Mss. Green described the original materials planned for the Marble Bridge (no. 9) as brownstone in his testimony before the senate committee, *World*, June 25, 1860, and suggested that the marble cost more. The mason John S. Howell testified (*Her.*, June 30, 1860) that he had bid on a granite and brick design for no. 9. See also Reed et al., *Bridges of Central Park*, 90–91. Butterworth's reference to bluestone apparently refers to the light bluish or gray sandstone used on the Greywacke and Balcony bridges and possibly to the variegated gneiss on the Greyshot bridge: Reed et al., 22–23, 32–33, 66–67. For Russell, see

BCCP *Min.*, Dec. 9, Nov. 23, 1858. The board also altered designs in order to reduce costs by, e.g., dropping urns from the Glade Arch (BCCP *Min.*, Apr. 11, 1859) and requiring "more economical" balustrades on the Dipway, Playmate, and Trefoil bridges (BCCP *Min.*, Apr. 26, July 10, 1860). By 1861 most balustrades were of iron. See also Reed et al., 26–27, 66–67, 64–65, 40–41, 44–45, 62–63.

5. For Belmont's effort to introduce more iron bridges, see BCCP *Min.*, June 24, July 21, 1859, May 9, 1860. For architects' debates over building materials, see Roger B. Stein, *John Ruskin and Aesthetic Thought in America, 1840–1900* (Cambridge, Mass., 1967), 69–72, 193, 199–200; John Ruskin, "The Work of Iron, in Nature, Art, and Policy," in *Unto This Last and Other Writings by John Ruskin*, ed. Clive Wilmer (1985), 115–39; *Crayon* 6 (Jan. 1859): 15–24 (Feb. 1859): 48–49. For the board's concern about stonecutters, see BCCP *Min.*, Aug. 18, 1859.

6. BCCP *Min.*, Aug. 18, 1859 (Stebbins), doc. 2 (1859): 13, 26. On Terrace, see BCCP *Min.*, Nov. 9, 1859, Oct. 18, 1860; FLO to CV, n.d. [ca. Nov. 1860], FLO Mss.; Reed et al., *Bridges of Central Park*, 56–59; on Jacob Wrey Mould, see M. M. Graff, *Central Park, Prospect Park: A New Perspective* (1985), 33–45. Vaux had also used New Brunswick sandstone on the Denesmouth, Dalehead, Green Gap, and Glade arches, but after 1859 he turned to brownstone, granite, gneiss, and fieldstone as well as brick.

7. FLO to BCCP, *Min.*, doc. 2 (May 24, 1860): 2, noted that the remaining bridges would be built on contract. See also BCCP *Min.*, July 21, Aug. 18, 1859, July 5, 1860 (restricting *total* expenditure on bridges north of the Reservoir to $25,000—the cost of two of Vaux's earlier bridges). For rustic bridges, see Reed et al., *Bridges of Central Park*, 78–79, 81, 86–87, and on iron bridges, 24–25, 60–61, 68–70, 74–75, 88–89.

8. Elliott to FLO, June 9, Sept. 2, 1859 FLO Mss.; BCCP *Min.*, June 16, 1859; FLO to BCCP, *FLOP* 3:221–28. A hefty portion of the $1,052,289 spent by July 1, 1859, had gone into grading and draining the park below 86th Street. Olmsted and Vaux had estimated only $42,000 for grading the Parade, Promenade, Playground, and lower park entrances: the laborers' payroll exceeded that amount in the month of June 1859 alone. Compare GP 152–61; BCCP *Min.*, doc. 2 (1859): 4–13; and Appendix A.

9. BCCP *Min.*, doc. 2 (1859): 9, 26–27. On tacit elimination of music hall and proposal to convert its site into a carriage concourse, see BCCP *Min.*, doc. 2 (1860): 2. The Casino later went up on the site.

10. Butterworth to FLO, Sept. 8, 1859, FLO Mss.; FLO to JO, Sept. 23, 1859, *FLOP* 3:230; BCCP *Min.*, Sept. 23, 1859.

11. FLO to John Bigelow, Feb. 9, 1861, *FLOP* 3:323, 325.

12. Samuel Swett Green, *Andrew Haswell Green: A Sketch of His Ancestry, Life, and Work* (Worcester, Mass. 1904); BCCP *Min.*, Sept. 23, 1859. See also George Alexander Mazaraki, "The Public Career of Andrew Haswell Green" (Ph.D. diss., New York University, 1966), 10–12 and passim; John Foord, *The Life and Public Service of Andrew Haswell Green* (Garden City, N.Y., 1913); Edward Hagaman Hall, "A Short Biography of Andrew Haswell Green," ASHPS *9AR* [1904], 11–122. Green "talked park nearly all the time but finished with Milton," Mary Olmsted reported to FLO, Oct. 10, 1859, FLO Mss.

13. BCCP *Min.*, Oct. 1, 6, 8, 1859; Mary Olmsted to FLO, Oct. 18 (quaking), 24, 1859, Alexander Dallas to FLO, Oct. 11, 1859, George Waring to FLO, Oct. 17, 1859, and see Dallas to FLO, Oct. 3, 1859, AHG to FLO, Oct. 21, 1859, and for earlier example of Green's style, AHG to FLO, July 15, 1859, all in FLO Mss.

14. Mary Olmsted to FLO, Oct. 24, 1859; Waring to FLO, Oct. 17, 1859. Green also had to contend with the common council's and mayor's resistance to appropriating bonds; see BCCP *Min.*, Sept. 5, 9, Dec. 1, 31, 1859; *NYT*, Jan. 4, 1860.

15. CV to FLO, n.d. [Sept. 1859], FLO Mss.; Dallas to FLO, Oct. 11, 1859.

16. *NYT*, Feb. 25, 1860; *Ir. N*, Mar. 24, 1860. The *Leader* headlined its articles Mar. 10, 17, 24, Apr. 7, 21, 1850, "The Central Park Swindle." See also *Leader*, Jan. 28, Feb. 11, 25, Mar. 3, 1860. Former reform mayors Ambrose Kingsland and Daniel Tiemann as well as Robert Dillon, who had resigned from the board the previous fall, all complained of mismanagement. On work planned for 1860, see *Her.*, Apr. 4, 1860; *NYT*, May 1, 1860.

17. *NYT*, Feb. 27, 28, 1860; *Leader*, Feb. 27, Mar. 14, 19, 1860. See also *Her.*, Jan. 26, Mar. 14, 19, 1860; *NYT*, Mar. 10, 13, 1860.

18. On passage of bill, see *NYT*, Mar. 3, 5, 1860; *Her.*, Mar. 19, 1860. Former commissioner

James Hogg and his brother Thomas Hogg presented charges against the board, including the unrefuted charge that other commissioners had persuaded James to resign in order to secure the appointment of Richard Blatchford, a well-connected Republican lawyer who became board president. For testimony, see *Her.*, June 19, 23, 27, 30, Nov. 24, 1860; *NYT,* June 23, Nov. 23 (bribe), 1860; *World,* June 25, 27 (tavern curse), 28, Nov. 24, 1860; *Trib.*, June 25, 27, 28, Nov. 23, 1860; *News,* Nov. 24, 1860. See also "Charges and Specifications Preferred by Thomas Hogg and Others," n.d. [Spring 1860], George Van Nort to Witnesses to reply to charges, June 26, 1860, Grant to FLO, July 14, 1860, all in FLO Mss.

19. Sen. *Docs.*, 84, no. 18 (Jan. 25, 1861): 5 and app. C, 54–56. "I think it is important to me that the public should know" Kellersberger's conclusion, Olmsted wrote his friend Brace on Dec. 8, 1860, "and that I should have the credit of it. I am anxious to remain Superintendent, that is" (*FLOP* 3:287).

20. Sen. Docs., 84, no. 18: 37 and passim.

21. *Ir. N,* Mar. 24, 1860.

22. Sen. *Docs.*, 84, no. 18: 39, and review of record-keeping system, 23–34. The *Leader,* Feb. 2, 1861, denounced the report as a whitewash.

23. FLO to BCCP, Jan. 22, Mar. 28, 1861, *FLOP* 3:297–323, 334–36.

24. FLO to BCCP, Jan. 22, 1861, *FLOP,* 3:316.

25. Ibid., 303–4. Olmsted was particularly envious of the status granted superintendents of European parks: 309–13.

26. Ibid., 307–9; AHG to FLO Feb. 1, 1860 (payroll), FLO Mss.; FLO to Bigelow, Feb. 9, 1861, *FLOP* 3:324. On Olmsted's relations with Green, see also Charles E. Beveridge, "Introduction," *FLOP* 3:30–31, 35–36.

27. On Olmsted's accident and relations with Green, see Laura Wood Roper, *FLO: A Biography of Frederick Law Olmsted* (Baltimore, 1973), 150–51, 153–55; on efforts to supervise construction, *Trib.*, Oct. 1, 8, 1861; on work done, Sen. *Docs.*, 84, no. 18: 12–14; BCCP *5AR* [1861], 8–16.

28. FLO to BCCP, Jan. 22, 1861, *FLOP* 3:305–7, 318–19.

29. Quoted in Green, *Andrew Haswell Green,* 10.

30. Green, Ibid., 20; FLO to CV, Mar. 25, 1864, *FLOP* 5:210. See also Foord, *Life and Public Service of Green,* 15–52; Mazaraki, "Public Career of Green," 8–24.

31. CV to FLO, May 12, July 6, 8, 31, 1865, and see June 3, July 6, 1865, *FLOP* 5:404, 363, 419, 377, 384–85, 402.

32. FLO to BCCP, Jan. 22, 1861, FLO to JO, Mar. 22, 1861, *FLOP* 3:314, 328. For claims of being the park's representative man, see FLO to CV, Nov. 26, 1863, *FLOP* 5:152. See also FLO to James T. Fields, Oct. 21, 1860, FLO to Richard Grant White, Mar. 9, 1861, *FLOP* 3:269–70, 327–28; [Henry Bellows], "Cities and Parks: With Special Reference to the New York Central Park," *Atlantic Monthly* (Apr. 1861): 416–29. On new appropriation bill, see *Post,* Feb. 28, Mar. 8, 1861; BCCP *5AR* [1861], 123–24. The board also faced a movement to abolish the commission and restore the park to the control of city officials; see, e.g., *NYT,* Feb. 5, Mar. 18, 1861; *World,* Mar. 7, 13, 1861.

33. FLO to JO, Mar. 22, 1861 (passage of bill), *FLOP* 3:328–29; BCCP *Min.,* June 6, 1861. For Olmsted's work with the Sanitary Commission, see *FLOP,* vol. 4. In addition to appropriations, the board won a far more significant point with the legislature: an amendment of an 1859 law that had restricted their term of office to five years and permitted the mayor thereafter to appoint new members. Not only were the commissioners' terms extended five years, but they also gained the right to fill any vacancy themselves. See laws in *FYLA,* 541–42, 543.

34. FLO to CV, Feb. 16, 1863, FLO Mss. On contracting out the transverse roads and grounds near the reservoir, see, e.g., *Min.,* Apr. 26, May 3, 5, 7, Sept. 5, 1860, Feb. 3, 1861, May 17, June 12, 1862. On workers laboring under contract, see, e.g., BCCP *5AR* [1861], 7; *6AR* [1862], 6.

35. Francis Hawks to William Grant, Feb. 1, 1861, J. H. Pieper to Grant, Feb. 4, 1861, FLO Mss.; Hawks to Pieper, July 20, 1861, FH Mss. See also Grant, Memorandum, May 14, 1861, FH Mss.

36. FLO to BCCP, Mar. 28, 1861, *FLOP* 3:335 (northern park). Modifications ranged from changing road grades to substituting quarry chips for screened gravel on the drives. See, e.g., Hawks to Pieper, Sept. 12, July 20, 1861, Pieper to Hawks, May 29, July 18, 1861, Grant to Assistant Engineers, July 15, 1861, FH Mss.

37. CV to FLO, Feb. 5, 1864, FLO Mss. (consulting with Pilat); FLO to Pilat, Sept. 26, 1863,

FLOP 5:85–92; CV to FLO, Dec. 1, 1863, FLO Mss. Pilat's spring 1863 reports to Olmsted can be found in the FLO Mss. For Pilat's approach to planting, see Graff, *Central Park*, 46–55; and Graff, *Tree Trails in Central Park* (1970), passim.

38. BA *Docs.*, 31, pt. 1, no. 8 (Feb. 1, 1864): 11; Eugene Baumann to AHG, Jan. 13, 1864. On temporary plantings, see FLO and CV to BDPP, Jan. 1872, in *FYLA*, 265–66; on early planting arrangements, FLO to W. L. Fischer, Apr. 10, 1874, FLO Mss. For debate over the park's dense plantings, see *Trib.*, Aug. 18, 1861.

39. CV to FLO, May 12, 1865, *FLOP* 5:361; FLO and CV to Pilat, July 26, 1865, copy in CV to FLO, July 31, 1865, FLO Mss.

40. CV to FLO, June 1, 1865, FLO to Mary Olmsted, Sept. 15, 1862 (fever), FLO Mss.; CV to FLO, June 3, 1865. On Terrace, see BA *Docs.*, 32, pt. 2 no. 8 (Feb. 13, 1865): 2.

41. "Request to Board of Aldermen," BCCP *Min.*, doc. 1 (Dec. 23, 1862). On contractors, see BA *Docs.*, 30, pt. 1, no. 6 (Feb. 2, 1863): 3; on wage reductions, BCCP *Min.*, Apr. 8, 1861; John Culyer to Hawks, Apr. 27, 1861, Grant to Hawks, Apr. 13, 1861, FH Mss.; BCCP *10AR* [1866], 13; on petitions, BCCP *Min.*, June 12, Dec. 11, 1862; *Trib.*, June 28, 1862; BA *Docs.*, 31, no. 8: 2. For aldermen's resistance to Green, see *Debates of the Board of Aldermen, 1862* (1862), 876–80, 905–17, 930–33, 942–45, 999–1010.

42. *NYT*, Aug. 14, 1863; *Sun*, Oct. 12, 1935. See also Iver Bernstein, *The New York City Draft Riots: Their Significance for American Society and Politics in the Age of the Civil War* (1990), chaps. 1–2.

43. See BCCP *8AR* [1864], 6–7; *9AR* [1865], 5–7, 39; *10AR* [1866], 9–10, 38–39, and passim; *Her.*, Aug. 13, 1866.

44. BA *Docs.*, 32, pt. 2, no. 8 (Feb. 13, 1865): 8, 10; James C. Mohr, *The Radical Republicans and Reform in New York during Reconstruction* (Ithaca, 1973), xiii. See also CV to FLO, Apr. 13, 1865, FLO Mss.

45. BCCP *Min.*, Apr. 19, 1864; Paul R. Baker, *Richard Morris Hunt* (Cambridge, Mass., 1980), 125, 146–47.

46. Baker, *Richard Morris Hunt*, 153 (quoting William J. Hoppin's articles in the *Post*, which were incorporated in the book Hunt published to make his designs known), and 146–56. See also Frank Kowsky, "The Central Park Gateways: Harbingers of French Urbanism Confront the American Landscape Tradition," in *The Architecture of Richard Morris Hunt*, ed. Susan R. Stein (Chicago, 1986), 78–89; David Schuyler, *The New Urban Landscape: The Redefinition of City Form in Nineteenth-Century America* (Baltimore, 1986), 96–99.

47. CV to FLO, Apr. 13, 1865, FLO Mss.; *Post*, May 9, 1865; CV to FLO, May 10, 1865, *FLOP* 5:359.

48. BCCP *Min.*, June 8, 1865; CV to Clarence Cook, June 6, 1865, FLO Mss. For Vaux's campaign against the Hunt gates, see CV to FLO, May 10, 12, 20, 22, 30, June 1, 3, 8, 10, 22, 1865, FLO Mss.

49. FLO to BCCP, Apr. 1860, *FYLA*, 396; CV to Cook, June 6, 1865. See also BCCP *Min.*, Mar. 3, 1861, Apr. 10, 1862, Jan. 26, 1863, and "Report of the Committee on Statuary and Enclosures," doc. 2 (Jan. 20, 1862).

50. *NYT*, Oct. 31, 1870; Committee on Statuary, Fountains, and Architecture to BCCP, BCCP *Min.*, doc. 2 (Apr. 10, 1862), rpt. in *FYLA*, 399. See also *NYT*, Aug. 19, 1866, Mar. 19, 1867, Mar. 5, 13, 1870; *World*, Mar. 15, Apr. 4, Oct. 2, 31, 1870; *Mail*, Jan. 14, 1878.

51. CV to FLO, May 12, 1865, and see CV to FLO, May 20, 22, 1865, *FLOP* 5:363, 374, 375. On Seventh Avenue improvement, see BCCP *8AR* [1864], 63–65; *9AR* [1865], 47–53; and Andrew H. Green, *Communication to the Commissioners of Central Park, Relative to the Improvement of Sixth and Seventh Avenues from Central Park to the Harlem River; the Laying Out of the Island above 155th Street; the Drive from 59th Street to 155 Street* (1866).

52. FLO to James Hoy, Mar. 5, 1864, CV to FLO, May 20, 1865, *FLOP* 5:205, 373.

53. CV to FLO, May 12 (Pilat), 22 (as artists), July 8 (fair subscription), 1865, FLO to CV, June 8, 1865, *FLOP* 5:361, 377, 403, 390; CV to FLO, June 1 (fair acknowledgment), 22 (Grant), 1865, FLO Mss. See also CV to FLO, May 30, June 1, 10, 1865, FLO Mss.

54. BCCP *Min.*, Feb. 26, May 3, 1866; BCCP *10AR* [1866], 38–39; *11AR* [1867], 22–23; *12AR* [1868], 7, 24–26; *13AR* [1869], 10, 13. On new features, see also Olmsted, Vaux & Company to Peter B. Sweeny, BDPP *Min.*, doc. 13 (June 6, 1870), rpt. in *FYLA*, 477–79; *Sun*, July 26, 1867; *HM*, Oct. 12, 1867; *NYT*, Nov. 8, 1868.

55. Schuyler, *New Urban Landscape*, 101–46. On Olmsted and Vaux consultation, see 107–8; on requests for the commission's reports, Mazaraki, "Public Career of Green," 109. The work of Olmsted, Vaux & Company is documented in *FLOP* 6 (forthcoming). On the influence of Central Park on the "American park movement," see also George F. Chadwick, *The Park and the Town* (1966), 160–220.

56. See *NYT*, Oct. 12, 1896 (Grant), Apr. 20, 1898 (Kellogg), Apr. 5, 1882 (Ryan), Oct. 30, 1898 (Waring), Apr. 26, 1920 (Bogart); Eugene T. Sawyer, *History of Santa Clara County, California* (Los Angeles, 1922), 412 (Pieper); *Engineering and Mining Journal* 64 (1897): 492 (Hogan); *DAB* 15:343–44 (Rand). See also *FLOP* 3:45 n. 76.

57. Green, "Communication of the Comptroller of the Park," BCCP *13AR* [1869]: app. H, 162. For the expansion of the commission's powers and jurisdiction, see BCCP *10AR* [1866], 52–60; *12AR* [1868], 121–28; *13AR* [1869], 37–40; and Mazaraki, "Public Career of Green," 91–112. On Green's planning vision, see David Hammack, "Comprehensive Planning before the Comprehensive Plan: A New Look at the Nineteenth-Century American City," in *Two Centuries of American Planning*, ed. Daniel Schaffer (Baltimore, 1988). See also, Robert Fogelsong, *Planning in the Capitalist City: The Colonial Era to the 1920s* (Princeton, 1986), 99–123; David Scobey, "The Streets and Social Order: Changing Relations of Class, Power, and Space in Gilded Age New York" (Ph.D. diss., Yale University, 1989), chaps. 4–5.

58. Bernstein, *New York City Draft Riots*, 195–236; Seymour Mandelbaum, *Boss Tweed's New York* (1965), 76–104. See Chapter 10.

59. *Her.*, July 23, 1895.

60. *News*, Apr. 29, 1933.

8. *"The Great Rendezvous of the Polite World"*

1. *Trib.*, Dec. 16, 1858; *Her.*, Dec. 20, 26, 27, 1858; *NYT*, Jan. 5, 1859.

2. *Her.*, July 25, Dec. 29, 1859; *Trib.*, Aug. 22, Oct. 17, 1859; *NYT*, Dec. 27, 1859; *FL*, Jan. 7, 1860; *Spirit*, Mar. 10, 1860. The annual reports from 1861 to 1873 provide detailed attendance records, which were compiled with great care by gatekeepers, who even made duplicate counts to check on accuracy. By 1865, attendance had reached 7.6 million; it remained relatively steady for the rest of the decade, reaching 8.52 million in 1870. Attendance data can be found in the BCCP *Annual Reports*.

3. *Her.*, Sept. 6, Dec. 27, 1858.

4. *NYT*, Dec. 27, 1859; *Trib.*, Sept. 3, 1860; *Her.*, Aug. 21, 1866. See also *Trib.*, Aug. 29, 1864; *S-Z*, Nov. 14, 1859; *Her.*, June 9, 1867; *NYT*, Aug. 13, 1865.

5. Dividing New York's population into class categories is difficult. We very loosely categorize about one-quarter as white-collar or middle and upper class and three-quarters as blue-collar or working class. Perhaps 5% of the population could be called "upper class," and 10% skilled working class. Thus about one-third could be classified as a "middling" group that includes skilled and white-collar workers but excludes wealthy New Yorkers. For efforts to untangle the problems of data and definition in talking about New York's midcentury class structure, see Edward K. Spann, *The New Metropolis: New York City, 1840–1857* (1981), 479–80; Carl F. Kaestle, *Evolution of an Urban School System: New York City, 1750–1850* (Cambridge, Mass. 1973), 100–11; Selma Berrol, "Who Went to School in the Mid-Nineteenth Century? An Essay in the New Urban History," in *Essays in the History of New York City: A Memorial to Sidney Pomerantz*, ed. Irwin Yellowitz (Port Washington, N.Y., 1978), 48. Although our main concern in this chapter is with the 1860s, our speculations on the meanings of the carriage parade draw from the subsequent two decades as well, since the patterns remained relatively unchanged.

6. *Her.*, July 15, 1850, Dec. 24, 1858, Mar. 13, 1859; *NYT*, June 21, 1853.

7. *A Guidebook to the Central Park* (1860), 37–39; "The Equipages of New York," *New York Coach-Maker's Magazine* 2 (Aug. 1859): 46–48, reprinted from the *Herald*. See also *Brewster and Baldwin's Illustrated Catalogue of Carriages* (1868). Percentages of visitors arriving by carriage were calculated from attendance tables in BCCP *Annual Reports*.

8. Newspaper quoted in "Equipages of New York," 47; expenses detailed in "The History and Mystery of Tandem Driving," *Hub* 19 (Jan. 1, 1878): 460–61.

9. *Her.*, Nov. 21, 1860, quoted in Henry Hope Reed and Sophia Duckworth, *Central Park: A*

History and Guide (1967; rpt. 1972), 93; Ezra M. Stratton, *The World on Wheels* (1878), 458. On inequality in New York, see Rufus S. Tucker, "The Distribution of Income among Taxpayers in the United States," *Quarterly Journal of Economics* 52 (1938): 547–62.

10. *Guidebook to the Central Park*, 1–2; Bayard Still, *A Mirror for Gotham: New York as Seen by Contemporaries from Dutch Days to the Present* (1956), 233–34; Oscar Hinrichs, *Guide to the Central Park* (1875), 9; "Central-Park Phaeton," *New York Coach-Maker's Magazine* 8 (June 1866): 8; *Post*, June 24, 1862.

11. Junius Henri Browne, *The Great Metropolis: A Mirror of New York* (Hartford, 1869), 568–69; "Photographs from Central Park," *New York Coach-Maker's Magazine* 12 (June 1870): 14.

12. *Her.*, Nov. 25, 1860.

13. Thorstein Veblen, *Theory of the Leisure Class: An Economic Study of Institutions* (1899; rpt. 1953).

14. Nellie Bly [Elizabeth Cochrane], *The Mystery of Central Park* (1889), 13; Stephen Birmingham, *"Our Crowd": The Great Jewish Families of New York* (1967), 245; Abby Maria Hall Ward, Diary, 1874–75, Ward Family Papers, NYHS. Ward's close connections to the Minturn "circle" can be traced in address books, clippings, and other diaries in these papers. On the Ward family, see Louise Hall Tharp, *Three Saints and a Sinner* (Boston, 1956).

15. *Her.*, Oct. 29, 1860, Sept. 21, 1864, and see Mar. 24, Sept. 24, Oct. 15, 1864, Sept. 17, 1865, Aug. 16, 1868, Oct. 4, 1880; *NYT*, Sept. 24, 1860. The lowest percentage of carriage visitors was in January (30%) and February (48.6%). These monthly figures are derived from an average of 1864–1866.

16. The percentage of visitors was at its highest in 1861 (2.2%); after that it generally declined and was below 1% after 1868.

17. *Her.*, Nov. 21, 1860, May 5, 1860; Arthur B. Maurice, *Fifth Avenue* (1918), 63–64. See also *NYT*, Apr. 30, 1864.

18. Frederic Cople Jaher, *The Urban Establishment: Upper Strata in Boston, New York, Charleston, Chicago, and Los Angeles* (Urbana, Ill., 1982), 205 (wealth figures); Browne, *Great Metropolis*, 35 (liveries); Allen Churchill, *The Upper Crust: An Informal History of New York's Highest Society* (Englewood Cliffs, N.J., 1970), 99–114; Steven D. Lyons, "James Gordon Bennett, Jr.," in *American Newspaper Journalists, 1873–1900*, ed. Perry J. Ashley (Detroit, 1983), 8. See also Robert Greenhalgh Albion, *The Rise of New York Port, 1815–1860* (1939), passim; and especially Jaher, 157–315.

19. Browne, *Great Metropolis*, 32; David Hammack, *Power and Society: Greater New York at the Turn of the Century* (1982), 65.

20. Edith Wharton, *The Age of Innocence* (1920; rpt. 1962), 89; Wharton, *A Backward Glance* (1934; rpt. 1964), 95, 158–60; Willis quoted in Reed and Duckworth, *Central Park*, 16. Archer's comment precisely echoes contemporary comments in, e.g., "Equipages of New York," 46; Abram C. Dayton, *Last Days of Knickerbocker Life* (1880), 314.

21. Robert Bowne Minturn, Jr., *Memoir of Robert Bowne Minturn* (1871), 239.

22. Jacques Offenbach, *Orpheus in America: Offenbach's Diary of His Journey to the New World* (Bloomington, Ind., 1957), 85. On new wealth, see Frederic Cople Jaher, "Style and Status: High Society in Late Nineteenth-Century New York," in *The Rich, the Well Born, and the Powerful: Elites and Upper Classes in History*, ed. Jaher (Urbana, Ill., 1973), 269, 283.

23. *Her.*, Nov. 25, 1860; Birmingham, *Our Crowd*, 128; Ward, Diary, Feb. 9, 1874. See also David Black, *The King of Fifth Avenue: The Fortunes of August Belmont* (1981), 271–77 and passim; *Her.*, Apr. 23, 1879.

24. Churchill, *Upper Crust*, 56; Jaher, *Urban Establishment*, 248; Birmingham, *Our Crowd*, 88.

25. *Her.*, May 24, 1875; Strong, *Diary*, 3:567; Anita Leslie, *The Remarkable Mr. Jerome* (1954), 80; Denis Tilden Lynch, *"Boss" Tweed: The Story of a Grim Generation* (1927), 183.

26. Browne, *Great Metropolis*, 124–26. See similarly *NYT*, June 3, 1866.

27. Mary Duffus Hardy, *Through Cities and Prairie Lands* (1881; rpt. 1974), 64.

28. Veblen, *Theory of the Leisure Class*, passim; Jaher, "Style and Status," 275; Leslie, *Remarkable Mr. Jerome*, 160–83. On marriage market, see Elizabeth Blackmar, *Manhattan for Rent, 1785–1850* (Ithaca, 1989), 128–32, 139–42.

29. Wharton, *Backward Glance*, 82, 57. On wealthy women in public, see, e.g., R. W. B. Lewis, *Edith Wharton: A Biography* (1975), 33, 37, 38; Churchill, *Upper Crust*, 33; William Leach, *True Love and Perfect Union: The Feminist Reform of Sex and Society* (1980), 220–35.

30. Lloyd Morris, *Incredible New York* (1951), 93; May King Van Rensselaer, *The Social Ladder* (1924), 40; Francis Ware, *Driving* (1903), 105; Churchill, *Upper Crust,* 72.

31. [Henry Bellows], "Cities and Parks: With Special Reference to the New York Central Park," *Atlantic Monthly* (Apr. 1861): 428; Ward, Diary, Apr. 6, 1875.

32. Browne, *Great Metropolis,* 123–28; *Her.,* Jan. 6, 1865, Jan 24, 1866, Nov. 17, 1862. See also *NYT,* Nov. 14, 1859, May 9, 1860; *Her.,* May 6, Nov. 1, 1860, Nov. 13, 1864, Aug. 13, 1865.

33. Browne, *Great Metropolis,* 126–27; *Her.,* Sept. 17 (horseflesh), 24 (criticisms), 1865; "Four-In-Hand Driving," *Hub* 19 (Mar. 1, 1878): 563 (*Tally-ho*); Ethel Nathalie Dana, *Young in New York: Memoir of a Victorian Girlhood* (Garden City, N.Y., 1963), 27. On Coaching Club, see Clarence Gohdes, "Driving a Drag in Old New York," *Bulletin of the New York Public Library* 66 (June 1962): 386–68.

34. Leslie, *Remarkable Mr. Jerome,* 68.

35. *NYT,* Aug. 15, 1860; *Leader,* June 30, 1860 (from Clippings Scrapbook, CP Arsenal); Walt Whitman, "Specimen Days" (May 16 to 22, 1879), in *Complete Prose Works* (Philadelphia, 1892), 135.

36. *NYT,* Mar. 13, 1870; *Trib.,* Oct. 8, 1860. On tourism and the park, see, e.g., BCCP *Min.,* Apr. 26, 1860; *Her.,* July 30, 1860, May 16, 1861, June 1, 20, 1863, Apr. 17, July 24, Aug. 2, Nov. 13, 1864, July 9, Aug. 5, 1865, Jan. 24, July 5, 1866, June 28, July 5, 1868; *NYT,* Apr. 30, 1864; *World,* Aug. 21, 1860; BCCP *5AR* [1861], 30; *7AR* [1863], 28. On tourism in this period, see Neil Harris, "On Vacation," in *Resorts of the Catskills* (1979), 101–8, and "Urban Tourism and the Commercial City," in *Inventing Times Square: Commerce and Culture at the Crossroads of the World,* ed. William R. Taylor (1991), 66–82. On extensive coverage of Central Park in illustrated weeklies, see, e.g., *FL* for the 1860s and 1870s. For early stereographs, lithographs, and photographs of the park, see, e.g., *FLOP* 3:371–449; David B. Stirk, "Photographs of Central Park," unpub. paper, 1984, copy in possession of authors.

37. *Her.,* May 16, 1861, June 20, 1863; *Sun,* June 11, 1866; *The Central Park: Explained and Illustrated in Familiar Form* (1871).

38. "Photographs from Central Park," 14; "Carriages in Central Park," *Hub and New York Coachmakers' Magazine* 13 (Dec. 15, 1871): 187.

39. Frank Fetherston, Diary, Oct. 2, 13, 30, Dec. 25, 1887, Feb. 12, 19, 22, 1888, NYHS. See note 5 for discussion of class divisions used here.

40. *NYT,* July 11, 1859; *Trib.,* July 12, 1859; *Her.,* July 31, 1859. See also *Her.,* Aug. 25, 1861; *Trib.,* Aug. 26, 1861; BCCP *7AR* [1863], 40. On bands and orchestras in this era, see Neil Harris, "John Philip Sousa and the Culture of Reassurance," in *Perspectives on John Philip Sousa,* ed. Jon Newsom (Washington, D.C., 1983), 11–40; Lawrence W. Levine, *Highbrow/Lowbrow: The Emergence of Cultural Hierarchy in America* (Cambridge, Mass., 1988), 104–46.

41. FLO to "Dear Sir," June 4, 1860, *FLOP* 3:254; *NYT,* July 11, 1859; *Post,* July 1, 1862; BCCP *7AR* [1863], 40; *10AR* [1866], 29.

42. FLO to "Dear Sir," *FLOP* 3:254; BCCP *9AR* [1865], 33; *Trib.,* Aug. 25, 1860.

43. *NYT,* Sept. 3, 1859; *Trib.,* July 12, 1859; *Her.,* Sept. 1, Aug. 25, 1861, Sept. 24, 1860. See also *Her.,* Aug. 28, Sept. 11, 1859; *NYT,* Aug. 15, 1860.

44. *Her.,* Sept. 1, 1861 (sit on grass), July 12, 1863 (classical), June 8, 1865 (danced); *NYT,* Aug. 1, 1859 (quiet enjoyment), Sept. 10 (drummed fingers), Oct. 9 (no reservation, seedy coat), 1860. On audience etiquette, see Levine, *Highbrow/Lowbrow,* passim; John F. Kasson, *Rudeness and Civility: Manners in Nineteenth-Century Urban America* (1990), 215–56.

45. *Her.,* July 31, 1859.

46. Ibid; *Trib.,* July 12, 1859; *Her.,* Aug. 28, 1859. See similarly *Trib.,* June 24, 1862; *Sun,* Aug. 8, 1869.

47. *Her.,* July 18, 1859; *Sun,* July 18, 1869. For coverage in the German press, see, e.g., *S-Z,* July 9, 30, Aug. 6, 1859.

48. *Her.,* June 3, 1866. On large numbers of women, see, e.g., *Her.,* June 17, 1866; *NYT,* July 4, 1871; on maids, *Sun,* July 18, 1869.

49. T. Addison Richards, "The Central Park," *HM* (Aug. 1861): 299; *Her.,* Oct. 30, 1864 (easy cushions). For carriage attendance at concerts, see BCCP *6AR* [1862], 40.

50. *Post,* Jan. 28, 1862. On enthusiasm for skating, see, e.g., *NYT,* Dec. 29, 1859, Jan. 2, 1860; *Ir. N,* Dec. 31, 1859; *Her.,* Jan. 14, 1861; *Sun,* Feb. 11, 1861; Melvin L. Adelman, *A Sporting Time: New York City and the Rise of Modern Athletics, 1820–70* (Urbana, Ill., 1986), 256–59; W. Porter

Ware, "Ice Skating in the United States in the Old Days," *Hobbies* (Jan. and Feb. 1961): 26, 60, 56–57; Henry Chadwick, *Beadle's Dime Guide to Skating and Curling* (1867); Edward L. Gill, *The Skater's Manual* (1862). The estimate of skating's effect on attendance is based on January attendance from 1862 to 1866 and the number of "skating days" (i.e., when the Lake was frozen), which varied from 1 (in 1863) to 26 (in 1865). Our calculations suggest that each skating day added about 30,000 pedestrians, more than 95% of all pedestrians coming to the park on those days. A similar calculation suggests that more than 41% of park pedestrians throughout the entire year came for skating.

51. *NYT,* Dec. 23, 1859; *NYT,* Jan. 4, 1860. On skating as "democratic," see, e.g., *NYT,* Dec. 27, 1859; *Her.,* Jan 24, 1866.

52. *Leader,* Jan. 11, 1862; *Guide Book to Central Park,* 37–38; FLO to BCCP, Jan. 3, 1861, FLO Mss. The distances and times on the two alternative street railway routes, the Sixth and Eighth Avenue cars, were roughly similar. On working-class neighborhoods, see Richard B. Stott, *Workers in the Metropolis: Class, Ethnicity, and Youth in Antebellum New York City* (Ithaca, 1990), 191–211.

53. *Post,* Jan. 28, 1862; *NYT,* Dec. 27, 1859.

54. *Her.,* Jan. 10, 1865; *Sun,* Nov. 19, 1867. On private ponds, see also *World,* Jan. 8, 1863; *Her.,* Jan. 8, 10, 1864, Jan. 20, 1865, Jan. 12, 1866; Adelman, *Sporting Time,* 257; Chadwick, *Beadle's,* 87. On social composition of park ponds, see, e.g., *Her.,* Jan. 28, 1866; *NYT,* Feb. 3, 1862.

55. *World,* Dec. 17, 1870; *Trib.,* Dec. 28, 1859. On middle-class public behavior, see, e.g., Kasson, *Rudeness and Civility;* Karen Halttunen, *Confidence Men and Painted Ladies: A Study of Middle-Class Culture in America, 1830–1870* (New Haven, 1982), 93–117, 191–97.

56. Dana, *Young in New York,* 9; *News,* Jan. 12, 1861; Richards, "The Central Park," 239; Thomas Lloyd, *Lloyd's Pocket Companion and Guide through New York City* (1866), 69. On women and skating, see, e.g., Gill, *Skater's Manual,* 22–23; *Her.,* Feb. 13, 1860, Jan. 22, 24, 1861. On conventions of women's dress, see, e.g., Leach, *True Love and Perfect Union,* 213–60; Halttunen, *Confidence Men,* 58–69; Lois Banner, *American Beauty* (Chicago, 1983), 66–105. For park hours, see BCCP *6AR* [1862], 28–29. In the summer the park was open until 11 P.M. and in the fall and spring until 9 P.M.

57. *Her.,* Feb. 15, 1869 (respectable), Dec. 26, 1861; *NYT,* Jan. 12, 1859 (order); Chadwick, *Beadle's,* 1.

58. *NYT,* Apr. 22, 1866, June 20, 1869; *Her.,* June 21, July 25, 1859. If workers were not among the carriage or horseback riders or tourists, were rare among those coming on weekdays, and were underrepresented among those skating, then only a small percentage of the remaining park visitors could have come from the city's artisan and laboring ranks. In 1865, for example, the increased number of pedestrian visitors on Sunday over the other days in the week (i.e., 20,000 pedestrian visitors on an average Sunday versus 9,200 pedestrian visitors on other days) would account for only 7.4% of annual park attendance. Even if we assume that *all* Sunday pedestrian visitors were working class—an extremely unlikely assumption—they still only constituted 13.7% of the annual park attendance in 1865. See data in BCCP *9AR* [1865], 24–27. Sunday attendance as a percentage of total attendance did not fluctuate widely between 1863 and 1870; the peak was 27.5% in 1868, the low, 24.0% in 1865. Carriage visitors as a percentage of Sunday visitors ranged from a peak of 50.6% in 1863 to a low of 36.0% in 1868.

59. BCCP *10AR* [1867], 13.

60. *Her.,* July 5, 1865, July 5, 1866. See also *Trib.,* July 6, 1865, July 5, 1870; *Her.,* July 6, 1860, July 6, 1869.

61. *Her.,* July 5, 1866; *Trib.,* July 5, 1870.

62. *NYT,* Apr. 11, 1857; Hopper Striker Mott, "Jones Wood," in *Valentine's Manual of the City of New York, 1917–1918,* ed., Henry Collins Brown (1917), 147.

63. Mott, "Jones Wood," 147–48, 151. See also *Her.,* July 30, 1860; *Trib.,* July 4, 1866.

64. Mott, "Jones Wood," 155; M. Despard, *Old New York from Battery to Bloomingdale* (1975), 167. On Germans and Jones Wood, see, e.g., Frank Harrison, *How to Have a Good Time in and about New York* (1885), 11; Stanley Nadel, *Little Germany: Ethnicity, Religion, and Class in New York City, 1845–1880* (Urbana, Ill., 1990), 107; *New York Illustrated* (1869), 43–44.

65. *World,* May 26, 1863; *Trib.,* July 16, 1859. For other German celebrations, see, e.g., *NYT,* May 25, June 30, 1858, June 24, 1859; *Her.,* June 29, 1858, June 8, 1859, July 30, 1860; *S-Z,* Aug. 14, 23, 1858; *Sun,* May 10, 1859.

66. *NYT,* June 24, 1859. On Caledonian Society, see, e.g., *Her.,* Sept. 24, 1858; *Leader,* Sept. 25, 1858; Adelman, *Sporting Time,* 215–17. On Irish Americans at Jones Wood, see, e.g., Patrick Joseph Dooley, *Fifty Years in Yorkville, 1866–1916; or, Annals of the Parish of St. Ignatius Loyola and St. Lawrence O'Toole* (1917), 8; *Ir. N,* July 27, 1863; *Ir. Am.,* June 4, 18, 20, July 4, 11, 18, Aug. 15, 1863, Aug. 19, Sept. 16, 1871, May 11, June 22, 1872, June 14, Aug. 23, 1873.

67. *Trib.,* July 4, 1866, July 6, 1859; *Her.,* July 6, 1866. See also *Trib.,* Sept. 8, 1859. On Heenan, see also Elliott J. Gorn, *The Manly Art: Bare-Knuckle Prize Fighting in America* (Ithaca, 1986), 156. On *Herald* and nativism, see James L. Crouthamel, *Bennett's "New York Herald" and the Rise of the Popular Press* (Syracuse, 1989), 96–98, 151.

68. On ethnic, working-class, and commercial cultures in this era, see, e.g., Gorn, *Manly Art;* Peter George Buckley, "To the Opera House: Culture and Society in New York City, 1820–1860" (Ph.D. diss., State University of New York, Stony Brook, 1984); Roy Rosenzweig, *Eight Hours for What We Will: Workers and Leisure in an Industrial City, 1870–1920* (1983); William Taylor, "The Launching of a Commercial Culture: New York City, 1860–1930," in *Power, Culture, and Place: Essays on New York City,* ed. John Hull Mollenkopf (1988), 107–34; Stott, *Workers in the Metropolis,* 212–46; Nadel, *Little Germany,* 104–21; Michael Denning, *Mechanic Accents: Dime Novels and Working-Class Culture in America* (1987).

69. Lawrence Costello, "The New York City Labor Movement, 1861–1873" (Ph.D. diss., Columbia University, 1967), 100; Thomas N. Brown, *Irish-American Nationalism, 1870–1890* (Philadelphia, 1966), 40–41.

70. *Her.,* June 21, 1859. On Germans, see, e.g., *NYT,* Aug. 15, 1860. On sex segregation in leisure time among the Irish in Ireland, see Hasia R. Diner, *Erin's Daughters in America: Irish Immigrant Women in the Nineteenth Century* (Baltimore, 1983), 25.

9. *"A Park Properly So-Called"*

1. *NYT,* Feb. 21, 1859.

2. FLO to CV, Nov. 26, 1863, *FLOP* 5:153; BCCP *Min.,* June 23, July 7, 21, Oct. 13, 20, 1857; Charles E. Beveridge, "Introduction," *FLOP* 3:38–39. See *FLOP* 6 (forthcoming) on Olmsted in the 1870s.

3. *FYLA,* 58–59.

4. *NYT,* Feb. 21, 1859.

5. "Description of the Central Park," Jan. 1859, BCCP *2AR* [1858], reprinted in *FLOP* 3:212–13, hereafter cited as "Description of CP: 1859," with page.

6. Olmsted quoted in David Schulyer, *The New Urban Landscape: The Redefinition of City Form in Nineteenth-Century America* (Baltimore, 1986), 28; "Description of CP: 1859," 212–13. On improper use, see, e.g., FLO to BCCP, ca. Nov. 13, 1860, *FLOP* 3:281; *FYLA,* 442; *NYT,* Feb. 21, 1859, May 9, 21, 1860.

7. FLO to Charles Brace, Dec. 1, 1853, *FLOP* 2:235. Olmsted speaks of the "fallacy of cowardly conservatism" in FLO to James T. Fields, Oct. 21, 1860, *FLOP* 3:270.

8. *FYLA,* 59; *Leader* quoted in *NYT,* Apr. 15, 1858; "Rules and Conditions of Service of the Central Park Keepers," Mar. 12, 1859, and "Notice Posted in Keepers' Room, Central Park," Nov. 10, 1860, *FLOP* 3:219–21, 279–80. See also *Sunday Atlas,* July 7, 1862.

9. *Her.,* Dec. 27, 1858; *NYT,* Jan. 12, Sept. 17, Feb. 21, 1859.

10. FLO to AHG, Apr. 29, 1860, *FLOP* 3:253. Calculations are based on arrest reports in BCCP, *Annual Reports;* the per capita figure for 1859 is based on estimate of attendance for that year.

11. BCCP *Min.,* July 21, Sept. 23, Dec. 29, 1859; *Trib.,* Nov. 14, Dec. 28, 1859; *Ir. N,* Nov. 29, 1859; "List of Signs in Use upon Central Park," ca. 1871, FLO Mss.

12. GP 151; *NYT,* Feb. 21, 1859; Melvin L. Adelman, *A Sporting Time: New York City and the Rise of Modern Athletics, 1820–70* (Urbana, Ill., 1986), 62–73; *Ir. N,* May 7, 1859. See also *NYT,* Nov. 8, 1859; *Trib.,* Nov. 14, 1859.

13. *Ir. N,* May 7, 1859; David Black. *The King of Fifth Avenue: The Fortunes of August Belmont* (1981), 34–35; BCCP *Min.,* Sept. 23, Nov. 9, Dec. 1, 1859.

14. Belmont to Matthew Perry, Mar. 12, 1856, Belmont Papers, Columbia University; Black, *King of Fifth Avenue*, 141; Adelman, *Sporting Time*, 59, 83.

15. *NYT*, Aug. 15, 1860; [Henry Bellows], "Cities and Parks: With Special Reference to the New York Central Park," *Atlantic Monthly* (Apr. 1861): 428; *Her.*, Mar. 13, 1859. Arrest figures from BCCP, *Annual Reports*.

16. *Her.*, Mar. 13, 1859; *FYLA*, 410; *Spirit*, June 2, 1860.

17. FLO to BCCP, May 24, 1860, FLO Mss.; *NYT*, May 30, 1860.

18. *Leader*, June 2, 1860; *FYLA*, 409–10; "Description of CP: 1859," 212–13.

19. BCCP *5AR* [1861], 107–9. On changing rules, see BCCP *Min.*, June 7, July 5, Nov. 1, 1860.

20. *Her.*, Sept. 4, 1859, Apr. 4, 1860; "Regulations of the Use of the Central Park," Nov. 3, 1860, *FLOP* 3:279; *News*, June 27, 1860. See also BCCP *Min.*, Dec. 8, 1864; BCCP *9AR* [1865], 40. Park reports from the 1860s list the Green (Sheep Meadow) at 15 acres, but the present-day Sheep Meadow measures 22 acres. Cf. BCCP *3AR* [1860], 44; *Rebuilding CP*, 133.

21. BCCP *Min.*, Dec. 9, 23, 1858, Jan. 6, Feb. 3, Dec. 29, 1859, June 21, 1860, Apr. 8, 1861; *NYT*, Nov. 11, 1858; *Ir. N*, May 7, 1859. See similarly *Her.*, July 20, 1859. On early ball clubs, see Adelman, *Sporting Time*, 127.

22. *A Guide to the Central Park* (1859); *A Guide Book to the Central Park* (1860), 29; GP 118, 127, 130; BCCP *2AR* [1858], 3. Two of the playgrounds were not developed immediately. On expectations of sports, see also "The Central Park," *HW*, Nov. 28, 1857, 757; T. Addison Richards, "The Central Park," *HM* (Aug. 1861): 301; *Spirit*, Mar. 10, 1860.

23. Elliott J. Gorn, *The Manly Art: Bare-Knuckle Prize Fighting in America* (Ithaca, 1986), 107; *Spirit*, Mar. 10, 1860; Adelman, *Sporting Time*, 126–27.

24. Adelman, *Sporting Time*, 141; Independent Baseball Club to BCCP, Dec. 31, 1859, FLO Mss.; George B. Kirsch, *The Creation of American Team Sports: Baseball and Cricket, 1838–72* (Urbana, Ill., 1989), 96, 114, 161.

25. *Spirit*, Mar. 10, 1860; Adelman, *Sporting Time*, 134; Gorn, *Manly Art*, 139.

26. BCCP *5AR* [1861], 48–49; *10AR* [1866], 36; *12AR* [1868], 25. See also FLO to Henry G. Stebbins, May 14, 1874, *FYLA*, 421–23.

27. BCCP *10AR* [1866], 36–37; *11AR* [1867], 113–14; *12AR* [1868], 24–25. On schooling, see David B. Tyack, *The One Best System: A History of Urban Education* (Cambridge, Mass., 1974), 56–58.

28. BCCP *10AR*, 37; *11AR*, 113. On women's playgrounds, see, e.g., Howard Daniels, plan 26, and "Arcadia," plan 23, in BCCP, *Description of Plans for Improvement of Central Park* (1858). On croquet, Adelman, *Sporting Time*, 255; on women and fitness, Martha Verbrugge, *Able-Bodied Womanhood: Personal Health and Social Change in Nineteenth-Century Boston* (1988); Harvey Green, *Fit for America: Health, Fitness, Sport, and American Society* (Baltimore, 1988), 91–98, 184–94.

29. BCCP *7AR* [1863], 36–37.

30. BCCP *7AR*, 38; *10AR*, 39. For categories of play, see Roger Caillois, *Man, Play, and Games* (1979), 14–26.

31. See, e.g., Clarence C. Cook, *A Description of the New York Central Park* (1869); *A Guide Book to the Central Park*.

32. "Description of CP: 1859," 214; BCCP *6AR* [1863], 61; *A Guide Book to the Central Park*, 29; BCCP *Min.*, Oct. 20, Nov. 17, Dec. 15, 1859, Jan. 5, 18, Nov. 23, 1860; Richard B. Stott, *Workers in the Metropolis: Class, Ethnicity, and Youth in Antebellum New York City* (Ithaca, 1990), 228–31.

33. FLO to J. P. Walker, Nov. 1, 1860, *FLOP* 3:276–78; AHG to FLO, Oct. 26, 1860, FLO Mss.; FLO to W. Reid, Mar. 2, 1877 (draft), transcript courtesy of Olmsted Papers Project, American University. For Olmsted's more favorable view of the different militia drills of his boyhood, see "Passages in the Life of an Unpractical Man," *FLOP* 1:104–5.

34. BCCP *Min.*, May 16, 1861, June 12, 1862, Jan. 9, Feb. 11, 1864; *Sunday Mercury*, June 1, 1862; BCCP *8AR* [1864], 27–29, 69; *NYT*, May 7, 1864. On sheep, see BCCP *8AR*, 40; *9AR*, 43; on controversy over parading in late 1860s, BCCP *13AR* [1869], 153–71.

35. *NYT*, Aug. 15, 1860.

36. BCCP *7AR*, 34–35.

37. *Ir. N*, Aug. 18, 1860; BCCP *Min.*, Apr. 26, June 7, 1860.

38. "Regulations of the Boat Service," *FYLA*, 415–16; BCCP *Min.*, Jan. 15, May 17, June 21, 1860, May 16, 1861, Feb. 6, 1862, July 13, 1865; FLO, form letter, n.d. [ca. 1860], FLO Mss. See also Olmsted, "Rules on Concessions," Dec. 19, 1860, FLO Mss, BCCP *Min.*, doc. 2 (July 21, 1859, printed Sept. 1, 1859): 16–18.

39. New York Sabbath Committee, *First Five Years of the Sabbath Reform, 1857–1862* (1862). We identified the leaders in the city directories and other biographical sources.

40. Stanley Nadel, *Little Germany: Ethnicity, Religion, and Class in New York City, 1845–1880* (Urbana, Ill., 1990), 132; *S-Z, Her., NYT*, Sept. 3, 1859. See also *Ir. N*, Sept. 10, 1859; *Her.*, Sept. 18, 1859.

41. N.Y. Sabbath Committee, *Our Central Park* (1860), 3–5, also printed in *NYT*, June 30, 1860.

42. *Her.*, June 30, 27, 1860; *World*, June 3, 1860.

43. For Olmsted's views on the sabbath, see FLO to A. D. White, June 2, 1873, in *FLOP* 6 (forthcoming); R. Grant White to FLO, July 3, 1860, FLO Mss. On Sunday malt liquor prohibition, see FLO to Richard M. Blatchford, Dec. 17, 1860, *FLOP* 3:290.

44. FLO to "Gardeners," ca. 1873, *FYLA*, 356; FLO to BCCP, ca. Nov. 13, 1860, *FLOP* 3:280–81. On violations of rules, see, e.g., *Her.*, July 25, 1859, Apr. 5, July 30, 1860.

45. *Express*, Aug. 20, 1860. See also Aug. 13, 27, Sept. 3, 10, 1860. On removing stands, see FLO to AHG, Nov. 8, 1860, FLO Mss.; BCCP *11AR* [1867], 26. On saloons, see Henry William Blair, *The Temperance Movement; or, The Conflict between Man and Alcohol* (Boston, 1888), map.

46. *NYT*, Aug. 13, 1865, May 9, 1860.

47. *Her.*, Sept. 6, 1857, July 31, 1859; Edward Winslow Martin [James Dabney McCabe, Jr.], *The Secrets of the Great City* (1868), 240.

48. *FYLA*, 61; Olmsted, "Patronage in Politics," Feb. 9, 1863, FLO Mss., transcript in Olmsted Papers Project; *Architects and Mechanics Journal*, Aug. 18, 1860.

49. FLO to AHG, Nov. 3, 1860, *FYLA*, 412–13.

50. *Her.*, Oct. 12, 13, 1860; *NYT*, Oct. 13, 1860. See also *World*, Oct. 12, 13, 1860; *Leader*, Oct. 13, 1860.

51. Both quoted in *Leader*, Oct. 20, 1860; *Evening Express*, Oct. 23, 1877. See also *Leader*, Oct. 13, 27, 1860; *Ir. N*, Oct. 13, 1860.

52. FLO to JO, Oct. 21, 1860, *FLOP* 3:274.

53. Robert Minturn to FLO, Feb. 14, 1860, FLO Mss.

10. The "Spoils of the Park"

1. BCCP *Min.*, Apr. 20, 1870. On the politics behind the 1870 charter, see Seymour J. Mandelbaum, *Boss Tweed's New York* (1965), 66–75; Alexander B. Callow, *The Tweed Ring* (1966), 222–35.

2. *NYT*, Mar. 13, 1870, Mar. 22, 1871; Eugene Kinkead, *Central Park, 1857–1995: The Birth, Decline, and Renewal of a National Treasure* (1990), 77; See also *NYT*, Apr. 5, 1870; *World*, Mar. 15, 18, Apr. 4, 1870.

3. *NYT*, Mar. 22, 1871; Kinkead, *Central Park*, 77; Herbert and Dorothy Fields, *Up in Central Park* (1945).

4. *SP*, 140, 144–45, 154.

5. Ibid., 127, 148, 131.

6. On genteel or liberal reformers, see John G. Sproat, *"The Best Men": Liberal Reformers in the Gilded Age* (1968); Eric Foner, *Reconstruction: America's Unfinished Revolution* (1989), 488–509; Geoffrey Blodgett, "Frederick Law Olmsted: Landscape Architecture as Conservative Reform," *Journal of American History* 62 (Mar. 1976): 869–89.

7. *Trib.*, Dec. 30, 1880.

8. Andrew H. Green, *Communication to the Commissioners of Central Park Relative to the Improvement of the Sixth and Seventh Avenues, from the Central Park to the Harlem River, the Laying Out of the Island from 155th Street, and Other Subjects* (1866), 68, and for uptown plan, 38–75. For Green's planning vision, see David Hammack, "Comprehensive Planning before the Comprehensive Plan:

A New Look at the Nineteenth-Century American City," in *Two Centuries of American Planning*, ed. Daniel Schaffer (Baltimore, 1988); David Scobey, "The Streets and Social Order: Changing Relations of Class, Power, and Space in Gilded Age New York" (Ph.D. diss., Yale University, 1989), chap. 6.

9. Green, *Communication*, 42; BCCP *11AR* [1867], 129–31; James C. Mohr, *The Radical Republicans and Reform in New York during Reconstruction* (Ithaca, 1973), 117–18 and passim; George Alexander Mazaraki, "The Public Career of Andrew Haswell Green" (Ph.D. diss., New York University, 1966), 101–12.

10. Green, *Communication*, 53; *RERBG*, Oct. 31, 1868; and for landowners taking credit, see, e.g., *RERBG*, Apr. 2, 1870. For typical landowners' petitions for improvements, see BCCP *Min.*, Jan. 9, Feb. 26, Mar. 26, Aug. 3, Nov. 12, 1868, Apr. 8, 1869. See also *Her.*, Nov. 23, 1864, Jan. 16, Apr. 22, 1865; Martha J. Lamb, "Riverside Park: The Fashionable Drive of the Future," *Manhattan* 4 (1884): 55–56, which credits uptown developer William R. Martin with first proposing Riverside Park.

11. Although the legislature authorized the park board to create the parks, delays developed when landowners objected to assessments. See, e.g., *RERBG*, June 4, 1870; *NYT*, Mar. 28, 1871; "Report of William R. Martin, President of the Department, on the Treatment of the Uptown Parks," BDPP *Min.*, doc. 70 (June 9, 1876).

12. Eugene Moehring, *Public Works and the Patterns of Urban Real Estate Growth in Manhattan, 1835–1894* (1981), 308, 283–87, 302–12; *NYT*, Mar. 11, 1868; Henry Stevens, *Recollections of Mr. James Lenox of New York and the Formation of His Library* (London, 1886), 4. See also *Trib.*, Apr. 11, 1863, June 3, 1867; *Her.*, Feb. 25, Nov. 23, 1864, Sept. 24, 1865; *Sun*, Sept. 4, 1867; *NYT*, Mar. 11, 1868, July 27, 1869; *RERBG*, Jan. 16, Feb. 13, 20, 1869; Real Estate Record and Guide, *A History of Real Estate, Building, and Architecture in New York City during the Last Quarter of a Century* (1898; rpt. 1967), 58–65; M. Christine Boyer, *Manhattan Manners: Architecture and Style, 1850–1900* (1985), 30–35.

13. Moehring, *Public Works*, 286; *RERBG*, Oct. 31, 1868; *Her.*, June 16, 1879.

14. *RERBG*, May 9, June 13, 27, 1868; Iver Bernstein, *The New York City Draft Riots: Their Significance for American Society and Politics in the Age of the Civil War* (1990), 206–9. See also West Side Association, *Proceedings of Six Public Meetings, 1870–1871* (1871).

15. On park wages and petitions, see BCCP *12AR* [1868], 13; BCCP *Min.*, Jan. 14, June 5, 1868; *Her.*, June 27, 1868. On labor movement and eight-hour day, see Bernstein, *New York City Draft Riots*, 209–15, 244–55; David Montgomery, *Beyond Equality: Labor and the Radical Republicans, 1862–1872* (1967; Urbana, Ill., 1981), 170–96, 237–49, 323–33; Mohr, *Radical Republicans and Reform*, 119–39; George Gorham Groat, "The Eight Hour and Prevailing Rate Movement in New York State," *Political Science Quarterly* 21 (Sept. 1906): 416–17. The parks department also formally adopted the eight-hour day: BDPP *Min.*, May 24, 1870.

16. Morton Keller as cited in Martin Shefter, *Political Crisis/Fiscal Crisis: The Collapse and Revival of New York City* (1987), 16.

17. *FYLA*, 536; BDPP *Min.*, Oct. 10, 1871. The Sweeny board served from April 20, 1870 to November 22, 1871. For its budgets, see "Communication of Commissioner William R. Martin," BDPP *Min.*, doc. 64 (Mar. 5, 1875): 13–14; Edward Dana Durand, *The Finances of New York City* (1898), 147, 148. Andrew Green estimated that the Sweeny board spent a total of $3.1 million on all parks in 17 months: *NYT*, Oct. 19, 1871.

18. For continuation of the earlier board's projects, see *NYT*, Apr. 30, July 31, Sept. 18, 1870; BDPP *Min.*, doc. 5 (Dec. 27, 1870); *FYLA*, 88 (Green), 265 (revisions), 266 (Sweeny board's program); *NYT*, June 29, 1870. For Green's isolation, see Mazaraki, "Public Career of Green," 119–29.

19. See BDPP, *1AR* [1870], 11–17, and report of Jacob Wrey Mould, 397–412; BDPP *Min.*, Dec. 6, 1870 (Dillon); on dismissal, BDPP *Min.*, Nov. 11, 1870; *NYT*, Dec. 21, 1870, *FYLA*, 88–89. See also *World*, June 19, 1870.

20. BDPP, *1AR* [1870], 295, 300 (quots.), and 26–27, 39–40, 296–99. For praise, see *Star*, Aug. 3, 1871; *Globe*, June 14, 1871; *CA*, June 14, July 22, 1871; *Mail*, June 14, 1871; *Turf, Field and Farm*, July 21, 1871; *Pomeroy's Democrat*, June 25, 1871; and Strong, *Diary*, 4:361, 373, 375, 377. Even the *NYT*, July 4, 1871, commended the park's "strikingly beautiful appearance" before returning to its drumbeat of criticism, e.g., on Sept. 1, 1871. For critique of the Sweeny board's

management of the natural features, see FLO and CV to BDPP, BDPP *2AR* [1871], app. B, rpt. in *FYLA*, 240–70; *SP*, 134–35.

21. *Her.*, Sept. 11, 1871; BDPP *1AR* [1870] 43–45; *Trib.*, June 12, 1871. See also *NYT*, Mar. 19, 1867, June 29, 1870; *Irish Democrat*, June 24, 1871; *World*, June 6, 1871; *Her*, July 30, 1871; *Post*, Aug. 23, 1871; BDPP *Min.*, Oct. 24, 1871; *NYT*, Aug. 9, 1871; and BDPP, doc. 64 (1875): 13–14.

22. For "honest graft," see Moehring, *Public Works*, 312–22; Callow, *Tweed Ring*, 179–81; *Her.*, Apr. 9, 1875 (Tweed's own holdings); and on West Siders' complaints, e.g., *World*, Mar. 3, Aug. 7, 1870. For "dishonest graft," see Callow, 164–65; Durand, *Finances of New York*, 139–40; BDPP, *1AR* [1870]; and for an alternative interpretation, Leo Hershkowitz, *Tweed's New York: Another Look* (1977).

23. Durand, *Finances of New York*, 373; BDPP, doc. 64 (1875): 31 (land values); Boyer, *Manhattan Manners*, 36 (new buildings). Even Andrew Green personally benefited from the postwar economic boom with a substantial salary raise, a free trip to Europe, and apparently an advance on a book on Central Park that he never wrote; see Report of the Committee of Law Department, BA *Docs.*, no. 5 (June 3, 1875), 28–29, 38–39; Report of the Commissioner of Accounts, ibid., no. 6 (June 17, 1875), 16–25. Charges of greater corruption implied in John Foley, *Andrew H. Green and Thomas C. Fields: Secret Management of the Central Park Commission* (1874) are unsubstantiated. Foley was a lobbyist unhappy with Green's actions as city comptroller, particularly his refusal to pay the Tweed regime's printing bills: Mazaraki, "Public Career of Green," 194–99. When Commissioner Fields left the country to avoid prosecution, it was for his shenanigans as a fire commissioner: *NYT*, Feb. 4, Oct. 26, 1872, Sept. 20, 1875, Jan. 26, 1885.

24. Durand, *Finances of New York*, 138, 146, 149; Mandelbaum, *Boss Tweed's New York*, 77–78; Shefter, *Political Crisis/Fiscal Crisis*, 18; Mandelbaum, *Boss Tweed's New York*, 78–85; Mazaraki, "Public Career of Green," 124–45. Green was made the city's deputy comptroller in September and took over the office alone in November.

25. *Municipal Debt of the City of New York: Communication from Andrew H. Green to William A. Booth and Others, Oct. 13, 1874* (1874), 5, 8–9, 24; Mazaraki, "Public Career of Green," 192–210, 212 (tighter); 225–29, 236–46. Charles O'Conor to Samuel Tilden, Sept. 29, 1871, in John Bigelow, *The Life of Samuel J. Tilden*, 2 vols. (1895), 1:281 (Handy Andy). See also Mandelbaum, *Boss Tweed's New York*, 87–113.

26. Mazaraki, "Public Career of Green," 218–22; *Ir. Am.*, Dec. 2, 1871 (Stebbins); *FYLA*, 92–94; *NYT*, Mar. 6, 1872; FLO to Henry Stebbins, Oct. 30, 1875, *FYLA*, 303–4. Sweeny and Hilton resigned from the park board: *NYT*, Nov. 8, 15, 1871. For restoration, see *NYT*, Nov. 28, 1871. Olmsted and Vaux served jointly as landscape architects until May 1872, when Vaux continued in that position and Olmsted became president of the park board while Stebbins was in Europe. In October 1872, when Stebbins returned, Olmsted and Vaux dissolved their partnership, and Olmsted then became landscape architect and superintendent (and after 1873, head of the Bureau of Design and Superintendence), and Vaux worked as consulting architect: chronology in *FLOP* 6 (forthcoming).

27. *Municipal Debt*, 16–20; *Public Improvements in the City of New York: Communication from Andrew H. Green to William A. Booth and Others, Sept. 28, 1874* (1874), 10 (quot.), 7–17; Mandelbaum, *Boss Tweed's New York*, 98–99 (reassessment). See also *World*, May 17, 1875.

28. *Sun*, May 17, 28, 1872; *Trib.*, June 5, 26, 1874; Charles Smith, Affidavit, Nov. 27, 1876, 81:23, MP (wage cuts in private sector). See also Bernstein, *New York City Draft Riots*, 237–57; Foner, *Reconstruction*, 521–22.

29. *RERBG*, Nov. 27, 1875; *Her.*, June 16, 1878. On panic, see also *RERBG*, Dec. 4, 11, 25, 1875, Jan. 1, 8, 15, 22, 1876.

30. "Report of the Committee of the Senate of the State of New York, Appointed to Investigate the Several Departments of the Government in the City and County of New York," Sen. *Docs.*, 99, vol. 7, no. 79 (Mar. 16, 1876): 419, 425, 385. See also *NYT*, Mar. 8, 1874.

31. "Action of the Board of Aldermen on the Subject of Laborers' Wages," exhibit G, 81:23, MP. On response to recession, see Jeffrey Sklansky, "The War on Pauperism: Responses to Poverty in New York City during the Depression" (M.A. thesis, Columbia University, 1990).

32. On 1874 law and appointments, see *NYT*, Apr. 24, May 5, 1874; *World*, *Her.*, Jan. 3, 1875; *Ir. Am.*, May 8, 1850. For debates over reducing the work force and wages, see *Trib.*, May 29, 1875; BDPP *Min.*, Jan. 18, 31, Feb. 2, 10, 18, Mar. 18, May 31, Aug. 4, 1876. See also Mandelbaum,

Boss Tweed's New York, 126–27; Mazaraki, "Public Career of Green," 249, 252–55. For biographical information on Martin, see Joshua Chamberlain, *Universities and Their Sons*, 5 vols. (Boston, 1898–1900), 21.

33. Rush Hawkins and Dorman Eaton, Testimony in the Matter of Charges against the Park Commission, Nov. 24, 1876, 81:24, MP. See also Petition to Mayor William Wickham, Sept. 23, 1876, 81:23, MP; *NYT*, Nov. 20, 21, 22, 24, 25, 1876.

34. *NYT*, Dec. 2, 1876; William Martin and Joseph O'Donohue to Wickham, Dec. 1, 1876, 81:24, MP. See also *NYT*, Dec. 1, 8, 1876; *Trib.*, Dec. 1, 1876.

35. Eaton, Testimony, Dec. 7, 1876, George Blair to Wickham, Dec. 5, 1876, both in 81:24, MP. See also Testimony, Dec. 1, 1876.

36. Martin and O'Donohue to Wickham, Dec. 1, 1876; "Communication of Commissioner William R. Martin," BDPP *Min.*, doc. 64 (1875). On relations with Green, see Mazaraki, "Public Career of Green," 249–57.

37. FLO, Memorandum, Mar. 11, 1875, FLO Mss. David Schuyler of the Olmsted Papers Project at American University has masterfully compiled a sequential transcript of what he has called Olmsted's "Patronage Notebook" and generously shared it with us. See *FLOP* 7 (forthcoming).

38. FLO, Memoranda, July 8, 1875, Mar. 19, 1874, Apr. 3, 1875, and see Mar. 25, Apr. 27, July 8, 1875, FLO Mss.

39. Despite his regular memoranda at this time, Olmsted wrote nothing explicit about the charges against Martin and O'Donohue. For his more positive view of Martin, see Memoranda, Apr. 28, May 1, 1875, May 30, June 7, 8, 1976, Dec. 1876, Mar. 1877, FLO Mss. Much of Olmsted's view of departmental politics was framed by his antipathy for Green. On Howard Martin, see *FLOP* 5: 142 n. 10, and Laura Wood Roper, *FLO: A Biography of Frederick Law Olmsted* (Baltimore, 1973), 350, 352–53, 360. On Riverdale plan, see BDPP *Min.*, doc. 72 (Dec. 20, 1876); and for criticism, see, e.g., "Report of Commissioner Stebbins upon Plans for Laying out That Part of the 24th Ward Lying West of the Riverdale Road," BDPP *Min.*, doc. 74 (Feb. 28, 1877); Albert Fein, ed., *Landscape into Cityscape: Frederick Law Olmsted's Plans for a Greater New York City* (Ithaca, 1968), 329; cf. *World*, May 20, 1877.

40. Mandelbaum, *Boss Tweed's New York*, 171; Clifton K. Yearley, *The Money Machines: The Breakdown and Reform of Government and Party Finance in the North, 1860–1920* (Albany, 1970), 3–35; Jon C. Teaford, *The Unheralded Triumph: City Government in America, 1870–1900* (Baltimore, 1984), 284–89.

41. "Report of the Commission to Devise a Plan for the Government of Cities in the State of New York," Ass. *Docs.*, 100, vol. 6, no. 68 (Mar. 6, 1877). See also Mandelbaum, *Boss Tweed's New York*, 169–71; Michael McGerr, *The Decline of Popular Politics: The American North, 1865–1928* (1986), 49–50, 65, 71–72.

42. Mandelbaum, *Boss Tweed's New York*, 170–71, 172 (municipal society); Calvert Vaux, *Villas and Cottages: A Series of Designs Prepared for Execution in the United States*, (1857; 2d ed., 1864; rpt. 1970), 50. Yearley, *Money Machines*, 27–28, argues that the middle class was particulary squeezed by taxes on real property.

43. Mandelbaum, *Boss Tweed's New York*, 172–81; John Kelly to William Martin, Dec. 4, 1877, FLO Mss.; *FYLA*, 110.

44. *Her.*, Jan. 10, 1878. For Olmsted's work on the Montreal and Buffalo parks, see Roper, *FLO*, 317–33, 348, 356–59, 384–85; *FLOP* 6 (forthcoming).

45. See, e.g., Howard Martin to FLO, Jan. 11, 15, 1878, Louisa Schuyler to FLO, Jan. 13, 1878, FLO Mss.; petition, *FYLA*, 112–13; *World*, Jan. 10, 13; 1878; *Her.*, Jan. 12, 14, 1878; *Post*, Jan. 11, 26, 1878; *Mail*, Jan. 14, 1878. The *Express*, Jan. 14, 1878, supported the firing.

46. *Trib.*, Jan. 11 (Godkin), CV to *Trib.* , Feb. 19, 1878.

47. *Trib.*, Feb. 20, 1878; CV to E. L. Godkin, n.d. [Mar. 1878], Mary Olmsted to John C. Olmsted, Feb. 24 (quots.), 25, 1878, all in FLO Mss. After the family's acknowledgment of the partners' "equal share" in the park's design, Vaux retracted his letter and urged that Olmsted be retained as superintendent: *Trib.*, Feb. 21, 1878.

48. CV to Godkin, n.d. [Mar. 1878]. For Vaux's "erasure," see, e.g., *Scribner's Monthly* (Sept. 1873), 523–39. For his lobbying efforts, see, e.g., *NYT*, Mar. 3, 1878, Sept. 9, 1879; and Chapter 11.

49. *Her.*, Aug. 22, 1875; *World,* Aug. 23, 1875 (Fuchs); *NYT,* Sept. 9, 1879 (suicides), June 29, 1880, Mar. 25, 1882 (Martin).

50. FLO to C. H. Dalton, Jan. 18, 1878, FLO Mss.; Olmsted, "Parks and the Enlargement of Towns" (1870), in *Civilizing American Cities: A Selection of Frederick Law Olmsted's Writings on City Landscapes,* ed. S. B. Sutton (Cambridge, Mass., 1971), 97–98. Olmsted's statistics on land values, stopping in 1876, did not register the depression's full impact.

51. *RERBG,* June 15, 29 (history), Dec. 7, 1878, Dec. 4, 1875, (beacon). See also June 29, 1878.

52. On deterioration, see, e.g., *NYT,* Nov. 15, 1875, Aug. 12, 1877, Feb. 1, Sept. 7, 8, 1879; *Trib.,* Mar. 3, 1879; *Her.,* May 28, 1877, May 26, Oct. 18, 1879. For budgets, see BDPP *Min.,* Sept. 24, 1879; *Trib.,* Dec. 31, 1877; an untitled report apparently prepared for a board of estimate hearing, Dec. 26, 1882, 84:12, MP; Commissioners of Account to Mayor Smith Ely, May 21, 1878, 81:24, MP.

53. *HW,* Oct. 11, 1879; Ass. *Docs.,* 100, no. 68: 11.

54. Ass. *Docs.,* 100, no. 68: 19. "People look back to the despised Ring Regime," the *Herald* noted on June 16, 1879, "and say no matter how the Ring plundered and robbed New York, it gave New York at least a splendid park."

55. Yearley, *Money Machines,* 275. The *Times* complained that the city was "starving this beautiful playground of the people," but advocated starving the party in the park: Nov. 7, 1874, Apr. 28, 1875, Nov. 22, 1876.

56. Charles Eliot Norton to FLO, Mar. 19, 1882, *FYLA,* 154.

11. Reshaping Park Politics

1. BDPP *Min.,* Dec. 15, 1880; *Trib.,* Mar. 15, 1883.

2. *NYT,* May 20, 1882; *World,* Dec. 19, 1880. See also *Trib.,* Dec. 19, 29, 30, 1880; *NYT,* Dec. 19, 29, 1880.

3. *World,* Jan. 1, 1881; W. L. Fischer to FLO, Mar. 10, 1882, FLO Mss.; *World,* Dec. 21, 1882. For McLean's ties to Green, see *Her., Trib.,* Jan. 1, 1881.

4. Louis F. Post and Frederick C. Leubuscher, *An Account of the George-Hewitt Campaign for the New York Municipal Election of 1886* (1886), 123; Henry George, *Poverty and Progress: An Inquiry into the Cause of Industrial Depression and of Increase of Want with the Increase of Wealth* (1879; rpt. 1929), 456, 470.

5. Biographical data on the commissioners are from *DAB, NCAB, NYT* obituaries, and articles in newspapers at the time of their appointment. Of 50 men who held 54 different appointments on the board between 1870 and 1898, 10 were Republicans, 34 were Democrats, 1 was an independent, and the party affiliation of 5 is unknown. On New York party politics in the second half of the 19th century, see Martin Shefter, "The Emergence of the Political Machine: An Alternative View," in *Theoretical Perspectives on Urban Politics,* ed. Willis Hawley (Englewood Cliffs, N.J., 1976), 14–44, and "The Electoral Foundations of City Machines: New York City, 1884–1897," in *American Electoral History: Quantitative Studies in Popular Voting Behavior,* ed. Joel Silbey et al. (Princeton, 1978), 263–98; David Hammack, *Power and Society: Greater New York at the Turn of the Century* (1982), 99–181 and passim. The four commissioners evenly divided park patronage: *Her.,* Apr. 9, 1877.

6. *World,* May 10, 1887, Jan. 10, 1883; *NYT,* Oct. 30, 1887. Of 50 commissioners, we could identify ethnicity for 43: 5 were first- or second-generation Irish, 3 were first- or second-generation German, 2 were second-generation Scottish; the rest were native stock, with at least 12 from old Yankee or Knickerbocker families. Sixteen commissioners gained their fortunes as professionals, primarily lawyers; 5 were artists or editors; 16 were in business; 8 were real estate investors or contractors; 4 were primarily politicians; the other's occupation is unknown.

7. On Viele and the West Side Association, see *NYT,* Feb. 6, 1881; on Olmsted's dismay at Viele's reappointment, see FLO to CV, Jan. 11, 1883, FLO Mss. On landowners' campaigns for a seat on the board, see, e.g., *RERBG,* Jan. 15, 1887; West Side Association to Mayor Abram Hewitt, Jan. 11, 1887, 87:23, MP; *NYT,* Jan. 27, 1895.

8. *NYT*, Dec. 29, 1880; *World*, Dec. 30, 1880. On budget, see *Trib.*, Jan. 1, 1881.

9. FLO and CV to BDPP, in BDPP *2AR* [1872], app. B, rpt. in *FYLA*, 241–42, 254–57; *NYT*, July 8, 1879 (Vaux). On the press and professionalism, see Michael Schudson, *Discovering the News: A Social History of American Newspapers* (1981), 61–87; Michael McGerr, *The Decline of Popular Politics: The American North, 1865–1928* (1986), 107–22.

10. *NYT*, Sept. 18, 1879. On Dawson, see *NYT*, June 17, July 21, 22, 25, 1880; on Halloran, *Trib.*, July 27, 1880, *NYT*, July 25, Dec. 24, 1880.

11. *NYT*, Sept. 7, 1879; Aneurin Jones to BDPP, Apr. 12, 1882, 84:12, MP; Fischer to FLO, Nov. 5, 1881, FLO Mss. For other complaints on the park's condition, see, e.g., *NYT*, Oct. 25, Nov. 13, 1881; on Jones's appointment, *Trib.*, Aug. 21, 1881.

12. Fischer to FLO, Nov. 5, 1881. On Jones, see also Fischer to FLO, Dec. 2, 1881, Feb. 21, Mar. 10, 1882, Jacob Weidenmann to FLO, Nov. 5, Dec. 12, 1881, CV to FLO, Oct. 9, 1883, FLO Mss.; Mabel Parsons, ed., *Memories of Samuel Parsons* (1926), 10, 18–22. The *Tribune* launched a running attack on Jones; see, e.g., Jan. 15, 1881. On Olmsted's work in Boston, see Cynthia Zaitzevsky, *Frederick Law Olmsted and the Boston Park System* (Cambridge, Mass., 1982), 52–57.

13. *Memories of Parsons*, 13; *NYT*, July 8, 1879. On *Tribune* editorial (Dec. 25, 1881), see Fischer to FLO, Dec. 31, Jan. 5, 1882, FLO Mss. For Vaux's efforts to mobilize the press and Olmsted, see, e.g., CV to FLO, Oct. 1, 9, Nov. 1, 14, 22, 25, Dec. 7, 1883, FLO mss.

14. CV to FLO, July 27, 1885, FLO Mss. On Vaux's campaign for his own and Parson's appointments, see *Sun*, Nov. 23, 1881; *Trib.*, Nov. 23, Dec. 25, 1881, Apr. 9, 1882; CV to FLO, Nov. 18, 1881, Fischer to FLO, Nov. 22, Dec. 2, 1881, Jan. 5, 1882, FLO Mss. For Vaux's relation to Green, see William R. Martin to FLO, Feb. 2, 1882 FLO Mss.; interview with AHG in *RERBG*, May 1, 1880. For Vaux's resignation, see CV to BDPP, Dec. 8, 1882, CV to FLO Jan. 6, [1883], FLO to CV, Jan. 11, 1883, FLO Mss.; *Trib.*, Dec. 28, 1882; *Memories of Parsons*, 15–16.

15. Weidenmann to FLO, Jan. 13, 1882; FLO to John C. Olmsted, Aug. 10, 1884, William A. Stiles to FLO, Aug. 10, 1887 (Vaux's reservations), FLO Mss. See also *Memories of Parsons*, 8–9.

16. *Memories of Parsons*, 23, 12. See also *Trib.*, Oct. 4, 1883; CV to FLO, July 27, 1885. Olmsted felt particularly frustrated by the "detente" among Vaux, Parsons, and Green and claimed that his former partner's political alliances prevented candor in the pamphlet on spoils: FLO to Charles Loring Brace, Mar. 7, 1882, *FYLA*, 155.

17. Theodore Roosevelt to FLO, Mar. 19, 1882, *FYLA*, 154; *Report of the Executive Committee of the New York Civil-Service Reform Association* (1885), 5, 8–11. For other responses to the pamphlet and the reform efforts it provoked, see also *NYT*, June 2, 1882; *Trib.* Mar. 12, 19, Apr. 2, 1882; Salem Wales to FLO, Mar. 14, 12, 1882, Martin to FLO, Jan. 27, Feb. 21, Mar. 22, 1882, FLO to E. Smith Lane, Mar. 4, 1882, Leopold Eidlitz to FLO, Mar. 21, 1882, FLO Mss. See also, Ari Hoogenboom, *Outlawing the Spoils: A History of the Civil Service Reform Movement, 1865–1883* (Urbana, Ill., 1961), 256–57.

18. For length of service, see testimony of park officers (including George Woolson, Montgomery Kellogg, Patrick St. John, and Thomas Beatty) and workers before the commissioners of accounts [hereafter, Comm. of Acc.] in the spring of 1887, 87:24–25, and Comm. of Acc. to Mayor Hugh Grant, July 8, 1890, both in MP. Fischer quoted in CV to FLO, Jan. 6, [1883]; *NYT*, Dec. 21, 1885 (Crimmins). For the use of "skilled workers" in civil service positions, see "Statement Showing Name, Occupation, and Actual Occupation of Employees of the Department of Parks for Year Ending Dec. 31, 1889," 88:38, MP. See also E. L. Godkin to FLO, Dec. 9, 1884, FLO Mss., on the difficulty of finding qualified examiners for the gardeners.

19. "Appropriations, 1885–1891 (provisional)," 88:38; Comm. of Acc. to Mayor Franklin Edson, June 21, 1884, 85:11, both in MP.

20. [Isaac Kendall], *The Growth of New York* (1865), 26–72.

21. *RERBG*, June 15, 1878; Robert M. Stern et al., *New York, 1900: Metropolitan Architecture and Urbanism, 1890–1915* (1983), 308 (Jones), 307–39, passim; M. Christine Boyer, *Manhattan Manners: Architecture and Style, 1850–1900* (1985), 170–73, 174–92; *NYT*, Dec. 27, 1878 (Vanderbilt and Bostwick). See also *NYT*, June 6, 1877, Feb. 27, 1878; *RERBG*, Dec. 7, 1878, Apr. 17, May 8, Oct. 9, 1880 (Lenox Hill), June 29, 1889.

22. *RERBG*, Dec. 27, 1879. On the West Side's uneven development, see *NYT*, Oct. 11, 1883; *Her.*, May 3, 1885. For Clark and the Dakota, see *Her.*, June 16, 1879; *RERBG*, Feb. 7, 1881;

Stephen Birmingham, *Life at the Dakota: New York's Most Unusual Address* (1979), 18–22; Elizabeth Cromley, *Alone Together: A History of New York's Early Apartments* (Ithaca, 1990), 134, 136–37, 142–43; Boyer, *Manhattan Manners*, 161, 201–202, and on renaming Central Park West, 210. On Upper West Side development, see also *RERBG*, June 28, 1884, Nov. 17, 1888, Nov. 11, June 1, 1889, Aug. 20, 1892, Feb. 11, 1893, supplement, Jan. 7, 1905; Peter Salwen, *Upper West Side Story: A History and a Guide* (1989), 63–75.

   23. *RERBG*, Dec. 27, 1879 (Clark), Feb. 28, Sept. 25, 1880, Feb. 19, 1881 (campaign against squatters), May 3, 1890 (vacant lots). See also "Squatter Life in New York," *HM* (Sept. 1880): 562–69; "Shantytown," *Scribner's Monthly* (Oct. 1880): 855–69; *World*, June 9, 1895.

   24. On renaming avenues, see *RERBG*, Mar. 22, 1890, and on Upper West Side construction, Nov. 17, 1888, May 3, 1890, and Supplement, Nov. 16, 1889. See also *History of Real Estate, Architecture, and Building Trades in New York*, 90–94, 153–54.

   25. *RERBG*, July 8, 1893. On apartments, see, e.g., *NYT*, June 8, 1881; Cromley, *Alone Together*, 128–72. See *NYT*, June 22, 1892, for dismay at buildings towering over the park.

   26. Howard Martin to FLO, Nov. 25, 1883, FLO Mss.

   27. John Crimmins to the Board of Estimate, Dec. 20, 1884, 85:11, MP. See also *Trib.*, Sept. 30, 1883, June 21, 1884; *NYT*, Feb. 8, 1883, Jan. 24, 1884, Feb. 8, Apr. 24, May 3, 5, 1885.

   28. *Memories of Parsons*, 27, 59. For ongoing complaints, see F. Scheider to Mayor Abram Hewitt, Apr. 1, 1887, Samuel Parsons to M. C. D. Borden, Apr. 8, 1887, both MP; *NYT*, Apr. 29, May 14, Aug. 18, 1891, May 18, 1893 (lake bottoms), June 27, 1896; *Trib.*, Mar. 17, 1892.

   29. On gates, *World*, May 2, 1886; BDPP *Min.*, July 6, 1888; *RERBG*, Jan. 19, 1889; Laura Lyman to Mayor Hewitt, June 14, 1888, Commissioner J. Hampden Robb to Hewitt, June 22, 1888, 87:25, MP. Petitions and approval of new entrances are indexed in the BDPP *Min.*, 1884–1897. For later petitions and new gates, see e.g. Pks. Dept. *AR* [1901], 18; [1902], 20; [1904], 28; [1905], 12; [1908], 159–60; [1909], 10–11. It is difficult to document the new entrances systematically; some were opened "temporarily" and later closed when new gates were introduced.

   30. Anonymous to Mayor Hewitt, Sept. 22, 1887, 87:23 (nuisance), H. Lauferty to Grant, Feb. 21, 1889, 88:37, MP. On crosstown roads, curfews, and lights see, e.g., Robb to Mayor Grant, Feb. 21, 1889, 88:37, West Side Improvement Association to Grant, Sept. 27, 1890, E. Delafield to Grant, Oct. 30, 1890, Petition of West Side Property Owners, 79th to 99th streets, to Grant, Dec. 27, 1890, all in 88:38, MP. On lights, see also BDPP *Min.*, Feb. 20, 1884, May 22, 1889, Mar. 19, 1890, Oct. 28, 1891, and on extending hours, Nov. 7, 1883, Sept. 24, 1890, Jan. 13, 1897; and *NYT*, Feb. 19, 1891. On request for new surface drives, *NYT*, July 11, 1883. After an 1884 law prohibited building street railways through parks, critics focused on securing a railway on the transverse roads; see Borden to Hewitt, Sept. 30, 1887, 87:23, MP; *RERBG*, Dec. 3, 1887, Mar. 24, Sept. 8, Dec. 1, 1888, Apr. 20, June 29, Sept. 28, 1889, Jan 11, 1890; *NYT*, May 7, 1890, Feb. 12, 1891; *Her.*, Sept. 18, 1893.

   31. East Harlem Improvement Association to Grant, Sept. 25, 1890, 88:38, MP. On flower beds, see *Trib.*, Dec. 26, 1884; BDPP *Min.*, Apr. 1, 1885; *World*, May 2, 1886; *RERBG*, Oct. 29, 1887; and Olmsted's distaste, *SP*, 147–48. On northern park, see, e.g., BDPP *Min.*, Apr. 5, 1888, Aug. 5, 1889, July 13, 1892, Apr. 26, 1893, Aug. 29, 1895, Jan. 20, Mar. 16, May 4, June 8, Oct. 12, 19, 1896, Aug. 2, 1898 (Conservatory). See also CV to Borden, Apr. 4, 1888, CV to FLO, Aug. 10, 1889, Stiles to FLO, Aug. 1, 1887, FLO Mss.; *RERBG*, Jan. 29, 1887; *Trib.*, Aug. 1, 1887, Feb. 21, 23, 1891, Jan. 22, 1895. For Olmsted on bedded gardens, see *SP*, 134, 143. Olmsted and Vaux's original proposal for such a conservatory on the site of the present Conservatory Water (between 73rd and 75th near Fifth Avenue) fell victim to budget pressures in the early 1860s; another plan was approved in the late 1860s, and the Sweeny board began building a conservatory in 1870, but this project was halted in 1871 when the Tweed Ring fell. See Olmsted, Vaux & Company to Peter Sweeny, BDPP *Min.*, doc. 13 (June 6, 1870), rpt. in *FYLA*, 477–79.

   32. Julia Robinson to Hewitt, May 22, 1888, 87:25, MP; *World*, July 17, 1886. See also Parsons to Robb, May 29, 1888, 87:25, Citizens of 68th and 69th streets to Grant, June 4, 1890, 88:33, MP.

   33. *RERBG*, May 3, 10, 1890; *NYT*, May 2, 5, 1890. See also BDPP *Min.*, Sept. 26, Oct. 9, 1883, Jan. 7, 1885, Feb. 18, 1887, Mar. 27, Apr. 9, 1890; *NYT*, Nov. 24, 29, 1883, Dec. 24, 1885; *Trib.*, Feb. 13, Oct. 8, 10, 14, 21, Dec. 12, 1883, Dec. 27, 1885. For Vaux's mobilizations on the zoo, see CV to FLO, Oct. 1, 9, Nov. 1, 14, 22, 25, Dec. 7, 1883.

34. *Memories of Parsons*, 14. On drives, see, e.g., BDPP *Min.*, May 12, 1883, Aug. 5, 1889; Secretary, BDPP to FLO, Aug. 5, 1889, Albert Gallup to CV, Aug. 7, 1889, CV to FLO, Aug. 10, 1889, FLO Mss.; *Sun*, May 23, 1886; *NYT*, Apr. 22, 1890. On the world's fair, see, e.g., *World*, Nov. 18, 1880; *Trib., Her., World, NYT*, Dec. 2, 1880; FLO to CV, June 3, 5, 1881, FLO Mss. Olmsted was on the committee to find a site for the world's fair in 1880 and joined in the effort to keep it out of the park.

35. See, e.g., Post and Leubuscher, *George-Hewitt Campaign*, 5, 9.

36. For cuts in skilled workers' wages, see *Trib.*, Feb. 3, 1876; for pay raises see *World*, June 22, 1882; BDPP *Min.*, Mar. 15, Apr. 5, 1882, Mar. 7, May 25, 1883, July 2, 1884, Mar. 31, 1886.

37. For petitions and layoffs, see BDPP *Min.*, Mar. 10, 29, 1880; *NYT*, Aug. 17, 1882, Mar. 3, 1883. For Grace's action, see *NYT*, July 27, 28, 1881. On attendants' wages, see William Oliffe to Mayor E. Franklin Edson, Jan. 20, 1883, 85:11, MP.

38. New York County Democracy, 22nd Assembly District, to Mayor Hewitt, Jan. 5, 1887, John Crimmins, Testimony before Comm. of Acc., Mar. 24, 1887, both in 87:23, MP. On Crimmins's business transactions and connections, see Thomas Crimmins, ed., *The Diary of John D. Crimmins from 1878 to 1917* (1925), passim; "Property owners and business men" to Hewitt, Jan. 6, 1887, 87:23, MP.

39. *NYT*, Jan. 15, 1887; Rush Hawkins to Hewitt, Mar. 12, 1887, "American Citizen" to Hewitt, Mar. 15, 1887, 87:23, MP; Crimmins, Testimony, Mar. 24, 1887.

40. Crimmins, Testimony, Mar. 24, 1887. The Council for Municipal Reform brought charges against the park board during the board of estimate hearings in December 1886. When the tax department took up these charges, Crimmins and Commissioner Matthew Borden resigned in protest. The commissioners of account conducted an investigation, which also took up charges that Crimmins's contracting company dumped soil on the park, and found the park's management "honest and capable." See *NYT*, Dec. 31, 1886, Jan. 2, 17, Mar. 13, 19, 25, July 20, 21, 1887; *Trib.*, Dec. 23, 1886, Jan. 5, 1887; *Her.*, July 20, 1887.

41. On the George campaign, see Post and Leubuscher, *George-Hewitt Campaign;* David Scobey, "Boycotting the Politics Factory: Labor Radicalism and the New York City Mayoral Election of 1886," *Radical History Review*, nos. 28–30 (1984): 280–325; Hammack, *Power and Society*, 112–13, 137, 174–76; Shefter, "Electoral Foundations of City Machines," 282, 286–92, and "Emergence of the Political Machine," 35; Thomas J. Condon, "Politics, Reform, and the New York City Election of 1886," *NYHSQ* 44 (Oct. 1960): 363–93.

42. George, *Poverty and Progress*, 461, 532; Post and Leubuscher, *George-Hewitt Campaign*, 10.

43. Post and Leubuscher, *George-Hewitt Campaign*, 13–14.

44. Ibid., 173. On impact of George campaign, see Shefter, "Electoral Foundations of the Political Machine," 289–96, and "Emergence of the Political Machine," 34–36; Hammack, *Power and Society*, 176–80; Irwin Yellowitz, *Labor and the Progressive Movement in New York State, 1897–1916* (Ithaca, 1965), 174–85.

45. Post and Leubuscher, *George-Hewitt Campaign*, 19, 14. For reformers' renewed campaign for budget and wage cuts, see *Trib.*, Jan. 5, 1887; note 40 herein; BDPP *Min.*, Dec. 15, 1886, Feb. 18, 1887, Feb. 27, 1888; Parsons, Testimony to Comm. of Acc., 87:24, MP. On the 1888 law, see George Gorham Groat, "The Eight Hour and Prevailing Rate Movement in New York State," *Political Science Quarterly* 21 (Sept. 1906): 417–18. For petitions of African Americans, see BDPP *Min.*, July 8, Sept., 10, 1873; *World*, July 11, 1873. On George's anti-Chinese sentiments, see Ronald Takaki, *Iron Cages: Race and Culture in 19th-Century America* (1990), 240–49.

46. Drivers of Central Park to Grant, May 29, 1889, Gardeners of Central Park to Grant, May 28, 1889, Parsons to Robb, June 12, 1889, 88:37, MP. On Sunday work, see also *Trib.*, Dec. 23, 1894.

47. Thomas Beatty, Michael Meany, and others to Grace, Feb. 23, 1885, 86:25, MP. On park keepers' benevolent association, see Beatty, Testimony, Mar. 30, 1887, 87:25, MP.

48. Crimmins to Grace, Feb. 27, 1885, 85:11, MP; City Reform Club, *Seventh AR of Assemblymen and Senators in the City of New York in the State Legislature, 1892* (1892), 127. Groat, "Eight Hour and Prevailing Rate Movement," 418–421; *Trib.*, Jan. 31, 1895. The legislature also authorized a special million-dollar bond issue for the parks department to provide work relief, but because of political in-fighting, few unemployed workers were hired by the department. See *NYT*,

Feb. 7, 9, 14, Mar. 14, June 7, 14, 15, Oct. 15, Dec. 13, 1894; *Trib.*, Feb. 8, 28, Mar. 7, 12, Apr. 3, June 7, 8, 1894; *Her.*, July 2, 1894.

49. On $2 wage, see City Reform Club, *Eighth AR of Assemblymen and Senators . . . 1893* (1893), 105. In 1896 the board lowered some laborers' wages back to $1.76: BDPP *Min.*, May 25, 1896. By 1913 park laborers earned $2.50 a day: Pks. Dept. *AR* [1913], 65. On the sanitation workers, see *Report of the Commissioner of Labor, 1913* (Albany, 1914), 155–57; *NYT*, Feb. 23, 1901; Yellowitz, *Labor and the Progressive Movement*, 189. On aging park workers, Pks. Dept. *AR* [1916], 68–69 (113 of 365 workers were over 61).

50. Joshua Freeman, *In Transit: The Transport Workers Union in New York City, 1933–1966* (1989), 11–15.

51. Unidentified newspaper clipping, Mar. 1887, in Comm. of Acc. investigation, Clippings File, exhibit L, 87:23, MP. On appropriations, see Edward Dana Durand, *The Finances of New York City* (1898), 290–91, 376–77, 383.

52. *Trib.*, Mar. 19, 1882, Feb. 19, 1885; *Sun*, Mar. 20, 1885. On the campaign for parks in the Bronx, see also John Mullaly, "The New Parks," *RERBG*, May 21, 28, June 4, July 9, 23, 30, Aug. 6, 13, 20, 27, Sept. 3, 1887; E. S. Nadal, "The New Parks of the City of New York," *Scribner's Magazine* (Apr. 1892): 439–55.

53. *Trib.*, Mar. 15, 1887; Post and Leubuscher, *George-Hewitt Campaign*, 27.

54. *Trib.*, Mar. 15, 1887; Richard F. Knapp, "Parks and Politics: The Rise of Municipal Responsibility for Playgrounds in New York City, 1887–1905" (M.A. thesis, Duke University, 1968), 47–48; Hammack, *Power and Society*, 178.

55. Knapp, "Parks and Politics," 49–56. On Tammany picnics, see Matthew and Hannah Josephson, *Al Smith: Hero of the Cities* (Boston, 1960), 54–55.

56. Durand, *Finances of New York*, 372–73. On tax inequities, see Clifton K. Yearley, *The Money Machines: The Breakdown and Reform of Governmental and Party Finance in the North, 1860–1920* (Albany, 1970), 43, 46, 68; Post and Leubuscher, *George-Hewitt Campaign*, 75. On late 19th-century economic growth, see Emanuel Tobier, "Manhattan's Business District in the Industrial Age," in *Power, Culture, and Place: Essays on New York City*, ed. John Hull Mollenkopf (1988), 77–105.

57. Durand, *Finances of New York*, 293.

58. Ibid., 376–77. A change in the portion of taxes the city paid the state also permitted this increase in per-capita expenditures without an increase in the tax rate.

59. Yearley, *Money Machines*, 177–79, 235–48.

12. The "Many Sided, Fluent, Thoroughly American" Park

1. *Ir. N*, Feb. 11, 1860.

2. Park attendance jumped to 10.8 million in 1870 and reached 11.26 million in 1874, the last year for which there is a specific figure. The 1874 attendance is in Oscar Hinrichs, *Guide to the Central Park* (New York, 1875), 7; the earlier years are in BDPP *Annual Reports*. For later estimate, see Moses King, *King's Handbook of New York City* (Boston, 1893), 162.

3. *Complete Guide to Central Park New York, with Map* (1877), 38–39; Robert C. Reed, *The New York Elevated* (South Brunswick, N.J. 1976), 50–61; *Ir. Am.*, May 11, 1878; *Her.*, July 7, 1884; Frank Harrison, *How to Have A Good Time in and about New York* (1885), 188. We have defined "uptown" as roughly the portion of Manhattan above 40th Street—the area encompassing the 19th-century wards 12, 19, and 22. Its population went from 117,935 in 1860 to approximately 859,000 in 1900. The ward figures are from the U.S. Bureau of the Census, decennial censuses. Ward population figures were not reported by ward after 1890. For 1900, we compiled an estimate based on the population of the roughly corresponding assembly districts.

4. *NYT*, May 15, 1871. See similarly *Turf, Field and Farm*, July 21, 1871; *Her.*, May 24, 1875; *NYT*, July 24, 1876. The proportion of Sunday visitors only rose from 26.2% for 1868–70 to 29.1% for 1871–73, but carriage riders dropped by 13% between 1870 and 1872 from 58.0% to 44.9%, although they rose by 6% the next year.

5. *Her.*, May 14, 21, June 4, 18, 25, Aug. 20, 1877. See also *World*, July 6, 1873; *NYT*, July 9, 1871, June 2, 1873; *Her.*, July 2, Aug. 13, 27, 1877; *Sun*, June 11, 1893.

6. *Irish Democrat*, June 24, 1871; Jacob Riis, *How the Other Half Lives: Studies among the Tenements of New York* (1890; rpt. 1971), 140; *World*, Aug. 18, 1902. See also *NYT*, July 23, 1884; *S-Z*, July 24, 1884. On wages, see U.S. Bureau of the Census, *Historical Statistics of the United States, Colonial Times to 1970, Part 1* (Washington, D.C., 1975), 165. On Sunday use, FLO to William Robinson, May 1872, *FYLA*, 96–97; BDPP *2AR* [1872], 9–10, 14.

7. *Her.*, Sept. 3, 1877; *NYT*, July 14, 1884; *S-Z*, July 15, 1884; BDPP *Min.*, July 2, 1884; *Her.*, July 20, 1884. On boats and animal rides, see *Sun*, Aug. 25, 1871; *Her.*, Aug. 1, 1870; BDPP *Min.*, June 10, 1871, May 22, June 5, Aug. 7, Sept. 1, 1872, May 20, June 17, 1874; BA *Proc.*, Aug. 8, 1872. On Beecher, see Altina L. Waller, *Reverend Beecher and Mrs. Tilton: Sex and Class in Victorian America* (Amherst, Mass., 1982), 12, 148.

8. *S-Z*, July 3, 7, 1884; *NYT*, July 15, 1884. On campaign for concerts, see *NYT*, July 7, 8, 14–16, 21, 23, 25, 1884; *Her.*, July 7, 8 14, 16, 17, 20–22, 1884; *S-Z*, July 7, 15, 24, 1884.

9. *NYT*, Sept. 3, 1859, July 4, 1884.

10. *S-Z*, July 7, 1884; *World*, Aug. 4, 1884. See also *NYT*, July 14, 1884.

11. *NYT*, July 7, 1884. See similarly *Her.*, *World*, July 7, 1884.

12. *Her.*, July 21, 1884; *World*, July 21, Aug. 4, 1884.

13. *NYT*, July 11, 1869, Aug. 7, 1871; *Her.*, Oct. 11, 1880. See also *Her.*, July 23, 1877; *NYT*, Aug. 21, 1871; *Trib.*, May 6, 1894. But the rule against commercial wagons remained in place: *NYT*, Nov. 3, 1899.

14. *Trib.*, May 20, 1886; *Sun*, May 20, 1886. The fourth commissioner abstained.

15. BDPP *Min.*, Sept. 12, 1871; *Sun*, May 22, July 29, 1871. On persistence of no-adults policy, see, e.g., *Her.*, May 17, June 10, 19, 1877; FLO to Henry G. Stebbins, July 10, 1873, *FLOP* 6 (forthcoming); *Trib.*, May 5, 1900; Pks. Dpt. *AR* [1899], 13; [1908], 84.

16. On tennis, see, e.g., BDPP *Min.*, May 7, 1884; *NYT*, May 23, 1892, July 3, 1893; *World*, May 2, 1886, May 12, 1895; *Sun*, June 11, 1893. James D. McCabe, Jr., *New York by Sunlight and Gaslight* (Philadelphia, 1882), 447, indicates that tennis was played as early as 1882, but the *Minutes* suggest that it was first approved in 1884. On permits, see, e.g., *NYT*, May 2, 1886; *Sun*, June 8, 1893.

17. *Her*, May 14, 1877; *NYT*, Nov. 15, 1875. See similarly *NYT*, Nov. 17, 1875, June 4, 1877, Nov. 27, 1881.

18. *Trib.*, June 5, 1873; *NYT*, June 21, 1884.

19. *Her.*, June 13, 1875.

20. Sign quoted in *NYT*, May 2, 1880. On lawns in 1870s, see *World*, June 13, 1873; *Her.*, Aug. 6, 1877. On May Day picnics, *Her.*, May 26, 1879, May 5, 1895; *Trib.*, May 23, 1886.

21. *NYT*, May 19, 20, 27, 28, June 6, 1895, July 11, 1897. The new park board that arrived with the consolidation of Greater New York reimposed some of the keep-off-the-grass rules in 1898 with only mixed success. The board also more readily offered permits for children's picnics. In 1898, for example, 2,500 permits allowed the lawns to be used by 250,000 people; Pks. Dpt. *AR* [1898], 11, 13; *AR* [1901], 16; *NYT*, July 8, 1901.

22. Samuel Reynolds Hole, *A Little Tour in America* (1895; rpt. Freeport, N.Y., 1971), 79; *World*, June 23, 1882. On festivals, see, e.g., *Ir. Am.*, June 2, 1872, May 10, 17, 24, June 7, Aug. 2, 16, 23, 1884, May 16, 30, 1885, July 3, 17, 1886; *S-Z*, June 15, July 7, 1884; *Star*, May 24, 1886; *New York Freeman*, Aug. 22, 1885.

23. *NYT*, July 7, 1884; Abraham Rosenberg, *Di Klotmakher un Zeyere Yumyons [Memoirs of a Cloakmaker]* (1920), 12, translated in Louis Levine [Lewis Levitzki Lorwin], *The Women Garment Workers* (1924), 42, reference courtesy of David Montgomery. On Labor Day, see Theodore F. Watts, *The First Labor Day Parade, Tuesday, September 5, 1882: Media Mirrors to Labor's Icons* (Silver Spring, Md., 1983), 33–34. On Labor Day picnics, see also, e.g., *Star*, May 17, 1886; *Her.*, Sept. 5, 1893.

24. Rhoda Hellman, *Henry George Reconsidered* (1987), 57. For dedications, see, e.g. *Her.*, Nov. 25, 26, 1876; *NYT*, May 13, 1894.

25. See BDPP *Min.*, doc. 14 (June 7, 1870), on licensing. See BCCP *Min.*, Mar. 1, 1870, on Carousel. For prices, see *Complete Guide to Central Park*, 20–25.

26. BCCP *13AR* [1869], 47–8; BDPP *Min.*, June 17, 1874; *City Record*, Aug. 12, 1875. On

Carousel, see Margaret Hunt, *The Children's District: A Central Park Walk: The Southern Section and the Park's Geology* (1986).

27. *NYT*, June 4, 1877; *Her.*, May 6, 1895; Neal Gabler, *An Empire of Their Own: How the Jews Invented Hollywood* (1988), 65; J. Joseph Huthmacher, *Senator Robert F. Wagner and the Rise of Urban Liberalism* (1968), 13.

28. *Trib.*, Oct. 8, 1883; *NYT*, Mar. 10, 1915; *Complete Guide to Central Park*, 26, 30. The Casino was intended as a "ladies refreshment salon," but it was open to both men and women from the start. See Henry Hope Reed and Sophia Duckworth, *Central Park: A History and a Guide* (1967; rpt. 1972), 100; *Her.*, Aug. 7, 1864; BCCP *Min.*, May 12, 1864. On Terrace, see *Her.*, Aug. 14, 1864; on Mount St. Vincent, BCCP *9AR* [1865], 38; BCCP *Min.*, May 3, 1866; on Mineral Springs Pavilion, *Rebuilding CP*, 133; BDPP *Min.*, doc. 14 (1870). After Olmsted returned to the park, the Dairy began dispensing fresh milk. On Dairy, see, e.g., FLO and CV to Stebbins, Jan. 1872, *FYLA*, 244–45; FLO, "A Handbill of 1872," *FYLA*, 417–18; *NYT*, Mar. 6, 1872; *Complete Guide to Central Park*, 26–27. On expansion of restaurants, see BDPP *2AR* [1872], 118; *3AR*, 58–60; *NYT*, Aug. 4, 1873; Columbus Ryan to FLO, Jan. 23, 1873, FLO Mss.

29. *NYT*, Jan. 27, 1884, Nov. 27, 1871; *Her.*, Apr. 3, 1882; Lloyd Morris, *Incredible New York* (1951), 93; Edward Hagaman Hall, "Central Park in the City of New York," ASHPS *16AR* [1911], 433–34. See also *NYT*, May 24, June 14, 1884, Apr. 26, 27, May 9, 12–14, 1890, July 1, Oct. 9, 1891, May 22, 1893; *Trib.*, Sept. 21, 1889; BDPP *Min.*, Apr. 16, 1884; *S-Z*, Apr. 17, 1884.

30. *NYT*, May 22, 1893; *Her.*, May 28, 1877.

31. *NYT*, May 14, 1891.

32. *Her.*, May 28, 1877; Alfred E. Smith, *Up to Now: An Autobiography* (1929), 18.

33. FLO to BDPP, Oct. 23, 1873, *FLOP* 6 (forthcoming).

34. *Trib.*, May 28, 1882 (barbarism). On picking flowers, see, e.g., *FL*, Sept. 4, 1880; *NYT*, July 17, 1889; *Trib.*, Sept. 7, 1884, *Her.*, May 27, 1877.

35. *Her.*, May 16, 1877; James Herbert Morse, Diary, May 17, 1877, Morse Papers, NYHS; FLO and Jules Munckwitz to William R. Martin, May 16, 1877, *FYLA*, 434–35; FLO to Stebbins, May 18, 1875, FLO Mss. See also *NYT*, May 16, 1877; Unidentified clipping, from May 17, 1877, Clipping File, Olmsted Papers Project, American University.

36. *Sun*, May 22, 1871; *NYT*, May 27, 1895.

37. *Trib.*, May 28, 1873; *The Illustrated Manners Book* (1855), quoted in John F. Kasson, *Rudeness and Civility: Manners in Nineteenth-Century Urban America* (1990), 116–17.

38. *Sun*, June 11, 1893; *Her.*, May 27, 31, 1877.

39. *World*, Aug. 4, 1884; Edith Wharton, *The Custom of the Country* (1913; rpt. 1981), 70. On chaperones, see Morris, *Incredible New York*, 93.

40. *Trib.*, May 28, 1873; *World*, Aug. 5, 1888.

41. *National Police Gazette*, Sept. 14, 1878.

42. For 1860s, see summary in BCCP *13AR* [1869], 60–61. For 1880s, see "Statement of the Business of the Police Force of the Department of Parks for 1879 to 1886 Inclusive," 87:24 MP. Note that, unlike those for the 1860s, these figures are for all city parks.

43. *NYT, Star*, Nov. 9, 1886. On prostitution, see Timothy Gilfoyle, "City of Eros: New York City, Prostitution, and the Commercialization of Sex, 1790–1920" (Ph.D. diss., Columbia University, 1987), chaps. 4–5.

44. *Trib.*, June 15, 1878; *NYT*, Oct. 7, 1872; *Police Gazette*, Sept. 14, 1878. See also *NYT*, Mar. 9, Apr. 27, 1872, Mar. 14, 1873; *Her.*, July 23, 1880; *Trib.*, May 12, 1877; *Police Gazette*, Oct. 19, 1878.

45. William Leach, *True Love and Perfect Union: The Feminist Reform of Sex and Society* (1980), 28–29, 40–43, 85–91, and passim. See also Mary Ryan, *Women in Public: Between Banners and Ballots, 1825–1880* (Baltimore, 1990), 76–88.

46. *NYT*, Apr. 27, 1872; *Police Gazette*, Sept. 14, 1878.

47. *Her.*, Oct. 17, 1880; "Pen-Sketches from Modern New-York on Wheels," *Hub* 33 (Apr. 1, 1891): 51.

48. Abby Maria Hall Ward, Diary, Nov. 27, 1874, Ward Family Papers, NYHS; Maria Emily Graham McKnight Ward, *The Common Sense of Bicycling: Bicycling for Ladies* (1896), 11–12; Annie Nathan Meyer, *My Park Book* (1898), 33–35, 111. The board initially permitted biking only on the West Drive: BDPP *Min.*, Nov. 21, 1884, Nov. 11, Dec. 1, 1886, July 20, 1887.

49. *Her.*, May 2, 1877; *NYT*, May 23, 1892. See also *Her.*, Apr. 29, June 20, 21, 1877; *World*, June 27, 1875; *Trib.*, July 7, 1871.

50. *NYT*, Jan. 26, 1893.

51. McCabe, *New York*, 652–53. On beggars, prostitutes, pickpockets, and tramps, see, e.g., *NYT*, May 14, 1873, May 24, Nov. 7, 1875, July 2, 1888; *Trib.*, May 24, 1873, Sept. 7, 1874, May 12, 1877, Mar. 20, 1882, June 30, 1893; *World*, June 4, 1882; Salem Wales to FLO, Mar. 24, 1874, FLO Mss.; Morse, Diary, May 5, 1877. On word "tramp," see Paul Rigenbach, *Tramps and Reformers, 1873–1916: The Discovery of Poverty in New York* (Westport, Conn., 1973), 5–18.

52. E. A. Hammond to M. C. Borden, Apr. 7, 1887, Samuel Parsons to Borden, Mar. 31, 1887, 87:23 MP; *Ir. Am.*, Mar. 23, 1878; Ethel Nathalie Dana, *Young in New York: Memoir of a Victorian Girlhood* (Garden City, N.Y., 1963), 26.

53. *Trib.*, May 12, 1877. Arrest figures are for all parks. One estimate suggests that 10 to 20% of all Americans belonged to families in which a member had "tramped" in search of work in these years: Eric Monkkonen, *Walking to Work* (Omaha, 1984), 8.

54. *Appleton's Journal*, Sept. 11, 1875.

55. Henry Koster to Stebbins, Sept. 12, 1874, FLO Mss.

56. For park regulations, see BDPP *Min.*, May 2, 1871. These generalizations about arrests are based on incomplete and imperfect statistics. The figures for the 1880s are for all city parks. Thus, the comparison with the 1860s assumes that about one-half of the arrests took place in Central Park (an estimate based on figures from the early 1870s which break down the statistics in that way). See note 42 above.

57. *SP*, 133; William Dean Howells, "Glimpses of New York," in *Impressions and Experiences* (1896; rpt. Freeport, N.Y., 1972), 226.

58. Olmsted and Vaux thought statuary was appropriate on the Mall and Terrace. For their views, see, e.g., Frederick Church, CV, and Stebbins to BDPP, Apr. 25, 1873, *FYLA*, 489; FLO and CV to Wales, Mar. 4, 1874, *FYLA*, 494–98.

59. Margot Gayle and Michele Cohen, *The Art Commission and Municipal Art Society Guide to Manhattan's Outdoor Sculpture* (1988), 187–246. On dedications, see, e.g., *NYT*, Sept. 15, 1869, May 30, 1878; *Trib.*, Sept. 15, 1869; BDPP *Min.*, Nov. 16, 1872.

60. Michele H. Bogart, *Public Sculpture and the Civic Ideal in New York City, 1890–1930* (Chicago, 1989), 61, 334 (*NYT* quot.). See also Gayle and Cohen, *Art Commission*, 263–64.

61. *NYT*, May 13, 1894; Gayle and Cohen, *Art Commission*, 204; Federal Writers' Project, *The WPA Guide to New York City* (1939; rpt. 1982), 268.

62. Criticism in *NYT*, June 1, 1873. See also *Her.*, June 1, 1873; Gayle and Cohen, *Art Commission*, 215–16; Lewis Sharp, "Changing Taste in Public Art," in Elizabeth Barlow [Rogers], *The Central Park Book* (1977), 39–40.

63. R. A. Hayward, *Cleopatra's Needle* (Buxton, Derbyshire, 1978), 92–109; *Her.*, Jan. 23, 1881; *Trib.*, Jan. 23, 1881; Gayle and Cohen, *Art Commission*, 226; McCabe, *New York*, 462–64. For examples of the guidebooks' emphasis on statuary, see *Complete Guide to Central Park*, 17–18; Carolyn Faville Ober and Cynthia M. Westover, *Manhattan Historic and Artistic: A Six Day Tour of New York City* (1892), 137–42.

64. Church, CV, and Stebbins to BDPP, Apr. 25, 1873, FLO and CV to Wales, Mar. 4, 1874, *FYLA*, 98, 498; Bogart, *Public Sculpture*, 61–68. For criticism of statues, see, e.g., "Vale," *Horrors in Architecture and So-Called Works of Art in Bronze in the City of New York* (1886); *World*, Aug. 21, 1873; *Trib.*, Nov. 27, 1876, July 20, Aug. 20, 1880; *NYT*, Feb. 19, 1893, May 13, 1894; CV to FLO, July 23, 1870, FLO Mss.

65. *Her.*, May 13, 1881; *HW*, Nov. 3, 1883; *Her.*, June 26, 1871, Aug. 20, 1877, and see June 7, 1886.

66. BDPP *Min.*, May 20, 1874; FLO to Junius Henri Browne, Nov. 12, 1874, FLO Mss.

67. Morse, Diary, June 28, 1875, Mar. 2, 8, 1881; Hole, *Little Tour in America*, 76, 78.

68. Morse, Diary, passim. On Met, see Winifred E. Howe, *A History of the Metropolitan Museum of Art* (1946), 231–32; *Her.* and *NYT*, Dec. 19, 1888.

69. Meyer, *My Park Book*, 32.

70. *NYT*, July 4, 1871.

71. *Sun*, June 11, 1893, May 23, 1886. On "Rotten Row," see Albert Gallup to CV, Aug. 7, 1889, FLO Mss.

72. *NYT,* May 31, 1896. Of the 75 people named in the article, at least 57 were German, and at least 11 in the liquor or brewery business. (Occupations were located in the city directory.) For gentlemen's riding club, see, e.g., BDPP *Min.,* Apr. 2, 1882.

73. On facilities for children, see *Appleton's Journal,* Aug. 3, 1872; Hunt, *Children's District.*

74. David Hapgood, "The Tax to End All Taxes," *American Heritage* 29 (Apr. 1978): 11; *World,* May 25, 1895; *NYT,* Oct. 16, 1898.

75. *Sun,* June 11, 1893.

76. Henry James, *The American Scene* (1907; rpt. 1946); 177; Israel Zangwill, *The Melting Pot* (1932), 102; "The Playground of the Metropolis," *Munsey's Magazine* (Sept. 1895): 576–77; J. Crawford Hamilton, "Snap Shots in Central Park," *Munsey's Magazine* (Oct. 1891): 5–6.

77. Howells, "Glimpses of New York," 131–32. For comparison of Howells with Curtis and Godkin, see Thomas Bender, *New York Intellect: A History of Intellectual Life in New York City, from 1750 to the Beginnings of Our Own Time* (Baltimore, 1987), 176–94.

78. *NYT,* July 14, 1870; *World,* July 14, 1870; *Trib.,* July 14, 1870, June 6, 1894.

79. *New York Freeman,* July 25, 1885; *NYT,* June 1, 1891. On African Americans in the park, see *Her.,* Sept. 4, 1870, July 5, 1877, Aug. 15, Sept. 5, 1887; *Globe,* Mar. 10, 16, 1883; *New York Freeman,* July 11, 1885.

80. *Her.,* July 7, 1884 (concert), Sept. 19, 1887 (German American).

81. Howells, "Glimpses of New York," 224.

13. *A Public Menagerie and Two Private Museums*

1. August Belmont to Matthew Perry, Mar. 12, 1856, Belmont Papers, Columbia University.

2. Ibid.

3. BCCP *Min.,* Nov. 17, 1859; BCCP *3AR* [1859], 17; John Foord, *The Life and Public Service of Andrew Haswell Green* (Garden City, N.Y., 1913), 203–4; BCCP *Min.,* doc. 3 (June 7, 1860). See also Frank Moore to FLO, May 10, 1860, FLO Mss.

4. BCCP *6AR* [1862], 23.

5. "An Act to Incorporate the American Zoological and Botanical Society," passed Apr. 10, 1860, *Laws of New York 1860,* 422; *Her.,* May 28, 1860; *Ir. N,* Mar. 17, 1860.

6. BCCP *6AR* [1862], 23. The annual reports, signed by board president Richard Blatchford and comptroller Green, were probably written by Green. For Green's interest in the park for public education, see, e.g., BCCP *9AR* [1865], 44; *12AR* [1868], 125–38; BCCP *Min.,* June 15, 1868, Apr. 18, Dec. 9, 1869, Jan. 13, 29, 1870.

7. BCCP *6AR* [1862], 15 (emphasis added). On early zoos, menageries, and animal shows, see Richard W. Flint, "Entrepreneurial and Cultural Aspects of the Early Nineteenth-Century Circus and Menagerie Business," in *Intinerancy in New England and New York,* ed. Peter Benes (Boston, 1986), 131–49; Peter George Buckley, "To the Opera House: Culture and Society in New York City, 1820–1860" (Ph.D. diss., State University of New York, Stony Brook, 1984), 31; Helen L. Horowitz, "Seeing Ourselves through the Bars," *Landscape* 25 (1981): 12–13, and "The National Zoological Park: 'City of Refuge' Or Zoo?" *Records of the Columbia Historical Society* 49 (1973–1974): 405–6.

8. *Ir. N,* Feb. 11, 1860; *FL,* May 23, 1868.

9. "Laws Relating to Central Park," *FYLA,* 544; BCCP *Min.,* doc. 3 (June 7, 1860); *NYT,* July 18, 1868; BCCP *12AR* [1868], 31–35; *13AR* [1869], 29–30; FLO and CV to the President of BCCP, 1866, *FYLA,* 500–503. The American Zoological and Botanical Society apparently lost interest in the project. See BCCP *7AR* [1863], 18–19; *8AR* [1864], 38.

10. FLO to Waldo Hutchins, Mar. 18, 1890, *FYLA,* 512; *NYT,* July 25, 1863. For list of animals and other gifts, see BCCP *9AR* [1865], 72–80.

11. BCCP *9AR* [1865], 72–80; Bernard Livingston, *Zoo: Animals, People, Places* (1974), 239; BCCP *Min.,* Apr. 10, 1865, May 9, 1867; John W. Smith, "Central Park Animals as Their Keeper Knows Them," *Outing* 42 (May 1903): 248; *Her.,* May 1, Aug. 5, 1865; Strong, *Diary,* 4:251.

12. BDPP *1AR* [1871], 20–21, 386; *NYT,* July 7, 1871; BDPP *2AR* [1872], 29. See description in *World,* May 28, 1871.

13. FLO and CV in *NYT,* Dec. 21, 1870; FLO to Hutchins, *FYLA,* 512. See also *NYT,* Dec. 22, 1870, July 1, 1871; BDPP *Min.,* June 7, Sept. 13, Nov. 22, 1870; BDPP *1AR* [1871], 20.

14. BCCP *13AR* [1869], 142; BDPP *2AR* [1872], 142; *3AR* [1873], 196; *NYT,* July 4, 1888. On the zoo's popularity, see also, e.g., *NYT,* Nov. 24, 1883, May 14, 1894; *Report of the Director of the Central Park Menagerie for 1876* (1877), 5. On Sunday visitors, see, e.g., *Her.,* June 7, 1875, July 16, 1877, June 16, 1879, May 14, 1894, May 6, 1895; *NYT,* Aug. 21, 1871, May 20, 1878, June 16, 1879, May 14, 1894, May 27, 1895; *World,* June 2, 1873; *Sun,* May 31, 1886.

15. *NYT,* June 5, 1881; BDPP *Min.,* Apr. 5, 1876. In the mid-1870s circus operators owned about one-quarter of the animals displayed at the zoo, including a disproportionate number of its most valuable specimens: *Report of the Director of the Menagerie for Years 1874 and 1875* (1876), 6–7; ibid., for 1877 (1878), 9. See also *NYT,* Jan. 6, 1878; *Her.,* June 25, 1877; BDPP *Min.,* July 3, 1874. For controversy over this practice, see *NYT,* Mar. 11, 17, 20, 24, June 10, 1892; *Trib.,* Mar. 26, 1892.

16. *Her.,* Nov. 9, 1874; *Sun,* Nov. 12, 1874; Don Carlos Seitz, *The James Gordon Bennetts— Father & Son, Proprietors of the "New York Herald"* (1928), 338. On press and zoo, see, e.g., *Star,* Oct. 19, Nov. 6, 27, 1886; *World,* July 11, 1886; *Trib.,* Aug. 11, 1895; *NYT,* Mar. 9, 1896.

17. *Report of the Director of the Menagerie for 1888* (1889), 5; Henry S. Fuller, *Mr. Crowley of Central Park: A Historie* (1888). See also John W. Smith, "The Central Park Animals as Their Keeper Knows Them," Part II, *Outing* 43 (Oct. 1903): 61; *Her.,* June 8, 1885; *NYT,* July 2, 11, 16, 23, 1888. Controversy over the use of Irish names for the zoo animals continued in the 1890s: *NYT,* Apr. 11, May 4, 1893; *Her.,* May 1, 1893.

18. Fuller, *Mr. Crowley,* 111–12.

19. FLO to Hutchins, *FYLA,* 511–17. On controversy over location of zoo in the 1880s, see, e.g., CV to FLO, Oct. 1, 9, 11, Nov. 1, 22, 25, Dec. 7, 9, 1883, E. C. Stedman to CV, Nov. 1883, FLO Mss. On 1890s, see BDPP *Min.,* Mar. 27, 1890; *NYT,* Apr. 6, 10, 11, 25, 29, May 2, 1890; *Her.,* May 5, June 27, 1895.

20. *RERBG,* May 3, 10, 1890; *Post,* Oct. 12, 1883. See similarly *Trib.,* Oct. 8, 1883. For other complaints about the zoo, see, e.g., *NYT,* June 5, 1881, Dec. 24, 1884, Mar. 18, 1887; BCCP *Min.,* Jan. 29, 1870; *World,* Oct. 9, 1883.

21. *Trib.,* June 3, 1883; *NYT,* Apr. 22, 1881.

22. William Bridges, *A Gathering of Animals: An Unconventional History of the New York Zoological Society* (1974), 4.

23. Ibid., 4–10.

24. Ibid., 10–11; Mabel Parsons, ed., *Memories of Samuel Parsons* (1926), 70. On Bronx Zoo, see also Helen L. Horowitz, "Animal and Man in the New York Zoological Park," *New York History* 56 (Oct. 1975): 426–55.

25. GP 128, 160; "Description of the Central Park," Jan. 1859, BCCP *2AR* [1858], rpt. in *FLOP* 3:218.

26. BCCP *3AR* [1859], 12. On founding of these institutions, see Lawrence W. Levine, *Highbrow/Lowbrow: The Emergence of Cultural Hierarchy in America* (Cambridge, Mass., 1988), 85– 168; Helen L. Horowitz, *Culture and the City: Cultural Philanthropy in Chicago from the 1880s to 1917* (Chicago, 1976).

27. Green also initially hoped that cultural institutions would contribute rent that could be applied toward park maintenance: BCCP *3AR* [1859], 12–13.

28. Robert Hendre Kelby, *The New York Historical Society, 1804–1904* (1893), 53–55; R. W. G. Vail, *Knickerbocker Birthday: A Sesqui-Centennial History of the New-York Historical Society* (1954), 119; Frederic De Peyster, *The Moral and Intellectual Influence of Libraries upon Social Progress* (1866); New York Historical Society, *Museum of History, Antiquities, and Art in the Central Park* (handwritten date of 1868), printed flier in collection of NYHS; Calvin Tompkins, *Merchants and Masterpieces: The Story of the Metropolitan Museum of Art* (rev. ed., 1989), 38. On observatory, see *NYT,* Feb. 9, 12, 22, 23, 26, 1859; *Her., Sun,* Feb. 26, 1859; Foord, *Life and Public Service,* 62. On the Hunt building, see Lewis I. Sharp, "Richard Morris Hunt and His Influence on American Beaux-Arts Sculpture," in *The Architecture of Richard Morris Hunt,* ed. Susan R. Stein (Chicago, 1986), 123; Rebecca Read Shanor, *The City That Never Was* (1988), 39–41; Paul R. Baker, *Richard Morris Hunt* (Cambridge, Mass., 1980), 154–55; BCCP *Min.,* Feb. 8, 15, 17, 26, Mar. 3, May 3, 1866, Mar. 26, 1868; BCCP *12AR* [1868], 47–48.

29. Quoted in Dixon Wechter, *The Saga of American Society* (1937), 198. On lack of progress, see BCCP *13AR* [1869], 27.

30. Albert Bickmore, "Autobiography," unpub. typescript, ca. 1900, in AMNH Archives, 1–8; Wolfe quoted in John M. Kennedy, "Philanthropy and Science in New York City: The American Museum of Natural History, 1868–1968" (Ph.D. diss., Yale University, 1968), 13. See also Geoffrey Hellman, *Bankers, Bones, and Beetles: The First Century of the American Museum of Natural History* (Garden City, N.Y., 1969), 9–17. Our account draws heavily on these two excellent histories of the museum, particularly Kennedy's well-documented study (see esp. pp. 1–43). Additional information on the founders comes from sketches in the *DAB* and *NCAB*.

31. *NYT*, Mar. 6, 1872; Gratcap quoted in Hellman, *Bankers*, 39. For receptions, see, e.g., *NYT*, May 16, 1883.

32. AHG to "Gentlemen," Jan. 13, 1869, reprinted in BCCP *13AR* [1869], 83; *NYT*, Feb. 7, 1869. See also Kennedy, "Philanthropy and Science," 40.

33. *NYT*, Mar. 18, 1868, *Her.*, July 12, 1866. On Barnum's museum, see Buckley, "To the Opera House," 477–97; Neil Harris, *Humbug: The Art of P. T. Barnum* (Chicago, 1985), 31–90.

34. *Her.*, July 12, 1866.

35. Ibid.; trustees quoted in Kennedy, "Philanthropy and Science," 43; Choate quoted in Tompkins, *Merchants and Masterpieces*, 16.

36. Thomas Bender, *New York Intellect: A History of Intellectual Life in New York City, from 1750 to the Beginnings of Our Own Time* (Baltimore, 1987), 77 (quot.), 62–64, 76–78, 82, 95. On early corporations performing public services, see L. Ray Gunn, *The Decline of Authority: Public Economic Policy and Political Development in New York State, 1800–1860* (Ithaca, 1988), 106–7, 111. On public money to private charities, see Edward K. Spann, *The New Metropolis: New York City, 1840–1857* (1981), 265–66; Michael Katz, *In the Shadow of the Poorhouse: A Social History of Welfare in America* (1986), 42–46. The city also briefly subsidized the Apprentices Library of the General Society of Mechanics and Tradesmen; Bender, p. 82.

37. On public education, see Spann, *New Metropolis*, 30–33, 257–60.

38. BCCP *13AR*, 82. Green quoted in David Hammack, "Comprehensive Planning before the Comprehensive Plan: A New Look at the Nineteenth-Century American City," in *Two Centuries of American Planning*, ed. Daniel Schaffer (Baltimore, 1988), 147.

39. Railroad executive quoted in Kennedy, "Philanthropy and Science," 44; Bickmore, "Autobiography," 9–12; Hellman, *Bankers*, 19–21.

40. Kennedy, "Philanthropy and Science," 45–58; Hellman, *Bankers*, 21–22; Bickmore, "Autobiography," 13–24; AMNH *1AR* [1870], 5–20; BDPP *Min.*, Sept. 13, 1870, Nov. 22, 1870; *NYT*, Apr. 28, 1871; *World*, May 28, 1871; AMNH *3AR* [1871], 33–35.

41. On Paleozoic museum, see BCCP *12AR* [1868], 30, 129–38; *13AR* [1869], 27–29, BDPP *1AR* [1870], 18–19; *NYT*, Mar. 17, 27, Apr. 23, 25, 29, 1868, Feb. 27, 1870, Mar. 7, 1871, Feb. 15, Mar. 1, Apr. 20, 1874, Apr. 28, 1875; *Star*, June 25, 1871; Richard C. Ryder, "Dusting Off America's First Dinosaur," *American Heritage* 39 (Mar. 1988): 68–73; Ryder, "Hawkins Hadrosaurs: The Stereographic Record," *The Mosasaur: The Journal of the Delaware Valley Paleontological Society* 3 (Nov. 1986): 169–80; Edwin H. Colbert and Katharine Beneker, "The Paleozoic Museum in Central Park; or, The Museum That Never Was," *Curator* 2 (1959): 137–50; Adrian J. Desmond, "Central Park's Fragile Dinosaurs," *Natural History* 83 (Oct. 1974): 65–71.

42. For attendance, see *Report of the Director of the Menagerie for 1876* (1877), 5; *Trib.*, Oct. 9, 1876; AMNH *7AR* [1875], 8–9 and unpaged insert.

43. Kennedy, "Philanthropy and Science," 49, 51, 59–60; J. F. Richmond, *New York and Its Institutions, 1609–1871* (1871), 161.

44. Bickmore quoted in Hellman, *Bankers*, 28–29; and *NYT*, May 19, 1881. On Bickmore's educational work, see AMNH *16AR* [1884–85], 8; *19AR* [1888–89], 8; *20AR* [1889–90], 14; on Jesup's efforts, Kennedy, "Philanthropy and Science," 78–79; on opening, *NYT*, Dec. 20, 22, 23, 1877; *New York Daily Graphic*, Dec. 22, 1877.

45. Kennedy, "Philanthropy and Science," 81, 99–100; Hellman, *Bankers*, 43; AMNH *18AR* [1886–87], 8.

46. Kennedy, "Philanthropy and Science," 45–58; Hellman, *Bankers*, 21–22; Bickmore, "Autobiography," 13–24; AMNH *1AR* [1870], 5–20; BDPP *Min.*, Sept. 13, Nov. 22, 1870; *NYT*, Apr. 28, 1871; *World*, May 28, 1871; AMNH *3AR* [1871], 33–35. On delays in construction, see *Trib.*,

July 17, 18, 25, 1873. For original plans of Metropolitan Museum, which were reduced because of budget constraints, see Shanor, *City That Never Was*, 48–49.

47. Leo Lerman, *The Museum: One Hundred Years of the Metropolitan Museum of Art* (1969), 12; Tompkins, *Merchants and Masterpieces*, 16 (Choate), 28–32; *NYT*, Nov. 25, 1869.

48. Choate and *Tribune* quoted in Tompkins, *Merchants and Masterpieces*, 23, 59.

49. Tompkins, *Merchants and Masterpieces*, 62–68; Michele H. Bogart, *Public Sculpture and the Civic Ideal in New York City, 1890–1930* (Chicago, 1989), 164–65, 351; "Sixteenth Annual Report . . . for the Year Ending December 31, 1885," in MMA, *Annual Reports of the Trustees of the Association, from 1871 to 1902* (1903), 321 (hereafter cited in form MMA *AR* [1885], 321); MMA *AR* [1892], 539–40.

50. Tompkins, *Merchants and Masterpieces*, 84–86. See also *NYT*, Sept. 24, 1892, Feb. 4, 1897; Levine, *Highbrow/Lowbrow*, 185–86.

51. *Her.*, May 27, 1877. Aldermen tried unsuccessfully in 1872 to force the museum to open on Sundays: BA *Proc.*, Aug. 8, 1872; *NYT*, Aug. 9, 1872. The Sweeny board may have briefly opened it on Sundays, but the evidence is ambiguous: *NYT*, Aug. 7, 21, 1871.

52. *NYT*, Mar. 31, 1880; BDPP *Min.*, Apr. 20, 1881; *Her.*, July 22, 1884; *NYT*, Jan. 17, Mar. 10, 1886. See also *NYT*, Sept. 29, 1884, Jan. 3, Feb. 9, Mar. 10, Apr. 5, 26, May 12, 23, Nov. 18, Dec. 18, 19, 27, 1886; *Her.*, Oct. 6, 1884.

53. *Her.*, Aug. 7, 1892; Tompkins, *Merchants and Masterpieces*, 33–34, 76–77. On museum boards, see Kennedy, "Philanthropy and Science," 55; Tompkins, 20, 76; on Stuart, *DAB*; Hellman, *Bankers*, 58–59.

54. MMA *AR* [1885], 324 (emphasis added); trustee quoted in Winifred E. Howe, *A History of the Metropolitan Museum of Art* (1946), 240; Morris K. Jesup, *The Museums in the Park: Should They Be Open on Sunday?* (1885), 5.

55. Kennedy, "Philanthropy and Science," 88–91, 104–6. On efforts to cut off funds, see *NYT*, Apr. 5, 1885, Dec. 29, 1886, Dec. 6, 12, 1889; Howe, *History of the Metropolitan*, 231, 238.

56. *NYT*, Dec. 27, 30, 1888, Dec. 30, 1886.

57. *NYT*, Aug. 7, 1892. On petition drive, see *NYT*, May 6, 18–20, 1891; MMA *AR* [1891], 501; James K. Paulding, *Charles B. Stover, July 14, 1861–April 24, 1929: His Life and Personality* (1938), 20, 159; Irving Howe, *World of Our Fathers* (1976), 214. On press, see Lerman, *Museum*, 71; on bill, Tompkins, *Merchants and Masterpieces*, 78.

58. AMNH *24AR* [1892], 8; MMA *AR* [1892], 537; [1894], 603; *NYT*, Dec. 22, 1891. The impact of Sunday opening on the Met's attendance is harder to gauge because of charges that the museum did not report its attendance accurately. See, e.g., *NYT*, May 15, Aug. 6, 1881, Sept. 22, 1882. Annual reports showed a drop in attendance between 1881 and 1892: MMA *AR* [1881], 193; [1892], 537. On membership, see MMA *AR* [1901], 844.

59. MMA *AR* [1892], 544; *Sun*, June 1, 1891. See also *NYT*, *Her.*, June 1, 1891.

60. *Her.*, June 1, 1891; Tompkins, *Merchants and Masterpieces*, 78; *Sun*, June 1, 1891.

61. *NYT*, Aug. 8, Oct. 24, 1892, and cf. May 19, 1881.

62. Tompkins, *Merchants and Masterpieces*, 78, 87 (Jesup). See also *NYT*, Feb. 16, 1895.

63. Quoted in Kennedy, "Philanthropy and Science," 106–8.

64. Tompkins, *Merchants and Masterpieces*, 75, 87; Morrison H. Heckscher, "Hunt and the Metropolitan Museum of Art," in *Architecture of Hunt*, 175–79; Baker, *Richard Morris Hunt*, 442–43.

65. Heckscher, "Hunt and the Metropolitan," 173–87; Baker, *Richard Morris Hunt*, 181–85. Lenox's "public library" restricted public access much more radically than the museums: patrons who formally applied might use the library on two days of the week: *NYT*, Jan. 6, 1878.

66. Heckscher, "Hunt and the Metropolitan," 175; Bogart, *Public Sculpture*, 160; Shanor, *City That Never Was*, 50.

67. On Hunt design, see Baker, *Richard Morris Hunt*, 442–49; Heckscher, "Hunt and the Metropolitan," 178–85. Hunt died on July 31, 1895, and the building was completed under his son's supervision. On the triumph of the French school, see Mardges Bacon, *Ernest Flagg: Beaux-Arts Architect and Urban Reformer* (1986), 49–52. Hunt won another symbolic triumph over Vaux and Olmsted when the Richard Morris Hunt Memorial was placed on the park's edge at Fifth Avenue between 70th and 71st streets. Despite various proposals, no memorial to the designers has been erected within the park.

68. FLO to Paul Dana, Dec. 22, 1890, *FYLA*, 527. For Vaux's willingness to make concessions, see Dana to FLO, Feb. 24, 1891, FLO Mss. For concerns that "the disciples of the Beaux Arts will get possession of the plan," see William Stiles to FLO, Mar. 16, 1891, FLO Mss.

69. *World*, Mar. 19, 1892; *Trib.*, Mar. 20, 1892.

70. *The Central Park Race Track Law Was Repealed by Public Sentiment* (1892), 7; Richard Welling, *As the Twig Is Bent* (1942), 52; *Trib.*, Mar. 18, 26, 1892; *World*, Mar. 26, 1892. For *Herald*'s position, see Mar. 18, 21, 22, 1892.

71. *World*, Mar. 21 (roughs), 23, 1892.

72. *World*, Mar. 21, 1892; *Trib.*, Mar. 26, 1892; Stiles to FLO, Mar. 22, 26, 1892, FLO Mss.

73. *Trib.*, Mar. 27, 29, 1892; *NYT*, Mar. 27, 1892.

74. Stiles to FLO, Apr. 18, 1892, FLO to Stiles, Sept. 18, 1894, Dana to FLO, Oct. 30, 1894, FLO Mss.

75. *NYT*, Mar. 27, 1892. See, for example, Stiles to FLO, Dec. 1, 1894, FLO Mss., for his linkage of raceway issue and Strong election.

14. The Fragmented Park

1. *Trib.*, *Sun*, Nov. 21, 1895; BDPP *Min.*, Aug. 21, 1895.

2. *Sun*, *World*, *Trib.*, Nov. 22, 1895. See also *NYT*, Nov. 21, 22, 1895; *Her.*, Nov. 21, 22, 1895; James Herbert Morse, Diary, Feb. 18, 1894, Morse Papers, NYHS; Laura Wood Roper, *FLO: A Biography of Frederick Law Olmsted* (Baltimore, 1973), 472. Frank Kowsky, who is the author of a forthcoming study of Vaux's architecture, generously shared information on Mary Vaux's death and Vaux's own health problems.

3. Roper, *FLO*, 469–75. See also Mary Olmsted to FLO, Jr., Feb. 23, 1896. On Olmsted's mental deterioration, see Charles Capen McLaughlin, "Frederick Law Olmsted: His Life and Work," *FLOP* 1:45; Melvin Kalfus, *Frederick Law Olmsted: The Passion of a Public Artist* (1990), 2, 12.

4. Accounts of the shooting vary. See Edward Hagaman Hall, "A Short Biography of Andrew Haswell Green," ASHPS *9AR* [1904], 214–16; *NYT*, Nov. 14, 1903; *Trib.*, Nov. 14, 15, 18, 1903; George Alexander Mazaraki, "The Public Career of Andrew Haswell Green" (Ph.D. diss., New York University, 1966), 375.

5. *NYT*, Nov. 14, 1903. On Viele, see Peter Salwen, *Upper West Side Story: A History and Guide* (1989), 65.

6. Robert Nathan, *Portrait of Jennie* (1940).

7. *NYT*, Feb. 15, 1947; Jack Finney, *Time and Again* (1970).

8. Sara Teasdale, "Central Park at Dusk" (1917), in *Chief Modern Poets of England and America*, ed. Gerald Sanders and John Nelson (1936), 539.

9. Carolyn Faville Ober and Cynthia M. Westover, *Manhattan Historic and Artistic: A Six Day Tour of New York City* (1892), 142; "The Hotel Majestic," *Illustrated American*, Jan. 26, 1895, 122. "Byron" was the joint imprint shared by the father-and-son team Joseph and Percy Byron.

10. John Tauranac, *Elegant New York: The Builders and the Buildings* (1985), 196–99, 204–9, 219 (Belmont); Allen Churchill, *The Upper Crust: An Informal History of New York's Highest Society* (Englewood Cliffs, N.J., 1970), 223. Both houses survive today, as the Frick and Cooper-Hewitt museums.

11. Tauranac, *Elegant New York*, 219–20 (998 Fifth and Elliman). See also Federal Writers' Project, *The WPA Guide to New York City* (1939; rpt. 1982), 234; Andrew Alpern, *New York's Fabulous Luxury Apartments* (1975), 74–75; W. Parker Chase, *New York, 1932: The Wonder City* (1932; rpt. 1983), 280–81 (Century Apartments).

12. *NYT*, Sept. 4, 1926, Aug. 21, Apr. 21, 1929.

13. FLO, Jr., to Thomas Adams, Apr. 29, 1925, OA Mss.; Herman W. Merkel, *Report on Survey of Central Park* (1927), 14; critics' views characterized in Olmsted, Jr., "The Park in Relation to the City Plan," in *FYLA*, 205.

14. Michele H. Bogart, *Public Sculpture and the Civic Ideal in New York City, 1890–1930* (Chicago, 1989), 185–217, provides an excellent account of the two monuments.

15. Bogart, *Public Sculpture*, 215.

16. For consolidation, see David Hammack, *Power and Society: Greater New York at the Turn of the Century* (1982), 185–229; for population, see Ira Rosenwaike, *Population History of New York City* (Syracuse, 1972), 58; for area, see Federal Writers' Project, *New York Panorama* (1938; rpt. 1984), 23.

17. Powers are outlined in Pks. Dpt. *AR* [1898], 3–4; some changes under the 1901 charter are noted in Pks. Dpt. *AR* [1903], 7–8. On 1895 law, see *NYT*, Feb. 14, 1895. For 1897 charter, see Clarence F. Birdseye, *The Greater New York Charter* (1897), 233–43. In 1911 Queens got its own commissioner, and in 1920 Staten Island was separated from Manhattan.

18. For political affiliations and occupations, see *NYT* obituaries; *DAB; NCAB;* and articles published at time of appointment. For calls for nonpartisan board, see, e.g., *NYT*, Mar. 25, 26, 29, July 27, 1929; *H-T*, June 3, 1934.

19. Birdseye, *Greater New York*, 234–35; Mabel Parsons, ed., *Memories of Samuel Parsons* (1926), 56–57. On creation of New York Art Commission, see Bogart, *Public Sculpture*, 61–68; Harvey A. Kantor, "Modern Urban Planning in New York City: Origins and Evolution, 1890–1933" (Ph.D. diss., New York University, 1971), 42–45. The board of estimate was added in the 1901 charter in order to decentralize power.

20. *NYT*, May 15, 1897; Pks. Dpt. *AR* [1898], 4; *AR* [1903], 7–8. See also *AR* [1930], 4.

21. Sulzberger quoted in Nathan Straus, "The Reminiscences of Nathan Straus" (transcript of an interview conducted by O. Bombard for the Oral History Research Office of Columbia University, 1950), 63.

22. Iphigene Ochs Sulzberger to Richard Welling, Feb. 12, 1930, B 12, RW Mss. See also Welling to Sulzberger, Feb. 5, 1930.

23. *Jour.*, July 7, 10, 1901; *NYT*, July 7, 10, 1901.

24. *World, Jour., NYT*, July 3, 1901; *Sun, Jour.*, July 8, 1901.

25. *Jour.*, July 10, 1910 (victory); *NYT*, July 10, 1901.

26. *Jour.*, June 26, 28, July 2–16, 1901; *Trib.*, June 27, July 5, 1901.

27. *Jour.*, July 2, 1901 (Cohen); *NYT*, July 5, 1901.

28. *NYT*, May 17, 1894; Sebastian de Grazia, *Of Time, Work, and Leisure* (1964), 419; U.S. Bureau of the Census, *Historical Statistics of the United States, Colonial Times to 1970, Part 1* (Washington, D.C., 1976), 164.

29. *Her.*, Sept. 20, 1880, June 12, 1893, July 30, 1894.

30. *Her.*, July 21, 1884, June 12, 1893, July 30, 1894. See also Kathy Peiss, *Cheap Amusements: Working Women and Leisure in Turn-of-the-Century New York* (Philadelphia, 1986), 122–38; John Kasson, *Amusing the Million: Coney Island at the Turn of the Century* (1978), 29–34, 87 (quot.); *WPA Guide*, 473 (empire).

31. Robert C. Allen, "Motion Picture Exhibition in Manhattan, 1906–1912: Beyond the Nickelodeon," *Cinema Journal* 17 (Spring 1979): 2–7. See also Robert Sklar, *Movie-Made America: A Social History of American Movies* (1975), 16. Only reading the newspaper and visiting with friends and families were more prevalent diversions: George Esdras Bevans, *How Workingmen Spend Their Spare Time* (1913), 20–21. On Radio City, Madison Square Garden, and sports stadiums, see *WPA Guide*, 297, 330–33, 337–38, 520.

32. Robert Coit Chapin, *The Standard of Living among Workingmen's Families in New York City* (1909), 210–13; Irving Bernstein, *The Lean Years: A History of the American Worker, 1920–1933* (1960; rpt. Baltimore, 1966), 63–65. Lizabeth Cohen discusses the uneven entrance of Chicago working-class families into the world of mass culture in *Making a New Deal: Industrial Workers in Chicago, 1919–1939* (1990), chap. 3.

33. See Lee F. Hanmer, *Public Recreation: A Study of Parks, Playgrounds and Other Outdoor Recreation Facilities* (1928; rpt. 1974), 30, 128, 131, 164.

34. *NYT*, Sept. 14, 1917. On concerts, see BDPP *3AR* [1873], 284; *NYT*, Apr. 4, 1889; Pks. Dpt. *AR* [1898], 13; *AR* [1913], 22; *NYT*, Apr. 6, 1924; *News*, May 12, 1925. On new bandstand, see *NYT*, Feb. 15, 1910, July 4, 1910, Pks. Dpt. *AR* [1910], 22. On German chorus, *NYT*, Aug. 31, 1914; on song and light, *Trib., Her., World, Post*, Sept. 14, 1917; *Trib.*, Sept. 15, 1917. See also Claude Bragdon (a Rochester architect who did the lighting effects), *More Lives Than One* (1938), 63–75, reference courtesy of William Leach.

35. Robert Wheelwright, "The Attacks on Central Park," *LA* 1 (1910–11): 17; Pks. Dpt. *AR* [1901], 18. See also Pks. Dpt. *AR* [1899], 4; *AR* [1902], 19; *AR* [1904], 33; *AR* [1907], 24.

36. Bogart, *Public Sculpture,* 164 (charter). For museum attendance, see AMNH and MMA annual reports. For addition of wings, see Leo Lerman, *The Museum: One Hundred Years of the Metropolitan Museum of Art* (1969), 122–27, 140, 149.

37. William Prendergast, *Report on the Maintenance of the Park Department of the City of New York in 1913 and 1914* (1915), 5; Pks. Dpt. *AR* [1927], 112; *NYT,* Jan. 21, 1887. Even accounting for inflation, the museum appropriation had increased about 15 times.

38. Pks. Dpt. *AR* [1902]; *NYT,* Mar. 19 (Yorkville children), 21, 1909; John W. Smith, "Central Park Animals as Their Keeper Knows Them," *Outing* 42 (May 1903): 248; *Forward* quoted in Irving Howe, *World of Our Fathers* (1976), 131.

39. On zoo's deterioration, see *NYT,* Aug. 24, 1919, Jan 26, 27, 1920; *World,* Jan. 27, 1920; Merkel, *Report,* 18. Budget comparison based on Prendergast, *Report,* 5, 16–17.

40. See, e.g., Pks. Dpt. *AR* [1906], 58.

41. *Trib.,* May 22, 1904. See similarly, e.g., *NYT,* May 30, 1902, June 18, 1905, May 31, 1916. *NYT,* Sept. 15, 1929; Arthur Mann, *La Guardia Comes to Power, 1933* (1965; rpt. Chicago, 1969), 55. On Farley, see Thomas M. Henderson, *Tammany Hall and the New Immigrants: The Progressive Years* (1976), 78.

42. Pks. Dpt. *AR* [1911], 12; Pks. Dpt., *Report of the Bureau of Recreation, for 1911–1912* (1913), 46–52; ASHPS *19AR* [1914], 169. For other festivals and pageants, see, e.g., Pks. Dpt. *AR* [1911], 12–13; *AR* [1913], 27; *AR* [1916], 77; *NYT,* Apr. 6, 17, 1913, May 23, 1920, May 12, 1929; *News,* May 10, 1920, Apr. 24, 1922. See also David Glassberg, *American Historical Pageantry: The Uses of Tradition in the Early Twentieth Century* (Chapel Hill, N.C., 1990).

43. *NYT,* Aug. 13, 16, 1927; *New York Call, Post,* May 2, 1914; ASHPS *22AR* [1917], 244.

44. *NYT,* Jan. 13, 1916; Pks. Dpt., *Report for 1911–1912,* 46–52. On the commercial aesthetic, see William R. Leach, "Transformation in a Culture of Consumption: Women and Department Stores, 1890–1925," *Journal of American History* 71 (Sept. 1984): 322–31.

45. Hanmer, *Public Recreation,* 39–40.

46. Roy Rosenzweig, *Eight Hours for What We Will: Workers and Leisure in an Industrial City, 1870–1920* (1983), 148. On playground movement, see Dominick Cavallo, *Muscles and Morals: Organized Playgrounds and Urban Reform, 1880–1920* (Philadelphia, 1981); Cary Goodman, *Choosing Sides: Playgrounds and Street Life on the Lower East Side* (1979); Galen Cranz, *The Politics of Park Design: A History of Urban Parks in America* (Cambridge, Mass., 1982), 61–99; Paul Boyer, *Urban Masses and Moral Order in America, 1820–1920* (Cambridge, Mass., 1978), 242–51; Rosenzweig, 143–52.

47. See Parks and Playgrounds Association, *Statement Relating to Recreation in Greater New York* (1910), 24–25; Hanmer, *Public Recreation,* 157. See also Richard F. Knapp, "Parks and Politics: The Rise of Municipal Responsibility for Playgrounds in New York City, 1887–1905" (M.A. thesis, Duke University, 1968), 61–75, 112–22; Pks. Dpt. *AR* [1910–13], passim; and esp. Pks. Dpt., *Report for 1911–1912.*

48. William A. Prendergast, *Report,* 7–8; Jennifer Cromley, "The First World War and Women's Work: A Case Study of the New York City Parks Department, 1900–1920," 66, 74–75, unpub. paper, in possession of authors; Pks. Dpt., *Report for 1911–1912,* 46.

49. Knapp, "Parks and Politics," 85; Paul Dana to FLO, Feb. 2, 24, 1891, FLO Mss.; Pks. Dpt. *AR* [1912], 54, 99; *NYT,* May 12, 1912; Hanmer, *Public Recreation,* 148. On tennis, see BDPP *Min.,* May 6, 1884; Pks. Dpt. *AR* [1912], 114; *AR* [1914], 20; *AR* [1916], 106; *NYT,* Nov. 1, 1914.

50. Calculations based on Hanmer, *Public Recreation,* 240. On rise of country clubs, see Casper W. Whitney, "Evolution of the Country Club," *HM* (Dec. 1894): 17–32, as reprinted in Neil Harris, ed., *The Land of Contrasts, 1880–1901* (1970), 135–46.

51. *Trib.* June 24, 1901; *NYT,* July 1, 4, 1910; Hanmer, *Public Recreation,* 76. On the influence of the country club on popular recreational facilities, see also Betsy Blackmar "Going to the Mountains: A Social History," in Alf Evers et al., *Resorts of the Catskills* (1979), 87–90.

52. *NYT,* Feb. 28, Apr. 25, 29, 30, May 1–3, 6, 8, 13, 20, June 3, Nov. 8, 1925, June 21 (description), 22, 1926. See also August Heckscher to Henry F. Osborn, Dec. 6, 1923, B 586r, AMNH Archives, New York; Albert Bard to William B. Roulstone, Apr. 30, 1925, B 6, Bard Papers, NYPL.

53. Hanmer, *Public Recreation,* 153–56.

54. Chapin, *Standard of Living,* 213. It should be noted, however, that Chapin did not use a random sample and that he also found only one Irish family mentioning use of parks, although the

number of black families in his study was larger. Census tracts for the blocks from which children at the playground came show a heavy concentration of black families.

55. On race riot, see Seth M. Scheiner, *Negro Mecca: A History of the Negro in New York City, 1865–1920* (1965), 121–27; Gilbert Osofsky, *Harlem: The Making of a Ghetto* (1966), 46–52; Mary White Ovington, *Half a Man: The Status of the Negro in New York* (1911; rpt. 1969), 40; Cromley, "First World War and Women's Work," 79.

56. Osofsky, *Harlem*, 170–72.

57. *NYT*, June 5, 1929.

58. Gene Fowler, *Beau James: The Life and Times of Jimmy Walker* (1949; rpt. Clifton, N.J., 1973), 246; *NYT*, May 14 (color), 15, 1929.

59. *News*, May 15, 1929; Fowler, *Beau James*, 248; *NYT*, June 4, 5, 1929. On Casino, see also Helen Lawrenson, *Stranger at the Party: A Memoir* (1975), 70–71, reference courtesy of Lewis Erenberg.

60. *NYT*, June 4, 5, 1929; Fowler, *Beau James*, 251.

61. *NYT*, June 4, 1929.

62. For commissioners' denial of permit, *NYT*, June, 30, 1899; for judge's ruling, *NYT*, Nov. 2, 3, 5, 1899; *Post*, Oct. 30, Nov. 11, 1899. For Clausen's drive through park, *Post*, Nov. 13, 1899; *NYT*, Feb. 3, 1924 (story of breakdown). See also Henry Hope Reed and Sophia Duckworth, *Central Park: A History and a Guide* (1967; rpt. 1972), 40–41.

63. *NYT*, Nov. 20, 22, 23, 1906. On conflicts over autos, see, e.g., *NYT*, July 29, Dec. 29, 1906, July 26, 1907, Apr. 18, 20, Aug. 3, Sept. 9, 16, 17, 19, 1908, Apr. 25, Sept. 8, 17, Oct. 20, 26, 1909; *World*, June 2, 1902; *Trib.*, Jan. 11, 1905, Dec. 29, 1906, May 23, 1910. Pks. Dpt. *AR* [1909], 25. On persistence of carriage parade in early twentieth century, see, e.g., James H. Tuckerman, "Park Driving," *Outing* 66 (June 1905): 259–66.

64. *NYT*, Oct. 22, 1909, Feb. 19 (auto row), Mar. 5 (test drives), June 22 (asphalting), 1911, Apr. 3, 1924 (country); Pks. Dpt. *AR* [1913], 5 (asphalt); *AR* [1916], 11 (speed limit); Edward S. Martin, "A Philosopher in Central Park," *HM* (Feb. 1914): 355–56.

65. Martin, "Philosopher in Central Park," 356. On women and tearooms, see Leach, "Transformation," 326–38.

66. FLO, Jr., to Adams, Apr. 26, 1926, OA Mss (traffic figures); *NYT*, Mar. 5, 1922 (lampposts); Hanmer, *Public Recreation*, 151. On increase in car ownership, see Robert A. Caro, *The Power Broker: Robert Moses and the Fall of New York* (1974), 144.

67. *NYT*, Feb. 3, 1924, Apr. 1, 1932. On car ban, see, e.g., *NYT*, Feb. 2, Apr. 3, 6, Nov. 16, 19, Dec. 14, 1924, Mar. 29, 1926, Jan. 7, 1927, June 19, 1927; *News*, Nov. 18, Dec. 1, 1924. On proposal for winding drives and lowering speed limit as well as widening Fifth and Eighth avenues, *NYT*, Sept. 22, 1931; on widening adjacent avenues by removing sidewalk on park side, *News*, Dec. 12, 1924; *NYT*, Dec. 27, 29, 1924, Apr. 9, 1926.

68. Walter Laidlaw, *Population of the City of New York, 1890–1930* (1932), 202, 233; Thomas Adams, Harold M. Lewis, and Theodore T. McCrosky, *Population, Land Values, and Government* (1929), 91.

69. Neil Harris, "Urban Tourism and the Commercial City," in *Inventing Times Square: Commerce and Culture at the Crossroads of the World*, ed. William R. Taylor (1991), 66–82; Sidney Skolsky, "Behind the News," *News*, May 20, 1933.

70. Hanmer, *Public Recreation*, 16. The population of Manhattan above 40th Street was 1,321,630 in 1930; it continued to grow over the next twenty years (to 1,391,199 in 1940 and 1,451,499 in 1950) before beginning to decline. These figures are calculated from the census tracts that roughly correspond to the 19th-century wards 12, 19, and 22. Census tract data are derived from Laidlaw, *Population*, and from U.S. Bureau of the Census, decennial censuses.

71. Chase, *New York, 1932*, 12.

72. Osofsky, *Harlem*, chaps. 5 and 6; *WPA Guide*, 256–57; Jeffrey S. Gurock, *When Harlem Was Jewish, 1870–1930* (1979), chap. 1–2. See also *WPA Guide*, 253, 268–69.

73. By 1930 Harlem had only 5,000 Jews but 165,000 African Americans, almost three-quarters of all black Manhattanites. See Osofsky, *Harlem*, 85, 92–149; Gurock, *When Harlem Was Jewish*, 137–57. Immigrants from the Caribbean may have constituted almost one-quarter of Harlem's black population.

74. Virginia E. Sánchez Korrol, *From Colonia to Community: The History of Puerto Ricans in New York City, 1917–1948* (Westport, Conn., 1983), 52–84. See also Lawrence R. Chenault, *The Puerto Rican Migrant in New York City* (1938).

75. *WPA Guide*, 265–68; U.S. Bureau of the Census, *Sixteenth Census, 1940: Population and Housing: Statistics for Health Areas: New York City* (Washington, D.C., 1942), 11–12.

76. Ibid., 130, 144; Craig Mitchell, "I Remember Fifth," *Town and Country* (Sept. 1989): 230. Lower Fifth is defined here as the "Health Area" running east from the park to Third Avenue and from 63rd to 77th streets.

77. These figures compare the Lower Fifth Avenue Health Area defined in text, Health Area 37 (79th–89th streets and First to Third avenues), and Health Area 40 (62nd to 74th streets and Central Park West to Amsterdam Avenue); *Sixteenth Census, 1940: Health Areas*, 129–30, 144. On Yorkville, see *WPA Guide*, 243–52; on Middle West Side, Otto G. Cartwright, *The Middle West Side: A Historical Sketch* (1914).

78. On bird watching, see, e.g., *NYT*, Apr. 19, 1885, Oct. 28, 1897; *World*, July 11, 1886; *Her.*, May 5, 1895; Pks. Dpt. *AR* [1903], 43; Agnes C. Stewart, "Paper-Bag People in Central Park," *Ladies Home Journal*, May 7, 1907, 57; *NYT*, May 29, 1927, Apr. 4, 1934; James Sheldon to George Woolsey, Jan. 24, 1931, B 12, RW Mss., NYPL. On interest in nature studies, see Pks. Dpt. *AR* [1902], 43; Louis H. Peets, *Trees and Shrubs of Central Park* (1903), directed at the "nontechnical city nature lover." On horseback riding, see, e.g., *NYT*, Sept. 30, 1934. On enthusiasm for nature in Progressive era, see David E. Shi, *The Simple Life: Plain Living and High Thinking in American Culture* (1985), 201–14. On fishing in the park, see *The Anglers' Club Story: Our First Fifty Years, 1906–1956* (1956), 17–18; *NYT*, Aug. 18, 1932; Scott Cohen, "A Fin's Notes: Fishing in Central Park," *VV*, Aug. 18, 1975, 84–85. As early as 1883 the park board had permitted an angler's tournament on the Harlem Meer: BDPP *Min.* Oct. 3, 1883. Skating championships on the Conservatory Water similarly drew crowds of up to 20,000 in the 1920s. See *Rebuilding CP: Draft*, 75.

79. George Austin Chauncey, Jr., "Gay New York: Urban Culture and the Making of a Gay Male World, 1890–1940" (Ph.d. diss., Yale University, 1989), 130–32.

80. *NYT*, May 28, 1909; *News*, Mar. 3, 1921.

81. *American*, June 11, 1905; *NYT*, Oct. 7, 1929; Investigator's Report, Aug. 27, 1920, Papers of the Committee of Fourteen, NYC, B 34, "1920" Folder, NYPL (reference courtesy of George Chauncey, Jr.). On Caruso, see, e.g., *NYT*, Nov. 17–19, 24, 26, Dec. 3, 1908, Jan. 7, 1909. There is some evidence that the singer may have been falsely accused: Michael Scott, *The Great Caruso* (1988), 93–96.

82. Dorothy Reed, *Leisure Time of Girls in a "Little Italy"* (Portland, Ore., 1932), 44–45, 51, 54–55.

83. Henry James, *The American Scene* (1907; rpt. 1946), 117–18, 174–77.

84. Howe, *World of Our Fathers*, 212; Joan Morrison and Charlotte Fox Zabusky, *American Mosaic: The Immigrant Experience in the Words of Those Who Lived It* (1980), 11; Valenti quoted in Elizabeth Ewen, *Immigrant Women in the Land of Dollars: Life and Culture on the Lower East Side, 1890–1925* (1985), 214–15. The names used in this and other oral histories quoted from Ewen are fictitious because of the conditions under which those interviews were deposited at the Tamiment Library, New York University.

85. *NYT*, May 21, 1914, June 30, 1913.

86. *NYT*, Dec. 29, 1921, Nov. 2, 1927, Feb. 15, Dec. 9, 1928; Allyn R. Jennings, "Feeding the Central Park Public," *LA* 26 (Apr. 1936): 112–13; *NYT*, June 9, 1928.

87. *NYT*, Apr. 15, Nov. 2, 1902 (litter), Nov. 7, 1927 (peanuts). See also Mary Ellen W. Hern, "Feast and Festivity: The Picnic Meal, 1840–1900," paper presented to American Studies Association, New York City, Nov. 24, 1987, copy in possession of authors.

88. Pks. Dpt. *AR* [1916], 74; *NYT*, Aug. 24, 1919.

89. On arrests and crackdowns, see *NYT*, June 2, 1908, Aug. 24, 1919 (Bolshevik); *Brooklyn Daily Times*, June 29, 1908; *New York Call*, July 16, 1908; Howe, *World of Our Fathers*, 212. On Manhattan magistrates, see *NYT*, June 30, 1913, Oct. 4, 1927, Apr. 4, 25, 1931; on signs and fliers, *NYT*, June 8, 1926, May 19, 1913.

90. For examples of epithets of "vandals" and "savages," see, e.g., *NYT*, May 19, 1913; Apr. 29,

1925. See also *Trib.*, May 24, 1873; *NYT*, Aug. 11, 1909; Christopher Stone, "Vandalism: Property, Gentility, and the Rhetoric of Crime in New York City, 1890–1920," *Radical History Review*, no. 26 (Oct. 1982): 13–34.

91. On park in crisis, see, e.g., *World*, June 1, 1902; *NYT*, Sept. 1, 1907; Max Schling and Wm. J. Pedrick to Board of Estimate and Apportionment, Mar. 26, 1926, Olmsted Brothers to Roulstone, July 6, 1926, both in OA Mss. For attendance estimates, see *NYT*, Mar. 5, 1914, Apr. 6, 1924, May 7, 1938; *Sun*, Apr. 27, 1919; *Mail*, Aug. 6, 1917; Eugene Kinkead and Russell Maloney, "Central Park III: What a *Nice* Municipal Park!" *NYer*, Sept. 27, 1941, 26.

92. See *NYT*, June 5, 1921, which notes decline since 1870 of carriages and skating. On urbanization and rising temperatures, see H. H. Lamb, *Climate: Present, Past, and Future* (London, 1972), 515, 517. For impact of paved streets on soils, see ASHPS *27AR* [1922], 81–82. On electric lights, see Pks. Dpt. *AR* [1908], 262; *AR* [1909], 25; *NYT*, Nov. 12, 1909; on new comfort stations, see, e.g., Pks. Dpt. *AR* [1902], 19–20.

93. On fiscal crisis, see David Hammack, "Social Instability and State Power: The Limits of Politics in New York City, 1880–1940," paper presented at Conference on the Comparative History of Budapest and New York, Budapest, Aug. 1988. Budget figures from Board of Estimate *Mins.* and Pks. Dpt. *AR*s; 7% based on calculations from Pks. Dpt. *AR* [1916], 126–39, 222–23, 264, 279.

94. *NYT*, Feb. 26, 1911 (grass), Nov. 2, 1918 (rhododendrons), June 30, 1922, Aug. 14, 1927 (trees); *World*, Jan. 27, 1920.

95. Merkel, *Report*, 4–5, 7.

96. FLO to Waldo Hutchins, Mar. 18, 1890, *FYLA*, 499.

97. *Mail*, Aug. 20, 1917; *NYT*, Dec. 9, 1928.

15. Will They Ever Drain the Reservoir? Modernizing the Park

1. *NYT*, Jan. 10, 1910; James K. Paulding, *Charles B. Stover, July 14, 1861–April 24, 1929: His Life and Personality* (1938), 21, 106, 139. See also A. J. Kennedy's "Biographical Notes" in the Stover Papers [hereafter Stover Mss.], State Historical Society of Wisconsin, Madison (available on microfilm); Allen F. Davis, *Spearheads for Reform: The Social Settlements and the Progressive Movement, 1890–1914* (1967), 9; Henry P. Kraus, *The Settlement Movement in New York City, 1886–1914* (1980), 59–60; *NYT*, Apr. 26, 1929.

2. Paulding, *Stover* (1938), 9–21.

3. Simkhovitch quoted in Kennedy, "Biographical Notes;" Paulding, *Stover*, 20, 22, 45–6, 139–40. See also Papers of the Outdoor Recreation League in Stover Mss. On early playgrounds, see Richard F. Knapp, "Parks and Politics: The Rise of Municipal Responsibility for Playgrounds in New York City, 1887–1905" (M.A. Thesis, Duke University, 1968).

4. *World*, Jan. 15, 1910; *Her.*, Jan. 20, 1910; *NYT*, Jan. 20, 25, 30, 1910.

5. On clash with Parsons and his firing, see *NYT*, July 3, 1910, Apr. 1–7, May 11–14, 16, 19, 1911; Raymond G. Fosdick, *Report on the Office of the Landscape Architect of the Park Department* (1911). The soil company's officers financed and helped write Parsons's book recommending its humus as best for Central Park: Parsons, *Landscape Gardening Studies* (1910). On press criticism, see Paulding, *Stover*, 78–81; on Stover's disappearance, *NYT*, Nov. 14, 18–20, 29, 30, 1913, Jan. 29, 1914, Apr. 26, 1929; Paulding, *Stover*, 85–86.

6. *NYT*, June 2, 10, July 4 (northern end) 1910. For Stover's views and opposition to him, see *NYT*, May 20, 21, July 1, 3, 4, 1910; *Her.*, May 20, 1910; *World*, July 2, 1910. For Crimmins's proposal, see *NYT*, Jan. 25, 1903, June 13, 27, 1903; Thomas Crimmins, ed., *The Diary of John D. Crimmins from 1878 to 1917* (1925), 499, 505, 507, 524. Even Olmsted—who had never liked the Lower Reservoir—proposed covering it over as part of a plan for holding the 1892 World's Fair in New York: *NYT*, Sept. 26, 1889.

7. *NYT*, Mar. 10, 1912.

8. On the City Beautiful in New York, see Harvey A. Kantor, "Modern Urban Planning in New York City: Origins and Evolution, 1890–1933" (Ph.D. diss., New York University, 1971), chap. 3;

Michele H. Bogart, *Public Sculpture and the Civic Ideal in New York City, 1890–1930* (Chicago, 1989), 56–59. On City Beautiful, in general, see William H. Wilson, *The City Beautiful Movement* (Baltimore, 1989); M. Christine Boyer, *Dreaming of the Rational City* (Cambridge, Mass., 1983), 43–56; Jon A. Peterson, "The City Beautiful Movement: Forgotten Origins, Lost Meanings," *Journal of Urban History* 2 (Aug. 1976): 415–34; Daniel M. Bluestone, "Detroit's City Beautiful and the Problem of Commerce," *Journal of the Society of Architectural Historians* 47 (Sept. 1988): 245–62.

9. Mardges Bacon, *Ernest Flagg: Beaux-Arts Architect and Urban Reformer* (1986), 223–24; Ernest Flagg, "The Plan of New York and How to Improve It," *Scribner's Magazine* (Aug. 1904): 253–56; Elbert Peets, "Central Park," *American Mercury* (Mar. 1925): 339–41.

10. On Pulitzer Fountain, see Bogart, *Public Sculpture*, 208; on Lenox Library, *NYT*, June 8, 1912; on paths, *NYT*, Feb. 26, 1911, Mar. 5, June 5, 1912.

11. *NYT*, Mar. 10, 13, 20, 1912.

12. On Hastings, see Curtis Channing Blake, "The Architecture of Carrère and Hastings" (Ph.D. diss., Columbia University, 1976); Bacon, *Flagg*, 53–61; *DAB*; Wayne Andrews, *Architecture, Ambition, and Americans: A Social History of American Architecture* (rev. ed., 1978), 188–90; David Gray, *Thomas Hastings, Architect: Collected Writings, Together with a Memoir* (Boston, 1932). The Union Theological connection may explain the apparent friendship between Hastings and Stover. See *NYT*, June 23, 29, 1912.

13. Gray, *Hastings*, 250. See also "Memorial to New York's New Water System in Central Park—A Great Sunken Garden," *Journal of the American Institute of Architects* 5 (July 1917): 399–400; *NYT*, July 20, 1917; Rebecca Read Shanor, *The City That Never Was* (1988), 210–12.

14. Thomas Hastings to FLO, Jr., Sept. 18, 1917, OA Mss.; *NYT*, July 22, 1917.

15. On McAneny and city planning, see Kantor, "Modern Urban Planning," chap. 4.

16. Gray, *Hastings*, 248; Hastings to Henry F. Osborn, Oct. 3, 1917, F 586d, AMNH Mss. On Osborn, see *DAB*; John M. Kennedy, "Philanthropy and Science in New York City: The American Museum of Natural History, 1868–1986" (Ph.D. diss., Yale University, 1968), 125–32, 156–224; Geoffrey Hellman, *Bankers, Bones, and Beetles: The First Century of the American Museum of Natural History* (Garden City, N.Y., 1969), chaps. 4, 7. On Osborn's early interest in the promenade, see Osborn to Grover A. Whalen, Feb. 20, 1924, F 959, Osborn, "Progress Report: Subject—Intermuseum Pathway," ca. Apr. 1926, F 1181.1, Osborn to Walter Herrick, Jan. 20, 1930, all in AMNH Archives (hereafter AMNH Mss.). We infer Osborn's role in persuading Hastings to modify the plan from the fact that earliest plans don't seem to emphasize the museum connector but that later ones do. Compare, for example, "Memorial to New York's New Water System" with "A Plan for the Lower Reservoir in Central Park, 1918," in Gray, *Hastings*, 247–51.

17. Osborn to Cass Gilbert, Feb. 26, 1917, F 586d, Osborn to John H. Finley, Jan. 23, 1930, F 1181.1, Osborn to John Sheehy, Aug. 4, 1933, F 1181.1, AMNH Mss.

18. *Mail*, Aug. 15, 1917. On McAneny, see *DAB*.

19. *Mail*, July 22 (plaything), 26 (Drescher), 31 (Bronx alderman), Aug. 8 (Farley and Conway), July 31, 1917.

20. *Mail*, Nov. 14, 1917. For Ward's support of City Beautiful goals, see, e.g, Pks. Dpt. *AR* [1916], 15–17, 27–34.

21. *NYT*, May 29, 1919; Hastings to FLO, Jr., Mar. 19, 1920, OA Mss. We have not located Hastings's plans for the Mitchel memorial; the connection to the earlier plan is inferred from the descriptions. For a similar conclusion, see Blake, "Hastings," 304. Around 1926 a gilded bronze bust of Mitchel (with an elaborate architectural setting designed by Hastings and Don Barber) was placed on the edge of Central Park at 90th Street and Fifth Avenue: Margot Gayle and Michele Cohen, *The Art Commission and Municipal Art Society Guide to Manhattan's Outdoor Sculpture* (1988), 229.

22. Hastings to FLO, Jr., Mar. 22, 1920, OA Mss.; Gray, *Hastings*, 68.

23. *Her.*, Apr. 29, 1900. See also Kantor, "Modern Urban Planning," 62–63.

24. *NYT*, June 24, 1922. See also Hastings to Osborn, Dec. 5, 6, 1923, Francis Gallatin to Henry Marshall, Dec. 5, 1923, Notes from Conference with Thomas Hastings, in the Office of President Osborn, Dec. 10, 1923, Osborn to Robert W. De Forest, Dec. 15, 1923, all in F 586r, AMNH Mss. The swimming pool and track were later dropped but the playgrounds remained:

Bogart, *Public Sculpture*, 287–88. For other World War I memorial designs, see *News*, Feb. 17, 1920.

25. *Mail*, Aug. 3, 1917; Osborn to Hastings, Dec. 4, 1923, F 586r, AMNH Mss.

26. This and the next paragraph draw heavily on the analysis in David Hammack, "Social Instability and State Power: The Limits of Politics in New York City, 1880–1940," paper presented at Conference on the Comparative History of Budapest and New York, Budapest, Aug. 1988. On Hylan, see W. Roger Biles, "Hylan, John F." in *Biographical Dictionary of American Mayors, 1820–1980: Big City Mayors*, ed. Melvin Holli and Peter d'A. Jones (Westport, Conn., 1981), 176; W. A. Swanberg, *Citizen Hearst: A Biography of William Randolph Hearst* (1961; rpt. New York, 1986), 366–70; Kantor, "Modern Urban Planning," 308–9. On spending by Low, see Kenneth Howard Finegold, "Progressivism, Electoral Change, and Public Policy: Reform Outcomes in New York, Cleveland, and Chicago" (Ph.D. diss., Harvard University, 1985), 68.

27. For voting analysis, see Finegold, "Progressivism," 77–101. Smith later retreated from this stance, and Robert Wagner became the prototypical "urban liberal." On urban populism, progressivism, and liberalism in this period generally, see, Finegold, 52–133; Thomas M. Henderson, *Tammany Hall and the New Immigrants: The Progressive Years* (1976); John D. Buenker, *Urban Liberalism and Progressive Reform* (1973); J. Joseph Huthmacher, *Senator Robert F. Wagner and the Rise of Urban Liberalism* (1968).

28. Finegold, "Progressivism," 101–27; W. Roger Biles, "Mitchel, John Purroy," in *Biographical Dictionary*, ed. Holli and Jones, 256–57.

29. For a useful summary of different progressive impulses, see Arthur S. Link and Richard L. McCormick, *Progressivism* (Arlington Heights, Ill., 1983), chap. 3.

30. George Esdras Bevans, *How Workingmen Spend Their Spare Time* (1913), 86–87; Charles B. Stover, "Playground Progress in Seward Park," *Charities* 6 (May 4, 1901): 393, copy in Stover Mss. See also David Scobey, "The Streets and the Social Order: The Class Politics of City-Building in Late Nineteenth-Century New York," paper presented at Conference on the Comparative History of Budapest and New York, Budapest, Aug. 1988.

31. *NYT*, Apr. 17, 1913 (emphasis added), Apr. 19, 1909. Cf. *Mail*, July 22, 1917.

32. *NYT*, July 4, 1910. See also *NYT*, Mar. 8, 1911.

33. Quoted in Robert A. Caro, *The Power Broker: Robert Moses and the Fall of New York* (1974), 169. Annual budget figures from Board of Estimate *Minutes* and Pks. Dpt. *Annual Reports*.

34. *News*, Oct. 29, 1924, Nov. 15, 1921, and see Mar. 15, 1924, May 4, 1927.

35. *News*, July 25, 1927. For different proposals, see, e.g., *News*, Dec. 3, 1925, Dec. 31, 1926, Jan. 8, 1927, Nov. 24, 1928, Apr. 15, 1929.

36. For publicity stunts, see *News*, June 12–15, 17–20, July 4, 9, 12, 22–24, 1928, Aug. 2, 1929. For inquiring photographer, see June 23, 1930, Feb. 12, 16, 23, 1931.

37. *News*, July 14, 1930.

38. For approval, see *NYT*, July 20, 1922, Apr. 12, 1924, Nov. 19, 1925; Board of Estimate and Apportionment *Min.*, July 19, 1922, Apr. 11, 1924; *News*, Apr. 11, 1924. Even the *News* turned against the war memorial in part out of its growing disillusionment with Hylan. Almost immediately after Walker was elected, the *News* reversed course and reaffirmed its support. See Apr. 4, 1924, Nov. 27, 1925. For the view of the memorial as "Hylan's scheme," see, e.g., *NYT*, Nov. 21, 1925, Mar. 11, 15, 1926. The art center did not have the clear-cut populist appeal that the war memorial offered, because of its wealthy backers. But what the *News* derided as "the exclusive art center," the *American* celebrated as "the People's Art Centre." Compare *News* Mar. 14, 21, Apr. 7, 14, 16, 1924 with *American*, Mar. 12, 14, 1924. For other coverage of the art center controversy, see, e.g., *NYT*, Dec. 9, 24, 1923, Jan. 14, 25, 27, Mar. 23, 30, Apr. 1, 10, 11, 15, 17, 1924; *World*, Mar. 8, 11, 14, 19, 23, 27, Apr. 2, 6, 1924; *Age*, Mar. 22, 1924; "The Art 'Raid' on Central Park," *Literary Digest*, Mar. 29, 1924, 29; *Greater New York* (publication of the Merchants' Association of New York), Mar. 17, 31, 1924; ASHPS *29AR* [1924], 25–29.

39. For goals of CPA, see *Central Park Association Incorporated*, pamphlet in OA Mss.; CPA, *The Central Park* (1926). On board's reversal, see *NYT*, Nov. 19, 21, 1925; *World*, Nov. 21, 1925. The board's preliminary step of approving the long-delayed payment of Hastings's $45,000 fee was understood as a go-ahead.

40. *NYT*, May 17, 1928.

41. For "crusade," see *NYT*, Jan. 12, 1926. The following discussion is based on biographical

information on 20 of the 21 CPA directors as found in the *DAB, NCAB, Who Was Who in America,* and *Times* obituaries. The directors are listed in CPA, *The Central Park,* 81.

42. Rollin Saltus to FLO, Jr., June 15, 1912, OA Mss.; *NYT,* June 22, 1912. On ASLA, Norman T. Newton, *Design on the Land: The Development of Landscape Architecture* (Cambridge, Mass., 1971), 385–92; Bremer W. Pond, "Fifty Years in Retrospect: Brief Account of the Origin and Development of the ASLA," *LA* 40 (Jan. 1950): 59–66. The one woman founder, Beatrix Cadwalader Jones (later Farrand), offspring of *the* Jones family and a leading landscape architect of her day, also had a connection to Central Park—or really Jones Wood. Another prominent New York landscape architect was Carl Pilat, nephew of Ignaz Pilat. On tensions with Hastings and architects, see also Saltus to Percival Gallagher, June 13, 1912, FLO, Jr., to Saltus, June 25, 1912; Saltus to FLO, Jr., June 27, 1912, OA Mss.; Harold A. Caparn, "Central Park, New York: A Work of Art," *LA* 2 (1911–12): 171–74.

43. Hastings to FLO, Jr., Sept. 18, 1917, Charles Downing Lay to FLO, Jr., Mar. 22, 1920, Saltus to FLO, Jr., Apr. 12, 1927, OA Mss. Lay was quoted in *H-T,* ca. Apr. 12, 1927, copy in OA Mss.

44. FLO, Jr., to Ferruccio Vitale, May 17, 1927, OA Mss. His father had talked of his reputation in landscape architecture as an "inheritance" that he could offer to Olmsted, Jr. See Laura Wood Roper, *FLO: A Biography of Frederick Law Olmsted* (Baltimore, 1973), 461. On the older Olmsted's renaming of his son (around age seven or eight) from Henry Perkins Olmsted to Frederick Law Olmsted, Jr., and on his expectations of his son's carrying on his legacy, see Melvin Kalfus, *Frederick Law Olmsted: The Passion of a Public Artist* (1990), 81–86. On FLO, Jr., see Sherry Page Berg, "Frederick Law Olmsted, Jr." in *American Landscape Architecture: Designers and Places,* ed. William H. Tishler (Washington, D.C., 1989), 60–65; Edward Clark Whiting and William Lyman Phillips, "Frederick Law Olmsted, 1870–1957: An Appreciation of the Man and His Achievements," *LA* 48 (Apr. 1958): 145–51.

45. Olmsted Brothers to William B. Roulstone, July 6, 1926, and see Roulstone to Olmsted Brothers, Apr. 9, 1926, OA Mss.

46. Olmsted Brothers to Roulstone, July 6, 1926. On Vaux's effort to persuade Olmsted, see CV to FLO, May 5, 1865, *FLOP* 5:363. Max Schling and Wm. J. Pedrick (of FAA) to Board of Estimate and Apportionment, Mar. 26, 1926, OA Mss.

47. Schling and Pedrick to Board of Estimate, Mar. 26, 1926.

48. *NYT,* Apr. 30, 1933.

49. Kantor, "Modern Urban Planning," 176–78; Fifth Avenue Association, *Fifty Years on Fifth, 1907–1957* (1957), 36. On early zoning, see also Mel Scott, *American City Planning Since 1890* (Berkeley, 1969), 153–60; Stanislaw J. Makielski, *The Politics of Zoning: The New York Experience* (1966), 11–40. On FAA's concerns with upper Fifth Avenue, see, e.g., *Avenue* (June 1919).

50. *Fifty Years on Fifth,* 36; *NYT,* July 15, 1922. See also *Avenue* (Apr. 1925); *NYT,* Apr. 28, 1925. For the association's lobbying, see *NYT,* Mar. 26, Oct. 3, 1926, Mar. 28, 1927; Schling and Pedrick to Board of Estimate, Mar. 26, 1926.

51. Schling and Pedrick to Board of Estimate, Mar. 26, 1926; Pedrick quoted in *Sun,* Apr. 15, 1927, typed copy in OA Mss. See also *NYT,* Apr. 15, 1927. Cf. the plan drawn up for the CPA by Olmsted Brothers in Olmsted Brothers to Roulstone, July 6, 1926. On tensions between the two groups, see, for example, Gallagher to A. A. Shurtleff, May 9, 1927, OA Mss.; and letter to Harold B. Stokes, July 3, 1928, B 5, Parks Council Papers, Avery Library, Columbia University, New York.

52. FLO, Jr., to Henry V. Hubbard, Apr. 6, 1926, OA Mss.; Richard Welling to Charles W. Gould, May 17, 1928, Box 32, RW Mss. On the preservationists' conflicts with the planners, see also Gallagher to FLO, Jr., Mar. 31, 1926, OA Mss.; Welling to Mrs. Arthur Hays Sulzberger, Feb. 5, 1930, B 32, RW Mss.

53. Welling to Osborn, May 16, 1928, Osborn to Welling, May 17, 1928, Osborn to George McAneny, Apr. 6, 1933, F 1181.1, AMNH Mss. On Osborn and Welling's friendship, see Robert H. Muccigrosso, "Richard W. G. Welling: A Reformer's Life" (Ph.D. diss., Columbia University, 1966), 9. This was not the only clash between Osborn and wealthy German Jews. In 1923 Jewish banker and museum trustee Felix Warburg had attacked as "scandalous" Osborn's cautiously approving introduction to *The Passing of the Great Race,* the racist and anti-Semitic tract by fellow museum trustee Madison Grant. See Kennedy, "Science and Philanthropy," 207–9; Hellman, *Bankers,* 195–96, 205.

54. *Mail*, Aug. 15, 1917; Richard Welling, *As the Twig Is Bent* (1942), 18–19; Welling to Walter Herrick, Apr. 30, May 21, 1930, B 12, RW Mss.; poem in *NYT*, May 13, 1933. Cf. letter to the *Globe*, Mar. 20, 1909; and Arthur Guiterman, "Central Park" *Literary Digest*, Jan. 9, 1926, 32.

55. Susan W. Dryfoos, *Iphigene: My Life and the "New York Times": The Memoirs of Iphigene Ochs Sulzberger* (1981), 29, 34, 36; *NYT*, Jan. 19, 1934, Feb. 27, 1990 (quot.).

56. On Hodgdon, see *NCAB* (under Frederick Hodgdon); on Matthews, *NYT*, Oct. 25, 1959; on Simkhovitch, *DAB;* on Parsons, *NYT*, Jan. 20, 1964; on Moskowitz, Elisabeth Isreals Perry, *Belle Moskowitz: Feminine Politics and the Exercise of Power in the Age of Alfred E. Smith* (1987).

57. Caro, *Power Broker*, 32–33; *News*, July 1, 1930.

58. Muccigrosso, "Welling," 16; Welling to James Sheldon, Feb. 2, 1931, Welling to Nathan Straus, Jr., July 8, 1932, B 12, RW Mss.

59. See Michael Wallace, "Reflections on the History of Historic Preservation," in *Presenting the Past: Essays on History and the Public*, ed. Susan Porter Benson, Stephen Brier, and Roy Rosenzweig (Philadelphia, 1986), 168–73. On ASHPS, see *9AR* [1904], 14–24; Charles B. Hosmer, Jr., *Presence of the Past: A History of the Preservation Movement in the United States before Williamsburg* (1965), 93–101.

60. Welling, "The Central Park Speedway," typed memo, ca. 1945, Welling to Iphigene Sulzberger, June 3, 1938, both in B 12, RW Mss.

61. Samuel H. Ordway, Jr., to Welling, Feb. 8, 1930, B 12, RW Mss. See also Ordway to Welling, Feb. 6, 1930, Welling to Ordway, Feb. 7, 1930, ibid. On racetrack as grab by special interest, see, e.g., *World*, Mar. 24, 1892. On park sacredness, see *World*, Apr. 2, 1909; *NYT*, Mar. 30, 1909.

62. Albert Bard to Joseph Howland Hunt, May 9, 1922, B 19, Bard Papers, NYPL; FLO, Jr., to Hunt, May 23, 1922, OA Mss. On Olmsted, Jr.'s, early interest in publishing his father's papers, see FLO, Jr., to George H. Putnam, May 16, 1913, OA Mss. On Van Ingen as authority on park history, see, e.g., *NYT*, Mar. 20, June 2, 17, 1912, Jan. 12, 1916, Jan 5, 1920, Mar. 16, 1924; *Mail*, Aug. 15, 1917. Another preservationist, Edward Hagaman Hall, published the first detailed history of the park in the annual report of the ASHPS, which he ran: Hall, "Central Park in the City of New York," ASHPS *16AR* [1911], 379–489.

63. On Hubbard and Kimball, see Kenneth I. Helphand, "Henry Vincent Hubbard," in *American Landscape Architecture*, ed. Tishler, 66–69; on publication of fragment, Putnam to FLO, Jr., July 8, 1913, OA Mss.

64. The story of the funding of the papers project can be traced in correspondence among Bard, Hunt, I. N. Phelps Stokes, De Forest, Olmsted, Jr., Thomas Adams, and Charles D. Norton in B 19, Bard Papers and F 252, B 32, Russell Sage Foundation Papers, Rockefeller Archives Center, North Tarrytown, N.Y. On Stokes and plan, see FLO, Jr., to Putnam, May 16, 1913. On Stokes and the Minturns, *NYT*, Mar. 17, 1918. For the published papers, see Frederick Law Olmsted, Jr., and Theodora Kimball, *Frederick Law Olmsted: Landscape Architect, 1822–1903: Forty Years of Landscape Architecture; Being the Professional Papers of Frederick Law Olmsted, Senior* (1922, 1928; rpt. 1970).

65. See note signed "TK" on CV to FLO, Feb. 5, 1864, FLO Mss. For acknowledgment, see *FYLA*, v, vii. On Vaux family assistance, see FLO, Jr., to C. Bowyer Vaux, Feb. 1, Mar. 1, 1921, Vaux to FLO, Jr., Mar. 1, 3, 1921, and Clippings File, all in Calvert Vaux Papers, NYPL. For two different examples of how early readers of the volume focused on Olmsted, see Abby A. Rockefeller to Moses, Sept. 11, 1935, B 97, Moses Papers, NYPL; Lewis Mumford, *The Brown Decades: A Study of the Arts in America, 1865–1895* (1931; rpt. 1971), 37–39, 118. Vaux's son Downing also became a landscape architect, but ill health forced him to retire early: Newton, *Design*, 391; *Her.*, Nov. 22, 1895. Bowyer Vaux wrote a short biographical article on his father, but in general the sons seem to have partaken of their father's modesty: "Calvert Vaux, Designer of Parks," *Parks International* 1 (Sept. 1920): 138–43.

66. See *News*, Jan. 29, 1928 (on initial appropriation of $871,000). On Walker parks program, see Judith Anne Davidson, "The Federal Government and the Democratization of Public Recreational Sport: New York City, 1933–1943" (Ph.D. diss., University of Massachusetts, 1983), 46–62; *NYT*, June 14, 18, 1926, Oct. 1, Mar. 30, 31, Apr. 4, 1928, Apr. 13, Oct. 8, 9, 1930.

67. Davidson, "Federal Government," 79–90; *NYT*, May 12, 1931; Gallagher to Shurtleff, May 9, 1927 (on firing Gallatin); Straus to Walter Herrick, June 11, 1928, B 12, RW Mss. For praise of the state of the park, see, e.g., *NYT*, Apr. 12, 1930, Jan. 18, 1931.

68. For *News* lobbying, see note 36 herein; for Osborn, see, e.g., Osborn to *H-T* editors, Sept. 20, 1929, Osborn to James Walker, Jan 20, 1930, F 1181.1, AMNH Mss.; *NYT,* Oct. 24, 1929, Apr. 11, 12, 18, 22, 1930. For earlier proposals for meadow, see, e.g., Lay to Bard, July 31, 1916, B 19, Bard Papers; Lay to FLO, Jr., Dec. 19, 1919, Mar. 22, 1930, OA Mss. For ASLA plan, see "Report to Accompany Plan of Development for the Lower Reservoir Site in Central Park," Apr. 22, 1930, F 1118.1, AMNH Mss.; *NYT,* Apr. 22, 23, June 3, 1930.

69. On Straus, see Nathan Straus, "The Reminiscences of Nathan Straus" (transcript of an interview conducted by O. Bombard for the Oral History Research Office of Columbia University, 1950), 60–61 and passim. On park activists and Walker, see Gallagher to Shurtleff, May 9, 1927; *NYT,* Oct. 17, 31, 1929. For Straus on the Casino, see *H-T,* Dec. 2, 4, 5, 1928; *Post, Sun,* Dec. 5, 1928; and on Walker, *NYT,* Jan. 12, 1926, Apr. 15, 1927.

70. On *Times* and park activism, see, e.g., Straus, "Reminiscences," 63; letter to Stokes, July 3, 1928; letters (June 15, 25, July 23, 1926, Dec. 20, 30, 1927) between CPA and *Times* editor John Finley in B 74, Finley Papers, NYPL. See *NYT,* Nov. 2, 1925 on impact of lobbying on board of estimate.

71. Gene Fowler, *Beau James: The Life and Times of Jimmy Walker* (1949; rpt. Clifton, N.J., 1973), 247.

72. See, e.g, *NYT,* July 20, Sept. 29, 1922.

73. For uses and versions of the map, see, e.g., *NYT,* Mar. 16, 1924, *News,* Mar. 30, 1924; "Saving the Parks for their Proper Purposes," *American City Magazine* 31 (Aug. 1924): 93; *FYLA,* 517; Henry Hope Reed and Sophia Duckworth, *Central Park: A History and a Guide* (1967; rpt. 1972), 42–43; *Rebuilding CP,* 6. For invocations of Coney Island, see, e.g., *NYT,* July 3, 1910.

16. Robert Moses and a New Deal

1. *NYT,* Jan. 23, 24, Apr. 12, 22, June 3, 1930.

2. *News,* July 5, 21, 1930; Roy Rosenzweig, "Organizing the Unemployed: The Early Years of the Great Depression, 1929–1933," *Radical America* 10 (July–Aug. 1976): 41, 57 n. 19; *NYT,* Apr. 4, 1933, Mar. 12, 1932. A delay caused by the shift to the ASLA plan, which altered the grade and triggered a dispute with the contractor, was not resolved until early 1931. See *NYT,* Feb. 24, 1931. The *News* protests may have also slowed the project. See *NYT,* Jan. 7, 1931.

3. *NYT, H-T,* Dec. 15, 1930; *News,* Dec. 16, 1930.

4. *NYT,* July 25, 1931; Robert Nathan, *One More Spring* (1933).

5. *NYT,* Dec. 12, 13, 1931; *News,* Dec. 14, 1931.

6. *Jour.,* Sept. 22, 1932. See also *NYT,* Sept. 22, 25, 1932.

7. *NYT,* Oct. 4, 1932; *W-T,* Mar. 30, 1933; *News, Jour., H-T.,* Sept. 22, 1932. See also *NYT,* Sept. 24, 25, 27, 1932; *News,* Sept. 23, 24, 26, 1932; *W-T,* Sept. 22, 24, 1932; *Jour., H-T.,* Sept. 23, 1932.

8. Joan Crouse, *The Homeless Transient in the Great Depression: New York State, 1929–1941* (Albany, 1986), 48, 71–73, 100–103; *NYT,* Mar. 26, 1933 (quots.); *News,* Sept. 24, 1932.

9. *NYT,* Apr. 3, 4, 6, 1933. Joseph V. McKee, president of the board of aldermen, served as acting mayor after Walker resigned in late 1932; O'Brien, running as the regular Democratic party candidate, defeated McKee and LaGuardia, who ran as a Republican. See Wallace S. Sayre and Herbert Kaufman, *Governing New York City: Politics in the Metropolis* (1965), 187.

10. *NYT,* Apr. 12, 13, 17, 18, 22, 23, 26, May 14, 1933; *News,* Apr. 25, May 3, 1933.

11. *NYT,* Apr. 26, 27, 1933. For lists of opponents, see *NYT,* May 1, 5, 12, 13, 1933. Straus later credited Sulzberger with leading the fight; *NYT,* Jan. 10, 1934.

12. *NYT,* Apr. 30 (injury and destroy) May 2, 3 (detrimental), 5, 12, 1933.

13. On Sheehy, see *NYT,* Apr. 7, 1933; *News,* May 2, 1933. For lists of supporters, *News,* May 2–4, 1933; *H-T,* Apr. 29, 1933; *NYT,* May 13, 1933.

14. *News,* May 2 (cartoon), 17, 1933. See also, e.g., *News,* Apr. 10, 25, 26, 28, 29, May 8, 17, 1933. The Hearst-owned *Journal* was the only other newspaper to side with the *News.* See May 13, 18, 1933.

15. *News,* Apr. 29, May 2 (googoos), 1933; "Memoranda of the Luncheon Discussion on Reform of the Administration of the New York City Parks at the City Club, Nov. 15, 1927," B 12,

RW Mss. See also Richard Welling to Nathan Straus, Jr., Jan. 18, 1934, Welling to Iphigene Sulzberger, June 3, 1938, ibid; Gustavus Kirby to Straus, Dec. 20, 1930, B 3, Parks Council Papers, Avery Library, Columbia University.

16. Welling to Robert Moses, Dec. 20, 1933, B 12, RW Mss.; *News*, Apr. 25, 1933. See also Straus to Welling, Sept. 20, 1928, B 12, RW Mss.

17. *News*, June 24, 1930 (hat), Apr. 25, 1933 (elsewhere); *NYT*, May 18, 19, 1933 (alternative sites). On Walker's parks, see *News*, Aug. 29, 1930; on Straus support of active recreation, *NYT*, Aug. 14, 1931, Jan. 13, 1932.

18. *NYT*, *News*, June 15, 1933 (emphasis added). See also *News*, June 30, 1933; *NYT*, June 25, 1933. For hearings, see *NYT*, Apr. 29, May 16, 1933; *News*, Apr. 29, May 16, 1933. Three ball fields remained in use through summer and fall: *News*, Jan. 10, 1934.

19. *News*, May 8, 1933; *NYT*, Feb. 13, 1927; James Sheldon to Welling, May 19, 1930, B 12, RW Mss.

20. *NYT*, May 11, 1933; *News*, May 12, 1933. On creation of Fusion party, see Arthur Mann, *La Guardia Comes to Power, 1933* (1965; rpt. Chicago, 1969), 68.

21. *NYT*, May 11, 1933; Mann, *La Guardia*, 79, 81–82, 88. Stanley Howe, the onetime managing director of the Central Park Association, was similarly a Republican party activist and leader of the Honest Ballot Association; after the election he became deputy commissioner of public welfare and, later, executive secretary to La Guardia: *NYT*, Mar. 31, 1955.

22. August Heckscher with Phyllis Robinson, *When LaGuardia Was Mayor: New York's Legendary Years* (1978), 30; Robert A. Caro, *The Power Broker: Robert Moses and the Fall of New York* (1974), 10, 308–11. Our discussion of Moses, while departing on some particulars, is deeply indebted to Caro's rich biography.

23. Caro, *Power Broker*, 358–62.

24. *NYT, American, Sun, H-T*, Apr. 6, 1934; *NYT*, May 14, 1936; Caro, *Power Broker*, 309; *News*, Feb. 2, 1935. On Clarke's role, see "Report to Accompany Plan of Development for the Lower Reservoir Site in Central Park," Apr. 22, 1930, F 1118.1, AMNH Papers, AMNH Archives, New York. On Clarke, see Norman T. Newton, *Design on the Land: The Development of Landscape Architecture* (Cambridge, Mass., 1971), 601–7, 611–12, 629; Caro, *Power Broker*, 365, 371–72. On Sulzberger and Moses, Caro, *Power Broker*, 458–62. Sulzberger became acting president of the park association in 1934 when Straus became head of National Recovery Administration for New York; Straus's dislike of Moses may have influenced his stepping down: *NYT*, Jan. 19, 1934; Susan W. Dryfoos, *Iphigene: My Life and the "New York Times": The Memoirs of Iphigene Ochs Sulzberger* (1981), 156. But the two had previous been friendly; see Nathan Straus, "The Reminiscences of Nathan Straus" (transcript of an interview conducted by O. Bombard for the Oral History Research Office of Columbia University, 1950), 62, 73.

25. *NYT*, May 14, 1936.

26. Caro, *Power Broker*, 59–60, 72–85, 159, 166–67, 243, 459; *H-T*, Mar. 12, 1935.

27. *NYT*, Dec. 30, 31, 1934, Jan. 10, Aug. 24, 1935, June 20, Oct. 29, 1941. See also *NYT*, Nov. 20, 1936, May 30, 1937. Moses had a penchant for quantifying his accomplishments, which the local press picked up. For summary, see Pks. Dpt., *Eight Years of Park Progress* (1941), 14–15, 21–23. Park acreage also increased because the parks department won control over all public recreational properties except those under the board of education under the 1938 charter. Moreover, the increases began during the Walker administration before Moses came to power. The *Times*, June 11, 1933, notes an addition of 2,440 acres of park land between 1928 and 1932, mostly in Queens and Staten Island.

28. *NYT*, Apr. 12, 1936. See also *NYT*, Sept. 13, 14, Nov. 17, 1935, June 20, 1941; *Eight Years of Park Progress*, 15. The idea of eight small perimeter playgrounds had first been floated by Herman Merkel in his 1927 report and then endorsed by the Regional Plan. Merkel, *Report on Survey of Central Park* (1927), 7, 17; Lee F. Hanmer, *Public Recreation: A Study of Parks, Playgrounds, and Other Outdoor Recreation Facilities* (1928; rpt. 1974), 98.

29. *NYT*, Apr. 6, 1934, Sept. 13, 24, 1935, Apr. 12, Sept. 12, Oct. 16, Nov. 22, 1936. In the 1930s the Great Hill was generally called the 106th Street Overlook. At other times, it has also been known as the Circle Lawn, the Circle, the Concourse, and Bogardus Hill. See *Rebuilding CP*, 96.

30. Eugene Kinkead and Russell Maloney, "Central Park III: What a *Nice* Municipal Park!" *NYer*, Sept. 27, 1941, 26; *NYT*, Apr. 12, 1936. We have been unable to date the rule change

precisely. See Pks. Dpt. *AR* [1915]; *NYT,* Aug. 20, 1924, for indications that the age restrictions were in effect. The 1928 regional plan report, however, notes that the fields are open to "older boys and younger men": Hanmer, *Public Recreation,* 149.

31. Caro, *Power Broker,* 459–60; *NYT,* Sept. 13, 14 (quot.), 1935.

32. Eugene Kinkead and Russell Maloney, "Central Park II: 'A Nasty Place,'" *NYer,* Sept. 20, 1941, 39. On these Moses-era changes in the park, see, e.g., Henry Hope Reed and Sophia Duckworth, *Central Park: A History and a Guide* (1967; rpt. 1972), 50; *Rebuilding CP,* 75–76, 92; Henry Hope Reed, Robert M. McGee, and Esther Mipaas, *Bridges of Central Park* (1990), 90–91; *American,* Apr. 6, 1934; *NYT,* Feb. 8, 1938; Bruce Kelly, Introduction to *Art of the Olmsted Landscape: His Works in New York City,* ed. Jeffrey Simpson and Mary Ellen W. Hern (1981), 3–4.

33. *NYT,* Feb. 11, 1934; Kinkead and Maloney, "Central Park II," 39; Allyn R. Jennings, "Feeding the Central Park Public," *LA* 26 (Apr. 1936): 112–13; *NYT,* Apr. 24, 1935. See also Mary Brown, "The Zoo and Kelly," *Survey Graphic* 24 (Sept. 1935): 429–31. On crackdown, see, e.g., *NYT,* May 21, 1935, June 2, 15, 29, 1937, May 7, 1938.

34. *News,* Apr. 25, 1934; *NYT,* Apr. 24–26, 1934. On tighter enforcement, see, e.g., *NYT,* July 22, 1934, June 12, 1938, May 21, 1939.

35. *NYT,* May 18, 19, 1934.

36. *News,* June 30, July 6, 1929; counsel quoted in Caro, *Power Broker,* 398, and see 320–21, 397–401.

37. *NYT,* Apr. 10, 1935, May 2, 6, 1936. See also *NYT,* Feb. 15, 1936; Caro, *Power Broker,* 397–401.

38. *NYT,* Mar. 1, 1934, Mar. 12, 1935. On sheep, see *NYT,* June 27, 1935.

39. Moses turned the Tavern into a small extension of Jones Beach, giving the concession to the company that had operated the seaside resort's restaurant. For prices and controversy, see, *News,* June 30, 1929; *NYT,* Nov. 3, 1934, Mar. 12, 1935; "Memo on Operation of the Tavern on the Green, Central Park," n.d.; William B. Herlands to W. Earle Andrews, Nov. 26, 1934; Moses to Dieppe Corporation, May 21, 1934; Andrews to Central Park Catering Corp., Oct. 16, 1934, all in B 97, Moses Papers, NYPL.

40. *NYT,* Dec. 25, 1935, Jan. 4, 1936; Caro, *Power Broker,* 460. The original letters are in B 97, Moses Papers. See also Dryfoos, *Iphigene,* 115, 157–58.

41. *News,* Feb. 7, 1935; *Times,* Apr. 6, May 28, Oct. 10, 1934, Feb. 7, May 26, July 4, 5, 25, 1935, Apr. 18, 1936, Mar. 22, May 5, Sept. 19, Nov. 14, 1937. One of the only discordant notes came from Henry Fairfield Osborn, who continued almost to his dying day in late 1935 to campaign for the intermuseum promenade. See, e.g., *NYT,* May 16, 1935; and letters in F 1181.1, AMNH Mss. For celebratory coverage of Moses, see, e.g., S. J. Woolf, "Robert Moses, New York's Park Expert," *Literary Digest,* Mar. 24, 1934, 11, 43; Hubert Herring, "Robert Moses and His Parks," *HM* (Dec. 1937): 26–37; "Robert Moses—Park Creator Extraordinary," *Recreation* 32 (Aug. 1938): 289–91; "Robert (Or-I'll-Resign) Moses," *Fortune* (June 1938): 71–77, 124, 126, 131, 136, 138, 141. One exception to the enthusiasm for Moses was Nathan Straus, Jr.,: Straus to Iphigene Sulzberger, Nov. 15, 1934, B 4, Parks Council Papers.

42. Paul B. Schumm, "The Central Park of New York City: Development of a Landmark in Landscape Architecture," *LA* 27 (Apr. 1937): 144.

43. Kinkead and Maloney, "Central Park II," 34, "Central Park III," 27–28. The second article mentioned Vaux but invariably subordinated his role: "Central Park II," 35. See FLO to CV, Nov. 26, 1863, *FLOP* 5:151.

44. Heckscher, *When LaGuardia Was Mayor,* 55 (quot.); John D. Millett, *The WPA in New York* (Chicago, 1938), 38–41, 47–49, 58–59.

45. Robert H. Muccigrosso, "Richard W. G. Welling: A Reformer's Life" (Ph.D. diss., Columbia University, 1966), 147; *NYT,* Oct. 15, 1934; Dryfoos, *Iphigene,* 154; Caro, *Power Broker,* 458–60.

46. Moses, Address to Meeting of Park Association of New York City, Oct. 23, 1945, B 12, RW Mss.

47. On the problem of municipal revenue, see, e.g., Kenneth Howard Finegold, "Progressivism, Electoral Change, and Public Policy: Reform Outcomes in New York, Cleveland, and Chicago" (Ph.D. diss., Harvard University, 1985), 130–32.

48. Caro, *Power Broker,* 426–43, 453–54; Thomas Kessner, *Fiorello H. La Guardia and the*

Making of Modern New York (1989), 304–19, 339–41. On state capacity, see Theda Skocpol and Kenneth Finegold, "State Capacity and Economic Intervention in the New Deal," *Political Science Quarterly* 97 (Summer 1982): 255–78; Alan Brinkley, "The New Deal and the Idea of the State," in *The Rise and Fall of the New Deal Order, 1930–1980*, ed., Steve Fraser and Gary Gerstle (Princeton, 1989), 102.

49. On Keynesianism, mass consumption, and the New Deal, see Brinkley, "New Deal," 94–98.

50. Judith Anne Davidson, "The Federal Government and the Democratization of Public Recreational Sport: New York City, 1933–1945" (Ph.D. diss., University of Massachusetts, 1983), 157–203; Barbara Blumberg, *The New Deal and the Unemployed: The View from New York City* (Lewisburg, Pa., 1979), 127; Millett, *WPA in New York*, 58–59.

51. J. J. Ladin to Moses, Dec. 9, 1936, B 12 RW Mss.; Caro, *Power Broker*, 368–69.

52. *NYT*, Jan. 20, 1940; Pks. Dept., *Six Years of Park Progress* (1939), 40–44; Dryfoos, *Iphigene*, 159. For other warnings from Moses, see, e.g., *NYT*, Sept. 4, 8, 1935, Sept. 22, Oct. 22, 1936, Aug. 25, Oct. 7, 1937.

53. Letter quoted in Davidson, "Federal Government," 189.

54. Davidson, "Federal Government," 16, 181, 200–201; Caro, *Power Broker*, 510, 513–14; *NYT*, June 19, 1935; *Amsterdam News*, June 20, 1935. See also Kessner, *La Guardia*, 374; *NYT*, June 29, 1935. Black workers did, however, receive substantial employment on the WPA, particularly as recreation workers. By the early 1940s, they made up about one-third of the city's WPA work force: Davidson, "Federal Government," 256. On northern park, *NYT*, Aug. 7, 1947. The renovations had been partially completed in 1943.

55. Kessner, *La Guardia*, 340; Millett, *WPA in New York*, 49, 59; Caro, *Power Broker*, 369–72; *NYT*, Feb. 15, 1936 (sleet); Davidson, "Federal Government," 128–29.

56. Caro, *Power Broker*, 318.

57. Kinkead and Maloney, "Central Park III," 27.

58. Davidson, "Federal Government," vii, and see 257–58, 268, 287. On sitdown, see *NYT*, Mar. 12, 13, 15, 1937; Davidson, "Federal Government," 190; Caro, *Power Broker*, 451–52; Kessner, *La Guardia*, 413; *NYT*, May 15, 1937. Caro points out that the crisis was manipulated by Moses, but the significant point is that the response shows how people had come to see public playgrounds as a "right."

17. Scenes from a Park, 1941–1980

1. Iphigene Sulzberger to Robert Moses, Mar. 27, 1950, B 102850, Pks. Dpt. Mss., MARC. On Sulzberger, see Susan W. Dryfoos, *Iphigene: My Life and the "New York Times": The Memoirs of Iphigene Ochs Sulzberger* (1981); *NYT*, Feb. 27, 1990.

2. Moses to Sulzberger, Apr. 5, 1950, B 102850, Pks. Dpt. Mss.

3. *NYT*, June 13, 1982; Donald Knowler, *The Falconer of Central Park* (1984), 82–85; *NYT*, May 1, 1946.

4. John Hull Mollenkopf, "Inequality and Political Mobilization in the Post-Crisis City," paper presented to Social Science Research Council, Research Committee on New York City, Oct. 30–Nov. 1, 1986; Gus Tyler, "A Tale of Three Cities: Upper Economy, Lower—and Under," *Dissent* 34 (Fall 1987): 463–64; Emanuel Tobier and Walter Stafford, "People and Income," in *Setting Municipal Priorities, 1986*, ed., Charles Brecher and Raymond Horton (1985), 57–58.

5. Ira Rosenwaike, *Population History of New York City* (Syracuse, 1972), 188–91, 198; U.S. Bureau of the Census, *1980 Census of Population and Housing: Census Tracts: New York, N.Y.-N.J.* (Washington, D.C., 1983), 452; Tobier and Stafford, "People and Income," 59.

6. Mollenkopf, "Inequality," 3; *1980 Census*, 452.

7. *News*, Nov. 3, 1941. For conviction, see *NYT*, Oct. 20, 1942, Jan. 16, 1943.

8. *News*, Nov. 3, 6, 8, 1941; *Mirror*, Nov. 7, 1941; *NYT*, Nov. 7, 1941, and cf. Nov. 8, 9, 1941.

9. *Am. S-N*, Nov. 15, 1941.

10. *Am. S-N*, *New York Age*, Nov. 15, 1941. On "crime waves" and the press, see Mark Fishman, *Manufacturing the News* (Austin, Tex., 1980), 8–9.